Core Java

Volume II—Advanced Features

Eleventh Edition

Core Java

Volume II—Advanced Features

Eleventh Edition

Cay S. Horstmann

Pearson

Boston • Columbus • New York • San Francisco • Amsterdam • Cape Town
Dubai • London • Madrid • Milan • Munich • Paris • Montreal • Toronto • Delhi • Mexico City
São Paulo • Sydney • Hong Kong • Seoul • Singapore • Taipei • Tokyo

Library of Congress Preassigned Control Number: 2018963595

ISBN-13: 978-0-13-516631-4
ISBN-10: 0-13-516631-4

1   19

Contents

Preface

To the Reader

The book you have in your hands is the second volume of the eleventh edition of *Core Java*, fully updated for Java SE 11. The first volume covers the essential features of the language; this volume deals with the advanced topics that a programmer needs to know for professional software development. Thus, as with the first volume and the previous editions of this book, we are still targeting programmers who want to put Java technology to work in real projects.

As is the case with any book, errors and inaccuracies are inevitable. Should you find any in this book, we would very much like to hear about them. Of course, we would prefer to hear about them only once. For this reason, we have put up a web site at http://horstmann.com/corejava with a FAQ, bug fixes, and workarounds. Strategically placed at the end of the bug report web page (to encourage you to read the previous reports) is a form that you can use to report bugs or problems and to send suggestions for improvements for future editions.

About This Book

The chapters in this book are, for the most part, independent of each other. You should be able to delve into whatever topic interests you the most and read the chapters in any order.

In **Chapter 1**, you will learn all about the Java stream library that brings a modern flavor to processing data, by specifying what you want without describing in detail how the result should be obtained. This allows the stream library to focus on an optimal evaluation strategy, which is particularly advantageous for optimizing concurrent computations.

The topic of **Chapter 2** is input and output handling (I/O). In Java, all input and output is handled through input/output streams. These streams (not to be confused with those in Chapter 1) let you deal, in a uniform manner, with communications among various sources of data, such as files, network connections, or memory blocks. We include detailed coverage of the reader and writer classes that make it easy to deal with Unicode. We show you what goes on under the hood when you use the object serialization mechanism, which makes saving and loading objects easy and convenient. We then move on to regular expressions and working with files and paths. Throughout this chapter, you will find welcome enhancements in recent Java versions.

Chapter 3 covers XML. We show you how to parse XML files, how to generate XML, and how to use XSL transformations. As a useful example, we show you how to specify the layout of a Swing form in XML. We also discuss the XPath API, which makes finding needles in XML haystacks much easier.

Chapter 4 covers the networking API. Java makes it phenomenally easy to do complex network programming. We show you how to make network connections to servers, how to implement your own servers, and how to make HTTP connections. This chapter includes coverage of the new HTTP client.

Chapter 5 covers database programming. The main focus is on JDBC, the Java database connectivity API that lets Java programs connect to relational databases. We show you how to write useful programs to handle realistic database chores, using a core subset of the JDBC API. (A complete treatment of the JDBC API would require a book almost as big as this one.) We finish the chapter with a brief introduction into hierarchical databases and discuss JNDI (the Java Naming and Directory Interface) and LDAP (the Lightweight Directory Access Protocol).

Java had two prior attempts at libraries for handling date and time. The third one was the charm in Java 8. In **Chapter 6**, you will learn how to deal with the complexities of calendars and time zones, using the new date and time library.

Chapter 7 discusses a feature that we believe can only grow in importance: internationalization. The Java programming language is one of the few languages designed from the start to handle Unicode, but the internationalization support on the Java platform goes much further. As a result, you can internationalize Java applications so that they cross not only platforms but country boundaries as well. For example, we show you how to write a retirement calculator that uses either English, German, or Chinese languages.

Chapter 8 discusses three techniques for processing code. The scripting and compiler APIs allow your program to call code in scripting languages such as JavaScript or Groovy, and to compile Java code. Annotations allow you to add arbitrary information (sometimes called metadata) to a Java program. We show you how annotation processors can harvest these annotations at the source or class file level, and how annotations can be used to influence the behavior of classes at runtime. Annotations are only useful with tools, and we hope that our discussion will help you select useful annotation processing tools for your needs.

In **Chapter 9**, you will learn about the Java Platform Module System that was introduced in Java 9 to facilitate an orderly evolution of the Java platform and core libraries. This module system provides encapsulation for packages and a mechanism for describing module requirements. You will learn the properties of modules so that you can decide whether to use them in your own applications. Even if you decide not to, you need to know the new rules so that you can interact with the Java platform and other modularized libraries.

Chapter 10 takes up the Java security model. The Java platform was designed from the ground up to be secure, and this chapter takes you under the hood to see how this design is implemented. We show you how to write your own class loaders and security managers for special-purpose applications. Then, we take up the security API that allows for such important features as message and code signing, authorization and authentication, and encryption. We conclude with examples that use the AES and RSA encryption algorithms.

Chapter 11 contains all the Swing material that didn't make it into Volume I, especially the important but complex tree and table components. We also cover the Java 2D API, which you can use to create realistic drawings and special effects. Of course, not many programmers need to program Swing user interfaces these days, so we pay particular attention to features that are useful for images that can be generated on a server.

Chapter 12 takes up native methods, which let you call methods written for a specific machine such as the Microsoft Windows API. Obviously, this feature is controversial: Use native methods, and the cross-platform nature of Java vanishes. Nonetheless, every serious programmer writing Java applications for specific platforms needs to know these techniques. At times, you need to turn to the operating system's API for your target platform when you interact with a device or service that is not supported by Java. We illustrate this by showing you how to access the registry API in Windows from a Java program.

As always, all chapters have been completely revised for the latest version of Java. Outdated material has been removed, and the new APIs of Java 9, 10, and 11 are covered in detail.

Conventions

As is common in many computer books, we use monospace type to represent computer code.

NOTE: Notes are tagged with "note" icons that look like this.

TIP: Tips are tagged with "tip" icons that look like this.

CAUTION: When there is danger ahead, we warn you with a "caution" icon.

C++ NOTE: There are a number of C++ notes that explain the difference between the Java programming language and C++. You can skip them if you aren't interested in C++.

Java comes with a large programming library, or Application Programming Interface (API). When using an API call for the first time, we add a short summary description at the end of the section. These descriptions are a bit more informal but, we hope, also a little more informative than those in the official online API documentation. The names of interfaces are in italics, just like in the official documentation. The number after a class, interface, or method name is the JDK version in which the feature was introduced.

Application Programming Interface 1.2

Programs whose source code is included in the companion code for this book are listed as examples, for instance

---

Listing 1.1 ScriptTest.java

You can download the companion code from http://horstmann.com/corejava.

Register your copy of *Core Java, Volume II—Advanced Features, Eleventh Edition,* on the InformIT site for convenient access to updates and/or corrections as they become available. To start the registration process, go to informit.com/register and log in or create an account. Enter the product ISBN (9780135166314) and click Submit. Look on the Registered Products tab for an Access Bonus Content link next to this product, and follow that link to access any available bonus materials. If you would like to be notified of exclusive offers on new editions and updates, please check the box to receive email from us.

Acknowledgments

Writing a book is always a monumental effort, and rewriting doesn't seem to be much easier, especially with such a rapid rate of change in Java technology. Making a book a reality takes many dedicated people, and it is my great pleasure to acknowledge the contributions of the entire *Core Java* team.

A large number of individuals at Pearson provided valuable assistance, but they managed to stay behind the scenes. I'd like them all to know how much I appreciate their efforts. As always, my warm thanks go to my editor, Greg Doench, for steering the book through the writing and production process, and for allowing me to be blissfully unaware of the existence of all those folks behind the scenes. I am very grateful to Julie Nahil for production support, and to Dmitry Kirsanov and Alina Kirsanova for copyediting and typesetting the manuscript.

Thanks to the many readers of earlier editions who reported embarrassing errors and made lots of thoughtful suggestions for improvement. I am particularly grateful to the excellent reviewing team that went over the manuscript with an amazing eye for detail and saved me from many more embarrassing errors.

Reviewers of this and earlier editions include Chuck Allison (Contributing Editor, C/C++ Users Journal), Lance Anderson (Oracle), Alec Beaton (Point-Base, Inc.), Cliff Berg (iSavvix Corporation), Joshua Bloch, David Brown, Corky Cartwright, Frank Cohen (PushToTest), Chris Crane (devXsolution), Dr. Nicholas J. De Lillo (Manhattan College), Rakesh Dhoopar (Oracle), Robert Evans (Senior Staff, The Johns Hopkins University Applied Physics Lab), David Geary (Sabreware), Jim Gish (Oracle), Brian Goetz (Oracle), Angela Gordon, Dan Gordon, Rob Gordon, John Gray (University of Hartford), Cameron Gregory (olabs.com), Steve Haines, Marty Hall (The Johns Hopkins University Applied Physics Lab), Vincent Hardy, Dan Harkey (San Jose State University), William Higgins (IBM), Vladimir Ivanovic (PointBase), Jerry Jackson (ChannelPoint Software), Tim Kimmet (Preview Systems), Chris Laffra, Charlie Lai, Angelika Langer, Doug Langston, Hang Lau (McGill University), Mark Lawrence, Doug Lea (SUNY Oswego), Gregory Longshore, Bob Lynch (Lynch Associates), Philip Milne (consultant), Mark Morrissey (The Oregon Graduate Institute), Mahesh Neelakanta (Florida Atlantic University), Hao Pham, Paul Philion, Blake Ragsdell, Ylber Ramadani (Ryerson University),

Stuart Reges (University of Arizona), Simon Ritter, Rich Rosen (Interactive Data Corporation), Peter Sanders (ESSI University, Nice, France), Dr. Paul Sanghera (San Jose State University and Brooks College), Paul Sevinc (Teamup AG), Yoshiki Shabata, Devang Shah, Richard Slywczak (NASA/Glenn Research Center), Bradley A. Smith, Steven Stelting, Christopher Taylor, Luke Taylor (Valtech), George Thiruvathukal, Kim Topley (author of *Core JFC, Second Edition*), Janet Traub, Paul Tyma (consultant), Christian Ullenboom, Peter van der Linden, Burt Walsh, Joe Wang (Oracle), and Dan Xu (Oracle).

Cay Horstmann
San Francisco, California
December 2018

Streams

In this chapter

Compared to collections, streams provide a view of data that lets you specify computations at a higher conceptual level. With a stream, you specify what you want to have done, not how to do it. You leave the scheduling of operations to the implementation. For example, suppose you want to compute the average of a certain property. You specify the source of data and the property, and the stream library can then optimize the computation, for example by using multiple threads for computing sums and counts and combining the results.

In this chapter, you will learn how to use the Java stream library, which was introduced in Java 8, to process collections in a "what, not how" style.

1.1 From Iterating to Stream Operations

When you process a collection, you usually iterate over its elements and do some work with each of them. For example, suppose we want to count all long words in a book. First, let's put them into a list:

```
var contents = new String(Files.readAllBytes(
   Paths.get("alice.txt")), StandardCharsets.UTF_8); // Read file into string
List<String> words = List.of(contents.split("\\PL+"));
   // Split into words; nonletters are delimiters
```

Now we are ready to iterate:

```
int count = 0;
for (String w : words) {
   if (w.length() > 12) count++;
}
```

With streams, the same operation looks like this:

```
long count = words.stream()
   .filter(w -> w.length() > 12)
   .count();
```

Now you don't have to scan the loop for evidence of filtering and counting. The method names tell you right away what the code intends to do. Moreover, where the loop prescribes the order of operations in complete detail, a stream is able to schedule the operations any way it wants, as long as the result is correct.

Simply changing stream to parallelStream allows the stream library to do the filtering and counting in parallel.

```
long count = words.parallelStream()
   .filter(w -> w.length() > 12)
   .count();
```

Streams follow the "what, not how" principle. In our stream example, we describe what needs to be done: get the long words and count them. We don't specify in which order, or in which thread, this should happen. In contrast, the loop at the beginning of this section specifies exactly how the computation should work, and thereby forgoes any chances of optimization.

A stream seems superficially similar to a collection, allowing you to transform and retrieve data. But there are significant differences:

1. A stream does not store its elements. They may be stored in an underlying collection or generated on demand.

2. Stream operations don't mutate their source. For example, the filter method does not remove elements from a stream but yields a new stream in which they are not present.

3. Stream operations are *lazy* when possible. This means they are not executed until their result is needed. For example, if you only ask for the first five long words instead of all, the filter method will stop filtering after the fifth match. As a consequence, you can even have infinite streams!

Let us have another look at the example. The stream and parallelStream methods yield a *stream* for the words list. The filter method returns another stream that contains only the words of length greater than twelve. The count method reduces that stream to a result.

This workflow is typical when you work with streams. You set up a pipeline of operations in three stages:

1. Create a stream.

2. Specify *intermediate operations* for transforming the initial stream into others, possibly in multiple steps.

3. Apply a *terminal operation* to produce a result. This operation forces the execution of the lazy operations that precede it. Afterwards, the stream can no longer be used.

In the example in Listing 1.1, the stream is created with the stream or parallelStream method. The filter method transforms it, and count is the terminal operation.

In the next section, you will see how to create a stream. The subsequent three sections deal with stream transformations. They are followed by five sections on terminal operations.

Listing 1.1 streams/CountLongWords.java

```
 1 package streams;
 2
 3 /**
 4  * @version 1.01 2018-05-01
 5  * @author Cay Horstmann
 6  */
 7
 8 import java.io.*;
 9 import java.nio.charset.*;
10 import java.nio.file.*;
11 import java.util.*;
12
13 public class CountLongWords
14 {
15    public static void main(String[] args) throws IOException
16    {
17       var contents = new String(Files.readAllBytes(
18          Paths.get("../gutenberg/alice30.txt")), StandardCharsets.UTF_8);
19       List<String> words = List.of(contents.split("\\PL+"));
20
21       long count = 0;
22       for (String w : words)
23       {
24          if (w.length() > 12) count++;
25       }
26       System.out.println(count);
27
28       count = words.stream().filter(w -> w.length() > 12).count();
29       System.out.println(count);
30
31       count = words.parallelStream().filter(w -> w.length() > 12).count();
32       System.out.println(count);
33    }
34 }
```

---

java.util.stream.Stream<T> 8

- Stream<T> filter(Predicate<? super T> p)

  yields a stream containing all elements of this stream fulfilling p.

- long count()

  yields the number of elements of this stream. This is a terminal operation.

---

java.util.Collection<E> 1.2

- default Stream<E> stream()
- default Stream<E> parallelStream()

  yields a sequential or parallel stream of the elements in this collection.

1.2 Stream Creation

You have already seen that you can turn any collection into a stream with the stream method of the Collection interface. If you have an array, use the static Stream.of method instead.

```
Stream<String> words = Stream.of(contents.split("\\PL+"));
   // split returns a String[] array
```

The of method has a varargs parameter, so you can construct a stream from any number of arguments:

```
Stream<String> song = Stream.of("gently", "down", "the", "stream");
```

Use Arrays.stream(array, from, to) to make a stream from a part of an array.

To make a stream with no elements, use the static Stream.empty method:

```
Stream<String> silence = Stream.empty();
   // Generic type <String> is inferred; same as Stream.<String>empty()
```

The Stream interface has two static methods for making infinite streams. The generate method takes a function with no arguments (or, technically, an object of the Supplier<T> interface). Whenever a stream value is needed, that function is called to produce a value. You can get a stream of constant values as

```
Stream<String> echos = Stream.generate(() -> "Echo");
```

or a stream of random numbers as

```
Stream<Double> randoms = Stream.generate(Math::random);
```

To produce sequences such as 0 1 2 3 . . ., use the iterate method instead. It takes a "seed" value and a function (technically, a UnaryOperator<T>) and repeatedly applies the function to the previous result. For example,

```
Stream<BigInteger> integers
   = Stream.iterate(BigInteger.ZERO, n -> n.add(BigInteger.ONE));
```

The first element in the sequence is the seed `BigInteger.ZERO`. The second element is `f(seed)` which yields 1 (as a big integer). The next element is `f(f(seed))` which yields 2, and so on.

To produce a finite stream instead, add a predicate that specifies when the iteration should finish:

```
var limit = new BigInteger("10000000");
Stream<BigInteger> integers
   = Stream.iterate(BigInteger.ZERO,
      n -> n.compareTo(limit) < 0,
      n -> n.add(BigInteger.ONE));
```

As soon as the predicate rejects an iteratively generated value, the stream ends.

Finally, the `Stream.ofNullable` method makes a really short stream from an object. The stream has length 0 if the object is `null` or length 1 otherwise, containing just the object. This is mostly useful in conjunction with `flatMap`—see Section 1.7.7, "Turning an Optional into a Stream," on p. 22 for an example.

NOTE: A number of methods in the Java API yield streams. For example, the `Pattern` class has a method `splitAsStream` that splits a `CharSequence` by a regular expression. You can use the following statement to split a string into words:

```
Stream<String> words = Pattern.compile("\\PL+").splitAsStream(contents);
```

The `Scanner.tokens` method yields a stream of tokens of a scanner. Another way to get a stream of words from a string is

```
Stream<String> words = new Scanner(contents).tokens();
```

The static `Files.lines` method returns a `Stream` of all lines in a file:

```
try (Stream<String> lines = Files.lines(path)) {
   Process lines
}
```

NOTE: If you have an `Iterable` that is not a collection, you can turn it into a stream by calling

```
StreamSupport.stream(iterable.spliterator(), false);
```

If you have an `Iterator` and want a stream of its results, use

```
StreamSupport.stream(Spliterators.spliteratorUnknownSize(
   iterator, Spliterator.ORDERED), false);
```

```
67
68    Iterator<Path> iterator = Paths.get("/usr/share/dict/words").iterator();
69    Stream<Path> pathComponents = StreamSupport.stream(Spliterators.spliteratorUnknownSize(
70        iterator, Spliterator.ORDERED), false);
71    show("pathComponents", pathComponents);
72  }
73 }
```

---

java.util.stream.Stream 8

- static <T> Stream<T> of(T... values)

  yields a stream whose elements are the given values.

- static <T> Stream<T> empty()

  yields a stream with no elements.

- static <T> Stream<T> generate(Supplier<T> s)

  yields an infinite stream whose elements are constructed by repeatedly invoking the function s.

- static <T> Stream<T> iterate(T seed, UnaryOperator<T> f)
- static <T> Stream<T> iterate(T seed, Predicate<? super T> hasNext, UnaryOperator<T> f)

  yields a stream whose elements are seed, f invoked on seed, f invoked on the preceding element, and so on. The first method yields an infinite stream. The stream of the second method comes to an end before the first element that doesn't fulfill the hasNext predicate.

- static <T> Stream<T> ofNullable(T t) 9

  returns an empty stream if t is null or a stream containing t otherwise.

---

java.util.Spliterators 8

- static <T> Spliterator<T> spliteratorUnknownSize(Iterator<? extends T> iterator, int characteristics)

  turns an iterator into a splittable iterator of unknown size with the given characteristics (a bit pattern containing constants such as Spliterator.ORDERED).

---

java.util.Arrays 1.2

- static <T> Stream<T> stream(T[] array, int startInclusive, int endExclusive) 8

  yields a stream whose elements are the specified range of the array.

---

java.util.regex.Pattern 1.4

- Stream<String> splitAsStream(CharSequence input) 8

  yields a stream whose elements are the parts of the input that are delimited by this pattern.

---

java.nio.file.Files 7

- static Stream<String> lines(Path path) 8
- static Stream<String> lines(Path path, Charset cs) 8

  yields a stream whose elements are the lines of the specified file, with the UTF-8 charset or the given charset.

---

java.util.stream.StreamSupport 8

- static <T> Stream<T> stream(Spliterator<T> spliterator, boolean parallel)

  yields a stream containing the values produced by the given splittable iterator.

---

java.lang.Iterable 5

- Spliterator<T> spliterator() 8

  yields a splittable iterator for this Iterable. The default implementation does not split and does not report a size.

---

java.util.Scanner 5

- public Stream<String> tokens() 9

  yields a stream of strings returned by calling the next method of this scanner.

---

java.util.function.Supplier<T> 8

- T get()

  supplies a value.

1.3 The `filter`, `map`, and `flatMap` Methods

A stream transformation produces a stream whose elements are derived from those of another stream. You have already seen the `filter` transformation that yields a new stream with those elements that match a certain condition. Here, we transform a stream of strings into another stream containing only long words:

```
List<String> words = . . .;
Stream<String> longWords = words.stream().filter(w -> w.length() > 12);
```

The argument of `filter` is a `Predicate<T>`—that is, a function from `T` to `boolean`.

Often, you want to transform the values in a stream in some way. Use the `map` method and pass the function that carries out the transformation. For example, you can transform all words to lowercase like this:

```
Stream<String> lowercaseWords = words.stream().map(String::toLowerCase);
```

Here, we used `map` with a method reference. Often, you will use a lambda expression instead:

```
Stream<String> firstLetters = words.stream().map(s -> s.substring(0, 1));
```

The resulting stream contains the first letter of each word.

When you use `map`, a function is applied to each element, and the result is a new stream with the results. Now, suppose you have a function that returns not just one value but a stream of values. Here is an example—a method that turns a string into a stream of strings, namely the individual code points:

```
public static Stream<String> codePoints(String s)
{
   var result = new ArrayList<String>();
   int i = 0;
   while (i < s.length())
   {
      int j = s.offsetByCodePoints(i, 1);
      result.add(s.substring(i, j));
      i = j;
   }
   return result.stream();
}
```

This method correctly handles Unicode characters that require two `char` values because that's the right thing to do. But you don't have to dwell on that.

For example, `codePoints("boat")` is the stream `["b", "o", "a", "t"]`.

Now let's map the `codePoints` method on a stream of strings:

```
Stream<Stream<String>> result = words.stream().map(w -> codePoints(w));
```

You will get a stream of streams, like [. . . ["y", "o", "u", "r"], ["b", "o", "a", "t"], . . .]. To flatten it out to a single stream [. . . "y", "o", "u", "r", "b", "o", "a", "t", . . .], use the `flatMap` method instead of `map`:

```
Stream<String> flatResult = words.stream().flatMap(w -> codePoints(w));
   // Calls codePoints on each word and flattens the results
```

NOTE: You will find a `flatMap` method in classes other than streams. It is a general concept in computer science. Suppose you have a generic type G (such as `Stream`) and functions f from some type T to G<U> and g from U to G<V>. Then you can compose them—that is, first apply f and then g, by using `flatMap`. This is a key idea in the theory of *monads*. But don't worry—you can use `flatMap` without knowing anything about monads.

---

java.util.stream.Stream 8

- `Stream<T> filter(Predicate<? super T> predicate)`

  yields a stream containing the elements of this stream that fulfill the predicate.

- `<R> Stream<R> map(Function<? super T,? extends R> mapper)`

  yields a stream containing the results of applying `mapper` to the elements of this stream.

- `<R> Stream<R> flatMap(Function<? super T,? extends Stream<? extends R>> mapper)`

  yields a stream obtained by concatenating the results of applying `mapper` to the elements of this stream. (Note that each result is a stream.)

1.4 Extracting Substreams and Combining Streams

The call *stream*`.limit(n)` returns a new stream that ends after n elements (or when the original stream ends if it is shorter). This method is particularly useful for cutting infinite streams down to size. For example,

```
Stream<Double> randoms = Stream.generate(Math::random).limit(100);
```

yields a stream with 100 random numbers.

The call *stream*`.skip(n)` does the exact opposite. It discards the first n elements. This is handy in our book reading example where, due to the way the `split` method works, the first element is an unwanted empty string. We can make it go away by calling `skip`:

```
Stream<String> words = Stream.of(contents.split("\\PL+")).skip(1);
```

The *stream*.takeWhile(*predicate*) call takes all elements from the stream while the predicate is true, and then stops.

For example, suppose we use the codePoints method of the preceding section to split a string into characters, and we want to collect all initial digits. The takeWhile method can do this:

```
Stream<String> initialDigits = codePoints(str).takeWhile(
    s -> "0123456789".contains(s));
```

The dropWhile method does the opposite, dropping elements while a condition is true and yielding a stream of all elements starting with the first one for which the condition was false. For example,

```
Stream<String> withoutInitialWhiteSpace = codePoints(str).dropWhile(
    s -> s.trim().length() == 0);
```

You can concatenate two streams with the static concat method of the Stream class:

```
Stream<String> combined = Stream.concat(
    codePoints("Hello"), codePoints("World"));
    // Yields the stream ["H", "e", "l", "l", "o", "W", "o", "r", "l", "d"]
```

Of course, the first stream should not be infinite—otherwise the second one wouldn't ever get a chance.

---

java.util.stream.Stream 8

- Stream<T> limit(long maxSize)

  yields a stream with up to maxSize of the initial elements from this stream.

- Stream<T> skip(long n)

  yields a stream whose elements are all but the initial n elements of this stream.

- Stream<T> takeWhile(Predicate<? super T> predicate) 9

  yields a stream whose elements are the initial elements of this stream that fulfill the predicate.

- Stream<T> dropWhile(Predicate<? super T> predicate) 9

  yields a stream whose elements are the elements of this stream except for the initial ones that do not fulfill the predicate.

- static <T> Stream<T> concat(Stream<? extends T> a, Stream<? extends T> b)

  yields a stream whose elements are the elements of a followed by the elements of b.

1.5 Other Stream Transformations

The distinct method returns a stream that yields elements from the original stream, in the same order, except that duplicates are suppressed. The duplicates need not be adjacent.

```
Stream<String> uniqueWords
    = Stream.of("merrily", "merrily", "merrily", "gently").distinct();
    // Only one "merrily" is retained
```

For sorting a stream, there are several variations of the sorted method. One works for streams of Comparable elements, and another accepts a Comparator. Here, we sort strings so that the longest ones come first:

```
Stream<String> longestFirst
    = words.stream().sorted(Comparator.comparing(String::length).reversed());
```

As with all stream transformations, the sorted method yields a new stream whose elements are the elements of the original stream in sorted order.

Of course, you can sort a collection without using streams. The sorted method is useful when the sorting process is part of a stream pipeline.

Finally, the peek method yields another stream with the same elements as the original, but a function is invoked every time an element is retrieved. That is handy for debugging:

```
Object[] powers = Stream.iterate(1.0, p -> p * 2)
    .peek(e -> System.out.println("Fetching " + e))
    .limit(20).toArray();
```

When an element is actually accessed, a message is printed. This way you can verify that the infinite stream returned by iterate is processed lazily.

 TIP: When you use a debugger to debug a stream computation, you can set a breakpoint in a method that is called from one of the transformations. With most IDEs, you can also set breakpoints in lambda expressions. If you just want to know what happens at a particular point in the stream pipeline, add

```
.peek(x -> {
    return; })
```

and set a breakpoint on the second line.

---

java.util.stream.Stream 8

- Stream<T> distinct()

  yields a stream of the distinct elements of this stream.

- Stream<T> sorted()
- Stream<T> sorted(Comparator<? super T> comparator)

  yields a stream whose elements are the elements of this stream in sorted order. The first method requires that the elements are instances of a class implementing Comparable.

- Stream<T> peek(Consumer<? super T> action)

  yields a stream with the same elements as this stream, passing each element to action as it is consumed.

1.6 Simple Reductions

Now that you have seen how to create and transform streams, we will finally get to the most important point—getting answers from the stream data. The methods covered in this section are called *reductions*. Reductions are *terminal operations*. They reduce the stream to a nonstream value that can be used in your program.

You have already seen a simple reduction: the count method that returns the number of elements of a stream.

Other simple reductions are max and min that return the largest or smallest value. There is a twist—these methods return an Optional<T> value that either wraps the answer or indicates that there is none (because the stream happened to be empty). In the olden days, it was common to return null in such a situation. But that can lead to null pointer exceptions when it happens in an incompletely tested program. The Optional type is a better way of indicating a missing return value. We discuss the Optional type in detail in the next section. Here is how you can get the maximum of a stream:

```
Optional<String> largest = words.max(String::compareToIgnoreCase);
System.out.println("largest: " + largest.orElse(""));
```

The findFirst returns the first value in a nonempty collection. It is often useful when combined with filter. For example, here we find the first word that starts with the letter Q, if it exists:

```
Optional<String> startsWithQ
    = words.filter(s -> s.startsWith("Q")).findFirst();
```

If you are OK with any match, not just the first one, use the `findAny` method. This is effective when you parallelize the stream, since the stream can report any match that it finds instead of being constrained to the first one.

```
Optional<String> startsWithQ
  = words.parallel().filter(s -> s.startsWith("Q")).findAny();
```

If you just want to know if there is a match, use `anyMatch`. That method takes a predicate argument, so you won't need to use `filter`.

```
boolean aWordStartsWithQ
  = words.parallel().anyMatch(s -> s.startsWith("Q"));
```

There are methods `allMatch` and `noneMatch` that return `true` if all or no elements match a predicate. These methods also benefit from being run in parallel.

---

java.util.stream.Stream 8

- `Optional<T> max(Comparator<? super T> comparator)`
- `Optional<T> min(Comparator<? super T> comparator)`

  yields a maximum or minimum element of this stream, using the ordering defined by the given comparator, or an empty `Optional` if this stream is empty. These are terminal operations.

- `Optional<T> findFirst()`
- `Optional<T> findAny()`

  yields the first, or any, element of this stream, or an empty `Optional` if this stream is empty. These are terminal operations.

- `boolean anyMatch(Predicate<? super T> predicate)`
- `boolean allMatch(Predicate<? super T> predicate)`
- `boolean noneMatch(Predicate<? super T> predicate)`

  returns `true` if any, all, or none of the elements of this stream match the given predicate. These are terminal operations.

1.7 The Optional Type

An `Optional<T>` object is a wrapper for either an object of type `T` or no object. In the former case, we say that the value is *present*. The `Optional<T>` type is intended as a safer alternative for a reference of type `T` that either refers to an object or is `null`. But it is only safer if you use it right. The next three sections shows you how.

1.7.1 Getting an Optional Value

The key to using Optional effectively is to use a method that either *produces an alternative* if the value is not present, or *consumes the value* only if it is present.

In this section, we look at the first strategy. Often, there is a default that you want to use when there was no match, perhaps the empty string:

```
String result = optionalString.orElse("");
   // The wrapped string, or "" if none
```

You can also invoke code to compute the default:

```
String result = optionalString.orElseGet(() -> System.getProperty("myapp.default"));
   // The function is only called when needed
```

Or you can throw an exception if there is no value:

```
String result = optionalString.orElseThrow(IllegalStateException::new);
   // Supply a method that yields an exception object
```

---

java.util.Optional 8

- T orElse(T other)

  yields the value of this Optional, or other if this Optional is empty.

- T orElseGet(Supplier<? extends T> other)

  yields the value of this Optional, or the result of invoking other if this Optional is empty.

- <X extends Throwable> T orElseThrow(Supplier<? extends X> exceptionSupplier)

  yields the value of this Optional, or throws the result of invoking exceptionSupplier if this Optional is empty.

1.7.2 Consuming an Optional Value

In the preceding section, you saw how to produce an alternative if no value is present. The other strategy for working with optional values is to consume the value only if it is present.

The ifPresent method accepts a function. If the optional value exists, it is passed to that function. Otherwise, nothing happens.

```
optionalValue.ifPresent(v -> Process v);
```

For example, if you want to add the value to a set if it is present, call

```
optionalValue.ifPresent(v -> results.add(v));
```

or simply

```
optionalValue.ifPresent(results::add);
```

If you want to take one action if the Optional has a value and another action if it doesn't, use ifPresentOrElse:

```
optionalValue.ifPresentOrElse(
    v -> System.out.println("Found " + v),
    () -> logger.warning("No match"));
```

---

java.util.Optional 8

- void ifPresent(Consumer<? super T> action)

  if this Optional is nonempty, passes its value to action.

- void ifPresentOrElse(Consumer<? super T> action, Runnable emptyAction) 9

  if this Optional is nonempty, passes its value to action, else invokes emptyAction.

1.7.3 Pipelining Optional Values

In the preceding sections, you saw how to get a value out of an Optional object. Another useful strategy is to keep the Optional intact. You can transform the value inside an Optional by using the map method:

```
Optional<String> transformed = optionalString.map(String::toUpperCase);
```

If optionalString is empty, then transformed is also empty.

Here is another example. We add a result to a list if it is present:

```
optionalValue.map(results::add);
```

If optionalValue is empty, nothing happens.

 NOTE: This map method is the analog of the map method of the Stream interface that you have seen in Section 1.3, "The filter, map, and flatMap Methods," on p. 11. Simply imagine an optional value as a stream of size zero or one. The result again has size zero or one, and in the latter case, the function has been applied.

Similarly, you can use the filter method to only consider Optional values that fulfill a certain property before or after transforming it. If the property is not fulfilled, the pipeline yields an empty result:

```
Optional<String> transformed = optionalString
    .filter(s -> s.length() >= 8)
    .map(String::toUpperCase);
```

You can substitute an alternative Optional for an empty Optional with the or method. The alternative is computed lazily.

```
Optional<String> result = optionalString.or(() -> // Supply an Optional
    alternatives.stream().findFirst());
```

If optionalString has a value, then result is optionalString. If not, the lambda expression is evaluated, and its result is used.

---

java.util.Optional 8

- `<U> Optional<U> map(Function<? super T,? extends U> mapper)`

  yields an Optional whose value is obtained by applying the given function to the value of this Optional if present, or an empty Optional otherwise.

- `Optional<T> filter(Predicate<? super T> predicate)`

  yields an Optional with the value of this Optional if it fulfills the given predicate, or an empty Optional otherwise.

- `Optional<T> or(Supplier<? extends Optional<? extends T>> supplier)` 9

  yields this Optional if it is nonempty, or the one produced by the supplier otherwise.

1.7.4 How Not to Work with Optional Values

If you don't use Optional values correctly, you have no benefit over the "something or null" approach of the past.

The get method gets the wrapped element of an Optional value if it exists, or throws a NoSuchElementException if it doesn't. Therefore,

```
Optional<T> optionalValue = . . .;
optionalValue.get().someMethod()
```

is no safer than

```
T value = . . .;
value.someMethod();
```

The isPresent method reports whether an Optional<T> object has a value. But

```
if (optionalValue.isPresent()) optionalValue.get().someMethod();
```

is no easier than

```
if (value != null) value.someMethod();
```

 NOTE: Java 10 introduces a scarier-sounding synonym for the get method. Call optionalValue.orElseThrow() to make explicit that the method will throw a NoSuchElementException if the optionalValue is empty. The hope is that programmers will only call that method when it is absolutely clear that the Optional is never empty.

Here are a few more tips for the proper use of the Optional type:

- A variable of type Optional should *never* be null.
- Don't use fields of type Optional. The cost is an additional object. Inside a class, using null for an absent field is manageable.
- Don't put Optional objects in a set, and don't use them as keys for a map. Collect the values instead.

---

java.util.Optional 8

- T get()
- T orElseThrow() 10

  yields the value of this Optional, or throws a NoSuchElementException if it is empty.

- boolean isPresent()

  returns true if this Optional is not empty.

1.7.5 Creating Optional Values

So far, we have discussed how to consume an Optional object someone else created. If you want to write a method that creates an Optional object, there are several static methods for that purpose, including Optional.of(result) and Optional.empty(). For example,

```
public static Optional<Double> inverse(Double x)
{
   return x == 0 ? Optional.empty() : Optional.of(1 / x);
}
```

The ofNullable method is intended as a bridge from possibly null values to optional values. Optional.ofNullable(obj) returns Optional.of(obj) if obj is not null and Optional.empty() otherwise.

---

java.util.Optional 8

- static <T> Optional<T> of(T value)
- static <T> Optional<T> ofNullable(T value)

  yields an Optional with the given value. If value is null, the first method throws a NullPointerException and the second method yields an empty Optional.

- static <T> Optional<T> empty()

  yields an empty Optional.

1.7.6 Composing Optional Value Functions with flatMap

Suppose you have a method f yielding an Optional<T>, and the target type T has a method g yielding an Optional<U>. If they were normal methods, you could compose them by calling s.f().g(). But that composition doesn't work since s.f() has type Optional<T>, not T. Instead, call

```
Optional<U> result = s.f().flatMap(T::g);
```

If s.f() is present, then g is applied to it. Otherwise, an empty Optional<U> is returned.

Clearly, you can repeat that process if you have more methods or lambdas that yield Optional values. You can then build a pipeline of steps, simply by chaining calls to flatMap, that will succeed only when all parts do.

For example, consider the safe inverse method of the preceding section. Suppose we also have a safe square root:

```
public static Optional<Double> squareRoot(Double x)
{
   return x < 0 ? Optional.empty() : Optional.of(Math.sqrt(x));
}
```

Then you can compute the square root of the inverse as

```
Optional<Double> result = inverse(x).flatMap(MyMath::squareRoot);
```

or, if you prefer,

```
Optional<Double> result
   = Optional.of(-4.0).flatMap(Demo::inverse).flatMap(Demo::squareRoot);
```

If either the inverse method or the squareRoot returns Optional.empty(), the result is empty.

 NOTE: You have already seen a flatMap method in the Stream interface (see Section 1.3, "The filter, map, and flatMap Methods," on p. 11). That method was used to compose two methods that yield streams, by flattening out the resulting stream of streams. The Optional.flatMap method works in the same way if you interpret an optional value as having zero or one element.

`java.util.Optional` 8

- `<U> Optional<U> flatMap(Function<? super T,? extends Optional<? extends U>> mapper)`

  yields the result of applying mapper to the value in this Optional if present, or an empty optional otherwise.

1.7.7 Turning an Optional into a Stream

The stream method turns an Optional<T> into a Stream<T> with zero or one element. Sure, why not, but why would you ever want that?

This becomes useful with methods that return an Optional result. Suppose you have a stream of user IDs and a method

```
Optional<User> lookup(String id)
```

How do you get a stream of users, skipping those IDs that are invalid?

Of course, you can filter out the invalid IDs and then apply get to the remaining ones:

```
Stream<String> ids = . . .;
Stream<User> users = ids.map(Users::lookup)
    .filter(Optional::isPresent)
    .map(Optional::get);
```

But that uses the isPresent and get methods that we warned about. It is more elegant to call

```
Stream<User> users = ids.map(Users::lookup)
    .flatMap(Optional::stream);
```

Each call to stream returns a stream with zero or one element. The flatMap method combines them all. That means the nonexistent users are simply dropped.

NOTE: In this section, we consider the happy scenario in which we have a method that returns an `Optional` value. These days, many methods return `null` when there is no valid result. Suppose `Users.classicLookup(id)` returns a `User` object or `null`, not an `Optional<User>`. Then you can of course filter out the `null` values:

```
Stream<User> users = ids.map(Users::classicLookup)
    .filter(Objects::nonNull);
```

But if you prefer the `flatMap` approach, you can use

```
Stream<User> users = ids.flatMap(
    id -> Stream.ofNullable(Users.classicLookup(id)));
```

or

```
Stream<User> users = ids.map(Users::classicLookup)
    .flatMap(Stream::ofNullable);
```

The call `Stream.ofNullable(obj)` yields an empty stream if `obj` is `null` or a stream just containing `obj` otherwise.

The example program in Listing 1.3 demonstrates the `Optional` API.

Listing 1.3 `optional/OptionalTest.java`

```
1  package optional;
2
3  /**
4   * @version 1.01 2018-05-01
5   * @author Cay Horstmann
6   */
7
8  import java.io.*;
9  import java.nio.charset.*;
10 import java.nio.file.*;
11 import java.util.*;
12
13 public class OptionalTest
14 {
15    public static void main(String[] args) throws IOException
16    {
17       var contents = new String(Files.readAllBytes(
18          Paths.get("../gutenberg/alice30.txt")), StandardCharsets.UTF_8);
19       List<String> wordList = List.of(contents.split("\\PL+"));
20
21       Optional<String> optionalValue = wordList.stream()
22          .filter(s -> s.contains("fred"))
23          .findFirst();
```

(Continues)

Listing 1.3 *(Continued)*

```
24        System.out.println(optionalValue.orElse("No word") + " contains fred");
25
26        Optional<String> optionalString = Optional.empty();
27        String result = optionalString.orElse("N/A");
28        System.out.println("result: " + result);
29        result = optionalString.orElseGet(() -> Locale.getDefault().getDisplayName());
30        System.out.println("result: " + result);
31        try
32        {
33           result = optionalString.orElseThrow(IllegalStateException::new);
34           System.out.println("result: " + result);
35        }
36        catch (Throwable t)
37        {
38           t.printStackTrace();
39        }
40
41        optionalValue = wordList.stream()
42           .filter(s -> s.contains("red"))
43           .findFirst();
44        optionalValue.ifPresent(s -> System.out.println(s + " contains red"));
45
46        var results = new HashSet<String>();
47        optionalValue.ifPresent(results::add);
48        Optional<Boolean> added = optionalValue.map(results::add);
49        System.out.println(added);
50
51        System.out.println(inverse(4.0).flatMap(OptionalTest::squareRoot));
52        System.out.println(inverse(-1.0).flatMap(OptionalTest::squareRoot));
53        System.out.println(inverse(0.0).flatMap(OptionalTest::squareRoot));
54        Optional<Double> result2 = Optional.of(-4.0)
55           .flatMap(OptionalTest::inverse).flatMap(OptionalTest::squareRoot);
56        System.out.println(result2);
57     }
58
59     public static Optional<Double> inverse(Double x)
60     {
61        return x == 0 ? Optional.empty() : Optional.of(1 / x);
62     }
63
64     public static Optional<Double> squareRoot(Double x)
65     {
66        return x < 0 ? Optional.empty() : Optional.of(Math.sqrt(x));
67     }
68  }
```

> **java.util.Optional 8**
>
> - `<U> Optional<U> flatMap(Function<? super T,Optional<U>> mapper)` 9
>
>   yields the result of applying `mapper` to the value of this `Optional`, or an empty `Optional` if this `Optional` is empty.

1.8 Collecting Results

When you are done with a stream, you will often want to look at the results. You can call the `iterator` method, which yields an old-fashioned iterator that you can use to visit the elements.

Alternatively, you can call the `forEach` method to apply a function to each element:

```
stream.forEach(System.out::println);
```

On a parallel stream, the `forEach` method traverses elements in arbitrary order. If you want to process them in stream order, call `forEachOrdered` instead. Of course, you might then give up some or all of the benefits of parallelism.

But more often than not, you will want to collect the result in a data structure. Call `toArray` to get an array of the stream elements.

Since it is not possible to create a generic array at runtime, the expression `stream.toArray()` returns an `Object[]` array. If you want an array of the correct type, pass in the array constructor:

```
String[] result = stream.toArray(String[]::new);
   // stream.toArray() has type Object[]
```

For collecting stream elements to another target, there is a convenient `collect` method that takes an instance of the `Collector` interface. A *collector* is an object that accumulates elements and produces a result. The `Collectors` class provides a large number of factory methods for common collectors. To collect stream elements into a list, use the collector produced by `Collectors.toList()`:

```
List<String> result = stream.collect(Collectors.toList());
```

Similarly, here is how you can collect stream elements into a set:

```
Set<String> result = stream.collect(Collectors.toSet());
```

If you want to control which kind of set you get, use the following call instead:

```
TreeSet<String> result = stream.collect(Collectors.toCollection(TreeSet::new));
```

Suppose you want to collect all strings in a stream by concatenating them. You can call

```
String result = stream.collect(Collectors.joining());
```

If you want a delimiter between elements, pass it to the joining method:

```
String result = stream.collect(Collectors.joining(", "));
```

If your stream contains objects other than strings, you need to first convert them to strings, like this:

```
String result = stream.map(Object::toString).collect(Collectors.joining(", "));
```

If you want to reduce the stream results to a sum, count, average, maximum, or minimum, use one of the summarizing(Int|Long|Double) methods. These methods take a function that maps the stream objects to numbers and yield a result of type (Int|Long|Double)SummaryStatistics, simultaneously computing the sum, count, average, maximum, and minimum.

```
IntSummaryStatistics summary = stream.collect(
   Collectors.summarizingInt(String::length));
double averageWordLength = summary.getAverage();
double maxWordLength = summary.getMax();
```

The example program in Listing 1.4 shows how to collect elements from a stream.

Listing 1.4 collecting/CollectingResults.java

```
1  package collecting;
2
3  /**
4   * @version 1.01 2018-05-01
5   * @author Cay Horstmann
6   */
7
8  import java.io.*;
9  import java.nio.charset.*;
10 import java.nio.file.*;
11 import java.util.*;
12 import java.util.stream.*;
13
14 public class CollectingResults
15 {
```

```
16    public static Stream<String> noVowels() throws IOException
17    {
18       var contents = new String(Files.readAllBytes(
19          Paths.get("../gutenberg/alice30.txt")),
20          StandardCharsets.UTF_8);
21       List<String> wordList = List.of(contents.split("\\PL+"));
22       Stream<String> words = wordList.stream();
23       return words.map(s -> s.replaceAll("[aeiouAEIOU]", ""));
24    }
25
26    public static <T> void show(String label, Set<T> set)
27    {
28       System.out.print(label + ": " + set.getClass().getName());
29       System.out.println("["
30          + set.stream().limit(10).map(Object::toString).collect(Collectors.joining(", "))
31          + "]");
32    }
33
34    public static void main(String[] args) throws IOException
35    {
36       Iterator<Integer> iter = Stream.iterate(0, n -> n + 1).limit(10).iterator();
37       while (iter.hasNext())
38          System.out.println(iter.next());
39
40       Object[] numbers = Stream.iterate(0, n -> n + 1).limit(10).toArray();
41       System.out.println("Object array:" + numbers);
42          // Note it's an Object[] array
43
44       try
45       {
46          var number = (Integer) numbers[0]; // OK
47          System.out.println("number: " + number);
48          System.out.println("The following statement throws an exception:");
49          var numbers2 = (Integer[]) numbers; // Throws exception
50       }
51       catch (ClassCastException ex)
52       {
53          System.out.println(ex);
54       }
55
56       Integer[] numbers3 = Stream.iterate(0, n -> n + 1)
57          .limit(10)
58          .toArray(Integer[]::new);
59       System.out.println("Integer array: " + numbers3);
60          // Note it's an Integer[] array
61
```

(Continues)

Listing 1.4 *(Continued)*

```
62      Set<String> noVowelSet = noVowels().collect(Collectors.toSet());
63      show("noVowelSet", noVowelSet);
64
65      TreeSet<String> noVowelTreeSet = noVowels().collect(
66          Collectors.toCollection(TreeSet::new));
67      show("noVowelTreeSet", noVowelTreeSet);
68
69      String result = noVowels().limit(10).collect(Collectors.joining());
70      System.out.println("Joining: " + result);
71      result = noVowels().limit(10)
72          .collect(Collectors.joining(", "));
73      System.out.println("Joining with commas: " + result);
74
75      IntSummaryStatistics summary = noVowels().collect(
76          Collectors.summarizingInt(String::length));
77      double averageWordLength = summary.getAverage();
78      double maxWordLength = summary.getMax();
79      System.out.println("Average word length: " + averageWordLength);
80      System.out.println("Max word length: " + maxWordLength);
81      System.out.println("forEach:");
82      noVowels().limit(10).forEach(System.out::println);
83    }
84 }
```

---

java.util.stream.BaseStream 8

- `Iterator<T> iterator()`

  yields an iterator for obtaining the elements of this stream. This is a terminal operation.

---

java.util.stream.Stream 8

- `void forEach(Consumer<? super T> action)`

  invokes action on each element of the stream. This is a terminal operation.
- `Object[] toArray()`
- `<A> A[] toArray(IntFunction<A[]> generator)`

  yields an array of objects, or of type A when passed a constructor reference A[]::new. These are terminal operations.
- `<R,A> R collect(Collector<? super T,A,R> collector)`

  collects the elements in this stream, using the given collector. The Collectors class has factory methods for many collectors.

---

java.util.stream.Collectors 8

- static <T> Collector<T,?,List<T>> toList()
- static <T> Collector<T,?,List<T>> toUnmodifiableList() 10
- static <T> Collector<T,?,Set<T>> toSet()
- static <T> Collector<T,?,Set<T>> toUnmodifiableSet() 10

  yield collectors that collect elements in a list or set.

- static <T,C extends Collection<T>> Collector<T,?,C> toCollection(Supplier<C> collectionFactory)

  yields a collector that collects elements into an arbitrary collection. Pass a constructor reference such as TreeSet::new.

- static Collector<CharSequence,?,String> joining()
- static Collector<CharSequence,?,String> joining(CharSequence delimiter)
- static Collector<CharSequence,?,String> joining(CharSequence delimiter, CharSequence prefix, CharSequence suffix)

  yields a collector that joins strings. The delimiter is placed between strings, and the prefix and suffix before the first and after the last string. When not specified, these are empty.

- static <T> Collector<T,?,IntSummaryStatistics> summarizingInt(ToIntFunction<? super T> mapper)
- static <T> Collector<T,?,LongSummaryStatistics> summarizingLong(ToLongFunction<? super T> mapper)
- static <T> Collector<T,?,DoubleSummaryStatistics> summarizingDouble(ToDoubleFunction<? super T> mapper)

  yields collectors that produce an (Int|Long|Double)SummaryStatistics object, from which you can obtain the count, sum, average, maximum, and minimum of the results of applying mapper to each element.

IntSummaryStatistics 8
LongSummaryStatistics 8
DoubleSummaryStatistics 8

- long getCount()

  yields the count of the summarized elements.

- (int|long|double) getSum()
- double getAverage()

  yields the sum or average of the summarized elements, or zero if there are no elements.

(Continues)

DoubleSummaryStatistics 8 *(Continued)*

- (int | long | double) getMax()
- (int | long | double) getMin()

  yields the maximum or minimum of the summarized elements, or (Integer | Long | Double).(MAX | MIN)_VALUE if there are no elements.

1.9 Collecting into Maps

Suppose you have a Stream<Person> and want to collect the elements into a map so that later you can look up people by their ID. The Collectors.toMap method has two function arguments that produce the map's keys and values. For example,

```
Map<Integer, String> idToName = people.collect(
   Collectors.toMap(Person::getId, Person::getName));
```

In the common case when the values should be the actual elements, use Function.identity() for the second function.

```
Map<Integer, Person> idToPerson = people.collect(
   Collectors.toMap(Person::getId, Function.identity()));
```

If there is more than one element with the same key, there is a conflict, and the collector will throw an IllegalStateException. You can override that behavior by supplying a third function argument that resolves the conflict and determines the value for the key, given the existing and the new value. Your function could return the existing value, the new value, or a combination of them.

Here, we construct a map that contains, for each language in the available locales, as key its name in your default locale (such as "German"), and as value its localized name (such as "Deutsch").

```
Stream<Locale> locales = Stream.of(Locale.getAvailableLocales());
Map<String, String> languageNames = locales.collect(
   Collectors.toMap(
      Locale::getDisplayLanguage,
      loc -> loc.getDisplayLanguage(loc),
      (existingValue, newValue) -> existingValue));
```

We don't care that the same language might occur twice (for example, German in Germany and in Switzerland), so we just keep the first entry.

NOTE: In this chapter, I use the Locale class as a source of an interesting data set. See Chapter 7 for more information on working with locales.

Now suppose we want to know all languages in a given country. Then we need a Map<String, Set<String>>. For example, the value for "Switzerland" is the set [French, German, Italian]. At first, we store a singleton set for each language. Whenever a new language is found for a given country, we form the union of the existing and the new set.

```
Map<String, Set<String>> countryLanguageSets = locales.collect(
   Collectors.toMap(
      Locale::getDisplayCountry,
      l -> Collections.singleton(l.getDisplayLanguage()),
      (a, b) -> { // Union of a and b
         var union = new HashSet<String>(a);
         union.addAll(b);
         return union; }));
```

You will see a simpler way of obtaining this map in the next section.

If you want a TreeMap, supply the constructor as the fourth argument. You must provide a merge function. Here is one of the examples from the beginning of the section, now yielding a TreeMap:

```
Map<Integer, Person> idToPerson = people.collect(
   Collectors.toMap(
      Person::getId,
      Function.identity(),
      (existingValue, newValue) -> { throw new IllegalStateException(); },
      TreeMap::new));
```

NOTE: For each of the toMap methods, there is an equivalent toConcurrentMap method that yields a concurrent map. A single concurrent map is used in the parallel collection process. When used with a parallel stream, a shared map is more efficient than merging maps. Note that elements are no longer collected in stream order, but that doesn't usually make a difference.

The program in Listing 1.5 gives examples of collecting stream results into maps.

Listing 1.5 collecting/CollectingIntoMaps.java

```
1  package collecting;
2
3  /**
4   * @version 1.00 2016-05-10
5   * @author Cay Horstmann
6   */
7
8  import java.io.*;
9  import java.util.*;
10 import java.util.function.*;
11 import java.util.stream.*;
12
13 public class CollectingIntoMaps
14 {
15
16    public static class Person
17    {
18       private int id;
19       private String name;
20
21       public Person(int id, String name)
22       {
23          this.id = id;
24          this.name = name;
25       }
26
27       public int getId()
28       {
29          return id;
30       }
31
32       public String getName()
33       {
34          return name;
35       }
36
37       public String toString()
38       {
39          return getClass().getName() + "[id=" + id + ",name=" + name + "]";
40       }
41    }
42
```

```
43  public static Stream<Person> people()
44  {
45     return Stream.of(new Person(1001, "Peter"), new Person(1002, "Paul"),
46        new Person(1003, "Mary")));
47  }
48
49  public static void main(String[] args) throws IOException
50  {
51     Map<Integer, String> idToName = people().collect(
52        Collectors.toMap(Person::getId, Person::getName));
53     System.out.println("idToName: " + idToName);
54
55     Map<Integer, Person> idToPerson = people().collect(
56        Collectors.toMap(Person::getId, Function.identity()));
57     System.out.println("idToPerson: " + idToPerson.getClass().getName()
58        + idToPerson);
59
60     idToPerson = people().collect(
61        Collectors.toMap(Person::getId, Function.identity(),
62           (existingValue, newValue) -> { throw new IllegalStateException(); },
63           TreeMap::new));
64     System.out.println("idToPerson: " + idToPerson.getClass().getName()
65        + idToPerson);
66
67     Stream<Locale> locales = Stream.of(Locale.getAvailableLocales());
68     Map<String, String> languageNames = locales.collect(
69        Collectors.toMap(
70           Locale::getDisplayLanguage,
71           l -> l.getDisplayLanguage(l),
72           (existingValue, newValue) -> existingValue));
73     System.out.println("languageNames: " + languageNames);
74
75     locales = Stream.of(Locale.getAvailableLocales());
76     Map<String, Set<String>> countryLanguageSets = locales.collect(
77        Collectors.toMap(
78           Locale::getDisplayCountry,
79           l -> Set.of(l.getDisplayLanguage()),
80           (a, b) ->
81           { // union of a and b
82              Set<String> union = new HashSet<>(a);
83              union.addAll(b);
84              return union;
85           }));
86     System.out.println("countryLanguageSets: " + countryLanguageSets);
87  }
88 }
```

`java.util.stream.Collectors` 8

- `static <T,K,U> Collector<T,?,Map<K,U>> toMap(Function<? super T,? extends K> keyMapper, Function<? super T,? extends U> valueMapper)`
- `static <T,K,U> Collector<T,?,Map<K,U>> toMap(Function<? super T,? extends K> keyMapper, Function<? super T,? extends U> valueMapper, BinaryOperator<U> mergeFunction)`
- `static <T,K,U,M extends Map<K,U>> Collector<T,?,M> toMap(Function<? super T,? extends K> keyMapper, Function<? super T,? extends U> valueMapper, BinaryOperator<U> mergeFunction, Supplier<M> mapSupplier)`
- `static <T,K,U> Collector<T,?,Map<K,U>> toUnmodifiableMap(Function<? super T,? extends K> keyMapper, Function<? super T,? extends U> valueMapper)` 10
- `static <T,K,U> Collector<T,?,Map<K,U>> toUnmodifiableMap(Function<? super T,? extends K> keyMapper, Function<? super T,? extends U> valueMapper, BinaryOperator<U> mergeFunction)` 10
- `static <T,K,U> Collector<T,?,ConcurrentMap<K,U>> toConcurrentMap(Function<? super T,? extends K> keyMapper, Function<? super T,? extends U> valueMapper)`
- `static <T,K,U> Collector<T,?,ConcurrentMap<K,U>> toConcurrentMap(Function<? super T,? extends K> keyMapper, Function<? super T,? extends U> valueMapper, BinaryOperator<U> mergeFunction)`
- `static <T,K,U,M extends ConcurrentMap<K,U>> Collector<T,?,M> toConcurrentMap(Function<? super T,? extends K> keyMapper, Function<? super T,? extends U> valueMapper, BinaryOperator<U> mergeFunction, Supplier<M> mapSupplier)`

yields a collector that produces a map, unmodifiable map, or concurrent map. The `keyMapper` and `valueMapper` functions are applied to each collected element, yielding a key/value entry of the resulting map. By default, an `IllegalStateException` is thrown when two elements give rise to the same key. You can instead supply a `mergeFunction` that merges values with the same key. By default, the result is a `HashMap` or `ConcurrentHashMap`. You can instead supply a `mapSupplier` that yields the desired map instance.

1.10 Grouping and Partitioning

In the preceding section, you saw how to collect all languages in a given country. But the process was a bit tedious. You had to generate a singleton set for each map value and then specify how to merge the existing and new values. Forming groups of values with the same characteristic is very common, so the `groupingBy` method supports it directly.

Let's look at the problem of grouping locales by country. First, form this map:

```
Map<String, List<Locale>> countryToLocales = locales.collect(
    Collectors.groupingBy(Locale::getCountry));
```

The function `Locale::getCountry` is the *classifier function* of the grouping. You can now look up all locales for a given country code, for example

```
List<Locale> swissLocales = countryToLocales.get("CH");
    // Yields locales de_CH, fr_CH, it_CH and maybe more
```

NOTE: A quick refresher on locales: Each locale has a language code (such as en for English) and a country code (such as US for the United States). The locale en_US describes English in the United States, and en_IE is English in Ireland. Some countries have multiple locales. For example, ga_IE is Gaelic in Ireland, and, as the preceding example shows, the JDK knows at least three locales in Switzerland.

When the classifier function is a predicate function (that is, a function returning a `boolean` value), the stream elements are partitioned into two lists: those where the function returns `true` and the complement. In this case, it is more efficient to use `partitioningBy` instead of `groupingBy`. For example, here we split all locales into those that use English and all others:

```
Map<Boolean, List<Locale>> englishAndOtherLocales = locales.collect(
    Collectors.partitioningBy(l -> l.getLanguage().equals("en")));
List<Locale> englishLocales = englishAndOtherLocales.get(true);
```

NOTE: If you call the `groupingByConcurrent` method, you get a concurrent map that, when used with a parallel stream, is concurrently populated. This is entirely analogous to the `toConcurrentMap` method.

---

java.util.stream.Collectors 8

- static <T,K> Collector<T,?,Map<K,List<T>>> groupingBy(Function<? super T,? extends K> classifier)
- static <T,K> Collector<T,?,ConcurrentMap<K,List<T>>> groupingByConcurrent(Function<? super T,? extends K> classifier)

  yields a collector that produces a map or concurrent map whose keys are the results of applying classifier to all collected elements, and whose values are lists of elements with the same key.

- static <T> Collector<T,?,Map<Boolean,List<T>>> partitioningBy(Predicate<? super T> predicate)

  yields a collector that produces a map whose keys are true/false, and whose values are lists of the elements that fulfill/do not fulfill the predicate.

1.11 Downstream Collectors

The `groupingBy` method yields a map whose values are lists. If you want to process those lists in some way, supply a *downstream collector*. For example, if you want sets instead of lists, you can use the `Collectors.toSet` collector that you saw in the preceding section:

```
Map<String, Set<Locale>> countryToLocaleSet = locales.collect(
    groupingBy(Locale::getCountry, toSet()));
```

 NOTE: In this example, as well as the remaining examples of this section, I assume a static import of `java.util.stream.Collectors.*` to make the expressions easier to read.

Several collectors are provided for reducing collected elements to numbers:

- `counting` produces a count of the collected elements. For example,

  ```
  Map<String, Long> countryToLocaleCounts = locales.collect(
      groupingBy(Locale::getCountry, counting()));
  ```

  counts how many locales there are for each country.

- `summing(Int|Long|Double)` takes a function argument, applies the function to the downstream elements, and produces their sum. For example,

  ```
  Map<String, Integer> stateToCityPopulation = cities.collect(
      groupingBy(City::getState, summingInt(City::getPopulation)));
  ```

  computes the sum of populations per state in a stream of cities.

- `maxBy` and `minBy` take a comparator and produce maximum and minimum of the downstream elements. For example,

  ```
  Map<String, Optional<City>> stateToLargestCity = cities.collect(
      groupingBy(City::getState,
          maxBy(Comparator.comparing(City::getPopulation))));
  ```

  produces the largest city per state.

The `collectingAndThen` collector adds a final processing step behind a collector. For example, if you want to know how many distinct results there are, collect them into a set and then compute the size:

```
Map<Character, Integer> stringCountsByStartingLetter = strings.collect(
    groupingBy(s -> s.charAt(0),
        collectingAndThen(toSet(), Set::size)));
```

The mapping collector does the opposite. It applies a function to each collected element and passes the results to a downstream collector.

```
Map<Character, Set<Integer>> stringLengthsByStartingLetter = strings.collect(
   groupingBy(s -> s.charAt(0),
      mapping(String::length, toSet())));
```

Here, we group strings by their first character. Within each group, we produce the lengths and collect them in a set.

The mapping method also yields a nicer solution to a problem from the preceding section—gathering a set of all languages in a country.

```
Map<String, Set<String>> countryToLanguages = locales.collect(
   groupingBy(Locale::getDisplayCountry,
      mapping(Locale::getDisplayLanguage,
         toSet())));
```

There is a flatMapping method as well, for use with functions that return streams.

If the grouping or mapping function has return type int, long, or double, you can collect elements into a summary statistics object, as discussed in Section 1.8, "Collecting Results," on p. 25. For example,

```
Map<String, IntSummaryStatistics> stateToCityPopulationSummary = cities.collect(
   groupingBy(City::getState,
      summarizingInt(City::getPopulation)));
```

Then you can get the sum, count, average, minimum, and maximum of the function values from the summary statistics objects of each group.

The filtering collector applies a filter to each group, for example:

```
Map<String, Set<City>> largeCitiesByState
   = cities.collect(
      groupingBy(City::getState,
         filtering(c -> c.getPopulation() > 500000,
            toSet()))); // States without large cities have empty sets
```

 NOTE: There are also three versions of a reducing method that apply general reductions, as described in the next section.

Composing collectors is powerful, but it can lead to very convoluted expressions. The best use is with groupingBy or partitioningBy to process the "downstream" map values. Otherwise, simply apply methods such as map, reduce, count, max, or min directly on streams.

The example program in Listing 1.6 demonstrates downstream collectors.

Listing 1.6 collecting/DownstreamCollectors.java

```
1  package collecting;
2
3  /**
4   * @version 1.00 2016-05-10
5   * @author Cay Horstmann
6   */
7
8  import static java.util.stream.Collectors.*;
9
10 import java.io.*;
11 import java.nio.file.*;
12 import java.util.*;
13 import java.util.stream.*;
14
15 public class DownstreamCollectors
16 {
17
18    public static class City
19    {
20       private String name;
21       private String state;
22       private int population;
23
24       public City(String name, String state, int population)
25       {
26          this.name = name;
27          this.state = state;
28          this.population = population;
29       }
30
31       public String getName()
32       {
33          return name;
34       }
35
36       public String getState()
37       {
38          return state;
39       }
40
41       public int getPopulation()
42       {
43          return population;
44       }
45    }
46
47    public static Stream<City> readCities(String filename) throws IOException
48    {
```

```
49    return Files.lines(Paths.get(filename))
50       .map(l -> l.split(", "))
51       .map(a -> new City(a[0], a[1], Integer.parseInt(a[2])));
52 }
53
54 public static void main(String[] args) throws IOException
55 {
56    Stream<Locale> locales = Stream.of(Locale.getAvailableLocales());
57    locales = Stream.of(Locale.getAvailableLocales());
58    Map<String, Set<Locale>> countryToLocaleSet = locales.collect(groupingBy(
59       Locale::getCountry, toSet()));
60    System.out.println("countryToLocaleSet: " + countryToLocaleSet);
61
62    locales = Stream.of(Locale.getAvailableLocales());
63    Map<String, Long> countryToLocaleCounts = locales.collect(groupingBy(
64       Locale::getCountry, counting()));
65    System.out.println("countryToLocaleCounts: " + countryToLocaleCounts);
66
67    Stream<City> cities = readCities("cities.txt");
68    Map<String, Integer> stateToCityPopulation = cities.collect(groupingBy(
69       City::getState, summingInt(City::getPopulation)));
70    System.out.println("stateToCityPopulation: " + stateToCityPopulation);
71
72    cities = readCities("cities.txt");
73    Map<String, Optional<String>> stateToLongestCityName = cities
74       .collect(groupingBy(City::getState,
75          mapping(City::getName, maxBy(Comparator.comparing(String::length)))));
76    System.out.println("stateToLongestCityName: " + stateToLongestCityName);
77
78    locales = Stream.of(Locale.getAvailableLocales());
79    Map<String, Set<String>> countryToLanguages = locales.collect(groupingBy(
80       Locale::getDisplayCountry, mapping(Locale::getDisplayLanguage, toSet())));
81    System.out.println("countryToLanguages: " + countryToLanguages);
82
83    cities = readCities("cities.txt");
84    Map<String, IntSummaryStatistics> stateToCityPopulationSummary = cities
85       .collect(groupingBy(City::getState, summarizingInt(City::getPopulation)));
86    System.out.println(stateToCityPopulationSummary.get("NY"));
87
88    cities = readCities("cities.txt");
89    Map<String, String> stateToCityNames = cities.collect(groupingBy(
90       City::getState,
91       reducing("", City::getName, (s, t) -> s.length() == 0 ? t : s + ", " + t)));
92
93    cities = readCities("cities.txt");
94    stateToCityNames = cities.collect(groupingBy(City::getState,
95       mapping(City::getName, joining(", "))));
96    System.out.println("stateToCityNames: " + stateToCityNames);
97 }
98 }
```

`java.util.stream.Collectors` 8

- `public static <T,K,A,D> Collector<T,?,Map<K,D>> groupingBy(Function<? super T,? extends K> classifier, Collector<? super T,A,D> downstream)`

  yields a collector that produces a map. The keys are the results of applying classifier to all collected elements. The values are the results of collecting elements with the same key, using the downstream collector.

- `static <T> Collector<T,?,Long> counting()`

  yields a collector that counts the collected elements.

- `static <T> Collector<T,?,Integer> summingInt(ToIntFunction<? super T> mapper)`
- `static <T> Collector<T,?,Long> summingLong(ToLongFunction<? super T> mapper)`
- `static <T> Collector<T,?,Double> summingDouble(ToDoubleFunction<? super T> mapper)`

  yields a collector that computes the sum of the results of applying mapper to the collected elements.

- `static <T> Collector<T,?,Optional<T>> maxBy(Comparator<? super T> comparator)`
- `static <T> Collector<T,?,Optional<T>> minBy(Comparator<? super T> comparator)`

  yields a collector that computes the maximum or minimum of the collected elements, using the ordering specified by comparator.

- `static <T,A,R,RR> Collector<T,A,RR> collectingAndThen(Collector<T,A,R> downstream, Function<R,RR> finisher)`

  yields a collector that sends elements to the downstream collector and then applies the finisher function to its result.

- `static <T,U,A,R> Collector<T,?,R> mapping(Function<? super T,? extends U> mapper, Collector<? super U,A,R> downstream)`

  yields a collector that calls mapper on each element and passes the results to the downstream collector.

- `static <T,U,A,R> Collector<T,?,R> flatMapping(Function<? super T,? extends Stream<? extends U>> mapper, Collector<? super U,A,R> downstream)`

  yields a collector that calls mapper on each element and passes the elements of the results to the downstream collector.

- `static <T,A,R> Collector<T,?,R> filtering(Predicate<? super T> predicate, Collector<? super T,A,R> downstream)`

  yields a collector that passes the elements fulfilling the predicate to the downstream collector.

1.12 Reduction Operations

The reduce method is a general mechanism for computing a value from a stream. The simplest form takes a binary function and keeps applying it, starting with the first two elements. It's easy to explain this if the function is the sum:

```
List<Integer> values = . . .;
Optional<Integer> sum = values.stream().reduce((x, y) -> x + y);
```

In this case, the reduce method computes $v_0 + v_1 + v_2 + \ldots$, where v_i are the stream elements. The method returns an Optional because there is no valid result if the stream is empty.

 NOTE: In this case, you can write reduce(Integer::sum) instead of reduce((x, y) -> x + y).

More generally, you can use any operation that combines a partial result x with the next value y to yield a new partial result.

Here is another way of looking at reductions. Given a reduction operation *op*, the reduction yields $v_0 \; op \; v_1 \; op \; v_2 \; op \; \ldots$, where $v_i \; op \; v_{i+1}$ denotes the function call $op(v_i, v_{i+1})$. There are many operations that might be useful in practice—such as sum, product, string concatenation, maximum and minimum, set union or intersection.

If you want to use reduction with parallel streams, the operation must be *associative*: It shouldn't matter in which order you combine the elements. In math notation, $(x \; op \; y) \; op \; z$ must be equal to $x \; op \; (y \; op \; z)$. An example of an operation that is not associative is subtraction. For example, $(6 - 3) - 2 \neq 6 - (3 - 2)$.

Often, there is an *identity e* such that $e \; op \; x = x$, and that element can be used as the start of the computation. For example, 0 is the identity for addition, and you can use the second form of reduce:

```
List<Integer> values = . . .;
Integer sum = values.stream().reduce(0, (x, y) -> x + y);
    // Computes 0 + v₀ + v₁ + v₂ + . . .
```

The identity value is returned if the stream is empty, and you no longer need to deal with the Optional class.

Now suppose you have a stream of objects and want to form the sum of some property, such as lengths in a stream of strings. You can't use the simple form of reduce. It requires a function (T, T) -> T, with the same types for the arguments and the result, but in this situation you have two types: The stream elements have type String, and the accumulated result is an integer. There is a form of reduce that can deal with this situation.

First, you supply an "accumulator" function (total, word) -> total + word.length(). That function is called repeatedly, forming the cumulative total. But when the computation is parallelized, there will be multiple computations of this kind, and you need to combine their results. You supply a second function for that purpose. The complete call is

```
int result = words.reduce(0,
    (total, word) -> total + word.length(),
    (total1, total2) -> total1 + total2);
```

 NOTE: In practice, you probably won't use the reduce method a lot. It is usually easier to map to a stream of numbers and use one of its methods to compute sum, maximum, or minimum. (We discuss streams of numbers in Section 1.13, "Primitive Type Streams," on p. 43.) In this particular example, you could have called words.mapToInt(String::length).sum(), which is both simpler and more efficient since it doesn't involve boxing.

 NOTE: There are times when reduce is not general enough. For example, suppose you want to collect the results in a BitSet. If the collection is parallelized, you can't put the elements directly into a single BitSet because a BitSet object is not thread-safe. For that reason, you can't use reduce. Each segment needs to start out with its own empty set, and reduce only lets you supply one identity value. Instead, use collect. It takes three arguments:

1. A *supplier* to make new instances of the target object—for example, a constructor for a hash set

2. An *accumulator* that adds an element to the target, such as an add method

3. A *combiner* that merges two objects into one, such as addAll

Here is how the collect method works for a bit set:

```
BitSet result = stream.collect(BitSet::new, BitSet::set, BitSet::or);
```

---

java.util.Stream 8

- Optional<T> reduce(BinaryOperator<T> accumulator)
- T reduce(T identity, BinaryOperator<T> accumulator)
- <U> U reduce(U identity, BiFunction<U,? super T,U> accumulator, BinaryOperator<U> combiner)

  forms a cumulative total of the stream elements with the given accumulator function. If identity is provided, then it is the first value to be accumulated. If combiner is provided, it can be used to combine totals of segments that are accumulated separately.

- <R> R collect(Supplier<R> supplier, BiConsumer<R,? super T> accumulator, BiConsumer<R,R> combiner)

  collects elements in a result of type R. On each segment, supplier is called to provide an initial result, accumulator is called to mutably add elements to it, and combiner is called to combine two results.

1.13 Primitive Type Streams

So far, we have collected integers in a Stream<Integer>, even though it is clearly inefficient to wrap each integer into a wrapper object. The same is true for the other primitive types—double, float, long, short, char, byte, and boolean. The stream library has specialized types IntStream, LongStream, and DoubleStream that store primitive values directly, without using wrappers. If you want to store short, char, byte, and boolean, use an IntStream; for float, use a DoubleStream.

To create an IntStream, call the IntStream.of and Arrays.stream methods:

```
IntStream stream = IntStream.of(1, 1, 2, 3, 5);
stream = Arrays.stream(values, from, to); // values is an int[] array
```

As with object streams, you can also use the static generate and iterate methods. In addition, IntStream and LongStream have static methods range and rangeClosed that generate integer ranges with step size one:

```
IntStream zeroToNinetyNine = IntStream.range(0, 100); // Upper bound is excluded
IntStream zeroToHundred = IntStream.rangeClosed(0, 100); // Upper bound is included
```

The CharSequence interface has methods codePoints and chars that yield an IntStream of the Unicode codes of the characters or of the code units in the UTF-16 encoding. (See Chapter 1 for the sordid details.)

```
String sentence = "\uD835\uDD46 is the set of octonions.";
   // \uD835\uDD46 is the UTF-16 encoding of the letter 𝕆, unicode U+1D546

IntStream codes = sentence.codePoints();
   // The stream with hex values 1D546 20 69 73 20 . . .
```

When you have a stream of objects, you can transform it to a primitive type stream with the `mapToInt`, `mapToLong`, or `mapToDouble` methods. For example, if you have a stream of strings and want to process their lengths as integers, you might as well do it in an `IntStream`:

```
Stream<String> words = . . .;
IntStream lengths = words.mapToInt(String::length);
```

To convert a primitive type stream to an object stream, use the `boxed` method:

```
Stream<Integer> integers = IntStream.range(0, 100).boxed();
```

Generally, the methods on primitive type streams are analogous to those on object streams. Here are the most notable differences:

- The `toArray` methods return primitive type arrays.
- Methods that yield an optional result return an `OptionalInt`, `OptionalLong`, or `OptionalDouble`. These classes are analogous to the `Optional` class, but they have methods `getAsInt`, `getAsLong`, and `getAsDouble` instead of the `get` method.
- There are methods `sum`, `average`, `max`, and `min` that return the sum, average, maximum, and minimum. These methods are not defined for object streams.
- The `summaryStatistics` method yields an object of type `IntSummaryStatistics`, `LongSummaryStatistics`, or `DoubleSummaryStatistics` that can simultaneously report the sum, count, average, maximum, and minimum of the stream.

 NOTE: The `Random` class has methods `ints`, `longs`, and `doubles` that return primitive type streams of random numbers. If you need random numbers in parallel streams, use the `SplittableRandom` class instead.

The program in Listing 1.7 gives examples for the API of primitive type streams.

Listing 1.7 `streams/PrimitiveTypeStreams.java`

```
1  package streams;
2
3  /**
4   * @version 1.01 2018-05-01
5   * @author Cay Horstmann
6   */
7
8  import java.io.IOException;
9  import java.nio.charset.StandardCharsets;
```

```java
10  import java.nio.file.Files;
11  import java.nio.file.Path;
12  import java.nio.file.Paths;
13  import java.util.stream.Collectors;
14  import java.util.stream.IntStream;
15  import java.util.stream.Stream;
16
17  public class PrimitiveTypeStreams
18  {
19      public static void show(String title, IntStream stream)
20      {
21          final int SIZE = 10;
22          int[] firstElements = stream.limit(SIZE + 1).toArray();
23          System.out.print(title + ": ");
24          for (int i = 0; i < firstElements.length; i++)
25          {
26              if (i > 0) System.out.print(", ");
27              if (i < SIZE) System.out.print(firstElements[i]);
28              else System.out.print("...");
29          }
30          System.out.println();
31      }
32
33      public static void main(String[] args) throws IOException
34      {
35          IntStream is1 = IntStream.generate(() -> (int) (Math.random() * 100));
36          show("is1", is1);
37          IntStream is2 = IntStream.range(5, 10);
38          show("is2", is2);
39          IntStream is3 = IntStream.rangeClosed(5, 10);
40          show("is3", is3);
41
42          Path path = Paths.get("../gutenberg/alice30.txt");
43          var contents = new String(Files.readAllBytes(path), StandardCharsets.UTF_8);
44
45          Stream<String> words = Stream.of(contents.split("\\PL+"));
46          IntStream is4 = words.mapToInt(String::length);
47          show("is4", is4);
48          var sentence = "\uD835\uDD46 is the set of octonions.";
49          System.out.println(sentence);
50          IntStream codes = sentence.codePoints();
51          System.out.println(codes.mapToObj(c -> String.format("%X ", c)).collect(
52              Collectors.joining()));
53
54          Stream<Integer> integers = IntStream.range(0, 100).boxed();
55          IntStream is5 = integers.mapToInt(Integer::intValue);
56          show("is5", is5);
57      }
58  }
```

---

java.util.stream.IntStream 8

- `static IntStream range(int startInclusive, int endExclusive)`
- `static IntStream rangeClosed(int startInclusive, int endInclusive)`

  yields an IntStream with the integers in the given range.

- `static IntStream of(int... values)`

  yields an IntStream with the given elements.

- `int[] toArray()`

  yields an array with the elements of this stream.

- `int sum()`
- `OptionalDouble average()`
- `OptionalInt max()`
- `OptionalInt min()`
- `IntSummaryStatistics summaryStatistics()`

  yields the sum, average, maximum, or minimum of the elements in this stream, or an object from which all four of these values can be obtained.

- `Stream<Integer> boxed()`

  yields a stream of wrapper objects for the elements in this stream.

---

java.util.stream.LongStream 8

- `static LongStream range(long startInclusive, long endExclusive)`
- `static LongStream rangeClosed(long startInclusive, long endInclusive)`

  yields a LongStream with the integers in the given range.

- `static LongStream of(long... values)`

  yields a LongStream with the given elements.

- `long[] toArray()`

  yields an array with the elements of this stream.

- `long sum()`
- `OptionalDouble average()`
- `OptionalLong max()`
- `OptionalLong min()`
- `LongSummaryStatistics summaryStatistics()`

  yields the sum, average, maximum, or minimum of the elements in this stream, or an object from which all four of these values can be obtained.

- `Stream<Long> boxed()`

  yields a stream of wrapper objects for the elements in this stream.

---

java.util.stream.DoubleStream 8

- `static DoubleStream of(double... values)`

  yields a DoubleStream with the given elements.

- `double[] toArray()`

  yields an array with the elements of this stream.

- `double sum()`
- `OptionalDouble average()`
- `OptionalDouble max()`
- `OptionalDouble min()`
- `DoubleSummaryStatistics summaryStatistics()`

  yields the sum, average, maximum, or minimum of the elements in this stream, or an object from which all four of these values can be obtained.

- `Stream<Double> boxed()`

  yields a stream of wrapper objects for the elements in this stream.

---

java.lang.CharSequence 1.0

- `IntStream codePoints()` 8

  yields a stream of all Unicode code points of this string.

`java.util.Random` 1.0

- `IntStream ints()`
- `IntStream ints(int randomNumberOrigin, int randomNumberBound)` 8
- `IntStream ints(long streamSize)` 8
- `IntStream ints(long streamSize, int randomNumberOrigin, int randomNumberBound)` 8
- `LongStream longs()` 8
- `LongStream longs(long randomNumberOrigin, long randomNumberBound)` 8
- `LongStream longs(long streamSize)` 8
- `LongStream longs(long streamSize, long randomNumberOrigin, long randomNumberBound)` 8
- `DoubleStream doubles()` 8
- `DoubleStream doubles(double randomNumberOrigin, double randomNumberBound)` 8
- `DoubleStream doubles(long streamSize)` 8
- `DoubleStream doubles(long streamSize, double randomNumberOrigin, double randomNumberBound)` 8

  yields streams of random numbers. If streamSize is provided, the stream is finite with the given number of elements. When bounds are provided, the elements are between randomNumberOrigin (inclusive) and randomNumberBound (exclusive).

---

java.util.Optional(Int|Long|Double) 8

- static Optional(Int|Long|Double) of((int|long|double) value)

  yields an optional object with the supplied primitive type value.

- (int|long|double) getAs(Int|Long|Double)()

  yields the value of this optional object, or throws a NoSuchElementException if it is empty.

- (int|long|double) orElse((int|long|double) other)
- (int|long|double) orElseGet((Int|Long|Double)Supplier other)

  yields the value of this optional object, or the alternative value if this object is empty.

- void ifPresent((Int|Long|Double)Consumer consumer)

  If this optional object is not empty, passes its value to consumer.

---

java.util.(Int|Long|Double)SummaryStatistics 8

- long getCount()
- (int|long|double) getSum()
- double getAverage()
- (int|long|double) getMax()
- (int|long|double) getMin()

  yields the count, sum, average, maximum, and minimum of the collected elements.

1.14 Parallel Streams

Streams make it easy to parallelize bulk operations. The process is mostly automatic, but you need to follow a few rules. First of all, you must have a parallel stream. You can get a parallel stream from any collection with the Collection.parallelStream() method:

```
Stream<String> parallelWords = words.parallelStream();
```

Moreover, the parallel method converts any sequential stream into a parallel one.

```
Stream<String> parallelWords = Stream.of(wordArray).parallel();
```

As long as the stream is in parallel mode when the terminal method executes, all intermediate stream operations will be parallelized.

When stream operations run in parallel, the intent is that the same result is returned as if they had run serially. It is important that the operations are *stateless* and can be executed in an arbitrary order.

Here is an example of something you cannot do. Suppose you want to count all short words in a stream of strings:

```
var shortWords = new int[12];
words.parallelStream().forEach(
    s -> { if (s.length() < 12) shortWords[s.length()]++; });
        // ERROR--race condition!
System.out.println(Arrays.toString(shortWords));
```

This is very, very bad code. The function passed to forEach runs concurrently in multiple threads, each updating a shared array. As you saw in Chapter 12 of Volume I, that's a classic *race condition*. If you run this program multiple times, you are quite likely to get a different sequence of counts in each run—each of them wrong.

It is your responsibility to ensure that any functions you pass to parallel stream operations are safe to execute in parallel. The best way to do that is to stay away from mutable state. In this example, you can safely parallelize the computation if you group strings by length and count them:

```
Map<Integer, Long> shortWordCounts
    = words.parallelStream()
        .filter(s -> s.length() < 12)
        .collect(groupingBy(
            String::length,
            counting()));
```

By default, streams that arise from ordered collections (arrays and lists), from ranges, generators, and iterators, or from calling Stream.sorted, are *ordered*. Results are accumulated in the order of the original elements, and are entirely predictable. If you run the same operations twice, you will get exactly the same results.

Ordering does not preclude efficient parallelization. For example, when computing stream.map(fun), the stream can be partitioned into *n* segments, each of which is concurrently processed. Then the results are reassembled in order.

Some operations can be more effectively parallelized when the ordering requirement is dropped. By calling the Stream.unordered method, you indicate that you are not interested in ordering. One operation that can benefit from this is Stream.distinct. On an ordered stream, distinct retains the first of all equal elements. That impedes parallelization—the thread processing a segment can't know which elements to discard until the preceding segment has been processed. If it is acceptable to retain *any* of the unique elements, all segments can be processed concurrently (using a shared set to track duplicates).

You can also speed up the `limit` method by dropping ordering. If you just want any n elements from a stream and you don't care which ones you get, call

```
Stream<String> sample = words.parallelStream().unordered().limit(n);
```

As discussed in Section 1.9, "Collecting into Maps," on p. 30, merging maps is expensive. For that reason, the `Collectors.groupingByConcurrent` method uses a shared concurrent map. To benefit from parallelism, the order of the map values will not be the same as the stream order.

```
Map<Integer, List<String>> result = words.parallelStream().collect(
   Collectors.groupingByConcurrent(String::length));
   // Values aren't collected in stream order
```

Of course, you won't care if you use a downstream collector that is independent of the ordering, such as

```
Map<Integer, Long> wordCounts
   = words.parallelStream()
      .collect(
         groupingByConcurrent(
            String::length,
            counting()));
```

Don't turn all your streams into parallel streams in the hope of speeding up operations. Keep these issues in mind:

- There is a substantial overhead to parallelization that will only pay off for very large data sets.
- Parallelizing a stream is only a win if the underlying data source can be effectively split into multiple parts.
- The thread pool that is used by parallel streams can be starved by blocking operations such as file I/O or network access.

Parallel streams work best with huge in-memory collections of data and computationally intensive processing.

 TIP: Prior to Java 9, parallelizing the stream returned by the `Files.lines` method made no sense. The data was not splittable—you had to read the first half of the file before the second half. Now the method uses a memory-mapped file, and splitting is effective. If you process the lines of a huge file, parallelizing the stream may improve performance.

NOTE: By default, parallel streams use the global fork-join pool returned by `ForkJoinPool.commonPool`. That is fine if your operations don't block and you don't share the pool with other tasks. There is a trick to substitute a different pool. Place your operations inside the `submit` method of a custom pool:

```
ForkJoinPool customPool = . . .;
result = customPool.submit(() ->
    stream.parallel().map(. . .).collect(. . .)).get();
```

Or, asynchronously:

```
CompletableFuture.supplyAsync(() ->
    stream.parallel().map(. . .).collect(. . .),
    customPool).thenAccept(result -> . . .);
```

 NOTE: If you want to parallelize stream computations based on random numbers, don't start out with a stream obtained from the `Random.ints`, `Random.longs`, or `Random.doubles` methods. Those streams don't split. Instead, use the `ints`, `longs`, or `doubles` methods of the `SplittableRandom` class.

The example program in Listing 1.8 demonstrates how to work with parallel streams.

Listing 1.8 parallel/ParallelStreams.java

```
1  package parallel;
2
3  /**
4   * @version 1.01 2018-05-01
5   * @author Cay Horstmann
6   */
7
8  import static java.util.stream.Collectors.*;
9
10 import java.io.*;
11 import java.nio.charset.*;
12 import java.nio.file.*;
13 import java.util.*;
14 import java.util.stream.*;
15
16 public class ParallelStreams
17 {
18     public static void main(String[] args) throws IOException
19     {
```

(Continues)

Listing 1.8 *(Continued)*

```
20    var contents = new String(Files.readAllBytes(
21        Paths.get("../gutenberg/alice30.txt")), StandardCharsets.UTF_8);
22    List<String> wordList = List.of(contents.split("\\PL+"));
23
24    // Very bad code ahead
25    var shortWords = new int[10];
26    wordList.parallelStream().forEach(s ->
27        {
28            if (s.length() < 10) shortWords[s.length()]++;
29        });
30    System.out.println(Arrays.toString(shortWords));
31
32    // Try again--the result will likely be different (and also wrong)
33    Arrays.fill(shortWords, 0);
34    wordList.parallelStream().forEach(s ->
35        {
36            if (s.length() < 10) shortWords[s.length()]++;
37        });
38    System.out.println(Arrays.toString(shortWords));
39
40    // Remedy: Group and count
41    Map<Integer, Long> shortWordCounts = wordList.parallelStream()
42        .filter(s -> s.length() < 10)
43        .collect(groupingBy(String::length, counting()));
44
45    System.out.println(shortWordCounts);
46
47    // Downstream order not deterministic
48    Map<Integer, List<String>> result = wordList.parallelStream().collect(
49        Collectors.groupingByConcurrent(String::length));
50
51    System.out.println(result.get(14));
52
53    result = wordList.parallelStream().collect(
54        Collectors.groupingByConcurrent(String::length));
55
56    System.out.println(result.get(14));
57
58    Map<Integer, Long> wordCounts = wordList.parallelStream().collect(
59        groupingByConcurrent(String::length, counting()));
60
61    System.out.println(wordCounts);
62    }
63 }
```

---

java.util.stream.BaseStream<T,S extends BaseStream<T,S>> 8

- S parallel()

  yields a parallel stream with the same elements as this stream.
- S unordered()

  yields an unordered stream with the same elements as this stream.

---

java.util.Collection<E> 1.2

- Stream<E> parallelStream() 8

  yields a parallel stream with the elements of this collection.

In this chapter, you have learned how to put the stream library of Java 8 to use. The next chapter covers another important topic: processing input and output.

2

Input and Output

In this chapter

In this chapter, we cover the Java Application Programming Interfaces (APIs) for input and output. You will learn how to access files and directories and how to read and write data in binary and text format. This chapter also shows you the object serialization mechanism that lets you store objects as easily as you can store text or numeric data. Next, we will turn to working with files and directories. We finish the chapter with a discussion of regular expressions, even though they are not actually related to input and output. We couldn't find a better place to handle that topic, and apparently neither could the Java team—the regular expression API specification was attached to a specification request for "new I/O" features.

2.1 Input/Output Streams

In the Java API, an object from which we can read a sequence of bytes is called an *input stream*. An object to which we can write a sequence of bytes is called an *output stream*. These sources and destinations of byte sequences can be—and often are—files, but they can also be network connections and even blocks of memory. The abstract classes InputStream and OutputStream are the basis for a hierarchy of input/output (I/O) classes.

NOTE: These input/output streams are unrelated to the streams that you saw in the preceding chapter. For clarity, we will use the terms input stream, output stream, or input/output stream whenever we discuss streams that are used for input and output.

Byte-oriented input/output streams are inconvenient for processing information stored in Unicode (recall that Unicode uses multiple bytes per character). Therefore, a separate hierarchy provides classes, inheriting from the abstract Reader and Writer classes, for processing Unicode characters. These classes have read and write operations that are based on two-byte char values (that is, UTF-16 code units) rather than byte values.

2.1.1 Reading and Writing Bytes

The InputStream class has an abstract method:

```
abstract int read()
```

This method reads one byte and returns the byte that was read, or -1 if it encounters the end of the input source. The designer of a concrete input stream class overrides this method to provide useful functionality. For example, in the FileInputStream class, this method reads one byte from a file. System.in is a predefined object of a subclass of InputStream that allows you to read information from "standard input," that is, the console or a redirected file.

The InputStream class also has nonabstract methods to read an array of bytes or to skip a number of bytes. Since Java 9, there is a very useful method to read all bytes of a stream:

```
byte[] bytes = in.readAllBytes();
```

There are also methods to read a given number of bytes—see the API notes.

These methods call the abstract read method, so subclasses need to override only one method.

Similarly, the OutputStream class defines the abstract method

```
abstract void write(int b)
```

which writes one byte to an output location.

If you have an array of bytes, you can write them all at once:

```
byte[] values = . . .;
out.write(values);
```

The transferTo method transfers all bytes from an input stream to an output stream:

```
in.transferTo(out);
```

Both the read and write methods *block* until the byte is actually read or written. This means that if the input stream cannot immediately be accessed (usually because of a busy network connection), the current thread blocks. This gives other threads the chance to do useful work while the method is waiting for the input stream to become available again.

The available method lets you check the number of bytes that are currently available for reading. This means a fragment like the following is unlikely to block:

```
int bytesAvailable = in.available();
if (bytesAvailable > 0)
{
   var data = new byte[bytesAvailable];
   in.read(data);
}
```

When you have finished reading or writing to an input/output stream, close it by calling the close method. This call frees up the operating system resources that are in limited supply. If an application opens too many input/output streams without closing them, system resources can become depleted. Closing an output stream also *flushes* the buffer used for the output stream: Any bytes that were temporarily placed in a buffer so that they could be delivered as a larger packet are sent off. In particular, if you do not close a file, the last packet of bytes might never be delivered. You can also manually flush the output with the flush method.

Even if an input/output stream class provides concrete methods to work with the raw read and write functions, application programmers rarely use them. The data that you are interested in probably contain numbers, strings, and objects, not raw bytes.

Instead of working with bytes, you can use one of many input/output classes that build upon the basic `InputStream` and `OutputStream` classes.

---

java.io.InputStream 1.0

- `abstract int read()`

  reads a byte of data and returns the byte read; returns -1 at the end of the input stream.

- `int read(byte[] b)`

  reads into an array of bytes and returns the actual number of bytes read, or -1 at the end of the input stream; this method reads at most `b.length` bytes.

- `int read(byte[] b, int off, int len)`
- `int readNBytes(byte[] b, int off, int len)` 9

  reads up to `len` bytes, if available without blocking (`read`), or blocking until all values have been read (`readNBytes`). Values are placed into `b`, starting at `off`. Returns the actual number of bytes read, or -1 at the end of the input stream.

- `byte[] readAllBytes()` 9

  yields an array of all bytes that can be read from this stream.

- `long transferTo(OutputStream out)` 9

  transfers all bytes from this input stream to the given output stream, returning the number of bytes transferred. Neither stream is closed.

- `long skip(long n)`

  skips n bytes in the input stream, returns the actual number of bytes skipped (which may be less than n if the end of the input stream was encountered).

- `int available()`

  returns the number of bytes available, without blocking (recall that blocking means that the current thread loses its turn).

- `void close()`

  closes the input stream.

- `void mark(int readlimit)`

  puts a marker at the current position in the input stream (not all streams support this feature). If more than `readlimit` bytes have been read from the input stream, the stream is allowed to forget the marker.

- `void reset()`

  returns to the last marker. Subsequent calls to `read` reread the bytes. If there is no current marker, the input stream is not reset.

- `boolean markSupported()`

  returns `true` if the input stream supports marking.

---

java.io.OutputStream 1.0

- abstract void write(int n)

  writes a byte of data.
- void write(byte[] b)
- void write(byte[] b, int off, int len)

  writes all bytes, or len bytes starting at off, in the array b.
- void close()

  flushes and closes the output stream.
- void flush()

  flushes the output stream—that is, sends any buffered data to its destination.

2.1.2 The Complete Stream Zoo

Unlike C, which gets by just fine with a single type FILE*, Java has a whole zoo of more than 60 (!) different input/output stream types (see Figures 2.1 and 2.2).

Let's divide the animals in the input/output stream zoo by how they are used. There are separate hierarchies for classes that process bytes and characters. As you saw, the InputStream and OutputStream classes let you read and write individual bytes and arrays of bytes. These classes form the basis of the hierarchy shown in Figure 2.1. To read and write strings and numbers, you need more capable subclasses. For example, DataInputStream and DataOutputStream let you read and write all the primitive Java types in binary format. Finally, there are input/output streams that do useful stuff; for example, the ZipInputStream and ZipOutputStream let you read and write files in the familiar ZIP compression format.

For Unicode text, on the other hand, you can use subclasses of the abstract classes Reader and Writer (see Figure 2.2). The basic methods of the Reader and Writer classes are similar to those of InputStream and OutputStream.

```
abstract int read()
abstract void write(int c)
```

The read method returns either a UTF-16 code unit (as an integer between 0 and 65535) or -1 when you have reached the end of the file. The write method is called with a Unicode code unit. (See Volume I, Chapter 3 for a discussion of Unicode code units.)

There are four additional interfaces: Closeable, Flushable, Readable, and Appendable (see Figure 2.3). The first two interfaces are very simple, with methods

```
void close() throws IOException
```

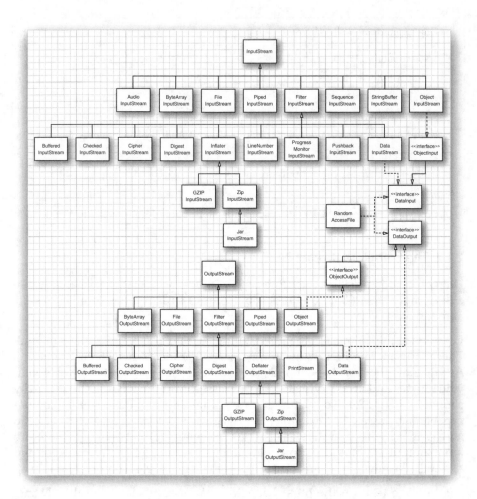

Figure 2.1 Input and output stream hierarchy

and

```
void flush()
```

respectively. The classes InputStream, OutputStream, Reader, and Writer all implement the Closeable interface.

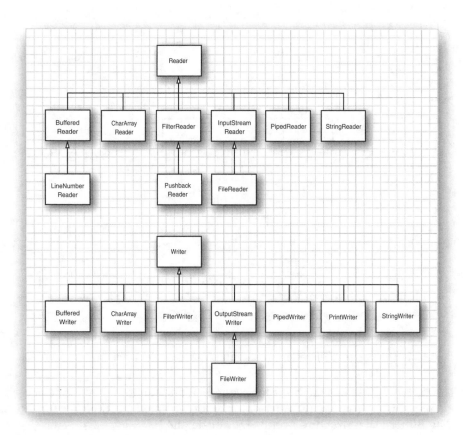

Figure 2.2 Reader and writer hierarchy

 NOTE: The java.io.Closeable interface extends the java.lang.AutoCloseable interface. Therefore, you can use the try-with-resources statement with any Closeable. Why have two interfaces? The close method of the Closeable interface only throws an IOException, whereas the AutoCloseable.close method may throw any exception.

OutputStream and Writer implement the Flushable interface.

The Readable interface has a single method

```
int read(CharBuffer cb)
```

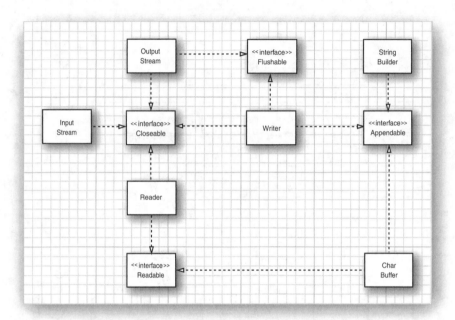

Figure 2.3 The Closeable, Flushable, Readable, and Appendable interfaces

The CharBuffer class has methods for sequential and random read/write access. It represents an in-memory buffer or a memory-mapped file. (See Section 2.5.2, "The Buffer Data Structure," on p. 132 for details.)

The Appendable interface has two methods for appending single characters and character sequences:

```
Appendable append(char c)
Appendable append(CharSequence s)
```

The CharSequence interface describes basic properties of a sequence of char values. It is implemented by String, CharBuffer, StringBuilder, and StringBuffer.

Of the input/output stream classes, only Writer implements Appendable.

---

java.io.Closeable 5.0

- void close()

  closes this Closeable. This method may throw an IOException.

---

java.io.Flushable 5.0

- void flush()

  flushes this Flushable.

---

java.lang.Readable 5.0

- int read(CharBuffer cb)

  attempts to read as many char values into cb as it can hold. Returns the number of values read, or -1 if no further values are available from this Readable.

---

java.lang.Appendable 5.0

- Appendable append(char c)
- Appendable append(CharSequence cs)

  appends the given code unit, or all code units in the given sequence, to this Appendable; returns this.

---

java.lang.CharSequence 1.4

- char charAt(int index)

  returns the code unit at the given index.

- int length()

  returns the number of code units in this sequence.

- CharSequence subSequence(int startIndex, int endIndex)

  returns a CharSequence consisting of the code units stored from index startIndex to endIndex - 1.

- String toString()

  returns a string consisting of the code units of this sequence.

2.1.3 Combining Input/Output Stream Filters

FileInputStream and FileOutputStream give you input and output streams attached to a disk file. You need to pass the file name or full path name of the file to the constructor. For example,

```
var fin = new FileInputStream("employee.dat");
```

looks in the user directory for a file named employee.dat.

 TIP: All the classes in java.io interpret relative path names as starting from the user's working directory. You can get this directory by a call to System .getProperty("user.dir").

 CAUTION: Since the backslash character is the escape character in Java strings, be sure to use \\ for Windows-style path names (for example, C:\\Windows\\win.ini). In Windows, you can also use a single forward slash (C:/Windows/win.ini) because most Windows file-handling system calls will interpret forward slashes as file separators. However, this is not recommended—the behavior of the Windows system functions is subject to change. Instead, for portable programs, use the file separator character for the platform on which your program runs. It is available as the constant string java.io.File.separator.

Like the abstract InputStream and OutputStream classes, these classes only support reading and writing at the byte level. That is, we can only read bytes and byte arrays from the object fin.

```
byte b = (byte) fin.read();
```

As you will see in the next section, if we just had a DataInputStream, we could read numeric types:

```
DataInputStream din = . . .;
double x = din.readDouble();
```

But just as the FileInputStream has no methods to read numeric types, the DataInputStream has no method to get data from a file.

Java uses a clever mechanism to separate two kinds of responsibilities. Some input streams (such as the FileInputStream and the input stream returned by the openStream method of the URL class) can retrieve bytes from files and other more exotic locations. Other input streams (such as the DataInputStream) can assemble bytes into more useful data types. The Java programmer has to combine the two. For example, to be able to read numbers from a file, first create a FileInputStream and then pass it to the constructor of a DataInputStream.

```
var fin = new FileInputStream("employee.dat");
var din = new DataInputStream(fin);
double x = din.readDouble();
```

If you look at Figure 2.1 again, you can see the classes FilterInputStream and FilterOutputStream. The subclasses of these classes are used to add capabilities to input/output streams that process bytes.

You can add multiple capabilities by nesting the filters. For example, by default, input streams are not buffered. That is, every call to read asks the operating system to dole out yet another byte. It is more efficient to request blocks of data instead and store them in a buffer. If you want buffering *and* the data input methods for a file, use the following rather monstrous sequence of constructors:

```
var din = new DataInputStream(
   new BufferedInputStream(
      new FileInputStream("employee.dat")));
```

Notice that we put the DataInputStream *last* in the chain of constructors because we want to use the DataInputStream methods, and we want *them* to use the buffered read method.

Sometimes you'll need to keep track of the intermediate input streams when chaining them together. For example, when reading input, you often need to peek at the next byte to see if it is the value that you expect. Java provides the PushbackInputStream for this purpose.

```
var pbin = new PushbackInputStream(
   new BufferedInputStream(
      new FileInputStream("employee.dat")));
```

Now you can speculatively read the next byte

```
int b = pbin.read();
```

and throw it back if it isn't what you wanted.

```
if (b != '<') pbin.unread(b);
```

However, reading and unreading are the *only* methods that apply to a pushback input stream. If you want to look ahead and also read numbers, then you need both a pushback input stream and a data input stream reference.

```
var din = new DataInputStream(
   pbin = new PushbackInputStream(
      new BufferedInputStream(
         new FileInputStream("employee.dat"))));
```

Of course, in the input/output libraries of other programming languages, niceties such as buffering and lookahead are automatically taken care of—so it is a bit of a hassle to resort, in Java, to combining stream filters. However, the ability to mix and match filter classes to construct useful sequences of input/output streams does give you an immense amount of flexibility. For example, you can read numbers from a compressed ZIP file by using the following sequence of input streams (see Figure 2.4):

```
var zin = new ZipInputStream(new FileInputStream("employee.zip"));
var din = new DataInputStream(zin);
```

(See Section 2.2.3, "ZIP Archives," on p. 85 for more on Java's handling of ZIP files.)

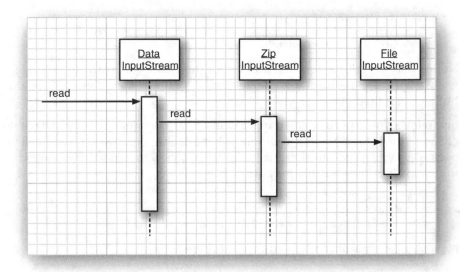

Figure 2.4 A sequence of filtered input streams

---

java.io.FileInputStream 1.0

- `FileInputStream(String name)`
- `FileInputStream(File file)`

creates a new file input stream using the file whose path name is specified by the `name` string or the `file` object. (The `File` class is described at the end of this chapter.) Path names that are not absolute are resolved relative to the working directory that was set when the VM started.

---

java.io.FileOutputStream 1.0

- FileOutputStream(String name)
- FileOutputStream(String name, boolean append)
- FileOutputStream(File file)
- FileOutputStream(File file, boolean append)

  creates a new file output stream specified by the name string or the file object. (The File class is described at the end of this chapter.) If the append parameter is true, an existing file with the same name will not be deleted and data will be added at the end of the file. Otherwise, this method deletes any existing file with the same name.

---

java.io.BufferedInputStream 1.0

- BufferedInputStream(InputStream in)

  creates a buffered input stream. A buffered input stream reads bytes from a stream without causing a device access every time. When the buffer is empty, a new block of data is read into the buffer.

---

java.io.BufferedOutputStream 1.0

- BufferedOutputStream(OutputStream out)

  creates a buffered output stream. A buffered output stream collects bytes to be written without causing a device access every time. When the buffer fills up or when the stream is flushed, the data are written.

---

java.io.PushbackInputStream 1.0

- PushbackInputStream(InputStream in)
- PushbackInputStream(InputStream in, int size)

  constructs an input stream with one-byte lookahead or a pushback buffer of specified size.

- void unread(int b)

  pushes back a byte, which is retrieved again by the next call to read.

2.1.4 Text Input and Output

When saving data, you have the choice between binary and text formats. For example, if the integer 1234 is saved in binary, it is written as the sequence of bytes 00 00 04 D2 (in hexadecimal notation). In text format, it is saved as the string "1234". Although binary I/O is fast and efficient, it is not easily readable by humans. We first discuss text I/O and cover binary I/O in Section 2.2, "Reading and Writing Binary Data," on p. 78.

When saving text strings, you need to consider the *character encoding*. In the UTF-16 encoding that Java uses internally, the string "José" is encoded as 00 4A 00 6F 00 73 00 E9 (in hex). However, many programs expect that text files use a different encoding. In UTF-8, the encoding most commonly used on the Internet, the string would be written as 4A 6F 73 C3 A9, without the zero bytes for the first three letters and with two bytes for the é character.

The OutputStreamWriter class turns an output stream of Unicode code units into a stream of bytes, using a chosen character encoding. Conversely, the InputStreamReader class turns an input stream that contains bytes (specifying characters in some character encoding) into a reader that emits Unicode code units.

For example, here is how you make an input reader that reads keystrokes from the console and converts them to Unicode:

```
var in = new InputStreamReader(System.in);
```

This input stream reader assumes the default character encoding used by the host system. On desktop operating systems, that can be an archaic encoding such as Windows 1252 or MacRoman. You should always choose a specific encoding in the constructor for the InputStreamReader, for example:

```
var in = new InputStreamReader(new FileInputStream("data.txt"), StandardCharsets.UTF_8);
```

See Section 2.1.8, "Character Encodings," on p. 75 for more information on character encodings.

The Reader and Writer classes have only basic methods to read and write individual characters. As with streams, you use subclasses for processing strings and numbers.

2.1.5 How to Write Text Output

For text output, use a PrintWriter. That class has methods to print strings and numbers in text format. In order to print to a file, construct a PrintStream from a file name and a character encoding:

```
var out = new PrintWriter("employee.txt", StandardCharsets.UTF_8);
```

To write to a print writer, use the same print, println, and printf methods that you used with System.out. You can use these methods to print numbers (int, short, long, float, double), characters, boolean values, strings, and objects.

For example, consider this code:

```
String name = "Harry Hacker";
double salary = 75000;
out.print(name);
out.print(' ');
out.println(salary);
```

This writes the characters

```
Harry Hacker 75000.0
```

to the writer out. The characters are then converted to bytes and end up in the file employee.txt.

The println method adds the correct end-of-line character for the target system ("\r\n" on Windows, "\n" on UNIX) to the line. This is the string obtained by the call System.getProperty("line.separator").

If the writer is set to *autoflush mode*, all characters in the buffer are sent to their destination whenever println is called. (Print writers are always buffered.) By default, autoflushing is *not* enabled. You can enable or disable autoflushing by using the PrintWriter(Writer writer, boolean autoFlush) constructor:

```
var out = new PrintWriter(
    new OutputStreamWriter(
        new FileOutputStream("employee.txt"), StandardCharsets.UTF_8),
    true); // autoflush
```

The print methods don't throw exceptions. You can call the checkError method to see if something went wrong with the output stream.

 NOTE: Java veterans might wonder whatever happened to the PrintStream class and to System.out. In Java 1.0, the PrintStream class simply truncated all Unicode characters to ASCII characters by dropping the top byte. (At the time, Unicode was still a 16-bit encoding.) Clearly, that was not a clean or portable approach, and it was fixed with the introduction of readers and writers in Java 1.1. For compatibility with existing code, System.in, System.out, and System.err are still input/output streams, not readers and writers. But now the PrintStream class internally converts Unicode characters to the default host encoding in the same way the PrintWriter does. Objects of type PrintStream act exactly like print writers when you use the print and println methods, but unlike print writers they allow you to output raw bytes with the write(int) and write(byte[]) methods.

---

java.io.PrintWriter 1.1

- PrintWriter(Writer out)
- PrintWriter(Writer writer)

  creates a new PrintWriter that writes to the given writer.

- PrintWriter(String filename, String encoding)
- PrintWriter(File file, String encoding)

  creates a new PrintWriter that writes to the given file, using the given character encoding.

- void print(Object obj)

  prints an object by printing the string resulting from toString.

- void print(String s)

  prints a string containing Unicode code units.

- void println(String s)

  prints a string followed by a line terminator. Flushes the output stream if it is in autoflush mode.

- void print(char[] s)

  prints all Unicode code units in the given array.

- void print(char c)

  prints a Unicode code unit.

- void print(int i)
- void print(long l)
- void print(float f)
- void print(double d)
- void print(boolean b)

  prints the given value in text format.

- void printf(String format, Object... args)

  prints the given values as specified by the format string. See Volume I, Chapter 3 for the specification of the format string.

- boolean checkError()

  returns true if a formatting or output error occurred. Once the output stream has encountered an error, it is tainted and all calls to checkError return true.

2.1.6 How to Read Text Input

The easiest way to process arbitrary text is the Scanner class that we used extensively in Volume I. You can construct a Scanner from any input stream.

Alternatively, you can read a short text file into a string like this:

```
var content = new String(Files.readAllBytes(path), charset);
```

But if you want the file as a sequence of lines, call

```
List<String> lines = Files.readAllLines(path, charset);
```

If the file is large, process the lines lazily as a Stream<String>:

```
try (Stream<String> lines = Files.lines(path, charset))
{
   . . .
}
```

You can also use a scanner to read *tokens*—strings that are separated by a delimiter. The default delimiter is white space. You can change the delimiter to any regular expression. For example,

```
Scanner in = . . .;
in.useDelimiter("\\PL+");
```

accepts any non-Unicode letters as delimiters. The scanner then accepts tokens consisting only of Unicode letters.

Calling the next method yields the next token:

```
while (in.hasNext())
{
   String word = in.next();
   . . .
}
```

Alternatively, you can obtain a stream of all tokens as

```
Stream<String> words = in.tokens();
```

In early versions of Java, the only game in town for processing text input was the BufferedReader class. Its readLine method yields a line of text, or null when no more input is available. A typical input loop looks like this:

```
InputStream inputStream = . . .;
try (var in = new BufferedReader(new InputStreamReader(inputStream, charset)))
{
   String line;
   while ((line = in.readLine()) != null)
   {
      do something with line
   }
}
```

Nowadays, the BufferedReader class also has a lines method that yields a Stream<String>. However, unlike a Scanner, a BufferedReader has no methods for reading numbers.

2.1.7 Saving Objects in Text Format

In this section, we walk you through an example program that stores an array of Employee records in a text file. Each record is stored in a separate line. Instance fields are separated from each other by delimiters. We use a vertical bar (|) as our delimiter. (A colon (:) is another popular choice. Part of the fun is that everyone uses a different delimiter.) Naturally, we punt on the issue of what might happen if a | actually occurs in one of the strings we save.

Here is a sample set of records:

```
Harry Hacker|35500|1989-10-01
Carl Cracker|75000|1987-12-15
Tony Tester|38000|1990-03-15
```

Writing records is simple. Since we write to a text file, we use the PrintWriter class. We simply write all fields, followed by either a | or, for the last field, a newline character. This work is done in the following writeData method that we add to our Employee class:

```
public static void writeEmployee(PrintWriter out, Employee e)
{
   out.println(e.getName() + "|" + e.getSalary() + "|" + e.getHireDay());
}
```

To read records, we read in a line at a time and separate the fields. We use a scanner to read each line and then split the line into tokens with the String.split method.

```
public static Employee readEmployee(Scanner in)
{
   String line = in.nextLine();
   String[] tokens = line.split("\\|");
   String name = tokens[0];
   double salary = Double.parseDouble(tokens[1]);
   LocalDate hireDate = LocalDate.parse(tokens[2]);
   int year = hireDate.getYear();
   int month = hireDate.getMonthValue();
   int day = hireDate.getDayOfMonth();
   return new Employee(name, salary, year, month, day);
}
```

The parameter of the split method is a regular expression describing the separator. We discuss regular expressions in more detail at the end of this chapter. As it happens, the vertical bar character has a special meaning in regular expressions, so it needs to be escaped with a \ character. That character needs to be escaped by another \, yielding the "\\|" expression.

The complete program is in Listing 2.1. The static method

```
void writeData(Employee[] e, PrintWriter out)
```

first writes the length of the array, then writes each record. The static method

```
Employee[] readData(BufferedReader in)
```

first reads in the length of the array, then reads in each record. This turns out to be a bit tricky:

```
int n = in.nextInt();
in.nextLine(); // consume newline
var employees = new Employee[n];
for (int i = 0; i < n; i++)
{
   employees[i] = new Employee();
   employees[i].readData(in);
}
```

The call to nextInt reads the array length but not the trailing newline character. We must consume the newline so that the readData method can get the next input line when it calls the nextLine method.

Listing 2.1 textFile/TextFileTest.java

```
1  package textFile;
2
3  import java.io.*;
4  import java.nio.charset.*;
5  import java.time.*;
6  import java.util.*;
7
8  /**
9   * @version 1.15 2018-03-17
10  * @author Cay Horstmann
11  */
12 public class TextFileTest
13 {
14    public static void main(String[] args) throws IOException
15    {
16       var staff = new Employee[3];
17
18       staff[0] = new Employee("Carl Cracker", 75000, 1987, 12, 15);
19       staff[1] = new Employee("Harry Hacker", 50000, 1989, 10, 1);
20       staff[2] = new Employee("Tony Tester", 40000, 1990, 3, 15);
```

(Continues)

Listing 2.1 *(Continued)*

```
21
22        // save all employee records to the file employee.dat
23        try (var out = new PrintWriter("employee.dat", StandardCharsets.UTF_8))
24        {
25            writeData(staff, out);
26        }
27
28        // retrieve all records into a new array
29        try (var in = new Scanner(
30            new FileInputStream("employee.dat"), "UTF-8"))
31        {
32            Employee[] newStaff = readData(in);
33
34            // print the newly read employee records
35            for (Employee e : newStaff)
36                System.out.println(e);
37        }
38    }
39
40    /**
41     * Writes all employees in an array to a print writer
42     * @param employees an array of employees
43     * @param out a print writer
44     */
45    private static void writeData(Employee[] employees, PrintWriter out)
46            throws IOException
47    {
48        // write number of employees
49        out.println(employees.length);
50
51        for (Employee e : employees)
52            writeEmployee(out, e);
53    }
54
55    /**
56     * Reads an array of employees from a scanner
57     * @param in the scanner
58     * @return the array of employees
59     */
60    private static Employee[] readData(Scanner in)
61    {
62        // retrieve the array size
63        int n = in.nextInt();
64        in.nextLine(); // consume newline
65
66        var employees = new Employee[n];
```

```
67          for (int i = 0; i < n; i++)
68          {
69              employees[i] = readEmployee(in);
70          }
71          return employees;
72      }
73
74      /**
75       * Writes employee data to a print writer
76       * @param out the print writer
77       */
78      public static void writeEmployee(PrintWriter out, Employee e)
79      {
80          out.println(e.getName() + "|" + e.getSalary() + "|" + e.getHireDay());
81      }
82
83      /**
84       * Reads employee data from a buffered reader
85       * @param in the scanner
86       */
87      public static Employee readEmployee(Scanner in)
88      {
89          String line = in.nextLine();
90          String[] tokens = line.split("\\|");
91          String name = tokens[0];
92          double salary = Double.parseDouble(tokens[1]);
93          LocalDate hireDate = LocalDate.parse(tokens[2]);
94          int year = hireDate.getYear();
95          int month = hireDate.getMonthValue();
96          int day = hireDate.getDayOfMonth();
97          return new Employee(name, salary, year, month, day);
98      }
99  }
```

2.1.8 Character Encodings

Input and output streams are for sequences of bytes, but in many cases you will work with texts—that is, sequences of characters. It then matters how characters are encoded into bytes.

Java uses the Unicode standard for characters. Each character, or "code point," has a 21-bit integer number. There are different *character encodings*—methods for packaging those 21-bit numbers into bytes.

The most common encoding is UTF-8, which encodes each Unicode code point into a sequence of one to four bytes (see Table 2.1). UTF-8 has the advantage that the characters of the traditional ASCII character set, which contains all characters used in English, only take up one byte each.

Table 2.1 UTF-8 Encoding

Character Range	Encoding
0. . .7F	$0a_6a_5a_4a_3a_2a_1a_0$
80. . .7FF	$110a_{10}a_9a_8a_7a_6\ 10a_5a_4a_3a_2a_1a_0$
800. . .FFFF	$1110a_{15}a_{14}a_{13}a_{12}\ 10a_{11}a_{10}a_9a_8a_7a_6\ 10a_5a_4a_3a_2a_1a_0$
10000. . .10FFFF	$11110a_{20}a_{19}a_{18}\ 10a_{17}a_{16}a_{15}a_{14}a_{13}a_{12}\ 10a_{11}a_{10}a_9a_8a_7a_6\ 10a_5a_4a_3a_2a_1a_0$

Table 2.2 UTF-16 Encoding

Character Range	Encoding
0. . .FFFF	$a_{15}a_{14}a_{13}a_{12}a_{11}a_{10}a_9a_8\ a_7a_6a_5a_4a_3a_2a_1a_0$
10000. . .10FFFF	$110110b_{19}b_{18}\ b_{17}b_{16}a_{15}a_{14}a_{13}a_{12}a_{11}a_{10}\ 110111a_9a_8\ a_7a_6a_5a_4a_3a_2a_1a_0$ where $b_{19}b_{18}b_{17}b_{16} = a_{20}a_{19}a_{18}a_{17}a_{16} - 1$

Another common encoding is UTF-16, which encodes each Unicode code point into one or two 16-bit values (see Table 2.2). This is the encoding used in Java strings. Actually, there are two forms of UTF-16, called "big-endian" and "little-endian." Consider the 16-bit value 0x2122. In the big-endian format, the more significant byte comes first: 0x21 followed by 0x22. In the little-endian format, it is the other way around: 0x22 0x21. To indicate which of the two is used, a file can start with the "byte order mark," the 16-bit quantity 0xFEFF. A reader can use this value to determine the byte order and then discard it.

 CAUTION: Some programs, including Microsoft Notepad, add a byte order mark at the beginning of UTF-8 encoded files. Clearly, this is unnecessary since there are no byte ordering issues in UTF-8. But the Unicode standard allows it, and even suggests that it's a pretty good idea since it leaves little doubt about the encoding. It is supposed to be removed when reading a UTF-8 en-coded file. Sadly, Java does not do that, and bug reports against this issue are closed as "will not fix." Your best bet is to strip out any leading \uFEFF that you find in your input.

In addition to the UTF encodings, there are partial encodings that cover a character range suitable for a given user population. For example, ISO 8859-1 is a one-byte code that includes accented characters used in Western European languages. Shift-JIS is a variable-length code for Japanese characters. A large number of these encodings are still in widespread use.

There is no reliable way to automatically detect the character encoding from a stream of bytes. Some API methods let you use the "default charset"—the character encoding preferred by the operating system of the computer. Is that the same encoding that is used by your source of bytes? These bytes may well originate from a different part of the world. Therefore, you should always explicitly specify the encoding. For example, when reading a web page, check the Content-Type header.

NOTE: The platform encoding is returned by the static method Charset .defaultCharset. The static method Charset.availableCharsets returns all available Charset instances, as a map from canonical names to Charset objects.

CAUTION: The Oracle implementation of Java has a system property file.encoding for overriding the platform default. This is not an officially supported property, and it is not consistently followed by all parts of Oracle's implementation of the Java library. You should not set it.

The StandardCharsets class has static variables of type Charset for the character encodings that every Java virtual machine must support:

```
StandardCharsets.UTF_8
StandardCharsets.UTF_16
StandardCharsets.UTF_16BE
StandardCharsets.UTF_16LE
StandardCharsets.ISO_8859_1
StandardCharsets.US_ASCII
```

To obtain the Charset for another encoding, use the static forName method:

```
Charset shiftJIS = Charset.forName("Shift-JIS");
```

Use the Charset object when reading or writing text. For example, you can turn an array of bytes into a string as

```
var str = new String(bytes, StandardCharsets.UTF_8);
```

TIP: As of Java 10, all methods in the java.io package allow you to specify a character encoding with a Charset object or a string. Choose the StandardCharsets constants, so that any spelling errors are caught at compile time.

CAUTION: Some methods (such as the String(byte[]) constructor) use the default platform encoding if you don't specify any; others (such as Files.readAllLines) use UTF-8.

2.2 Reading and Writing Binary Data

Text format is convenient for testing and debugging because it is humanly readable, but it is not as efficient as transmitting data in binary format. In the following sections, you will learn how to perform input and output with binary data.

2.2.1 The DataInput and DataOutput interfaces

The DataOutput interface defines the following methods for writing a number, a character, a boolean value, or a string in binary format:

```
writeChars        writeFloat
writeByte         writeDouble
writeInt          writeChar
writeShort        writeBoolean
writeLong         writeUTF
```

For example, writeInt always writes an integer as a 4-byte binary quantity regardless of the number of digits, and writeDouble always writes a double as an 8-byte binary quantity. The resulting output is not human-readable, but it will use the same space for each value of a given type and reading it back in will be faster than parsing text.

 NOTE: There are two different methods of storing integers and floating-point numbers in memory, depending on the processor you are using. Suppose, for example, you are working with a 4-byte int, such as the decimal number 1234, or 4D2 in hexadecimal ($1234 = 4 \times 256 + 13 \times 16 + 2$). This value can be stored in such a way that the first of the four bytes in memory holds the most significant byte (MSB) of the value: 00 00 04 D2. This is the so-called big-endian method. Or, we can start with the least significant byte (LSB) first: D2 04 00 00. This is called, naturally enough, the little-endian method. For example, the SPARC uses big-endian; the Pentium, little-endian. This can lead to problems. When a file is saved from C or C++ file, the data are saved exactly as the processor stores them. That makes it challenging to move even the simplest data files from one platform to another. In Java, all values are written in the big-endian fashion, regardless of the processor. That makes Java data files platform-independent.

The writeUTF method writes string data using a modified version of the 8-bit Unicode Transformation Format. Instead of simply using the standard UTF-8 encoding, sequences of Unicode code units are first represented in UTF-16, and then the result is encoded using the UTF-8 rules. This modified encoding is different for characters with codes higher than 0xFFFF. It is used for backward compatibility with virtual machines that were built when Unicode had not yet grown beyond 16 bits.

Since nobody else uses this modification of UTF-8, you should only use the writeUTF method to write strings intended for a Java virtual machine—for example, in a program that generates bytecodes. Use the writeChars method for other purposes.

To read the data back in, use the following methods defined in the DataInput interface:

```
readInt          readDouble
readShort        readChar
readLong         readBoolean
readFloat        readUTF
```

The DataInputStream class implements the DataInput interface. To read binary data from a file, combine a DataInputStream with a source of bytes such as a FileInputStream:

```
var in = new DataInputStream(new FileInputStream("employee.dat"));
```

Similarly, to write binary data, use the DataOutputStream class that implements the DataOutput interface:

```
var out = new DataOutputStream(new FileOutputStream("employee.dat"));
```

---

java.io.DataInput 1.0

- boolean readBoolean()
- byte readByte()
- char readChar()
- double readDouble()
- float readFloat()
- int readInt()
- long readLong()
- short readShort()

  reads in a value of the given type.

- void readFully(byte[] b)

  reads bytes into the array b, blocking until all bytes are read.

- void readFully(byte[] b, int off, int len)

  places up to len bytes into the array b, starting at off, blocking until all bytes are read.

(Continues)

---

java.io.DataInput 1.0 *(Continued)*

- `String readUTF()`

  reads a string of characters in the "modified UTF-8" format.

- `int skipBytes(int n)`

  skips n bytes, blocking until all bytes are skipped.

---

java.io.DataOutput 1.0

- `void writeBoolean(boolean b)`
- `void writeByte(int b)`
- `void writeChar(int c)`
- `void writeDouble(double d)`
- `void writeFloat(float f)`
- `void writeInt(int i)`
- `void writeLong(long l)`
- `void writeShort(int s)`

  writes a value of the given type.

- `void writeChars(String s)`

  writes all characters in the string.

- `void writeUTF(String s)`

  writes a string of characters in the "modified UTF-8" format.

2.2.2 Random-Access Files

The `RandomAccessFile` class lets you read or write data anywhere in a file. Disk files are random-access, but input/output streams that communicate with a network socket are not. You can open a random-access file either for reading only or for both reading and writing; specify the option by using the string `"r"` (for read access) or `"rw"` (for read/write access) as the second argument in the constructor.

```
var in = new RandomAccessFile("employee.dat", "r");
var inOut = new RandomAccessFile("employee.dat", "rw");
```

When you open an existing file as a `RandomAccessFile`, it does not get deleted.

A random-access file has a *file pointer* that indicates the position of the next byte to be read or written. The `seek` method can be used to set the file pointer to an arbitrary byte position within the file. The argument to `seek` is a `long` integer between zero and the length of the file in bytes.

The getFilePointer method returns the current position of the file pointer.

The RandomAccessFile class implements both the DataInput and DataOutput interfaces. To read and write from a random-access file, use methods such as readInt/ writeInt and readChar/writeChar that we discussed in the preceding section.

Let's walk through an example program that stores employee records in a random-access file. Each record will have the same size. This makes it easy to read an arbitrary record. Suppose you want to position the file pointer to the third record. Simply set the file pointer to the appropriate byte position and start reading.

```
long n = 3;
in.seek((n - 1) * RECORD_SIZE);
var e = new Employee();
e.readData(in);
```

If you want to modify the record and save it back into the same location, remember to set the file pointer back to the beginning of the record:

```
in.seek((n - 1) * RECORD_SIZE);
e.writeData(out);
```

To determine the total number of bytes in a file, use the length method. The total number of records is the length divided by the size of each record.

```
long nbytes = in.length(); // length in bytes
int nrecords = (int) (nbytes / RECORD_SIZE);
```

Integers and floating-point values have a fixed size in binary format, but we have to work harder for strings. We provide two helper methods to write and read strings of a fixed size.

The writeFixedString writes the specified number of code units, starting at the beginning of the string. If there are too few code units, the method pads the string, using zero values.

```
public static void writeFixedString(String s, int size, DataOutput out)
      throws IOException
{
   for (int i = 0; i < size; i++)
   {
      char ch = 0;
      if (i < s.length()) ch = s.charAt(i);
      out.writeChar(ch);
   }
}
```

The readFixedString method reads characters from the input stream until it has consumed size code units or until it encounters a character with a zero value.

Then, it skips past the remaining zero values in the input field. For added efficiency, this method uses the StringBuilder class to read in a string.

```
public static String readFixedString(int size, DataInput in)
      throws IOException
{
   var b = new StringBuilder(size);
   int i = 0;
   var done = false;
   while (!done && i < size)
   {
      char ch = in.readChar();
      i++;
      if (ch == 0) done = true;
      else b.append(ch);
   }
   in.skipBytes(2 * (size - i));
   return b.toString();
}
```

We placed the writeFixedString and readFixedString methods inside the DataIO helper class.

To write a fixed-size record, we simply write all fields in binary.

```
DataIO.writeFixedString(e.getName(), Employee.NAME_SIZE, out);
out.writeDouble(e.getSalary());
LocalDate hireDay = e.getHireDay();
out.writeInt(hireDay.getYear());
out.writeInt(hireDay.getMonthValue());
out.writeInt(hireDay.getDayOfMonth());
```

Reading the data back is just as simple.

```
String name = DataIO.readFixedString(Employee.NAME_SIZE, in);
double salary = in.readDouble();
int y = in.readInt();
int m = in.readInt();
int d = in.readInt();
```

Let us compute the size of each record. We will use 40 characters for the name strings. Therefore, each record will contain 100 bytes:

- 40 characters = 80 bytes for the name
- 1 double = 8 bytes for the salary
- 3 int = 12 bytes for the date

The program shown in Listing 2.2 writes three records into a data file and then reads them from the file in reverse order. To do this efficiently requires random access—we need to get to the last record first.

Listing 2.2 randomAccess/RandomAccessTest.java

```java
1  package randomAccess;
2
3  import java.io.*;
4  import java.time.*;
5
6  /**
7   * @version 1.14 2018-05-01
8   * @author Cay Horstmann
9   */
10 public class RandomAccessTest
11 {
12    public static void main(String[] args) throws IOException
13    {
14       var staff = new Employee[3];
15
16       staff[0] = new Employee("Carl Cracker", 75000, 1987, 12, 15);
17       staff[1] = new Employee("Harry Hacker", 50000, 1989, 10, 1);
18       staff[2] = new Employee("Tony Tester", 40000, 1990, 3, 15);
19
20       try (var out = new DataOutputStream(new FileOutputStream("employee.dat")))
21       {
22          // save all employee records to the file employee.dat
23          for (Employee e : staff)
24             writeData(out, e);
25       }
26
27       try (var in = new RandomAccessFile("employee.dat", "r"))
28       {
29          // retrieve all records into a new array
30
31          // compute the array size
32          int n = (int)(in.length() / Employee.RECORD_SIZE);
33          var newStaff = new Employee[n];
34
35          // read employees in reverse order
36          for (int i = n - 1; i >= 0; i--)
37          {
38             newStaff[i] = new Employee();
39             in.seek(i * Employee.RECORD_SIZE);
40             newStaff[i] = readData(in);
41          }
42
43          // print the newly read employee records
44          for (Employee e : newStaff)
45             System.out.println(e);
46       }
47    }
```

(Continues)

Listing 2.2 *(Continued)*

```
48
49    /**
50     * Writes employee data to a data output
51     * @param out the data output
52     * @param e the employee
53     */
54    public static void writeData(DataOutput out, Employee e) throws IOException
55    {
56       DataIO.writeFixedString(e.getName(), Employee.NAME_SIZE, out);
57       out.writeDouble(e.getSalary());
58
59       LocalDate hireDay = e.getHireDay();
60       out.writeInt(hireDay.getYear());
61       out.writeInt(hireDay.getMonthValue());
62       out.writeInt(hireDay.getDayOfMonth());
63    }
64
65    /**
66     * Reads employee data from a data input
67     * @param in the data input
68     * @return the employee
69     */
70    public static Employee readData(DataInput in) throws IOException
71    {
72       String name = DataIO.readFixedString(Employee.NAME_SIZE, in);
73       double salary = in.readDouble();
74       int y = in.readInt();
75       int m = in.readInt();
76       int d = in.readInt();
77       return new Employee(name, salary, y, m - 1, d);
78    }
79 }
```

---

java.io.RandomAccessFile 1.0

- RandomAccessFile(String file, String mode)
- RandomAccessFile(File file, String mode)

  opens the given file for random access. The mode string is "r" for read-only mode, "rw" for read/write mode, "rws" for read/write mode with synchronous disk writes of data and metadata for every update, and "rwd" for read/write mode with synchronous disk writes of data only.

- long getFilePointer()

  returns the current location of the file pointer.

(Continues)

---

java.io.RandomAccessFile 1.0 *(Continued)*

- void seek(long pos)

  sets the file pointer to pos bytes from the beginning of the file.
- long length()

  returns the length of the file in bytes.

2.2.3 ZIP Archives

ZIP archives store one or more files in a (usually) compressed format. Each ZIP archive has a header with information such as the name of each file and the compression method that was used. In Java, you can use a ZipInputStream to read a ZIP archive. You need to look at the individual *entries* in the archive. The getNextEntry method returns an object of type ZipEntry that describes the entry. Read from the stream until the end, which is actually the end of the current entry. Then call closeEntry to read the next entry. Do not close zin until you read the last entry. Here is a typical code sequence to read through a ZIP file:

```
var zin = new ZipInputStream(new FileInputStream(zipname));
ZipEntry entry;
while ((entry = zin.getNextEntry()) != null)
{
   read the contents of zin
   zin.closeEntry();
}
zin.close();
```

To write a ZIP file, use a ZipOutputStream. For each entry that you want to place into the ZIP file, create a ZipEntry object. Pass the file name to the ZipEntry constructor; it sets the other parameters such as file date and decompression method. You can override these settings if you like. Then, call the putNextEntry method of the ZipOutputStream to begin writing a new file. Send the file data to the ZIP output stream. When done, call closeEntry. Repeat for all the files you want to store. Here is a code skeleton:

```
var fout = new FileOutputStream("test.zip");
var zout = new ZipOutputStream(fout);
for all files
{
   var ze = new ZipEntry(filename);
   zout.putNextEntry(ze);
   send data to zout
   zout.closeEntry();
}
zout.close();
```

NOTE: JAR files (which were discussed in Volume I, Chapter 4) are simply ZIP files with a special entry—the so-called manifest. Use the `JarInputStream` and `JarOutputStream` classes to read and write the manifest entry.

ZIP input streams are a good example of the power of the stream abstraction. When you read data stored in compressed form, you don't need to worry that the data are being decompressed as they are being requested. Moreover, the source of the bytes in a ZIP stream need not be a file—the ZIP data can come from a network connection.

 NOTE: Section 2.4.8, "ZIP File Systems," on p. 123 shows how to access a ZIP archive without a special API, using the `FileSystem` class of Java 7.

`java.util.zip.ZipInputStream` `1.1`

- `ZipInputStream(InputStream in)`

  creates a `ZipInputStream` that allows you to inflate data from the given `InputStream`.

- `ZipEntry getNextEntry()`

  returns a `ZipEntry` object for the next entry, or `null` if there are no more entries.

- `void closeEntry()`

  closes the current open entry in the ZIP file. You can then read the next entry by using `getNextEntry()`.

`java.util.zip.ZipOutputStream` `1.1`

- `ZipOutputStream(OutputStream out)`

  creates a `ZipOutputStream` that you can use to write compressed data to the specified `OutputStream`.

- `void putNextEntry(ZipEntry ze)`

  writes the information in the given `ZipEntry` to the output stream and positions the stream for the data. The data can then be written by calling the `write()` method.

(Continues)

---

java.util.zip.ZipOutputStream 1.1 *(Continued)*

- void closeEntry()

  closes the currently open entry in the ZIP file. Use the putNextEntry method to start the next entry.

- void setLevel(int level)

  sets the default compression level of subsequent DEFLATED entries to a value from Deflater.NO_COMPRESSION to Deflater.BEST_COMPRESSION. The default value is Deflater.DEFAULT_COMPRESSION. Throws an IllegalArgumentException if the level is not valid.

- void setMethod(int method)

  sets the default compression method for this ZipOutputStream for any entries that do not specify a method; can be either DEFLATED or STORED.

---

java.util.zip.ZipEntry 1.1

- ZipEntry(String name)

  constructs a ZIP entry with a given name.

- long getCrc()

  returns the CRC32 checksum value for this ZipEntry.

- String getName()

  returns the name of this entry.

- long getSize()

  returns the uncompressed size of this entry, or -1 if the uncompressed size is not known.

- boolean isDirectory()

  returns true if this entry is a directory.

- void setMethod(int method)

  sets the compression method for the entry to DEFLATED or STORED.

- void setSize(long size)

  sets the size of this entry. Only required if the compression method is STORED.

- void setCrc(long crc)

  sets the CRC32 checksum of this entry. Use the CRC32 class to compute this checksum. Only required if the compression method is STORED.

---

java.util.zip.ZipFile 1.1

- ZipFile(String name)
- ZipFile(File file)

  creates a ZipFile for reading from the given string or File object.

- Enumeration entries()

  returns an Enumeration object that enumerates the ZipEntry objects that describe the entries of the ZipFile.

- ZipEntry getEntry(String name)

  returns the entry corresponding to the given name, or null if there is no such entry.

- InputStream getInputStream(ZipEntry ze)

  returns an InputStream for the given entry.

- String getName()

  returns the path of this ZIP file.

2.3 Object Input/Output Streams and Serialization

Using a fixed-length record format is a good choice if you need to store data of the same type. However, objects that you create in an object-oriented program are rarely all of the same type. For example, you might have an array called staff that is nominally an array of Employee records but contains objects that are actually instances of a subclass such as Manager.

It is certainly possible to come up with a data format that allows you to store such polymorphic collections—but, fortunately, we don't have to. The Java language supports a very general mechanism, called *object serialization*, that makes it possible to write any object to an output stream and read it again later. (You will see in this chapter where the term "serialization" comes from.)

2.3.1 Saving and Loading Serializable Objects

To save object data, you first need to open an ObjectOutputStream object:

```
var out = new ObjectOutputStream(new FileOutputStream("employee.dat"));
```

Now, to save an object, simply use the writeObject method of the ObjectOutputStream class as in the following fragment:

```
var harry = new Employee("Harry Hacker", 50000, 1989, 10, 1);
var boss = new Manager("Carl Cracker", 80000, 1987, 12, 15);
```

```
out.writeObject(harry);
out.writeObject(boss);
```

To read the objects back in, first get an `ObjectInputStream` object:

```
var in = new ObjectInputStream(new FileInputStream("employee.dat"));
```

Then, retrieve the objects in the same order in which they were written, using the `readObject` method:

```
var e1 = (Employee) in.readObject();
var e2 = (Employee) in.readObject();
```

There is, however, one change you need to make to any class that you want to save to an output stream and restore from an object input stream. The class must implement the `Serializable` interface:

```
class Employee implements Serializable { . . . }
```

The `Serializable` interface has no methods, so you don't need to change your classes in any way. In this regard, it is similar to the `Cloneable` interface that we discussed in Volume I, Chapter 6. However, to make a class cloneable, you still had to override the `clone` method of the `Object` class. To make a class serializable, you do not need to do anything else.

 NOTE: You can write and read only *objects* with the `writeObject`/`readObject` methods. For primitive type values, use methods such as `writeInt`/`readInt` or `writeDouble`/`readDouble`. (The object input/output stream classes implement the `DataInput`/`DataOutput` interfaces.)

Behind the scenes, an `ObjectOutputStream` looks at all the fields of the objects and saves their contents. For example, when writing an `Employee` object, the name, date, and salary fields are written to the output stream.

However, there is one important situation to consider: What happens when one object is shared by several objects as part of their state?

To illustrate the problem, let us make a slight modification to the `Manager` class. Let's assume that each manager has a secretary:

```
class Manager extends Employee
{
   private Employee secretary;
   . . .
}
```

Each Manager object now contains a reference to an Employee object that describes the secretary. Of course, two managers can share the same secretary, as is the case in Figure 2.5 and the following code:

```
var harry = new Employee("Harry Hacker", . . .);
var carl = new Manager("Carl Cracker", . . .);
carl.setSecretary(harry);
var tony = new Manager("Tony Tester", . . .);
tony.setSecretary(harry);
```

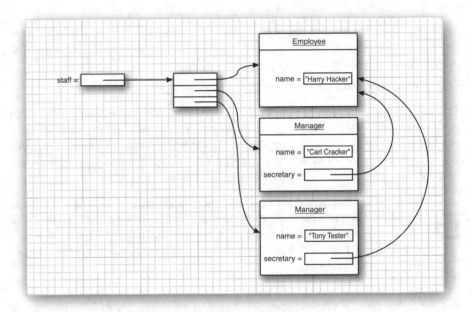

Figure 2.5 Two managers can share a mutual employee.

Saving such a network of objects is a challenge. Of course, we cannot save and restore the memory addresses for the secretary objects. When an object is reloaded, it will likely occupy a completely different memory address than it originally did.

Instead, each object is saved with the *serial number*—hence the name *object serialization* for this mechanism. Here is the algorithm:

1. Associate a serial number with each object reference that you encounter (as shown in Figure 2.6).

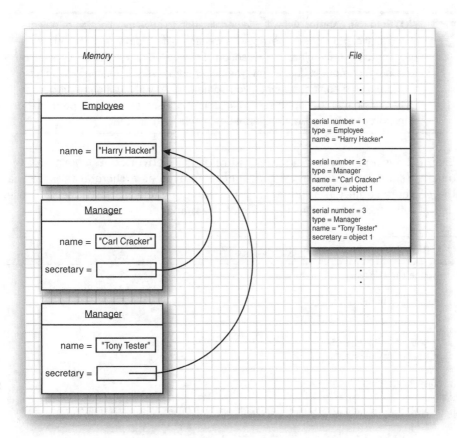

Figure 2.6 An example of object serialization

2. When encountering an object reference for the first time, save the object data to the output stream.

3. If it has been saved previously, just write "same as the previously saved object with serial number *x*."

When reading the objects back, the procedure is reversed.

1. When an object is specified in an object input stream for the first time, construct it, initialize it with the stream data, and remember the association between the serial number and the object reference.

2. When the tag "same as the previously saved object with serial number *x*" is encountered, retrieve the object reference for the sequence number.

NOTE: In this chapter, we will use serialization to save a collection of objects to a disk file and retrieve it exactly as we stored it. Another very important application is the transmittal of a collection of objects across a network connection to another computer. Just as raw memory addresses are meaningless in a file, they are also meaningless when you communicate with a different processor. By replacing memory addresses with serial numbers, serialization permits the transport of object collections from one machine to another.

Listing 2.3 is a program that saves and reloads a network of Employee and Manager objects (some of which share the same employee as a secretary). Note that the secretary object is unique after reloading—when newStaff[1] gets a raise, that is reflected in the secretary fields of the managers.

Listing 2.3 objectStream/ObjectStreamTest.java

```java
1  package objectStream;
2
3  import java.io.*;
4
5  /**
6   * @version 1.11 2018-05-01
7   * @author Cay Horstmann
8   */
9  class ObjectStreamTest
10 {
11    public static void main(String[] args) throws IOException, ClassNotFoundException
12    {
13       var harry = new Employee("Harry Hacker", 50000, 1989, 10, 1);
14       var carl = new Manager("Carl Cracker", 80000, 1987, 12, 15);
15       carl.setSecretary(harry);
16       var tony = new Manager("Tony Tester", 40000, 1990, 3, 15);
17       tony.setSecretary(harry);
18
19       var staff = new Employee[3];
20
21       staff[0] = carl;
22       staff[1] = harry;
23       staff[2] = tony;
24
25       // save all employee records to the file employee.dat
26       try (var out = new ObjectOutputStream(new FileOutputStream("employee.dat")))
27       {
28          out.writeObject(staff);
29       }
30
```

```
31      try (var in = new ObjectInputStream(new FileInputStream("employee.dat")))
32      {
33         // retrieve all records into a new array
34
35         var newStaff = (Employee[]) in.readObject();
36
37         // raise secretary's salary
38         newStaff[1].raiseSalary(10);
39
40         // print the newly read employee records
41         for (Employee e : newStaff)
42            System.out.println(e);
43      }
44   }
45 }
```

---

java.io.ObjectOutputStream 1.1

- ObjectOutputStream(OutputStream out)

  creates an ObjectOutputStream so you can write objects to the specified OutputStream.

- void writeObject(Object obj)

  writes the specified object to the ObjectOutputStream. This method saves the class of the object, the signature of the class, and the values of any nonstatic, nontransient fields of the class and its superclasses.

---

java.io.ObjectInputStream 1.1

- ObjectInputStream(InputStream in)

  creates an ObjectInputStream to read back object information from the specified InputStream.

- Object readObject()

  reads an object from the ObjectInputStream. In particular, this method reads back the class of the object, the signature of the class, and the values of the nontransient and nonstatic fields of the class and all its superclasses. It does deserializing so that multiple object references can be recovered.

2.3.2 Understanding the Object Serialization File Format

Object serialization saves object data in a particular file format. Of course, you can use the writeObject/readObject methods without having to know the exact sequence of bytes that represents objects in a file. Nonetheless, we found studying the data format extremely helpful for gaining insight into the object serialization process. As the details are somewhat technical, feel free to skip this section if you are not interested in the implementation.

Every file begins with the two-byte "magic number"

```
AC ED
```

followed by the version number of the object serialization format, which is currently

```
00 05
```

(We use hexadecimal numbers throughout this section to denote bytes.) Then, it contains a sequence of objects, in the order in which they were saved.

String objects are saved as

74	two-byte length	characters

For example, the string "Harry" is saved as

```
74 00 05 Harry
```

The Unicode characters of the string are saved in the "modified UTF-8" format.

When an object is saved, the class of that object must be saved as well. The class description contains

- The name of the class
- The *serial version unique ID*, which is a fingerprint of the data field types and method signatures
- A set of flags describing the serialization method
- A description of the data fields

The fingerprint is obtained by ordering the descriptions of the class, superclass, interfaces, field types, and method signatures in a canonical way, and then applying the so-called Secure Hash Algorithm (SHA) to that data.

SHA is a fast algorithm that gives a "fingerprint" of a larger block of information. This fingerprint is always a 20-byte data packet, regardless of the size of the original data. It is created by a clever sequence of bit operations on the data that makes it essentially 100 percent certain that the fingerprint will change if the information is altered in any way. (For more details on SHA, see, for example, *Cryptography and Network Security, Seventh Edition* by William Stallings, Prentice Hall, 2016.) However, the serialization mechanism uses only the first eight bytes of the SHA code as a class fingerprint. It is still very likely that the class fingerprint will change if the data fields or methods change.

When reading an object, its fingerprint is compared against the current fingerprint of the class. If they don't match, it means the class definition has changed after the object was written, and an exception is generated. Of course, in practice, classes do evolve, and it might be necessary for a program to read in older versions of objects. We will discuss this in Section 2.3.5, "Versioning," on p. 103.

Here is how a class identifier is stored:

* 72
* 2-byte length of class name
* Class name
* 8-byte fingerprint
* 1-byte flag
* 2-byte count of data field descriptors
* Data field descriptors
* 78 (end marker)
* Superclass type (70 if none)

The flag byte is composed of three bit masks, defined in java.io.ObjectStreamConstants:

```
static final byte SC_WRITE_METHOD = 1;
   // class has a writeObject method that writes additional data
static final byte SC_SERIALIZABLE = 2;
   // class implements the Serializable interface
static final byte SC_EXTERNALIZABLE = 4;
   // class implements the Externalizable interface
```

We discuss the Externalizable interface later in this chapter. Externalizable classes supply custom read and write methods that take over the output of their instance fields. The classes that we write implement the Serializable interface and will have a flag value of 02. The serializable java.util.Date class defines its own readObject/writeObject methods and has a flag of 03.

Each data field descriptor has the format:

* 1-byte type code
* 2-byte length of field name
* Field name
* Class name (if the field is an object)

The type code is one of the following:

B	byte
C	char
D	double
F	float
I	int
J	long
L	object
S	short
Z	boolean
[	array

When the type code is L, the field name is followed by the field type. Class and field name strings do not start with the string code 74, but field types do. Field types use a slightly different encoding of their names—namely, the format used by native methods.

For example, the salary field of the Employee class is encoded as

```
D 00 06 salary
```

Here is the complete class descriptor of the Employee class:

```
72 00 08 Employee
```
E6 D2 86 7D AE AC 18 1B 02	Fingerprint and flags
00 03	Number of instance fields
D 00 06 salary	Instance field type and name
L 00 07 hireDay	Instance field type and name
74 00 10 Ljava/util/Date;	Instance field class name: Date
L 00 04 name	Instance field type and name
74 00 12 Ljava/lang/String;	Instance field class name: String
78	End marker
70	No superclass

These descriptors are fairly long. If the *same* class descriptor is needed again in the file, an abbreviated form is used:

71	4-byte serial number

The serial number refers to the previous explicit class descriptor. We discuss the numbering scheme later.

An object is stored as

73	class descriptor	object data

For example, here is how an Employee object is stored:

```
40 E8 6A 00 00 00 00 00          salary field value: double
73                               hireDay field value: new object
   71 00 7E 00 08                Existing class java.util.Date
   77 08 00 00 00 91 1B 4E B1 80 78    External storage (details later)
74 00 0C Harry Hacker            name field value: String
```

As you can see, the data file contains enough information to restore the Employee object.

Arrays are saved in the following format:

```
75            class descriptor       4-byte number of     entries
                                     entries
```

The array class name in the class descriptor is in the same format as that used by native methods (which is slightly different from the format used by class names in other class descriptors). In this format, class names start with an L and end with a semicolon.

For example, an array of three Employee objects starts out like this:

```
75                               Array
   72 00 0B [LEmployee;          New class, string length, class name
                                 Employee[]
      FC BF 36 11 C5 91 11 C7 02 Fingerprint and flags
      00 00                      Number of instance fields
      78                         End marker
      70                         No superclass
   00 00 00 03                   Number of array entries
```

Note that the fingerprint for an array of Employee objects is different from a fingerprint of the Employee class itself.

All objects (including arrays and strings) and all class descriptors are given serial numbers as they are saved in the output file. The numbers start at 00 7E 00 00.

We already saw that a full class descriptor for any given class occurs only once. Subsequent descriptors refer to it. For example, in our previous example, a repeated reference to the Date class was coded as

```
71 00 7E 00 08
```

The same mechanism is used for objects. If a reference to a previously saved object is written, it is saved in exactly the same way—that is, 71 followed by the serial number. It is always clear from the context whether a particular serial reference denotes a class descriptor or an object.

Finally, a null reference is stored as

    70

Here is the commented output of the `ObjectRefTest` program of the preceding section. Run the program, look at a hex dump of its data file `employee.dat`, and compare it with the commented listing. The important lines toward the end of the output show a reference to a previously saved object.

AC ED 00 05	File header
75	Array `staff` (serial #1)
72 00 0B [LEmployee;	New class, string length, class name `Employee[]` (serial #0)
FC BF 36 11 C5 91 11 C7 02	Fingerprint and flags
00 00	Number of instance fields
78	End marker
70	No superclass
00 00 00 03	Number of array entries
73	`staff[0]`— new object (serial #7)
72 00 07 Manager	New class, string length, class name (serial #2)
36 06 AE 13 63 8F 59 B7 02	Fingerprint and flags
00 01	Number of data fields
L 00 09 secretary	Instance field type and name
74 00 0A LEmployee;	Instance field class name: `String` (serial #3)
78	End marker
72 00 08 Employee	Superclass: new class, string length, class name (serial #4)
E6 D2 86 7D AE AC 18 1B 02	Fingerprint and flags
00 03	Number of instance fields
D 00 06 salary	Instance field type and name
L 00 07 hireDay	Instance field type and name
74 00 10 Ljava/util/Date;	Instance field class name: `String` (serial #5)
L 00 04 name	Instance field type and name
74 00 12 Ljava/lang/String;	Instance field class name: `String` (serial #6)
78	End marker
70	No superclass

40 F3 88 00 00 00 00 00	salary field value: double
73	hireDay field value: new object (serial #9)
72 00 0E java.util.Date	New class, string length, class name (serial #8)
68 6A 81 01 4B 59 74 19 03	Fingerprint and flags
00 00	No instance variables
78	End marker
70	No superclass
77 08	External storage, number of bytes
00 00 00 83 E9 39 E0 00	Date
78	End marker
74 00 0C Carl Cracker	name field value: String (serial #10)
73	secretary field value: new object (serial #11)
71 00 7E 00 04	existing class (use serial #4)
40 E8 6A 00 00 00 00 00	salary field value: double
73	hireDay field value: new object (serial #12)
71 00 7E 00 08	Existing class (use serial #8)
77 08	External storage, number of bytes
00 00 00 91 1B 4E B1 80	Date
78	End marker
74 00 0C Harry Hacker	name field value: String (serial #13)
71 00 7E 00 0B	staff[1]: existing object (use serial #11)
73	staff[2]: new object (serial #14)
71 00 7E 00 02	Existing class (use serial #2)
40 E3 88 00 00 00 00 00	salary field value: double
73	hireDay field value: new object (serial #15)
71 00 7E 00 08	Existing class (use serial #8)
77 08	External storage, number of bytes
00 00 00 94 6D 3E EC 00 00	Date
78	End marker
74 00 0B Tony Tester	name field value: String (serial #16)
71 00 7E 00 0B	secretary field value: existing object (use serial #11)

Of course, studying these codes can be about as exciting as reading a phone book. It is not important to know the exact file format (unless you are trying to create an evil effect by modifying the data), but it is still instructive to know that the serialized format has a detailed description of all the objects it contains, with sufficient detail to allow reconstruction of both objects and arrays of objects.

What you should remember is this:

- The serialized format contains the types and data fields of all objects.
- Each object is assigned a serial number.
- Repeated occurrences of the same object are stored as references to that serial number.

2.3.3 Modifying the Default Serialization Mechanism

Certain data fields should never be serialized—for example, integer values that store file handles or handles of windows that are only meaningful to native methods. Such information is guaranteed to be useless when you reload an object at a later time or transport it to a different machine. In fact, improper values for such fields can actually cause native methods to crash. Java has an easy mechanism to prevent such fields from ever being serialized: Mark them with the keyword transient. You also need to tag fields as transient if they belong to nonserializable classes. Transient fields are always skipped when objects are serialized.

The serialization mechanism provides a way for individual classes to add validation or any other desired action to the default read and write behavior. A serializable class can define methods with the signature

```
private void readObject(ObjectInputStream in)
    throws IOException, ClassNotFoundException;
private void writeObject(ObjectOutputStream out)
    throws IOException;
```

Then, the data fields are no longer automatically serialized—these methods are called instead.

Here is a typical example. A number of classes in the java.awt.geom package, such as Point2D.Double, are not serializable. Now, suppose you want to serialize a class LabeledPoint that stores a String and a Point2D.Double. First, you need to mark the Point2D.Double field as transient to avoid a NotSerializableException.

```
public class LabeledPoint implements Serializable
{
   private String label;
   private transient Point2D.Double point;
   . . .
}
```

In the writeObject method, we first write the object descriptor and the String field, label, by calling the defaultWriteObject method. This is a special method of the ObjectOutputStream class that can only be called from within a writeObject method of a serializable class. Then we write the point coordinates, using the standard DataOutput calls.

```
private void writeObject(ObjectOutputStream out)
      throws IOException
{
   out.defaultWriteObject();
   out.writeDouble(point.getX());
   out.writeDouble(point.getY());
}
```

In the readObject method, we reverse the process:

```
private void readObject(ObjectInputStream in)
      throws IOException
{
   in.defaultReadObject();
   double x = in.readDouble();
   double y = in.readDouble();
   point = new Point2D.Double(x, y);
}
```

Another example is the java.util.Date class that supplies its own readObject and writeObject methods. These methods write the date as a number of milliseconds from the epoch (January 1, 1970, midnight UTC). The Date class has a complex internal representation that stores both a Calendar object and a millisecond count to optimize lookups. The state of the Calendar is redundant and does not have to be saved.

The readObject and writeObject methods only need to save and load their data fields. They should not concern themselves with superclass data or any other class information.

Instead of letting the serialization mechanism save and restore object data, a class can define its own mechanism. To do this, a class must implement the Externalizable interface. This, in turn, requires it to define two methods:

```
public void readExternal(ObjectInputStream in)
      throws IOException, ClassNotFoundException;
public void writeExternal(ObjectOutputStream out)
      throws IOException;
```

Unlike the readObject and writeObject methods that were described in the previous section, these methods are fully responsible for saving and restoring the entire object, *including the superclass data*. When writing an object, the serialization mechanism merely records the class of the object in the output stream. When reading an externalizable object, the object input stream creates an object with the no-argument constructor and then calls the readExternal method. Here is how you can implement these methods for the Employee class:

```
public void readExternal(ObjectInput s)
      throws IOException
{
   name = s.readUTF();
   salary = s.readDouble();
   hireDay = LocalDate.ofEpochDay(s.readLong());
}

public void writeExternal(ObjectOutput s)
      throws IOException
{
   s.writeUTF(name);
   s.writeDouble(salary);
   s.writeLong(hireDay.toEpochDay());
}
```

CAUTION: Unlike the readObject and writeObject methods, which are private and can only be called by the serialization mechanism, the readExternal and writeExternal methods are public. In particular, readExternal potentially permits modification of the state of an existing object.

2.3.4 Serializing Singletons and Typesafe Enumerations

You have to pay particular attention to serializing and deserializing objects that are assumed to be unique. This commonly happens when you are implementing singletons and typesafe enumerations.

If you use the enum construct of the Java language, you need not worry about serialization—it just works. However, suppose you maintain legacy code that contains an enumerated type such as

```
public class Orientation
{
   public static final Orientation HORIZONTAL = new Orientation(1);
   public static final Orientation VERTICAL   = new Orientation(2);

   private int value;

   private Orientation(int v) { value = v; }
}
```

This idiom was common before enumerations were added to the Java language. Note that the constructor is private. Thus, no objects can be created beyond Orientation.HORIZONTAL and Orientation.VERTICAL. In particular, you can use the == operator to test for object equality:

```
if (orientation == Orientation.HORIZONTAL) . . .
```

There is an important twist that you need to remember when a typesafe enumeration implements the Serializable interface. The default serialization mechanism is not appropriate. Suppose we write a value of type Orientation and read it in again:

```
Orientation original = Orientation.HORIZONTAL;
ObjectOutputStream out = . . .;
out.write(original);
out.close();
ObjectInputStream in = . . .;
var saved = (Orientation) in.read();
```

Now the test

```
if (saved == Orientation.HORIZONTAL) . . .
```

will fail. In fact, the saved value is a completely new object of the Orientation type that is not equal to any of the predefined constants. Even though the constructor is private, the serialization mechanism can create new objects!

To solve this problem, you need to define another special serialization method, called readResolve. If the readResolve method is defined, it is called after the object is deserialized. It must return an object which then becomes the return value of the readObject method. In our case, the readResolve method will inspect the value field and return the appropriate enumerated constant:

```
protected Object readResolve() throws ObjectStreamException
{
    if (value == 1) return Orientation.HORIZONTAL;
    if (value == 2) return Orientation.VERTICAL;
    throw new ObjectStreamException(); // this shouldn't happen
}
```

Remember to add a readResolve method to all typesafe enumerations in your legacy code and to all classes that follow the singleton design pattern.

2.3.5 Versioning

If you use serialization to save objects, you need to consider what happens when your program evolves. Can version 1.1 read the old files? Can the users who still use 1.0 read the files that the new version is producing? Clearly, it would be desirable if object files could cope with the evolution of classes.

At first glance, it seems that this would not be possible. When a class definition changes in any way, its SHA fingerprint also changes, and you know that object input streams will refuse to read in objects with different fingerprints. However, a class can indicate that it is *compatible* with an earlier version of itself. To do this, you must first obtain the fingerprint of the *earlier* version of the class. Use the standalone serialver program that is part of the JDK to obtain this number. For example, running

```
serialver Employee
```

prints

```
Employee: static final long serialVersionUID = -1814239825517340645L;
```

All *later* versions of the class must define the serialVersionUID constant to the same fingerprint as the original.

```
class Employee implements Serializable // version 1.1
{
    . . .
    public static final long serialVersionUID = -1814239825517340645L;
}
```

When a class has a static data member named serialVersionUID, it will not compute the fingerprint manually but will use that value instead.

Once that static data member has been placed inside a class, the serialization system is now willing to read in different versions of objects of that class.

If only the methods of the class change, there is no problem with reading the new object data. However, if the data fields change, you may have problems. For example, the old file object may have more or fewer data fields than the one in the program, or the types of the data fields may be different. In that case, the object input stream makes an effort to convert the serialized object to the current version of the class.

The object input stream compares the data fields of the current version of the class with those of the version in the serialized object. Of course, the object input stream considers only the nontransient and nonstatic data fields. If two fields have matching names but different types, the object input stream makes no effort to convert one type to the other—the objects are incompatible. If the serialized object has data fields that are not present in the current version, the object input stream ignores the additional data. If the current version has data fields that are not present in the serialized object, the added fields are set to their default (null for objects, zero for numbers, and false for boolean values).

Here is an example. Suppose we have saved a number of employee records on disk, using the original version (1.0) of the class. Now we change the Employee class to version 2.0 by adding a data field called department. Figure 2.7 shows what happens when a 1.0 object is read into a program that uses 2.0 objects. The department field is set to null. Figure 2.8 shows the opposite scenario: A program using 1.0 objects reads a 2.0 object. The additional department field is ignored.

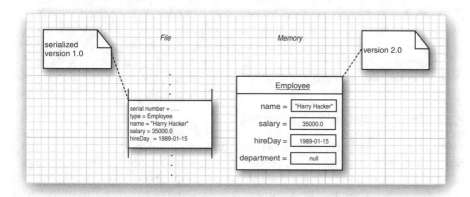

Figure 2.7 Reading an object with fewer data fields

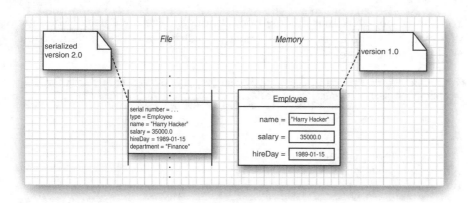

Figure 2.8 Reading an object with more data fields

Is this process safe? It depends. Dropping a data field seems harmless—the recipient still has all the data that it knows how to manipulate. Setting a data field to null might not be so safe. Many classes work hard to initialize all data fields in all constructors to non-null values, so that the methods don't have to be prepared to handle null data. It is up to the class designer to implement additional code in the readObject method to fix version incompatibilities or to make sure the methods are robust enough to handle null data.

 TIP: Before you add a serialVersionUID field to a class, ask yourself why you made your class serializable. If serialization is used only for short-term persistence, such as distributed method calls in an application server, there is no need to worry about versioning and the serialVersionUID. The same applies if you extend a class that happens to be serializable, but you have no intent to ever persist its instances. If your IDE gives you pesky warnings, change the IDE preferences to turn them off, or add an annotation @SuppressWarnings("serial"). This is safer than adding a serialVersionUID that you may later forget to change.

2.3.6 Using Serialization for Cloning

There is an amusing use for the serialization mechanism: It gives you an easy way to clone an object, provided the class is serializable. Simply serialize it to an output stream and then read it back in. The result is a new object that is a deep copy of the existing object. You don't have to write the object to a file—you can use a ByteArrayOutputStream to save the data into a byte array.

As Listing 2.4 shows, to get clone for free, simply extend the SerialCloneable class, and you are done.

You should be aware that this method, although clever, will usually be much slower than a clone method that explicitly constructs a new object and copies or clones the data fields.

Listing 2.4 serialClone/SerialCloneTest.java

```
1 package serialClone;
2
3 /**
4  * @version 1.22 2018-05-01
5  * @author Cay Horstmann
6  */
7
8 import java.io.*;
9 import java.time.*;
10
11 public class SerialCloneTest
12 {
13    public static void main(String[] args) throws CloneNotSupportedException
14    {
```

```
15       var harry = new Employee("Harry Hacker", 35000, 1989, 10, 1);
16       // clone harry
17       var harry2 = (Employee) harry.clone();
18
19       // mutate harry
20       harry.raiseSalary(10);
21
22       // now harry and the clone are different
23       System.out.println(harry);
24       System.out.println(harry2);
25    }
26 }
27
28 /**
29  * A class whose clone method uses serialization.
30  */
31 class SerialCloneable implements Cloneable, Serializable
32 {
33    public Object clone() throws CloneNotSupportedException
34    {
35       try {
36          // save the object to a byte array
37          var bout = new ByteArrayOutputStream();
38          try (var out = new ObjectOutputStream(bout))
39          {
40             out.writeObject(this);
41          }
42
43          // read a clone of the object from the byte array
44          try (var bin = new ByteArrayInputStream(bout.toByteArray()))
45          {
46             var in = new ObjectInputStream(bin);
47             return in.readObject();
48          }
49       }
50       catch (IOException | ClassNotFoundException e)
51       {
52          var e2 = new CloneNotSupportedException();
53          e2.initCause(e);
54          throw e2;
55       }
56    }
57 }
58
59 /**
60  * The familiar Employee class, redefined to extend the
61  * SerialCloneable class.
62  */
```

(Continues)

Listing 2.4 *(Continued)*

```java
63  class Employee extends SerialCloneable
64  {
65     private String name;
66     private double salary;
67     private LocalDate hireDay;
68
69     public Employee(String n, double s, int year, int month, int day)
70     {
71        name = n;
72        salary = s;
73        hireDay = LocalDate.of(year, month, day);
74     }
75
76     public String getName()
77     {
78        return name;
79     }
80
81     public double getSalary()
82     {
83        return salary;
84     }
85
86     public LocalDate getHireDay()
87     {
88        return hireDay;
89     }
90
91     /**
92        Raises the salary of this employee.
93        @byPercent the percentage of the raise
94     */
95     public void raiseSalary(double byPercent)
96     {
97        double raise = salary * byPercent / 100;
98        salary += raise;
99     }
100
101    public String toString()
102    {
103       return getClass().getName()
104          + "[name=" + name
105          + ",salary=" + salary
106          + ",hireDay=" + hireDay
107          + "]";
108    }
109 }
```

2.4 Working with Files

You have learned how to read and write data from a file. However, there is more to file management than reading and writing. The Path interface and Files class encapsulate the functionality required to work with the file system on the user's machine. For example, the Files class can be used to remove or rename a file, or to find out when a file was last modified. In other words, the input/output stream classes are concerned with the contents of files, whereas the classes that we discuss here are concerned with the storage of files on a disk.

The Path interface and Files class were added in Java 7. They are much more convenient to use than the File class which dates back all the way to JDK 1.0. We expect them to be very popular with Java programmers and discuss them in depth.

2.4.1 Paths

A Path is a sequence of directory names, optionally followed by a file name. The first component of a path may be a *root component* such as / or C:\. The permissible root components depend on the file system. A path that starts with a root component is *absolute*. Otherwise, it is *relative*. For example, here we construct an absolute and a relative path. For the absolute path, we assume a UNIX-like file system.

```
Path absolute = Paths.get("/home", "harry");
Path relative = Paths.get("myprog", "conf", "user.properties");
```

The static Paths.get method receives one or more strings, which it joins with the path separator of the default file system (/ for a UNIX-like file system, \ for Windows). It then parses the result, throwing an InvalidPathException if the result is not a valid path in the given file system. The result is a Path object.

The get method can get a single string containing multiple components. For example, you can read a path from a configuration file like this:

```
String baseDir = props.getProperty("base.dir");
   // May be a string such as /opt/myprog or c:\Program Files\myprog
Path basePath = Paths.get(baseDir); // OK that baseDir has separators
```

 NOTE: A path does not have to correspond to a file that actually exists. It is merely an abstract sequence of names. As you will see in the next section, when you want to create a file, you first make a path and then call a method to create the corresponding file.

It is very common to combine or *resolve* paths. The call p.resolve(q) returns a path according to these rules:

- If q is absolute, then the result is q.
- Otherwise, the result is "p then q," according to the rules of the file system.

For example, suppose your application needs to find its working directory relative to a given base directory that is read from a configuration file, as in the preceding example.

```
Path workRelative = Paths.get("work");
Path workPath = basePath.resolve(workRelative);
```

There is a shortcut for the resolve method that takes a string instead of a path:

```
Path workPath = basePath.resolve("work");
```

There is a convenience method resolveSibling that resolves against a path's parent, yielding a sibling path. For example, if workPath is /opt/myapp/work, the call

```
Path tempPath = workPath.resolveSibling("temp");
```

creates /opt/myapp/temp.

The opposite of resolve is relativize. The call p.relativize(r) yields the path q which, when resolved with p, yields r. For example, relativizing /home/harry against /home/fred/input.txt yields ../fred/input.txt. Here, we assume that .. denotes the parent directory in the file system.

The normalize method removes any redundant . and .. components (or whatever the file system may deem redundant). For example, normalizing the path /home/harry/../fred/./input.txt yields /home/fred/input.txt.

The toAbsolutePath method yields the absolute path of a given path, starting at a root component, such as /home/fred/input.txt or c:\Users\fred\input.txt.

The Path interface has many useful methods for taking paths apart. This code sample shows some of the most useful ones:

```
Path p = Paths.get("/home", "fred", "myprog.properties");
Path parent = p.getParent(); // the path /home/fred
Path file = p.getFileName(); // the path myprog.properties
Path root = p.getRoot(); // the path /
```

As you have already seen in Volume I, you can construct a Scanner from a Path object:

```
var in = new Scanner(Paths.get("/home/fred/input.txt"));
```

NOTE: Occasionally, you may need to interoperate with legacy APIs that use the File class instead of the Path interface. The Path interface has a toFile method, and the File class has a toPath method.

---

java.nio.file.Paths 7

- static Path get(String first, String... more)

  makes a path by joining the given strings.

---

java.nio.file.Path 7

- Path resolve(Path other)
- Path resolve(String other)

  if other is absolute, returns other; otherwise, returns the path obtained by joining this and other.

- Path resolveSibling(Path other)
- Path resolveSibling(String other)

  if other is absolute, returns other; otherwise, returns the path obtained by joining the parent of this and other.

- Path relativize(Path other)

  returns the relative path that, when resolved with this, yields other.

- Path normalize()

  removes redundant path elements such as . and ..

- Path toAbsolutePath()

  returns an absolute path that is equivalent to this path.

- Path getParent()

  returns the parent, or null if this path has no parent.

- Path getFileName()

  returns the last component of this path, or null if this path has no components.

- Path getRoot()

  returns the root component of this path, or null if this path has no root components.

- toFile()

  makes a File from this path.

---

java.io.File 1.0

- Path toPath() 7

  makes a Path from this file.

2.4.2 Reading and Writing Files

The Files class makes quick work of common file operations. For example, you can easily read the entire contents of a file:

```
byte[] bytes = Files.readAllBytes(path);
```

If you want to read the file as a string, call readAllBytes followed by

```
var content = new String(bytes, charset);
```

But if you want the file as a sequence of lines, call

```
List<String> lines = Files.readAllLines(path, charset);
```

Conversely, if you want to write a string, call

```
Files.write(path, content.getBytes(charset));
```

To append to a given file, use

```
Files.write(path, content.getBytes(charset), StandardOpenOption.APPEND);
```

You can also write a collection of lines with

```
Files.write(path, lines);
```

These simple methods are intended for dealing with text files of moderate length. If your files are large or binary, you can still use the familiar input/output streams or readers/writers:

```
InputStream in = Files.newInputStream(path);
OutputStream out = Files.newOutputStream(path);
Reader in = Files.newBufferedReader(path, charset);
Writer out = Files.newBufferedWriter(path, charset);
```

These convenience methods save you from dealing with FileInputStream, FileOutputStream, BufferedReader, or BufferedWriter.

---

java.nio.file.Files 7

- `static byte[] readAllBytes(Path path)`
- `static List<String> readAllLines(Path path, Charset charset)`

  reads the contents of a file.

- `static Path write(Path path, byte[] contents, OpenOption... options)`
- `static Path write(Path path, Iterable<? extends CharSequence> contents, OpenOption options)`

  writes the given contents to a file and returns path.

- `static InputStream newInputStream(Path path, OpenOption... options)`
- `static OutputStream newOutputStream(Path path, OpenOption... options)`
- `static BufferedReader newBufferedReader(Path path, Charset charset)`
- `static BufferedWriter newBufferedWriter(Path path, Charset charset, OpenOption... options)`

  opens a file for reading or writing.

2.4.3 Creating Files and Directories

To create a new directory, call

```
Files.createDirectory(path);
```

All but the last component in the path must already exist. To create intermediate directories as well, use

```
Files.createDirectories(path);
```

You can create an empty file with

```
Files.createFile(path);
```

The call throws an exception if the file already exists. The check for existence and creation are atomic. If the file doesn't exist, it is created before anyone else has a chance to do the same.

There are convenience methods for creating a temporary file or directory in a given or system-specific location.

```
Path newPath = Files.createTempFile(dir, prefix, suffix);
Path newPath = Files.createTempFile(prefix, suffix);
Path newPath = Files.createTempDirectory(dir, prefix);
Path newPath = Files.createTempDirectory(prefix);
```

Here, `dir` is a `Path`, and `prefix`/`suffix` are strings which may be `null`. For example, the call `Files.createTempFile(null, ".txt")` might return a path such as `/tmp/12344055522364837194.txt`.

When you create a file or directory, you can specify attributes, such as owners or permissions. However, the details depend on the file system, and we won't cover them here.

---

java.nio.file.Files 7

- `static Path createFile(Path path, FileAttribute<?>... attrs)`
- `static Path createDirectory(Path path, FileAttribute<?>... attrs)`
- `static Path createDirectories(Path path, FileAttribute<?>... attrs)`

creates a file or directory. The `createDirectories` method creates any intermediate directories as well.

- `static Path createTempFile(String prefix, String suffix, FileAttribute<?>... attrs)`
- `static Path createTempFile(Path parentDir, String prefix, String suffix, FileAttribute<?>... attrs)`
- `static Path createTempDirectory(String prefix, FileAttribute<?>... attrs)`
- `static Path createTempDirectory(Path parentDir, String prefix, FileAttribute<?>... attrs)`

creates a temporary file or directory, in a location suitable for temporary files or in the given parent directory. Returns the path to the created file or directory.

2.4.4 Copying, Moving, and Deleting Files

To copy a file from one location to another, simply call

```
Files.copy(fromPath, toPath);
```

To move the file (that is, copy and delete the original), call

```
Files.move(fromPath, toPath);
```

The copy or move will fail if the target exists. If you want to overwrite an existing target, use the `REPLACE_EXISTING` option. If you want to copy all file attributes, use the `COPY_ATTRIBUTES` option. You can supply both like this:

```
Files.copy(fromPath, toPath, StandardCopyOption.REPLACE_EXISTING,
    StandardCopyOption.COPY_ATTRIBUTES);
```

You can specify that a move should be atomic. Then you are assured that either the move completed successfully, or the source continues to be present. Use the ATOMIC_MOVE option:

```
Files.move(fromPath, toPath, StandardCopyOption.ATOMIC_MOVE);
```

You can also copy an input stream to a Path, which just means saving the input stream to disk. Similarly, you can copy a Path to an output stream. Use the following calls:

```
Files.copy(inputStream, toPath);
Files.copy(fromPath, outputStream);
```

As with the other calls to copy, you can supply copy options as needed.

Finally, to delete a file, simply call

```
Files.delete(path);
```

This method throws an exception if the file doesn't exist, so instead you may want to use

```
boolean deleted = Files.deleteIfExists(path);
```

The deletion methods can also be used to remove an empty directory.

See Table 2.3 for a summary of the options that are available for file operations.

---

java.nio.file.Files 7

- static Path copy(Path from, Path to, CopyOption... options)
- static Path move(Path from, Path to, CopyOption... options)

  copies or moves from to the given target location and returns to.

- static long copy(InputStream from, Path to, CopyOption... options)
- static long copy(Path from, OutputStream to, CopyOption... options)

  copies from an input stream to a file, or from a file to an output stream, returning the number of bytes copied.

- static void delete(Path path)
- static boolean deleteIfExists(Path path)

  deletes the given file or empty directory. The first method throws an exception if the file or directory doesn't exist. The second method returns false in that case.

Table 2.3 Standard Options for File Operations

Option	Description
StandardOpenOption; use with newBufferedWriter, newInputStream, newOutputStream, write	
READ	Open for reading
WRITE	Open for writing
APPEND	If opened for writing, append to the end of the file
TRUNCATE_EXISTING	If opened for writing, remove existing contents
CREATE_NEW	Create a new file and fail if it exists
CREATE	Atomically create a new file if it doesn't exist
DELETE_ON_CLOSE	Make a "best effort" to delete the file when it is closed
SPARSE	A hint to the file system that this file will be sparse
DSYNC or SYNC	Requires that each update to the file data or data and metadata be written synchronously to the storage device
StandardCopyOption; use with copy, move	
ATOMIC_MOVE	Move the file atomically
COPY_ATTRIBUTES	Copy the file attributes
REPLACE_EXISTING	Replace the target if it exists
LinkOption; use with all of the above methods and exists, isDirectory, isRegularFile	
NOFOLLOW_LINKS	Do not follow symbolic links
FileVisitOption; use with find, walk, walkFileTree	
FOLLOW_LINKS	Follow symbolic links

2.4.5 Getting File Information

The following static methods return a boolean value to check a property of a path:

- exists
- isHidden
- isReadable, isWritable, isExecutable
- isRegularFile, isDirectory, isSymbolicLink

The size method returns the number of bytes in a file.

```
long fileSize = Files.size(path);
```

The getOwner method returns the owner of the file, as an instance of java.nio .file.attribute.UserPrincipal.

All file systems report a set of basic attributes, encapsulated by the BasicFileAttributes interface, which partially overlaps with that information. The basic file attributes are

- The times at which the file was created, last accessed, and last modified, as instances of the class java.nio.file.attribute.FileTime
- Whether the file is a regular file, a directory, a symbolic link, or none of these
- The file size
- The file key—an object of some class, specific to the file system, that may or may not uniquely identify a file

To get these attributes, call

```
BasicFileAttributes attributes = Files.readAttributes(path, BasicFileAttributes.class);
```

If you know that the user's file system is POSIX-compliant, you can instead get an instance of PosixFileAttributes:

```
PosixFileAttributes attributes = Files.readAttributes(path, PosixFileAttributes.class);
```

Then you can find out the group owner and the owner, group, and world access permissions of the file. We won't dwell on the details since so much of this information is not portable across operating systems.

---

java.nio.file.Files 7

- static boolean exists(Path path)
- static boolean isHidden(Path path)
- static boolean isReadable(Path path)
- static boolean isWritable(Path path)
- static boolean isExecutable(Path path)
- static boolean isRegularFile(Path path)
- static boolean isDirectory(Path path)
- static boolean isSymbolicLink(Path path)

  checks for the given property of the file given by the path.

- static long size(Path path)

  gets the size of the file in bytes.

- A readAttributes(Path path, Class<A> type, LinkOption... options)

  reads the file attributes of type A.

---

java.nio.file.attribute.BasicFileAttributes 7

- FileTime creationTime()
- FileTime lastAccessTime()
- FileTime lastModifiedTime()
- boolean isRegularFile()
- boolean isDirectory()
- boolean isSymbolicLink()
- long size()
- Object fileKey()

  gets the requested attribute.

2.4.6 Visiting Directory Entries

The static `Files.list` method returns a `Stream<Path>` that reads the entries of a directory. The directory is read lazily, making it possible to efficiently process directories with huge numbers of entries.

Since reading a directory involves a system resource that needs to be closed, you should use a `try` block:

```
try (Stream<Path> entries = Files.list(pathToDirectory))
{
   . . .
}
```

The `list` method does not enter subdirectories. To process all descendants of a directory, use the `Files.walk` method instead.

```
try (Stream<Path> entries = Files.walk(pathToRoot))
{
   // Contains all descendants, visited in depth-first order
}
```

Here is a sample traversal of the unzipped `src.zip` tree:

```
java
java/nio
java/nio/DirectCharBufferU.java
java/nio/ByteBufferAsShortBufferRL.java
java/nio/MappedByteBuffer.java

  . . .

java/nio/ByteBufferAsDoubleBufferB.java
java/nio/charset
java/nio/charset/CoderMalfunctionError.java
java/nio/charset/CharsetDecoder.java
java/nio/charset/UnsupportedCharsetException.java
```

```
java/nio/charset/spi
java/nio/charset/spi/CharsetProvider.java
java/nio/charset/StandardCharsets.java
java/nio/charset/Charset.java
. . .
java/nio/charset/CoderResult.java
java/nio/HeapFloatBufferR.java
. . .
```

As you can see, whenever the traversal yields a directory, it is entered before continuing with its siblings.

You can limit the depth of the tree that you want to visit by calling Files.walk(pathToRoot, depth). Both walk methods have a varargs parameter of type FileVisitOption..., but there is only one option you can supply: FOLLOW_LINKS to follow symbolic links.

 NOTE: If you filter the paths returned by walk and your filter criterion involves the file attributes stored with a directory, such as size, creation time, or type (file, directory, symbolic link), then use the find method instead of walk. Call that method with a predicate function that accepts a path and a BasicFileAttributes object. The only advantage is efficiency. Since the directory is being read anyway, the attributes are readily available.

This code fragment uses the Files.walk method to copy one directory to another:

```
Files.walk(source).forEach(p ->
    {
        try
        {
            Path q = target.resolve(source.relativize(p));
            if (Files.isDirectory(p))
                Files.createDirectory(q);
            else
                Files.copy(p, q);
        }
        catch (IOException ex)
        {
            throw new UncheckedIOException(ex);
        }
    });
```

Unfortunately, you cannot easily use the Files.walk method to delete a tree of directories since you need to delete the children before deleting the parent. The next section shows you how to overcome that problem.

2.4.7 Using Directory Streams

As you saw in the preceding section, the Files.walk method produces a Stream<Path>
that traverses the descendants of a directory. Sometimes, you need more
fine-grained control over the traversal process. In that case, use the Files
.newDirectoryStream object instead. It yields a DirectoryStream. Note that this is not
a subinterface of java.util.stream.Stream but an interface that is specialized for
directory traversal. It is a subinterface of Iterable so that you can use directory
stream in an enhanced for loop. Here is the usage pattern:

```
try (DirectoryStream<Path> entries = Files.newDirectoryStream(dir))
{
    for (Path entry : entries)
        Process entries
}
```

The try-with-resources block ensures that the directory stream is properly
closed.

There is no specific order in which the directory entries are visited.

You can filter the files with a glob pattern:

```
try (DirectoryStream<Path> entries = Files.newDirectoryStream(dir, "*.java"))
```

Table 2.4 shows all glob patterns.

Table 2.4 Glob Patterns

Pattern	Description	Example
*	Matches zero or more characters of a path component.	*.java matches all Java files in the current directory.
**	Matches zero or more characters, crossing directory boundaries.	**.java matches all Java files in any subdirectory.
?	Matches one character.	????.java matches all four-character (not counting the extension) Java files.
[. . .]	Matches a set of characters. You can use hyphens [0-9] and negation [!0-9].	Test[0-9A-F].java matches Test$x$.java, where x is one hexadecimal digit.
{. . .}	Matches alternatives, separated by commas.	*.{java,class} matches all Java and class files.
\	Escapes any of the above as well as \.	*** matches all files with a * in their name.

CAUTION: If you use the glob syntax on Windows, you have to escape back-slashes *twice*: once for the glob syntax, and once for the Java string syntax: `Files.newDirectoryStream(dir, "C:\\\\")`.

If you want to visit all descendants of a directory, call the `walkFileTree` method instead and supply an object of type `FileVisitor`. That object gets notified

- When a file is encountered: `FileVisitResult visitFile(T path, BasicFileAttributes attrs)`
- Before a directory is processed: `FileVisitResult preVisitDirectory(T dir, IOException ex)`
- After a directory is processed: `FileVisitResult postVisitDirectory(T dir, IOException ex)`
- When an error occurred trying to visit a file or directory, such as trying to open a directory without the necessary permissions: `FileVisitResult visitFileFailed(T path, IOException ex)`

In each case, you can specify whether you want to

- Continue visiting the next file: `FileVisitResult.CONTINUE`
- Continue the walk, but without visiting the entries in this directory: `FileVisitResult.SKIP_SUBTREE`
- Continue the walk, but without visiting the siblings of this file: `FileVisitResult.SKIP_SIBLINGS`
- Terminate the walk: `FileVisitResult.TERMINATE`

If any of the methods throws an exception, the walk is also terminated, and that exception is thrown from the `walkFileTree` method.

 NOTE: The `FileVisitor` interface is a generic type, but it isn't likely that you'll ever want something other than a `FileVisitor<Path>`. The `walkFileTree` method is willing to accept a `FileVisitor<? super Path>`, but `Path` does not have an abundance of supertypes.

A convenience class `SimpleFileVisitor` implements the `FileVisitor` interface. All methods except `visitFileFailed` do nothing and continue. The `visitFileFailed` method throws the exception that caused the failure, thereby terminating the visit.

For example, here is how to print out all subdirectories of a given directory:

```
Files.walkFileTree(Paths.get("/"), new SimpleFileVisitor<Path>()
   {
      public FileVisitResult preVisitDirectory(Path path, BasicFileAttributes attrs)
            throws IOException
      {
         System.out.println(path);
         return FileVisitResult.CONTINUE;
      }

      public FileVisitResult postVisitDirectory(Path dir, IOException exc)
      {
         return FileVisitResult.CONTINUE;
      }

      public FileVisitResult visitFileFailed(Path path, IOException exc)
            throws IOException
      {
         return FileVisitResult.SKIP_SUBTREE;
      }
   });
```

Note that we need to override postVisitDirectory and visitFileFailed. Otherwise, the visit would fail as soon as it encounters a directory that it's not allowed to open or a file it's not allowed to access.

Also note that the attributes of the path are passed as a parameter to the preVisitDirectory and visitFile methods. The visitor already had to make an OS call to get the attributes, since it needs to distinguish between files and directories. This way, you don't need to make another call.

The other methods of the FileVisitor interface are useful if you need to do some work when entering or leaving a directory. For example, when you delete a directory tree, you need to remove the current directory after you have removed all of its files. Here is the complete code for deleting a directory tree:

```
// Delete the directory tree starting at root
Files.walkFileTree(root, new SimpleFileVisitor<Path>()
   {
      public FileVisitResult visitFile(Path file, BasicFileAttributes attrs)
            throws IOException
      {
         Files.delete(file);
         return FileVisitResult.CONTINUE;
      }
```

```
public FileVisitResult postVisitDirectory(Path dir, IOException e) throws IOException
{
    if (e != null) throw e;
    Files.delete(dir);
    return FileVisitResult.CONTINUE;
}
});
```

---

java.nio.file.Files 7

- static DirectoryStream<Path> newDirectoryStream(Path path)
- static DirectoryStream<Path> newDirectoryStream(Path path, String glob)

  gets an iterator over the files and directories in a given directory. The second method only accepts those entries matching the given glob pattern.

- static Path walkFileTree(Path start, FileVisitor<? super Path> visitor)

  walks all descendants of the given path, applying the visitor to all descendants.

---

java.nio.file.SimpleFileVisitor<T> 7

- static FileVisitResult visitFile(T path, BasicFileAttributes attrs)

  is called when a file or directory is visited; returns one of CONTINUE, SKIP_SUBTREE, SKIP_SIBLINGS, or TERMINATE. The default implementation does nothing and continues.

- static FileVisitResult preVisitDirectory(T dir, BasicFileAttributes attrs)
- static FileVisitResult postVisitDirectory(T dir, BasicFileAttributes attrs)

  are called before and after visiting a directory. The default implementation does nothing and continues.

- static FileVisitResult visitFileFailed(T path, IOException exc)

  is called if an exception was thrown in an attempt to get information about the given file. The default implementation rethrows the exception, which causes the visit to terminate with that exception. Override the method if you want to continue.

2.4.8 ZIP File Systems

The Paths class looks up paths in the default file system—the files on the user's local disk. You can have other file systems. One of the more useful ones is a *ZIP file system*. If zipname is the name of a ZIP file, then the call

```
FileSystem fs = FileSystems.newFileSystem(Paths.get(zipname), null);
```

establishes a file system that contains all files in the ZIP archive. It's an easy matter to copy a file out of that archive if you know its name:

```
Files.copy(fs.getPath(sourceName), targetPath);
```

Here, `fs.getPath` is the analog of `Paths.get` for an arbitrary file system.

To list all files in a ZIP archive, walk the file tree:

```
FileSystem fs = FileSystems.newFileSystem(Paths.get(zipname), null);
Files.walkFileTree(fs.getPath("/"), new SimpleFileVisitor<Path>()
    {
        public FileVisitResult visitFile(Path file, BasicFileAttributes attrs)
            throws IOException
        {
            System.out.println(file);
            return FileVisitResult.CONTINUE;
        }
    });
```

That is nicer than the API described in Section 2.2.3, "ZIP Archives," on p. 85 which required a set of new classes just to deal with ZIP archives.

---

java.nio.file.FileSystems 7

- `static FileSystem newFileSystem(Path path, ClassLoader loader)`

  iterates over the installed file system providers and, provided that `loader` is not null, the file systems that the given class loader can load. Returns the file system created by the first file system provider that accepts the given path. By default, there is a provider for ZIP file systems that accepts files whose names end in .zip or .jar.

---

java.nio.file.FileSystem 7

- `static Path getPath(String first, String... more)`

  makes a path by joining the given strings.

2.5 Memory-Mapped Files

Most operating systems can take advantage of a virtual memory implementation to "map" a file, or a region of a file, into memory. Then the file can be accessed as if it were an in-memory array, which is much faster than the traditional file operations.

2.5.1 Memory–Mapped File Performance

At the end of this section, you can find a program that computes the CRC32 checksum of a file using traditional file input and a memory-mapped file. On one machine, we got the timing data shown in Table 2.5 when computing the checksum of the 37MB file rt.jar in the jre/lib directory of the JDK.

Table 2.5 Timing Data for File Operations

Method	Time
Plain input stream	110 seconds
Buffered input stream	9.9 seconds
Random access file	162 seconds
Memory-mapped file	7.2 seconds

As you can see, on this particular machine, memory mapping is a bit faster than using buffered sequential input and dramatically faster than using a RandomAccessFile.

Of course, the exact values will differ greatly from one machine to another, but it is obvious that the performance gain, compared to random access, can be substantial. For sequential reading of files of moderate size, on the other hand, there is no reason to use memory mapping.

The java.nio package makes memory mapping quite simple. Here is what you do.

First, get a *channel* for the file. A channel is an abstraction for a disk file that lets you access operating system features such as memory mapping, file locking, and fast data transfers between files.

```
FileChannel channel = FileChannel.open(path, options);
```

Then, get a ByteBuffer from the channel by calling the map method of the FileChannel class. Specify the area of the file that you want to map and a *mapping mode*. Three modes are supported:

* FileChannel.MapMode.READ_ONLY: The resulting buffer is read-only. Any attempt to write to the buffer results in a ReadOnlyBufferException.

* FileChannel.MapMode.READ_WRITE: The resulting buffer is writable, and the changes will be written back to the file at some time. Note that other programs that have mapped the same file might not see those changes immediately. The exact behavior of simultaneous file mapping by multiple programs depends on the operating system.

- `FileChannel.MapMode.PRIVATE`: The resulting buffer is writable, but any changes are private to this buffer and not propagated to the file.

Once you have the buffer, you can read and write data using the methods of the `ByteBuffer` class and the `Buffer` superclass.

Buffers support both sequential and random data access. A buffer has a *position* that is advanced by `get` and `put` operations. For example, you can sequentially traverse all bytes in the buffer as

```
while (buffer.hasRemaining())
{
   byte b = buffer.get();
   . . .
}
```

Alternatively, you can use random access:

```
for (int i = 0; i < buffer.limit(); i++)
{
   byte b = buffer.get(i);
   . . .
}
```

You can also read and write arrays of bytes with the methods

```
get(byte[] bytes)
get(byte[], int offset, int length)
```

Finally, there are methods

```
getInt        getChar
getLong       getFloat
getShort      getDouble
```

to read primitive-type values that are stored as *binary* values in the file. As we already mentioned, Java uses big-endian ordering for binary data. However, if you need to process a file containing binary numbers in little-endian order, simply call

```
buffer.order(ByteOrder.LITTLE_ENDIAN);
```

To find out the current byte order of a buffer, call

```
ByteOrder b = buffer.order();
```

 CAUTION: This pair of methods does not use the set/get naming convention.

To write numbers to a buffer, use one of the methods

```
putInt          putChar
putLong         putFloat
putShort        putDouble
```

At some point, and certainly when the channel is closed, these changes are written back to the file.

Listing 2.5 computes the 32-bit cyclic redundancy checksum (CRC32) of a file. That checksum is often used to determine whether a file has been corrupted. Corruption of a file makes it very likely that the checksum has changed. The java.util.zip package contains a class CRC32 that computes the checksum of a sequence of bytes, using the following loop:

```
var crc = new CRC32();
while (more bytes)
    crc.update(next byte);
long checksum = crc.getValue();
```

The details of the CRC computation are not important. We just use it as an example of a useful file operation. (In practice, you would read and update data in larger blocks, not a byte at a time. Then the speed differences are not as dramatic.)

Run the program as

```
java memoryMap.MemoryMapTest filename
```

Listing 2.5 memoryMap/MemoryMapTest.java

```
1 package memoryMap;
2
3 import java.io.*;
4 import java.nio.*;
5 import java.nio.channels.*;
6 import java.nio.file.*;
7 import java.util.zip.*;
8
9 /**
10  * This program computes the CRC checksum of a file in four ways. <br>
11  * Usage: java memoryMap.MemoryMapTest filename
12  * @version 1.02 2018-05-01
13  * @author Cay Horstmann
14  */
```

(Continues)

Listing 2.5 *(Continued)*

```
15  public class MemoryMapTest
16  {
17     public static long checksumInputStream(Path filename) throws IOException
18     {
19        try (InputStream in = Files.newInputStream(filename))
20        {
21           var crc = new CRC32();
22
23           int c;
24           while ((c = in.read()) != -1)
25              crc.update(c);
26           return crc.getValue();
27        }
28     }
29
30     public static long checksumBufferedInputStream(Path filename) throws IOException
31     {
32        try (var in = new BufferedInputStream(Files.newInputStream(filename)))
33        {
34           var crc = new CRC32();
35
36           int c;
37           while ((c = in.read()) != -1)
38              crc.update(c);
39           return crc.getValue();
40        }
41     }
42
43     public static long checksumRandomAccessFile(Path filename) throws IOException
44     {
45        try (var file = new RandomAccessFile(filename.toFile(), "r"))
46        {
47           long length = file.length();
48           var crc = new CRC32();
49
50           for (long p = 0; p < length; p++)
51           {
52              file.seek(p);
53              int c = file.readByte();
54              crc.update(c);
55           }
56           return crc.getValue();
57        }
58     }
59
```

```java
60  public static long checksumMappedFile(Path filename) throws IOException
61  {
62     try (FileChannel channel = FileChannel.open(filename))
63     {
64        var crc = new CRC32();
65        int length = (int) channel.size();
66        MappedByteBuffer buffer = channel.map(FileChannel.MapMode.READ_ONLY, 0, length);
67
68        for (int p = 0; p < length; p++)
69        {
70           int c = buffer.get(p);
71           crc.update(c);
72        }
73        return crc.getValue();
74     }
75  }
76
77  public static void main(String[] args) throws IOException
78  {
79     System.out.println("Input Stream:");
80     long start = System.currentTimeMillis();
81     Path filename = Paths.get(args[0]);
82     long crcValue = checksumInputStream(filename);
83     long end = System.currentTimeMillis();
84     System.out.println(Long.toHexString(crcValue));
85     System.out.println((end - start) + " milliseconds");
86
87     System.out.println("Buffered Input Stream:");
88     start = System.currentTimeMillis();
89     crcValue = checksumBufferedInputStream(filename);
90     end = System.currentTimeMillis();
91     System.out.println(Long.toHexString(crcValue));
92     System.out.println((end - start) + " milliseconds");
93
94     System.out.println("Random Access File:");
95     start = System.currentTimeMillis();
96     crcValue = checksumRandomAccessFile(filename);
97     end = System.currentTimeMillis();
98     System.out.println(Long.toHexString(crcValue));
99     System.out.println((end - start) + " milliseconds");
100
101     System.out.println("Mapped File:");
102     start = System.currentTimeMillis();
103     crcValue = checksumMappedFile(filename);
104     end = System.currentTimeMillis();
105     System.out.println(Long.toHexString(crcValue));
106     System.out.println((end - start) + " milliseconds");
107  }
108 }
```

---

java.io.FileInputStream 1.0

- FileChannel getChannel() 1.4

  returns a channel for accessing this input stream.

---

java.io.FileOutputStream 1.0

- FileChannel getChannel() 1.4

  returns a channel for accessing this output stream.

---

java.io.RandomAccessFile 1.0

- FileChannel getChannel() 1.4

  returns a channel for accessing this file.

---

java.nio.channels.FileChannel 1.4

- static FileChannel open(Path path, OpenOption... options) 7

  opens a file channel for the given path. By default, the channel is opened for reading. The parameter options is one of the values WRITE, APPEND,TRUNCATE_EXISTING, CREATE in the StandardOpenOption enumeration.

- MappedByteBuffer map(FileChannel.MapMode mode, long position, long size)

  maps a region of the file to memory. The parameter mode is one of the constants READ_ONLY, READ_WRITE, or PRIVATE in the FileChannel.MapMode class.

---

java.nio.Buffer 1.4

- boolean hasRemaining()

  returns true if the current buffer position has not yet reached the buffer's limit position.

- int limit()

  returns the limit position of the buffer—that is, the first position at which no more values are available.

---

java.nio.ByteBuffer 1.4

- byte get()

  gets a byte from the current position and advances the current position to the next byte.

- byte get(int index)

  gets a byte from the specified index.

- ByteBuffer put(byte b)

  puts a byte at the current position and advances the current position to the next byte. Returns a reference to this buffer.

- ByteBuffer put(int index, byte b)

  puts a byte at the specified index. Returns a reference to this buffer.

- ByteBuffer get(byte[] destination)
- ByteBuffer get(byte[] destination, int offset, int length)

  fills a byte array, or a region of a byte array, with bytes from the buffer, and advances the current position by the number of bytes read. If not enough bytes remain in the buffer, then no bytes are read, and a BufferUnderflowException is thrown. Returns a reference to this buffer.

- ByteBuffer put(byte[] source)
- ByteBuffer put(byte[] source, int offset, int length)

  puts all bytes from a byte array, or the bytes from a region of a byte array, into the buffer, and advances the current position by the number of bytes read. If not enough bytes remain in the buffer, then no bytes are written, and a BufferOverflowException is thrown. Returns a reference to this buffer.

- *Xxx* get*Xxx*()
- *Xxx* get*Xxx*(int index)
- ByteBuffer put*Xxx*(*Xxx* value)
- ByteBuffer put*Xxx*(int index, *Xxx* value)

  gets or puts a binary number. *Xxx* is one of Int, Long, Short, Char, Float, or Double.

- ByteBuffer order(ByteOrder order)
- ByteOrder order()

  sets or gets the byte order. The value for order is one of the constants BIG_ENDIAN or LITTLE_ENDIAN of the ByteOrder class.

- static ByteBuffer allocate(int capacity)

  constructs a buffer with the given capacity.

(Continues)

`java.nio.ByteBuffer` 1.4 *(Continued)*

- `static ByteBuffer wrap(byte[] values)`

  constructs a buffer that is backed by the given array.

- `CharBuffer asCharBuffer()`

  constructs a character buffer that is backed by this buffer. Changes to the character buffer will show up in this buffer, but the character buffer has its own position, limit, and mark.

`java.nio.CharBuffer` 1.4

- `char get()`
- `CharBuffer get(char[] destination)`
- `CharBuffer get(char[] destination, int offset, int length)`

  gets one `char` value, or a range of `char` values, starting at the buffer's position and moving the position past the characters that were read. The last two methods return this.

- `CharBuffer put(char c)`
- `CharBuffer put(char[] source)`
- `CharBuffer put(char[] source, int offset, int length)`
- `CharBuffer put(String source)`
- `CharBuffer put(CharBuffer source)`

  puts one `char` value, or a range of `char` values, starting at the buffer's position and advancing the position past the characters that were written. When reading from a `CharBuffer`, all remaining characters are read. All methods return this.

2.5.2 The Buffer Data Structure

When you use memory mapping, you make a single buffer that spans the entire file or the area of the file that you're interested in. You can also use buffers to read and write more modest chunks of information.

In this section, we briefly describe the basic operations on `Buffer` objects. A buffer is an array of values of the same type. The `Buffer` class is an abstract class with concrete subclasses `ByteBuffer`, `CharBuffer`, `DoubleBuffer`, `FloatBuffer`, `IntBuffer`, `LongBuffer`, and `ShortBuffer`.

 NOTE: The `StringBuffer` class is not related to these buffers.

In practice, you will most commonly use ByteBuffer and CharBuffer. As shown in Figure 2.9, a buffer has

- A *capacity* that never changes
- A *position* at which the next value is read or written
- A *limit* beyond which reading and writing is meaningless
- Optionally, a *mark* for repeating a read or write operation

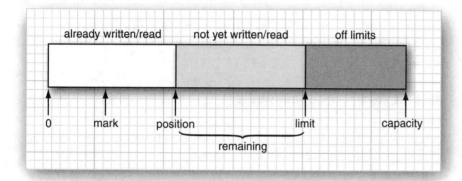

Figure 2.9 A buffer

These values fulfill the condition

$$0 = mark = position = limit = capacity$$

The principal purpose of a buffer is a "write, then read" cycle. At the outset, the buffer's position is 0 and the limit is the capacity. Keep calling put to add values to the buffer. When you run out of data or reach the capacity, it is time to switch to reading.

Call flip to set the limit to the current position and the position to 0. Now keep calling get while the remaining method (which returns *limit – position*) is positive. When you have read all values in the buffer, call clear to prepare the buffer for the next writing cycle. The clear method resets the position to 0 and the limit to the capacity.

If you want to reread the buffer, use rewind or mark/reset (see the API notes for details).

To get a buffer, call a static method such as ByteBuffer.allocate or ByteBuffer.wrap.

Then, you can fill a buffer from a channel, or write its contents to a channel. For example,

```
ByteBuffer buffer = ByteBuffer.allocate(RECORD_SIZE);
channel.read(buffer);
channel.position(newpos);
buffer.flip();
channel.write(buffer);
```

This can be a useful alternative to a random-access file.

---

java.nio.Buffer   1.4

- Buffer clear()

  prepares this buffer for writing by setting the position to 0 and the limit to the capacity; returns this.

- Buffer flip()

  prepares this buffer for reading after writing, by setting the limit to the position and the position to 0; returns this.

- Buffer rewind()

  prepares this buffer for rereading the same values by setting the position to 0 and leaving the limit unchanged; returns this.

- Buffer mark()

  sets the mark of this buffer to the position; returns this.

- Buffer reset()

  sets the position of this buffer to the mark, thus allowing the marked portion to be read or written again; returns this.

- int remaining()

  returns the remaining number of readable or writable values—that is, the difference between the limit and position.

- int position()
- void position(int newValue)

  gets and sets the position of this buffer.

- int capacity()

  returns the capacity of this buffer.

2.6 File Locking

When multiple simultaneously executing programs need to modify the same file, they need to communicate in some way, or the file can easily become damaged. File locks can solve this problem. A file lock controls access to a file or a range of bytes within a file.

Suppose your application saves a configuration file with user preferences. If a user invokes two instances of the application, it could happen that both of them want to write the configuration file at the same time. In that situation, the first instance should lock the file. When the second instance finds the file locked, it can decide to wait until the file is unlocked or simply skip the writing process.

To lock a file, call either the lock or tryLock methods of the FileChannel class.

```
FileChannel = FileChannel.open(path);
FileLock lock = channel.lock();
```

or

```
FileLock lock = channel.tryLock();
```

The first call blocks until the lock becomes available. The second call returns immediately, either with the lock or with null if the lock is not available. The file remains locked until the channel is closed or the release method is invoked on the lock.

You can also lock a portion of the file with the call

```
FileLock lock(long start, long size, boolean shared)
```

or

```
FileLock tryLock(long start, long size, boolean shared)
```

The shared flag is false to lock the file for both reading and writing. It is true for a *shared* lock, which allows multiple processes to read from the file, while preventing any process from acquiring an exclusive lock. Not all operating systems support shared locks. You may get an exclusive lock even if you just asked for a shared one. Call the isShared method of the FileLock class to find out which kind you have.

 NOTE: If you lock the tail portion of a file and the file subsequently grows beyond the locked portion, the additional area is not locked. To lock all bytes, use a size of Long.MAX_VALUE.

Be sure to unlock the lock when you are done. As always, this is best done with a try-with-resources statement:

```
try (FileLock lock = channel.lock())
{
    access the locked file or segment
}
```

Keep in mind that file locking is system-dependent. Here are some points to watch for:

- On some systems, file locking is merely *advisory*. If an application fails to get a lock, it may still write to a file that another application has currently locked.
- On some systems, you cannot simultaneously lock a file and map it into memory.
- File locks are held by the entire Java virtual machine. If two programs are launched by the same virtual machine (such as an applet or application launcher), they can't each acquire a lock on the same file. The `lock` and `tryLock` methods will throw an `OverlappingFileLockException` if the virtual machine already holds another overlapping lock on the same file.
- On some systems, closing a channel releases all locks on the underlying file held by the Java virtual machine. You should therefore avoid multiple channels on the same locked file.
- Locking files on a networked file system is highly system-dependent and should probably be avoided.

---

java.nio.channels.FileChannel `1.4`

- `FileLock lock()`

  acquires an exclusive lock on the entire file. This method blocks until the lock is acquired.

- `FileLock tryLock()`

  acquires an exclusive lock on the entire file, or returns `null` if the lock cannot be acquired.

- `FileLock lock(long position, long size, boolean shared)`
- `FileLock tryLock(long position, long size, boolean shared)`

  acquires a lock on a region of the file. The first method blocks until the lock is acquired, and the second method returns `null` if the lock cannot be acquired. The parameter `shared` is `true` for a shared lock, `false` for an exclusive lock.

---

java.nio.channels.FileLock `1.4`

- `void close()` `1.7`

  releases this lock.

2.7 Regular Expressions

Regular expressions are used to specify string patterns. You can use regular expressions whenever you need to locate strings that match a particular pattern. For example, one of our sample programs locates all hyperlinks in an HTML file by looking for strings of the pattern <a href="...">.

Of course, when specifying a pattern, the . . . notation is not precise enough. You need to specify exactly what sequence of characters is a legal match, using a special syntax to describe a pattern.

In the following sections, we cover the regular expression syntax used by the Java API and discuss how to put regular expressions to work.

2.7.1 The Regular Expression Syntax

Let us start with a simple example. The regular expression

```
[Jj]ava.+
```

matches any string of the following form:

- The first letter is a J or j.
- The next three letters are ava.
- The remainder of the string consists of one or more arbitrary characters.

For example, the string "javanese" matches this particular regular expression, but the string "Core Java" does not.

As you can see, you need to know a bit of syntax to understand the meaning of a regular expression. Fortunately, for most purposes, a few straightforward constructs are sufficient.

- A *character class* is a set of character alternatives, enclosed in brackets, such as [Jj], [0-9], [A-Za-z], or [^0-9]. Here the - denotes a range (all characters whose Unicode values fall between the two bounds), and ^ denotes the complement (all characters except those specified).
- To include a - inside a character class, make it the first or last item. To include a], make it the first item. To include a ^, put it anywhere but the beginning. You only need to escape [and \.
- There are many predefined character classes such as \d (digits) or \p{Sc} (Unicode currency symbol). See Tables 2.6 and 2.7.

Table 2.6 Regular Expression Syntax

Expression	Description	Example
Characters		
c, not one of . * + ? { | ( ) [\ ^ $	The character c	J
.	Any character except line terminators, or any character if the DOTALL flag is set	
\x{p}	The Unicode code point with hex code p	\x{1D546}
\u$hhhh$, \x$hh$, \0o, \0oo, \0ooo	The UTF-16 code unit with the given hex or octal value	\uFEFF
\a, \e, \f, \n, \r, \t	Alert (\x{7}), escape (\x{1B}), form feed (\x{B}), newline (\x{A}), carriage return (\x{D}), tab (\x{9})	\n
\c$c$, where c is in [A-Z] or one of @ [\ ] ^ _ ?	The control character corresponding to the character c	\cH is a backspace (\x{8})
\c, where c is not in [A-Za-z0-9]	The character c	\\
\Q. . .\E	Everything between the start and the end of the quotation	\Q(. . .)\E matches the string (. . .)
Character Classes		
[C_1C_2. . .], where C_i are characters, ranges c-d, or character classes	Any of the characters represented by C_1, C_2, . . .	[0-9+-]
[^. . .]	Complement of a character class	[^\d\s]
[. . .&&. . .]	Intersection of character classes	[\p{L}&&[^A-Za-z]]
\p{. . .}, \P{. . .}	A predefined character class (see Table 2.7); its complement	\p{L} matches a Unicode letter, and so does \pL—you can omit braces around a single letter

(Continues)

Table 2.6 *(Continued)*

Expression	Description	Example
\d, \D	Digits ([0-9], or \p{Digit} when the UNICODE_CHARACTER_CLASS flag is set); the complement	\d+ is a sequence of digits
\w, \W	Word characters ([a-zA-Z0-9_], or Unicode word characters when the UNICODE_CHARACTER_CLASS flag is set); the complement	
\s, \S	Spaces ([\n\r\t\f\x{B}], or \p{IsWhite_Space} when the UNICODE_CHARACTER_CLASS flag is set); the complement	\s*,\s* is a comma surrounded by optional white space
\h, \v, \H, \V	Horizontal whitespace, vertical whitespace, their complements	
Sequences and Alternatives		
XY	Any string from X, followed by any string from Y	[1-9][0-9]* is a positive number without leading zero
X|Y	Any string from X or Y	http|ftp
Grouping		
(X)	Captures the match of X	'([^']*)' captures the quoted text
\n	The nth group	(['"]).*\1 matches 'Fred' or "Fred" but not "Fred'
(?<name>X)	Captures the match of X with the given name	'(?<id>[A-Za-z0-9]+)' captures the match with name id
\k<name>	The group with the given name	\k<id> matches the group with name id
(?:X)	Use parentheses without capturing X	In (?:http|ftp)://(.*), the match after :// is \1

(Continues)

Table 2.6 (Continued)

Expression	Description	Example
$(?f_1f_2\ldots:X)$, $(?f_1\ldots-f_k\ldots:X)$, with f_i in [dimsuUx]	Matches, but does not capture, X with the given flags on or off (after -)	(?i:jpe?g) is a case-insensitive match
Other (?. . .)	See the Pattern API documentation	
Quantifiers		
$X?$	Optional X	\+? is an optional + sign
$X*$, $X+$	0 or more X, 1 or more X	[1-9][0-9]+ is an integer ≥ 10
$X\{n\}$, $X\{n,\}$, $X\{m,n\}$	n times X, at least n times X, between m and n times X	[0-7]{1,3} are one to three octal digits
$Q?$, where Q is a quantified expression	Reluctant quantifier, attempting the shortest match before trying longer matches	.*(<.+?>).* captures the shortest sequence enclosed in angle brackets
$Q+$, where Q is a quantified expression	Possessive quantifier, taking the longest match without backtracking	'[^']*+' matches strings enclosed in single quotes and fails quickly on strings without a closing quote
Boundary Matches		
^, $	Beginning, end of input (or beginning, end of line in multiline mode)	^Java$ matches the input or line Java
\A, \Z, \z	Beginning of input, end of input, absolute end of input (unchanged in multiline mode)	
\b, \B	Word boundary, nonword boundary	\bJava\b matches the word Java
\R	A Unicode line break	
\G	The end of the previous match	

Table 2.7 Predefined Character Class Names Used with \p

Character Class Name	Explanation
posixClass	*posixClass* is one of Lower, Upper, Alpha, Digit, Alnum, Punct, Graph, Print, Cntrl, XDigit, Space, Blank, ASCII, interpreted as POSIX or Unicode class, depending on the UNICODE_CHARACTER_CLASS flag
Is*Script*, sc=*Script*, script=*Script*	A script accepted by Character.UnicodeScript.forName
In*Block*, blk=*Block*, block=*Block*	A block accepted by Character.UnicodeBlock.forName
Category, In*Category*, gc=*Category*, general_category=*Category*	A one- or two-letter name for a Unicode general category
Is*Property*	*Property* is one of Alphabetic, Ideographic, Letter, Lowercase, Uppercase, Titlecase, Punctuation, Control, White_Space, Digit, Hex_Digit, Join_Control, Noncharacter_Code_Point, Assigned
java*Method*	Invokes the method Character.is*Method* (must not be deprecated)

- Most characters match themselves, such as the ava characters in the preceding example.

- The . symbol matches any character (except possibly line terminators, depending on flag settings).

- Use \ as an escape character. For example, \. matches a period and \\ matches a backslash.

- ^ and $ match the beginning and end of a line, respectively.

- If *X* and *Y* are regular expressions, then *XY* means "any match for *X* followed by a match for *Y*." *X | Y* means "any match for *X* or *Y*."

- You can apply *quantifiers* X+ (1 or more), X* (0 or more), and X? (0 or 1) to an expression *X*.

- By default, a quantifier matches the largest possible repetition that makes the overall match succeed. You can modify that behavior with suffixes ? (reluctant, or stingy, match: match the smallest repetition count) and + (possessive, or greedy, match: match the largest count even if that makes the overall match fail).

For example, the string cab matches [a-z]*ab but not [a-z]*+ab. In the first case, the expression [a-z]* only matches the character c, so that the characters ab match the remainder of the pattern. But the greedy version [a-z]*+ matches the characters cab, leaving the remainder of the pattern unmatched.

- You can use *groups* to define subexpressions. Enclose the groups in ( ), for example, ([+-]?)([0-9]+). You can then ask the pattern matcher to return the match of each group or to refer back to a group with \n where n is the group number, starting with \1.

For example, here is a somewhat complex but potentially useful regular expression that describes decimal or hexadecimal integers:

```
[+-]?[0-9]+|0[Xx][0-9A-Fa-f]+
```

Unfortunately, the regular expression syntax is not completely standardized between various programs and libraries; there is a consensus on the basic constructs but many maddening differences in the details. The Java regular expression classes use a syntax that is similar to, but not quite the same as, the one used in the Perl language. Table 2.6 shows all constructs of the Java syntax. For more information on the regular expression syntax, consult the API documentation for the Pattern class or the book *Mastering Regular Expressions* by Jeffrey E. F. Friedl (O'Reilly and Associates, 2006).

2.7.2 Matching a String

The simplest use for a regular expression is to test whether a particular string matches it. Here is how you program that test in Java. First, construct a Pattern object from a string containing the regular expression. Then, get a Matcher object from the pattern and call its matches method:

```
Pattern pattern = Pattern.compile(patternString);
Matcher matcher = pattern.matcher(input);
if (matcher.matches()) . . .
```

The input of the matcher is an object of any class that implements the CharSequence interface, such as a String, StringBuilder, or CharBuffer.

When compiling the pattern, you can set one or more flags, for example:

```
Pattern pattern = Pattern.compile(expression,
    Pattern.CASE_INSENSITIVE + Pattern.UNICODE_CASE);
```

Or you can specify them inside the pattern:

```
String regex = "(?iU:expression)";
```

Here are the flags:

- Pattern.CASE_INSENSITIVE or i: Match characters independently of the letter case. By default, this flag takes only US ASCII characters into account.

- `Pattern.UNICODE_CASE` or u: When used in combination with `CASE_INSENSITIVE`, use Unicode letter case for matching.
- `Pattern.UNICODE_CHARACTER_CLASS` or U: Select Unicode character classes instead of POSIX. Implies `UNICODE_CASE`.
- `Pattern.MULTILINE` or m: Make ^ and $ match the beginning and end of a line, not the entire input.
- `Pattern.UNIX_LINES` or d: Only '\n' is a line terminator when matching ^ and $ in multiline mode.
- `Pattern.DOTALL` or s: Make the . symbol match all characters, including line terminators.
- `Pattern.COMMENTS` or x: Whitespace and comments (from # to the end of a line) are ignored.
- `Pattern.LITERAL`: The pattern is taken literally and must be matched exactly, except possibly for letter case.
- `Pattern.CANON_EQ`: Take canonical equivalence of Unicode characters into account. For example, u followed by ¨ (diaeresis) matches ü.

The last two flags cannot be specified inside a regular expression.

If you want to match elements in a collection or stream, turn the pattern into a predicate:

```
Stream<String> strings = . . .;
Stream<String> result = strings.filter(pattern.asPredicate());
```

The result contains all strings that match the regular expression.

If the regular expression contains groups, the `Matcher` object can reveal the group boundaries. The methods

```
int start(int groupIndex)
int end(int groupIndex)
```

yield the starting index and the past-the-end index of a particular group.

You can simply extract the matched string by calling

```
String group(int groupIndex)
```

Group 0 is the entire input; the group index for the first actual group is 1. Call the `groupCount` method to get the total group count. For named groups, use the methods

```
int start(String groupName)
int end(String groupName)
String group(String groupName)
```

Nested groups are ordered by the opening parentheses. For example, given the pattern

```
((([1-9]|1[0-2]):([0-5][0-9]))[ap]m
```

and the input

```
11:59am
```

the matcher reports the following groups

Group Index	Start	End	String
0	0	7	11:59am
1	0	5	11:59
2	0	2	11
3	3	5	59

Listing 2.6 prompts for a pattern, then for strings to match. It prints out whether or not the input matches the pattern. If the input matches and the pattern contains groups, the program prints the group boundaries as parentheses, for example:

```
((11):(59))am
```

Listing 2.6 regex/RegexTest.java

```java
1  package regex;
2
3  import java.util.*;
4  import java.util.regex.*;
5
6  /**
7   * This program tests regular expression matching. Enter a pattern and strings to match,
8   * or hit Cancel to exit. If the pattern contains groups, the group boundaries are displayed
9   * in the match.
10  * @version 1.03 2018-05-01
11  * @author Cay Horstmann
12  */
13 public class RegexTest
14 {
15    public static void main(String[] args) throws PatternSyntaxException
16    {
17       var in = new Scanner(System.in);
18       System.out.println("Enter pattern: ");
19       String patternString = in.nextLine();
20
```

```
21        Pattern pattern = Pattern.compile(patternString);
22
23        while (true)
24        {
25           System.out.println("Enter string to match: ");
26           String input = in.nextLine();
27           if (input == null || input.equals("")) return;
28           Matcher matcher = pattern.matcher(input);
29           if (matcher.matches())
30           {
31              System.out.println("Match");
32              int g = matcher.groupCount();
33              if (g > 0)
34              {
35                 for (int i = 0; i < input.length(); i++)
36                 {
37                    // Print any empty groups
38                    for (int j = 1; j <= g; j++)
39                       if (i == matcher.start(j) && i == matcher.end(j))
40                          System.out.print("()");
41                    // Print ( for non-empty groups starting here
42                    for (int j = 1; j <= g; j++)
43                       if (i == matcher.start(j) && i != matcher.end(j))
44                          System.out.print('(');
45                    System.out.print(input.charAt(i));
46                    // Print ) for non-empty groups ending here
47                    for (int j = 1; j <= g; j++)
48                       if (i + 1 != matcher.start(j) && i + 1 == matcher.end(j))
49                          System.out.print(')');
50                 }
51                 System.out.println();
52              }
53           }
54           else
55              System.out.println("No match");
56        }
57     }
58 }
```

2.7.3 Finding Multiple Matches

Usually, you don't want to match the entire input against a regular expression, but to find one or more matching substrings in the input. Use the find method of the Matcher class to find the next match. If it returns true, use the start and end methods to find the extent of the match or the group method without an argument to get the matched string.

```
while (matcher.find())
{
   int start = matcher.start();
   int end = matcher.end();
   String match = input.group();
   . . .
}
```

In this way, you can process each match in turn. As shown in the code fragment, you can get the matched string as well as its position in the input string.

More elegantly, you can call the `results` method to get a `Stream<MatchResult>`. The `MatchResult` interface has methods `group`, `start`, and `end`, just like `Matcher`. (In fact, the `Matcher` class implements this interface.) Here is how you get a list of all matches:

```
List<String> matches = pattern.matcher(input)
   .results()
   .map(Matcher::group)
   .collect(Collectors.toList());
```

If you have the data in a file, you can use the `Scanner.findAll` method to get a `Stream<MatchResult>`, without first having to read the contents into a string. You can pass a `Pattern` or a pattern string:

```
var in = new Scanner(path, StandardCharsets.UTF_8);
Stream<String> words = in.findAll("\\pL+")
   .map(MatchResult::group);
```

Listing 2.7 puts this mechanism to work. It locates all hypertext references in a web page and prints them. To run the program, supply a URL on the command line, such as

```
java match.HrefMatch http://horstmann.com
```

Listing 2.7 match/HrefMatch.java

```
1  package match;
2
3  import java.io.*;
4  import java.net.*;
5  import java.nio.charset.*;
6  import java.util.regex.*;
7
8  /**
9   * This program displays all URLs in a web page by matching a regular expression that
10  * describes the <a href=...> HTML tag. Start the program as <br>
11  * java match.HrefMatch URL
```

```
12    * @version 1.03 2018-03-19
13    * @author Cay Horstmann
14    */
15   public class HrefMatch
16   {
17      public static void main(String[] args)
18      {
19         try
20         {
21            // get URL string from command line or use default
22            String urlString;
23            if (args.length > 0) urlString = args[0];
24            else urlString = "http://openjdk.java.net/";
25
26            // read contents of URL
27            InputStream in = new URL(urlString).openStream();
28            var input = new String(in.readAllBytes(), StandardCharsets.UTF_8);
29
30            // search for all occurrences of pattern
31            var patternString = "<a\\s+href\\s*=\\s*(\"[^\"]*\"|[^\\s>]*)\\s*>";
32            Pattern pattern = Pattern.compile(patternString, Pattern.CASE_INSENSITIVE);
33            pattern.matcher(input)
34               .results()
35               .map(MatchResult::group)
36               .forEach(System.out::println);
37         }
38         catch (IOException | PatternSyntaxException e)
39         {
40            e.printStackTrace();
41         }
42      }
43   }
```

2.7.4 Splitting along Delimiters

Sometimes, you want to break an input along matched delimiters and keep everything else. The Pattern.split method automates this task. You obtain an array of strings, with the delimiters removed:

```
String input = . . .;
Pattern commas = Pattern.compile("\\s*,\\s*");
String[] tokens = commas.split(input);
   // "1, 2, 3" turns into ["1", "2", "3"]
```

If there are many tokens, you can fetch them lazily:

```
Stream<String> tokens = commas.splitAsStream(input);
```

If you don't care about precompiling the pattern or lazy fetching, you can just use the String.split method:

```
String[] tokens = input.split("\\s*,\\s*");
```

If the input is in a file, use a scanner:

```
var in = new Scanner(path, StandardCharsets.UTF_8);
in.useDelimiter("\\s*,\\s*");
Stream<String> tokens = in.tokens();
```

2.7.5 Replacing Matches

The replaceAll method of the Matcher class replaces all occurrences of a regular expression with a replacement string. For example, the following instructions replace all sequences of digits with a # character:

```
Pattern pattern = Pattern.compile("[0-9]+");
Matcher matcher = pattern.matcher(input);
String output = matcher.replaceAll("#");
```

The replacement string can contain references to the groups in the pattern: $n is replaced with the *n*th group, and ${*name*} is replaced with the group that has the given name. Use \$ to include a $ character in the replacement text.

If you have a string that may contain $ and \, and you don't want them to be interpreted as group replacements, call matcher.replaceAll(Matcher.quoteReplacement(str)).

If you want to carry out a more complex operation than splicing in group matches, you can provide a replacement function instead of a replacement string. The function accepts a MatchResult and yields a string. For example, here we replace all words with at least four letters with their uppercase version:

```
String result = Pattern.compile("\\pL{4,}")
    .matcher("Mary had a little lamb")
    .replaceAll(m -> m.group().toUpperCase());
    // Yields "MARY had a LITTLE LAMB"
```

The replaceFirst method replaces only the first occurrence of the pattern.

---

java.util.regex.Pattern 1.4

- static Pattern compile(String expression)
- static Pattern compile(String expression, int flags)

    compiles the regular expression string into a pattern object for fast processing of matches. The flags parameter has one or more of the bits CASE_INSENSITIVE, UNICODE_CASE, MULTILINE, UNIX_LINES, DOTALL, and CANON_EQ set.

(Continues)

---

java.util.regex.Pattern 1.4 *(Continued)*

- `Matcher matcher(CharSequence input)`

  returns a matcher object that you can use to locate the matches of the pattern in the input.

- `String[] split(CharSequence input)`
- `String[] split(CharSequence input, int limit)`
- `Stream<String> splitAsStream(CharSequence input)` 8

  splits the input string into tokens, with the pattern specifying the form of the delimiters. Returns an array or stream of tokens. The delimiters are not part of the tokens. The second form has a parameter limit denoting the maximum number of strings to produce. If limit - 1 matching delimiters have been found, then the last entry of the returned array contains the remaining unsplit input. If limit is ≤ 0, then the entire input is split. If limit is 0, then trailing empty strings are not placed in the returned array.

---

java.util.regex.Matcher 1.4

- `boolean matches()`

  returns true if the input matches the pattern.

- `boolean lookingAt()`

  returns true if the beginning of the input matches the pattern.

- `boolean find()`
- `boolean find(int start)`

  attempts to find the next match and returns true if another match is found.

- `int start()`
- `int end()`

  returns the start or past-the-end position of the current match.

- `String group()`

  returns the current match.

- `int groupCount()`

  returns the number of groups in the input pattern.

(Continues)

---

java.util.regex.Matcher 1.4 *(Continued)*

- `int start(int groupIndex)`
- `int start(String name)` 8
- `int end(int groupIndex)`
- `int end(String name)` 8

  returns the start or past-the-end position of a group in the current match. The group is specified by an index starting with 1, or 0 to indicate the entire match, or by a string identifying a named group.

- `String group(int groupIndex)`
- `String group(String name)` 7

  returns the string matching a given group, denoted by an index starting with 1, or 0 to indicate the entire match, or by a string identifying a named group.

- `String replaceAll(String replacement)`
- `String replaceFirst(String replacement)`

  returns a string obtained from the matcher input by replacing all matches, or the first match, with the replacement string. The replacement string can contain references to pattern groups as $n. Use \$ to include a $ symbol.

- `static String quoteReplacement(String str)` 5.0

  quotes all \ and $ in str.

- `String replaceAll(Function<MatchResult,String> replacer)` 9

  replaces every match with the result of the `replacer` function applied to the `MatchResult`.

- `Stream<MatchResult> results()` 9

  yields a stream of all match results.

---

java.util.regex.MatchResult 5

- `String group()`
- `String group(int group)`

  yields the matched string or the string matched by the given group.

- `int start()`
- `int end()`
- `int start(int group)`
- `int end(int group)`

  yields the start and end offsets of the matched string or the string matched by the given group.

---

java.util.Scanner 5.0

- `Stream<MatchResult> findAll(Pattern pattern)` 9

  yields a stream of all matches of the given pattern in the input produced by this scanner.

You have now seen how to carry out input and output operations in Java, and had an overview of the regular expression package that was a part of the "new I/O" specification. In the next chapter, we turn to the processing of XML data.

3

XML

In this chapter

The preface of the book *Essential XML* by Don Box et al. (Addison-Wesley, 2000) stated only half-jokingly: "The Extensible Markup Language (XML) has replaced Java, Design Patterns, and Object Technology as the software industry's solution to world hunger." This kind of hype is long gone but, as you will see in this chapter, XML is still a very useful technology for describing structured information. XML tools make it easy to process and transform that information. However, XML is not a silver bullet. You need domain-specific standards and code libraries to use it effectively. Moreover, far from making Java obsolete, XML works very well with Java. Since the late 1990s, IBM, Apache, and others have been instrumental in producing high-quality Java libraries for XML processing. Many of these libraries have now been integrated into the Java platform.

This chapter introduces XML and covers the XML features of the Java library. As always, we'll point out along the way when using XML is justified—and when you have to take it with a grain of salt and try solving your problems the old-fashioned way: through good design and code.

3.1 Introducing XML

In Chapter 13 of Volume I, you have seen the use of *property files* to describe the configuration of a program. A property file contains a set of name/value pairs, such as

```
fontname=Times Roman
fontsize=12
windowsize=400 200
color=0 50 100
```

You can use the Properties class to read in such a file with a single method call. That's a nice feature, but it doesn't really go far enough. In many cases, the information you want to describe has more structure than the property file format can comfortably handle. Consider the fontname/fontsize entries in the example. It would be more object-oriented to have a single entry:

```
font=Times Roman 12
```

But then, parsing the font description gets ugly as you have to figure out when the font name ends and the font size starts.

Property files have a single flat hierarchy. You can often see programmers work around that limitation with key names like

```
title.fontname=Helvetica
title.fontsize=36
body.fontname=Times Roman
body.fontsize=12
```

Another shortcoming of the property file format is the requirement that keys must be unique. To store a sequence of values, you need another workaround, such as

```
menu.item.1=Times Roman
menu.item.2=Helvetica
menu.item.3=Goudy Old Style
```

The XML format solves these problems. It can express hierarchical structures and is thus more flexible than the flat table structure of a property file.

An XML file for describing a program configuration might look like this:

```
<config>
   <entry id="title">
      <font>
         <name>Helvetica</name>
         <size>36</size>
      </font>
   </entry>
   <entry id="body">
      <font>
         <name>Times Roman</name>
         <size>12</size>
      </font>
   </entry>
   <entry id="background">
      <color>
         <red>0</red>
         <green>50</green>
         <blue>100</blue>
      </color>
   </entry>
</config>
```

The XML format allows you to express the hierarchy and record repeated elements without contortions.

The format of an XML file is straightforward. It looks similar to an HTML file. There is a good reason for that—both XML and HTML are descendants of the venerable Standard Generalized Markup Language (SGML).

SGML has been around since the 1970s for describing the structure of complex documents. It has been used with success in some industries that require ongoing maintenance of massive documentation—in particular, the aircraft industry. However, SGML is quite complex, so it has never caught on in a big way. Much of that complexity arises because SGML has two conflicting goals. SGML wants to make sure that documents are formed according to the rules for their document type, but it also wants to make data entry easy by allowing shortcuts that reduce typing. XML was designed as a simplified version of SGML for use on the Internet. As is often true, simpler is better, and XML has enjoyed the immediate and enthusiastic reception that has eluded SGML for so long.

 NOTE: You can find a very nice version of the XML standard, with annotations by Tim Bray, at www.xml.com/axml/axml.html.

Even though XML and HTML have common roots, there are important differences between the two.

- Unlike HTML, XML is case-sensitive. For example, `<H1>` and `<h1>` are different XML tags.

- In HTML, you can omit end tags, such as `</p>` or `</li>`, if it is clear from the context where a paragraph or list item ends. In XML, you can never omit an end tag.

- In XML, elements that have a single tag without a matching end tag must end in a `/`, as in `<img src="coffeecup.png"/>`. That way, the parser knows not to look for a `</img>` tag.

- In XML, attribute values must be enclosed in quotation marks. In HTML, quotation marks are optional. For example, `<applet code="MyApplet.class" width=300 height=300>` is legal HTML but not legal XML. In XML, you have to use quotation marks: `width="300"`.

- In HTML, you can have attribute names without values, such as `<input type="radio" name="language" value="Java" checked>`. In XML, all attributes must have values, such as `checked="true"` or (ugh) `checked="checked"`.

- There are XML formulations for HTML versions 4 and 5 that are known as XHTML.

3.2 The Structure of an XML Document

An XML document should start with a header such as

```
<?xml version="1.0"?>
```

or

```
<?xml version="1.0" encoding="UTF-8"?>
```

Strictly speaking, a header is optional, but it is highly recommended.

 NOTE: Since SGML was created for processing of real documents, XML files are called *documents* even though many of them describe data sets that one would not normally call documents.

The header can be followed by a *document type definition* (DTD), such as

```
<!DOCTYPE web-app PUBLIC
    "-//Sun Microsystems, Inc.//DTD Web Application 2.2//EN"
    "http://java.sun.com/j2ee/dtds/web-app_2_2.dtd">
```

DTDs are an important mechanism to ensure the correctness of a document, but they are not required. We will discuss them later in this chapter.

Finally, the body of the XML document contains the *root element*, which can contain other elements. For example,

```
<?xml version="1.0"?>
<!DOCTYPE config . . .>
<config>
   <entry id="title">
      <font>
         <name>Helvetica</name>
         <size>36</size>
      </font>
   </entry>
   . . .
</config>
```

An element can contain *child elements*, text, or both. In the preceding example, the font element has two child elements, name and size. The name element contains the text "Helvetica".

 TIP: It is best to structure your XML documents so that an element contains *either* child elements *or* text. Here's an example of what you should avoid:

```
<font>
   Helvetica
   <size>36</size>
</font>
```

This is called *mixed content* in the XML specification. As you will see later in this chapter, you can simplify parsing if you avoid mixed content.

XML elements can contain attributes, such as

```
<size unit="pt">36</size>
```

There is some disagreement among XML designers about when to use elements and when to use attributes. For example, it would seem easier to describe a font as

```
<font name="Helvetica" size="36"/>
```

compared to

```
<font>
   <name>Helvetica</name>
   <size>36</size>
</font>
```

However, attributes are much less flexible. Suppose you want to add units to the size value. If you use attributes, you will have to add the unit to the attribute value:

```
<font name="Helvetica" size="36 pt"/>
```

Ugh! Now you have to parse the string "36 pt", just the kind of hassle that XML was designed to avoid. Adding an attribute to the size element is much cleaner:

```
<font>
   <name>Helvetica</name>
   <size unit="pt">36</size>
</font>
```

A commonly used rule of thumb is that attributes should be used only to modify the interpretation of a value, not to specify values. If you find yourself engaged in a metaphysical discussion about whether a particular setting is a modification of the interpretation of a value or not, just say "no" to attributes and use elements throughout. Many useful XML documents don't use attributes at all.

 NOTE: In HTML, the rule for attribute usage is simple: If it isn't displayed on the web page, it's an attribute. For example, consider the hyperlink

```
<a href="http://java.sun.com">Java Technology</a>
```

The string Java Technology is displayed on the web page, but the URL of the link is not a part of the displayed page. However, the rule isn't all that helpful for most XML files because the data in an XML file aren't normally meant to be viewed by humans.

Elements and text are the "bread and butter" of XML documents. Here are a few other markup instructions that you might encounter:

- *Character references* have the form &#*decimalValue*; or &#x*hexValue*;. For example, the é character can be denoted with either of the following:

  ```
  &#233; &#xE9;
  ```

- *Entity references* have the form &*name*;. The entity references

  ```
  &lt; &gt; &amp; &quot; &apos;
  ```

  have predefined meanings: the less-than, greater-than, ampersand, quotation mark, and apostrophe characters. You can define other entity references in a DTD.

- *CDATA sections* are delimited by <![CDATA[and]]>. They are a special form of character data. You can use them to include strings that contain characters such as < > & without having them interpreted as markup, for example:

  ```
  <![CDATA[< & > are my favorite delimiters]]>
  ```

  CDATA sections cannot contain the string]]>. Use this feature with caution! It is too often used as a back door for smuggling legacy data into XML documents.

- *Processing instructions* are instructions for applications that process XML documents. They are delimited by <? and ?>, for example

  ```
  <?xml-stylesheet href="mystyle.css" type="text/css"?>
  ```

  Every XML document starts with a processing instruction

  ```
  <?xml version="1.0"?>
  ```

- *Comments* are delimited by <!-- and -->, for example

  ```
  <!-- This is a comment. -->
  ```

Comments should not contain the string --. Comments should only be information for human readers. They should never contain hidden commands; use processing instructions for commands.

3.3 Parsing an XML Document

To process an XML document, you need to *parse* it. A parser is a program that reads a file, confirms that the file has the correct format, breaks it up into the constituent elements, and lets a programmer access those elements. The Java library supplies two kinds of XML parsers:

- Tree parsers, such as a Document Object Model (DOM) parser, that read an XML document into a tree structure.
- Streaming parsers, such as a Simple API for XML (SAX) parser, that generate events as they read an XML document.

DOM parsers are easier to use for most purposes, so we explain them first. You may consider a streaming parser if you process very long documents whose tree structures would use up a lot of memory, or if you are only interested in a few elements and don't care about their context. For more information, see Section 3.7, "Streaming Parsers," on p. 196.

The DOM parser interface is standardized by the World Wide Web Consortium (W3C). The org.w3c.dom package contains the definitions of interface types such as Document and Element. Different suppliers, such as the Apache Organization and IBM, have written DOM parsers whose classes implement these interfaces. The Java API for XML Processing (JAXP) library actually makes it possible to plug in any of these parsers. But the JDK also comes with a DOM parser that is derived from the Apache parser.

To read an XML document, you need a DocumentBuilder object that you get from a DocumentBuilderFactory like this:

```
DocumentBuilderFactory factory = DocumentBuilderFactory.newInstance();
DocumentBuilder builder = factory.newDocumentBuilder();
```

You can now read a document from a file:

```
File f = . . .;
Document doc = builder.parse(f);
```

Alternatively, you can use a URL:

```
URL u = . . .;
Document doc = builder.parse(u);
```

You can even specify an arbitrary input stream:

```
InputStream in = . . .;
Document doc = builder.parse(in);
```

 NOTE: If you use an input stream as an input source, the parser will not be able to locate other files that are referenced relative to the location of the document, such as a DTD in the same directory. You can install an "entity resolver" to overcome that problem. See www.xml.com/pub/a/2004/03/03/catalogs.html or www.ibm.com/developerworks/xml/library/x-mxd3.html for more information.

A Document object is an in-memory representation of the tree structure of an XML document. It is composed of objects whose classes implement the Node interface and its various subinterfaces. Figure 3.1 shows the inheritance hierarchy of the subinterfaces.

Start analyzing the contents of a document by calling the getDocumentElement method. It returns the root element.

```
Element root = doc.getDocumentElement();
```

For example, if you are processing a document

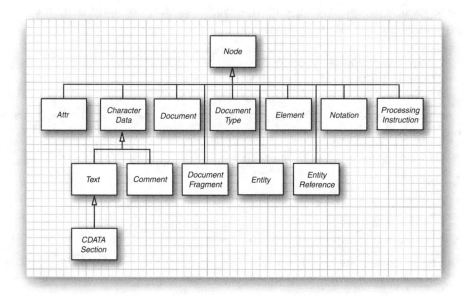

Figure 3.1 The Node interface and its subinterfaces

```
<?xml version="1.0"?>
<font>
    . . .
</font>
```

then calling getDocumentElement returns the font element.

The getTagName method returns the tag name of an element. In the preceding example, root.getTagName() returns the string "font".

To get an element's children (which may be subelements, text, comments, or other nodes), use the getChildNodes method. That method returns a collection of type NodeList. That type was standardized before the standard Java collections, so it has a different access protocol. The item method gets the item with a given index, and the getLength method gives the total count of the items. You can enumerate all children like this:

```
NodeList children = root.getChildNodes();
for (int i = 0; i < children.getLength(); i++)
{
    Node child = children.item(i);
    . . .
}
```

Be careful when analyzing children. Suppose, for example, that you are processing the document

```
<font>
   <name>Helvetica</name>
   <size>36</size>
</font>
```

You would expect the font element to have two children, but the parser reports five:

- The whitespace between <font> and <name>
- The name element
- The whitespace between </name> and <size>
- The size element
- The whitespace between </size> and </font>

Figure 3.2 shows the DOM tree.

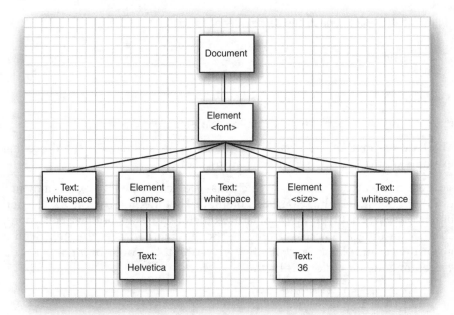

Figure 3.2 A simple DOM tree

If you expect only subelements, you can ignore the whitespace:

```
for (int i = 0; i < children.getLength(); i++)
{
   Node child = children.item(i);
   if (child instanceof Element)
   {
      var childElement = (Element) child;
      . . .
   }
}
```

Now you look at only two elements, with tag names name and size.

As you will see in the next section, you can do even better if your document has a DTD. Then the parser knows which elements don't have text nodes as children, and it can suppress the whitespace for you.

When analyzing the name and size elements, you want to retrieve the text strings that they contain. Those text strings are themselves contained in child nodes of type Text. You know that these Text nodes are the only children, so you can use the getFirstChild method without having to traverse another NodeList. Then, use the getData method to retrieve the string stored in a Text node:

```
for (int i = 0; i < children.getLength(); i++)
{
   Node child = children.item(i);
   if (child instanceof Element)
   {
      var childElement = (Element) child;
      var textNode = (Text) childElement.getFirstChild();
      String text = textNode.getData().trim();
      if (childElement.getTagName().equals("name"))
         name = text;
      else if (childElement.getTagName().equals("size"))
         size = Integer.parseInt(text);
   }
}
```

 TIP: It is a good idea to call trim on the return value of the getData method. If the author of an XML file puts the beginning and the ending tags on separate lines, such as

```
<size>
   36
</size>
```

then the parser will include all line breaks and spaces in the text node data. Calling the trim method removes the whitespace surrounding the actual data.

You can also get the last child with the getLastChild method, and the next sibling of a node with getNextSibling. Therefore, another way of traversing a node's children is

```
for (Node childNode = element.getFirstChild();
     childNode != null;
     childNode = childNode.getNextSibling())
{
   . . .
}
```

To enumerate the attributes of a node, call the getAttributes method. It returns a NamedNodeMap object that contains Node objects describing the attributes. You can traverse the nodes in a NamedNodeMap the same way as in a NodeList. Then, call the getNodeName and getNodeValue methods to get the attribute names and values.

```
NamedNodeMap attributes = element.getAttributes();
for (int i = 0; i < attributes.getLength(); i++)
{
   Node attribute = attributes.item(i);
   String name = attribute.getNodeName();
   String value = attribute.getNodeValue();
   . . .
}
```

Alternatively, if you know the name of an attribute, you can retrieve the corresponding value directly:

```
String unit = element.getAttribute("unit");
```

You have now seen how to analyze a DOM tree. The program in Listing 3.1 puts these techniques to work by converting an XML document to JSON format.

The tree display clearly shows how child elements are surrounded by text containing whitespace and comments. You can clearly see the newline and return characters as \n.

You don't have to be familiar with JSON to understand how the program works with the DOM tree. Simply observe the following:

- We use a DocumentBuilder to read a Document from a file.
- For each element, we print the tag name, attributes, and elements.
- For character data, we produce a string with the data. If the data comes from a comment, we add a "Comment: " prefix.

Listing 3.1 dom/JSONConverter.java

```java
1  package dom;
2
3  import java.io.*;
4  import java.util.*;
5
6  import javax.xml.parsers.*;
7
8  import org.w3c.dom.*;
9  import org.w3c.dom.CharacterData;
10 import org.xml.sax.*;
11
12 /**
13  * This program displays an XML document as a tree in JSON format.
14  * @version 1.2 2018-04-02
15  * @author Cay Horstmann
16  */
17 public class JSONConverter
18 {
19    public static void main(String[] args)
20          throws SAXException, IOException, ParserConfigurationException
21    {
22       String filename;
23       if (args.length == 0)
24       {
25          try (var in = new Scanner(System.in))
26          {
27             System.out.print("Input file: ");
28             filename = in.nextLine();
29          }
30       }
31       else
32          filename = args[0];
33       DocumentBuilderFactory factory = DocumentBuilderFactory.newInstance();
34       DocumentBuilder builder = factory.newDocumentBuilder();
35
36       Document doc = builder.parse(filename);
37       Element root = doc.getDocumentElement();
38       System.out.println(convert(root, 0));
39    }
40
41    public static StringBuilder convert(Node node, int level)
42    {
43       if (node instanceof Element)
44       {
45          return elementObject((Element) node, level);
46       }
```

(Continues)

Listing 3.1 *(Continued)*

```
47       else if (node instanceof CharacterData)
48       {
49          return characterString((CharacterData) node, level);
50       }
51       else
52       {
53          return pad(new StringBuilder(), level).append(
54             jsonEscape(node.getClass().getName()));
55       }
56    }
57
58    private static Map<Character, String> replacements = Map.of('\b', "\\b", '\f', "\\f",
59       '\n', "\\n", '\r', "\\r", '\t', "\\t", '"', "\\\"", '\\', "\\\\");
60
61    private static StringBuilder jsonEscape(String str)
62    {
63       var result = new StringBuilder("\"");
64       for (int i = 0; i < str.length(); i++)
65       {
66          char ch = str.charAt(i);
67          String replacement = replacements.get(ch);
68          if (replacement == null) result.append(ch);
69          else result.append(replacement);
70       }
71       result.append("\"");
72       return result;
73    }
74
75    private static StringBuilder characterString(CharacterData node, int level)
76    {
77       var result = new StringBuilder();
78       StringBuilder data = jsonEscape(node.getData());
79       if (node instanceof Comment) data.insert(1, "Comment: ");
80       pad(result, level).append(data);
81       return result;
82    }
83
84    private static StringBuilder elementObject(Element elem, int level)
85    {
86       var result = new StringBuilder();
87       pad(result, level).append("{\n");
88       pad(result, level + 1).append("\"name\": ");
89       result.append(jsonEscape(elem.getTagName()));
90       NamedNodeMap attrs = elem.getAttributes();
```

```
 91       if (attrs.getLength() > 0)
 92       {
 93          pad(result.append(",\n"), level + 1).append("\"attributes\": ");
 94          result.append(attributeObject(attrs));
 95       }
 96       NodeList children = elem.getChildNodes();
 97       if (children.getLength() > 0)
 98       {
 99          pad(result.append(",\n"), level + 1).append("\"children\": [\n");
100          for (int i = 0; i < children.getLength(); i++)
101          {
102             if (i > 0) result.append(",\n");
103             result.append(convert(children.item(i), level + 2));
104          }
105          result.append("\n");
106          pad(result, level + 1).append("]\n");
107       }
108       pad(result, level).append("}");
109       return result;
110    }
111
112    private static StringBuilder pad(StringBuilder builder, int level)
113    {
114       for (int i = 0; i < level; i++) builder.append("  ");
115       return builder;
116    }
117
118    private static StringBuilder attributeObject(NamedNodeMap attrs)
119    {
120       var result = new StringBuilder("{");
121       for (int i = 0; i < attrs.getLength(); i++)
122       {
123          if (i > 0) result.append(", ");
124          result.append(jsonEscape(attrs.item(i).getNodeName()));
125          result.append(": ");
126          result.append(jsonEscape(attrs.item(i).getNodeValue()));
127       }
128       result.append("}");
129       return result;
130    }
131 }
```

---

javax.xml.parsers.DocumentBuilderFactory 1.4

- static DocumentBuilderFactory newInstance()

  returns an instance of the DocumentBuilderFactory class.

- DocumentBuilder newDocumentBuilder()

  returns an instance of the DocumentBuilder class.

---

javax.xml.parsers.DocumentBuilder 1.4

- Document parse(File f)
- Document parse(String url)
- Document parse(InputStream in)

  parses an XML document from the given file, URL, or input stream and returns the parsed document.

---

org.w3c.dom.Document 1.4

- Element getDocumentElement()

  returns the root element of the document.

---

org.w3c.dom.Element 1.4

- String getTagName()

  returns the name of the element.

- String getAttribute(String name)

  returns the value of the attribute with the given name, or an empty string if there is no such attribute.

---

org.w3c.dom.Node 1.4

- NodeList getChildNodes()

  returns a node list that contains all children of this node.

- Node getFirstChild()
- Node getLastChild()

  gets the first or last child node of this node, or null if this node has no children.

- Node getNextSibling()
- Node getPreviousSibling()

  gets the next or previous sibling of this node, or null if this node has no siblings.

- Node getParentNode()

  gets the parent of this node, or null if this node is the document node.

- NamedNodeMap getAttributes()

  returns a node map that contains Attr nodes that describe all attributes of this node.

(Continues)

---

org.w3c.dom.Node 1.4 *(Continued)*

- `String getNodeName()`

  returns the name of this node. If the node is an `Attr` node, the name is the attribute name.

- `String getNodeValue()`

  returns the value of this node. If the node is an `Attr` node, the value is the attribute value.

---

org.w3c.dom.CharacterData 1.4

- `String getData()`

  returns the text stored in this node.

---

org.w3c.dom.NodeList 1.4

- `int getLength()`

  returns the number of nodes in this list.

- `Node item(int index)`

  returns the node with the given index. The index is between 0 and `getLength()` - 1.

---

org.w3c.dom.NamedNodeMap 1.4

- `int getLength()`

  returns the number of nodes in this map.

- `Node item(int index)`

  returns the node with the given index. The index is between 0 and `getLength()` - 1.

3.4 Validating XML Documents

In the previous section, you saw how to traverse the tree structure of a DOM document. However, with that approach, you'll have to do quite a bit of tedious programming and error checking. It's not just having to deal with whitespace between elements; you will also need to check whether the document contains the nodes that you expect. For example, suppose you are reading this element:

```
<font>
   <name>Helvetica</name>
   <size>36</size>
</font>
```

You get the first child. Oops . . . it is a text node containing whitespace "\n ". You skip text nodes and find the first element node. Then, you need to check that its tag name is "name" and that it has one child node of type Text. You move on to the next nonwhitespace child and make the same check. What if the author of the document switched the order of the children or added another child element? It is tedious to code all this error checking—but reckless to skip the checks.

Fortunately, one of the major benefits of an XML parser is that it can automatically verify that a document has the correct structure. That makes parsing much simpler. For example, if you know that the font fragment has passed validation, you can simply get the two grandchildren, cast them as Text nodes, and get the text data, without any further checking.

To specify the document structure, you can supply a DTD or an XML Schema definition. A DTD or schema contains rules that explain how a document should be formed, by specifying the legal child elements and attributes for each element. For example, a DTD might contain a rule:

```
<!ELEMENT font (name,size)>
```

This rule expresses that a font element must always have two children, which are name and size elements. The XML Schema language expresses the same constraint as

```
<xsd:element name="font">
   <xsd:sequence>
      <xsd:element name="name" type="xsd:string"/>
      <xsd:element name="size" type="xsd:int"/>
   </xsd:sequence>
</xsd:element>
```

XML Schema can express more sophisticated validation conditions (such as the fact that the size element must contain an integer) than can DTDs. Unlike the DTD syntax, the XML Schema syntax itself uses XML, which is a benefit if you need to process schema files.

In the next section, we will discuss DTDs in detail, then briefly cover the basics of XML Schema support. Finally, we will present a complete application that demonstrates how validation simplifies XML programming.

3.4.1 Document Type Definitions

There are several methods for supplying a DTD. You can include a DTD in an XML document like this:

```
<?xml version="1.0"?>
<!DOCTYPE config [
   <!ELEMENT config . . .>
   more rules
   . . .
]>
<config>
   . . .
</config>
```

As you can see, the rules are included inside a DOCTYPE declaration, in a block delimited by [. . .]. The document type must match the name of the root element, such as config in our example.

Supplying a DTD inside an XML document is somewhat uncommon because DTDs can grow lengthy. It makes more sense to store the DTD externally. The SYSTEM declaration can be used for that purpose. Specify a URL that contains the DTD, for example:

```
<!DOCTYPE config SYSTEM "config.dtd">
```

or

```
<!DOCTYPE config SYSTEM "http://myserver.com/config.dtd">
```

CAUTION: If you use a relative URL for the DTD (such as "config.dtd"), give the parser a File or URL object, not an InputStream. If you must parse from an input stream, supply an entity resolver (see the following note).

The mechanism for identifying well-known DTDs has its origin in SGML. Here is an example:

```
<!DOCTYPE web-app
    PUBLIC "-//Sun Microsystems, Inc.//DTD Web Application 2.2//EN"
    "http://java.sun.com/j2ee/dtds/web-app_2_2.dtd">
```

If an XML processor knows how to locate the DTD with the public identifier, it need not go to the URL.

NOTE: The system identifier URL of a DTD may not actually be working, or be purposefully slowed down. An example for the latter is the system identifier of the XHTML 1.0 Strict DTD, `http://www.w3.org/TR/xhtml1/DTD/xhtml1-strict.dtd`. If you parse an XHTML file, it may take a minute or two for the DTD to be served.

The remedy is to use an *entity resolver* that maps public identifiers to local files. Prior to Java 9, you had to provide an object of a class that implements the `EntityResolver` interface and provides a `resolveEntity` method.

Nowadays, you can use *XML catalogs* to manage the mapping. Provide one or more *catalog files* of the form

```
<?xml version="1.0"?>
<!DOCTYPE catalog PUBLIC "-//OASIS//DTD XML Catalogs V1.0//EN"
     "http://www.oasis-open.org/committees/entity/release/1.0/catalog.dtd">
<catalog xmlns="urn:oasis:names:tc:entity:xmlns:xml:catalog" prefer="public">
  <public publicId=". . ." uri=". . ."/>
  . . .
</catalog>
```

Then construct and install a resolver like this:

```
builder.setEntityResolver(CatalogManager.catalogResolver(
   CatalogFeatures.defaults(),
   Paths.get("catalog.xml").toAbsolutePath().toUri()));
```

See Listing 3.6 for a complete example.

Instead of setting the catalog file locations in your program, you can specify them on the command line with the `javax.xml.catalog.files` system property. Provide absolute `file` URLs separated by semicolons.

Now that you have seen how the parser locates the DTD, let us consider the various kinds of rules.

The `ELEMENT` rule specifies what children an element can have. Use a regular expression, made up of the components shown in Table 3.1.

Here are several simple but typical examples. The following rule states that a `menu` element contains 0 or more `item` elements:

```
<!ELEMENT menu (item)*>
```

This set of rules states that a font is described by a `name` followed by a `size`, each of which contain text:

```
<!ELEMENT font (name,size)>
<!ELEMENT name (#PCDATA)>
<!ELEMENT size (#PCDATA)>
```

Table 3.1 Rules for Element Content

Rule	Meaning
$E*$	0 or more occurrences of E
$E+$	1 or more occurrences of E
$E?$	0 or 1 occurrences of E
$E_1|E_2|...|E_n$	One of $E_1, E_2, ..., E_n$
$E_1, E_2, ..., E_n$	E_1 followed by $E_2, ..., E_n$
#PCDATA	Text
$(\text{\#PCDATA}|E_1|E_2|...|E_n)*$	0 or more occurrences of text and $E_1, E_2, ..., E_n$ in any order (mixed content)
ANY	Any children allowed
EMPTY	No children allowed

The abbreviation PCDATA denotes *parsed character data*. It is "parsed" because the parser interprets the text string, looking for < characters that denote the start of a new tag, or & characters that denote the start of an entity.

An element specification can contain regular expressions that are nested and complex. For example, here is a rule that describes the makeup of a chapter in a book:

```
<!ELEMENT chapter (intro,(heading,(para|image|table|note)+)+)
```

Each chapter starts with an introduction, which is followed by one or more sections consisting of a heading and one or more paragraphs, images, tables, or notes.

However, in one common case you can't define the rules to be as flexible as you might like. Whenever an element can contain text, there are only two valid cases. Either the element contains nothing but text, such as

```
<!ELEMENT name (#PCDATA)>
```

or the element contains *any combination of text and tags in any order*, such as

```
<!ELEMENT para (#PCDATA|em|strong|code)*>
```

It is not legal to specify any other types of rules that contain #PCDATA. For example, the following is illegal:

```
<!ELEMENT captionedImage (image,#PCDATA)>
```

You have to rewrite such a rule, either by introducing another caption element or by allowing any combination of image elements and text.

This restriction simplifies the job of the XML parser when parsing *mixed content* (a mixture of tags and text). Since you lose some control by allowing mixed content, it is best to design DTDs so that all elements contain either other elements or nothing but text.

 NOTE: Actually, it isn't quite true that you can specify arbitrary regular expressions of elements in a DTD rule. An XML parser may reject certain complex rule sets that lead to nondeterministic parsing. For example, a regular expression ((x,y)|(x,z)) is nondeterministic. When the parser sees x, it doesn't know which of the two alternatives to take. This expression can be rewritten in a deterministic form as (x,(y|z)). However, some expressions can't be reformulated, such as ((x,y)*|x?). The parser in the Java XML library gives no warnings when presented with an ambiguous DTD; it simply picks the first matching alternative when parsing, which causes it to reject some correct inputs. The parser is well within its rights to do so because the XML standard allows a parser to assume that the DTD is unambiguous.

You can also specify rules to describe the legal attributes of elements. The general syntax is

<!ATTLIST *element attribute type default*>

Table 3.2 shows the legal attribute types, and Table 3.3 shows the syntax for the defaults.

Table 3.2 Attribute Types

Type	Meaning
CDATA	Any character string
$(A_1|A_2| \ldots |A_n)$	One of the string attributes $A_1, A_2, \ldots, A_n$
NMTOKEN, NMTOKENS	One or more name tokens
ID	A unique ID
IDREF, IDREFS	One or more references to a unique ID
ENTITY, ENTITIES	One or more unparsed entities

Table 3.3 Attribute Defaults

Default	Meaning
#REQUIRED	Attribute is required.
#IMPLIED	Attribute is optional.
A	Attribute is optional; the parser reports it to be *A* if it is not specified.
#FIXED *A*	The attribute must either be unspecified or *A*; in either case, the parser reports it to be *A*.

Here are two typical attribute specifications:

```
<!ATTLIST font style (plain|bold|italic|bold-italic) "plain">
<!ATTLIST size unit CDATA #IMPLIED>
```

The first specification describes the style attribute of a font element. There are four legal attribute values, and the default value is plain. The second specification expresses that the unit attribute of the size element can contain any character data sequence.

 NOTE: We generally recommend the use of elements, not attributes, to describe data. Thus, the font style should be a separate element, such as <font><style>plain</style>. . .</font>. However, attributes have an undeniable advantage for enumerated types because the parser can verify that the values are legal. For example, if the font style is an attribute, the parser checks that it is one of the four allowed values, and supplies a default if no value was given.

The handling of a CDATA attribute value is subtly different from the processing of #PCDATA that you have seen before, and quite unrelated to the <![CDATA[. . .]]> sections. The attribute value is first *normalized*—that is, the parser processes character and entity references (such as é or <) and replaces whitespace with spaces.

An NMTOKEN (or name token) is similar to CDATA, but most nonalphanumeric characters and internal whitespace are disallowed, and the parser removes leading and trailing whitespace. NMTOKENS is a whitespace-separated list of name tokens.

The ID construct is quite useful. An ID is a name token that must be unique in the document—the parser checks the uniqueness. You will see an application in the next sample program. An IDREF is a reference to an ID that exists in the same document, which the parser also checks. IDREFS is a whitespace-separated list of ID references.

An ENTITY attribute value refers to an "unparsed external entity." That is a holdover from SGML that is rarely used in practice. The annotated XML specification at www.xml.com/axml/axml.html has an example.

A DTD can also define *entities*, or abbreviations that are replaced during parsing. You can find a good example for the use of entities in the user interface descriptions of the Firefox browser. Those descriptions are formatted in XML and contain entity definitions such as

```
<!ENTITY back.label "Back">
```

Elsewhere, text can contain an entity reference, for example:

```
<menuitem label="&back.label;"/>
```

The parser replaces the entity reference with the replacement string. To internationalize the application, only the string in the entity definition needs to be changed. Other uses of entities are more complex and less common; look at the XML specification for details.

This concludes the introduction to DTDs. Now that you have seen how to use DTDs, you can configure your parser to take advantage of them.

First, tell the document builder factory to turn on validation:

```
factory.setValidating(true);
```

All builders produced by this factory validate their input against a DTD. The most useful benefit of validation is ignoring whitespace in element content. For example, consider the XML fragment

```
<font>
   <name>Helvetica</name>
   <size>36</size>
</font>
```

A nonvalidating parser reports the whitespace between the font, name, and size elements because it has no way of knowing if the children of font are

```
(name,size)
(#PCDATA,name,size)*
```

or perhaps

```
ANY
```

Once the DTD specifies that the children are (name,size), the parser knows that the whitespace between them is not text. Call

```
factory.setIgnoringElementContentWhitespace(true);
```

and the builder will stop reporting the whitespace in text nodes. That means you can now *rely on* the fact that a font node has two children. You no longer need to program a tedious loop:

```
for (int i = 0; i < children.getLength(); i++)
{
   Node child = children.item(i);
   if (child instanceof Element)
   {
      var childElement = (Element) child;
      if (childElement.getTagName().equals("name")) . . .;
      else if (childElement.getTagName().equals("size")) . . .;
   }
}
```

Instead, you can simply access the first and second child:

```
var nameElement = (Element) children.item(0);
var sizeElement = (Element) children.item(1);
```

That is why DTDs are so useful. You don't overload your program with rule-checking code—the parser has already done that work by the time you get the document.

When the parser reports an error, your application will want to do something about it—log it, show it to the user, or throw an exception to abandon the parsing. Therefore, you should install an error handler whenever you use validation. Supply an object that implements the ErrorHandler interface. That interface has three methods:

```
void warning(SAXParseException exception)
void error(SAXParseException exception)
void fatalError(SAXParseException exception)
```

Install the error handler with the setErrorHandler method of the DocumentBuilder class:

```
builder.setErrorHandler(handler);
```

---

javax.xml.parsers.DocumentBuilder 1.4

- void setEntityResolver(EntityResolver resolver)

  sets the resolver to locate entities that are referenced in the XML documents being parsed.

- void setErrorHandler(ErrorHandler handler)

  sets the handler to report errors and warnings that occur during parsing.

---

org.xml.sax.EntityResolver 1.4

- `public InputSource resolveEntity(String publicID, String systemID)`

  returns an input source that contains the data referenced by the given ID(s), or null to indicate that this resolver doesn't know how to resolve the particular name. The publicID parameter may be null if no public ID was supplied.

---

org.xml.sax.InputSource 1.4

- `InputSource(InputStream in)`
- `InputSource(Reader in)`
- `InputSource(String systemID)`

  constructs an input source from a stream, reader, or system ID (usually a relative or absolute URL).

---

org.xml.sax.ErrorHandler 1.4

- `void fatalError(SAXParseException exception)`
- `void error(SAXParseException exception)`
- `void warning(SAXParseException exception)`

  Override these methods to provide handlers for fatal errors, nonfatal errors, and warnings.

---

org.xml.sax.SAXParseException 1.4

- `int getLineNumber()`
- `int getColumnNumber()`

  returns the line and column numbers of the end of the processed input that caused the exception.

---

javax.xml.catalog.CatalogManager 9

- `static CatalogResolver catalogResolver(CatalogFeatures features, URI... uris)`

  produces a resolver that uses the catalog files located at the provided URIs. This class implements EntityResolver as well as the resolver classes used by StAX, schema validation, and XSL transforms.

> **javax.xml.catalog.CatalogFeatures 9**
>
> • static CatalogFeatures defaults()
>
> yields an instance with default settings.

> **javax.xml.parsers.DocumentBuilderFactory 1.4**
>
> • boolean isValidating()
> • void setValidating(boolean value)
>
> gets or sets the validating property of the factory. If set to true, the parsers that this factory generates validate their input.
>
> • boolean isIgnoringElementContentWhitespace()
> • void setIgnoringElementContentWhitespace(boolean value)
>
> gets or sets the ignoringElementContentWhitespace property of the factory. If set to true, the parsers that this factory generates ignore whitespace between element nodes that don't have mixed content (i.e., a mixture of elements and #PCDATA).

3.4.2 XML Schema

XML Schema is quite a bit more complex than the DTD syntax, so we will only cover the basics. For more information, we recommend the tutorial at www.w3.org/TR/xmlschema-0.

To reference a schema file in a document, add attributes to the root element, for example:

```
<?xml version="1.0"?>
<config xmlns:xsi="http://www.w3.org/2001/XMLSchema-instance"
      xsi:noNamespaceSchemaLocation="config.xsd">
   . . .
</config>
```

This declaration states that the schema file config.xsd should be used to validate the document. If your document uses namespaces, the syntax is a bit more complex—see the XML Schema tutorial for details. (The prefix xsi is a *namespace alias*; see Section 3.6, "Using Namespaces," on p. 193 for more information.)

A schema defines a *type* for each element and attribute. A *simple type* is a string, perhaps with restrictions on its contents. Everything else is a *complex* type. An element with a simple type can have no attributes and no child elements. Otherwise, it must have a complex type. Conversely, attributes always have a simple type.

Some simple types are built into XML Schema, including

```
xsd:string
xsd:int
xsd:boolean
```

 NOTE: We use the prefix xsd: to denote the XML Schema Definition namespace. Some authors use the prefix xs: instead.

You can define your own simple types. For example, here is an enumerated type:

```
<xsd:simpleType name="StyleType">
   <xsd:restriction base="xsd:string">
      <xsd:enumeration value="PLAIN" />
      <xsd:enumeration value="BOLD" />
      <xsd:enumeration value="ITALIC" />
      <xsd:enumeration value="BOLD_ITALIC" />
   </xsd:restriction>
</xsd:simpleType>
```

When you define an element, you specify its type:

```
<xsd:element name="name" type="xsd:string"/>
<xsd:element name="size" type="xsd:int"/>
<xsd:element name="style" type="StyleType"/>
```

The type constrains the element content. For example, the elements

```
<size>10</size>
<style>PLAIN</style>
```

will validate correctly, but the elements

```
<size>default</size>
<style>SLANTED</style>
```

will be rejected by the parser.

You can compose types into complex types, for example:

```
<xsd:complexType name="FontType">
   <xsd:sequence>
      <xsd:element ref="name"/>
      <xsd:element ref="size"/>
      <xsd:element ref="style"/>
   </xsd:sequence>
</xsd:complexType>
```

A FontType is a sequence of name, size, and style elements. In this type definition, we use the ref attribute and refer to definitions that are located elsewhere in the schema. You can also nest definitions, like this:

```
<xsd:complexType name="FontType">
   <xsd:sequence>
      <xsd:element name="name" type="xsd:string"/>
      <xsd:element name="size" type="xsd:int"/>
      <xsd:element name="style">
         <xsd:simpleType>
            <xsd:restriction base="xsd:string">
               <xsd:enumeration value="PLAIN" />
               <xsd:enumeration value="BOLD" />
               <xsd:enumeration value="ITALIC" />
               <xsd:enumeration value="BOLD_ITALIC" />
            </xsd:restriction>
         </xsd:simpleType>
      </xsd:element>
   </xsd:sequence>
</xsd:complexType>
```

Note the *anonymous type definition* of the style element.

The xsd:sequence construct is the equivalent of the concatenation notation in DTDs. The xsd:choice construct is the equivalent of the | operator. For example,

```
<xsd:complexType name="contactinfo">
   <xsd:choice>
      <xsd:element ref="email"/>
      <xsd:element ref="phone"/>
   </xsd:choice>
</xsd:complexType>
```

This is the equivalent of the DTD type email|phone.

To allow repeated elements, use the minoccurs and maxoccurs attributes. For example, the equivalent of the DTD type item* is

```
<xsd:element name="item" type=". . ." minoccurs="0" maxoccurs="unbounded">
```

To specify attributes, add xsd:attribute elements to complexType definitions:

```
<xsd:element name="size">
   <xsd:complexType>
      . . .
      <xsd:attribute name="unit" type="xsd:string" use="optional" default="cm"/>
   </xsd:complexType>
</xsd:element>
```

This is the equivalent of the DTD statement

```
<!ATTLIST size unit CDATA #IMPLIED "cm">
```

Enclose element and type definitions of your schema inside an `xsd:schema` element:

```
<xsd:schema xmlns:xsd="http://www.w3.org/2001/XMLSchema">
    . . .
</xsd:schema>
```

Parsing an XML file with a schema is similar to parsing a file with a DTD, but with two differences:

1. You need to turn on support for namespaces, even if you don't use them in your XML files.

    ```
    factory.setNamespaceAware(true);
    ```

2. You need to prepare the factory for handling schemas, with the following magic incantation:

    ```
    final String JAXP_SCHEMA_LANGUAGE =
        "http://java.sun.com/xml/jaxp/properties/schemaLanguage";
    final String W3C_XML_SCHEMA = "http://www.w3.org/2001/XMLSchema";
    factory.setAttribute(JAXP_SCHEMA_LANGUAGE, W3C_XML_SCHEMA);
    ```

3.4.3 A Practical Example

In this section, we work through a practical example that shows the use of XML in a realistic setting.

Suppose an application needs configuration data that specifies arbitrary objects, not just text strings. We provide two mechanisms for instantiating the object: with a constructor, and with a factory method. Here is how to make a `Color` object using a constructor:

```
<construct class="java.awt.Color">
    <int>55</int>
    <int>200</int>
    <int>100</int>
</construct>
```

Here is an example with a factory method:

```
<factory class="java.util.logging.Logger" method="getLogger">
    <string>com.horstmann.corejava</string>
</factory>
```

If the factory method name is omitted, it defaults to `getInstance`.

As you can see, there are elements for describing strings and integers. We also support the `boolean` type, and other primitive types can be added in the same way.

Just to show off the syntax, there is a second mechanism for primitive types:

```
<value type="int">30</value>
```

A configuration is a sequence of entries. Each entry has an ID and an object:

```
<config>
   <entry id="background">
      <construct class="java.awt.Color">
         <value type="int">55</value>
         <value type="int">200</value>
         <value type="int">100</value>
      </construct>
   </entry>
   . . .
</config>
```

The parser checks that IDs are unique.

The DTD, shown in Listing 3.4, is straightforward.

Listing 3.5 contains the equivalent schema. In the schema, we can provide additional checking: an `int` or `boolean` element can only contain integer or boolean content. Note the use of the `xsd:group` construct to define parts of complex types that are used repeatedly.

The program in Listing 3.2 shows how to parse a configuration file. A sample configuration is defined in Listing 3.3.

The program uses the schema instead of the DTD if you choose a file that contains the string `-schema`.

This example is a typical use of XML. The XML format is robust enough to express complex relationships. The XML parser adds value by taking over the routine job of validity checking and supplying defaults.

Listing 3.2 read/XMLReadTest.java

```
 1 package read;
 2
 3 import java.io.*;
 4 import java.lang.reflect.*;
 5 import java.util.*;
 6
 7 import javax.xml.parsers.*;
 8
 9 import org.w3c.dom.*;
10 import org.xml.sax.*;
11
```

(Continues)

Listing 3.2 *(Continued)*

```java
12  /**
13   * This program shows how to use an XML file to describe Java objects
14   * @version 1.0 2018-04-03
15   * @author Cay Horstmann
16   */
17  public class XMLReadTest
18  {
19     public static void main(String[] args) throws ParserConfigurationException,
20           SAXException, IOException, ReflectiveOperationException
21     {
22        String filename;
23        if (args.length == 0)
24        {
25           try (var in = new Scanner(System.in))
26           {
27              System.out.print("Input file: ");
28              filename = in.nextLine();
29           }
30        }
31        else
32           filename = args[0];
33
34        DocumentBuilderFactory factory = DocumentBuilderFactory.newInstance();
35        factory.setValidating(true);
36
37        if (filename.contains("-schema"))
38        {
39           factory.setNamespaceAware(true);
40           final String JAXP_SCHEMA_LANGUAGE =
41                 "http://java.sun.com/xml/jaxp/properties/schemaLanguage";
42           final String W3C_XML_SCHEMA = "http://www.w3.org/2001/XMLSchema";
43           factory.setAttribute(JAXP_SCHEMA_LANGUAGE, W3C_XML_SCHEMA);
44        }
45
46        factory.setIgnoringElementContentWhitespace(true);
47
48        DocumentBuilder builder = factory.newDocumentBuilder();
49
50        builder.setErrorHandler(new ErrorHandler()
51           {
52              public void warning(SAXParseException e) throws SAXException
53              {
54                 System.err.println("Warning: " + e.getMessage());
55              }
56
57              public void error(SAXParseException e) throws SAXException
58              {
```

```
59              System.err.println("Error: " + e.getMessage());
60              System.exit(0);
61           }
62
63           public void fatalError(SAXParseException e) throws SAXException
64           {
65              System.err.println("Fatal error: " + e.getMessage());
66              System.exit(0);
67           }
68        });
69
70     Document doc = builder.parse(filename);
71     Map<String, Object> config = parseConfig(doc.getDocumentElement());
72     System.out.println(config);
73  }
74
75  private static Map<String, Object> parseConfig(Element e)
76        throws ReflectiveOperationException
77  {
78     var result = new HashMap<String, Object>();
79     NodeList children = e.getChildNodes();
80     for (int i = 0; i < children.getLength(); i++)
81     {
82        var child = (Element) children.item(i);
83        String name = child.getAttribute("id");
84        Object value = parseObject((Element) child.getFirstChild());
85        result.put(name, value);
86     }
87     return result;
88  }
89
90  private static Object parseObject(Element e)
91        throws ReflectiveOperationException
92  {
93     String tagName = e.getTagName();
94     if (tagName.equals("factory")) return parseFactory(e);
95     else if (tagName.equals("construct")) return parseConstruct(e);
96     else
97     {
98        String childData = ((CharacterData) e.getFirstChild()).getData();
99        if (tagName.equals("int"))
100          return Integer.valueOf(childData);
101       else if (tagName.equals("boolean"))
102          return Boolean.valueOf(childData);
103       else
104          return childData;
105    }
106 }
107
```

(Continues)

Listing 3.2 *(Continued)*

```
108   private static Object parseFactory(Element e)
109        throws ReflectiveOperationException
110   {
111      String className = e.getAttribute("class");
112      String methodName = e.getAttribute("method");
113      Object[] args = parseArgs(e.getChildNodes());
114      Class<?>[] parameterTypes = getParameterTypes(args);
115      Method method = Class.forName(className).getMethod(methodName, parameterTypes);
116      return method.invoke(null, args);
117   }
118
119   private static Object parseConstruct(Element e)
120        throws ReflectiveOperationException
121   {
122      String className = e.getAttribute("class");
123      Object[] args = parseArgs(e.getChildNodes());
124      Class<?>[] parameterTypes = getParameterTypes(args);
125      Constructor<?> constructor = Class.forName(className).getConstructor(parameterTypes);
126      return constructor.newInstance(args);
127   }
128
129   private static Object[] parseArgs(NodeList elements)
130        throws ReflectiveOperationException
131   {
132      var result = new Object[elements.getLength()];
133      for (int i = 0; i < result.length; i++)
134         result[i] = parseObject((Element) elements.item(i));
135      return result;
136   }
137
138   private static Map<Class<?>, Class<?>> toPrimitive = Map.of(
139        Integer.class, int.class,
140        Boolean.class, boolean.class);
141
142   private static Class<?>[] getParameterTypes(Object[] args)
143   {
144      var result = new Class<?>[args.length];
145      for (int i = 0; i < result.length; i++)
146      {
147         Class<?> cl = args[i].getClass();
148         result[i] = toPrimitive.get(cl);
149         if (result[i] == null) result[i] = cl;
150      }
151      return result;
152   }
153 }
```

Listing 3.3 read/config.xml

```xml
1  <?xml version="1.0"?>
2  <!DOCTYPE config SYSTEM "config.dtd">
3  <config>
4    <entry id="background">
5      <construct class="java.awt.Color">
6        <int>55</int>
7        <int>200</int>
8        <int>100</int>
9      </construct>
10   </entry>
11   <entry id="currency">
12     <factory class="java.util.Currency">
13       <string>USD</string>
14     </factory>
15   </entry>
16 </config>
```

Listing 3.4 read/config.dtd

```
1  <!ELEMENT config (entry)*>
2
3  <!ELEMENT entry (string|int|boolean|construct|factory)>
4  <!ATTLIST entry id ID #IMPLIED>
5
6  <!ELEMENT construct (string|int|boolean|construct|factory)*>
7  <!ATTLIST construct class CDATA #IMPLIED>
8
9  <!ELEMENT factory (string|int|boolean|construct|factory)*>
10 <!ATTLIST factory class CDATA #IMPLIED>
11 <!ATTLIST factory method CDATA "getInstance">
12
13 <!ELEMENT string (#PCDATA)>
14 <!ELEMENT int (#PCDATA)>
15 <!ELEMENT boolean (#PCDATA)>
```

Listing 3.5 read/config.xsd

```xml
1  <xsd:schema xmlns:xsd="http://www.w3.org/2001/XMLSchema">
2    <xsd:element name="config">
3      <xsd:complexType>
4        <xsd:sequence>
5          <xsd:element name="entry" minOccurs="0" maxOccurs="unbounded">
6            <xsd:complexType>
7              <xsd:group ref="Object"/>
8              <xsd:attribute name="id" type="xsd:ID"/>
```

(Continues)

Listing 3.5 *(Continued)*

```
9              </xsd:complexType>
10            </xsd:element>
11          </xsd:sequence>
12        </xsd:complexType>
13      </xsd:element>
14
15      <xsd:element name="construct">
16        <xsd:complexType>
17          <xsd:group ref="Arguments"/>
18          <xsd:attribute name="class" type="xsd:string"/>
19        </xsd:complexType>
20      </xsd:element>
21
22      <xsd:element name="factory">
23        <xsd:complexType>
24          <xsd:group ref="Arguments"/>
25          <xsd:attribute name="class" type="xsd:string"/>
26          <xsd:attribute name="method" type="xsd:string" default="getInstance"/>
27        </xsd:complexType>
28      </xsd:element>
29
30      <xsd:group name="Object">
31        <xsd:choice>
32          <xsd:element ref="construct"/>
33          <xsd:element ref="factory"/>
34          <xsd:element name="string" type="xsd:string"/>
35          <xsd:element name="int" type="xsd:int"/>
36          <xsd:element name="boolean" type="xsd:boolean"/>
37        </xsd:choice>
38      </xsd:group>
39
40      <xsd:group name="Arguments">
41        <xsd:sequence>
42          <xsd:group ref="Object" minOccurs="0" maxOccurs="unbounded"/>
43        </xsd:sequence>
44      </xsd:group>
45    </xsd:schema>
```

3.5 Locating Information with XPath

If you want to locate a specific piece of information in an XML document, it can be a bit of a hassle to navigate the nodes of the DOM tree. The XPath language makes it simple to access tree nodes. For example, suppose you have this XHTML document:

```
<html>
   <head>
      . . .
      <title>. . .</title>
      . . .
   </database>
   . . .
</html>
```

You can get the title text by evaluating the XPath expression

```
/html/head/title/text()
```

That's a lot simpler than the plain DOM approach:

1. Get the document root.
2. Get the first child and cast is as an Element.
3. Locate the title element among its children.
4. Get its first child and cast it as a CharacterData node.
5. Get its data.

An XPath can describe *a set of nodes* in an XML document. For example, the XPath

```
/html/body/form
```

describes the set of all form elements that are children of the body element in an XHTML file. You can select a particular element with the [] operator:

```
/html/body/form[1]
```

is the first form. (The index values start at 1.)

Use the @ operator to get attribute values. The XPath expression

```
/html/body/form[1]/@action
```

describes the action attribute of the first table. The XPath expression

```
/html/body/form/@action
```

describes all action attribute nodes of all form elements that are children of the body element.

There are a number of useful XPath functions. For example,

```
count(/html/body/form)
```

returns the number of form children of the body element. There are many more elaborate XPath expressions; see the specification at www.w3c.org/TR/xpath or the online tutorial at www.zvon.org/xxl/XPathTutorial/General/examples.html.

To evaluate XPath expressions, first create an XPath object from an XPathFactory:

```
XPathFactory xpfactory = XPathFactory.newInstance();
path = xpfactory.newXPath();
```

Then, call the evaluate method to evaluate XPath expressions:

```
String username = path.evaluate("/html/head/title/text()", doc);
```

You can use the same XPath object to evaluate multiple expressions.

This form of the evaluate method returns a string result. It is suitable for retrieving text, such as the text child of the title element in the preceding example. If an XPath expression yields multiple nodes, make a call such as the following:

```
XPathNodes result = path.evaluateExpression("/html/body/form", doc, XPathNodes.class);
```

The XPathNodes class is similar to a NodeList, but it extends the Iterable interface, allowing you to use an enhanced for loop.

This method was added in Java 9. In older releases, use the following call instead:

```
var nodes = (NodeList) path.evaluate("/html/body/form", doc, XPathConstants.NODESET);
```

If the result is a single node, use one of the following calls:

```
Node node = path.evaluateExpression("/html/body/form[1]", doc, Node.class);
node = (Node) path.evaluate("/html/body/form[1]", doc, XPathConstants.NODE);
```

If the result is a number, use:

```
int count = path.evaluateExpression("count(/html/body/form)", doc, Integer.class);
count = ((Number) path.evaluate("count(/html/body/form)",
    doc, XPathConstants.NUMBER)).intValue();
```

You don't have to start the search at the document root; you can start at any node or node list. For example, if you have a node from a previous evaluation, you can call

```
String result = path.evaluate(expression, node);
```

If you do not know the result of evaluating an XPath expression (perhaps because it comes from a user), then call

```
XPathEvaluationResult<?> result = path.evaluateExpression(expression, doc);
```

The expression result.type() is one of the constants

```
STRING
NODESET
NODE
```

NUMBER
BOOLEAN

of the `XPathEvaluationResult.XPathResultType` enumeration. Call `result.value()` to get the value.

The program in Listing 3.6 demonstrates evaluation of arbitrary XPath expressions. Load an XML file and type an expression. The result of the expression is displayed.

Listing 3.6 `xpath/XPathTest.java`

```
1  package xpath;
2
3  import java.io.*;
4  import java.nio.file.*;
5  import java.util.*;
6
7  import javax.xml.catalog.*;
8  import javax.xml.parsers.*;
9  import javax.xml.xpath.*;
10
11 import org.w3c.dom.*;
12 import org.xml.sax.*;
13
14 /**
15  * This program evaluates XPath expressions.
16  * @version 1.1 2018-04-06
17  * @author Cay Horstmann
18  */
19 public class XPathTest
20 {
21    public static void main(String[] args) throws Exception
22    {
23       DocumentBuilderFactory factory = DocumentBuilderFactory.newInstance();
24       DocumentBuilder builder = factory.newDocumentBuilder();
25
26       // Avoid a delay in parsing an XHTML file--see the first note in
27       // Section 3.3.1
28       builder.setEntityResolver(CatalogManager.catalogResolver(
29             CatalogFeatures.defaults(),
30             Paths.get("xpath/catalog.xml").toAbsolutePath().toUri()));
31
32       XPathFactory xpfactory = XPathFactory.newInstance();
33       XPath path = xpfactory.newXPath();
34       try (var in = new Scanner(System.in))
35       {
```

(Continues)

Listing 3.6 *(Continued)*

```
36          String filename;
37          if (args.length == 0)
38          {
39             System.out.print("Input file: ");
40             filename = in.nextLine();
41          }
42          else
43             filename = args[0];
44
45          Document doc = builder.parse(filename);
46          var done = false;
47          while (!done)
48          {
49             System.out.print("XPath expression (empty line to exit): " );
50             String expression = in.nextLine();
51             if (expression.trim().isEmpty()) done = true;
52             else
53             {
54                try
55                {
56                   XPathEvaluationResult<?> result
57                         = path.evaluateExpression(expression, doc);
58                   if (result.type() == XPathEvaluationResult.XPathResultType.NODESET)
59                   {
60                      for (Node n : (XPathNodes) result.value())
61                         System.out.println(description(n));
62                   }
63                   else if (result.type() == XPathEvaluationResult.XPathResultType.NODESET)
64                      System.out.println((Node) result.value());
65                   else
66                      System.out.println(result.value());
67                }
68                catch (XPathExpressionException e)
69                {
70                   System.out.println(e.getMessage());
71                }
72             }
73          }
74       }
75    }
76
77    public static String description(Node n)
78    {
79       if (n instanceof Element) return "Element " + n.getNodeName();
80       else if (n instanceof Attr) return "Attribute " + n;
81       else return n.toString();
82    }
83 }
```

---

javax.xml.xpath.XPathFactory 5.0

- static XPathFactory newInstance()

  returns an XPathFactory instance for creating XPath objects.
- XPath newXpath()

  constructs an XPath object for evaluating XPath expressions.

---

javax.xml.xpath.XPath 5.0

- String evaluate(String expression, Object startingPoint)

  evaluates an expression, beginning at the given starting point. The starting point can be a node or node list. If the result is a node or node set, the returned string consists of the data of all text node children.
- Object evaluate(String expression, Object startingPoint, QName resultType)

  evaluates an expression, beginning at the given starting point. The starting point can be a node or node list. The resultType is one of the constants STRING, NODE, NODESET, NUMBER, or BOOLEAN in the XPathConstants class. The return value is a String, Node, NodeList, Number, or Boolean.
- <T> T evaluateExpression(String expression, Object item, Class<T> type) 9

  evaluates the given expression and yields the result as a value of the given type.
- XPathEvaluationResult<?> evaluateExpression(String expression, InputSource source) 9

  evaluates the given expression.

---

javax.xml.xpath.XPathEvaluationResult<T> 9

- XPathEvaluationResult.XPathResultType type()

  returns one of the enumeration constants STRING, NODESET, NODE, NUMBER, BOOLEAN.
- T value()

  returns the result value.

3.6 Using Namespaces

The Java language uses packages to avoid name clashes. Programmers can use the same name for different classes as long as they aren't in the same package. XML has a similar *namespace* mechanism for element and attribute names.

A namespace is identified by a Uniform Resource Identifier (URI), such as

```
http://www.w3.org/2001/XMLSchema
uuid:1c759aed-b748-475c-ab68-10679700c4f2
urn:com:books-r-us
```

The HTTP URL form is the most common. Note that the URL is just used as an identifier string, not as a locator for a document. For example, the namespace identifiers

```
http://www.horstmann.com/corejava
http://www.horstmann.com/corejava/index.html
```

denote *different* namespaces, even though a web server would serve the same document for both URLs.

There need not be any document at a namespace URL—the XML parser doesn't attempt to find anything at that location. However, as a help to programmers who encounter a possibly unfamiliar namespace, it is customary to place a document explaining the purpose of the namespace at the URL location. For example, if you point your browser to the namespace URL for the XML Schema namespace (`http://www.w3.org/2001/XMLSchema`), you will find a document describing the XML Schema standard.

Why use HTTP URLs for namespace identifiers? It is easy to ensure that they are unique. If you choose a real URL, the host part's uniqueness is guaranteed by the domain name system. Your organization can then arrange for the uniqueness of the remainder of the URL. This is the same rationale that underlies the use of reversed domain names in Java package names.

Of course, although long namespace identifiers are good for uniqueness, you don't want to deal with long identifiers any more than you have to. In the Java programming language, you use the `import` mechanism to specify the long names of packages, and then use just the short class names. In XML, there is a similar mechanism:

```
<element xmlns="namespaceURI">
   children
</element>
```

The element and its children are now part of the given namespace.

A child can provide its own namespace, for example:

```
<element xmlns="namespaceURI1">
   <child xmlns="namespaceURI2">
      grandchildren
   </child>
   more children
</element>
```

Then the first child and the grandchildren are part of the second namespace.

This simple mechanism works well if you need only a single namespace or if the namespaces are naturally nested. Otherwise, you will want to use a second mechanism that has no analog in Java. You can have a *prefix* for a namespace—a short identifier that you choose for a particular document. Here is a typical example—the xsd prefix in an XML Schema file:

```
<xsd:schema xmlns:xsd="http://www.w3.org/2001/XMLSchema">
  <xsd:element name="config"/>
  . . .
</xsd:schema>
```

The attribute

```
xmlns:prefix="namespaceURI"
```

defines a namespace and a prefix. In our example, the prefix is the string xsd. Thus, xsd:schema really means schema in the namespace http://www.w3.org/2001/XMLSchema.

 NOTE: Only child elements inherit the namespace of their parent. Attributes without an explicit prefix are never part of a namespace. Consider this contrived example:

```
<configuration xmlns="http://www.horstmann.com/corejava"
    xmlns:si="http://www.bipm.fr/enus/3_SI/si.html">
    <size value="210" si:unit="mm"/>
    . . .
  </configuration>
```

In this example, the elements configuration and size are part of the namespace with URI http://www.horstmann.com/corejava. The attribute si:unit is part of the namespace with URI http://www.bipm.fr/enus/3_SI/si.html. However, the attribute value is not part of any namespace.

You can control how the parser deals with namespaces. By default, the DOM parser of the Java XML library is not namespace-aware.

To turn on namespace handling, call the setNamespaceAware method of the DocumentBuilderFactory:

```
factory.setNamespaceAware(true);
```

Now, all builders the factory produces support namespaces. Each node has three properties:

- The *qualified name*, with a prefix, returned by getNodeName, getTagName, and so on
- The namespace URI, returned by the getNamespaceURI method

- The *local name*, without a prefix or a namespace, returned by the getLocalName method

Here is an example. Suppose the parser sees the following element:

```
<xsd:schema xmlns:xsd="http://www.w3.org/2001/XMLSchema">
```

It then reports the following:

- Qualified name = xsd:schema
- Namespace URI = http://www.w3.org/2001/XMLSchema
- Local name = schema

 NOTE: If namespace awareness is turned off, getNamespaceURI and getLocalName return null.

---

org.w3c.dom.Node 1.4

- String getLocalName()

  returns the local name (without prefix), or null if the parser is not namespace-aware.

- String getNamespaceURI()

  returns the namespace URI, or null if the node is not part of a namespace or if the parser is not namespace-aware.

---

javax.xml.parsers.DocumentBuilderFactory 1.4

- boolean isNamespaceAware()
- void setNamespaceAware(boolean value)

  gets or sets the namespaceAware property of the factory. If set to true, the parsers that this factory generates are namespace-aware.

3.7 Streaming Parsers

The DOM parser reads an XML document in its entirety into a tree data structure. For most practical applications, DOM works fine. However, it can be inefficient if the document is large and if your processing algorithm is simple enough that you can analyze nodes on the fly, without having to see all of the tree structure. In these cases, you should use a streaming parser.

In the following sections, we discuss the streaming parsers supplied by the Java library: the venerable SAX parser and the more modern StAX parser that was added to Java 6. The SAX parser uses event callbacks, and the StAX parser provides an iterator through the parsing events. The latter is usually a bit more convenient.

3.7.1 Using the SAX Parser

The SAX parser reports events as it parses the components of the XML input, but it does not store the document in any way—it is up to the event handlers to build a data structure. In fact, the DOM parser is built on top of the SAX parser. It builds the DOM tree as it receives the parser events.

Whenever you use a SAX parser, you need a handler that defines the event actions for the various parse events. The ContentHandler interface defines several callback methods that the parser executes as it parses the document. Here are the most important ones:

- startElement and endElement are called each time a start tag or end tag is encountered.

- characters is called whenever character data are encountered.

- startDocument and endDocument are called once each, at the start and the end of the document.

For example, when parsing the fragment

```
<font>
    <name>Helvetica</name>
    <size units="pt">36</size>
</font>
```

the parser makes the following callbacks:

1. startElement, element name: font
2. startElement, element name: name
3. characters, content: Helvetica
4. endElement, element name: name
5. startElement, element name: size, attributes: units="pt"
6. characters, content: 36
7. endElement, element name: size
8. endElement, element name: font

Your handler needs to override these methods and have them carry out whatever action you want to carry out as you parse the file. The program at the end of this section prints all links <a href=". . ."> in an HTML file. It simply overrides the startElement method of the handler to check for links with name a and an attribute with name href. This is potentially useful for implementing a "web crawler"—a program that reaches more and more web pages by following links.

 NOTE: HTML doesn't have to be valid XML, and many web pages deviate so much from proper XML that the example programs will not be able to parse them. However, most pages authored by the W3C are written in XHTML (an HTML dialect that is proper XML). You can use those pages to test the example program. For example, if you run

```
java SAXTest http://www.w3c.org/MarkUp
```

you will see a list of the URLs of all links on that page.

The sample program is a good example for the use of SAX. We don't care at all in which context the a elements occur, and there is no need to store a tree structure.

Here is how you get a SAX parser:

```
SAXParserFactory factory = SAXParserFactory.newInstance();
SAXParser parser = factory.newSAXParser();
```

You can now process a document:

```
parser.parse(source, handler);
```

Here, source can be a file, URL string, or input stream. The handler belongs to a subclass of DefaultHandler. The DefaultHandler class defines do-nothing methods for the four interfaces:

```
ContentHandler
DTDHandler
EntityResolver
ErrorHandler
```

The example program defines a handler that overrides the startElement method of the ContentHandler interface to watch out for a elements with an href attribute:

```
var handler = new DefaultHandler()
    {
        public void startElement(String namespaceURI, String lname, String qname,
            Attributes attrs) throws SAXException
        {
            if (lname.equalsIgnoreCase("a") && attrs != null)
            {
```

```
        for (int i = 0; i < attrs.getLength(); i++)
        {
           String aname = attrs.getLocalName(i);
           if (aname.equalsIgnoreCase("href"))
              System.out.println(attrs.getValue(i));
        }
     }
  }
};
```

The startElement method has three parameters that describe the element name. The qname parameter reports the qualified name of the form prefix:localname. If namespace processing is turned on, then the namespaceURI and lname parameters provide the namespace and local (unqualified) name.

As with the DOM parser, namespace processing is turned off by default. To activate namespace processing, call the setNamespaceAware method of the factory class:

```
SAXParserFactory factory = SAXParserFactory.newInstance();
factory.setNamespaceAware(true);
SAXParser saxParser = factory.newSAXParser();
```

In this program, we cope with another common issue. An XHTML file starts with a tag that contains a DTD reference, and the parser will want to load it. Understandably, the W3C isn't too happy to serve billions of copies of files such as www.w3.org/TR/xhtml1/DTD/xhtml1-strict.dtd. At one point, they refused altogether, but at the time of this writing, they serve the DTD at a glacial pace. If you don't need to validate the document, just call

```
factory.setFeature("http://apache.org/xml/features/nonvalidating/load-external-dtd", false);
```

Listing 3.7 contains the code for the web crawler program. Later in this chapter, you will see another interesting use of SAX. An easy way of turning a non-XML data source into XML is to report the SAX events that an XML parser would report. See Section 3.9, "XSL Transformations," on p. 216 for details.

Listing 3.7 sax/SAXTest.java

```
1 package sax;
2
3 import java.io.*;
4 import java.net.*;
5 import javax.xml.parsers.*;
6 import org.xml.sax.*;
7 import org.xml.sax.helpers.*;
```

(Continues)

Listing 3.7 *(Continued)*

```
8
9  /**
10 * This program demonstrates how to use a SAX parser. The program prints all
11 * hyperlinks of an XHTML web page. <br>
12 * Usage: java sax.SAXTest URL
13 * @version 1.01 2018-05-01
14 * @author Cay Horstmann
15 */
16 public class SAXTest
17 {
18    public static void main(String[] args) throws Exception
19    {
20       String url;
21       if (args.length == 0)
22       {
23          url = "http://www.w3c.org";
24          System.out.println("Using " + url);
25       }
26       else url = args[0];
27
28       var handler = new DefaultHandler()
29          {
30             public void startElement(String namespaceURI, String lname,
31                   String qname, Attributes attrs)
32             {
33                if (lname.equals("a") && attrs != null)
34                {
35                   for (int i = 0; i < attrs.getLength(); i++)
36                   {
37                      String aname = attrs.getLocalName(i);
38                      if (aname.equals("href"))
39                         System.out.println(attrs.getValue(i));
40                   }
41                }
42             }
43          };
44
45       SAXParserFactory factory = SAXParserFactory.newInstance();
46       factory.setNamespaceAware(true);
47       factory.setFeature(
48          "http://apache.org/xml/features/nonvalidating/load-external-dtd",
49          false);
50       SAXParser saxParser = factory.newSAXParser();
51       InputStream in = new URL(url).openStream();
52       saxParser.parse(in, handler);
53    }
54 }
```

---

javax.xml.parsers.SAXParserFactory 1.4

- `static SAXParserFactory newInstance()`

  returns an instance of the SAXParserFactory class.

- `SAXParser newSAXParser()`

  returns an instance of the SAXParser class.

- `boolean isNamespaceAware()`
- `void setNamespaceAware(boolean value)`

  gets or sets the `namespaceAware` property of the factory. If set to `true`, the parsers that this factory generates are namespace-aware.

- `boolean isValidating()`
- `void setValidating(boolean value)`

  gets or sets the `validating` property of the factory. If set to `true`, the parsers that this factory generates validate their input.

---

javax.xml.parsers.SAXParser 1.4

- `void parse(File f, DefaultHandler handler)`
- `void parse(String url, DefaultHandler handler)`
- `void parse(InputStream in, DefaultHandler handler)`

  parses an XML document from the given file, URL, or input stream and reports parse events to the given handler.

---

org.xml.sax.*ContentHandler* 1.4

- `void startDocument()`
- `void endDocument()`

  is called at the start or the end of the document.

- `void startElement(String uri, String lname, String qname, Attributes attr)`
- `void endElement(String uri, String lname, String qname)`

  is called at the start or the end of an element. If the parser is namespace-aware, it reports the URI of the namespace, the local name without prefix, and the qualified name with prefix.

- `void characters(char[] data, int start, int length)`

  is called when the parser reports character data.

---

org.xml.sax.Attributes 1.4

- `int getLength()`

  returns the number of attributes stored in this attribute collection.

- `String getLocalName(int index)`

  returns the local name (without prefix) of the attribute with the given index, or the empty string if the parser is not namespace-aware.

- `String getURI(int index)`

  returns the namespace URI of the attribute with the given index, or the empty string if the node is not part of a namespace or if the parser is not namespace-aware.

- `String getQName(int index)`

  returns the qualified name (with prefix) of the attribute with the given index, or the empty string if the qualified name is not reported by the parser.

- `String getValue(int index)`
- `String getValue(String qname)`
- `String getValue(String uri, String lname)`

  returns the attribute value from a given index, qualified name, or namespace URI + local name. Returns `null` if the value doesn't exist.

3.7.2 Using the StAX Parser

The StAX parser is a "pull parser." Instead of installing an event handler, you simply iterate through the events, using this basic loop:

```
InputStream in = url.openStream();
XMLInputFactory factory = XMLInputFactory.newInstance();
XMLStreamReader parser = factory.createXMLStreamReader(in);
while (parser.hasNext())
{
   int event = parser.next();
   Call parser methods to obtain event details
}
```

For example, when parsing the fragment

```
<font>
   <name>Helvetica</name>
   <size units="pt">36</size>
</font>
```

the parser yields the following events:

1. START_ELEMENT, element name: font
2. CHARACTERS, content: white space
3. START_ELEMENT, element name: name
4. CHARACTERS, content: Helvetica
5. END_ELEMENT, element name: name
6. CHARACTERS, content: white space
7. START_ELEMENT, element name: size
8. CHARACTERS, content: 36
9. END_ELEMENT, element name: size
10. CHARACTERS, content: white space
11. END_ELEMENT, element name: font

To analyze the attribute values, call the appropriate methods of the XMLStreamReader class. For example,

```
String units = parser.getAttributeValue(null, "units");
```

gets the units attribute of the current element.

By default, namespace processing is enabled. You can deactivate it by modifying the factory:

```
XMLInputFactory factory = XMLInputFactory.newInstance();
factory.setProperty(XMLInputFactory.IS_NAMESPACE_AWARE, false);
```

Listing 3.8 contains the code for the web crawler program implemented with the StAX parser. As you can see, the code is simpler than the equivalent SAX code because you don't have to worry about event handling.

Listing 3.8 stax/StAXTest.java

```
1  package stax;
2
3  import java.io.*;
4  import java.net.*;
5  import javax.xml.stream.*;
6
7  /**
8   * This program demonstrates how to use a StAX parser. The program prints all
9   * hyperlinks links of an XHTML web page. <br>
10  * Usage: java stax.StAXTest URL
11  * @author Cay Horstmann
12  * @version 1.1 2018-05-01
13  */
```

(Continues)

Listing 3.8 *(Continued)*

```
14  public class StAXTest
15  {
16     public static void main(String[] args) throws Exception
17     {
18        String urlString;
19        if (args.length == 0)
20        {
21           urlString = "http://www.w3c.org";
22           System.out.println("Using " + urlString);
23        }
24        else urlString = args[0];
25        var url = new URL(urlString);
26        InputStream in = url.openStream();
27        XMLInputFactory factory = XMLInputFactory.newInstance();
28        XMLStreamReader parser = factory.createXMLStreamReader(in);
29        while (parser.hasNext())
30        {
31           int event = parser.next();
32           if (event == XMLStreamConstants.START_ELEMENT)
33           {
34              if (parser.getLocalName().equals("a"))
35              {
36                 String href = parser.getAttributeValue(null, "href");
37                 if (href != null)
38                    System.out.println(href);
39              }
40           }
41        }
42     }
43  }
```

---

javax.xml.stream.XMLInputFactory 6

- static XMLInputFactory newInstance()

  returns an instance of the XMLInputFactory class.

- void setProperty(String name, Object value)

  sets a property for this factory, or throws an IllegalArgumentException if the property is not supported or cannot be set to the given value. The JDK implementation supports the following Boolean-valued properties:

(Continues)

---

javax.xml.stream.XMLInputFactory 6   *(Continued)*

`"javax.xml.stream.isValidating"`	When false (the default), the document is not validated. Not required by the specification.
`"javax.xml.stream.isNamespaceAware"`	When true (the default), namespaces are processed. Not required by the specification.
`"javax.xml.stream.isCoalescing"`	When false (the default), adjacent character data are not coalesced.
`"javax.xml.stream.isReplacingEntityReferences"`	When true (the default), entity references are replaced and reported as character data.
`"javax.xml.stream.isSupportingExternalEntities"`	When true (the default), external entities are resolved. The specification gives no default for this property.
`"javax.xml.stream.supportDTD"`	When true (the default), DTDs are reported as events.

- `XMLStreamReader createXMLStreamReader(InputStream in)`
- `XMLStreamReader createXMLStreamReader(InputStream in, String characterEncoding)`
- `XMLStreamReader createXMLStreamReader(Reader in)`
- `XMLStreamReader createXMLStreamReader(Source in)`

creates a parser that reads from the given stream, reader, or JAXP source.

---

javax.xml.stream.XMLStreamReader 6

- `boolean hasNext()`

returns true if there is another parse event.

- `int next()`

sets the parser state to the next parse event and returns one of the following constants: START_ELEMENT, END_ELEMENT, CHARACTERS, START_DOCUMENT, END_DOCUMENT, CDATA, COMMENT, SPACE (ignorable whitespace), PROCESSING_INSTRUCTION, ENTITY_REFERENCE, DTD.

- `boolean isStartElement()`
- `boolean isEndElement()`
- `boolean isCharacters()`
- `boolean isWhiteSpace()`

returns true if the current event is a start element, end element, character data, or whitespace.

(Continues)

---

javax.xml.stream.XMLStreamReader 6   *(Continued)*

- QName getName()
- String getLocalName()

  gets the name of the element in a START_ELEMENT or END_ELEMENT event.

- String getText()

  returns the characters of a CHARACTERS, COMMENT, or CDATA event, the replacement value for an ENTITY_REFERENCE, or the internal subset of a DTD.

- int getAttributeCount()
- QName getAttributeName(int index)
- String getAttributeLocalName(int index)
- String getAttributeValue(int index)

  gets the attribute count and the names and values of the attributes, provided the current event is START_ELEMENT.

- String getAttributeValue(String namespaceURI, String name)

  gets the value of the attribute with the given name, provided the current event is START_ELEMENT. If namespaceURI is null, the namespace is not checked.

3.8 Generating XML Documents

You now know how to write Java programs that read XML. Let us now turn to the opposite process: producing XML output. Of course, you could write an XML file simply by making a sequence of print calls, printing the elements, attributes, and text content, but that would not be a good idea. The code is rather tedious, and you can easily make mistakes if you don't pay attention to special symbols (such as " or <) in the attribute values and text content.

A better approach is to build up a DOM tree with the contents of the document and then write out the tree contents. The following sections discuss the details.

3.8.1 Documents without Namespaces

To build a DOM tree, you start out with an empty document. You can get an empty document by calling the newDocument method of the DocumentBuilder class:

```
Document doc = builder.newDocument();
```

Use the createElement method of the Document class to construct the elements of your document:

```
Element rootElement = doc.createElement(rootName);
Element childElement = doc.createElement(childName);
```

Use the `createTextNode` method to construct text nodes:

```
Text textNode = doc.createTextNode(textContents);
```

Add the root element to the document, and add the child nodes to their parents:

```
doc.appendChild(rootElement);
rootElement.appendChild(childElement);
childElement.appendChild(textNode);
```

As you build up the DOM tree, you may also need to set element attributes. Simply call the `setAttribute` method of the `Element` class:

```
rootElement.setAttribute(name, value);
```

3.8.2 Documents with Namespaces

If you use namespaces, the procedure for creating a document is slightly different.

First, set the builder factory to be namespace-aware, then create the builder:

```
DocumentBuilderFactory factory = DocumentBuilderFactory.newInstance();
factory.setNamespaceAware(true);
builder = factory.newDocumentBuilder();
```

Then use `createElementNS` instead of `createElement` to create any nodes:

```
String namespace = "http://www.w3.org/2000/svg";
Element rootElement = doc.createElementNS(namespace, "svg");
```

If your node has a qualified name with a namespace prefix, then any necessary `xmlns`-prefixed attributes are created automatically. For example, if you need SVG inside XHTML, you can construct an element like this:

```
Element svgElement = doc.createElement(namespace, "svg:svg")
```

When the element is written, it turns into

```
<svg:svg xmlns:svg="http://www.w3.org/2000/svg">
```

If you need to set element attributes whose names are in a namespace, use the `setAttributeNS` method of the `Element` class:

```
rootElement.setAttributeNS(namespace, qualifiedName, value);
```

3.8.3 Writing Documents

Somewhat curiously, it is not so easy to write a DOM tree to an output stream. The easiest approach is to use the Extensible Stylesheet Language Transformations (XSLT) API. For more information about XSLT, turn to Section 3.9, "XSL Transformations," on p. 216. Right now, consider the code that follows a magic incantation to produce XML output.

We apply the do-nothing transformation to the document and capture its output. To include a DOCTYPE node in the output, we also need to set the SYSTEM and PUBLIC identifiers as output properties.

```
// construct the do-nothing transformation
Transformer t = TransformerFactory.newInstance().newTransformer();
// set output properties to get a DOCTYPE node
t.setOutputProperty(OutputKeys.DOCTYPE_SYSTEM, systemIdentifier);
t.setOutputProperty(OutputKeys.DOCTYPE_PUBLIC, publicIdentifier);
// set indentation
t.setOutputProperty(OutputKeys.INDENT, "yes");
t.setOutputProperty(OutputKeys.METHOD, "xml");
t.setOutputProperty("{http://xml.apache.org/xslt}indent-amount", "2");
// apply the do-nothing transformation and send the output to a file
t.transform(new DOMSource(doc), new StreamResult(new FileOutputStream(file)));
```

Another approach is to use the LSSerializer interface. To get an instance, you have to use the following magic incantation:

```
DOMImplementation impl = doc.getImplementation();
var implLS = (DOMImplementationLS) impl.getFeature("LS", "3.0");
LSSerializer ser = implLS.createLSSerializer();
```

If you want spaces and line breaks, set this flag:

```
ser.getDomConfig().setParameter("format-pretty-print", true);
```

Then it's simple enough to convert a document to a string:

```
String str = ser.writeToString(doc);
```

If you want to write the output directly to a file, you need an LSOutput:

```
LSOutput out = implLS.createLSOutput();
out.setEncoding("UTF-8");
out.setByteStream(Files.newOutputStream(path));
ser.write(doc, out);
```

---

javax.xml.parsers.DocumentBuilder 1.4

• Document newDocument()

   returns an empty document.

---

org.w3c.dom.Document 1.4

- Element createElement(String name)
- Element createElementNS(String uri, String qname)

  creates an element with the given name.

- Text createTextNode(String data)

  creates a text node with the given data.

---

org.w3c.dom.Node 1.4

- Node appendChild(Node child)

  appends a node to the list of children of this node. Returns the appended node.

---

org.w3c.dom.Element 1.4

- void setAttribute(String name, String value)
- void setAttributeNS(String uri, String qname, String value)

  sets the attribute with the given name to the given value. If the qualified name has an alias prefix, then uri must not be null.

---

javax.xml.transform.TransformerFactory 1.4

- static TransformerFactory newInstance()

  returns an instance of the TransformerFactory class.

- Transformer newTransformer()

  returns an instance of the Transformer class that carries out an identity (do-nothing) transformation.

---

javax.xml.transform.Transformer 1.4

- void setOutputProperty(String name, String value)

  sets an output property. See www.w3.org/TR/xslt#output for a listing of the standard output properties. The most useful ones are shown here:

doctype-public	The public ID to be used in the DOCTYPE declaration
doctype-system	The system ID to be used in the DOCTYPE declaration
indent	"yes" or "no"
method	"xml", "html", "text", or a custom string

- void transform(Source from, Result to)

  transforms an XML document.

---

javax.xml.transform.dom.DOMSource 1.4

* DOMSource(Node n)

    constructs a source from the given node. Usually, n is a document node.

---

javax.xml.transform.stream.StreamResult 1.4

* StreamResult(File f)
* StreamResult(OutputStream out)
* StreamResult(Writer out)
* StreamResult(String systemID)

    constructs a stream result from a file, stream, writer, or system ID (usually a relative or absolute URL).

3.8.4 Writing an XML Document with StAX

In the preceding section, you saw how to produce an XML document by writing a DOM tree. If you have no other use for the DOM tree, that approach is not very efficient.

The StAX API lets you write an XML tree directly. Construct an XMLStreamWriter from an OutputStream:

```
XMLOutputFactory factory = XMLOutputFactory.newInstance();
XMLStreamWriter writer = factory.createXMLStreamWriter(out);
```

To produce the XML header, call

```
writer.writeStartDocument()
```

Then call

```
writer.writeStartElement(name);
```

Add attributes by calling

```
writer.writeAttribute(name, value);
```

Now you can add child elements by calling writeStartElement again, or write characters with

```
writer.writeCharacters(text);
```

When you have written all child nodes, call

```
writer.writeEndElement();
```

This causes the current element to be closed.

To write an element without children (such as <img . . ./>), use the call

```
writer.writeEmptyElement(name);
```

Finally, at the end of the document, call

```
writer.writeEndDocument();
```

This call closes any open elements.

You still need to close the XMLStreamWriter, and you need to do it manually since the XMLStreamWriter interface does not extend the AutoCloseable interface.

As with the DOM/XSLT approach, you don't have to worry about escaping characters in attribute values and character data. However, it is possible to produce malformed XML, such as a document with multiple root nodes. Also, the current version of StAX has no support for producing indented output.

The program in Listing 3.9 shows you both approaches for writing XML.

Listing 3.9 write/XMLWriteTest.java

```
 1  package write;
 2
 3  import java.io.*;
 4  import java.nio.file.*;
 5  import java.util.*;
 6
 7  import javax.xml.parsers.*;
 8  import javax.xml.stream.*;
 9  import javax.xml.transform.*;
10  import javax.xml.transform.dom.*;
11  import javax.xml.transform.stream.*;
12
13  import org.w3c.dom.*;
14
15  /**
16   * This program shows how to write an XML file. It produces modern art in SVG
17   * format.
18   * @version 1.12 2016-04-27
19   * @author Cay Horstmann
20   */
21  public class XMLWriteTest
22  {
23     public static void main(String[] args) throws Exception
24     {
25        Document doc = newDrawing(600, 400);
26        writeDocument(doc, "drawing1.svg");
27        writeNewDrawing(600, 400, "drawing2.svg");
28     }
```

(Continues)

Listing 3.9   *(Continued)*

```
29
30    private static Random generator = new Random();
31
32    /**
33     * Creates a new random drawing.
34     * @return the DOM tree of the SVG document
35     */
36    public static Document newDrawing(int drawingWidth, int drawingHeight)
37          throws ParserConfigurationException
38    {
39       DocumentBuilderFactory factory = DocumentBuilderFactory.newInstance();
40       factory.setNamespaceAware(true);
41       DocumentBuilder builder = factory.newDocumentBuilder();;
42       var namespace = "http://www.w3.org/2000/svg";
43       Document doc = builder.newDocument();
44       Element svgElement = doc.createElementNS(namespace, "svg");
45       doc.appendChild(svgElement);
46       svgElement.setAttribute("width", "" + drawingWidth);
47       svgElement.setAttribute("height", "" + drawingHeight);
48       int n = 10 + generator.nextInt(20);
49       for (int i = 1; i <= n; i++)
50       {
51          int x = generator.nextInt(drawingWidth);
52          int y = generator.nextInt(drawingHeight);
53          int width = generator.nextInt(drawingWidth - x);
54          int height = generator.nextInt(drawingHeight - y);
55          int r = generator.nextInt(256);
56          int g = generator.nextInt(256);
57          int b = generator.nextInt(256);
58
59          Element rectElement = doc.createElementNS(namespace, "rect");
60          rectElement.setAttribute("x", "" + x);
61          rectElement.setAttribute("y", "" + y);
62          rectElement.setAttribute("width", "" + width);
63          rectElement.setAttribute("height", "" + height);
64          rectElement.setAttribute("fill",
65                String.format("#%02x%02x%02x", r, g, b));
66          svgElement.appendChild(rectElement);
67       }
68       return doc;
69    }
70
71    /**
72     * Saves a document using DOM/XSLT
73     */
74    public static void writeDocument(Document doc, String filename)
75          throws TransformerException, IOException
76    {
```

```
77      Transformer t = TransformerFactory.newInstance().newTransformer();
78      t.setOutputProperty(OutputKeys.DOCTYPE_SYSTEM,
79          "http://www.w3.org/TR/2000/CR-SVG-20000802/DTD/svg-20000802.dtd");
80      t.setOutputProperty(OutputKeys.DOCTYPE_PUBLIC,
81          "-//W3C//DTD SVG 20000802//EN");
82      t.setOutputProperty(OutputKeys.INDENT, "yes");
83      t.setOutputProperty(OutputKeys.METHOD, "xml");
84      t.setOutputProperty("{http://xml.apache.org/xslt}indent-amount", "2");
85      t.transform(new DOMSource(doc), new StreamResult(
86          Files.newOutputStream(Paths.get(filename))));
87   }
88
89   /**
90    * Writes an SVG document of the current drawing.
91    * @param writer the document destination
92    * @throws IOException
93    */
94   public static void writeNewDrawing(int drawingWidth, int drawingHeight,
95          String filename) throws XMLStreamException, IOException
96   {
97      XMLOutputFactory factory = XMLOutputFactory.newInstance();
98      XMLStreamWriter writer = factory.createXMLStreamWriter(
99          Files.newOutputStream(Paths.get(filename)));
100     writer.writeStartDocument();
101     writer.writeDTD("<!DOCTYPE svg PUBLIC \"-//W3C//DTD SVG 20000802//EN\" "
102         + "\"http://www.w3.org/TR/2000/CR-SVG-20000802/DTD/svg-20000802.dtd\">");
103     writer.writeStartElement("svg");
104     writer.writeDefaultNamespace("http://www.w3.org/2000/svg");
105     writer.writeAttribute("width", "" + drawingWidth);
106     writer.writeAttribute("height", "" + drawingHeight);
107     int n = 10 + generator.nextInt(20);
108     for (int i = 1; i <= n; i++)
109     {
110        int x = generator.nextInt(drawingWidth);
111        int y = generator.nextInt(drawingHeight);
112        int width = generator.nextInt(drawingWidth - x);
113        int height = generator.nextInt(drawingHeight - y);
114        int r = generator.nextInt(256);
115        int g = generator.nextInt(256);
116        int b = generator.nextInt(256);
117        writer.writeEmptyElement("rect");
118        writer.writeAttribute("x", "" + x);
119        writer.writeAttribute("y", "" + y);
120        writer.writeAttribute("width", "" + width);
121        writer.writeAttribute("height", "" + height);
122        writer.writeAttribute("fill", String.format("#%02x%02x%02x", r, g, b));
123     }
124     writer.writeEndDocument(); // closes svg element
125  }
126 }
```

---

javax.xml.stream.XMLOutputFactory 6

- `static XMLOutputFactory newInstance()`

  returns an instance of the XMLOutputFactory class.

- `XMLStreamWriter createXMLStreamWriter(OutputStream in)`
- `XMLStreamWriter createXMLStreamWriter(OutputStream in, String characterEncoding)`
- `XMLStreamWriter createXMLStreamWriter(Writer in)`
- `XMLStreamWriter createXMLStreamWriter(Result in)`

  creates a writer that writes to the given stream, writer, or JAXP result.

---

javax.xml.stream.XMLStreamWriter 6

- `void writeStartDocument()`
- `void writeStartDocument(String xmlVersion)`
- `void writeStartDocument(String encoding, String xmlVersion)`

  writes the XML processing instruction at the top of the document. Note that the encoding parameter is only used to write the attribute. It does not set the character encoding of the output.

- `void setDefaultNamespace(String namespaceURI)`
- `void setPrefix(String prefix, String namespaceURI)`

  sets the default namespace or the namespace associated with a prefix. The declaration is scoped to the current element or, if no element has been written, to the document root.

- `void writeStartElement(String localName)`
- `void writeStartElement(String namespaceURI, String localName)`

  writes a start tag, replacing the namespaceURI with the associated prefix.

- `void writeEndElement()`

  closes the current element.

- `void writeEndDocument()`

  closes all open elements.

- `void writeEmptyElement(String localName)`
- `void writeEmptyElement(String namespaceURI, String localName)`

  writes a self-closing tag, replacing the namespaceURI with the associated prefix.

- `void writeAttribute(String localName, String value)`
- `void writeAttribute(String namespaceURI, String localName, String value)`

  writes an attribute for the current element, replacing the namespaceURI with the associated prefix.

(Continues)

---

javax.xml.stream.XMLStreamWriter 6 *(Continued)*

- void writeCharacters(String text)

  writes character data.

- void writeCData(String text)

  writes a CDATA block.

- void writeDTD(String dtd)

  writes the dtd string, which is assumed to contain a DOCTYPE declaration.

- void writeComment(String comment)

  writes a comment.

- void close()

  closes this writer.

3.8.5 An Example: Generating an SVG File

Listing 3.9 is a typical program that produces XML output. The program draws a modernist painting—a random set of colored rectangles (see Figure 3.3). To save our masterpiece, we use the Scalable Vector Graphics (SVG) format. SVG is an XML format to describe complex graphics in a device-independent fashion. You can find more information about SVG at www.w3.org/Graphics/SVG. To view SVG files, simply use any modern browser.

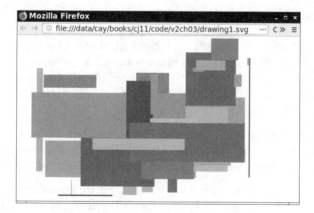

Figure 3.3 Generating modern art

The program demonstrates two ways of producing XML: by constructing and saving a DOM tree, and by directly writing the XML with the StAX API.

We don't need to go into details about SVG; for our purposes, we just need to know how to express a set of colored rectangles. Here is a sample:

```
<?xml version="1.0" encoding="UTF-8"?>
<!DOCTYPE svg PUBLIC "-//W3C//DTD SVG 20000802//EN"
   "http://www.w3.org/TR/2000/CR-SVG-20000802/DTD/svg-20000802.dtd">
<svg xmlns="http://www.w3.org/2000/svg" width="300" height="150">
   <rect x="231" y="61" width="9" height="12" fill="#6e4a13"/>
   <rect x="107" y="106" width="56" height="5" fill="#c406be"/>
   . . .
</svg>
```

As you can see, each rectangle is described as a rect node. The position, width, height, and fill color are attributes. The fill color is an RGB value in hexadecimal.

 NOTE: SVG uses attributes heavily. In fact, some attributes are quite complex. For example, here is a path element:

```
<path d="M 100 100 L 300 100 L 200 300 z">
```

The M denotes a "moveto" command, L is "lineto," and z is "closepath" (!). Apparently, the designers of this data format didn't have much confidence in using XML for structured data. In your own XML formats, you might want to use elements instead of complex attributes.

3.9 XSL Transformations

The XSL Transformations (XSLT) mechanism allows you to specify rules for transforming XML documents into other formats, such as plain text, XHTML, or any other XML format. XSLT is commonly used to translate from one machine-readable XML format to another, or to translate XML into a presentation format for human consumption.

You need to provide an XSLT stylesheet that describes the conversion of XML documents into some other format. An XSLT processor reads an XML document and the stylesheet and produces the desired output (see Figure 3.4).

The XSLT specification is quite complex, and entire books have been written on the subject. We can't possibly discuss all the features of XSLT, so we will just work through a representative example. You can find more information in the book *Essential XML* by Don Box et al. The XSLT specification is available at www.w3.org/TR/xslt.

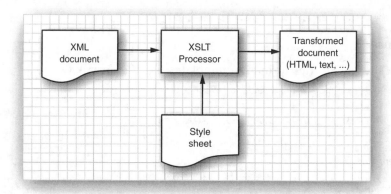

Figure 3.4 Applying XSL transformations

Suppose we want to transform XML files with employee records into HTML documents. Consider this input file:

```
<staff>
  <employee>
    <name>Carl Cracker</name>
    <salary>75000</salary>
    <hiredate year="1987" month="12" day="15"/>
  </employee>
  <employee>
    <name>Harry Hacker</name>
    <salary>50000</salary>
    <hiredate year="1989" month="10" day="1"/>
  </employee>
  <employee>
    <name>Tony Tester</name>
    <salary>40000</salary>
    <hiredate year="1990" month="3" day="15"/>
  </employee>
</staff>
```

The desired output is an HTML table:

```
<table border="1">
<tr>
<td>Carl Cracker</td><td>$75000.0</td><td>1987-12-15</td>
</tr>
<tr>
<td>Harry Hacker</td><td>$50000.0</td><td>1989-10-1</td>
</tr>
```

```
<tr>
<td>Tony Tester</td><td>$40000.0</td><td>1990-3-15</td>
</tr>
</table>
```

A stylesheet with transformation templates has this form:

```
<?xml version="1.0" encoding="ISO-8859-1"?>
<xsl:stylesheet
      xmlns:xsl="http://www.w3.org/1999/XSL/Transform"
      version="1.0">
   <xsl:output method="html"/>
   template₁

   template₂
   . . .
</xsl:stylesheet>
```

In our example, the xsl:output element specifies the method as HTML. Other valid method settings are xml and text.

Here is a typical template:

```
<xsl:template match="/staff/employee">
   <tr><xsl:apply-templates/></tr>
</xsl:template>
```

The value of the match attribute is an XPath expression. The template states: Whenever you see a node in the XPath set /staff/employee, do the following:

1. Emit the string <tr>.
2. Keep applying templates as you process its children.
3. Emit the string </tr> after you are done with all children.

In other words, this template generates the HTML table row markers around every employee record.

The XSLT processor starts processing by examining the root element. Whenever a node matches one of the templates, it applies the template. (If multiple templates match, the best matching one is used; see the specification at www.w3.org/TR/xslt for the gory details.) If no template matches, the processor carries out a default action. For text nodes, the default is to include the contents in the output. For elements, the default action is to create no output but to keep processing the children.

Here is a template for transforming name nodes in an employee file:

```
<xsl:template match="/staff/employee/name">
   <td><xsl:apply-templates/></td>
</xsl:template>
```

As you can see, the template produces the <td>. . .</td> delimiters, and it asks the processor to recursively visit the children of the name element. There is just one child—the text node. When the processor visits that node, it emits the text contents (provided, of course, that there is no other matching template).

You have to work a little harder if you want to copy attribute values into the output. Here is an example:

```
<xsl:template match="/staff/employee/hiredate">
   <td><xsl:value-of select="@year"/>-<xsl:value-of
   select="@month"/>-<xsl:value-of select="@day"/></td>
</xsl:template>
```

When processing a hiredate node, this template emits

1. The string <td>
2. The value of the year attribute
3. A hyphen
4. The value of the month attribute
5. A hyphen
6. The value of the day attribute
7. The string </td>

The xsl:value-of statement computes the string value of a node set. The node set is specified by the XPath value of the select attribute. In this case, the path is relative to the currently processed node. The node set is converted to a string by concatenation of the string values of all nodes. The string value of an attribute node is its value. The string value of a text node is its contents. The string value of an element node is the concatenation of the string values of its child nodes (but not its attributes).

Listing 3.10 contains the stylesheet for turning an XML file with employee records into an HTML table.

Listing 3.11 shows a different set of transformations. The input is the same XML file, and the output is plain text in the familiar property file format:

```
employee.1.name=Carl Cracker
employee.1.salary=75000.0
employee.1.hiredate=1987-12-15
employee.2.name=Harry Hacker
employee.2.salary=50000.0
employee.2.hiredate=1989-10-1
employee.3.name=Tony Tester
employee.3.salary=40000.0
employee.3.hiredate=1990-3-15
```

That example uses the position() function which yields the position of the current node as seen from its parent. We thus get an entirely different output simply by switching the stylesheet. This means you can safely use XML to describe your data; if some applications need the data in another format, just use XSLT to generate the alternative format.

It is simple to generate XSL transformations on the Java platform. Set up a transformer factory for each stylesheet. Then, get a transformer object and tell it to transform a source to a result:

```
var styleSheet = new File(filename);
var styleSource = new StreamSource(styleSheet);
Transformer t = TransformerFactory.newInstance().newTransformer(styleSource);
t.transform(source, result);
```

The parameters of the transform method are objects of classes that implement the Source and Result interfaces. Several classes implement the Source interface:

```
DOMSource
SAXSource
StAXSource
StreamSource
```

You can construct a StreamSource from a file, stream, reader, or URL, and a DOMSource from the node of a DOM tree. For example, in the preceding section, we invoked the identity transformation as

```
t.transform(new DOMSource(doc), result);
```

In our example program, we do something slightly more interesting. Instead of starting out with an existing XML file, we produce a SAX XML reader that gives the illusion of parsing an XML file by emitting appropriate SAX events. Actually, our XML reader reads a flat file, as described in Chapter 1. The input file looks like this:

```
Carl Cracker|75000.0|1987|12|15
Harry Hacker|50000.0|1989|10|1
Tony Tester|40000.0|1990|3|15
```

Our XML reader generates SAX events as it processes the input. Here is a part of the parse method of the EmployeeReader class that implements the XMLReader interface:

```
var attributes = new AttributesImpl();
handler.startDocument();
handler.startElement("", "staff", "staff", attributes);
while ((line = in.readLine()) != null)
{
    handler.startElement("", "employee", "employee", attributes);
    var tokenizer = new StringTokenizer(line, "|");
```

```
    handler.startElement("", "name", "name", attributes);
    String s = tokenizer.nextToken();
    handler.characters(s.toCharArray(), 0, s.length());
    handler.endElement("", "name", "name");
    . . .
    handler.endElement("", "employee", "employee");
  }
  handler.endElement("", rootElement, rootElement);
  handler.endDocument();
```

The SAXSource for the transformer is constructed from the XML reader:

```
t.transform(new SAXSource(new EmployeeReader(),
    new InputSource(new FileInputStream(filename))), result);
```

This is an ingenious trick to convert non-XML legacy data into XML. Of course, most XSLT applications will already have XML input data, and you can simply invoke the transform method on a StreamSource:

```
t.transform(new StreamSource(file), result);
```

The transformation result is an object of a class that implements the Result interface. The Java library supplies three classes:

```
DOMResult
SAXResult
StreamResult
```

To store the result in a DOM tree, use a DocumentBuilder to generate a new document node and wrap it into a DOMResult:

```
Document doc = builder.newDocument();
t.transform(source, new DOMResult(doc));
```

To save the output in a file, use a StreamResult:

```
t.transform(source, new StreamResult(file));
```

Listing 3.12 contains the complete source code.

Listing 3.10 transform/makehtml.xsl

```
1  <?xml version="1.0" encoding="ISO-8859-1"?>
2
3  <xsl:stylesheet
4     xmlns:xsl="http://www.w3.org/1999/XSL/Transform"
5     version="1.0">
6
7     <xsl:output method="html"/>
8
```

(Continues)

Listing 3.10 *(Continued)*

```
9    <xsl:template match="/staff">
10       <table border="1"><xsl:apply-templates/></table>
11    </xsl:template>
12
13    <xsl:template match="/staff/employee">
14       <tr><xsl:apply-templates/></tr>
15    </xsl:template>
16
17    <xsl:template match="/staff/employee/name">
18       <td><xsl:apply-templates/></td>
19    </xsl:template>
20
21    <xsl:template match="/staff/employee/salary">
22       <td>$<xsl:apply-templates/></td>
23    </xsl:template>
24
25    <xsl:template match="/staff/employee/hiredate">
26       <td><xsl:value-of select="@year"/>-<xsl:value-of
27       select="@month"/>-<xsl:value-of select="@day"/></td>
28    </xsl:template>
29
30 </xsl:stylesheet>
```

Listing 3.11 `transform/makeprop.xsl`

```
1  <?xml version="1.0"?>
2
3  <xsl:stylesheet
4     xmlns:xsl="http://www.w3.org/1999/XSL/Transform"
5     version="1.0">
6
7     <xsl:output method="text" omit-xml-declaration="yes"/>
8
9     <xsl:template match="/staff/employee">
10 employee.<xsl:value-of select="position()"
11 />.name=<xsl:value-of select="name/text()"/>
12 employee.<xsl:value-of select="position()"
13 />.salary=<xsl:value-of select="salary/text()"/>
14 employee.<xsl:value-of select="position()"
15 />.hiredate=<xsl:value-of select="hiredate/@year"
16 />-<xsl:value-of select="hiredate/@month"
17 />-<xsl:value-of select="hiredate/@day"/>
18    </xsl:template>
19
20 </xsl:stylesheet>
```

Listing 3.12 transform/TransformTest.java

```java
1  package transform;
2
3  import java.io.*;
4  import java.nio.file.*;
5  import java.util.*;
6  import javax.xml.transform.*;
7  import javax.xml.transform.sax.*;
8  import javax.xml.transform.stream.*;
9  import org.xml.sax.*;
10 import org.xml.sax.helpers.*;
11
12 /**
13  * This program demonstrates XSL transformations. It applies a transformation to a set of
14  * employee records. The records are stored in the file employee.dat and turned into XML
15  * format. Specify the stylesheet on the command line, e.g.<br>
16  *    java transform.TransformTest transform/makeprop.xsl
17  * @version 1.04 2018-04-10
18  * @author Cay Horstmann
19  */
20 public class TransformTest
21 {
22    public static void main(String[] args) throws Exception
23    {
24       Path path;
25       if (args.length > 0) path = Paths.get(args[0]);
26       else path = Paths.get("transform", "makehtml.xsl");
27       try (InputStream styleIn = Files.newInputStream(path))
28       {
29          var styleSource = new StreamSource(styleIn);
30
31          Transformer t = TransformerFactory.newInstance().newTransformer(styleSource);
32          t.setOutputProperty(OutputKeys.INDENT, "yes");
33          t.setOutputProperty(OutputKeys.METHOD, "xml");
34          t.setOutputProperty("{http://xml.apache.org/xslt}indent-amount", "2");
35
36          try (InputStream docIn = Files.newInputStream(Paths.get("transform", "employee.dat")))
37          {
38             t.transform(new SAXSource(new EmployeeReader(), new InputSource(docIn)),
39                new StreamResult(System.out));
40          }
41       }
42    }
43 }
44
45 /**
46  * This class reads the flat file employee.dat and reports SAX parser events to act as if it
47  * was parsing an XML file.
```

(Continues)

Listing 3.12 *(Continued)*

```
48   */
49   class EmployeeReader implements XMLReader
50   {
51      private ContentHandler handler;
52
53      public void parse(InputSource source) throws IOException, SAXException
54      {
55         InputStream stream = source.getByteStream();
56         var in = new BufferedReader(new InputStreamReader(stream));
57         String rootElement = "staff";
58         var atts = new AttributesImpl();
59
60         if (handler == null) throw new SAXException("No content handler");
61
62         handler.startDocument();
63         handler.startElement("", rootElement, rootElement, atts);
64         String line;
65         while ((line = in.readLine()) != null)
66         {
67            handler.startElement("", "employee", "employee", atts);
68            var t = new StringTokenizer(line, "|");
69
70            handler.startElement("", "name", "name", atts);
71            String s = t.nextToken();
72            handler.characters(s.toCharArray(), 0, s.length());
73            handler.endElement("", "name", "name");
74
75            handler.startElement("", "salary", "salary", atts);
76            s = t.nextToken();
77            handler.characters(s.toCharArray(), 0, s.length());
78            handler.endElement("", "salary", "salary");
79
80            atts.addAttribute("", "year", "year", "CDATA", t.nextToken());
81            atts.addAttribute("", "month", "month", "CDATA", t.nextToken());
82            atts.addAttribute("", "day", "day", "CDATA", t.nextToken());
83            handler.startElement("", "hiredate", "hiredate", atts);
84            handler.endElement("", "hiredate", "hiredate");
85            atts.clear();
86
87            handler.endElement("", "employee", "employee");
88         }
89
90         handler.endElement("", rootElement, rootElement);
91         handler.endDocument();
92      }
93
```

```
94    public void setContentHandler(ContentHandler newValue)
95    {
96       handler = newValue;
97    }
98
99    public ContentHandler getContentHandler()
100   {
101      return handler;
102   }
103
104   // the following methods are just do-nothing implementations
105   public void parse(String systemId) throws IOException, SAXException {}
106   public void setErrorHandler(ErrorHandler handler) {}
107   public ErrorHandler getErrorHandler() { return null; }
108   public void setDTDHandler(DTDHandler handler) {}
109   public DTDHandler getDTDHandler() { return null; }
110   public void setEntityResolver(EntityResolver resolver) {}
111   public EntityResolver getEntityResolver() { return null; }
112   public void setProperty(String name, Object value) {}
113   public Object getProperty(String name) { return null; }
114   public void setFeature(String name, boolean value) {}
115   public boolean getFeature(String name) { return false; }
116 }
```

---

javax.xml.transform.TransformerFactory 1.4

- Transformer newTransformer(Source styleSheet)

  returns an instance of the Transformer class that reads a stylesheet from the given source.

---

javax.xml.transform.stream.StreamSource 1.4

- StreamSource(File f)
- StreamSource(InputStream in)
- StreamSource(Reader in)
- StreamSource(String systemID)

  constructs a stream source from a file, stream, reader, or system ID (usually a relative or absolute URL).

---

javax.xml.transform.sax.SAXSource 1.4

- SAXSource(XMLReader reader, InputSource source)

  constructs a SAX source that obtains data from the given input source and uses the given reader to parse the input.

---

org.xml.sax.XMLReader 1.4

- void setContentHandler(ContentHandler handler)

  sets the handler that is notified of parse events as the input is parsed.

- void parse(InputSource source)

  parses the input from the given input source and sends parse events to the content handler.

---

javax.xml.transform.dom.DOMResult 1.4

- DOMResult(Node n)

  constructs a source from the given node. Usually, n is a new document node.

---

org.xml.sax.helpers.AttributesImpl 1.4

- void addAttribute(String uri, String lname, String qname, String type, String value)

  adds an attribute to this attribute collection. The lname parameter is the local name without prefix, and qname is the qualified name with prefix. The type parameter is one of "CDATA", "ID", "IDREF", "IDREFS", "NMTOKEN", "NMTOKENS", "ENTITY", "ENTITIES", or "NOTATION".

- void clear()

  removes all attributes from this attribute collection.

This example concludes our discussion of XML support in the Java library. You should now have a good perspective on the major strengths of XML—in particular, its automated parsing and validation as well as its powerful transformation mechanism. Of course, all this technology is only going to work for you if you design your XML formats well. You need to make sure that the formats are rich enough to express all your business needs, that they are stable over time, and that your business partners are willing to accept your XML documents. Those issues can be far more challenging than dealing with parsers, DTDs, or transformations.

In the next chapter, we will discuss network programming on the Java platform, starting with the basics of network sockets and moving on to higher-level protocols for e-mail and the World Wide Web.

Networking

In this chapter

We begin this chapter by reviewing basic networking concepts, then move on to writing Java programs that connect to network services. We will show you how network clients and servers are implemented. Finally, you will see how to send e-mail from a Java program and how to harvest information from a web server.

4.1 Connecting to a Server

In the following sections, you will connect to a server, first by hand and with telnet, and then with a Java program.

4.1.1 Using Telnet

The telnet program is a great debugging tool for network programming. You should be able to launch it by typing telnet from a command shell.

NOTE: In Windows, you need to activate telnet. Go to the Control Panel, select Programs, click Turn Windows Features On or Off, and select the Telnet client checkbox. The Windows firewall also blocks quite a few network ports that we use in this chapter; you might need an administrator account to unblock them.

You may have used telnet to connect to a remote computer, but you can use it to communicate with other services provided by Internet hosts as well. Here is an example of what you can do. Type

```
telnet time-a.nist.gov 13
```

As Figure 4.1 shows, you should get back a line like this:

```
57488 16-04-10 04:23:00 50 0 0 610.5 UTC(NIST) *
```

```
Terminal                                                    _ □ ×
~$ telnet time-a.nist.gov 13
Trying 129.6.15.28...
Connected to time-a.nist.gov.
Escape character is '^]'.

57488 16-04-10 04:23:00 50 0 0 610.5 UTC(NIST) *
Connection closed by foreign host.
~$ █
```

Figure 4.1 Output of the "time of day" service

What is going on? You have connected to the "time of day" service that most UNIX machines constantly run. The particular server that you connected to is operated by the National Institute of Standards and Technology and gives the measurement of a Cesium atomic clock. (Of course, the reported time is not completely accurate due to network delays.)

By convention, the "time of day" service is always attached to "port" number 13.

NOTE: In network parlance, a port is not a physical device, but an abstraction facilitating communication between a server and a client (see Figure 4.2).

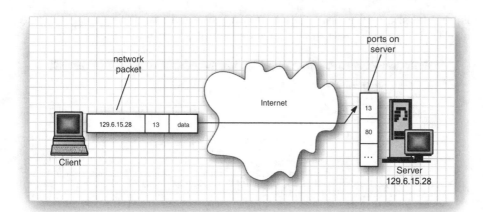

Figure 4.2 A client connecting to a server port

The server software is continuously running on the remote machine, waiting for any network traffic that wants to chat with port 13. When the operating system on the remote computer receives a network package that contains a request to connect to port number 13, it wakes up the listening server process and establishes the connection. The connection stays up until it is terminated by one of the parties.

When you began the telnet session with time-a.nist.gov at port 13, a piece of network software knew enough to convert the string "time-a.nist.gov" to its correct Internet Protocol (IP) address, 129.6.15.28. The telnet software then sent a connection request to that address, asking for a connection to port 13. Once the connection was established, the remote program sent back a line of data and closed the connection. In general, of course, clients and servers engage in a more extensive dialog before one or the other closes the connection.

Here is another experiment along the same lines—but a bit more interesting. Type

```
telnet horstmann.com 80
```

Then type very carefully the following:

```
GET / HTTP/1.1
Host: horstmann.com
blank line
```

That is, hit the Enter key twice at the end.

Figure 4.3 shows the response. It should look eerily familiar—you got a page of HTML-formatted text, namely Cay Horstmann's home page.

```
Terminal                                                                    _ □ ×
~$ telnet horstmann.com 80
Trying 67.210.118.65...
Connected to horstmann.com.
Escape character is '^]'.
GET / HTTP/1.1
Host: horstmann.com

HTTP/1.1 200 OK
Date: Sun, 10 Apr 2016 04:36:27 GMT
Server: Apache/2.2.24 (Unix) mod_ssl/2.2.24 OpenSSL/0.9.8e-fips-rhel5 mod_auth_p
assthrough/2.1 mod_bwlimited/1.4 mod_fcgid/2.3.6 Sun-ONE-ASP/4.0.3
Last-Modified: Thu, 17 Mar 2016 18:32:18 GMT
ETag: "2590e1c-1c47-52e42d9a8f080"
Accept-Ranges: bytes
Content-Length: 7239
Content-Type: text/html

<?xml version="1.0" encoding="UTF-8"?>
<!DOCTYPE html PUBLIC "-//W3C//DTD XHTML 1.0 Strict//EN" "http://www.w3.org/TR/x
html1/DTD/xhtml1-strict.dtd">
<html xmlns="http://www.w3.org/1999/xhtml"><head>
  <title>Cay Horstmann's Home Page</title>
  <link href="styles.css" rel="stylesheet" type="text/css"/>
```

Figure 4.3 Using telnet to access an HTTP port

This is exactly the same process that your web browser goes through to get a web page. It uses HTTP to request web pages from servers. Of course, the browser displays the HTML code more nicely.

NOTE: The Host key/value pair is required when you connect to a web server that hosts multiple domains at the same IP address. You can omit it if the server hosts a single domain.

4.1.2 Connecting to a Server with Java

Our first network program in Listing 4.1 will do the same thing we did using telnet—connect to a port and print out what it finds.

The key statements of this simple program are these:

```
var s = new Socket("time-a.nist.gov", 13);
InputStream inStream = s.getInputStream();
```

Listing 4.1 socket/SocketTest.java

```
1  package socket;
2
3  import java.io.*;
4  import java.net.*;
5  import java.nio.charset.*;
6  import java.util.*;
7
8  /**
9   * This program makes a socket connection to the atomic clock in Boulder, Colorado, and prints
10  * the time that the server sends.
11  * @version 1.22 2018-03-17
12  * @author Cay Horstmann
13  */
14  public class SocketTest
15  {
16     public static void main(String[] args) throws IOException
17     {
18        try (var s = new Socket("time-a.nist.gov", 13);
19             var in = new Scanner(s.getInputStream(), StandardCharsets.UTF_8))
20        {
21           while (in.hasNextLine())
22           {
23              String line = in.nextLine();
24              System.out.println(line);
25           }
26        }
27     }
28  }
```

The first line opens a *socket*, which is a network software abstraction that enables communication out of and into this program. We pass the remote address and the port number to the socket constructor. If the connection fails, an UnknownHostException is thrown. If there is another problem, an IOException occurs. Since UnknownHostException is a subclass of IOException and this is a sample program, we just catch the superclass.

Once the socket is open, the getInputStream method in java.net.Socket returns an InputStream object that you can use just like any other stream. Once you have grabbed the stream, this program simply prints each input line to standard output. This process continues until the stream is finished and the server disconnects.

This program works only with very simple servers, such as a "time of day" service. In more complex networking programs, the client sends request data to the server, and the server might not immediately disconnect at the end of a response. You will see how to implement that behavior in several examples throughout this chapter.

The Socket class is pleasant and easy to use because the Java library hides the complexities of establishing a networking connection and sending data across it. The java.net package essentially gives you the same programming interface you would use to work with a file.

> **NOTE:** In this book, we cover only the Transmission Control Protocol (TCP). The Java platform also supports the User Datagram Protocol (UDP), which can be used to send packets (also called *datagrams*) with much less overhead than TCP. The drawback is that packets need not be delivered in sequential order to the receiving application and can even be dropped altogether. It is up to the recipient to put the packets in order and to request retransmission of missing packets. UDP is well suited for applications in which missing packets can be tolerated—for example, for audio or video streams or continuous measurements.

---

java.net.Socket 1.0

- Socket(String host, int port)

  constructs a socket to connect to the given host and port.
- InputStream getInputStream()
- OutputStream getOutputStream()

  gets the stream to read data from the socket or write data to the socket.

4.1.3 Socket Timeouts

Reading from a socket blocks until data are available. If the host is unreachable, your application waits for a long time and you are at the mercy of the underlying operating system to eventually time out.

You can decide what timeout value is reasonable for your particular application. Then, call the setSoTimeout method to set a timeout value (in milliseconds).

```
var s = new Socket(. . .);
s.setSoTimeout(10000); // time out after 10 seconds
```

If the timeout value has been set for a socket, all subsequent read operations throw a SocketTimeoutException when the timeout has been reached before the operation has completed its work. You can catch that exception and react to the timeout.

```
try
{
   InputStream in = s.getInputStream(); // read from in
   . . .
}
catch (SocketTimeoutException e)
{
   react to timeout
}
```

There is no timeout for write operations.

There is one additional timeout issue that you need to address. The constructor

```
Socket(String host, int port)
```

can block indefinitely until an initial connection to the host is established.

You can overcome this problem by first constructing an unconnected socket and then connecting it with a timeout:

```
var s = new Socket();
s.connect(new InetSocketAddress(host, port), timeout);
```

See Section 4.2.4, "Interruptible Sockets," on p. 244 for how to allow users to interrupt a socket connection at any time.

---

java.net.Socket 1.0

- Socket() 1.1

  creates a socket that has not yet been connected.

- void connect(SocketAddress address) 1.4

  connects this socket to the given address.

- void connect(SocketAddress address, int timeoutInMilliseconds) 1.4

  connects this socket to the given address, or returns if the time interval expired.

- void setSoTimeout(int timeoutInMilliseconds) 1.1

  sets the blocking time for read requests on this socket. If the timeout is reached, a SocketTimeoutException is raised.

- boolean isConnected() 1.4

  returns true if the socket is connected.

- boolean isClosed() 1.4

  returns true if the socket is closed.

4.1.4 Internet Addresses

Usually, you don't have to worry too much about Internet addresses—the numerical host addresses that consist of 4 bytes (or, with IPv6, 16 bytes) such as 129.6.15.28. However, you can use the InetAddress class if you need to convert between host names and Internet addresses.

The java.net package supports IPv6 Internet addresses, provided the host operating system does.

The static getByName method returns an InetAddress object of a host. For example,

```
InetAddress address = InetAddress.getByName("time-a.nist.gov");
```

returns an InetAddress object that encapsulates the sequence of four bytes 129.6.15.28. You can access the bytes with the getAddress method.

```
byte[] addressBytes = address.getAddress();
```

Some host names with a lot of traffic correspond to multiple Internet addresses, to facilitate load balancing. For example, at the time of this writing, the host name google.com corresponds to twelve different Internet addresses. One of them is picked at random when the host is accessed. You can get all hosts with the getAllByName method.

```
InetAddress[] addresses = InetAddress.getAllByName(host);
```

Finally, you sometimes need the address of the local host. If you simply ask for the address of localhost, you always get the local loopback address 127.0.0.1, which cannot be used by others to connect to your computer. Instead, use the static getLocalHost method to get the address of your local host.

```
InetAddress address = InetAddress.getLocalHost();
```

Listing 4.2 is a simple program that prints the Internet address of your local host if you do not specify any command-line parameters, or all Internet addresses of another host if you specify the host name on the command line, such as

```
java inetAddress/InetAddressTest www.horstmann.com
```

Listing 4.2 inetAddress/InetAddressTest.java

```
1  package inetAddress;
2
3  import java.io.*;
4  import java.net.*;
```

```
5
6  /**
7   * This program demonstrates the InetAddress class. Supply a host name as command-line
8   * argument, or run without command-line arguments to see the address of the local host.
9   * @version 1.02 2012-06-05
10  * @author Cay Horstmann
11  */
12 public class InetAddressTest
13 {
14    public static void main(String[] args) throws IOException
15    {
16       if (args.length > 0)
17       {
18          String host = args[0];
19          InetAddress[] addresses = InetAddress.getAllByName(host);
20          for (InetAddress a : addresses)
21             System.out.println(a);
22       }
23       else
24       {
25          InetAddress localHostAddress = InetAddress.getLocalHost();
26          System.out.println(localHostAddress);
27       }
28    }
29 }
```

---

java.net.InetAddress 1.0

- static InetAddress getByName(String host)
- static InetAddress[] getAllByName(String host)

  constructs an InetAddress, or an array of all Internet addresses, for the given host name.

- static InetAddress getLocalHost()

  constructs an InetAddress for the local host.

- byte[] getAddress()

  returns an array of bytes that contains the numerical address.

- String getHostAddress()

  returns a string with decimal numbers, separated by periods, for example "129.6.15.28".

- String getHostName()

  returns the host name.

4.2 Implementing Servers

Now that we have implemented a basic network client that receives data from the Internet, let's program a simple server that can send information to clients.

4.2.1 Server Sockets

A server program, when started, waits for a client to attach to its port. For our example program, we chose port number 8189, which is not used by any of the standard services. The ServerSocket class establishes a socket. In our case, the command

```
var s = new ServerSocket(8189);
```

establishes a server that monitors port 8189. The command

```
Socket incoming = s.accept();
```

tells the program to wait indefinitely until a client connects to that port. Once someone connects to this port by sending the correct request over the network, this method returns a Socket object that represents the connection that was made. You can use this object to get input and output streams, as is shown in the following code:

```
InputStream inStream = incoming.getInputStream();
OutputStream outStream = incoming.getOutputStream();
```

Everything that the server sends to the server output stream becomes the input of the client program, and all the output from the client program ends up in the server input stream.

In all the examples in this chapter, we transmit text through sockets. We therefore turn the streams into scanners and writers.

```
var in = new Scanner(inStream, StandardCharsets.UTF_8);
var out = new PrintWriter(new OutputStreamWriter(outStream, StandardCharsets.UTF_8),
    true /* autoFlush */);
```

Let's send the client a greeting:

```
out.println("Hello! Enter BYE to exit.");
```

When you use telnet to connect to this server program at port 8189, you will see this greeting on the terminal screen.

In this simple server, we just read the client's input, a line at a time, and echo it. This demonstrates that the program receives the input. An actual server would obviously compute and return an answer depending on the input.

```
String line = in.nextLine();
out.println("Echo: " + line);
if (line.trim().equals("BYE")) done = true;
```

In the end, we close the incoming socket.

```
incoming.close();
```

That is all there is to it. Every server program, such as an HTTP web server, continues performing this loop:

1. It receives a command from the client ("get me this information") through an incoming data stream.

2. It decodes the client command.

3. It gathers the information that the client requested.

4. It sends the information to the client through the outgoing data stream.

Listing 4.3 is the complete program.

Listing 4.3 server/EchoServer.java

```java
1  package server;
2
3  import java.io.*;
4  import java.net.*;
5  import java.nio.charset.*;
6  import java.util.*;
7
8  /**
9   * This program implements a simple server that listens to port 8189 and echoes back all
10  * client input.
11  * @version 1.22 2018-03-17
12  * @author Cay Horstmann
13  */
14 public class EchoServer
15 {
16    public static void main(String[] args) throws IOException
17    {
```

(Continues)

Listing 4.3   *(Continued)*

```
18        // establish server socket
19        try (var s = new ServerSocket(8189))
20        {
21           // wait for client connection
22           try (Socket incoming = s.accept())
23           {
24              InputStream inStream = incoming.getInputStream();
25              OutputStream outStream = incoming.getOutputStream();
26
27              try (var in = new Scanner(inStream, StandardCharsets.UTF_8))
28              {
29                 var out = new PrintWriter(
30                    new OutputStreamWriter(outStream, StandardCharsets.UTF_8),
31                    true /* autoFlush */);
32
33                 out.println("Hello! Enter BYE to exit.");
34
35                 // echo client input
36                 var done = false;
37                 while (!done && in.hasNextLine())
38                 {
39                    String line = in.nextLine();
40                    out.println("Echo: " + line);
41                    if (line.trim().equals("BYE")) done = true;
42                 }
43              }
44           }
45        }
46     }
47  }
```

To try it out, compile and run the program. Then use telnet to connect to the server localhost (or IP address 127.0.0.1) and port 8189.

If you are connected directly to the Internet, anyone in the world can access your echo server, provided they know your IP address and the magic port number.

When you connect to the port, you will see the message shown in Figure 4.4:

```
Hello! Enter BYE to exit.
```

Type anything and watch the input echo on your screen. Type BYE (all uppercase letters) to disconnect. The server program will terminate as well.

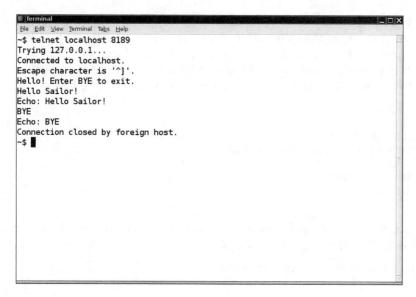

Figure 4.4 Accessing an echo server

---

java.net.ServerSocket 1.0

- ServerSocket(int port)

  creates a server socket that monitors a port.

- Socket accept()

  waits for a connection. This method blocks (i.e., idles) the current thread until the connection is made. The method returns a Socket object through which the program can communicate with the connecting client.

- void close()

  closes the server socket.

4.2.2 Serving Multiple Clients

There is one problem with the simple server in the preceding example. Suppose we want to allow multiple clients to connect to our server at the same time. Typically, a server runs constantly on a server computer, and clients from all over the Internet might want to use it at the same time. Without support for multiple connections, any one client can monopolize the service by connecting to it for a long time. We can do much better through the magic of threads.

Every time we know the program has established a new socket connection—that is, every time the call to accept() returns a socket—we will launch a new thread to take care of the connection between the server and *that* client. The main program will just go back and wait for the next connection. For this to happen, the main loop of the server should look like this:

```
while (true)
{
   Socket incoming = s.accept();
   var r = new ThreadedEchoHandler(incoming);

   var t = new Thread(r);
   t.start();
}
```

The ThreadedEchoHandler class implements Runnable and contains the communication loop with the client in its run method.

```
class ThreadedEchoHandler implements Runnable
{
   . . .
   public void run()
   {
      try (InputStream inStream = incoming.getInputStream();
           OutputStream outStream = incoming.getOutputStream())
      {
         Process input and send response
      }
      catch(IOException e)
      {
         Handle exception
      }
   }
}
```

When each connection starts a new thread, multiple clients can connect to the server at the same time. You can easily check this out.

1. Compile and run the server program (Listing 4.4).

2. Open several telnet windows as we have in Figure 4.5.

3. Switch between windows and type commands. Note that you can communicate through all of them simultaneously.

4. When done, switch to the window from which you launched the server program and press Ctrl+C to kill it.

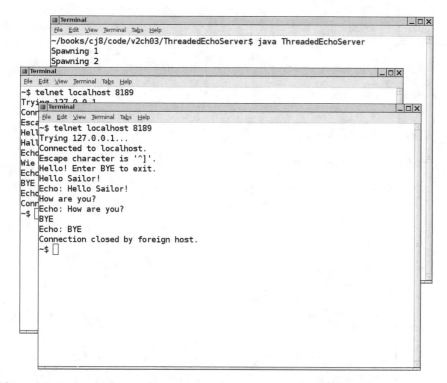

Figure 4.5 Several telnet windows communicating simultaneously

 NOTE: In this program, we spawn a separate thread for each connection. This approach is not satisfactory for high-performance servers. You can achieve greater server throughput by using features of the java.nio package. See www.ibm.com/developerworks/java/library/j-javaio for more information.

Listing 4.4 threaded/ThreadedEchoServer.java

```java
1  package threaded;
2
3  import java.io.*;
4  import java.net.*;
5  import java.nio.charset.*;
6  import java.util.*;
7
```

(Continues)

Listing 4.4 *(Continued)*

```
 8   /**
 9    * This program implements a multithreaded server that listens to port 8189 and echoes back
10    * all client input.
11    * @author Cay Horstmann
12    * @version 1.23 2018-03-17
13    */
14   public class ThreadedEchoServer
15   {
16      public static void main(String[] args )
17      {
18         try (var s = new ServerSocket(8189))
19         {
20            int i = 1;
21
22            while (true)
23            {
24               Socket incoming = s.accept();
25               System.out.println("Spawning " + i);
26               Runnable r = new ThreadedEchoHandler(incoming);
27               var t = new Thread(r);
28               t.start();
29               i++;
30            }
31         }
32         catch (IOException e)
33         {
34            e.printStackTrace();
35         }
36      }
37   }
38
39   /**
40    * This class handles the client input for one server socket connection.
41    */
42   class ThreadedEchoHandler implements Runnable
43   {
44      private Socket incoming;
45
46      /**
47         Constructs a handler.
48         @param incomingSocket the incoming socket
49      */
50      public ThreadedEchoHandler(Socket incomingSocket)
51      {
52         incoming = incomingSocket;
53      }
54
```

```
55    public void run()
56    {
57       try (InputStream inStream = incoming.getInputStream();
58             OutputStream outStream = incoming.getOutputStream();
59             var in = new Scanner(inStream, StandardCharsets.UTF_8);
60             var out = new PrintWriter(
61                new OutputStreamWriter(outStream, StandardCharsets.UTF_8),
62                true /* autoFlush */))
63       {
64          out.println( "Hello! Enter BYE to exit." );
65
66          // echo client input
67          var done = false;
68          while (!done && in.hasNextLine())
69          {
70             String line = in.nextLine();
71             out.println("Echo: " + line);
72             if (line.trim().equals("BYE"))
73                done = true;
74          }
75       }
76       catch (IOException e)
77       {
78          e.printStackTrace();
79       }
80    }
81 }
```

4.2.3 Half-Close

The *half-close* allows one end of a socket connection to terminate its output while still receiving data from the other end.

Here is a typical situation. Suppose you transmit data to the server but you don't know at the outset how much data you have. With a file, you'd just close the file at the end of the data. However, if you close a socket, you immediately disconnect from the server and cannot read the response.

The half-close solves this problem. You can close the output stream of a socket, thereby indicating to the server the end of the requested data, but keep the input stream open.

The client side looks like this:

```
try (var socket = new Socket(host, port))
{
   var in = new Scanner(socket.getInputStream(), StandardCharsets.UTF_8);
   var writer = new PrintWriter(socket.getOutputStream());
   // send request data
   writer.print(. . .);
```

```
   writer.flush();
   socket.shutdownOutput();
   // now socket is half-closed
   // read response data
   while (in.hasNextLine() != null)
   {
      String line = in.nextLine();
      . . .
   }
}
```

The server side simply reads input until the end of the input stream is reached. Then it sends the response.

Of course, this protocol is only useful for one-shot services such as HTTP where the client connects, issues a request, catches the response, and then disconnects.

---

java.net.Socket 1.0

- void shutdownOutput() 1.3

  sets the output stream to "end of stream."

- void shutdownInput() 1.3

  sets the input stream to "end of stream."

- boolean isOutputShutdown() 1.4

  returns true if output has been shut down.

- boolean isInputShutdown() 1.4

  returns true if input has been shut down.

4.2.4 Interruptible Sockets

When you connect to a socket, the current thread blocks until the connection has been established or a timeout has elapsed. Similarly, when you read data through a socket, the current thread blocks until the operation is successful or has timed out. (There is no timeout for writing data.)

In interactive applications, you would like to give users an option to simply cancel a socket connection that does not appear to produce results. However, if a thread blocks on an unresponsive socket, you cannot unblock it by calling interrupt.

To interrupt a socket operation, use a SocketChannel, a feature of the java.nio package. Open the SocketChannel like this:

```
SocketChannel channel = SocketChannel.open(new InetSocketAddress(host, port));
```

A channel does not have associated streams. Instead, it has read and write methods that make use of Buffer objects. (See Chapter 1 for more information about NIO buffers.) These methods are declared in the interfaces ReadableByteChannel and WritableByteChannel.

If you don't want to deal with buffers, you can use the Scanner class to read from a SocketChannel because Scanner has a constructor with a ReadableByteChannel parameter:

```
var in = new Scanner(channel, StandardCharsets.UTF_8);
```

To turn a channel into an output stream, use the static Channels.newOutputStream method.

```
OutputStream outStream = Channels.newOutputStream(channel);
```

That's all you need to do. Whenever a thread is interrupted during an open, read, or write operation, the operation does not block, but is terminated with an exception.

The program in Listing 4.5 contrasts interruptible and blocking sockets. A server sends numbers and pretends to be stuck after the tenth number. Click on either button, and a thread is started that connects to the server and prints the output. The first thread uses an interruptible socket; the second thread uses a blocking socket. If you click the Cancel button within the first ten numbers, you can interrupt either thread.

However, after the first ten numbers, you can only interrupt the first thread. The second thread keeps blocking until the server finally closes the connection (see Figure 4.6).

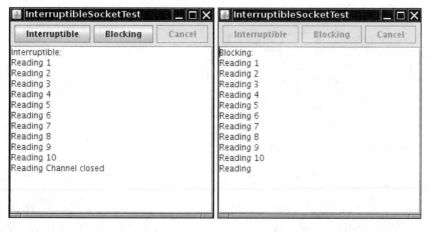

Figure 4.6 Interrupting a socket

Listing 4.5 interruptible/InterruptibleSocketTest.java

```java
1  package interruptible;
2
3  import java.awt.*;
4  import java.awt.event.*;
5  import java.util.*;
6  import java.net.*;
7  import java.io.*;
8  import java.nio.charset.*;
9  import java.nio.channels.*;
10 import javax.swing.*;
11
12 /**
13  * This program shows how to interrupt a socket channel.
14  * @author Cay Horstmann
15  * @version 1.05 2018-03-17
16  */
17 public class InterruptibleSocketTest
18 {
19    public static void main(String[] args)
20    {
21       EventQueue.invokeLater(() ->
22          {
23             var frame = new InterruptibleSocketFrame();
24             frame.setTitle("InterruptibleSocketTest");
25             frame.setDefaultCloseOperation(JFrame.EXIT_ON_CLOSE);
26             frame.setVisible(true);
27          });
28    }
29 }
30
31 class InterruptibleSocketFrame extends JFrame
32 {
33    private Scanner in;
34    private JButton interruptibleButton;
35    private JButton blockingButton;
36    private JButton cancelButton;
37    private JTextArea messages;
38    private TestServer server;
39    private Thread connectThread;
40
41    public InterruptibleSocketFrame()
42    {
43       var northPanel = new JPanel();
44       add(northPanel, BorderLayout.NORTH);
45
46       final int TEXT_ROWS = 20;
47       final int TEXT_COLUMNS = 60;
48       messages = new JTextArea(TEXT_ROWS, TEXT_COLUMNS);
```

```
49      add(new JScrollPane(messages));
50
51      interruptibleButton = new JButton("Interruptible");
52      blockingButton = new JButton("Blocking");
53
54      northPanel.add(interruptibleButton);
55      northPanel.add(blockingButton);
56
57      interruptibleButton.addActionListener(event ->
58         {
59            interruptibleButton.setEnabled(false);
60            blockingButton.setEnabled(false);
61            cancelButton.setEnabled(true);
62            connectThread = new Thread(() ->
63               {
64                  try
65                  {
66                     connectInterruptibly();
67                  }
68                  catch (IOException e)
69                  {
70                     messages.append("\nInterruptibleSocketTest.connectInterruptibly: " + e);
71                  }
72               });
73            connectThread.start();
74         });
75
76      blockingButton.addActionListener(event ->
77         {
78            interruptibleButton.setEnabled(false);
79            blockingButton.setEnabled(false);
80            cancelButton.setEnabled(true);
81            connectThread = new Thread(() ->
82               {
83                  try
84                  {
85                     connectBlocking();
86                  }
87                  catch (IOException e)
88                  {
89                     messages.append("\nInterruptibleSocketTest.connectBlocking: " + e);
90                  }
91               });
92            connectThread.start();
93         });
94
95      cancelButton = new JButton("Cancel");
96      cancelButton.setEnabled(false);
97      northPanel.add(cancelButton);
```

(Continues)

Listing 4.5 *(Continued)*

```
 98        cancelButton.addActionListener(event ->
 99           {
100              connectThread.interrupt();
101              cancelButton.setEnabled(false);
102           });
103        server = new TestServer();
104        new Thread(server).start();
105        pack();
106     }
107
108     /**
109      * Connects to the test server, using interruptible I/O
110      */
111     public void connectInterruptibly() throws IOException
112     {
113        messages.append("Interruptible:\n");
114        try (SocketChannel channel
115              = SocketChannel.open(new InetSocketAddress("localhost", 8189)))
116        {
117           in = new Scanner(channel, StandardCharsets.UTF_8);
118           while (!Thread.currentThread().isInterrupted())
119           {
120              messages.append("Reading ");
121              if (in.hasNextLine())
122              {
123                 String line = in.nextLine();
124                 messages.append(line);
125                 messages.append("\n");
126              }
127           }
128        }
129        finally
130        {
131           EventQueue.invokeLater(() ->
132              {
133                 messages.append("Channel closed\n");
134                 interrruptibleButton.setEnabled(true);
135                 blockingButton.setEnabled(true);
136              });
137        }
138     }
139
140     /**
141      * Connects to the test server, using blocking I/O
142      */
143     public void connectBlocking() throws IOException
144     {
```

```
145    messages.append("Blocking:\n");
146    try (var sock = new Socket("localhost", 8189))
147    {
148       in = new Scanner(sock.getInputStream(), StandardCharsets.UTF_8);
149       while (!Thread.currentThread().isInterrupted())
150       {
151          messages.append("Reading ");
152          if (in.hasNextLine())
153          {
154             String line = in.nextLine();
155             messages.append(line);
156             messages.append("\n");
157          }
158       }
159    }
160    finally
161    {
162       EventQueue.invokeLater(() ->
163          {
164             messages.append("Socket closed\n");
165             interruptibleButton.setEnabled(true);
166             blockingButton.setEnabled(true);
167          });
168    }
169 }
170
171 /**
172  * A multithreaded server that listens to port 8189 and sends numbers to the client,
173  * simulating a hanging server after 10 numbers.
174  */
175 class TestServer implements Runnable
176 {
177    public void run()
178    {
179       try (var s = new ServerSocket(8189))
180       {
181          while (true)
182          {
183             Socket incoming = s.accept();
184             Runnable r = new TestServerHandler(incoming);
185             new Thread(r).start();
186          }
187       }
188       catch (IOException e)
189       {
190          messages.append("\nTestServer.run: " + e);
191       }
192    }
193 }
```

(Continues)

Listing 4.5 *(Continued)*

```
194
195    /**
196     * This class handles the client input for one server socket connection.
197     */
198    class TestServerHandler implements Runnable
199    {
200       private Socket incoming;
201       private int counter;
202
203       /**
204        * Constructs a handler.
205        * @param i the incoming socket
206        */
207       public TestServerHandler(Socket i)
208       {
209          incoming = i;
210       }
211
212       public void run()
213       {
214          try
215          {
216             try
217             {
218                OutputStream outStream = incoming.getOutputStream();
219                var out = new PrintWriter(
220                   new OutputStreamWriter(outStream, StandardCharsets.UTF_8),
221                   true /* autoFlush */);
222                while (counter < 100)
223                {
224                   counter++;
225                   if (counter <= 10) out.println(counter);
226                   Thread.sleep(100);
227                }
228             }
229             finally
230             {
231                incoming.close();
232                messages.append("Closing server\n");
233             }
234          }
235          catch (Exception e)
236          {
237             messages.append("\nTestServerHandler.run: " + e);
238          }
239       }
240    }
241 }
```

```
java.net.InetSocketAddress 1.4
```

- `InetSocketAddress(String hostname, int port)`

  constructs an address object with the given host and port, resolving the host name during construction. If the host name cannot be resolved, the address object's unresolved property is set to true.

- `boolean isUnresolved()`

  returns true if this address object could not be resolved.

```
java.nio.channels.SocketChannel 1.4
```

- `static SocketChannel open(SocketAddress address)`

  opens a socket channel and connects it to a remote address.

```
java.nio.channels.Channels 1.4
```

- `static InputStream newInputStream(ReadableByteChannel channel)`

  constructs an input stream that reads from the given channel.

- `static OutputStream newOutputStream(WritableByteChannel channel)`

  constructs an output stream that writes to the given channel.

4.3 Getting Web Data

To access web servers in a Java program, you will want to work at a higher level than socket connections and HTTP requests. In the following sections, we discuss the classes that the Java library provides for this purpose.

4.3.1 URLs and URIs

The URL and URLConnection classes encapsulate much of the complexity of retrieving information from a remote site. You can construct a URL object from a string:

```
var url = new URL(urlString);
```

If you simply want to fetch the contents of the resource, use the openStream method of the URL class. This method yields an InputStream object. Use it in the usual way—for example, to construct a Scanner:

```
InputStream inStream = url.openStream();
var in = new Scanner(inStream, StandardCharsets.UTF_8);
```

The `java.net` package makes a useful distinction between URLs (uniform resource *locators*) and URIs (uniform resource *identifiers*).

A URI is a purely syntactical construct that contains the various parts of the string specifying a web resource. A URL is a special kind of URI, namely, one with sufficient information to *locate* a resource. Other URIs, such as

```
mailto:cay@horstmann.com
```

are not locators—there is no data to locate from this identifier. Such a URI is called a URN (uniform resource *name*).

In the Java library, the `URI` class has no methods for accessing the resource that the identifier specifies—its sole purpose is parsing. In contrast, the `URL` class can open a stream to the resource. For that reason, the `URL` class only works with schemes that the Java library knows how to handle, such as `http:`, `https:`, `ftp:`, the local file system (`file:`), and JAR files (`jar:`).

To see why parsing is not trivial, consider how complex URIs can be. For example,

```
http:/google.com?q=Beach+Chalet
ftp://username:password@ftp.yourserver.com/pub/file.txt
```

The URI specification gives the rules for the makeup of these identifiers. A URI has the syntax

[*scheme*:]*schemeSpecificPart*[#*fragment*]

Here, the [. . .] denotes an optional part, and the : and # are included literally in the identifier.

If the *scheme*: part is present, the URI is called *absolute*. Otherwise, it is called *relative*.

An absolute URI is *opaque* if the *schemeSpecificPart* does not begin with a / such as

```
mailto:cay@horstmann.com
```

All absolute nonopaque URIs and all relative URIs are *hierarchical*. Examples are

```
http://horstmann.com/index.html
../../java/net/Socket.html#Socket()
```

The *schemeSpecificPart* of a hierarchical URI has the structure

[//*authority*][*path*][?*query*]

where, again, [. . .] denotes optional parts.

For server-based URIs, the *authority* part has the form

    [*user-info@*]*host*[*:port*]

The *port* must be an integer.

RFC 2396, which standardizes URIs, also supports a registry-based mechanism in which the *authority* has a different format, but this is not in common use.

One of the purposes of the URI class is to parse an identifier and break it up into its components. You can retrieve them with the methods

```
getScheme
getSchemeSpecificPart
getAuthority
getUserInfo
getHost
getPort
getPath
getQuery
getFragment
```

The other purpose of the URI class is the handling of absolute and relative identifiers. If you have an absolute URI such as

```
http://docs.mycompany.com/api/java/net/ServerSocket.html
```

and a relative URI such as

```
../../java/net/Socket.html#Socket()
```

then you can combine the two into an absolute URI.

```
http://docs.mycompany.com/api/java/net/Socket.html#Socket()
```

This process is called *resolving* a relative URL.

The opposite process is called *relativization*. For example, suppose you have a *base* URI

```
http://docs.mycompany.com/api
```

and a URI

```
http://docs.mycompany.com/api/java/lang/String.html
```

Then the relativized URI is

```
java/lang/String.html
```

The URI class supports both of these operations:

```
relative = base.relativize(combined);
combined = base.resolve(relative);
```

4.3.2 Using a `URLConnection` to Retrieve Information

If you want additional information about a web resource, you should use the `URLConnection` class, which gives you much more control than the basic `URL` class.

When working with a `URLConnection` object, you must carefully schedule your steps.

1. Call the `openConnection` method of the `URL` class to obtain the `URLConnection` object:

   ```
   URLConnection connection = url.openConnection();
   ```

2. Set any request properties, using the methods

   ```
   setDoInput
   setDoOutput
   setIfModifiedSince
   setUseCaches
   setAllowUserInteraction
   setRequestProperty
   setConnectTimeout
   setReadTimeout
   ```

   We discuss these methods later in this section and in the API notes.

3. Connect to the remote resource by calling the `connect` method:

   ```
   connection.connect();
   ```

   Besides making a socket connection to the server, this method also queries the server for *header information.*

4. After connecting to the server, you can query the header information. Two methods, `getHeaderFieldKey` and `getHeaderField`, enumerate all fields of the header. The method `getHeaderFields` gets a standard `Map` object containing the header fields. For your convenience, the following methods query standard fields:

   ```
   getContentType
   getContentLength
   getContentEncoding
   getDate
   getExpiration
   getLastModified
   ```

5. Finally, you can access the resource data. Use the `getInputStream` method to obtain an input stream for reading the information. (This is the same input stream that the `openStream` method of the `URL` class returns.) The other method, `getContent`, isn't very useful in practice. The objects that are returned by standard content types such as `text/plain` and `image/gif` require

classes in the com.sun hierarchy for processing. You could register your own content handlers, but we do not discuss this technique in our book.

 CAUTION: Some programmers form a wrong mental image when using the URLConnection class, thinking that the getInputStream and getOutputStream methods are similar to those of the Socket class. But that isn't quite true. The URLConnection class does quite a bit of magic behind the scenes—in particular, the handling of request and response headers. For that reason, it is important that you follow the setup steps for the connection.

Let us now look at some of the URLConnection methods in detail. Several methods set properties of the connection before connecting to the server. The most important ones are setDoInput and setDoOutput. By default, the connection yields an input stream for reading from the server but no output stream for writing. If you want an output stream (for example, for posting data to a web server), you need to call

```
connection.setDoOutput(true);
```

Next, you may want to set some of the request headers. The request headers are sent together with the request command to the server. Here is an example:

```
GET www.server.com/index.html HTTP/1.0
Referer: http://www.somewhere.com/links.html
Proxy-Connection: Keep-Alive
User-Agent: Mozilla/5.0 (X11; U; Linux i686; en-US; rv:1.8.1.4)
Host: www.server.com
Accept: text/html, image/gif, image/jpeg, image/png, */*
Accept-Language: en
Accept-Charset: iso-8859-1,*,utf-8
Cookie: orangemilano=192218887821987
```

The setIfModifiedSince method tells the connection that you are only interested in data modified since a certain date.

Finally, you can use the catch-all setRequestProperty method to set any name/value pair that is meaningful for the particular protocol. For the format of the HTTP request headers, see RFC 2616. Some of these parameters are not well documented and are passed around by word of mouth from one programmer to the next. For example, if you want to access a password-protected web page, you must do the following:

1. Concatenate the user name, a colon, and the password.

```
String input = username + ":" + password;
```

2. Compute the Base64 encoding of the resulting string. (The Base64 encoding encodes a sequence of bytes into a sequence of printable ASCII characters.)

```
Base64.Encoder encoder = Base64.getEncoder();
String encoding = encoder.encodeToString(input.getBytes(StandardCharsets.UTF_8));
```

3. Call the `setRequestProperty` method with a name of `"Authorization"` and the value `"Basic "` + encoding.

```
connection.setRequestProperty("Authorization", "Basic " + encoding);
```

 TIP: You just saw how to access a password-protected web page. To access a password-protected file by FTP, use an entirely different method: Construct a URL of the form

```
ftp://username:password@ftp.yourserver.com/pub/file.txt
```

Once you call the `connect` method, you can query the response header information. First, let's see how to enumerate all response header fields. The implementors of this class felt a need to express their individuality by introducing yet another iteration protocol. The call

```
String key = connection.getHeaderFieldKey(n);
```

gets the nth key from the response header, where n starts from 1! It returns `null` if n is zero or greater than the total number of header fields. There is no method to return the number of fields; you simply keep calling `getHeaderFieldKey` until you get `null`. Similarly, the call

```
String value = connection.getHeaderField(n);
```

returns the nth value.

The method `getHeaderFields` returns a `Map` of response header fields.

```
Map<String,List<String>> headerFields = connection.getHeaderFields();
```

Here is a set of response header fields from a typical HTTP request:

```
Date: Wed, 27 Aug 2008 00:15:48 GMT
Server: Apache/2.2.2 (Unix)
Last-Modified: Sun, 22 Jun 2008 20:53:38 GMT
Accept-Ranges: bytes
Content-Length: 4813
Connection: close
Content-Type: text/html
```

NOTE: You can obtain the response status line (such as "HTTP/1.1 200 OK") as connection.getHeaderField(0) or headerFields.get(null).

As a convenience, six methods query the values of the most common header types and convert them to numeric types when appropriate. Table 4.1 shows these convenience methods. The methods with return type long return the number of seconds since January 1, 1970 GMT.

Table 4.1 Convenience Methods for Response Header Values

Key Name	Method Name	Return Type
Date	getDate	long
Expires	getExpiration	long
Last-Modified	getLastModified	long
Content-Length	getContentLength	int
Content-Type	getContentType	String
Content-Encoding	getContentEncoding	String

The program in Listing 4.6 lets you experiment with URL connections. Supply a URL and an optional user name and password on the command line when running the program, for example:

```
java urlConnection.URLConnectionTest http://www.yourserver.com user password
```

The program prints

- All keys and values of the header
- The return values of the six convenience methods in Table 4.1
- The first ten lines of the requested resource

Listing 4.6 urlConnection/URLConnectionTest.java

```
1 package urlConnection;
2
3 import java.io.*;
4 import java.net.*;
5 import java.nio.charset.*;
6 import java.util.*;
7
```

(Continues)

Listing 4.6 *(Continued)*

```
 8  /**
 9   * This program connects to an URL and displays the response header data and the first
10   * 10 lines of the requested data.
11   *
12   * Supply the URL and an optional username and password (for HTTP basic authentication) on the
13   * command line.
14   * @version 1.12 2018-03-17
15   * @author Cay Horstmann
16   */
17  public class URLConnectionTest
18  {
19     public static void main(String[] args)
20     {
21        try
22        {
23           String urlName;
24           if (args.length > 0) urlName = args[0];
25           else urlName = "http://horstmann.com";
26
27           var url = new URL(urlName);
28           URLConnection connection = url.openConnection();
29
30           // set username, password if specified on command line
31
32           if (args.length > 2)
33           {
34              String username = args[1];
35              String password = args[2];
36              String input = username + ":" + password;
37              Base64.Encoder encoder = Base64.getEncoder();
38              String encoding = encoder.encodeToString(input.getBytes(StandardCharsets.UTF_8));
39              connection.setRequestProperty("Authorization", "Basic " + encoding);
40           }
41
42           connection.connect();
43
44           // print header fields
45
46           Map<String, List<String>> headers = connection.getHeaderFields();
47           for (Map.Entry<String, List<String>> entry : headers.entrySet())
48           {
49              String key = entry.getKey();
50              for (String value : entry.getValue())
51                 System.out.println(key + ": " + value);
52           }
53
54           // print convenience functions
```

```
55
56          System.out.println("----------");
57          System.out.println("getContentType: " + connection.getContentType());
58          System.out.println("getContentLength: " + connection.getContentLength());
59          System.out.println("getContentEncoding: " + connection.getContentEncoding());
60          System.out.println("getDate: " + connection.getDate());
61          System.out.println("getExpiration: " + connection.getExpiration());
62          System.out.println("getLastModifed: " + connection.getLastModified());
63          System.out.println("----------");
64
65          String encoding = connection.getContentEncoding();
66          if (encoding == null) encoding = "UTF-8";
67          try (var in = new Scanner(connection.getInputStream(), encoding))
68          {
69             // print first ten lines of contents
70
71             for (int n = 1; in.hasNextLine() && n <= 10; n++)
72                System.out.println(in.nextLine());
73             if (in.hasNextLine()) System.out.println(". . .");
74          }
75       }
76       catch (IOException e)
77       {
78          e.printStackTrace();
79       }
80    }
81 }
```

---

java.net.URL 1.0

- `InputStream openStream()`

  opens an input stream for reading the resource data.

- `URLConnection openConnection()`

  returns a URLConnection object that manages the connection to the resource.

---

java.net.URLConnection 1.0

- `void setDoInput(boolean doInput)`
- `boolean getDoInput()`

  If doInput is true, the user can receive input from this URLConnection.

- `void setDoOutput(boolean doOutput)`
- `boolean getDoOutput()`

  If doOutput is true, the user can send output to this URLConnection.

(Continues)

---

java.net.URLConnection 1.0 *(Continued)*

- void setIfModifiedSince(long time)
- long getIfModifiedSince()

  The ifModifiedSince property configures this URLConnection to fetch only data modified since a given time. The time is given in seconds since midnight, GMT, January 1, 1970.

- void setConnectTimeout(int timeout) 5.0
- int getConnectTimeout() 5.0

  sets or gets the timeout for the connection (in milliseconds). If the timeout has elapsed before a connection was established, the connect method of the associated input stream throws a SocketTimeoutException.

- void setReadTimeout(int timeout) 5.0
- int getReadTimeout() 5.0

  sets or gets the timeout for reading data (in milliseconds). If the timeout has elapsed before a read operation was successful, the read method throws a SocketTimeoutException.

- void setRequestProperty(String key, String value)

  sets a request header field.

- Map<String,List<String>> getRequestProperties() 1.4

  returns a map of request properties. All values for the same key are placed in a list.

- void connect()

  connects to the remote resource and retrieves the response header information.

- Map<String,List<String>> getHeaderFields() 1.4

  returns a map of response headers. All values for the same key are placed in a list.

- String getHeaderFieldKey(int n)

  gets the key for the nth response header field, or null if n is ≤ 0 or greater than the number of response header fields.

- String getHeaderField(int n)

  gets value of the nth response header field, or null if n is ≤ 0 or greater than the number of response header fields.

- int getContentLength()

  gets the content length if available, or -1 if unknown.

(Continues)

---

java.net.URLConnection 1.0 *(Continued)*

- `String getContentType()`

  gets the content type, such as text/plain or image/gif.

- `String getContentEncoding()`

  gets the content encoding, such as gzip. This value is not commonly used, because the default identity encoding is not supposed to be specified with a Content-Encoding header.

- `long getDate()`
- `long getExpiration()`
- `long getLastModifed()`

  gets the date of creation, expiration, and last modification of the resource. The dates are specified as seconds since midnight, GMT, January 1, 1970.

- `InputStream getInputStream()`
- `OutputStream getOutputStream()`

  returns a stream for reading from the resource or writing to the resource.

- `Object getContent()`

  selects the appropriate content handler to read the resource data and convert it into an object. This method is not useful for reading standard types such as text/plain or image/gif unless you install your own content handler.

4.3.3 Posting Form Data

In the preceding section, you saw how to read data from a web server. Now we will show you how your programs can send data back to a web server and to programs that the web server invokes.

To send information from a web browser to the web server, a user fills out a *form*, like the one in Figure 4.7.

When the user clicks the Submit button, the text in the text fields and the settings of any checkboxes, radio buttons, and other input elements are sent back to the web server. The web server invokes a program that processes the user input.

Many technologies enable web servers to invoke programs. Among the best known ones are Java servlets, JavaServer Faces, Microsoft Active Server Pages (ASP), and Common Gateway Interface (CGI) scripts.

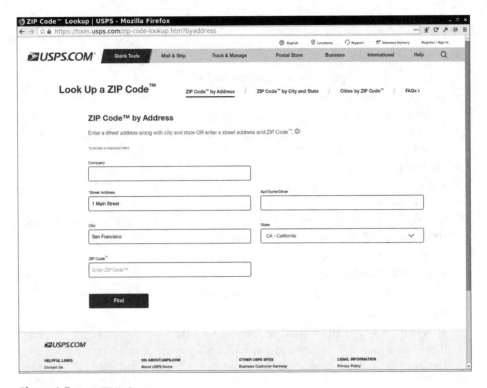

Figure 4.7 An HTML form

The server-side program processes the form data and produces another HTML page that the web server sends back to the browser. This sequence is illustrated in Figure 4.8. The response page can contain new information (for example, in an information-search program) or just an acknowledgment. The web browser then displays the response page.

We do not discuss the implementation of server-side programs in this book. Our interest is merely in writing client programs that interact with existing server-side programs.

When form data are sent to a web server, it does not matter whether the data are interpreted by a servlet, a CGI script, or some other server-side technology. The client sends the data to the web server in a standard format, and the web server takes care of passing it on to the program that generates the response.

Two commands, called GET and POST, are commonly used to send information to a web server.

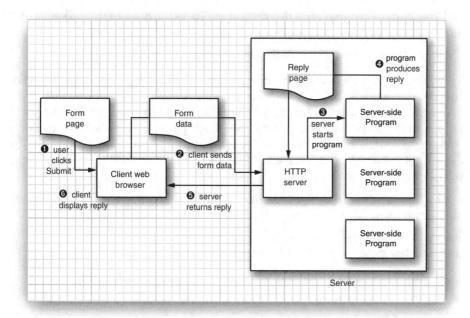

Figure 4.8 Data flow during execution of a server-side program

In the GET command, you simply attach query parameters to the end of the URL. The URL has the form

http://*host*/*path*?*query*

Each parameter has the form *name=value*. Parameters are separated by & characters. Parameter values are encoded using the *URL encoding* scheme, following these rules:

- Leave the characters A through Z, a through z, 0 through 9, and . - ~ _ unchanged.
- Replace all spaces with + characters.
- Encode all other characters into UTF-8 and encode each byte by a %, followed by a two-digit hexadecimal number.

For example, to transmit *San Francisco, CA*, you use San+Francisco%2c+CA, as the hexadecimal number 2c is the UTF-8 code of the ',' character.

This encoding keeps any intermediate programs from messing with spaces and other special characters.

At the time of this writing, the Google Maps site (www.google.com/maps) accepts query parameters with names q and hl whose values are the location query and the human language of the response. To get a map of 1 Market Street in San Francisco, with a response in German, use the following URL:

```
http://www.google.com/maps?q=1+Market+Street+San+Francisco&hl=de
```

Very long query strings can look unattractive in browsers, and older browsers and proxies have a limit on the number of characters that you can include in a GET request. For that reason, a POST request is often used for forms with a lot of data. In a POST request, you do not attach parameters to a URL; instead, you get an output stream from the URLConnection and write name/value pairs to the output stream. You still have to URL-encode the values and separate them with & characters.

Let us look at this process in detail. To post data to a server-side program, first establish a URLConnection:

```
var url = new URL("http://host/path");
URLConnection connection = url.openConnection();
```

Then, call the setDoOutput method to set up the connection for output:

```
connection.setDoOutput(true);
```

Next, call getOutputStream to get a stream through which you can send data to the server. If you are sending text to the server, it is convenient to wrap that stream into a PrintWriter.

```
var out = new PrintWriter(connection.getOutputStream(), StandardCharsets.UTF_8);
```

Now you are ready to send data to the server:

```
out.print(name1 + "=" + URLEncoder.encode(value1, StandardCharsets.UTF_8) + "&");
out.print(name2 + "=" + URLEncoder.encode(value2, StandardCharsets.UTF_8));
```

Close the output stream:

```
out.close();
```

Finally, call getInputStream and read the server response.

Let's run through a practical example. The web site at https://tools.usps.com /zip-code-lookup.htm?byaddress contains a form to find the zip code for a street address (see Figure 4.7). To use this form in a Java program, you need to know the URL and the parameters of the POST request.

You could get that information by looking at the HTML code of the form, but it is usually easier to "spy" on a request with a network monitor. Most browsers have a network monitor as part of their development toolkit. For example, Figure 4.9 shows a screen capture of the Firefox network monitor when submitting data to our example web site. You can find out the submission URL as well as the parameter names and values.

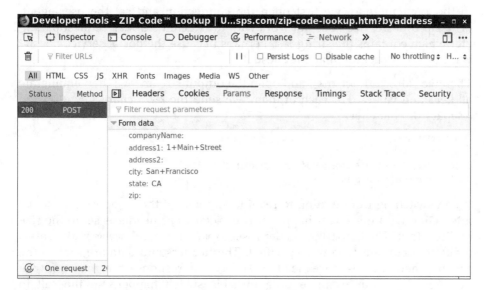

Figure 4.9 Monitoring the submission of a form

When posting form data, the HTTP header includes the content type:

```
Content-Type: application/x-www-form-urlencoded
```

You can also post data in other formats. For example, when sending data in JavaScript Object Notation (JSON), set the content type to application/json.

The header for a POST must also include the content length, for example

```
Content-Length: 124
```

The program in Listing 4.7 sends POST form data to any server-side program. Place the data into a .properties file such as the following:

```
url=https://tools.usps.com/tools/app/ziplookup/zipByAddress
User-Agent=HTTPie/0.9.2
address1=1 Market Street
address2=
city=San Francisco
state=CA
companyName=
. . .
```

The program removes the url and User-Agent entries and sends all others to the doPost method.

In the doPost method, we first open the connection and set the user agent. (The zip code service does not work with the default User-Agent request parameter which contains the string Java, perhaps because the postal service doesn't want to serve programmatic requests.)

Then we call setDoOutput(true), and open the output stream. We then enumerate all keys and values. For each of them, we send the key, = character, value, and & separator character:

```
out.print(key);
out.print('=');
out.print(URLEncoder.encode(value, StandardCharsets.UTF_8));
if (more pairs) out.print('&');
```

When switching from writing to reading any part of the response, the actual interaction with the server happens. The Content-Length header is set to the size of the output. The Content-Type header is set to application/x-www-form-urlencoded unless a different content type was specified. The headers and data are sent to the server. Then the response headers and server response are read and can be queried. In our example program, this switch happens in the call to connection.getContentEncoding().

There is one twist with reading the response. If a server-side error occurs, the call to connection.getInputStream() throws a FileNotFoundException. However, the server still sends an error page back to the browser (such as the ubiquitous "Error 404—page not found"). To capture this error page, call the getErrorStream method:

```
InputStream err = connection.getErrorStream();
```

 NOTE: The getErrorStream method, as well as several other methods in this program, belong to the HttpURLConnection subclass of URLConnection. If you make a request to an URL that starts with http:// or https://, you can cast the resulting connection object to HttpURLConnection.

When you send POST data to a server, it can happen that the server-side program responds with a *redirect*: a different URL that should be called to get the actual information. The server could do that because the information is available elsewhere, or to provide a bookmarkable URL. The HttpURLConnection class can handle redirects in most cases.

NOTE: If cookies need to be sent from one site to another in a redirect, you can configure the global cookie handler like this:

```
CookieHandler.setDefault(new CookieManager(null, CookiePolicy.ACCEPT_ALL));
```

Then cookies will be properly included in the redirect.

Even though redirects are usually automatically handled, there are some situations where you need to do them yourself. Automatic redirects between HTTP and HTTPS are not supported for security reasons. Redirects can also fail for more subtle reasons. For example, an earlier version of the zip code service used a redirect. Recall that we set the User-Agent request parameter so that the post office didn't think we made a request via the Java API. While it is possible to set the user agent to a different string in the initial request, that setting is not used in automatic redirects. Instead, automatic redirects always send a generic user agent string that contains the word Java.

In such situations, you can manually carry out the redirects. Before connecting the server, turn off automatic redirects:

```
connection.setInstanceFollowRedirects(false);
```

After making the request, get the response code:

```
int responseCode = connection.getResponseCode();
```

Check if it is one of

```
HttpURLConnection.HTTP_MOVED_PERM
HttpURLConnection.HTTP_MOVED_TEMP
HttpURLConnection.HTTP_SEE_OTHER
```

In that case, get the Location response header to obtain the URL for the redirect. Then disconnect and make another connection to the new URL:

```
String location = connection.getHeaderField("Location");
if (location != null)
{
   URL base = connection.getURL();
   connection.disconnect();
   connection = (HttpURLConnection) new URL(base, location).openConnection();
   . . .
}
```

The techniques that this program illustrates can be useful whenever you need to query information from an existing web site. Simply find out the parameters that you need to send, and then strip out the HTML tags and other unnecessary information from the reply.

Listing 4.7 post/PostTest.java

```
1  package post;
2
3  import java.io.*;
4  import java.net.*;
5  import java.nio.charset.*;
6  import java.nio.file.*;
7  import java.util.*;
8
9  /**
10  * This program demonstrates how to use the URLConnection class for a POST request.
11  * @version 1.42 2018-03-17
12  * @author Cay Horstmann
13  */
14  public class PostTest
15  {
16     public static void main(String[] args) throws IOException
17     {
18        String propsFilename = args.length > 0 ? args[0] : "post/post.properties";
19        var props = new Properties();
20        try (InputStream in = Files.newInputStream(Paths.get(propsFilename)))
21        {
22           props.load(in);
23        }
24        String urlString = props.remove("url").toString();
25        Object userAgent = props.remove("User-Agent");
26        Object redirects = props.remove("redirects");
27        CookieHandler.setDefault(new CookieManager(null, CookiePolicy.ACCEPT_ALL));
28        String result = doPost(new URL(urlString), props,
29           userAgent == null ? null : userAgent.toString(),
30           redirects == null ? -1 : Integer.parseInt(redirects.toString()));
31        System.out.println(result);
32     }
33
34     /**
35      * Do an HTTP POST.
36      * @param url the URL to post to
37      * @param nameValuePairs the query parameters
38      * @param userAgent the user agent to use, or null for the default user agent
39      * @param redirects the number of redirects to follow manually, or -1 for automatic
40      * redirects
41      * @return the data returned from the server
42      */
43     public static String doPost(URL url, Map<Object, Object> nameValuePairs, String userAgent,
44           int redirects) throws IOException
45     {
46        var connection = (HttpURLConnection) url.openConnection();
47        if (userAgent != null)
48           connection.setRequestProperty("User-Agent", userAgent);
```

```
49
50       if (redirects >= 0)
51          connection.setInstanceFollowRedirects(false);
52
53       connection.setDoOutput(true);
54
55       try (var out = new PrintWriter(connection.getOutputStream()))
56       {
57          var first = true;
58          for (Map.Entry<Object, Object> pair : nameValuePairs.entrySet())
59          {
60             if (first) first = false;
61             else out.print('&');
62             String name = pair.getKey().toString();
63             String value = pair.getValue().toString();
64             out.print(name);
65             out.print('=');
66             out.print(URLEncoder.encode(value, StandardCharsets.UTF_8));
67          }
68       }
69       String encoding = connection.getContentEncoding();
70       if (encoding == null) encoding = "UTF-8";
71
72       if (redirects > 0)
73       {
74          int responseCode = connection.getResponseCode();
75          if (responseCode == HttpURLConnection.HTTP_MOVED_PERM
76                || responseCode == HttpURLConnection.HTTP_MOVED_TEMP
77                || responseCode == HttpURLConnection.HTTP_SEE_OTHER)
78          {
79             String location = connection.getHeaderField("Location");
80             if (location != null)
81             {
82                URL base = connection.getURL();
83                connection.disconnect();
84                return doPost(new URL(base, location), nameValuePairs, userAgent,
85                   redirects - 1);
86             }
87          }
88       }
89       else if (redirects == 0)
90       {
91          throw new IOException("Too many redirects");
92       }
93
94       var response = new StringBuilder();
95       try (var in = new Scanner(connection.getInputStream(), encoding))
96       {
```

(Continues)

Listing 4.7 *(Continued)*

```
 97         while (in.hasNextLine())
 98         {
 99            response.append(in.nextLine());
100            response.append("\n");
101         }
102      }
103      catch (IOException e)
104      {
105         InputStream err = connection.getErrorStream();
106         if (err == null) throw e;
107         try (var in = new Scanner(err))
108         {
109            response.append(in.nextLine());
110            response.append("\n");
111         }
112      }
113
114      return response.toString();
115   }
116 }
```

---

java.net.HttpURLConnection 1.0

- InputStream getErrorStream()

  returns a stream from which you can read web server error messages.

---

java.net.URLEncoder 1.0

- static String encode(String s, String encoding) 1.4

  returns the URL-encoded form of the string s, using the given character encoding scheme. (The recommended scheme is "UTF-8".) In URL encoding, the characters A–Z, a–z, 0–9, - _ . ~ are left unchanged. Space is encoded into +, and all other characters are encoded into sequences of encoded bytes of the form %XY, where 0xXY is the hexadecimal value of the byte.

---

java.net.URLDecoder 1.2

- static string decode(String s, String encoding) 1.4

  returns the decoding of the URL encoded string s under the given character encoding scheme.

4.4 The HTTP Client

The URLConnection class was designed before HTTP was the universal protocol of the Web. It provides support for a number of protocols, but its HTTP support is somewhat cumbersome. When the decision was made to support HTTP/2, it became clear that it would be best to provide a modern client interface instead of reworking the existing API. The HttpClient provides a more convenient API and HTTP/2 support. In Java 9 and 10, the API classes are located in the jdk.incubator.http package, to give the API a chance to evolve as a result of user feedback. As of Java 11, the HttpClient is in the java.net.http package.

 NOTE: With Java 9 and 10, you need to run your program with the command-line option

```
--add-modules jdk.incubator.httpclient
```

The HTTP client API provides a simpler mechanism for connecting to a web server than the URLConnection class with its rather fussy set of stages.

An HttpClient can issue requests and receive responses. You get a client by calling

```
HttpClient client = HttpClient.newHttpClient()
```

Alternatively, if you need to configure the client, you use a builder API, like this:

```
HttpClient client = HttpClient.newBuilder()
    .followRedirects(HttpClient.Redirect.ALWAYS)
    .build();
```

That is, you get a builder, call methods to customize the item that is going to be built, and then call the build method to finalize the building process. This is a common pattern for constructing immutable objects.

You also follow the builder pattern for formulating requests. Here is a GET request:

```
HttpRequest request = HttpRequest.newBuilder()
    .uri(new URI("http://horstmann.com"))
    .GET()
    .build();
```

The URI is the "uniform resource identifier" which is, when using HTTP, the same as a URL. However, in Java, the URL class has methods for actually opening a connection to a URL, whereas the URI class is only concerned with the syntax (scheme, host, port, path, query, fragment, and so on).

With a POST request, you need a "body publisher" that turns the request data into the data that is being posted. There are body publishers for strings, byte arrays, and files. For example, if your request is in JSON, you just provide the JSON string to a string body publisher.

```
HttpRequest request = HttpRequest.newBuilder()
    .uri(new URI(url))
    .header("Content-Type", "application/json")
    .POST(HttpRequest.BodyPublishers.ofString(jsonString))
    .build();
```

It is unfortunate that the API does not support the required formatting for common content types. The sample program in Listing 4.8 provides body publishers for form data and file uploads.

When sending the request, you have to tell the client how to handle the response. If you just want the body as a string, send the request with a HttpResponse.BodyHandlers.ofString(), like this:

```
HttpResponse<String> response = client.send(request, HttpResponse.BodyHandlers.ofString());
```

The HttpResponse class is a generic type whose type parameter denotes the type of the body. You get the response body string simply as

```
String bodyString = response.body();
```

There are other response body handlers that get the response as a byte array or input stream. BodyHandlers.ofFile(filePath) yields a handler that saves the response to the given file, and BodyHandlers.ofFileDownload(directoryPath) saves the response in the given directory, using the file name from the Content-Disposition header. Finally, the handler obtained from BodyHandlers.discarding() simply discards the response.

Processing the contents of the response is not considered part of the API. For example, if you receive JSON data, you need a JSON library to parse the contents.

The HttpResponse object also yields the status code and the response headers.

```
int status = response.statusCode();
HttpHeaders responseHeaders = response.headers();
```

You can turn the HttpHeaders object into a map:

```
Map<String, List<String>> headerMap = responseHeaders.map();
```

The map values are lists since in HTTP, each key can have multiple values.

If you just want the value of a particular key, and you know that there won't be multiple values, call the firstValue method:

```
Optional<String> lastModified = headerMap.firstValue("Last-Modified");
```

You get the response value or an empty optional if none was supplied.

You can process the response asynchronously. When building the client, provide an executor:

```
ExecutorService executor = Executors.newCachedThreadPool();
HttpClient client = HttpClient.newBuilder().executor(executor).build();
```

Build a request and then invoke the sendAsync method on the client. You receive a CompletableFuture<HttpResponse<T>>, where T is the type of the body handler. Use the CompletableFuture API as described in Chapter 12 of Volume I:

```
HttpRequest request = HttpRequest.newBuilder().uri(uri).GET().build();
client.sendAsync(request, HttpResponse.BodyHandlers.ofString())
    thenAccept(response -> . . .);
```

 TIP: To enable logging for the HttpClient, add this line to net.properties in your JDK:

```
jdk.httpclient.HttpClient.log=all
```

Instead of all, you can specify a comma-separated list of headers, requests, content, errors, ssl, trace, and frames, optionally followed by :control, :data, :window, or :all. Don't use any spaces.

Then, set the logging level for the logger with name jdk.httpclient.HttpClient to INFO, for example by adding this line to the logging.properties file in your JDK:

```
jdk.httpclient.HttpClient.level=INFO
```

Listing 4.8 client/HttpClientTest.java

```
1  package client;
2
3  import java.io.*;
4  import java.math.*;
5  import java.net.*;
6  import java.nio.charset.*;
7  import java.nio.file.*;
8  import java.util.*;
9
10 import java.net.http.*;
```

(Continues)

Listing 4.8   *(Continued)*

```java
11  import java.net.http.HttpRequest.*;
12
13  class MoreBodyPublishers
14  {
15     public static BodyPublisher ofFormData(Map<Object, Object> data)
16     {
17        var first = true;
18        var builder = new StringBuilder();
19        for (Map.Entry<Object, Object> entry : data.entrySet())
20        {
21           if (first) first = false;
22           else builder.append("&");
23           builder.append(URLEncoder.encode(entry.getKey().toString(),
24              StandardCharsets.UTF_8));
25           builder.append("=");
26           builder.append(URLEncoder.encode(entry.getValue().toString(),
27              StandardCharsets.UTF_8));
28        }
29        return BodyPublishers.ofString(builder.toString());
30     }
31
32     private static byte[] bytes(String s) { return s.getBytes(StandardCharsets.UTF_8); }
33
34     public static BodyPublisher ofMimeMultipartData(Map<Object, Object> data, String boundary)
35           throws IOException
36     {
37        var byteArrays = new ArrayList<byte[]>();
38        byte[] separator = bytes("--" + boundary + "\nContent-Disposition: form-data; name=");
39        for (Map.Entry<Object, Object> entry : data.entrySet())
40        {
41           byteArrays.add(separator);
42
43           if (entry.getValue() instanceof Path)
44           {
45              var path = (Path) entry.getValue();
46              String mimeType = Files.probeContentType(path);
47              byteArrays.add(bytes("\"" + entry.getKey() + "\"; filename=\"" + path.getFileName()
48                 + "\"\nContent-Type: " + mimeType + "\n\n"));
49              byteArrays.add(Files.readAllBytes(path));
50           }
51           else
52              byteArrays.add(bytes("\"" + entry.getKey() + "\"\n\n" + entry.getValue() + "\n"));
53        }
54        byteArrays.add(bytes("--" + boundary + "--"));
55        return BodyPublishers.ofByteArrays(byteArrays);
56     }
57
```

```
58    public static BodyPublisher ofSimpleJSON(Map<Object, Object> data)
59    {
60       var builder = new StringBuilder();
61       builder.append("{");
62       var first = true;
63       for (Map.Entry<Object, Object> entry : data.entrySet())
64       {
65          if (first) first = false;
66          else
67             builder.append(",");
68          builder.append(jsonEscape(entry.getKey().toString())).append(": ")
69             .append(jsonEscape(entry.getValue().toString()));
70       }
71       builder.append("}");
72       return BodyPublishers.ofString(builder.toString());
73    }
74
75    private static Map<Character, String> replacements = Map.of('\b', "\\b", '\f', "\\f",
76       '\n', "\\n", '\r', "\\r", '\t', "\\t", '"', "\\\"", '\\', "\\\\");
77
78    private static StringBuilder jsonEscape(String str)
79    {
80       var result = new StringBuilder("\"");
81       for (int i = 0; i < str.length(); i++)
82       {
83          char ch = str.charAt(i);
84          String replacement = replacements.get(ch);
85          if (replacement == null) result.append(ch);
86          else result.append(replacement);
87       }
88       result.append("\"");
89       return result;
90    }
91 }
92
93 public class HttpClientTest
94 {
95    public static void main(String[] args)
96          throws IOException, URISyntaxException, InterruptedException
97    {
98       System.setProperty("jdk.httpclient.HttpClient.log", "headers,errors");
99       String propsFilename = args.length > 0 ? args[0] : "client/post.properties";
100      Path propsPath = Paths.get(propsFilename);
101      var props = new Properties();
102      try (InputStream in = Files.newInputStream(propsPath))
103      {
104         props.load(in);
105      }
```

(Continues)

Listing 4.8 *(Continued)*

```
106    String urlString = "" + props.remove("url");
107    String contentType = "" + props.remove("Content-Type");
108    if (contentType.equals("multipart/form-data"))
109    {
110       var generator = new Random();
111       String boundary = new BigInteger(256, generator).toString();
112       contentType += ";boundary=" + boundary;
113       props.replaceAll((k, v) ->
114          v.toString().startsWith("file://")
115             ? propsPath.getParent().resolve(Paths.get(v.toString().substring(7)))
116             : v);
117    }
118    String result = doPost(urlString, contentType, props);
119    System.out.println(result);
120 }
121
122 public static String doPost(String url, String contentType, Map<Object, Object> data)
123       throws IOException, URISyntaxException, InterruptedException
124 {
125    HttpClient client = HttpClient.newBuilder()
126       .followRedirects(HttpClient.Redirect.ALWAYS).build();
127
128    BodyPublisher publisher = null;
129    if (contentType.startsWith("multipart/form-data"))
130    {
131       String boundary = contentType.substring(contentType.lastIndexOf("=") + 1);
132       publisher = MoreBodyPublishers.ofMimeMultipartData(data, boundary);
133    }
134    else if (contentType.equals("application/x-www-form-urlencoded"))
135       publisher = MoreBodyPublishers.ofFormData(data);
136    else
137    {
138       contentType = "application/json";
139       publisher = MoreBodyPublishers.ofSimpleJSON(data);
140    }
141
142    HttpRequest request  = HttpRequest.newBuilder()
143       .uri(new URI(url))
144       .header("Content-Type", contentType)
145       .POST(publisher)
146       .build();
147    HttpResponse<String> response
148       = client.send(request, HttpResponse.BodyHandlers.ofString());
149    return response.body();
150 }
151 }
```

---

java.net.http.HttpClient 11

- static HttpClient newHttpClient()

  yields an HttpClient with a default configuration.

- static HttpClient.Builder newBuilder()

  yields a builder for building an HttpClient.

- `<T>` HttpResponse`<T>` send(HttpRequest request, HttpResponse.BodyHandler`<T>` responseBodyHandler)
- `<T>` CompletableFuture`<HttpResponse<T>>` sendAsync(HttpRequest request, HttpResponse
  .BodyHandler`<T>` responseBodyHandler)

  makes a synchronous or asynchronous request and processes the response body with the given handler.

---

java.net.http.HttpClient.Builder 11

- HttpClient build()

  yields an HttpClient with the properties configured by this builder.

- HttpClient.Builder followRedirects(HttpClient.Redirect policy)

  sets the redirect policy to one of the values ALWAYS, NEVER, or NORMAL (only refuse redirects from HTTPS to HTTP) of the HttpClient.Redirect enumeration.

- HttpClient.Builder executor(Executor executor)

  sets the executor for asynchronous requests.

---

java.net.http.HttpRequest 11

- HttpRequest.Builder newBuilder()

  yields a builder for building an HttpRequest.

---

java.net.http.HttpRequest.Builder 11

- HttpRequest build()

  yields an HttpRequest with the properties configured by this builder.

- HttpRequest.Builder uri(URI uri)

  sets the URI for this request.

- HttpRequest.Builder header(String name, String value)

  sets a request header for this request.

(Continues)

---

java.net.http.HttpRequest.Builder 11 *(Continued)*

- `HttpRequest.Builder GET()`
- `HttpRequest.Builder DELETE()`
- `HttpRequest.Builder POST(HttpRequest.BodyPublisher bodyPublisher)`
- `HttpRequest.Builder PUT(HttpRequest.BodyPublisher bodyPublisher)`

  sets the request method and body for this request.

---

java.net.http.HttpResponse<T> 11

- `T body()`

  yields the body of this response.
- `int statusCode()`

  yields the status code for this response.
- `HttpHeaders headers()`

  yields the response headers.

---

java.net.http.HttpHeaders 11

- `Map<String,List<String>> map()`

  yields a `Map` of these headers.
- `Optional<String> firstValue(String name)`

  the first value with the given name in these headers, if present.

4.5 Sending E-Mail

In the past, it was simple to write a program that sends e-mail by making a socket connection to port 25, the SMTP port, of a mail server. The Simple Mail Transport Protocol (SMTP) describes the format for e-mail messages. Once you are connected to the server, send a mail header (in the SMTP format, which is easy to generate), followed by the mail message.

Here are the details:

1. Open a socket to your host.

    ```
    var s = new Socket("mail.yourserver.com", 25); // 25 is SMTP
    var out = new PrintWriter(s.getOutputStream(), StandardCharsets.UTF_8);
    ```

2. Send the following information to the print stream:

    ```
    HELO sending host
    MAIL FROM: sender e-mail address
    RCPT TO: recipient e-mail address
    DATA
    Subject: subject
    (blank line)
    mail message (any number of lines)
    .
    QUIT
    ```

The SMTP specification (RFC 821) states that lines must be terminated with \r followed by \n.

It used to be that SMTP servers were often willing to route e-mail from anyone. However, in these days of spam floods, most servers have built-in checks and only accept requests from users or IP address ranges that they trust. Authentication usually happens over secure socket connections.

Implementing these authentication schemes manually would be very tedious. Instead, we will show you how to use the JavaMail API to send e-mail from a Java program.

Download JavaMail from www.oracle.com/technetwork/java/javamail and unzip it somewhere on your hard disk.

To use JavaMail, you need to set up some properties that depend on your mail server. For example, with GMail, you use

```
mail.transport.protocol=smtps
mail.smtps.auth=true
mail.smtps.host=smtp.gmail.com
mail.smtps.user=accountname@gmail.com
```

Our sample program reads these from a property file.

For security reasons, we don't put the password into the property file but instead prompt for it.

Read in the property file, then get a mail session like this:

```
Session mailSession = Session.getDefaultInstance(props);
```

Make a message with the desired sender, recipient, subject, and message text:

```
var message = new MimeMessage(mailSession);
message.setFrom(new InternetAddress(from));
message.addRecipient(RecipientType.TO, new InternetAddress(to));
message.setSubject(subject);
message.setText(builder.toString());
```

Then send it off:

```
Transport tr = mailSession.getTransport();
tr.connect(null, password);
tr.sendMessage(message, message.getAllRecipients());
tr.close();
```

The program in Listing 4.9 reads the message from a text file of the format

Sender
Recipient
Subject
Message text (any number of lines)

To run the program, download the JavaMail implementation from `https://javaee` `.github.io/javamail`. You also need the JAR file for the Java Activation Framework—get it from `http://www.oracle.com/technetwork/java/javase/jaf-135115.html` or search on Maven Central. Then run

```
java -classpath .:javax.mail.jar:activation-1.1.1.jar path/to/message.txt
```

At the time of this writing, GMail does not check the veracity of the information—you can supply any sender you like. (Keep this in mind the next time you get an e-mail message from `president@whitehouse.gov` inviting you to a black-tie affair on the front lawn.)

TIP: If you can't figure out why your mail connection isn't working, call

```
mailSession.setDebug(true);
```

and check out the messages. Also, the JavaMail API FAQ has some useful debugging hints.

Listing 4.9 mail/MailTest.java

```
1  package mail;
2
3  import java.io.*;
4  import java.nio.charset.*;
5  import java.nio.file.*;
6  import java.util.*;
7  import javax.mail.*;
8  import javax.mail.internet.*;
9  import javax.mail.internet.MimeMessage.RecipientType;
10
11 /**
12  * This program shows how to use JavaMail to send mail messages.
13  * @author Cay Horstmann
14  * @version 1.01 2018-03-17
```

```
15   */
16   public class MailTest
17   {
18      public static void main(String[] args) throws MessagingException, IOException
19      {
20         var props = new Properties();
21         try (InputStream in = Files.newInputStream(Paths.get("mail", "mail.properties")))
22         {
23            props.load(in);
24         }
25         List<String> lines = Files.readAllLines(Paths.get(args[0]), StandardCharsets.UTF_8);
26
27         String from = lines.get(0);
28         String to = lines.get(1);
29         String subject = lines.get(2);
30
31         var builder = new StringBuilder();
32         for (int i = 3; i < lines.size(); i++)
33         {
34            builder.append(lines.get(i));
35            builder.append("\n");
36         }
37
38         Console console = System.console();
39         var password = new String(console.readPassword("Password: "));
40
41         Session mailSession = Session.getDefaultInstance(props);
42         // mailSession.setDebug(true);
43         var message = new MimeMessage(mailSession);
44         message.setFrom(new InternetAddress(from));
45         message.addRecipient(RecipientType.TO, new InternetAddress(to));
46         message.setSubject(subject);
47         message.setText(builder.toString());
48         Transport tr = mailSession.getTransport();
49         try
50         {
51            tr.connect(null, password);
52            tr.sendMessage(message, message.getAllRecipients());
53         }
54         finally
55         {
56            tr.close();
57         }
58      }
59   }
```

In this chapter, you have seen how to write network clients and servers in Java and how to harvest information from web servers. The next chapter covers database connectivity. You will learn how to work with relational databases in Java, using the JDBC API.

Database Programming

In this chapter

In 1996, Sun released the first version of the JDBC API. This API lets programmers connect to a database to query or update it using the Structured Query Language (SQL). (SQL, usually pronounced "sequel," is an industry standard for relational database access.) JDBC has since become one of the most commonly used APIs in the Java library.

JDBC has been updated several times. As this book is published, JDBC 4.3, the version included with Java 9, is the most current version.

In this chapter, we will explain the key ideas behind JDBC. We will introduce you to (or refresh your memory of) SQL, the industry-standard Structured Query Language for relational databases. We will then provide enough details and examples to let you start using JDBC for common programming situations.

> **NOTE:** According to Oracle, JDBC is a trademarked term and not an acronym for Java Database Connectivity. It was named to be reminiscent of ODBC, a standard database API pioneered by Microsoft and since incorporated into the SQL standard.

5.1 The Design of JDBC

From the start, the developers of the Java technology were aware of the potential that Java showed for working with databases. In 1995, they began work on extending the standard Java library to deal with SQL access to databases. What they first hoped to do was to extend Java so that a program could talk to any random database using only "pure" Java. It didn't take them long to realize that this is an impossible task: There are simply too many databases out there, using too many protocols. Moreover, although database vendors were all in favor of Java providing a standard network protocol for database access, they were only in favor of it if Java used *their* network protocol.

What all the database vendors and tool vendors *did* agree on was that it would be useful for Java to provide a pure Java API for SQL access along with a driver manager to allow third-party drivers to connect to specific databases. Database vendors could provide their own drivers to plug into the driver manager. There would then be a simple mechanism for registering third-party drivers with the driver manager.

This organization follows the very successful model of Microsoft's ODBC which provided a C programming language interface for database access. Both JDBC and ODBC are based on the same idea: Programs written according to the API talk to the driver manager, which, in turn, uses a driver to talk to the actual database.

This means the JDBC API is all that most programmers will ever have to deal with.

5.1.1 JDBC Driver Types

The JDBC specification classifies drivers into the following *types*:

- A *type 1 driver* translates JDBC to ODBC and relies on an ODBC driver to communicate with the database. Early versions of Java included one such driver, the *JDBC/ODBC bridge*. However, the bridge requires deployment and proper configuration of an ODBC driver. When JDBC was first released, the bridge was handy for testing, but it was never intended for production use. At this point, many better drivers are available, and the JDK no longer provides the JDBC/ODBC bridge.

- A *type 2 driver* is written partly in Java and partly in native code; it communicates with the client API of a database. To use such a driver, you must install some platform-specific code onto the client in addition to a Java library.

- A *type 3 driver* is a pure Java client library that uses a database-independent protocol to communicate database requests to a server component, which then translates the requests into a database-specific protocol. This simplifies deployment because the platform-specific code is located only on the server.

- A *type 4 driver* is a pure Java library that translates JDBC requests directly to a database-specific protocol.

NOTE: The JDBC specification is available at https://jcp.org/aboutJava /communityprocess/mrel/jsr221/index3.html.

Most database vendors supply either a type 3 or type 4 driver with their database. Furthermore, a number of third-party companies specialize in producing drivers with better standards conformance, support for more platforms, better performance, or, in some cases, simply better reliability than the drivers provided by the database vendors.

In summary, the ultimate goal of JDBC is to make possible the following:

- Programmers can write applications in the Java programming language to access any database using standard SQL statements (or even specialized extensions of SQL) while still following Java language conventions.

- Database vendors and database tool vendors can supply the low-level drivers. Thus, they can optimize their drivers for their specific products.

NOTE: If you are curious as to why Java just didn't adopt the ODBC model, the reason, as given at the JavaOne conference in 1996, was this:

- ODBC is hard to learn.

- ODBC has a few commands with lots of complex options. The preferred style in the Java programming language is to have simple and intuitive methods, but to have lots of them.

- ODBC relies on the use of void* pointers and other C features that are not natural in the Java programming language.

- An ODBC-based solution is inherently less safe and harder to deploy than a pure Java solution.

5.1.2 Typical Uses of JDBC

The traditional client/server model has a rich GUI on the client and a database on the server (see Figure 5.1). In this model, a JDBC driver is deployed on the client.

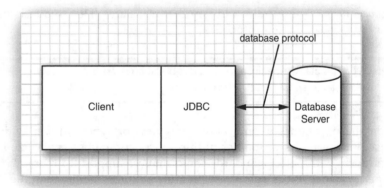

Figure 5.1 A traditional client/server application

However, nowadays it is far more common to have a three-tier model where the client application does not make database calls. Instead, it calls on a middleware layer on the server that in turn makes the database queries. The three-tier model has a couple of advantages. It separates *visual presentation* (on the client) from the *business logic* (in the middle tier) and the raw data (in the database). Therefore, it becomes possible to access the same data and the same business rules from multiple clients, such as a Java desktop application, a web browser, or a mobile app.

Communication between the client and the middle tier typically occurs through HTTP. JDBC manages the communication between the middle tier and the back-end database. Figure 5.2 shows the basic architecture.

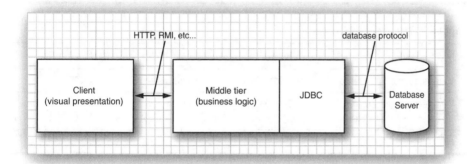

Figure 5.2 A three-tier application

5.2 The Structured Query Language

JDBC lets you communicate with databases using SQL, which is the command language for essentially all modern relational databases. Desktop databases usually have a GUI that lets users manipulate the data directly, but server-based databases are accessed purely through SQL.

The JDBC package can be thought of as nothing more than an API for communicating SQL statements to databases. We will briefly introduce SQL in this section. If you have never seen SQL before, you might not find this material sufficient. If so, turn to one of the many learning resources on the topic; we recommend *Learning SQL* by Alan Beaulieu (O'Reilly, 2009) or the online book *Learn SQL The Hard Way* at http://sql.learncodethehardway.org.

You can think of a database as a bunch of named tables with rows and columns. Each column has a *column name*. Each row contains a set of related data.

As an example database for this book, we use a set of database tables that describe a collection of classic computer science books (see Tables 5.1 through 5.4).

Table 5.1 The Authors Table

Author_ID	Name	Fname
ALEX	Alexander	Christopher
BROO	Brooks	Frederick P.
. . .	. . .	. . .

Table 5.2 The Books Table

Title	ISBN	Publisher_ID	Price
A Guide to the SQL Standard	0-201-96426-0	0201	47.95
A Pattern Language: Towns, Buildings, Construction	0-19-501919-9	019	65.00
. . .	. . .	. . .	. . .

Table 5.3 The BooksAuthors Table

ISBN	Author_ID	Seq_No
0-201-96426-0	DATE	1
0-201-96426-0	DARW	2
0-19-501919-9	ALEX	1
. . .	. . .	. . .

Table 5.4 The Publishers Table

Publisher_ID	Name	URL
0201	Addison-Wesley	www.aw-bc.com
0407	John Wiley & Sons	www.wiley.com
. . .	. . .	. . .

Figure 5.3 shows a view of the Books table. Figure 5.4 shows the result of *joining* this table with the Publishers table. The Books and the Publishers tables each contain an identifier for the publisher. When we join both tables on the publisher code, we obtain a *query result* made up of values from the joined tables. Each

row in the result contains the information about a book, together with the publisher name and web page URL. Note that the publisher names and URLs are duplicated across several rows because we have several books with the same publisher.

Title	ISBN	Publisher_ID	Price
UNIX System Administration Handbook	0-13-020601-6	013	68.00
The C Programming Language	0-13-110362-8	013	42.00
A Pattern Language: Towns, Buildings, Construction	0-19-501919-9	019	65.00
Introduction to Automata Theory, Languages, and Computation	0-201-44124-1	0201	105.00
Design Patterns	0-201-63361-2	0201	54.99
The C++ Programming Language	0-201-70073-5	0201	64.99
The Mythical Man-Month	0-201-83595-9	0201	29.95
Computer Graphics: Principles and Practice	0-201-84840-6	0201	79.99
The Art of Computer Programming vol. 1	0-201-89683-4	0201	59.99
The Art of Computer Programming vol. 2	0-201-89684-2	0201	59.99
The Art of Computer Programming vol. 3	0-201-89685-0	0201	59.99
A Guide to the SQL Standard	0-201-96426-0	0201	47.95
Introduction to Algorithms	0-262-03293-7	0262	80.00
Applied Cryptography	0-471-11709-9	0471	60.00
JavaScript: The Definitive Guide	0-596-00048-0	0596	44.95
The Cathedral and the Bazaar	0-596-00108-8	0596	16.95
The Soul of a New Machine	0-679-60261-5	0679	18.95
The Codebreakers	0-684-83130-9	07434	70.00
Cuckoo's Egg	0-7434-1146-3	07434	13.95
The UNIX Hater"s Handbook	1-56884-203-1	0471	16.95

Record 1   of   20

Figure 5.3 Sample table containing books

The benefit of joining tables is avoiding unnecessary duplication of data in the database tables. For example, a naive database design might have had columns for the publisher name and URL right in the Books table. But then the database itself, and not just the query result, would have many duplicates of these entries. If a publisher's web address changed, *all* entries would need to be updated. Clearly, this is somewhat error-prone. In the relational model, we distribute data into multiple tables so that no information is unnecessarily duplicated. For example, each publisher's URL is contained only once in the publisher table. If the information needs to be combined, the tables are joined.

In the figures, you can see a graphical tool to inspect and link the tables. Many vendors have tools to express queries in a simple form by connecting column names and filling information into forms. Such tools are often called *query by example* (QBE) tools. In contrast, a query that uses SQL is written out in text, using SQL syntax, for example:

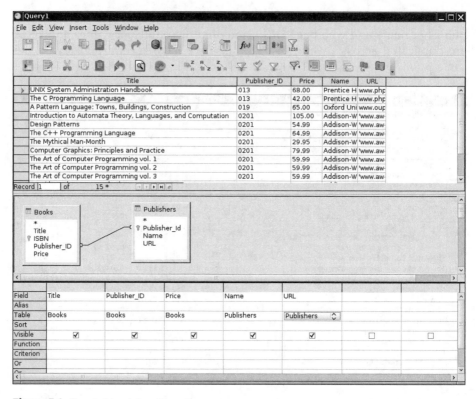

Figure 5.4 Two tables joined together

```
SELECT Books, Books.Publisher_Id, Books.Price, Publishers.Name, Publishers.URL
FROM Books, Publishers
WHERE Books.Publisher_Id = Publishers.Publisher_Id
```

In the remainder of this section, you will learn how to write such queries. If you are already familiar with SQL, just skip this section.

By convention, SQL keywords are written in capital letters, although this is not necessary.

The SELECT statement is quite flexible. You can simply select all rows in the Books table with the following query:

```
SELECT * FROM Books
```

The FROM clause is required in every SQL SELECT statement. It tells the database which tables to examine to find the data.

You can choose the columns that you want:

```
SELECT ISBN, Price, Title
FROM Books
```

You can restrict the rows in the answer with the WHERE clause:

```
SELECT ISBN, Price, Title
FROM Books
WHERE Price <= 29.95
```

Be careful with the "equals" comparison. SQL uses = and <>, rather than == or != as in the Java programming language, for equality testing.

 NOTE: Some database vendors support the use of != for inequality testing. This is not standard SQL, so we recommend against such use.

The WHERE clause can also use pattern matching by means of the LIKE operator. The wildcard characters are not the usual * and ?, however. Use a % for zero or more characters and an underscore for a single character. For example,

```
SELECT ISBN, Price, Title
FROM Books
WHERE Title NOT LIKE '%n_x%'
```

excludes books with titles that contain words such as Unix or Linux.

Note that strings are enclosed in single quotes, not double quotes. A single quote inside a string is represented by a pair of single quotes. For example,

```
SELECT Title
FROM Books
WHERE Title LIKE '%''%'
```

reports all titles that contain a single quote.

You can select data from multiple tables:

```
SELECT * FROM Books, Publishers
```

Without a WHERE clause, this query is not very interesting. It lists *all combinations* of rows from both tables. In our case, where Books has 20 rows and Publishers has 8 rows, the result is a set of rows with 20 × 8 entries and lots of duplications. We really want to constrain the query to say that we are only interested in *matching* books with their publishers:

```
SELECT * FROM Books, Publishers
WHERE Books.Publisher_Id = Publishers.Publisher_Id
```

This query result has 20 rows, one for each book, because each book has one publisher in the Publisher table.

Whenever you have multiple tables in a query, the same column name can occur in two different places. That happened in our example. There is a column called Publisher_Id in both the Books and the Publishers tables. When an ambiguity would otherwise result, you must prefix each column name with the name of the table to which it belongs, such as Books.Publisher_Id.

You can use SQL to change the data inside a database as well. For example, suppose you want to reduce by $5.00 the current price of all books that have "C++" in their title:

```
UPDATE Books
SET Price = Price - 5.00
WHERE Title LIKE '%C++%'
```

Similarly, to delete all C++ books, use a DELETE query:

```
DELETE FROM Books
WHERE Title LIKE '%C++%'
```

SQL comes with built-in functions for taking averages, finding maximums and minimums in a column, and so on, which we do not discuss here.

Typically, to insert values into a table, you can use the INSERT statement:

```
INSERT INTO Books
VALUES ('A Guide to the SQL Standard', '0-201-96426-0', '0201', 47.95)
```

You need a separate INSERT statement for every row being inserted in the table.

Of course, before you can query, modify, and insert data, you must have a place to store data. Use the CREATE TABLE statement to make a new table. Specify the name and data type for each column. For example,

```
CREATE TABLE Books
(
    Title CHAR(60),
    ISBN CHAR(13),
    Publisher_Id CHAR(6),
    Price DECIMAL(10,2)
)
```

Table 5.5 shows the most common SQL data types.

In this book, we do not discuss the additional clauses, such as keys and constraints, that you can use with the CREATE TABLE statement.

Table 5.5 Common SQL Data Types

Data Types	Description
INTEGER or INT	Typically, a 32-bit integer
SMALLINT	Typically, a 16-bit integer
NUMERIC(m,n), DECIMAL(m,n) or DEC(m,n)	Fixed-point decimal number with m total digits and n digits after the decimal point
FLOAT(n)	A floating-point number with n binary digits of precision
REAL	Typically, a 32-bit floating-point number
DOUBLE	Typically, a 64-bit floating-point number
CHARACTER(n) or CHAR(n)	Fixed-length string of length n
VARCHAR(n)	Variable-length strings of maximum length n
BOOLEAN	A Boolean value
DATE	Calendar date, implementation-dependent
TIME	Time of day, implementation-dependent
TIMESTAMP	Date and time of day, implementation-dependent
BLOB	A binary large object
CLOB	A character large object

5.3 JDBC Configuration

Of course, you need a database program for which a JDBC driver is available. There are many excellent choices, such as IBM DB2, Microsoft SQL Server, MySQL, Oracle, and PostgreSQL.

You must also create a database for your experimental use. We assume you name it COREJAVA. Create a new database, or have your database administrator create one with the appropriate permissions. You need to be able to create, update, and drop tables in the database.

If you have never installed a client/server database before, you might find setting up the database to be somewhat complex—diagnosing causes of failure can be difficult. It might be best to seek expert help if your setup is not working correctly.

If this is your first experience with databases, we recommend that you use the Apache Derby database, which is available from http://db.apache.org/derby.

You need to gather a number of items before you can write your first database program. The following sections cover these items.

5.3.1 Database URLs

When connecting to a database, you must use various database-specific parameters such as host names, port numbers, and database names.

JDBC uses a syntax similar to that of ordinary URLs to describe data sources. Here are examples of the syntax:

```
jdbc:derby://localhost:1527/COREJAVA;create=true
jdbc:postgresql:COREJAVA
```

These JDBC URLs specify a Derby database and a PostgreSQL database named COREJAVA.

The general syntax is

```
jdbc:subprotocol:other stuff
```

where a subprotocol selects the specific driver for connecting to the database.

The format for the *other stuff* depends on the subprotocol used. You will need to look up your vendor's documentation for the specific format.

5.3.2 Driver JAR Files

You need to obtain the JAR file in which the driver for your database is located. If you use Derby, you need the file derbyclient.jar. With another database, you need to locate the appropriate driver. For example, the PostgreSQL drivers are available at http://jdbc.postgresql.org.

Include the driver JAR file on the class path when running a program that accesses the database. (You don't need the JAR file for compiling.)

When you launch programs from the command line, simply use the command

```
java -classpath driverPath:. ProgramName
```

On Windows, use a semicolon to separate the current directory (denoted by the . character) from the driver JAR location.

5.3.3 Starting the Database

The database server needs to be started before you can connect to it. The details depend on your database.

With the Derby database, follow these steps:

1. Open a command shell and change to a directory that will hold the database files.

2. Locate the file `derbyrun.jar`. With some versions of the JDK, it is contained in the *jdk/db/lib* directory. If it's not there, install Apache Derby and locate the JAR file in the installation directory. We will denote the directory containing lib/derbyrun.jar with *derby*.

3. Run the command

   ```
   java -jar derby/lib/derbyrun.jar server start
   ```

4. Double-check that the database is working correctly. Create a file `ij.properties` that contains these lines:

   ```
   ij.driver=org.apache.derby.jdbc.ClientDriver
   ij.protocol=jdbc:derby://localhost:1527/
   ij.database=COREJAVA;create=true
   ```

   From another command shell, run Derby's interactive scripting tool (called ij) by executing

   ```
   java -jar derby/lib/derbyrun.jar ij -p ij.properties
   ```

   Now you can issue SQL commands such as

   ```
   CREATE TABLE Greetings (Message CHAR(20));
   INSERT INTO Greetings VALUES ('Hello, World!');
   SELECT * FROM Greetings;
   DROP TABLE Greetings;
   ```

   Note that each command must be terminated by a semicolon. To exit, type

   ```
   EXIT;
   ```

5. When you are done using the database, stop the server with the command

   ```
   java -jar derby/lib/derbyrun.jar server shutdown
   ```

If you use another database, you need to consult the documentation to find out how to start and stop your database server, and how to connect to it and issue SQL commands.

5.3.4 Registering the Driver Class

Many JDBC JAR files (such as the Apache Derby driver) automatically register the driver class. In that case, you can skip the manual registration step that we describe in this section. A JAR file can automatically register the driver class if it contains a file META-INF/services/java.sql.Driver. You can simply unzip your driver's JAR file to check.

If your driver's JAR file doesn't support automatic registration, you need to find out the name of the JDBC driver classes used by your vendor. Typical driver names are

```
org.apache.derby.jdbc.ClientDriver
org.postgresql.Driver
```

There are two ways to register the driver with the DriverManager. One way is to load the driver class in your Java program. For example,

```
Class.forName("org.postgresql.Driver"); // force loading of driver class
```

This statement causes the driver class to be loaded, thereby executing a static initializer that registers the driver.

Alternatively, you can set the jdbc.drivers property. You can specify the property with a command-line argument, such as

```
java -Djdbc.drivers=org.postgresql.Driver ProgramName
```

Or, your application can set the system property with a call such as

```
System.setProperty("jdbc.drivers", "org.postgresql.Driver");
```

You can also supply multiple drivers; separate them with colons, for example:

```
org.postgresql.Driver:org.apache.derby.jdbc.ClientDriver
```

5.3.5 Connecting to the Database

In your Java program, open a database connection like this:

```
String url = "jdbc:postgresql:COREJAVA";
String username = "dbuser";
String password = "secret";
Connection conn = DriverManager.getConnection(url, username, password);
```

The driver manager iterates through the registered drivers to find a driver that can use the subprotocol specified in the database URL.

The getConnection method returns a Connection object. In the following sections, you will see how to use the Connection object to execute SQL statements.

To connect to the database, you will need a user name and password for your database.

 NOTE: By default, Derby lets you connect with any user name, and it does not check passwords. A separate set of tables is generated for each user. The default user name is app.

The test program in Listing 5.1 puts these steps to work. It loads connection parameters from a file named database.properties and connects to the database. The database.properties file supplied with the sample code contains connection information for the Derby database. If you use a different database, put your database-specific connection information into that file. Here is an example for connecting to a PostgreSQL database:

```
jdbc.drivers=org.postgresql.Driver
jdbc.url=jdbc:postgresql:COREJAVA
jdbc.username=dbuser
jdbc.password=secret
```

After connecting to the database, the test program executes the following SQL statements:

```
CREATE TABLE Greetings (Message CHAR(20))
INSERT INTO Greetings VALUES ('Hello, World!')
SELECT * FROM Greetings
```

The result of the SELECT statement is printed, and you should see an output of

```
Hello, World!
```

Then the table is removed by executing the statement

```
DROP TABLE Greetings
```

To run this test, start your database as described previously, and launch the program as

```
java -classpath .:driverJAR test.TestDB
```

(As always, Windows users need to use ; instead of : to separate the path elements.)

 TIP: One way to debug JDBC-related problems is to enable JDBC tracing. Call the DriverManager.setLogWriter method to send trace messages to a PrintWriter. The trace output contains a detailed listing of the JDBC activity. Most JDBC driver implementations provide additional mechanisms for tracing. For example, with Derby, you can add a traceFile option to the JDBC URL: jdbc:derby:// localhost:1527/COREJAVA;create=true;traceFile=trace.out.

---

java.sql.DriverManager 1.1

- static Connection getConnection(String url, String user, String password)

  establishes a connection to the given database and returns a Connection object.

Listing 5.1 test/TestDB.java

```java
1  package test;
2
3  import java.nio.file.*;
4  import java.sql.*;
5  import java.io.*;
6  import java.util.*;
7
8  /**
9   * This program tests that the database and the JDBC driver are correctly configured.
10  * @version 1.03 2018-05-01
11  * @author Cay Horstmann
12  */
13 public class TestDB
14 {
15    public static void main(String args[]) throws IOException
16    {
17       try
18       {
19          runTest();
20       }
21       catch (SQLException ex)
22       {
23          for (Throwable t : ex)
24             t.printStackTrace();
25       }
26    }
27
28    /**
29     * Runs a test by creating a table, adding a value, showing the table contents, and
30     * removing the table.
31     */
32    public static void runTest() throws SQLException, IOException
33    {
34       try (Connection conn = getConnection();
35            Statement stat = conn.createStatement())
36       {
37          stat.executeUpdate("CREATE TABLE Greetings (Message CHAR(20))");
38          stat.executeUpdate("INSERT INTO Greetings VALUES ('Hello, World!')");
39
40          try (ResultSet result = stat.executeQuery("SELECT * FROM Greetings"))
41          {
42             if (result.next())
43                System.out.println(result.getString(1));
44          }
45          stat.executeUpdate("DROP TABLE Greetings");
46       }
47    }
48
```

```
49    /**
50     * Gets a connection from the properties specified in the file database.properties.
51     * @return the database connection
52     */
53    public static Connection getConnection() throws SQLException, IOException
54    {
55       var props = new Properties();
56       try (InputStream in = Files.newInputStream(Paths.get("database.properties")))
57       {
58          props.load(in);
59       }
60       String drivers = props.getProperty("jdbc.drivers");
61       if (drivers != null) System.setProperty("jdbc.drivers", drivers);
62       String url = props.getProperty("jdbc.url");
63       String username = props.getProperty("jdbc.username");
64       String password = props.getProperty("jdbc.password");
65
66       return DriverManager.getConnection(url, username, password);
67    }
68 }
```

5.4 Working with JDBC Statements

In the following sections, you will see how to use the JDBC Statement to execute
SQL statements, obtain results, and deal with errors. Then we show you a
simple program for populating a database.

5.4.1 Executing SQL Statements

To execute a SQL statement, you first create a Statement object. To create
statement objects, use the Connection object that you obtained from the call to
DriverManager.getConnection.

```
Statement stat = conn.createStatement();
```

Next, place the statement that you want to execute into a string, for example:

```
String command = "UPDATE Books"
   + " SET Price = Price - 5.00"
   + " WHERE Title NOT LIKE '%Introduction%'";
```

Then, call the executeUpdate method of the Statement interface:

```
stat.executeUpdate(command);
```

The executeUpdate method returns a count of the rows that were affected by the
SQL statement, or zero for statements that do not return a row count. For

example, the call to executeUpdate in the preceding example returns the number of rows where the price was lowered by $5.00.

The executeUpdate method can execute actions such as INSERT, UPDATE, and DELETE, as well as data definition statements such as CREATE TABLE and DROP TABLE. However, you need to use the executeQuery method to execute SELECT queries. There is also a catch-all execute statement to execute arbitrary SQL statements. It's commonly used only for queries that a user supplies interactively.

When you execute a query, you are interested in the result. The executeQuery object returns an object of type ResultSet that you can use to walk through the result one row at a time.

```
ResultSet rs = stat.executeQuery("SELECT * FROM Books");
```

The basic loop for analyzing a result set looks like this:

```
while (rs.next())
{
    look at a row of the result set
}
```

 CAUTION: The iteration protocol of the ResultSet interface is subtly different from that of the java.util.Iterator interface. Here, the iterator is initialized to a position *before* the first row. You must call the next method once to move the iterator to the first row. Also, there is no hasNext method; keep calling next until it returns false.

The order of the rows in a result set is completely arbitrary. Unless you specifically ordered the result with an ORDER BY clause, you should not attach any significance to the row order.

When inspecting an individual row, you will want to know the contents of the fields. A large number of accessor methods give you this information.

```
String isbn = rs.getString(1);
double price = rs.getDouble("Price");
```

There are accessors for various *types*, such as getString and getDouble. Each accessor has two forms, one taking a numeric argument, and the other, a string argument. When you supply a numeric argument, you refer to the column with that number. For example, rs.getString(1) returns the value of the first column in the current row.

 CAUTION: Unlike array indexes, database column numbers start at 1.

When you supply a string argument, you refer to the column in the result set with that name. For example, rs.getDouble("Price") returns the value of the column with label Price. Using the numeric argument is a bit more efficient, but string arguments make the code easier to read and maintain.

Each get method makes reasonable type conversions when the type of the method doesn't match the type of the column. For example, the call rs.getString("Price") converts the floating-point value of the Price column to a string.

---

java.sql.Connection 1.1

- Statement createStatement()

  creates a Statement object that can be used to execute SQL queries and updates without parameters.

- void close()

  immediately closes the current connection and the JDBC resources that it created.

---

java.sql.Statement 1.1

- ResultSet executeQuery(String sqlQuery)

  executes the SQL statement given in the string and returns a ResultSet object to view the query result.

- int executeUpdate(String sqlStatement)
- long executeLargeUpdate(String sqlStatement) 8

  executes the SQL INSERT, UPDATE, or DELETE statement specified by the string. Also executes Data Definition Language (DDL) statements such as CREATE TABLE. Returns the number of rows affected, or 0 for a statement without an update count.

- boolean execute(String sqlStatement)

  executes the SQL statement specified by the string. Multiple result sets and update counts may be produced. Returns true if the first result is a result set, false otherwise. Call getResultSet or getUpdateCount to retrieve the first result. See Section 5.5.4, "Multiple Results," on p. 321 for details on processing multiple results.

(Continues)

---

java.sql.Statement 1.1 *(Continued)*

- ResultSet getResultSet()

  returns the result set of the preceding query statement, or null if the preceding statement did not have a result set. Call this method only once per executed statement.

- int getUpdateCount()
- long getLargeUpdateCount() 8

  returns the number of rows affected by the preceding update statement, or -1 if the preceding statement was a statement without an update count. Call this method only once per executed statement.

- void close()

  closes this statement object and its associated result set.

- boolean isClosed() 6

  returns true if this statement is closed.

- void closeOnCompletion() 7

  causes this statement to be closed once all of its result sets have been closed.

---

java.sql.ResultSet 1.1

- boolean next()

  makes the current row in the result set move forward by one. Returns false after the last row. Note that you must call this method to advance to the first row.

- *Xxx* get*Xxx*(int columnNumber)
- *Xxx* get*Xxx*(String columnLabel)

  (*Xxx* is a type such as int, double, String, Date, etc.)

- <T> T getObject(int columnIndex, Class<T> type) 7
- <T> T getObject(String columnLabel, Class<T> type) 7
- void updateObject(int columnIndex, Object x, SQLType targetSqlType) 8
- void updateObject(String columnLabel, Object x, SQLType targetSqlType) 8

  returns or updates the value of the column with the given column index or label, converted to the specified type. The column label is the label specified in the SQL AS clause or the column name if AS is not used.

- int findColumn(String columnName)

  gives the column index associated with a column name.

---

java.sql.ResultSet 1.1 *(Continued)*

- void close()

  immediately closes the current result set.
- boolean isClosed() 6

  returns true if this statement is closed.

5.4.2 Managing Connections, Statements, and Result Sets

Every Connection object can create one or more Statement objects. You can use the same Statement object for multiple unrelated commands and queries. However, a statement has *at most one* open result set. If you issue multiple queries whose results you analyze concurrently, you need multiple Statement objects.

Be forewarned, though, that there is a limit to the number of statements per connection. Use the getMaxStatements method of the DatabaseMetaData interface to find out the number of concurrently open statements that your JDBC driver supports.

In practice, you should probably not fuss with multiple concurrent result sets. If the result sets are related, you should be able to issue a combined query and analyze a single result. It is much more efficient to let the database combine queries than it is for a Java program to iterate through multiple result sets.

Be sure to finish processing of any result set before you issue a new query or update on a Statement object. The result sets of prior queries are automatically closed.

When you are done using a ResultSet, Statement, or Connection, it is a good idea to call the close method immediately. These objects use large data structures that draw on the finite resources of the database server.

The close method of a Statement object closes any associated result sets. Similarly, the close method of the Connection class closes all statements of the connection.

Conversely, you can call the closeOnCompletion method on a Statement, and it will close automatically as soon as all its result sets have closed.

If your connections are short-lived, don't worry about closing statements and result sets. To make sure a connection object cannot possibly remain open, use a try-with-resources statement:

```
try (Connection conn = . . .)
{
   Statement stat = conn.createStatement();
   ResultSet result = stat.executeQuery(queryString);
   process query result
}
```

5.4.3 Analyzing SQL Exceptions

Each SQLException has a chain of SQLException objects that are retrieved with the
getNextException method. This exception chain is in addition to the "cause" chain
of Throwable objects that every exception has. (See Volume I, Chapter 7 for details about Java exceptions.) One would need two nested loops to fully enumerate all these exceptions. Fortunately, the SQLException class has been enhanced
to implement the Iterable<Throwable> interface. The iterator() method yields an
Iterator<Throwable> that iterates through both chains: It starts by going through
the cause chain of the first SQLException, then moves on to the next SQLException,
and so on. You can simply use an enhanced for loop:

```
for (Throwable t : sqlException)
{
   do something with t
}
```

You can call getSQLState and getErrorCode on a SQLException to analyze it further. The
first method yields a string that is standardized by either X/Open or SQL:2003.
(Call the getSQLStateType method of the DatabaseMetaData interface to find out which
standard is used by your driver.) The error code is vendor-specific.

The SQL exceptions are organized into an inheritance tree (shown in
Figure 5.5). This allows you to catch specific error types in a vendor-
independent way.

In addition, the database driver can report nonfatal conditions as warnings.
You can retrieve warnings from connections, statements, and result sets. The
SQLWarning class is a subclass of SQLException (even though a SQLWarning is not thrown
as an exception). Call getSQLState and getErrorCode to get further information about
the warnings. Similar to SQL exceptions, warnings are chained. To retrieve
all warnings, use this loop:

```
SQLWarning w = stat.getWarning();
while (w != null)
{
   do something with w
   w = w.nextWarning();
}
```

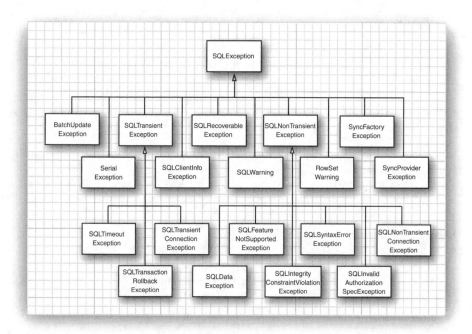

Figure 5.5 SQL exception types

The DataTruncation subclass of SQLWarning is used when data being read from the database are unexpectedly truncated. If data truncation happens in an update statement, a DataTruncation is thrown as an exception.

---

java.sql.SQLException 1.1

- SQLException getNextException()

  gets the next SQL exception chained to this one, or null at the end of the chain.

- Iterator<Throwable> iterator() 6

  gets an iterator that yields the chained SQL exceptions and their causes.

- String getSQLState()

  gets the "SQL state"—a standardized error code.

- int getErrorCode()

  gets the vendor-specific error code.

---

java.sql.SQLWarning 1.1

- SQLWarning getNextWarning()

  returns the next warning chained to this one, or null at the end of the chain.

---

java.sql.Connection 1.1
java.sql.Statement 1.1
java.sql.ResultSet 1.1

- SQLWarning getWarnings()

  returns the first of the pending warnings, or null if no warnings are pending.

---

java.sql.DataTruncation 1.1

- boolean getParameter()

  returns true if the data truncation applies to a parameter, false if it applies to a column.

- int getIndex()

  returns the index of the truncated parameter or column.

- int getDataSize()

  returns the number of bytes that should have been transferred, or -1 if the value is unknown.

- int getTransferSize()

  returns the number of bytes that were actually transferred, or -1 if the value is unknown.

5.4.4 Populating a Database

We are now ready to write our first real JDBC program. Sure, it would be nice to try some of the fancy queries discussed earlier, but we have a problem: Right now, there are no data in the database. We need to populate the database, and a simple way of doing that is with a set of SQL instructions to create tables and insert data into them. Most database programs can process a set of SQL instructions from a text file, but there are pesky differences about statement terminators and other syntactical issues.

For that reason, we will use JDBC in a simple program that reads a file with SQL instructions, one instruction per line, and executes them.

Specifically, the program reads data from a text file in a format such as

```
CREATE TABLE Publishers (Publisher_Id CHAR(6), Name CHAR(30), URL CHAR(80));
INSERT INTO Publishers VALUES ('0201', 'Addison-Wesley', 'www.aw-bc.com');
INSERT INTO Publishers VALUES ('0471', 'John Wiley & Sons', 'www.wiley.com');
. . .
```

Listing 5.2 contains the code for the program that reads a file with SQL statements and executes them. You don't have to read through the code; simply use the program so you can populate your database and run the examples in the remainder of this chapter.

Make sure that your database server is running, and run the program as follows:

```
java -classpath driverPath:. exec.ExecSQL Books.sql
java -classpath driverPath:. exec.ExecSQL Authors.sql
java -classpath driverPath:. exec.ExecSQL Publishers.sql
java -classpath driverPath:. exec.ExecSQL BooksAuthors.sql
```

Before running the program, check that the file database.properties is set up properly for your environment (see Section 5.3.5, "Connecting to the Database," on p. 296).

 NOTE: Your database may also have a utility to read SQL files directly. For example, with Derby, you can run

```
java -jar derby/lib/derbyrun.jar ij -p ij.properties Books.sql
```

(The ij.properties file is described in Section 5.3.3, "Starting the Database," on p. 294.)

In the data format for the ExecSQL command, we allow an optional semicolon at the end of each line because most database utilities expect this format.

The following steps briefly describe the ExecSQL program:

1. Connect to the database. The getConnection method reads the properties in the file database.properties and adds the jdbc.drivers property to the system properties. The driver manager uses the jdbc.drivers property to load the appropriate database driver. The getConnection method uses the jdbc.url, jdbc.username, and jdbc.password properties to open the database connection.

2. Open the file with the SQL statements. If no file name was supplied, prompt the user to enter the statements on the console.

3. Execute each statement with the generic execute method. If it returns true, the statement had a result set. The four SQL files that we provide for the book database all end in a SELECT * statement so that you can see that the data were successfully inserted.

4. If there was a result set, print out the result. Since this is a generic result set, we need to use metadata to find out how many columns the result has. For more information, see Section 5.8, "Metadata," on p. 334.

5. If there is any SQL exception, print the exception and any chained exceptions that may be contained in it.

6. Close the connection to the database.

Listing 5.2 shows the code for the program.

Listing 5.2 exec/ExecSQL.java

```
1  package exec;
2
3  import java.io.*;
4  import java.nio.charset.*;
5  import java.nio.file.*;
6  import java.util.*;
7  import java.sql.*;
8
9  /**
10  * Executes all SQL statements in a file. Call this program as <br>
11  * java -classpath driverPath:. ExecSQL commandFile
12  *
13  * @version 1.33 2018-05-01
14  * @author Cay Horstmann
15  */
16  class ExecSQL
17  {
18     public static void main(String args[]) throws IOException
19     {
20        try (Scanner in = args.length == 0 ? new Scanner(System.in)
21              : new Scanner(Paths.get(args[0]), StandardCharsets.UTF_8))
22        {
23           try (Connection conn = getConnection();
24                Statement stat = conn.createStatement())
25           {
26              while (true)
27              {
28                 if (args.length == 0) System.out.println("Enter command or EXIT to exit:");
29
30                 if (!in.hasNextLine()) return;
31
32                 String line = in.nextLine().trim();
33                 if (line.equalsIgnoreCase("EXIT")) return;
34                 if (line.endsWith(";")) // remove trailing semicolon
35                    line = line.substring(0, line.length() - 1);
36                 try
37                 {
```

```
38                    boolean isResult = stat.execute(line);
39                    if (isResult)
40                    {
41                       try (ResultSet rs = stat.getResultSet())
42                       {
43                          showResultSet(rs);
44                       }
45                    }
46                    else
47                    {
48                       int updateCount = stat.getUpdateCount();
49                       System.out.println(updateCount + " rows updated");
50                    }
51                 }
52                 catch (SQLException e)
53                 {
54                    for (Throwable t : e)
55                       t.printStackTrace();
56                 }
57              }
58           }
59        }
60        catch (SQLException e)
61        {
62           for (Throwable t : e)
63              t.printStackTrace();
64        }
65     }
66
67     /**
68      * Gets a connection from the properties specified in the file database.properties
69      * @return the database connection
70      */
71     public static Connection getConnection() throws SQLException, IOException
72     {
73        var props = new Properties();
74        try (InputStream in = Files.newInputStream(Paths.get("database.properties")))
75        {
76           props.load(in);
77        }
78        String drivers = props.getProperty("jdbc.drivers");
79        if (drivers != null) System.setProperty("jdbc.drivers", drivers);
80
81        String url = props.getProperty("jdbc.url");
82        String username = props.getProperty("jdbc.username");
83        String password = props.getProperty("jdbc.password");
84
85        return DriverManager.getConnection(url, username, password);
86     }
```

(Continues)

Listing 5.2 *(Continued)*

```
87
88    /**
89     * Prints a result set.
90     * @param result the result set to be printed
91     */
92    public static void showResultSet(ResultSet result) throws SQLException
93    {
94       ResultSetMetaData metaData = result.getMetaData();
95       int columnCount = metaData.getColumnCount();
96
97       for (int i = 1; i <= columnCount; i++)
98       {
99          if (i > 1) System.out.print(", ");
100         System.out.print(metaData.getColumnLabel(i));
101      }
102      System.out.println();
103
104      while (result.next())
105      {
106         for (int i = 1; i <= columnCount; i++)
107         {
108            if (i > 1) System.out.print(", ");
109            System.out.print(result.getString(i));
110         }
111         System.out.println();
112      }
113   }
114 }
```

5.5 Query Execution

In this section, we write a program that executes queries against the COREJAVA
database. For this program to work, you must have a COREJAVA database
populated with tables as described in the preceding section.

When querying the database, you can select the author and the publisher or
leave either of them as Any.

You can also change the data in the database. Select a publisher and type an
amount. All prices of that publisher are adjusted by the amount you entered,
and the program displays how many rows were changed. After a price change,
you might want to run a query to verify the new prices.

5.5.1 Prepared Statements

In this program, we use one new feature, *prepared statements*. Consider the SQL query for all books by a particular publisher, regardless of the author:

```
SELECT Books.Price, Books
FROM Books, Publishers
WHERE Books.Publisher_Id = Publishers.Publisher_Id
AND Publishers.Name = the name from the list box
```

Instead of building a separate query statement every time the user launches such a query, we can *prepare* a query with a host variable and use it many times, each time filling in a different string for the variable. That technique improves performance. Whenever the database executes a query, it first computes a strategy of how to do it efficiently. By preparing the query and reusing it, you ensure that the planning step is done only once.

Each host variable in a prepared query is indicated with a ?. If there is more than one variable, you must keep track of the positions of the ? when setting the values. For example, our prepared query becomes

```
String publisherQuery
   = "SELECT Books.Price, Books"
   + " FROM Books, Publishers"
   + " WHERE Books.Publisher_Id = Publishers.Publisher_Id AND Publishers.Name = ?";
PreparedStatement stat = conn.prepareStatement(publisherQuery);
```

Before executing the prepared statement, you must bind the host variables to actual values with a set method. As with the get methods of the ResultSet interface, there are different set methods for the various types. Here, we want to set a string to a publisher name:

```
stat.setString(1, publisher);
```

The first argument is the position number of the host variable that we want to set. The position 1 denotes the first ?. The second argument is the value that we want to assign to the host variable.

If you reuse a prepared query that you have already executed, all host variables stay bound unless you change them with a set method or call the clearParameters method. That means you only need to call a set*Xxx* method on those host variables that change from one query to the next.

Once all variables have been bound to values, you can execute the prepared statement:

```
ResultSet rs = stat.executeQuery();
```

TIP: Building a query manually, by concatenating strings, is tedious and potentially dangerous. You have to worry about special characters such as quotes—and, if your query involves user input, you have to guard against injection attacks. Therefore, use prepared statements whenever your query involves variables.

The price update feature is implemented as an UPDATE statement. Note that we call executeUpdate, not executeQuery, because the UPDATE statement does not return a result set. The return value of executeUpdate is the count of changed rows.

```
int r = stat.executeUpdate();
System.out.println(r + " rows updated");
```

 NOTE: A PreparedStatement object becomes invalid after the associated Connection object is closed. However, many databases automatically *cache* prepared statements. If the same query is prepared twice, the database simply reuses the query strategy. Therefore, don't worry about the overhead of calling prepareStatement.

The following list briefly describes the structure of the example program:

- The author and publisher array lists are populated by running two queries that return all author and publisher names in the database.
- The queries involving authors are complex. A book can have multiple authors, so the BooksAuthors table stores the correspondence between authors and books. For example, the book with ISBN 0-201-96426-0 has two authors with codes DATE and DARW. The BooksAuthors table has the rows

```
0-201-96426-0, DATE, 1
0-201-96426-0, DARW, 2
```

to indicate this fact. The third column lists the order of the authors. (We can't just use the position of the rows in the table. There is no fixed row ordering in a relational table.) Thus, the query has to join the Books, BooksAuthors, and Authors tables to compare the author name with the one selected by the user.

```
SELECT Books.Price, Books FROM Books, BooksAuthors, Authors, Publishers
WHERE Authors.Author_Id = BooksAuthors.Author_Id AND BooksAuthors.ISBN = Books.ISBN
AND Books.Publisher_Id = Publishers.Publisher_Id AND Authors.Name = ?
AND Publishers.Name = ?
```

TIP: Some Java programmers avoid complex SQL statements such as this one. A surprisingly common, but very inefficient, workaround is to write lots of Java code that iterates through multiple result sets. But the database is *a lot* better at executing query code than a Java program can be—that's the core competency of a database. A rule of thumb: If you can do it in SQL, don't do it in Java.

- The changePrices method executes an UPDATE statement. Note that the WHERE clause of the UPDATE statement needs the publisher *code* and we only know the publisher *name*. This problem is solved with a nested subquery:

```
UPDATE Books
SET Price = Price + ?
WHERE Books.Publisher_Id = (SELECT Publisher_Id FROM Publishers WHERE Name = ?)
```

Listing 5.3 is the complete program code.

Listing 5.3 query/QueryTest.java

```
1  package query;
2
3  import java.io.*;
4  import java.nio.file.*;
5  import java.sql.*;
6  import java.util.*;
7
8  /**
9   * This program demonstrates several complex database queries.
10  * @version 1.31 2018-05-01
11  * @author Cay Horstmann
12  */
13 public class QueryTest
14 {
15    private static final String allQuery = "SELECT Books.Price, Books.Title FROM Books";
16
17    private static final String authorPublisherQuery = "SELECT Books.Price, Books.Title"
18       + " FROM Books, BooksAuthors, Authors, Publishers"
19       + " WHERE Authors.Author_Id = BooksAuthors.Author_Id AND BooksAuthors.ISBN = Books.ISBN"
20       + " AND Books.Publisher_Id = Publishers.Publisher_Id AND Authors.Name = ?"
21       + " AND Publishers.Name = ?";
22
23    private static final String authorQuery
24       = "SELECT Books.Price, Books.Title FROM Books, BooksAuthors, Authors"
25       + " WHERE Authors.Author_Id = BooksAuthors.Author_Id"
26       + " AND BooksAuthors.ISBN = Books.ISBN"
27       + " AND Authors.Name = ?";
28
```

(Continues)

Listing 5.3 *(Continued)*

```java
29   private static final String publisherQuery
30      = "SELECT Books.Price, Books.Title FROM Books, Publishers"
31      + " WHERE Books.Publisher_Id = Publishers.Publisher_Id AND Publishers.Name = ?";
32
33   private static final String priceUpdate = "UPDATE Books SET Price = Price + ? "
34      + " WHERE Books.Publisher_Id = (SELECT Publisher_Id FROM Publishers WHERE Name = ?)";
35
36   private static Scanner in;
37   private static ArrayList<String> authors = new ArrayList<>();
38   private static ArrayList<String> publishers = new ArrayList<>();
39
40   public static void main(String[] args) throws IOException
41   {
42      try (Connection conn = getConnection())
43      {
44         in = new Scanner(System.in);
45         authors.add("Any");
46         publishers.add("Any");
47         try (Statement stat = conn.createStatement())
48         {
49            // Fill the authors array list
50            var query = "SELECT Name FROM Authors";
51            try (ResultSet rs = stat.executeQuery(query))
52            {
53               while (rs.next())
54                  authors.add(rs.getString(1));
55            }
56
57            // Fill the publishers array list
58            query = "SELECT Name FROM Publishers";
59            try (ResultSet rs = stat.executeQuery(query))
60            {
61               while (rs.next())
62                  publishers.add(rs.getString(1));
63            }
64         }
65         var done = false;
66         while (!done)
67         {
68            System.out.print("Q)uery C)hange prices E)xit: ");
69            String input = in.next().toUpperCase();
70            if (input.equals("Q"))
71               executeQuery(conn);
72            else if (input.equals("C"))
73               changePrices(conn);
74            else
75               done = true;
76         }
```

```
77          }
78          catch (SQLException e)
79          {
80             for (Throwable t : e)
81                System.out.println(t.getMessage());
82          }
83       }
84
85       /**
86        * Executes the selected query.
87        * @param conn the database connection
88        */
89       private static void executeQuery(Connection conn) throws SQLException
90       {
91          String author = select("Authors:", authors);
92          String publisher = select("Publishers:", publishers);
93          PreparedStatement stat;
94          if (!author.equals("Any") && !publisher.equals("Any"))
95          {
96             stat = conn.prepareStatement(authorPublisherQuery);
97             stat.setString(1, author);
98             stat.setString(2, publisher);
99          }
100         else if (!author.equals("Any") && publisher.equals("Any"))
101         {
102             stat = conn.prepareStatement(authorQuery);
103             stat.setString(1, author);
104         }
105         else if (author.equals("Any") && !publisher.equals("Any"))
106         {
107             stat = conn.prepareStatement(publisherQuery);
108             stat.setString(1, publisher);
109         }
110         else
111             stat = conn.prepareStatement(allQuery);
112
113         try (ResultSet rs = stat.executeQuery())
114         {
115             while (rs.next())
116                System.out.println(rs.getString(1) + ", " + rs.getString(2));
117         }
118      }
119
120      /**
121       * Executes an update statement to change prices.
122       * @param conn the database connection
123       */
```

(Continues)

Listing 5.3 *(Continued)*

```java
124   public static void changePrices(Connection conn) throws SQLException
125   {
126      String publisher = select("Publishers:", publishers.subList(1, publishers.size()));
127      System.out.print("Change prices by: ");
128      double priceChange = in.nextDouble();
129      PreparedStatement stat = conn.prepareStatement(priceUpdate);
130      stat.setDouble(1, priceChange);
131      stat.setString(2, publisher);
132      int r = stat.executeUpdate();
133      System.out.println(r + " records updated.");
134   }
135
136   /**
137    * Asks the user to select a string.
138    * @param prompt the prompt to display
139    * @param options the options from which the user can choose
140    * @return the option that the user chose
141    */
142   public static String select(String prompt, List<String> options)
143   {
144      while (true)
145      {
146         System.out.println(prompt);
147         for (int i = 0; i < options.size(); i++)
148            System.out.printf("%2d) %s%n", i + 1, options.get(i));
149         int sel = in.nextInt();
150         if (sel > 0 && sel <= options.size())
151            return options.get(sel - 1);
152      }
153   }
154
155   /**
156    * Gets a connection from the properties specified in the file database.properties.
157    * @return the database connection
158    */
159   public static Connection getConnection() throws SQLException, IOException
160   {
161      var props = new Properties();
162      try (InputStream in = Files.newInputStream(Paths.get("database.properties")))
163      {
164         props.load(in);
165      }
166
167      String drivers = props.getProperty("jdbc.drivers");
168      if (drivers != null) System.setProperty("jdbc.drivers", drivers);
169
```

```
170     String url = props.getProperty("jdbc.url");
171     String username = props.getProperty("jdbc.username");
172     String password = props.getProperty("jdbc.password");
173
174     return DriverManager.getConnection(url, username, password);
175   }
176 }
```

---

java.sql.Connection 1.1

- PreparedStatement prepareStatement(String sql)

  returns a PreparedStatement object containing the precompiled statement. The string sql contains a SQL statement with one or more parameter placeholders denoted by ? characters.

---

java.sql.PreparedStatement 1.1

- void set*Xxx*(int n, *Xxx* x)

  (*Xxx* is a type such as int, double, String, Date, etc.)

  sets the value of the nth parameter to x.

- void clearParameters()

  clears all current parameters in the prepared statement.

- ResultSet executeQuery()

  executes a prepared SQL query and returns a ResultSet object.

- int executeUpdate()

  executes the prepared SQL INSERT, UPDATE, or DELETE statement represented by the PreparedStatement object. Returns the number of rows affected, or 0 for DDL statements such as CREATE TABLE.

5.5.2 Reading and Writing LOBs

In addition to numbers, strings, and dates, many databases can store *large objects* (LOBs) such as images or other data. In SQL, binary large objects are called BLOBs, and character large objects are called CLOBs.

To read a LOB, execute a SELECT statement and call the getBlob or getClob method on the ResultSet. You will get an object of type Blob or Clob. To get the binary data from a Blob, call the getBytes or getBinaryStream. For example, if you have a table with book cover images, you can retrieve an image like this:

```
PreparedStatement stat = conn.prepareStatement("SELECT Cover FROM BookCovers WHERE ISBN=?");
. . .
stat.set(1, isbn);
try (ResultSet result = stat.executeQuery())
{
   if (result.next())
   {
      Blob coverBlob = result.getBlob(1);
      Image coverImage = ImageIO.read(coverBlob.getBinaryStream());
   }
}
```

Similarly, if you retrieve a Clob object, you can get character data by calling the getSubString or getCharacterStream method.

To place a LOB into a database, call createBlob or createClob on your Connection object, get an output stream or writer to the LOB, write the data, and store the object in the database. For example, here is how you store an image:

```
Blob coverBlob = connection.createBlob();
int offset = 0;
OutputStream out = coverBlob.setBinaryStream(offset);
ImageIO.write(coverImage, "PNG", out);
PreparedStatement stat = conn.prepareStatement("INSERT INTO Cover VALUES (?, ?)");
stat.set(1, isbn);
stat.set(2, coverBlob);
stat.executeUpdate();
```

---

java.sql.ResultSet 1.1

- Blob getBlob(int columnIndex) 1.2
- Blob getBlob(String columnLabel) 1.2
- Clob getClob(int columnIndex) 1.2
- Clob getClob(String columnLabel) 1.2

   gets the BLOB or CLOB at the given column.

---

java.sql.Blob 1.2

- long length()

   gets the length of this BLOB.

- byte[] getBytes(long startPosition, long length)

   gets the data in the given range from this BLOB.

(Continues)

---

java.sql.Blob 1.2 *(Continued)*

- InputStream getBinaryStream()
- InputStream getBinaryStream(long startPosition, long length)

  returns a stream to read the data from this BLOB or from the given range.

- OutputStream setBinaryStream(long startPosition) 1.4

  returns an output stream for writing into this BLOB, starting at the given position.

---

java.sql.Clob 1.4

- long length()

  gets the number of characters of this CLOB.

- String getSubString(long startPosition, long length)

  gets the characters in the given range from this CLOB.

- Reader getCharacterStream()
- Reader getCharacterStream(long startPosition, long length)

  returns a reader (not a stream) to read the characters from this CLOB or from the given range.

- Writer setCharacterStream(long startPosition) 1.4

  returns a writer (not a stream) for writing into this CLOB, starting at the given position.

---

java.sql.Connection 1.1

- Blob createBlob() 6
- Clob createClob() 6

  creates an empty BLOB or CLOB.

5.5.3 SQL Escapes

The "escape" syntax features are commonly supported by databases but use database-specific syntax variations. It is the job of the JDBC driver to translate the escape syntax to the syntax of a particular database.

Escapes are provided for the following features:

- Date and time literals
- Calling scalar functions

- Calling stored procedures
- Outer joins
- The escape character in LIKE clauses

Date and time literals vary widely among databases. To embed a date or time literal, specify the value in the ISO 8601 format (www.cl.cam.ac.uk/~mgk25/iso-time.html). The driver will then translate it into the native format. Use d, t, ts for DATE, TIME, or TIMESTAMP values:

```
{d '2008-01-24'}
{t '23:59:59'}
{ts '2008-01-24 23:59:59.999'}
```

A *scalar function* is a function that returns a single value. Many functions are widely available in databases, but with varying names. The JDBC specification provides standard names and translates them into the database-specific names. To call a function, embed the standard function name and arguments like this:

```
{fn left(?, 20)}
{fn user()}
```

You can find a complete list of supported function names in the JDBC specification.

A *stored procedure* is a procedure that executes in the database, written in a database-specific language. To call a stored procedure, use the call escape. You need not supply parentheses if the procedure has no parameters. Use = to capture a return value:

```
{call PROC1(?, ?)}
{call PROC2}
{call ? = PROC3(?)}
```

An *outer join* of two tables does not require that the rows of each table match according to the join condition. For example, the query

```
SELECT * FROM {oj Books LEFT OUTER JOIN Publishers
ON Books.Publisher_Id = Publisher.Publisher_Id}
```

contains books for which Publisher_Id has no match in the Publishers table, with NULL values to indicate that no match exists. You would need a RIGHT OUTER JOIN to include publishers without matching books, or a FULL OUTER JOIN to return both. The escape syntax is needed because not all databases use a standard notation for these joins.

Finally, the _ and % characters have special meanings in a LIKE clause—to match a single character or a sequence of characters. There is no standard way to use them literally. If you want to match all strings containing a _, use this construct:

```
. . . WHERE ? LIKE %!_% {escape '!'}
```

Here we define ! as the escape character. The combination !_ denotes a literal underscore.

5.5.4 Multiple Results

It is possible for a query to return multiple results. This can happen when executing a stored procedure, or with databases that also allow submission of multiple SELECT statements in a single query. Here is how you retrieve all result sets:

1. Use the execute method to execute the SQL statement.
2. Retrieve the first result or update count.
3. Repeatedly call the getMoreResults method to move on to the next result set.
4. Finish when there are no more result sets or update counts.

The execute and getMoreResults methods return true if the next item in the chain is a result set. The getUpdateCount method returns -1 if the next item in the chain is not an update count.

The following loop traverses all results:

```
boolean isResult = stat.execute(command);
boolean done = false;
while (!done)
{
   if (isResult)
   {
      ResultSet result = stat.getResultSet();
      do something with result
   }
   else
   {
      int updateCount = stat.getUpdateCount();
      if (updateCount >= 0)
         do something with updateCount
      else
         done = true;
   }
   if (!done) isResult = stat.getMoreResults();
}
```

---

java.sql.Statement 1.1

- boolean getMoreResults()
- boolean getMoreResults(int current) 6

    gets the next result for this statement. The current parameter is one of CLOSE_CURRENT_RESULT (default), KEEP_CURRENT_RESULT, or CLOSE_ALL_RESULTS. Returns true if the next result exists and is a result set.

5.5.5 Retrieving Autogenerated Keys

Most databases support some mechanism for autonumbering rows in a database. Unfortunately, the mechanisms differ widely among vendors. These automatic numbers are often used as primary keys. Although JDBC doesn't offer a vendor-independent solution for generating keys, it does provide an efficient way of retrieving them. When you insert a new row into a table and a key is automatically generated, you can retrieve it with the following code:

```
stat.executeUpdate(insertStatement, Statement.RETURN_GENERATED_KEYS);
ResultSet rs = stat.getGeneratedKeys();
if (rs.next())
{
   int key = rs.getInt(1);
   . . .
}
```

---

java.sql.Statement 1.1

- boolean execute(String statement, int autogenerated) 1.4
- int executeUpdate(String statement, int autogenerated) 1.4

    executes the given SQL statement, as previously described. If autogenerated is set to Statement.RETURN_GENERATED_KEYS and the statement is an INSERT statement, the first column contains the autogenerated key.

5.6 Scrollable and Updatable Result Sets

As you have seen, the next method of the ResultSet interface iterates over the rows in a result set. That is certainly adequate for a program that needs to analyze the data. However, consider a visual data display that shows a table or query results (such as Figure 5.4). You usually want the user to be able to move both forward and backward in the result set. In a *scrollable* result, you can move forward and backward through a result set and even jump to any position.

Furthermore, once users see the contents of a result set displayed, they may be tempted to edit it. In an *updatable* result set, you can programmatically update entries so that the database is automatically updated. We discuss these capabilities in the following sections.

5.6.1 Scrollable Result Sets

By default, result sets are not scrollable or updatable. To obtain scrollable result sets from your queries, you must obtain a different Statement object with the method

```
Statement stat = conn.createStatement(type, concurrency);
```

For a prepared statement, use the call

```
PreparedStatement stat = conn.prepareStatement(command, type, concurrency);
```

The possible values of type and concurrency are listed in Tables 5.6 and 5.7. You have the following choices:

- Do you want the result set to be scrollable? If not, use ResultSet.TYPE_FORWARD_ONLY.

- If the result set is scrollable, do you want it to reflect changes in the database that occurred after the query that yielded it? (In our discussion, we assume the ResultSet.TYPE_SCROLL_INSENSITIVE setting for scrollable result sets. This assumes that the result set does not "sense" database changes that occurred after execution of the query.)

- Do you want to be able to update the database by editing the result set? (See the next section for details.)

Table 5.6 ResultSet Type Values

Value	Explanation
TYPE_FORWARD_ONLY	The result set is not scrollable (default).
TYPE_SCROLL_INSENSITIVE	The result set is scrollable but not sensitive to database changes.
TYPE_SCROLL_SENSITIVE	The result set is scrollable and sensitive to database changes.

Table 5.7 ResultSet Concurrency Values

Value	Explanation
CONCUR_READ_ONLY	The result set cannot be used to update the database (default).
CONCUR_UPDATABLE	The result set can be used to update the database.

For example, if you simply want to be able to scroll through a result set but don't want to edit its data, use

```
Statement stat = conn.createStatement(
   ResultSet.TYPE_SCROLL_INSENSITIVE, ResultSet.CONCUR_READ_ONLY);
```

All result sets that are returned by calls

```
ResultSet rs = stat.executeQuery(query);
```

are now scrollable. A scrollable result set has a *cursor* that indicates the current position.

 NOTE: Not all database drivers support scrollable or updatable result sets. (The supportsResultSetType and supportsResultSetConcurrency methods of the DatabaseMetaData interface will tell you which types and concurrency modes are supported by a particular database using a particular driver.) Even if a database supports all result set modes, a particular query might not be able to yield a result set with all the properties that you requested. (For example, the result set of a complex query might not be updatable.) In that case, the executeQuery method returns a ResultSet of lesser capabilities and adds a SQLWarning to the connection object. (Section 5.4.3, "Analyzing SQL Exceptions," on p. 304 shows how to retrieve the warning.) Alternatively, you can use the getType and getConcurrency methods of the ResultSet interface to find out what mode a result set actually has. If you do not check the result set capabilities and issue an unsupported operation, such as previous on a result set that is not scrollable, the operation will throw a SQLException.

Scrolling is very simple. Use

```
if (rs.previous()) . . .;
```

to scroll backward. The method returns true if the cursor is positioned on an actual row, or false if it is now positioned before the first row.

You can move the cursor backward or forward by any number of rows with the call

```
rs.relative(n);
```

If n is positive, the cursor moves forward. If n is negative, it moves backward. If n is zero, the call has no effect. If you attempt to move the cursor outside the current set of rows, it is set to point either after the last row or before the first row, depending on the sign of n. Then, the method returns false and the cursor does not move. The method returns true if the cursor is positioned on an actual row.

Alternatively, you can set the cursor to a particular row number:

```
rs.absolute(n);
```

To get the current row number, call

```
int currentRow = rs.getRow();
```

The first row in the result set has number 1. If the return value is 0, the cursor is not currently on a row—it is either before the first row or after the last row.

The convenience methods first, last, beforeFirst, and afterLast move the cursor to the first, to the last, before the first, or after the last position.

Finally, the methods isFirst, isLast, isBeforeFirst, and isAfterLast test whether the cursor is at one of these special positions.

Using a scrollable result set is very simple. The hard work of caching the query data is carried out behind the scenes by the database driver.

5.6.2 Updatable Result Sets

If you want to edit the data in the result set and have the changes automatically reflected in the database, create an updatable result set. Updatable result sets don't have to be scrollable, but if you present data to a user for editing, you usually want to allow scrolling as well.

To obtain updatable result sets, create a statement as follows:

```
Statement stat = conn.createStatement(
    ResultSet.TYPE_SCROLL_INSENSITIVE, ResultSet.CONCUR_UPDATABLE);
```

The result sets returned by a call to executeQuery are then updatable.

 NOTE: Not all queries return updatable result sets. If your query is a join that involves multiple tables, the result might not be updatable. However, if your query involves only a single table or if it joins multiple tables by their primary keys, you should expect the result set to be updatable. Call the getConcurrency method of the ResultSet interface to find out for sure.

For example, suppose you want to raise the prices of some books, but you don't have a simple criterion for issuing an UPDATE statement. Then, you can iterate through all books and update prices based on arbitrary conditions.

```
String query = "SELECT * FROM Books";
ResultSet rs = stat.executeQuery(query);
```

```
while (rs.next())
{
   if (. . .)
   {
      double increase = . . .;
      double price = rs.getDouble("Price");
      rs.updateDouble("Price", price + increase);
      rs.updateRow(); // make sure to call updateRow after updating fields
   }
}
```

There are updateXxx methods for all data types that correspond to SQL types, such as updateDouble, updateString, and so on; specify the name or the number of the column (as with the getXxx methods), then the new value for the field.

 NOTE: If you use the updateXxx method whose first parameter is the column number, be aware that this is the column number in the *result set*. It could well be different from the column number in the database.

The updateXxx method changes only the row values, not the database. When you are done with the field updates in a row, you must call the updateRow method. That method sends all updates in the current row to the database. If you move the cursor to another row without calling updateRow, this row's updates are discarded from the row set and never communicated to the database. You can also call the cancelRowUpdates method to cancel the updates to the current row.

The preceding example shows how to modify an existing row. If you want to add a new row to the database, first use the moveToInsertRow method to move the cursor to a special position, called the *insert row*. Then, build up a new row in the insert row position by issuing updateXxx instructions. When you are done, call the insertRow method to deliver the new row to the database. When you are done inserting, call moveToCurrentRow to move the cursor back to the position before the call to moveToInsertRow. Here is an example:

```
rs.moveToInsertRow();
rs.updateString("Title", title);
rs.updateString("ISBN", isbn);
rs.updateString("Publisher_Id", pubid);
rs.updateDouble("Price", price);
rs.insertRow();
rs.moveToCurrentRow();
```

Note that you cannot influence *where* the new data is added in the result set or the database.

If you don't specify a column value in the insert row, it is set to a SQL NULL. However, if the column has a NOT NULL constraint, an exception is thrown and the row is not inserted.

Finally, you can delete the row under the cursor:

```
rs.deleteRow();
```

The deleteRow method immediately removes the row from both the result set and the database.

The updateRow, insertRow, and deleteRow methods of the ResultSet interface give you the same power as executing UPDATE, INSERT, and DELETE SQL statements. However, Java programmers might find it more natural to manipulate the database contents through result sets than by constructing SQL statements.

CAUTION: If you are not careful, you can write staggeringly inefficient code with updatable result sets. It is *much* more efficient to execute an UPDATE statement than to make a query and iterate through the result, changing data along the way. Updatable result sets make sense for interactive programs in which a user can make arbitrary changes, but for most programmatic changes, a SQL UPDATE is more appropriate.

NOTE: JDBC 2 delivered further enhancements to result sets, such as the capability to update a result set with the most recent data if the data have been modified by another concurrent database connection. JDBC 3 added yet another refinement, specifying the behavior of result sets when a transaction is committed. However, these advanced features are outside the scope of this introductory chapter. We refer you to the *JDBC™ API Tutorial and Reference, Third Edition*, by Maydene Fisher, Jon Ellis, and Jonathan Bruce (Addison-Wesley, 2003) and the JDBC specification for more information.

---

java.sql.Connection 1.1

- Statement createStatement(int type, int concurrency) 1.2
- PreparedStatement prepareStatement(String command, int type, int concurrency) 1.2

  creates a statement or prepared statement that yields result sets with the given type and concurrency. The type parameter is of the constants TYPE_FORWARD_ONLY, TYPE_SCROLL_INSENSITIVE, or TYPE_SCROLL_SENSITIVE, and concurrency is one of the constants CONCUR_READ_ONLY or CONCUR_UPDATABLE, all defined in the ResultSet interface.

---

java.sql.ResultSet 1.1

- int getType() 1.2

  returns the type of this result set—one of TYPE_FORWARD_ONLY, TYPE_SCROLL_INSENSITIVE, or TYPE_SCROLL_SENSITIVE.

- int getConcurrency() 1.2

  returns the concurrency setting of this result set—one of CONCUR_READ_ONLY or CONCUR_UPDATABLE.

- boolean previous() 1.2

  moves the cursor to the preceding row. Returns true if the cursor is positioned on a row, or false if the cursor is positioned before the first row.

- int getRow() 1.2

  gets the number of the current row. Rows are numbered starting with 1.

- boolean absolute(int r) 1.2

  moves the cursor to row r. Returns true if the cursor is positioned on a row.

- boolean relative(int d) 1.2

  moves the cursor by d rows. If d is negative, the cursor is moved backward. Returns true if the cursor is positioned on a row.

- boolean first() 1.2
- boolean last() 1.2

  moves the cursor to the first or last row. Returns true if the cursor is positioned on a row.

- void beforeFirst() 1.2
- void afterLast() 1.2

  moves the cursor before the first or after the last row.

- boolean isFirst() 1.2
- boolean isLast() 1.2

  tests whether the cursor is at the first or last row.

- boolean isBeforeFirst() 1.2
- boolean isAfterLast() 1.2

  tests whether the cursor is before the first or after the last row.

- void moveToInsertRow() 1.2

  moves the cursor to the insert row. The insert row is a special row for inserting new data with the update*Xxx* and insertRow methods.

(Continues)

---

java.sql.ResultSet 1.1   *(Continued)*

- void moveToCurrentRow() 1.2

  moves the cursor back from the insert row to the row that it occupied when the moveToInsertRow method was called.

- void insertRow() 1.2

  inserts the contents of the insert row into the database and the result set.

- void deleteRow() 1.2

  deletes the current row from the database and the result set.

- void update*Xxx*(int column, *Xxx* data) 1.2
- void update*Xxx*(String columnName, *Xxx* data) 1.2

  (*Xxx* is a type such as int, double, String, Date, etc.)

  updates a field in the current row of the result set.

- void updateRow() 1.2

  sends the current row updates to the database.

- void cancelRowUpdates() 1.2

  cancels the current row updates.

---

java.sql.DatabaseMetaData 1.1

- boolean supportsResultSetType(int type) 1.2

  returns true if the database can support result sets of the given type; type is one of the constants TYPE_FORWARD_ONLY, TYPE_SCROLL_INSENSITIVE, or TYPE_SCROLL_SENSITIVE of the ResultSet interface.

- boolean supportsResultSetConcurrency(int type, int concurrency) 1.2

  returns true if the database can support result sets of the given combination of type and concurrency. The type parameter is one of the constants TYPE_FORWARD_ONLY, TYPE_SCROLL_INSENSITIVE, or TYPE_SCROLL_SENSITIVE, and concurrency is one of the constants CONCUR_READ_ONLY or CONCUR_UPDATABLE, all defined in the ResultSet interface.

5.7 Row Sets

Scrollable result sets are powerful, but they have a major drawback. You need to keep the database connection open during the entire user interaction. However, a user can walk away from the computer for a long time, leaving the connection occupied. That is not good—database connections are scarce resources. In this situation, use a *row set*. The RowSet interface extends the ResultSet interface, but row sets don't have to be tied to a database connection.

Row sets are also suitable if you need to move a query result to a different tier of a complex application, or to another device such as a cell phone. You would never want to move a result set—its data structures can be huge, and it is tethered to the database connection.

5.7.1 Constructing Row Sets

The javax.sql.rowset package provides the following interfaces that extend the RowSet interface:

- A CachedRowSet allows disconnected operation. We will discuss cached row sets in the following section.
- A WebRowSet is a cached row set that can be saved to an XML file. The XML file can be moved to another tier of a web application where it is opened by another WebRowSet object.
- The FilteredRowSet and JoinRowSet interfaces support lightweight operations on row sets that are equivalent to SQL SELECT and JOIN operations. These operations are carried out on the data stored in row sets, without having to make a database connection.
- A JdbcRowSet is a thin wrapper around a ResultSet. It adds useful methods from the RowSet interface.

As of Java 7, there is a standard way for obtaining a row set:

```
RowSetFactory factory = RowSetProvider.newFactory();
CachedRowSet crs = factory.createCachedRowSet();
```

There are similar methods for obtaining the other row set types.

5.7.2 Cached Row Sets

A cached row set contains all data from a result set. Since CachedRowSet is a subinterface of the ResultSet interface, you can use a cached row set exactly as you would use a result set. Cached row sets confer an important benefit: You can close the connection and still use the row set. As you will see in our sample program in Listing 5.4, this greatly simplifies the implementation of interactive applications. Each user command simply opens the database connection, issues a query, puts the result in a cached row set, and then closes the database connection.

It is even possible to modify the data in a cached row set. Of course, the modifications are not immediately reflected in the database; you need to make an explicit request to accept the accumulated changes. The CachedRowSet then reconnects to the database and issues SQL statements to write the accumulated changes.

You can populate a CachedRowSet from a result set:

```
ResultSet result = . . .;
RowSetFactory factory = RowSetProvider.newFactory();
CachedRowSet crs = factory.createCachedRowSet();
crs.populate(result);
conn.close(); // now OK to close the database connection
```

Alternatively, you can let the CachedRowSet object establish a connection automatically. Set up the database parameters:

```
crs.setURL("jdbc:derby://localhost:1527/COREJAVA");
crs.setUsername("dbuser");
crs.setPassword("secret");
```

Then set the query statement and any parameters:

```
crs.setCommand("SELECT * FROM Books WHERE Publisher_ID = ?");
crs.setString(1, publisherId);
```

Finally, populate the row set with the query result:

```
crs.execute();
```

This call establishes a database connection, issues the query, populates the row set, and disconnects.

If your query result is very large, you would not want to put it into the row set in its entirety. After all, your users will probably only look at a few rows. In that case, specify a page size:

```
CachedRowSet crs = . . .;
crs.setCommand(command);
crs.setPageSize(20);
. . .
crs.execute();
```

Now you will only get 20 rows. To get the next batch of rows, call

```
crs.nextPage();
```

You can inspect and modify the row set with the same methods you use for result sets. If you modified the row set contents, you must write it back to the database by calling

```
crs.acceptChanges(conn);
```

or

```
crs.acceptChanges();
```

The second call works only if you configured the row set with the information required to connect to a database (such as the URL, user name, and password).

In Section 5.6.2, "Updatable Result Sets," on p. 325, you saw that not all result sets are updatable. Similarly, a row set that contains the result of a complex query will not be able to write its changes back to the database. You should be safe if your row set contains data from a single table.

 CAUTION: If you populated the row set from a result set, the row set does not know the name of the table to update. You need to call `setTableName` to set the table name.

Another complexity arises if the data in the database have changed after you populated the row set. This is clearly a sign of trouble that could lead to inconsistent data. The reference implementation checks whether the original row set values (that is, the values before editing) are identical to the current values in the database. If so, they are replaced with the edited values; otherwise, a `SyncProviderException` is thrown and none of the changes are written. Other implementations may use other strategies for synchronization.

---

javax.sql.RowSet 1.4

- `String getURL()`
- `void setURL(String url)`

  gets or sets the database URL.

- `String getUsername()`
- `void setUsername(String username)`

  gets or sets the user name for connecting to the database.

- `String getPassword()`
- `void setPassword(String password)`

  gets or sets the password for connecting to the database.

- `String getCommand()`
- `void setCommand(String command)`

  gets or sets the command that is executed to populate this row set.

- `void execute()`

  populates this row set by issuing the statement set with `setCommand`. For the driver manager to obtain a connection, the URL, user name, and password must be set.

---

javax.sql.rowset.CachedRowSet 5.0

- void execute(Connection conn)

  populates this row set by issuing the statement set with setCommand. This method uses the given connection *and closes it.*

- void populate(ResultSet result)

  populates this cached row set with the data from the given result set.

- String getTableName()
- void setTableName(String tableName)

  gets or sets the name of the table from which this cached row set was populated.

- int getPageSize()
- void setPageSize(int size)

  gets or sets the page size.

- boolean nextPage()
- boolean previousPage()

  loads the next or previous page of rows. Returns true if there is a next or previous page.

- void acceptChanges()
- void acceptChanges(Connection conn)

  reconnects to the database and writes the changes that are the result of editing the row set. May throw a SyncProviderException if the data cannot be written back because the database data have changed.

---

javax.sql.rowset.RowSetProvider 7

- static RowSetFactory newFactory()

  creates a row set factory.

---

javax.sql.rowset.RowSetFactory 7

- CachedRowSet createCachedRowSet()
- FilteredRowSet createFilteredRowSet()
- JdbcRowSet createJdbcRowSet()
- JoinRowSet createJoinRowSet()
- WebRowSet createWebRowSet()

  creates a row set of the specified type.

5.8 Metadata

In the preceding sections, you saw how to populate, query, and update database tables. However, JDBC can give you additional information about the *structure* of a database and its tables. For example, you can get a list of the tables in a particular database or the column names and types of a table. This information is not useful when you are implementing a business application with a predefined database. After all, if you design the tables, you know their structure. Structural information is, however, extremely useful for programmers who write tools that work with any database.

In SQL, data that describe the database or one of its parts are called *metadata* (to distinguish them from the actual data stored in the database). You can get three kinds of metadata: about a database, about a result set, and about parameters of prepared statements.

To find out more about the database, request an object of type DatabaseMetaData from the database connection.

```
DatabaseMetaData meta = conn.getMetaData();
```

Now you are ready to get some metadata. For example, the call

```
ResultSet mrs = meta.getTables(null, null, null, new String[] { "TABLE" });
```

returns a result set that contains information about all tables in the database. (See the API note at the end of this section for other parameters to this method.)

Each row in the result set contains information about a table in the database. The third column is the name of the table. (Again, see the API note for the other columns.) The following loop gathers all table names:

```
while (mrs.next())
    tableNames.addItem(mrs.getString(3));
```

There is a second important use for database metadata. Databases are complex, and the SQL standard leaves plenty of room for variability. Well over a hundred methods in the DatabaseMetaData interface can inquire about the database, including calls with such exotic names as

```
meta.supportsCatalogsInPrivilegeDefinitions()
```

and

```
meta.nullPlusNonNullIsNull()
```

Clearly, these are geared toward advanced users with special needs—in particular, those who need to write highly portable code that works with multiple databases.

The DatabaseMetaData interface gives data about the database. A second metadata interface, ResultSetMetaData, reports information about a result set. Whenever you have a result set from a query, you can inquire about the number of columns and each column's name, type, and field width. Here is a typical loop:

```
ResultSet rs = stat.executeQuery("SELECT * FROM " + tableName);
ResultSetMetaData meta = rs.getMetaData();
for (int i = 1; i <= meta.getColumnCount(); i++)
{
    String columnName = meta.getColumnLabel(i);
    int columnWidth = meta.getColumnDisplaySize(i);
    . . .
}
```

In this section, we will show you how to write such a simple tool. The program in Listing 5.4 uses metadata to let you browse all tables in a database. The program also illustrates the use of a cached row set.

The combo box on top displays all tables in the database. Select one of them, and the center of the frame is filled with the field names of that table and the values of the first row, as shown in Figure 5.6. Click Next and Previous to scroll through the rows in the table. You can also delete a row and edit the row values. Click the Save button to save the changes to the database.

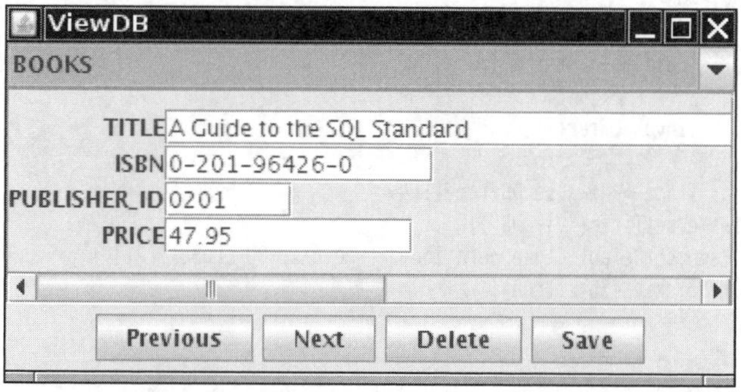

Figure 5.6 The ViewDB application

NOTE: Many databases come with much more sophisticated tools for viewing and editing tables. If your database doesn't, check out DBeaver (https://dbeaver.io) or SQuirreL (http://squirrel-sql.sourceforge.net). These programs can view the tables in any JDBC database. Our example program is not intended as a replacement for these tools—it just shows you how to implement a tool for working with arbitrary tables.

Listing 5.4 view/ViewDB.java

```java
1  package view;
2
3  import java.awt.*;
4  import java.awt.event.*;
5  import java.io.*;
6  import java.nio.file.*;
7  import java.sql.*;
8  import java.util.*;
9
10 import javax.sql.*;
11 import javax.sql.rowset.*;
12 import javax.swing.*;
13
14 /**
15  * This program uses metadata to display arbitrary tables in a database.
16  * @version 1.34 2018-05-01
17  * @author Cay Horstmann
18  */
19 public class ViewDB
20 {
21    public static void main(String[] args)
22    {
23       EventQueue.invokeLater(() ->
24          {
25             var frame = new ViewDBFrame();
26             frame.setTitle("ViewDB");
27             frame.setDefaultCloseOperation(JFrame.EXIT_ON_CLOSE);
28             frame.setVisible(true);
29          });
30    }
31 }
32
33 /**
34  * The frame that holds the data panel and the navigation buttons.
35  */
36 class ViewDBFrame extends JFrame
37 {
```

```
38    private JButton previousButton;
39    private JButton nextButton;
40    private JButton deleteButton;
41    private JButton saveButton;
42    private DataPanel dataPanel;
43    private Component scrollPane;
44    private JComboBox<String> tableNames;
45    private Properties props;
46    private CachedRowSet crs;
47    private Connection conn;
48
49    public ViewDBFrame()
50    {
51       tableNames = new JComboBox<String>();
52
53       try
54       {
55          readDatabaseProperties();
56          conn = getConnection();
57          DatabaseMetaData meta = conn.getMetaData();
58          try (ResultSet mrs = meta.getTables(null, null, null, new String[] { "TABLE" }))
59          {
60             while (mrs.next())
61                tableNames.addItem(mrs.getString(3));
62          }
63       }
64       catch (SQLException ex)
65       {
66          for (Throwable t : ex)
67             t.printStackTrace();
68       }
69       catch (IOException ex)
70       {
71          ex.printStackTrace();
72       }
73
74       tableNames.addActionListener(
75          event -> showTable((String) tableNames.getSelectedItem(), conn));
76       add(tableNames, BorderLayout.NORTH);
77       addWindowListener(new WindowAdapter()
78          {
79             public void windowClosing(WindowEvent event)
80             {
81                try
82                {
83                   if (conn != null) conn.close();
84                }
```

(Continues)

Listing 5.4 *(Continued)*

```
85              catch (SQLException ex)
86              {
87                  for (Throwable t : ex)
88                      t.printStackTrace();
89              }
90          }
91      });
92
93      var buttonPanel = new JPanel();
94      add(buttonPanel, BorderLayout.SOUTH);
95
96      previousButton = new JButton("Previous");
97      previousButton.addActionListener(event -> showPreviousRow());
98      buttonPanel.add(previousButton);
99
100     nextButton = new JButton("Next");
101     nextButton.addActionListener(event -> showNextRow());
102     buttonPanel.add(nextButton);
103
104     deleteButton = new JButton("Delete");
105     deleteButton.addActionListener(event -> deleteRow());
106     buttonPanel.add(deleteButton);
107
108     saveButton = new JButton("Save");
109     saveButton.addActionListener(event -> saveChanges());
110     buttonPanel.add(saveButton);
111     if (tableNames.getItemCount() > 0)
112         showTable(tableNames.getItemAt(0), conn);
113  }
114
115  /**
116   * Prepares the text fields for showing a new table, and shows the first row.
117   * @param tableName the name of the table to display
118   * @param conn the database connection
119   */
120  public void showTable(String tableName, Connection conn)
121  {
122      try (Statement stat = conn.createStatement();
123          ResultSet result = stat.executeQuery("SELECT * FROM " + tableName))
124      {
125          // get result set
126
127          // copy into cached row set
128          RowSetFactory factory = RowSetProvider.newFactory();
129          crs = factory.createCachedRowSet();
130          crs.setTableName(tableName);
131          crs.populate(result);
132
```

```
133        if (scrollPane != null) remove(scrollPane);
134        dataPanel = new DataPanel(crs);
135        scrollPane = new JScrollPane(dataPanel);
136        add(scrollPane, BorderLayout.CENTER);
137        pack();
138        showNextRow();
139     }
140     catch (SQLException ex)
141     {
142        for (Throwable t : ex)
143           t.printStackTrace();
144     }
145  }
146
147  /**
148   * Moves to the previous table row.
149   */
150  public void showPreviousRow()
151  {
152     try
153     {
154        if (crs == null || crs.isFirst()) return;
155        crs.previous();
156        dataPanel.showRow(crs);
157     }
158     catch (SQLException ex)
159     {
160        for (Throwable t : ex)
161           t.printStackTrace();
162     }
163  }
164
165  /**
166   * Moves to the next table row.
167   */
168  public void showNextRow()
169  {
170     try
171     {
172        if (crs == null || crs.isLast()) return;
173        crs.next();
174        dataPanel.showRow(crs);
175     }
176     catch (SQLException ex)
177     {
178        for (Throwable t : ex)
179           t.printStackTrace();
180     }
181  }
```

(Continues)

Listing 5.4 *(Continued)*

```
182
183    /**
184     * Deletes current table row.
185     */
186    public void deleteRow()
187    {
188       if (crs == null) return;
189       new SwingWorker<Void, Void>()
190       {
191          public Void doInBackground() throws SQLException
192          {
193             crs.deleteRow();
194             crs.acceptChanges(conn);
195             if (crs.isAfterLast())
196                if (!crs.last()) crs = null;
197             return null;
198          }
199          public void done()
200          {
201             dataPanel.showRow(crs);
202          }
203       }.execute();
204    }
205    /**
206     * Saves all changes.
207     */
208    public void saveChanges()
209    {
210       if (crs == null) return;
211       new SwingWorker<Void, Void>()
212       {
213          public Void doInBackground() throws SQLException
214          {
215             dataPanel.setRow(crs);
216             crs.acceptChanges(conn);
217             return null;
218          }
219       }.execute();
220    }
221
222    private void readDatabaseProperties() throws IOException
223    {
224       props = new Properties();
225       try (InputStream in = Files.newInputStream(Paths.get("database.properties")))
226       {
227          props.load(in);
228       }
```

```
229       String drivers = props.getProperty("jdbc.drivers");
230       if (drivers != null) System.setProperty("jdbc.drivers", drivers);
231    }
232
233    /**
234     * Gets a connection from the properties specified in the file database.properties.
235     * @return the database connection
236     */
237    private Connection getConnection() throws SQLException
238    {
239       String url = props.getProperty("jdbc.url");
240       String username = props.getProperty("jdbc.username");
241       String password = props.getProperty("jdbc.password");
242
243       return DriverManager.getConnection(url, username, password);
244    }
245 }
246
247 /**
248  * This panel displays the contents of a result set.
249  */
250 class DataPanel extends JPanel
251 {
252    private java.util.List<JTextField> fields;
253
254    /**
255     * Constructs the data panel.
256     * @param rs the result set whose contents this panel displays
257     */
258    public DataPanel(RowSet rs) throws SQLException
259    {
260       fields = new ArrayList<>();
261       setLayout(new GridBagLayout());
262       var gbc = new GridBagConstraints();
263       gbc.gridwidth = 1;
264       gbc.gridheight = 1;
265
266       ResultSetMetaData rsmd = rs.getMetaData();
267       for (int i = 1; i <= rsmd.getColumnCount(); i++)
268       {
269          gbc.gridy = i - 1;
270
271          String columnName = rsmd.getColumnLabel(i);
272          gbc.gridx = 0;
273          gbc.anchor = GridBagConstraints.EAST;
274          add(new JLabel(columnName), gbc);
275
276          int columnWidth = rsmd.getColumnDisplaySize(i);
277          var tb = new JTextField(columnWidth);
```

(Continues)

Listing 5.4 *(Continued)*

```
278          if (!rsmd.getColumnClassName(i).equals("java.lang.String"))
279             tb.setEditable(false);
280
281          fields.add(tb);
282
283          gbc.gridx = 1;
284          gbc.anchor = GridBagConstraints.WEST;
285          add(tb, gbc);
286       }
287    }
288
289    /**
290     * Shows a database row by populating all text fields with the column values.
291     */
292    public void showRow(ResultSet rs)
293    {
294       try
295       {
296          if (rs == null) return;
297          for (int i = 1; i <= fields.size(); i++)
298          {
299             String field = rs == null ? "" : rs.getString(i);
300             JTextField tb = fields.get(i - 1);
301             tb.setText(field);
302          }
303       }
304       catch (SQLException ex)
305       {
306          for (Throwable t : ex)
307             t.printStackTrace();
308       }
309    }
310
311    /**
312     * Updates changed data into the current row of the row set.
313     */
314    public void setRow(RowSet rs) throws SQLException
315    {
316       for (int i = 1; i <= fields.size(); i++)
317       {
318          String field = rs.getString(i);
319          JTextField tb = fields.get(i - 1);
320          if (!field.equals(tb.getText()))
321             rs.updateString(i, tb.getText());
322       }
323       rs.updateRow();
324    }
325 }
```

---

java.sql.Connection 1.1

- DatabaseMetaData getMetaData()

  returns the metadata for the connection as a DatabaseMetaData object.

---

java.sql.DatabaseMetaData 1.1

- ResultSet getTables(String catalog, String schemaPattern, String tableNamePattern, String types[])

  returns a description of all tables in a catalog that match the schema and table name patterns and the type criteria. (A *schema* describes a group of related tables and access permissions. A *catalog* describes a related group of schemas. These concepts are important for structuring large databases.)

  The catalog and schemaPattern parameters can be "" to retrieve those tables without a catalog or schema, or null to return tables regardless of catalog or schema.

  The types array contains the names of the table types to include. Typical types are TABLE, VIEW, SYSTEM TABLE, GLOBAL TEMPORARY, LOCAL TEMPORARY, ALIAS, and SYNONYM. If types is null, tables of all types are returned.

  The result set has five columns, all of which are of type String.

Column	Name	Explanation
1	TABLE_CAT	Table catalog (may be null)
2	TABLE_SCHEM	Table schema (may be null)
3	TABLE_NAME	Table name
4	TABLE_TYPE	Table type
5	REMARKS	Comment on the table

- int getJDBCMajorVersion() 1.4
- int getJDBCMinorVersion() 1.4

  returns the major or minor JDBC version numbers of the driver that established the database connection. For example, a JDBC 3.0 driver has major version number 3 and minor version number 0.

- int getMaxConnections()

  returns the maximum number of concurrent connections allowed to this database.

- int getMaxStatements()

  returns the maximum number of concurrently open statements allowed per database connection, or 0 if the number is unlimited or unknown.

---

java.sql.ResultSet 1.1

• ResultSetMetaData getMetaData()

  returns the metadata associated with the current ResultSet columns.

---

java.sql.ResultSetMetaData 1.1

• int getColumnCount()

  returns the number of columns in the current ResultSet object.

• int getColumnDisplaySize(int column)

  returns the maximum width of the column specified by the index parameter.

• String getColumnLabel(int column)

  returns the suggested title for the column.

• String getColumnName(int column)

  returns the column name associated with the column index specified.

5.9 Transactions

You can group a set of statements to form a *transaction*. The transaction can be *committed* when all has gone well—or, if an error has occurred in one of them, it can be *rolled back* as if none of the statements had been issued.

The major reason for grouping statements into transactions is *database integrity*. For example, suppose we want to transfer money from one bank account to another. Then, it is important that we simultaneously debit one account and credit another. If the system fails after debiting the first account but before crediting the other account, the debit needs to be undone.

If you group update statements into a transaction, the transaction either succeeds in its entirety and can be *committed,* or it fails somewhere in the middle. In that case, you can carry out a *rollback* and the database automatically undoes the effect of all updates that occurred since the last committed transaction.

5.9.1 Programming Transactions with JDBC

By default, a database connection is in *autocommit mode,* and each SQL statement is committed to the database as soon as it is executed. Once a statement is committed, you cannot roll it back. Turn off this default so you can use transactions:

```
conn.setAutoCommit(false);
```

Create a statement object in the normal way:

```
Statement stat = conn.createStatement();
```

Call executeUpdate any number of times:

```
stat.executeUpdate(command₁);
stat.executeUpdate(command₂);
stat.executeUpdate(command₃);
. . .
```

If all statements have been executed without error, call the commit method:

```
conn.commit();
```

However, if an error occurred, call

```
conn.rollback();
```

Then, all statements since the last commit are automatically reversed. You typically issue a rollback when your transaction was interrupted by a SQLException.

5.9.2 Save Points

With some databases and drivers, you can gain finer-grained control over the rollback process by using *save points*. Creating a save point marks a point to which you can later return without having to abandon the entire transaction. For example,

```
Statement stat = conn.createStatement(); // start transaction; rollback() goes here
stat.executeUpdate(command1);
Savepoint svpt = conn.setSavepoint(); // set savepoint; rollback(svpt) goes here
stat.executeUpdate(command2);

if (. . .) conn.rollback(svpt); // undo effect of command2
. . .
conn.commit();
```

When you no longer need a save point, you should release it:

```
conn.releaseSavepoint(svpt);
```

5.9.3 Batch Updates

Suppose a program needs to execute many INSERT statements to populate a database table. You can improve the performance of the program by using a *batch update*. In a batch update, a sequence of statements is collected and submitted as a batch.

NOTE: Use the `supportsBatchUpdates` method of the `DatabaseMetaData` interface to find out if your database supports this feature.

The statements in a batch can be actions such as INSERT, UPDATE, or DELETE as well as data definition statements such as CREATE TABLE or DROP TABLE. An exception is thrown if you add a SELECT statement to a batch. (Conceptually, a SELECT statement makes no sense in a batch because it returns a result set without updating the database.)

To execute a batch, first create a Statement object in the usual way:

```
Statement stat = conn.createStatement();
```

Now, instead of calling executeUpdate, call the addBatch method:

```
String command = "CREATE TABLE . . ."
stat.addBatch(command);

while (. . .)
{
   command = "INSERT INTO . . . VALUES (" + . . . + ")";
   stat.addBatch(command);
}
```

Finally, submit the entire batch:

```
int[] counts = stat.executeBatch();
```

The call to executeBatch returns an array of the row counts for all submitted statements.

For proper error handling in batch mode, treat the batch execution as a single transaction. If a batch fails in the middle, you want to roll back to the state before the beginning of the batch.

First, turn the autocommit mode off, then collect the batch, execute it, commit it, and finally restore the original autocommit mode:

```
boolean autoCommit = conn.getAutoCommit();
conn.setAutoCommit(false);
Statement stat = conn.getStatement();
. . .
// keep calling stat.addBatch(. . .);
. . .
stat.executeBatch();
conn.commit();
conn.setAutoCommit(autoCommit);
```

---

java.sql.Connection 1.1

- boolean getAutoCommit()
- void setAutoCommit(boolean b)

  gets or sets the autocommit mode of this connection to b. If autocommit is true, all statements are committed as soon as their execution is completed.

- void commit()

  commits all statements that were issued since the last commit.

- void rollback()

  undoes the effect of all statements that were issued since the last commit.

- Savepoint setSavepoint() 1.4
- Savepoint setSavepoint(String name) 1.4

  sets an unnamed or named save point.

- void rollback(Savepoint svpt) 1.4

  rolls back until the given save point.

- void releaseSavepoint(Savepoint svpt) 1.4

  releases the given save point.

---

java.sql.Savepoint 1.4

- int getSavepointId()

  gets the ID of this unnamed save point, or throws a SQLException if this is a named save point.

- String getSavepointName()

  gets the name of this save point, or throws a SQLException if this is an unnamed save point.

---

java.sql.Statement 1.1

- void addBatch(String command) 1.2

  adds the command to the current batch of commands for this statement.

- int[] executeBatch() 1.2
- long[] executeLargeBatch() 8

  executes all commands in the current batch. Each value in the returned array corresponds to one of the batch statements. If it is non-negative, it is a row count. If it is the value SUCCESS_NO_INFO, the statement succeeded, but no row count is available. If it is EXECUTE_FAILED, the statement failed.

> ***java.sql.DatabaseMetaData*** 1.1
>
> • boolean supportsBatchUpdates() 1.2
>
> returns true if the driver supports batch updates.

5.9.4 Advanced SQL Types

Table 5.8 lists the SQL data types supported by JDBC and their equivalents in the Java programming language.

Table 5.8 SQL Data Types and Their Corresponding Java Types

SQL Data Type	Java Data Type
INTEGER or INT	int
SMALLINT	short
NUMERIC(m,n), DECIMAL(m,n) or DEC(m,n)	java.math.BigDecimal
FLOAT(n)	double
REAL	float
DOUBLE	double
CHARACTER(n) or CHAR(n)	String
VARCHAR(n), LONG VARCHAR	String
BOOLEAN	boolean
DATE	java.sql.Date
TIME	java.sql.Time
TIMESTAMP	java.sql.Timestamp
BLOB	java.sql.Blob
CLOB	java.sql.Clob
ARRAY	java.sql.Array
ROWID	java.sql.RowId
NCHAR(n), NVARCHAR(n), LONG NVARCHAR	String
NCLOB	java.sql.NClob
SQLXML	java.sql.SQLXML

A SQL ARRAY is a sequence of values. For example, in a Student table, you can have a Scores column that is an ARRAY OF INTEGER. The getArray method returns an object of the interface type java.sql.Array. That interface has methods to fetch the array values.

When you get a LOB or an array from a database, the actual contents are fetched from the database only when you request individual values. This is a useful performance enhancement, as the data can be quite voluminous.

Some databases support ROWID values that describe the location of a row so that it can be retrieved very rapidly. JDBC 4 introduced an interface java.sql.RowId and the methods to supply the row ID in queries and retrieve it from results.

A *national character string* (NCHAR and its variants) stores strings in a local character encoding and sorts them using a local sorting convention. JDBC 4 provided methods for converting between Java String objects and national character strings in queries and results.

Some databases can store user-defined structured types. JDBC 3 provides a mechanism for automatically mapping structured SQL types to Java objects.

Some databases provide native storage for XML data. JDBC 4 introduced a SQLXML interface that can mediate between the internal XML representation and the DOM Source/Result interfaces, as well as binary streams. See the API documentation for the SQLXML class for details.

We do not discuss these advanced SQL types any further. You can find more information on these topics in the *JDBC API Tutorial and Reference* and the JDBC specification.

5.10 Connection Management in Web and Enterprise Applications

The simplistic database connection setup with a database.properties file, as described in the preceding sections, is suitable for small test programs but won't scale for larger applications.

When a JDBC application is deployed in a web or enterprise environment, the management of database connections is integrated with the JNDI. The properties of data sources across the enterprise can be stored in a directory. Using a directory allows for centralized management of user names, passwords, database names, and JDBC URLs.

In such an environment, you can use the following code to establish a database connection:

```
var jndiContext = new InitialContext();
var source = (DataSource) jndiContext.lookup("java:comp/env/jdbc/corejava");
Connection conn = source.getConnection();
```

Note that the DriverManager is no longer involved. Instead, the JNDI service locates a *data source*. A data source is an interface that allows for simple JDBC connections as well as more advanced services, such as executing distributed transactions that involve multiple databases. The DataSource interface is defined in the javax.sql standard extension package.

 NOTE: In a Java EE container, you don't even have to program the JNDI lookup. Simply use the Resource annotation on a DataSource field, and the data source reference will be set when your application is loaded:

```
@Resource(name="jdbc/corejava")
private DataSource source;
```

Of course, the data source needs to be configured somewhere. If you write database programs that execute in a servlet container such as Apache Tomcat or in an application server such as GlassFish, place the database configuration (including the JNDI name, JDBC URL, user name, and password) in a configuration file, or set it in an admin GUI.

Management of user names and logins is just one of the issues that require special attention. Another issue involves the cost of establishing database connections. Our sample database programs used two strategies for obtaining a database connection. The QueryDB program in Listing 5.3 established a single database connection at the start of the program and closed it at the end of the program. The ViewDB program in Listing 5.4 opened a new connection whenever one was needed.

However, neither of these approaches is satisfactory. Database connections are a finite resource. If a user walks away from an application for some time, the connection should not be left open. Conversely, obtaining a connection for each query and closing it afterward is very costly.

The solution is to *pool* connections. This means that database connections are not physically closed but are kept in a queue and reused. Connection pooling is an important service, and the JDBC specification provides hooks for implementors to supply it. However, the JDK itself does not provide any implementation, and database vendors don't usually include one with their JDBC drivers either. Instead, vendors of web containers and application servers supply connection pool implementations.

Using a connection pool is completely transparent to the programmer. Acquire a connection from a source of pooled connections by obtaining a data source and calling getConnection. When you are done using the connection, call close. That doesn't close the physical connection but tells the pool that you are done using it. The connection pool typically makes an effort to pool prepared statements as well.

You have now learned about the JDBC fundamentals and know enough to implement simple database applications. However, as we mentioned at the beginning of this chapter, databases are complex and quite a few advanced topics are beyond the scope of this introductory chapter. For an overview of advanced JDBC capabilities, refer to the *JDBC API Tutorial and Reference* or the JDBC specification.

In this chapter, you have learned how to work with relational databases in Java. The next chapter covers the Java 8 date and time library.

The Date and Time API

In this chapter

Time flies like an arrow, and we can easily set a starting point and count forward and backward in seconds. So why is it so hard to deal with time? The problem is humans. All would be easy if we could just tell each other: "Meet me at 1523793600, and don't be late!" But we want time to relate to daylight and the seasons. That's where things get complicated. Java 1.0 had a Date class that was, in hindsight, naïve, and had most of its methods deprecated in Java 1.1 when a Calendar class was introduced. Its API wasn't stellar, its instances were mutable, and it didn't deal with issues such as leap seconds. The third time is a charm, and the java.time API introduced in Java 8 has remedied the flaws of the past and should serve us for quite some time. In this chapter, you will learn what makes time computations so vexing, and how the Date and Time API solves these issues.

6.1 The Time Line

Historically, the fundamental time unit—the second—was derived from Earth's rotation around its axis. There are 24 hours or $24 \times 60 \times 60 = 86400$ seconds in a full revolution, so it seems just a question of astronomical measurements to precisely define a second. Unfortunately, Earth wobbles slightly, and a more precise definition was needed. In 1967, a new precise definition of a second, matching the historical definition, was derived from an intrinsic property of atoms of caesium-133. Since then, a network of atomic clocks keeps the official time.

Ever so often, the official time keepers synchronize the absolute time with the rotation of Earth. At first, the official seconds were slightly adjusted, but starting in 1972, "leap seconds" were occasionally inserted. (In theory, a second might need to be removed once in a while, but that has not yet happened.) There is talk of changing the system again. Clearly, leap seconds are a pain, and many computer systems instead use "smoothing" where time is artificially slowed down or sped up just before the leap second, keeping 86,400 seconds per day. This works because the local time on a computer isn't all that precise, and computers are used to synchronizing themselves with an external time service.

The Java Date and Time API specification requires that Java uses a time scale that

- Has 86,400 seconds per day
- Exactly matches the official time at noon each day
- Closely matches it elsewhere, in a precisely defined way

That gives Java the flexibility to adjust to future changes in the official time.

In Java, an Instant represents a point on the time line. An origin, called the *epoch*, is arbitrarily set at midnight of January 1, 1970 at the prime meridian that passes through the Greenwich Royal Observatory in London. This is the same convention used in the UNIX/POSIX time. Starting from that origin, time is measured in 86,400 seconds per day, forward and backward, to nanosecond precision. The Instant values go back as far as a billion years (Instant.MIN). That's not quite enough to express the age of the universe (around 13.5 billion years) but it should be enough for all practical purposes. After all, a billion years ago, the earth was covered in ice and populated by microscopic ancestors of today's plants and animals. The largest value, Instant.MAX, is December 31 of the year 1,000,000,000.

The static method call Instant.now() gives the current instant. You can compare two instants with the equals and compareTo methods in the usual way, so you can use instants as timestamps.

To find out the difference between two instants, use the static method Duration.between. For example, here is how you can measure the running time of an algorithm:

```
Instant start = Instant.now();
runAlgorithm();
Instant end = Instant.now();
Duration timeElapsed = Duration.between(start, end);
long millis = timeElapsed.toMillis();
```

A Duration is the amount of time between two instants. You can get the length of a Duration in conventional units by calling toNanos, toMillis, toSeconds, toMinutes, toHours, or toDays.

NOTE: In Java 8, you had to call getSeconds instead of toSeconds.

If you need nanosecond precision, be aware of overflow. A long value can hold almost 300 years of nanoseconds. If your durations are shorter than that, simply convert them to nanoseconds. You can use longer durations—a Duration object stores the number of seconds in a long, and the number of nanoseconds in an additional int. The Duration API has a number of methods, shown at the end of this section, for carrying out arithmetic.

For example, if you want to check whether an algorithm is at least ten times faster than another, you can compute

```
Duration timeElapsed2 = Duration.between(start2, end2);
boolean overTenTimesFaster
  = timeElapsed.multipliedBy(10).minus(timeElapsed2).isNegative();
```

This is just to show the syntax. Since the algorithms aren't going to run for hundreds of years, you can simply use

```
boolean overTenTimesFaster = timeElapsed.toNanos() * 10 < timeElapsed2.toNanos();
```

NOTE: The Instant and Duration classes are immutable, and all methods, such as multipliedBy or minus, return a new instance.

In the example program in Listing 6.1, you can see how to use the `Instant` and `Duration` classes for timing two algorithms.

Listing 6.1 `timeline/TimeLine.java`

```java
1  package timeline;
2
3  /**
4   * @version 1.0 2016-05-10
5   * @author Cay Horstmann
6   */
7
8  import java.time.*;
9  import java.util.*;
10 import java.util.stream.*;
11
12 public class Timeline
13 {
14    public static void main(String[] args)
15    {
16       Instant start = Instant.now();
17       runAlgorithm();
18       Instant end = Instant.now();
19       Duration timeElapsed = Duration.between(start, end);
20       long millis = timeElapsed.toMillis();
21       System.out.printf("%d milliseconds\n", millis);
22
23       Instant start2 = Instant.now();
24       runAlgorithm2();
25       Instant end2 = Instant.now();
26       Duration timeElapsed2 = Duration.between(start2, end2);
27       System.out.printf("%d milliseconds\n", timeElapsed2.toMillis());
28       boolean overTenTimesFaster = timeElapsed.multipliedBy(10)
29          .minus(timeElapsed2).isNegative();
30       System.out.printf("The first algorithm is %smore than ten times faster",
31          overTenTimesFaster ? "" : "not ");
32    }
33
34    public static void runAlgorithm()
35    {
36       int size = 10;
37       List<Integer> list = new Random().ints().map(i -> i % 100).limit(size)
38          .boxed().collect(Collectors.toList());
39       Collections.sort(list);
40       System.out.println(list);
41    }
```

```
42
43   public static void runAlgorithm2()
44   {
45      int size = 10;
46      List<Integer> list = new Random().ints().map(i -> i % 100).limit(size)
47         .boxed().collect(Collectors.toList());
48      while (!IntStream.range(1, list.size())
49            .allMatch(i -> list.get(i - 1).compareTo(list.get(i)) <= 0))
50         Collections.shuffle(list);
51      System.out.println(list);
52   }
53 }
```

---

java.time.Instant 8

- static Instant now()

gets the current instant from the best available system clock.

- Instant plus(TemporalAmount amountToAdd)
- Instant minus(TemporalAmount amountToSubtract)

yields an instant that is the given amount away from this Instant. The classes Duration and Period (see Section 6.2, "Local Dates," on p. 358) implement the TemporalAmount interface.

- Instant (plus|minus)(Nanos|Millis|Seconds)(long number)

yields an Instant that is the given number of nanoseconds, milliseconds, or seconds away from this Instant.

---

java.time.Duration 8

- static Duration of(Nanos|Millis|Seconds|Minutes|Hours|Days)(long number)

yields a duration of the given number of time units.

- static Duration between(Temporal startInclusive, Temporal endExclusive)

yields a duration between the given points in time. The Temporal interface is implemented by the Instant class as well as LocalDate/LocalDateTime/LocalTime (see Section 6.4, "Local Time," on p. 365) and ZonedDateTime (see Section 6.5, "Zoned Time," on p. 367).

(Continues)

---

java.time.Duration 8 *(Continued)*

- long toNanos()
- long toMillis()
- long toSeconds() 9
- long toMinutes()
- long toHours()
- long toSeconds()
- long toSeconds()
- long toDays()

  gets the number of the time units in the method name for this Duration.

- int to(Nanos|Millis|Seconds|Minutes|Hours)Part() 9
- long to(Days|Hours|Minutes|Seconds|Millis|Nanos)Part() 9

  the part of the given time unit in this Duration. For example, in a duration of 100 seconds, the minutes part is 1 and the seconds part is 40.

- Instant plus(TemporalAmount amountToAdd)
- Instant minus(TemporalAmount amountToSubtract)

  yields an instant that is the given amount away from this Instant. The classes Duration and Period (see Section 6.2, "Local Dates," on p. 358) implement the TemporalAmount interface.

- Duration multipliedBy(long multiplicand)
- Duration dividedBy(long divisor)
- Duration negated()

  yields a duration that is obtained by multiplying or dividing this Duration by the given amount, or by −1.

- boolean isZero()
- boolean isNegative()

  returns true if this Duration is zero or negative.

- Duration (plus|minus)(Nanos|Millis|Seconds|Minutes|Hours|Days)(long number)

  yields a Duration obtained by adding or subtracting the given number of time units.

6.2 Local Dates

Now let us turn from absolute time to human time. There are two kinds of human time in the Java API, *local date/time* and *zoned time*. Local date/time has a date and/or time of day, but no associated time zone information. An example of a local date is June 14, 1903 (the day on which Alonzo Church, inventor of the lambda calculus, was born). Since that date has neither a time of day nor time zone information, it does not correspond to a precise instant of time. In contrast, July 16, 1969, 09:32:00 EDT (the launch of Apollo 11) is a zoned date/time, representing a precise instant on the time line.

There are many calculations where time zones are not required, and in some cases they can even be a hindrance. Suppose you schedule a meeting every week at 10:00. If you add 7 days (that is, $7 \times 24 \times 60 \times 60$ seconds) to the last zoned time, and you happen to cross the daylight savings time boundary, the meeting will be an hour too early or too late!

For that reason, the API designers recommend that you do not use zoned time unless you really want to represent absolute time instances. Birthdays, holidays, schedule times, and so on are usually best represented as local dates or times.

A LocalDate is a date with a year, month, and day of the month. To construct one, you can use the now or of static methods:

```
LocalDate today = LocalDate.now(); // Today's date
LocalDate alonzosBirthday = LocalDate.of(1903, 6, 14);
alonzosBirthday = LocalDate.of(1903, Month.JUNE, 14);
    // Uses the Month enumeration
```

Unlike the irregular conventions in UNIX and java.util.Date, where months are zero-based and years are counted from 1900, here you supply the usual numbers for the month of year. Alternatively, you can use the Month enumeration.

The API notes at the end of this section show the most useful methods for working with LocalDate objects.

For example, *Programmer's Day* is the 256th day of the year. Here is how you can easily compute it:

```
LocalDate programmersDay = LocalDate.of(2014, 1, 1).plusDays(255);
    // September 13, but in a leap year it would be September 12
```

Recall that the difference between two time instants is a Duration. The equivalent for local dates is a Period, which expresses a number of elapsed years, months, or days. You can call birthday.plus(Period.ofYears(1)) to get the birthday next year. Of course, you can also just call birthday.plusYears(1). But birthday.plus(Period .ofDays(365)) won't produce the correct result in a leap year.

The until method yields the difference between two local dates. For example,

```
independenceDay.until(christmas)
```

yields a period of 5 months and 21 days. That is actually not terribly useful because the number of days per month varies. To find the number of days, use

```
independenceDay.until(christmas, ChronoUnit.DAYS) // 174 days
```

 CAUTION: Some methods in the LocalDate API could potentially create nonexistent dates. For example, adding one month to January 31 should not yield February 31. Instead of throwing an exception, these methods return the last valid day of the month. For example,

```
LocalDate.of(2016, 1, 31).plusMonths(1)
```

and

```
LocalDate.of(2016, 3, 31).minusMonths(1)
```

yield February 29, 2016.

The getDayOfWeek yields the weekday, as a value of the DayOfWeek enumeration. DayOfWeek.MONDAY has the numerical value 1, and DayOfWeek.SUNDAY has the value 7. For example,

```
LocalDate.of(1900, 1, 1).getDayOfWeek().getValue()
```

yields 1. The DayOfWeek enumeration has convenience methods plus and minus to compute weekdays modulo 7. For example, DayOfWeek.SATURDAY.plus(3) yields DayOfWeek.TUESDAY.

 NOTE: The weekend days actually come at the end of the week. This is different from java.util.Calendar where Sunday has value 1 and Saturday value 7.

Java 9 adds two useful methods datesUntil that yield streams of LocalDate objects.

```
LocalDate start = LocalDate.of(2000, 1, 1);
LocalDate endExclusive = LocalDate.now();
Stream<LocalDate> allDays = start.datesUntil(endExclusive);
Stream<LocalDate> firstDaysInMonth = start.datesUntil(endExclusive, Period.ofMonths(1));
```

In addition to LocalDate, there are also classes MonthDay, YearMonth, and Year to describe partial dates. For example, December 25 (with the year unspecified) can be represented as a MonthDay.

The example program in Listing 6.2 shows how to work with the LocalDate class.

Listing 6.2 localdates/LocalDates.java

```java
1  package localdates;
2
3  /**
4   * @version 1.0 2016-05-10
5   * @author Cay Horstmann
6   */
7  import java.time.*;
8  import java.time.temporal.*;
9  import java.util.stream.*;
10
11  public class LocalDates
12  {
13     public static void main(String[] args)
14     {
15        LocalDate today = LocalDate.now(); // Today's date
16        System.out.println("today: " + today);
17
18        LocalDate alonzosBirthday = LocalDate.of(1903, 6, 14);
19        alonzosBirthday = LocalDate.of(1903, Month.JUNE, 14);
20        // Uses the Month enumeration
21        System.out.println("alonzosBirthday: " + alonzosBirthday);
22
23        LocalDate programmersDay = LocalDate.of(2018, 1, 1).plusDays(255);
24        // September 13, but in a leap year it would be September 12
25        System.out.println("programmersDay: " + programmersDay);
26
27        LocalDate independenceDay = LocalDate.of(2018, Month.JULY, 4);
28        LocalDate christmas = LocalDate.of(2018, Month.DECEMBER, 25);
29
30        System.out.println("Until christmas: " + independenceDay.until(christmas));
31        System.out.println("Until christmas: "
32           + independenceDay.until(christmas, ChronoUnit.DAYS));
33
34        System.out.println(LocalDate.of(2016, 1, 31).plusMonths(1));
35        System.out.println(LocalDate.of(2016, 3, 31).minusMonths(1));
36
37        DayOfWeek startOfLastMillennium = LocalDate.of(1900, 1, 1).getDayOfWeek();
38        System.out.println("startOfLastMillennium: " + startOfLastMillennium);
39        System.out.println(startOfLastMillennium.getValue());
40        System.out.println(DayOfWeek.SATURDAY.plus(3));
41
42        LocalDate start = LocalDate.of(2000, 1, 1);
43        LocalDate endExclusive = LocalDate.now();
44        Stream<LocalDate> firstDaysInMonth = start.datesUntil(endExclusive, Period.ofMonths(1));
45        System.out.println("firstDaysInMonth: "
46           + firstDaysInMonth.collect(Collectors.toList()));
47     }
48  }
```

`java.time.LocalDate` 8

- `static LocalDate now()`

  gets the current `LocalDate`.

- `static LocalDate of(int year, int month, int dayOfMonth)`
- `static LocalDate of(int year, Month month, int dayOfMonth)`

  yields a local date with the given year, month (as integer between 1 and 12 or a value of the `Month` enumeration), and day of the month (between 1 and 31).

- `LocalDate (plus|minus)(Days|Weeks|Months|Years)(long number)`

  yields a `LocalDate` obtained by adding or subtracting the given number of time units.

- `LocalDate plus(TemporalAmount amountToAdd)`
- `LocalDate minus(TemporalAmount amountToSubtract)`

  yields an instant that is the given amount away from this `Instant`. The classes `Duration` and `Period` implement the `TemporalAmount` interface.

- `LocalDate withDayOfMonth(int dayOfMonth)`
- `LocalDate withDayOfYear(int dayOfYear)`
- `LocalDate withMonth(int month)`
- `LocalDate withYear(int year)`

  returns a new `LocalDate` with the day of month, day of year, month, or year changed to the given value.

- `int getDayOfMonth()`

  gets the day of the month (between 1 and 31).

- `int getDayOfYear()`

  gets the day of the year (between 1 and 366).

- `DayOfWeek getDayOfWeek()`

  gets the day of the week, returning a value of the `DayOfWeek` enumeration.

- `Month getMonth()`
- `int getMonthValue()`

  gets the month as a value of the `Month` enumeration, or as a number between 1 and 12.

- `int getYear()`

  gets the year, between −999,999,999 and 999,999,999.

- `Period until(ChronoLocalDate endDateExclusive)`

  gets the period until the given end date. The `ChronoLocalDate` interface is implemented by `LocalDate` and date classes for non-Gregorian calendars.

---

java.time.LocalDate 8   *(Continued)*

- boolean isBefore(ChronoLocalDate other)
- boolean isAfter(ChronoLocalDate other)

  returns true if this date is before or after the given date.

- boolean isLeapYear()

  returns true if the year is a leap year—that is, if it is divisible by 4 but not by 100, or divisible by 400. The algorithm is applied for all past years, even though that is historically inaccurate. (Leap years were invented in the year −46, and the rules involving divisibility by 100 and 400 were introduced in the Gregorian calendar reform of 1582. The reform took over 300 years to become universal.)

- Stream<LocalDate> datesUntil(LocalDate endExclusive) 9
- Stream<LocalDate> datesUntil(LocalDate endExclusive, Period step) 9

  yields a stream of dates from this LocalDate until the end, with step size 1 or the given period.

---

java.time.Period 8

- static Period of(int years, int months, int days)
- Period of(Days|Weeks|Months|Years)(int number)

  yields a Period with the given number of time units.

- int get(Days|Months|Years)()

  gets the days, months, or years of this Period.

- Period (plus|minus)(Days|Months|Years)(long number)

  yields a LocalDate obtained by adding or subtracting the given number of time units.

- Period plus(TemporalAmount amountToAdd)
- Period minus(TemporalAmount amountToSubtract)

  yields an instant that is the given amount away from this Instant. The classes Duration and Period implement the TemporalAmount interface.

- Period with(Days|Months|Years)(int number)

  returns a new Period with the days, months, or years changed to the given number.

6.3 Date Adjusters

For scheduling applications, you often need to compute dates such as "the first Tuesday of every month." The TemporalAdjusters class provides a number of static methods for common adjustments. You pass the result of an adjustment method to the with method. For example, the first Tuesday of a month can be computed like this:

```
LocalDate firstTuesday = LocalDate.of(year, month, 1).with(
    TemporalAdjusters.nextOrSame(DayOfWeek.TUESDAY));
```

As always, the with method returns a new LocalDate object without modifying the original. The API notes at the end of this section show the available adjusters.

You can also make your own adjuster by implementing the TemporalAdjuster interface. Here is an adjuster for computing the next weekday:

```
TemporalAdjuster NEXT_WORKDAY = w ->
    {
        var result = (LocalDate) w;
        do
        {
            result = result.plusDays(1);
        }
        while (result.getDayOfWeek().getValue() >= 6);
        return result;
    };

LocalDate backToWork = today.with(NEXT_WORKDAY);
```

Note that the parameter of the lambda expression has type Temporal, and it must be cast to LocalDate. You can avoid this cast with the ofDateAdjuster method that expects a lambda of type UnaryOperator<LocalDate>.

```
TemporalAdjuster NEXT_WORKDAY = TemporalAdjusters.ofDateAdjuster(w ->
    {
        LocalDate result = w; // No cast
        do
        {
            result = result.plusDays(1);
        }
        while (result.getDayOfWeek().getValue() >= 6);
        return result;
    });
```

---

java.time.LocalDate 9

- LocalDate with(TemporalAdjuster adjuster)

  returns the result of adjusting this date by the given adjuster.

---

java.time.temporal.TemporalAdjusters 9

- static TemporalAdjuster next(DayOfWeek dayOfWeek)
- static TemporalAdjuster nextOrSame(DayOfWeek dayOfWeek)
- static TemporalAdjuster previous(DayOfWeek dayOfWeek)
- static TemporalAdjuster previousOrSame(DayOfWeek dayOfWeek)

  returns an adjuster that adjusts a date to the given day of the week.

- static TemporalAdjuster dayOfWeekInMonth(int n, DayOfWeek dayOfWeek)
- static TemporalAdjuster lastInMonth(DayOfWeek dayOfWeek)

  returns an adjuster that adjusts a date to the nth or last given weekday on the month.

- static TemporalAdjuster firstDayOfMonth()
- static TemporalAdjuster firstDayOfNextMonth()
- static TemporalAdjuster firstDayOfYear()
- static TemporalAdjuster firstDayOfNextYear()
- static TemporalAdjuster lastDayOfMonth()
- static TemporalAdjuster lastDayOfYear()

  returns an adjuster that adjusts a date to the given day of the month or year.

6.4 Local Time

A LocalTime represents a time of day, such as 15:30:00. You can create an instance with the now or of methods:

```
LocalTime rightNow = LocalTime.now();
LocalTime bedtime = LocalTime.of(22, 30); // or LocalTime.of(22, 30, 0)
```

The API notes show common operations with local times. The plus and minus operations wrap around a 24-hour day. For example,

```
LocalTime wakeup = bedtime.plusHours(8); // wakeup is 6:30:00
```

 NOTE: LocalTime doesn't concern itself with AM/PM. That silliness is left to a formatter—see Section 6.6, "Formatting and Parsing," on p. 371.

There is a LocalDateTime class representing a date and time. That class is suitable for storing points in time in a fixed time zone—for example, for a schedule of classes or events. However, if you need to make calculations that span the daylight savings time, or if you need to deal with users in different time zones, you should use the ZonedDateTime class that we discuss next.

---

java.time.LocalTime   8

- static LocalTime now()

  gets the current LocalTime.

- static LocalTime of(int hour, int minute)
- static LocalTime of(int hour, int minute, int second)
- static LocalTime of(int hour, int minute, int second, int nanoOfSecond)

  yields a local time with the given hour (between 0 and 23), minute, second (between 0 and 59), and nanosecond (between 0 and 999,999,999).

- LocalTime (plus|minus)(Hours|Minutes|Seconds|Nanos)(long number)

  yields a LocalTime obtained by adding or subtracting the given number of time units.

- LocalTime plus(TemporalAmount amountToAdd)
- LocalTime minus(TemporalAmount amountToSubtract)

  yields an instant that is the given amount away from this Instant.

- LocalTime with(Hour|Minute|Second|Nano)(int value)

  returns a new LocalTime with the hour, minute, second, or nanosecond changed to the given value.

- int getHour()

  gets the hour (between 0 and 23).

- int getMinute()
- int getSecond()

  gets the minute or second (between 0 and 59).

- int getNano()

  gets the nanoseconds (between 0 and 999,999,999).

- int toSecondOfDay()
- long toNanoOfDay()

  yields the seconds or nanoseconds since midnight.

- boolean isBefore(LocalTime other)
- boolean isAfter(LocalTime other)

  returns true if this date is before or after the given date.

6.5 Zoned Time

Time zones, perhaps because they are an entirely human creation, are even messier than the complications caused by the earth's irregular rotation. In a rational world, we'd all follow the clock in Greenwich, and some of us would eat our lunch at 02:00, others at 22:00. Our stomachs would figure it out. This is actually done in China, which spans four conventional time zones. Elsewhere, we have time zones with irregular and shifting boundaries and, to make matters worse, the daylight savings time.

As capricious as the time zones may appear to the enlightened, they are a fact of life. When you implement a calendar application, it needs to work for people who fly from one country to another. When you have a conference call at 10:00 in New York, but happen to be in Berlin, you expect to be alerted at the correct local time.

The Internet Assigned Numbers Authority (IANA) keeps a database of all known time zones around the world (www.iana.org/time-zones), which is updated several times per year. The bulk of the updates deals with the changing rules for daylight savings time. Java uses the IANA database.

Each time zone has an ID, such as America/New_York or Europe/Berlin. To find out all available time zones, call ZoneId.getAvailableZoneIds. At the time of this writing, there are almost 600 IDs.

Given a time zone ID, the static method ZoneId.of(id) yields a ZoneId object. You can use that object to turn a LocalDateTime object into a ZonedDateTime object by calling local.atZone(zoneId), or you can construct a ZonedDateTime by calling the static method ZonedDateTime.of(year, month, day, hour, minute, second, nano, zoneId). For example,

```
ZonedDateTime apollo11launch = ZonedDateTime.of(1969, 7, 16, 9, 32, 0, 0,
    ZoneId.of("America/New_York"));
    // 1969-07-16T09:32-04:00[America/New_York]
```

This is a specific instant in time. Call apollo11launch.toInstant to get the Instant. Conversely, if you have an instant in time, call instant.atZone(ZoneId.of("UTC")) to get the ZonedDateTime at the Greenwich Royal Observatory, or use another ZoneId to get it elsewhere on the planet.

 NOTE: UTC stands for "Coordinated Universal Time," and the acronym is a compromise between the aforementioned English and the French "Temps Universel Coordiné," having the distinction of being incorrect in either language. UTC is the time at the Greenwich Royal Observatory, without daylight savings time.

Many of the methods of ZonedDateTime are the same as those of LocalDateTime (see the API notes at the end of this section). Most are straightforward, but daylight savings time introduces some complications.

When daylight savings time starts, clocks advance by an hour. What happens when you construct a time that falls into the skipped hour? For example, in 2013, Central Europe switched to daylight savings time on March 31 at 2:00. If you try to construct nonexistent time March 31 2:30, you actually get 3:30.

```
ZonedDateTime skipped = ZonedDateTime.of(
   LocalDate.of(2013, 3, 31),
   LocalTime.of(2, 30),
   ZoneId.of("Europe/Berlin"));
   // Constructs March 31 3:30
```

Conversely, when daylight time ends, clocks are set back by an hour, and there are two instants with the same local time! When you construct a time within that span, you get the earlier of the two.

```
ZonedDateTime ambiguous = ZonedDateTime.of(
   LocalDate.of(2013, 10, 27), // End of daylight savings time
   LocalTime.of(2, 30),
   ZoneId.of("Europe/Berlin"));
   // 2013-10-27T02:30+02:00[Europe/Berlin]
ZonedDateTime anHourLater = ambiguous.plusHours(1);
   // 2013-10-27T02:30+01:00[Europe/Berlin]
```

An hour later, the time has the same hours and minutes, but the zone offset has changed.

You also need to pay attention when adjusting a date across daylight savings time boundaries. For example, if you set a meeting for next week, don't add a duration of seven days:

```
ZonedDateTime nextMeeting = meeting.plus(Duration.ofDays(7));
   // Caution! Won't work with daylight savings time
```

Instead, use the Period class.

```
ZonedDateTime nextMeeting = meeting.plus(Period.ofDays(7)); // OK
```

The example program in Listing 6.3 demonstrates the ZonedDateTime class.

 CAUTION: There is also an OffsetDateTime class that represents times with an offset from UTC, but without time zone rules. That class is intended for specialized applications that specifically require the absence of those rules, such as certain network protocols. For human time, use ZonedDateTime.

Listing 6.3 zonedtimes/ZonedTimes.java

```
 1  package zonedtimes;
 2
 3  /**
 4   * @version 1.0 2016-05-10
 5   * @author Cay Horstmann
 6   */
 7
 8  import java.time.*;
 9
10  public class ZonedTimes
11  {
12     public static void main(String[] args)
13     {
14        ZonedDateTime apollo11launch = ZonedDateTime.of(1969, 7, 16, 9, 32, 0, 0,
15           ZoneId.of("America/New_York")); // 1969-07-16T09:32-04:00[America/New_York]
16        System.out.println("apollo11launch: " + apollo11launch);
17
18        Instant instant = apollo11launch.toInstant();
19        System.out.println("instant: " + instant);
20
21        ZonedDateTime zonedDateTime = instant.atZone(ZoneId.of("UTC"));
22        System.out.println("zonedDateTime: " + zonedDateTime);
23
24        ZonedDateTime skipped = ZonedDateTime.of(LocalDate.of(2013, 3, 31),
25           LocalTime.of(2, 30), ZoneId.of("Europe/Berlin")); // Constructs March 31 3:30
26        System.out.println("skipped: " + skipped);
27
28        ZonedDateTime ambiguous = ZonedDateTime.of(
29           LocalDate.of(2013, 10, 27), // End of daylight savings time
30           LocalTime.of(2, 30), ZoneId.of("Europe/Berlin"));
31           // 2013-10-27T02:30+02:00[Europe/Berlin]
32        ZonedDateTime anHourLater = ambiguous.plusHours(1);
33           // 2013-10-27T02:30+01:00[Europe/Berlin]
34        System.out.println("ambiguous: " + ambiguous);
35        System.out.println("anHourLater: " + anHourLater);
36
37        ZonedDateTime meeting = ZonedDateTime.of(LocalDate.of(2013, 10, 31),
38           LocalTime.of(14, 30), ZoneId.of("America/Los_Angeles"));
39        System.out.println("meeting: " + meeting);
40        ZonedDateTime nextMeeting = meeting.plus(Duration.ofDays(7));
41           // Caution! Won't work with daylight savings time
42        System.out.println("nextMeeting: " + nextMeeting);
43        nextMeeting = meeting.plus(Period.ofDays(7)); // OK
44        System.out.println("nextMeeting: " + nextMeeting);
45     }
46  }
```

---

java.time.ZonedDateTime 8

- `static ZonedDateTime now()`

  gets the current ZonedDateTime.

- `static ZonedDateTime of(int year, int month, int dayOfMonth, int hour, int minute, int second, int nanoOfSecond, ZoneId zone)`
- `static ZonedDateTime of(LocalDate date, LocalTime time, ZoneId zone)`
- `static ZonedDateTime of(LocalDateTime localDateTime, ZoneId zone)`
- `static ZonedDateTime ofInstant(Instant instant, ZoneId zone)`

  yields a ZonedDateTime with the given parameters and time zone.

- `ZonedDateTime    (plus|minus)(Days|Weeks|Months|Years|Hours|Minutes|Seconds|Nanos)(long number)`

  yields a ZonedDateTime obtained by adding or subtracting the given number of time units.

- `ZonedDateTime plus(TemporalAmount amountToAdd)`
- `ZonedDateTime minus(TemporalAmount amountToSubtract)`

  yields an instant that is the given amount away from this Instant.

- `ZonedDateTime with(DayOfMonth|DayOfYear|Month|Year|Hour|Minute|Second|Nano)(int value)`

  returns a new ZonedDateTime with the given temporal unit replaced by the given value.

- `ZonedDateTime withZoneSameInstant(ZoneId zone)`
- `ZonedDateTime withZoneSameLocal(ZoneId zone)`

  returns a new ZonedDateTime in the given time zone, either representing the same instant or the same local time.

- `int getDayOfMonth()`

  gets the day of the month (between 1 and 31).

- `int getDayOfYear()`

  gets the day of the year (between 1 and 366).

- `DayOfWeek getDayOfWeek()`

  gets the day of the week, returning a value of the DayOfWeek enumeration.

- `Month getMonth()`
- `int getMonthValue()`

  gets the month as a value of the Month enumeration, or as a number between 1 and 12.

- `int getYear()`

  gets the year, between −999,999,999 and 999,999,999.

(Continues)

---

java.time.ZonedDateTime 8 *(Continued)*

- `int getHour()`

  gets the hour (between 0 and 23).

- `int getMinute()`
- `int getSecond()`

  gets the minute or second (between 0 and 59).

- `int getNano()`

  gets the nanoseconds (between 0 and 999,999,999).

- `public ZoneOffset getOffset()`

  gets the offset from UTC. Offsets can vary from −12:00 to +14:00. Some time zones have fractional offsets. Offsets change with daylight savings time.

- `LocalDate toLocalDate()`
- `LocalTime toLocalTime()`
- `LocalDateTime toLocalDateTime()`
- `Instant toInstant()`

  yields the local date, time, or date/time, or the corresponding instant.

- `boolean isBefore(ChronoZonedDateTime other)`
- `boolean isAfter(ChronoZonedDateTime other)`

  returns true if this zoned date/time is before or after the given zoned date/time.

6.6 Formatting and Parsing

The `DateTimeFormatter` class provides three kinds of formatters to print a date/time value:

- Predefined standard formatters (see Table 6.1)
- Locale-specific formatters
- Formatters with custom patterns

To use one of the standard formatters, simply call its `format` method:

```
String formatted = DateTimeFormatter.ISO_OFFSET_DATE_TIME.format(apollo11launch);
   // 1969-07-16T09:32:00-04:00"
```

The standard formatters are mostly intended for machine-readable time-stamps. To present dates and times to human readers, use a locale-specific formatter. There are four styles, `SHORT`, `MEDIUM`, `LONG`, and `FULL`, for both date and time—see Table 6.2.

Table 6.1 Predefined Formatters

Formatter	Description	Example
BASIC_ISO_DATE	Year, month, day, zone offset without separators	19690716-0500
ISO_LOCAL_DATE, ISO_LOCAL_TIME, ISO_LOCAL_DATE_TIME	Separators -, :, T	1969-07-16, 09:32:00, 1969-07-16T09:32:00
ISO_OFFSET_DATE, ISO_OFFSET_TIME, ISO_OFFSET_DATE_TIME	Like ISO_LOCAL_*XXX*, but with zone offset	1969-07-16-05:00, 09:32:00-05:00, 1969-07-16T09:32:00-05:00
ISO_ZONED_DATE_TIME	With zone offset and zone ID	1969-07-16T09:32:00-05:00[America/New_York]
ISO_INSTANT	In UTC, denoted by the Z zone ID	1969-07-16T14:32:00Z
ISO_DATE, ISO_TIME, ISO_DATE_TIME	Like ISO_OFFSET_DATE, ISO_OFFSET_TIME, and ISO_ZONED_DATE_TIME, but the zone information is optional	1969-07-16-05:00, 09:32:00-05:00, 1969-07-16T09:32:00-05:00[America/New_York]
ISO_ORDINAL_DATE	The year and day of year, for LocalDate	1969-197
ISO_WEEK_DATE	The year, week, and day of week, for LocalDate	1969-W29-3
RFC_1123_DATE_TIME	The standard for email timestamps, codified in RFC 822 and updated to four digits for the year in RFC 1123	Wed, 16 Jul 1969 09:32:00 -0500

The static methods ofLocalizedDate, ofLocalizedTime, and ofLocalizedDateTime create such a formatter. For example:

```
DateTimeFormatter formatter = DateTimeFormatter.ofLocalizedDateTime(FormatStyle.LONG);
String formatted = formatter.format(apollo11launch);
   // July 16, 1969 9:32:00 AM EDT
```

These methods use the default locale. To change to a different locale, simply use the withLocale method.

Table 6.2 Locale-Specific Formatting Styles

Style	Date	Time
SHORT	7/16/69	9:32 AM
MEDIUM	Jul 16, 1969	9:32:00 AM
LONG	July 16, 1969	9:32:00 AM EDT
FULL	Wednesday, July 16, 1969	9:32:00 AM EDT

```
formatted = formatter.withLocale(Locale.FRENCH).format(apollo11launch);
    // 16 juillet 1969 09:32:00 EDT
```

The `DayOfWeek` and `Month` enumerations have methods `getDisplayName` for giving the names of weekdays and months in different locales and formats.

```
for (DayOfWeek w : DayOfWeek.values())
    System.out.print(w.getDisplayName(TextStyle.SHORT, Locale.ENGLISH) + " ");
    // Prints Mon Tue Wed Thu Fri Sat Sun
```

See Chapter 7 for more information about locales.

 NOTE: The `java.time.format.DateTimeFormatter` class is intended as a replacement for `java.util.DateFormat`. If you need an instance of the latter for backward compatibility, call `formatter.toFormat()`.

Finally, you can roll your own date format by specifying a pattern. For example,

```
formatter = DateTimeFormatter.ofPattern("E yyyy-MM-dd HH:mm");
```

formats a date in the form `Wed 1969-07-16 09:32`. Each letter denotes a different time field, and the number of times the letter is repeated selects a particular format, according to rules that are arcane and seem to have organically grown over time. Table 6.3 shows the most useful pattern elements.

To parse a date/time value from a string, use one of the static `parse` methods. For example,

```
LocalDate churchsBirthday = LocalDate.parse("1903-06-14");
ZonedDateTime apollo11launch =
    ZonedDateTime.parse("1969-07-16 03:32:00-0400",
        DateTimeFormatter.ofPattern("yyyy-MM-dd HH:mm:ssxx"));
```

The first call uses the standard `ISO_LOCAL_DATE` formatter, the second one a custom formatter.

Table 6.3 Commonly Used Formatting Symbols for Date/Time Formats

ChronoField or Purpose	Examples
ERA	G: AD, GGGG: Anno Domini, GGGGG: A
YEAR_OF_ERA	yy: 69, yyyy: 1969
MONTH_OF_YEAR	M: 7, MM: 07, MMM: Jul, MMMM: July, MMMMM: J
DAY_OF_MONTH	d: 6, dd: 06
DAY_OF_WEEK	e: 3, E: Wed, EEEE: Wednesday, EEEEE: W
HOUR_OF_DAY	H: 9, HH: 09
CLOCK_HOUR_OF_AM_PM	K: 9, KK: 09
AMPM_OF_DAY	a: AM
MINUTE_OF_HOUR	mm: 02
SECOND_OF_MINUTE	ss: 00
NANO_OF_SECOND	nnnnnn: 000000
Time zone ID	VV: America/New_York
Time zone name	z: EDT, zzzz: Eastern Daylight Time, v: ET, vvvv: Eastern Time
Zone offset	x: -04, xx: -0400, xxx: -04:00, XXX: same, but use Z for zero
Localized zone offset	O: GMT-4, OOOO: GMT-04:00
Modified Julian Day	g: 58243

The program in Listing 6.4 shows how to format and parse dates and times.

Listing 6.4 formatting/Formatting.java

```
1 package formatting;
2
3 /**
4  * @version 1.0 2016-05-10
5  * @author Cay Horstmann
6  */
7
8 import java.time.*;
9 import java.time.format.*;
10 import java.util.*;
11
12 public class Formatting
13 {
```

```
14    public static void main(String[] args)
15    {
16        ZonedDateTime apollo11launch = ZonedDateTime.of(1969, 7, 16, 9, 32, 0, 0,
17            ZoneId.of("America/New_York"));
18
19        String formatted = DateTimeFormatter.ISO_OFFSET_DATE_TIME.format(apollo11launch);
20        // 1969-07-16T09:32:00-04:00
21        System.out.println(formatted);
22
23        DateTimeFormatter formatter = DateTimeFormatter.ofLocalizedDateTime(FormatStyle.LONG);
24        formatted = formatter.format(apollo11launch);
25        // July 16, 1969 9:32:00 AM EDT
26        System.out.println(formatted);
27        formatted = formatter.withLocale(Locale.FRENCH).format(apollo11launch);
28        // 16 juillet 1969 09:32:00 EDT
29        System.out.println(formatted);
30
31        formatter = DateTimeFormatter.ofPattern("E yyyy-MM-dd HH:mm");
32        formatted = formatter.format(apollo11launch);
33        System.out.println(formatted);
34
35        LocalDate churchsBirthday = LocalDate.parse("1903-06-14");
36        System.out.println("churchsBirthday: " + churchsBirthday);
37        apollo11launch = ZonedDateTime.parse("1969-07-16 03:32:00-0400",
38            DateTimeFormatter.ofPattern("yyyy-MM-dd HH:mm:ssxx"));
39        System.out.println("apollo11launch: " + apollo11launch);
40
41        for (DayOfWeek w : DayOfWeek.values())
42            System.out.print(w.getDisplayName(TextStyle.SHORT, Locale.ENGLISH) + " ");
43    }
44 }
```

---

java.time.format.DateTimeFormatter 8

- `String format(TemporalAccessor temporal)`

  formats the given value. The classes Instant, LocalDate, LocalTime, LocalDateTime, and ZonedDateTime, as well as many others, implement the TemporalAccessor interface.

- `static DateTimeFormatter ofLocalizedDate(FormatStyle dateStyle)`
- `static DateTimeFormatter ofLocalizedTime(FormatStyle timeStyle)`
- `static DateTimeFormatter ofLocalizedDateTime(FormatStyle dateTimeStyle)`
- `static DateTimeFormatter ofLocalizedDateTime(FormatStyle dateStyle, FormatStyle timeStyle)`

  yields a formatter for the given styles. The FormatStyle enumeration has values SHORT, MEDIUM, LONG, and FULL.

(Continues)

---

java.time.format.DateTimeFormatter 8   *(Continued)*

- `DateTimeFormatter withLocale(Locale locale)`

  yields a formatter equal to this formatter, using the given locale.
- `static DateTimeFormatter ofPattern(String pattern)`
- `static DateTimeFormatter ofPattern(String pattern, Locale locale)`

  yields a formatter using the given pattern and locale. See Table 6.3 for the pattern syntax.

---

java.time.LocalDate 8

- `static LocalDate parse(CharSequence text)`
- `static LocalDate parse(CharSequence text, DateTimeFormatter formatter)`

  yields a `LocalDate` using the default formatter, or the given formatter.

---

java.time.ZonedDateTime 8

- `static ZonedDateTime parse(CharSequence text)`
- `static ZonedDateTime parse(CharSequence text, DateTimeFormatter formatter)`

  yields a `ZonedDateTime` using the default formatter, or the given formatter.

6.7 Interoperating with Legacy Code

As a new creation, the Java Date and Time API will have to interoperate with existing classes—in particular, the ubiquitous `java.util.Date`, `java.util .GregorianCalendar`, and `java.sql.Date/Time/Timestamp`.

The `Instant` class is a close analog to `java.util.Date`. In Java 8, that class has two added methods: the `toInstant` method that converts a `Date` to an `Instant`, and the static `from` method that converts in the other direction.

Similarly, `ZonedDateTime` is a close analog to `java.util.GregorianCalendar`, and that class has gained conversion methods in Java 8. The `toZonedDateTime` method converts a `GregorianCalendar` to a `ZonedDateTime`, and the static `from` method does the opposite conversion.

Another set of conversions is available for the date and time classes in the `java.sql` package. You can also pass a `DateTimeFormatter` to legacy code that uses `java.text.Format`. Table 6.4 summarizes these conversions.

Table 6.4 Conversions between `java.time` Classes and Legacy Classes

Classes	To Legacy Class	From Legacy Class
Instant ↔ java.util.Date	Date.from(instant)	date.toInstant()
ZonedDateTime ↔ java.util.GregorianCalendar	GregorianCalendar.from(zonedDateTime)	cal.toZonedDateTime()
Instant ↔ java.sql.Timestamp	Timestamp.from(instant)	timestamp.toInstant()
LocalDateTime ↔ java.sql.Timestamp	Timestamp.valueOf(localDateTime)	timestamp.toLocalDateTime()
LocalDate ↔ java.sql.Date	Date.valueOf(localDate)	date.toLocalDate()
LocalTime ↔ java.sql.Time	Time.valueOf(localTime)	time.toLocalTime()
DateTimeFormatter → java.text.DateFormat	formatter.toFormat()	None
java.util.TimeZone ↔ ZoneId	TimeZone.getTimeZone(id)	timeZone.toZoneId()
java.nio.file.attribute.FileTime ↔ Instant	FileTime.from(instant)	fileTime.toInstant()

You now know how to use the Java 8 date and time library to work with date and time values around the world. The next chapter takes the discussion of programming for an international audience further. You will see how to format program messages, numbers, and currencies in the way that makes sense for your customers, wherever they may be.

CHAPTER 7

Internationalization

In this chapter

There's a big world out there; we hope that lots of its inhabitants will be interested in your software. The Internet, after all, effortlessly spans the barriers between countries. On the other hand, when you pay no attention to an international audience, *you* are putting up a barrier.

The Java programming language was the first language designed from the ground up to support internationalization. From the beginning, it had the one essential feature needed for effective internationalization: It used Unicode for all strings. Unicode support makes it easy to write Java programs that manipulate strings in most of the world's languages.

Many programmers believe that all they need to do to internationalize their application is to support Unicode and to translate the messages in the user interface. However, as this chapter demonstrates, there is a lot more to internationalizing programs than just Unicode support. Dates, times, currencies, even numbers are formatted differently in different parts of the world. You need an easy way to configure menu and button names, message strings, and keyboard shortcuts for different languages.

In this chapter, we will show you how to write internationalized Java programs and how to localize dates, times, numbers, text, and GUIs. We will show you the tools that Java offers for writing internationalized programs. We will close this chapter with a complete example—a retirement calculator with a user interface in English, German, and Chinese.

7.1 Locales

When you look at an application that is adapted to an international market, the most obvious difference you notice is the language. This observation is actually a bit too limiting for true internationalization, since countries can share a common language, but you might still need to do some work to make computer users of both countries happy. As Oscar Wilde famously said: "We have really everything in common with America nowadays, except, of course, language."

7.1.1 Why Locales?

When you provide international versions of a program, all program messages need to be translated to the local language. However, simply translating the user interface text is not sufficient. There are many more subtle differences—for example, numbers are formatted quite differently in English and in German. The number

123,456.78

should be displayed as

123.456,78

for a German user—that is, the roles of the decimal point and the decimal comma separator are reversed. There are similar variations in the display of dates. In the United States, dates are (somewhat irrationally) displayed as month/day/year. Germany uses the more sensible order of day/month/year, whereas in China, the usage is year/month/day. Thus, the date

3/22/61

should be presented as

22.03.1961

to a German user. Of course, if the month names are written out explicitly, the difference in languages becomes apparent. The English

March 22, 1961

should be presented as

22. März 1961

in German, or

1961年3月22日

in Chinese.

A *locale* captures local preferences such as these. Whenever you present numbers, dates, currency values, and other items whose formatting varies by language or location, you need to use locale-aware APIs.

7.1.2 Specifying Locales

A locale is made up of up to five components:

1. A language, specified by two or three lowercase letters, such as en (English), de (German), or zh (Chinese). Table 7.1 shows common codes.

2. Optionally, a script, specified by four letters with an initial uppercase, such as Latn (Latin), Cyrl (Cyrillic), or Hant (traditional Chinese characters). This can be useful because some languages, such as Serbian, are written in Latin or Cyrillic, and some Chinese readers prefer the traditional over the simplified characters.

3. Optionally, a country or region, specified by two uppercase letters or three digits, such as US (United States) or CH (Switzerland). Table 7.2 shows common codes.

4. Optionally, a variant, specifying miscellaneous features such as dialects or spelling rules. Variants are rarely used nowadays. There used to be a "Nynorsk" variant of Norwegian, but it is now expressed with a different language code, nn. What used to be variants for the Japanese imperial calendar and Thai numerals are now expressed as extensions (see the next item).

5. Optionally, an extension. Extensions describe local preferences for calendars (such as the Japanese calendar), numbers (Thai instead of Western digits), and so on. The Unicode standard specifies some of these extensions. Extensions start with u- and a two-letter code specifying whether the extension deals with the calendar (ca), numbers (nu), and so on. For example, the extension u-nu-thai denotes the use of Thai numerals. Other extensions are entirely arbitrary and start with x-, such as x-java.

Rules for locales are formulated in the "Best Current Practices" memo BCP 47 of the Internet Engineering Task Force (http://tools.ietf.org/html/bcp47). You can find a more accessible summary at www.w3.org/International/articles/language-tags.

Table 7.1 Common ISO 639-1 Language Codes

Language	Code	Language	Code
Chinese	zh	Italian	it
Danish	da	Japanese	ja
Dutch	nl	Korean	ko
English	en	Norwegian	no
French	fr	Portuguese	pt
Finnish	fi	Spanish	es
German	de	Swedish	sv
Greek	el	Turkish	tr

Table 7.2 Common ISO 3166-1 Country Codes

Country	Code	Country	Code
Austria	AT	Japan	JP
Belgium	BE	Korea	KR
Canada	CA	The Netherlands	NL
China	CN	Norway	NO
Denmark	DK	Portugal	PT
Finland	FI	Spain	ES
Germany	DE	Sweden	SE
Great Britain	GB	Switzerland	CH
Greece	GR	Taiwan	TW
Ireland	IE	Turkey	TR
Italy	IT	United States	US

The codes for languages and countries seem a bit random because some of them are derived from local languages. German in German is Deutsch, Chinese in Chinese is zhongwen: hence de and zh. And Switzerland is CH, deriving from the Latin term *Confoederatio Helvetica* for the Swiss confederation.

Locales are described by tags—hyphenated strings of locale elements such as en-US.

In Germany, you would use a locale de-DE. Switzerland has four official languages (German, French, Italian, and Rhaeto-Romance). A German speaker in Switzerland would want to use a locale de-CH. This locale uses the rules for the German language, but currency values are expressed in Swiss francs, not euros.

If you only specify the language, say, de, then the locale cannot be used for country-specific issues such as currencies.

You can construct a Locale object from a tag string like this:

```
Locale usEnglish = Locale.forLanguageTag("en-US");
```

The toLanguageTag method yields the language tag for a given locale. For example, Locale.US.toLanguageTag() is the string "en-US".

For your convenience, there are predefined locale objects for various countries:

```
Locale.CANADA
Locale.CANADA_FRENCH
Locale.CHINA
Locale.FRANCE
Locale.GERMANY
Locale.ITALY
Locale.JAPAN
Locale.KOREA
Locale.PRC
Locale.TAIWAN
Locale.UK
Locale.US
```

A number of predefined locales specify just a language without a location:

```
Locale.CHINESE
Locale.ENGLISH
Locale.FRENCH
Locale.GERMAN
Locale.ITALIAN
Locale.JAPANESE
Locale.KOREAN
Locale.SIMPLIFIED_CHINESE
Locale.TRADITIONAL_CHINESE
```

Finally, the static getAvailableLocales method returns an array of all locales known to the virtual machine.

NOTE: You can get all language codes as `Locale.getISOLanguages()` and all country codes as `Locale.getISOCountries()`.

7.1.3 The Default Locale

The static `getDefault` method of the `Locale` class initially gets the default locale as stored by the local operating system. You can change the default Java locale by calling the `setDefault` method with a different locale.

Some operating systems allow the user to specify different locales for displayed messages and for formatting. For example, a French speaker living in the United States can have French menus but currency values in dollar.

To obtain these preferences, call

```
Locale displayLocale = Locale.getDefault(Locale.Category.DISPLAY);
Locale formatLocale = Locale.getDefault(Locale.Category.FORMAT);
```

NOTE: In UNIX, you can specify separate locales for numbers, currencies, and dates, by setting the `LC_NUMERIC`, `LC_MONETARY`, and `LC_TIME` environment variables. Java does not pay attention to these settings.

TIP: If you want to test a locale that just has language and country settings, you can supply them on the command line when you launch your program. For example, here we set the default locale to `de-CH`:

```
java -Duser.language=de -Duser.region=CH MyProgram
```

7.1.4 Display Names

Once you have a locale, what can you do with it? Initially, not much, as it turns out. The only useful methods in the `Locale` class are those for identifying the language and country codes. The most important one is `getDisplayName`. It returns a string describing the locale. This string does not contain the cryptic two-letter codes, but is in a form that can be presented to a user, such as

```
German (Switzerland)
```

Actually, there is a problem here. The display name is issued in the default locale. That might not be appropriate. If your user already selected German as the preferred language, you probably want to present the string in German. You can do just that by giving the German locale as a parameter. The code

```
var loc = new Locale("de", "CH");
System.out.println(loc.getDisplayName(Locale.GERMAN));
```

prints

```
Deutsch (Schweiz)
```

This example shows why you need Locale objects. You feed them to locale-aware methods that produce text that is presented to users in different locations. You will see many examples of this in the following sections.

CAUTION: Even such mundane operations as turning a string into lowercase or uppercase can be locale-specific. For example, in the Turkish locale, the lowercase of the letter I is a dotless ı. Programs that tried to normalize strings by storing them in lowercase have mysteriously failed for Turkish customers where I and the dotted i don't have the same lowercase version. It is a good idea to always use the variants of toUpperCase and toLowerCase that take a Locale argument. For example, try out:

```
String cmd = "QUIT".toLowerCase(Locale.forLanguageTag("tr"));
    // "quıt" with a dotless ı
```

Of course, in Turkey, where Locale.getDefault() yields just that locale, "QUIT".toLowerCase() is not the same as "quit".

If you want to normalize English language strings to lowercase, you should pass an English locale to the toLowerCase method.

NOTE: You can explicitly set the locale for input and output operations.

- When reading numbers from a Scanner, you can set its locale with the useLocale method.

- The String.format and PrintWriter.printf methods optionally take a Locale argument.

---

java.util.Locale 1.1

- Locale(String language)
- Locale(String language, String country)
- Locale(String language, String country, String variant)

  constructs a locale with the given language, country, and variant. Don't use variants in new code—use the IETF BCP 47 language tags instead.

(Continues)

---

java.util.Locale 1.1 *(Continued)*

- `static Locale forLanguageTag(String languageTag)` 7

  constructs a locale corresponding to the given language tag.

- `static Locale getDefault()`

  returns the default locale.

- `static void setDefault(Locale loc)`

  sets the default locale.

- `String getDisplayName()`

  returns a name describing the locale, expressed in the current locale.

- `String getDisplayName(Locale loc)`

  returns a name describing the locale, expressed in the given locale.

- `String getLanguage()`

  returns the language code—a lowercase two-letter ISO 639 code.

- `String getDisplayLanguage()`

  returns the name of the language, expressed in the current locale.

- `String getDisplayLanguage(Locale loc)`

  returns the name of the language, expressed in the given locale.

- `String getCountry()`

  returns the country code as an uppercase two-letter ISO 3166 code.

- `static String[] getISOCountries()`
- `static Set<String> getISOCountries(Locale.IsoCountryCode type)` 9

  gets all two-letter country codes, or all country codes with 2, 3, or 4 letters. The type is one of the enumeration constants `PART1_ALPHA2`, `PART1_ALPHA3`, and `PART3`.

- `String getDisplayCountry()`

  returns the name of the country, expressed in the current locale.

- `String getDisplayCountry(Locale loc)`

  returns the name of the country, expressed in the given locale.

- `String toLanguageTag()` 7

  returns the IETF BCP 47 language tag for this locale, e.g., `"de-CH"`.

- `String toString()`

  returns a description of the locale, with the language and country separated by underscores (e.g., `"de_CH"`). Use this method only for debugging.

7.2 Number Formats

We already mentioned how number and currency formatting is highly locale-dependent. The Java library supplies a collection of formatter objects that can format and parse numeric values in the java.text package.

7.2.1 Formatting Numeric Values

Go through the following steps to format a number for a particular locale:

1. Get the locale object, as described in the preceding section.
2. Use a "factory method" to obtain a formatter object.
3. Use the formatter object for formatting and parsing.

The factory methods are static methods of the NumberFormat class that take a Locale argument. There are three factory methods: getNumberInstance, getCurrencyInstance, and getPercentInstance. These methods return objects that can format and parse numbers, currency amounts, and percentages, respectively. For example, here is how you can format a currency value in German:

```
Locale loc = Locale.GERMAN;
NumberFormat currFmt = NumberFormat.getCurrencyInstance(loc);
double amt = 123456.78;
String result = currFmt.format(amt);
```

The result is

123.456,78 €

Note that the currency symbol is € and that it is placed at the end of the string. Also, note the reversal of decimal points and decimal commas.

Conversely, to read in a number that was entered or stored with the conventions of a certain locale, use the parse method. For example, the following code parses the value that the user typed into a text field. The parse method can deal with decimal points and commas, as well as digits in other languages.

```
TextField inputField;
. . .
NumberFormat fmt = NumberFormat.getNumberInstance();
// get the number formatter for default locale
Number input = fmt.parse(inputField.getText().trim());
double x = input.doubleValue();
```

The return type of parse is the abstract type Number. The returned object is either a Double or a Long wrapper object, depending on whether the parsed number was a floating-point number. If you don't care about the distinction, you can simply use the doubleValue method of the Number class to retrieve the wrapped number.

 CAUTION: Objects of type Number are not automatically unboxed—you cannot simply assign a Number object to a primitive type. Instead, use the doubleValue or intValue method.

If the text for the number is not in the correct form, the method throws a ParseException. For example, leading whitespace in the string is *not* allowed. (Call trim to remove it.) However, any characters that follow the number in the string are simply ignored, so no exception is thrown.

Note that the classes returned by the get*Xxx*Instance factory methods are not actually of type NumberFormat. The NumberFormat type is an abstract class, and the actual formatters belong to one of its subclasses. The factory methods merely know how to locate the object that belongs to a particular locale.

You can get a list of the currently supported locales with the static getAvailableLocales method. That method returns an array of the locales for which number formatter objects can be obtained.

The sample program for this section lets you experiment with number formatters (see Figure 7.1). The combo box at the top of the figure contains all locales with number formatters. You can choose between number, currency, and percentage formatters. Each time you make another choice, the number in the text field is reformatted. If you go through a few locales, you can get a good impression of the many ways that a number or currency value can be formatted. You can also type a different number and click the Parse button to call the parse method, which tries to parse what you entered. If your input is successfully parsed, it is passed to format and the result is displayed. If parsing fails, a "Parse error" message is displayed in the text field.

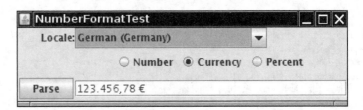

Figure 7.1 The NumberFormatTest program

The code, shown in Listing 7.1, is fairly straightforward. In the constructor, we call NumberFormat.getAvailableLocales. For each locale, we call getDisplayName and fill a combo box with the strings that the getDisplayName method returns. (The strings are not sorted; we tackle this issue in Section 7.4, "Collation and Normalization," on p. 402.) Whenever the user selects another locale or clicks one of the radio buttons, we create a new formatter object and update the text field. When the user clicks the Parse button, we call the parse method to do the actual parsing, based on the locale selected.

 NOTE: You can use a Scanner to read localized integers and floating-point numbers. Call the useLocale method to set the locale.

Listing 7.1 numberFormat/NumberFormatTest.java

```
1  package numberFormat;
2
3  import java.awt.*;
4  import java.awt.event.*;
5  import java.text.*;
6  import java.util.*;
7
8  import javax.swing.*;
9
10 /**
11  * This program demonstrates formatting numbers under various locales.
12  * @version 1.15 2018-05-01
13  * @author Cay Horstmann
14  */
15 public class NumberFormatTest
16 {
17    public static void main(String[] args)
18    {
19       EventQueue.invokeLater(() ->
20          {
21             var frame = new NumberFormatFrame();
22             frame.setTitle("NumberFormatTest");
23             frame.setDefaultCloseOperation(JFrame.EXIT_ON_CLOSE);
24             frame.setVisible(true);
25          });
26    }
27 }
28
29 /**
30  * This frame contains radio buttons to select a number format, a combo box to pick a locale,
31  * a text field to display a formatted number, and a button to parse the text field contents.
32  */
```

(Continues)

Listing 7.1 *(Continued)*

```
33  class NumberFormatFrame extends JFrame
34  {
35     private Locale[] locales;
36     private double currentNumber;
37     private JComboBox<String> localeCombo = new JComboBox<>();
38     private JButton parseButton = new JButton("Parse");
39     private JTextField numberText = new JTextField(30);
40     private JRadioButton numberRadioButton = new JRadioButton("Number");
41     private JRadioButton currencyRadioButton = new JRadioButton("Currency");
42     private JRadioButton percentRadioButton = new JRadioButton("Percent");
43     private ButtonGroup rbGroup = new ButtonGroup();
44     private NumberFormat currentNumberFormat;
45
46     public NumberFormatFrame()
47     {
48        setLayout(new GridBagLayout());
49
50        ActionListener listener = event -> updateDisplay();
51
52        var p = new JPanel();
53        addRadioButton(p, numberRadioButton, rbGroup, listener);
54        addRadioButton(p, currencyRadioButton, rbGroup, listener);
55        addRadioButton(p, percentRadioButton, rbGroup, listener);
56
57        add(new JLabel("Locale:"), new GBC(0, 0).setAnchor(GBC.EAST));
58        add(p, new GBC(1, 1));
59        add(parseButton, new GBC(0, 2).setInsets(2));
60        add(localeCombo, new GBC(1, 0).setAnchor(GBC.WEST));
61        add(numberText, new GBC(1, 2).setFill(GBC.HORIZONTAL));
62        locales = (Locale[]) NumberFormat.getAvailableLocales().clone();
63        Arrays.sort(locales, Comparator.comparing(Locale::getDisplayName));
64        for (Locale loc : locales)
65           localeCombo.addItem(loc.getDisplayName());
66        localeCombo.setSelectedItem(Locale.getDefault().getDisplayName());
67        currentNumber = 123456.78;
68        updateDisplay();
69
70        localeCombo.addActionListener(listener);
71
72        parseButton.addActionListener(event ->
73           {
74              String s = numberText.getText().trim();
75              try
76              {
77                 Number n = currentNumberFormat.parse(s);
78                 currentNumber = n.doubleValue();
79                 updateDisplay();
80              }
```

```
81          catch (ParseException e)
82          {
83             numberText.setText(e.getMessage());
84          }
85       });
86    pack();
87  }
88
89  /**
90   * Adds a radio button to a container.
91   * @param p the container into which to place the button
92   * @param b the button
93   * @param g the button group
94   * @param listener the button listener
95   */
96  public void addRadioButton(Container p, JRadioButton b, ButtonGroup g,
97        ActionListener listener)
98  {
99     b.setSelected(g.getButtonCount() == 0);
100    b.addActionListener(listener);
101    g.add(b);
102    p.add(b);
103  }
104
105  /**
106   * Updates the display and formats the number according to the user settings.
107   */
108  public void updateDisplay()
109  {
110    Locale currentLocale = locales[localeCombo.getSelectedIndex()];
111    currentNumberFormat = null;
112    if (numberRadioButton.isSelected())
113       currentNumberFormat = NumberFormat.getNumberInstance(currentLocale);
114    else if (currencyRadioButton.isSelected())
115       currentNumberFormat = NumberFormat.getCurrencyInstance(currentLocale);
116    else if (percentRadioButton.isSelected())
117       currentNumberFormat = NumberFormat.getPercentInstance(currentLocale);
118    String formatted = currentNumberFormat.format(currentNumber);
119    numberText.setText(formatted);
120  }
121 }
```

---

java.text.NumberFormat 1.1

- static Locale[] getAvailableLocales()

  returns an array of Locale objects for which NumberFormat formatters are available.

(Continues)

---

java.text.NumberFormat 1.1 *(Continued)*

- static NumberFormat getNumberInstance()
- static NumberFormat getNumberInstance(Locale l)
- static NumberFormat getCurrencyInstance()
- static NumberFormat getCurrencyInstance(Locale l)
- static NumberFormat getPercentInstance()
- static NumberFormat getPercentInstance(Locale l)

returns a formatter for numbers, currency amounts, or percentage values for the current locale or for the given locale.

- String format(double x)
- String format(long x)

returns the string resulting from formatting the given floating-point number or integer.

- Number parse(String s)

parses the given string and returns the number value, as a Double if the input string describes a floating-point number or as a Long otherwise. The beginning of the string must contain a number; no leading whitespace is allowed. The number can be followed by other characters, which are ignored. Throws ParseException if parsing was not successful.

- void setParseIntegerOnly(boolean b)
- boolean isParseIntegerOnly()

sets or gets a flag to indicate whether this formatter should parse only integer values.

- void setGroupingUsed(boolean b)
- boolean isGroupingUsed()

sets or gets a flag to indicate whether this formatter emits and recognizes decimal separators (such as 100,000).

- void setMinimumIntegerDigits(int n)
- int getMinimumIntegerDigits()
- void setMaximumIntegerDigits(int n)
- int getMaximumIntegerDigits()
- void setMinimumFractionDigits(int n)
- int getMinimumFractionDigits()
- void setMaximumFractionDigits(int n)
- int getMaximumFractionDigits()

sets or gets the maximum or minimum number of digits allowed in the integer or fractional part of a number.

7.2.2 Currencies

To format a currency value, you can use the `NumberFormat.getCurrencyInstance` method. However, that method is not very flexible—it returns a formatter for a single currency. Suppose you prepare an invoice for an American customer in which some amounts are in dollars and others are in euros. You can't just use two formatters:

```
NumberFormat dollarFormatter = NumberFormat.getCurrencyInstance(Locale.US);
NumberFormat euroFormatter = NumberFormat.getCurrencyInstance(Locale.GERMANY);
```

Your invoice would look very strange, with some values shown as $100,000 and others as 100.000 €. (Note that the euro value uses a decimal point, not a comma.)

Instead, use the `Currency` class to control the currency used by the formatters. You can get a `Currency` object by passing a currency identifier to the static `Currency.getInstance` method. Then call the `setCurrency` method for each formatter. Here is how you would set up the euro formatter for your American customer:

```
NumberFormat euroFormatter = NumberFormat.getCurrencyInstance(Locale.US);
euroFormatter.setCurrency(Currency.getInstance("EUR"));
```

The currency identifiers are defined by ISO 4217 (see `https://www.iso.org /iso-4217-currency-codes.html`). Table 7.3 provides a partial list.

Table 7.3 Currency Identifiers

Currency Value	Identifier	Numeric Code
U.S. Dollar	USD	840
Euro	EUR	978
British Pound	GBP	826
Japanese Yen	JPY	392
Chinese Renminbi (Yuan)	CNY	156
Indian Rupee	INR	356
Russian Ruble	RUB	643

---

java.util.Currency 1.4

- static Currency getInstance(String currencyCode)
- static Currency getInstance(Locale locale)

  returns the Currency instance for the given ISO 4217 currency code or the country of the given locale.

- String toString()
- String getCurrencyCode()
- String getNumericCode() 7
- String getNumericCodeAsString() 9

  gets the ISO 4217 alphabetic or numeric currency code of this currency.

- String getSymbol()
- String getSymbol(Locale locale)

  gets the formatting symbol of this currency for the default locale or the given locale. For example, the symbol for USD can be "$" or "US$", depending on the locale.

- int getDefaultFractionDigits()

  gets the default number of fraction digits of this currency.

- static Set<Currency> getAvailableCurrencies() 7

  gets all available currencies.

7.3 Date and Time

When you are formatting date and time, you should be concerned with four locale-dependent issues:

- The names of months and weekdays should be presented in the local language.
- There will be local preferences for the order of year, month, and day.
- The Gregorian calendar might not be the local preference for expressing dates.
- The time zone of the location must be taken into account.

The DateTimeFormatter class from the java.time package handles these issues. Pick one of the formatting styles shown in Tables 7.4. Then, get a formatter:

```
FormatStyle style = . . .; // One of FormatStyle.SHORT, FormatStyle.MEDIUM, . . .
DateTimeFormatter dateFormatter = DateTimeFormatter.ofLocalizedDate(style);
DateTimeFormatter timeFormatter = DateTimeFormatter.ofLocalizedTime(style);
```

```
DateTimeFormatter dateTimeFormatter = DateTimeFormatter.ofLocalizedDateTime(style);
   // or DateTimeFormatter.ofLocalizedDateTime(style1, style2)
```

These formatters use the current locale. To use a different locale, use the withLocale method:

```
DateTimeFormatter dateFormatter =
   DateTimeFormatter.ofLocalizedDate(style).withLocale(locale);
```

Now you can format a LocalDate, LocalDateTime, LocalTime, or ZonedDateTime:

```
ZonedDateTime appointment = . . .;
String formatted = formatter.format(appointment);
```

Table 7.4 Date and Time Formatting Styles

Style	Date	Time
SHORT	7/16/69	9:32 AM
MEDIUM	Jul 16, 1969	9:32:00 AM
LONG	July 16, 1969	9:32:00 AM EDT in en-US, 9:32:00 MSZ in de-DE (only for ZonedDateTime)
FULL	Wednesday, July 16, 1969	9:32:00 AM EDT in en-US, 9:32 Uhr MSZ in de-DE (only for ZonedDateTime)

 NOTE: Here we use the DateTimeFormatter class from the java.time package. There is also a legacy java.text.DateFormatter class from Java 1.1 that works with Date and Calendar objects.

You can use one of the static parse methods of LocalDate, LocalDateTime, LocalTime, or ZonedDateTime to parse a date or time in a string:

```
LocalTime time = LocalTime.parse("9:32 AM", formatter);
```

These methods are not suitable for parsing human input, at least not without preprocessing. For example, the short time formatter for the United States will parse "9:32 AM" but not "9:32AM" or "9:32 am".

 CAUTION: Date formatters parse nonexistent dates, such as November 31, and adjust them to the last date in the given month.

Sometimes, you need to display just the names of weekdays and months, for example, in a calendar application. Call the getDisplayName method of the DayOfWeek and Month enumerations.

```
for (Month m : Month.values())
   System.out.println(m.getDisplayName(textStyle, locale) + " ");
```

Tables 7.5 shows the text styles. The STANDALONE versions are for display outside a formatted date. For example, in Finnish, January is "tammikuuta" inside a date, but "tammikuu" standalone.

Table 7.5 Values of the java.time.format.TextStyle Enumeration

Style	Example
FULL / FULL_STANDALONE	January
SHORT / SHORT_STANDALONE	Jan
NARROW / NARROW_STANDALONE	J

 NOTE: The first day of the week can be Saturday, Sunday, or Monday, depending on the locale. You can obtain it like this:

```
DayOfWeek first = WeekFields.of(locale).getFirstDayOfWeek();
```

Listing 7.2 shows the DateFormat class in action. You can select a locale and see how the date and time are formatted in different places around the world.

Figure 7.2 shows the program (after Chinese fonts were installed). As you can see, it correctly displays the output.

Figure 7.2 The DateFormatTest program

You can also experiment with parsing. Enter a date, time, or date/time and click the Parse button.

We use a helper class EnumCombo to solve a technical problem (see Listing 7.3). We wanted to fill a combo with values such as Short, Medium, and Long and then automatically convert the user's selection to values FormatStyle.SHORT, FormatStyle.MEDIUM, and FormatStyle.LONG. Instead of writing repetitive code, we use reflection: We convert the user's choice to upper case, replace all spaces with underscores, and then find the value of the static field with that name. (See Volume I, Chapter 5 for more details about reflection.)

Listing 7.2 dateFormat/DateTimeFormatterTest.java

```java
1  package dateFormat;
2
3  import java.awt.*;
4  import java.awt.event.*;
5  import java.time.*;
6  import java.time.format.*;
7  import java.util.*;
8
9  import javax.swing.*;
10
11 /**
12  * This program demonstrates formatting dates under various locales.
13  * @version 1.01 2018-05-01
14  * @author Cay Horstmann
15  */
16 public class DateTimeFormatterTest
17 {
18    public static void main(String[] args)
19    {
20       EventQueue.invokeLater(() ->
21          {
22             var frame = new DateTimeFormatterFrame();
23             frame.setTitle("DateFormatTest");
24             frame.setDefaultCloseOperation(JFrame.EXIT_ON_CLOSE);
25             frame.setVisible(true);
26          });
27    }
28 }
29
30 /**
31  * This frame contains combo boxes to pick a locale, date and time formats, text fields to
32  * display formatted date and time, buttons to parse the text field contents, and a "lenient"
33  * check box.
34  */
35 class DateTimeFormatterFrame extends JFrame
36 {
37    private Locale[] locales;
38    private LocalDate currentDate;
39    private LocalTime currentTime;
40    private ZonedDateTime currentDateTime;
41    private DateTimeFormatter currentDateFormat;
42    private DateTimeFormatter currentTimeFormat;
43    private DateTimeFormatter currentDateTimeFormat;
44    private JComboBox<String> localeCombo = new JComboBox<>();
```

(Continues)

Listing 7.2 *(Continued)*

```java
45    private JButton dateParseButton = new JButton("Parse");
46    private JButton timeParseButton = new JButton("Parse");
47    private JButton dateTimeParseButton = new JButton("Parse");
48    private JTextField dateText = new JTextField(30);
49    private JTextField timeText = new JTextField(30);
50    private JTextField dateTimeText = new JTextField(30);
51    private EnumCombo<FormatStyle> dateStyleCombo = new EnumCombo<>(FormatStyle.class,
52       "Short", "Medium", "Long", "Full");
53    private EnumCombo<FormatStyle> timeStyleCombo = new EnumCombo<>(FormatStyle.class,
54       "Short", "Medium");
55    private EnumCombo<FormatStyle> dateTimeStyleCombo = new EnumCombo<>(FormatStyle.class,
56       "Short", "Medium", "Long", "Full");
57
58    public DateTimeFormatterFrame()
59    {
60       setLayout(new GridBagLayout());
61       add(new JLabel("Locale"), new GBC(0, 0).setAnchor(GBC.EAST));
62       add(localeCombo, new GBC(1, 0, 2, 1).setAnchor(GBC.WEST));
63
64       add(new JLabel("Date"), new GBC(0, 1).setAnchor(GBC.EAST));
65       add(dateStyleCombo, new GBC(1, 1).setAnchor(GBC.WEST));
66       add(dateText, new GBC(2, 1, 2, 1).setFill(GBC.HORIZONTAL));
67       add(dateParseButton, new GBC(4, 1).setAnchor(GBC.WEST));
68
69       add(new JLabel("Time"), new GBC(0, 2).setAnchor(GBC.EAST));
70       add(timeStyleCombo, new GBC(1, 2).setAnchor(GBC.WEST));
71       add(timeText, new GBC(2, 2, 2, 1).setFill(GBC.HORIZONTAL));
72       add(timeParseButton, new GBC(4, 2).setAnchor(GBC.WEST));
73
74       add(new JLabel("Date and time"), new GBC(0, 3).setAnchor(GBC.EAST));
75       add(dateTimeStyleCombo, new GBC(1, 3).setAnchor(GBC.WEST));
76       add(dateTimeText, new GBC(2, 3, 2, 1).setFill(GBC.HORIZONTAL));
77       add(dateTimeParseButton, new GBC(4, 3).setAnchor(GBC.WEST));
78
79       locales = (Locale[]) Locale.getAvailableLocales().clone();
80       Arrays.sort(locales, Comparator.comparing(Locale::getDisplayName));
81       for (Locale loc : locales)
82          localeCombo.addItem(loc.getDisplayName());
83       localeCombo.setSelectedItem(Locale.getDefault().getDisplayName());
84       currentDate = LocalDate.now();
85       currentTime = LocalTime.now();
86       currentDateTime = ZonedDateTime.now();
87       updateDisplay();
88
89       ActionListener listener = event -> updateDisplay();
90       localeCombo.addActionListener(listener);
91       dateStyleCombo.addActionListener(listener);
92       timeStyleCombo.addActionListener(listener);
```

```
93          dateTimeStyleCombo.addActionListener(listener);
94
95          addAction(dateParseButton, () ->
96             {
97                currentDate = LocalDate.parse(dateText.getText().trim(), currentDateFormat);
98             });
99          addAction(timeParseButton, () ->
100            {
101               currentTime = LocalTime.parse(timeText.getText().trim(), currentTimeFormat);
102            });
103         addAction(dateTimeParseButton, () ->
104            {
105               currentDateTime = ZonedDateTime.parse(
106                  dateTimeText.getText().trim(), currentDateTimeFormat);
107            });
108
109         pack();
110     }
111
112     /**
113      * Adds the given action to the button and updates the display upon completion.
114      * @param button the button to which to add the action
115      * @param action the action to carry out when the button is clicked
116      */
117     public void addAction(JButton button, Runnable action)
118     {
119         button.addActionListener(event ->
120            {
121               try
122               {
123                  action.run();
124                  updateDisplay();
125               }
126               catch (Exception e)
127               {
128                  JOptionPane.showMessageDialog(null, e.getMessage());
129               }
130            });
131     }
132
133     /**
134      * Updates the display and formats the date according to the user settings.
135      */
136     public void updateDisplay()
137     {
138         Locale currentLocale = locales[localeCombo.getSelectedIndex()];
139         FormatStyle dateStyle = dateStyleCombo.getValue();
140         currentDateFormat = DateTimeFormatter.ofLocalizedDate(
141            dateStyle).withLocale(currentLocale);
```

(Continues)

Listing 7.2 *(Continued)*

```
142        dateText.setText(currentDateFormat.format(currentDate));
143        FormatStyle timeStyle = timeStyleCombo.getValue();
144        currentTimeFormat = DateTimeFormatter.ofLocalizedTime(
145            timeStyle).withLocale(currentLocale);
146        timeText.setText(currentTimeFormat.format(currentTime));
147        FormatStyle dateTimeStyle = dateTimeStyleCombo.getValue();
148        currentDateTimeFormat = DateTimeFormatter.ofLocalizedDateTime(
149            dateTimeStyle).withLocale(currentLocale);
150        dateTimeText.setText(currentDateTimeFormat.format(currentDateTime));
151    }
152 }
```

Listing 7.3 dateFormat/EnumCombo.java

```
1 package dateFormat;
2
3 import java.util.*;
4 import javax.swing.*;
5
6 /**
7  * A combo box that lets users choose from among static field
8  * values whose names are given in the constructor.
9  * @version 1.15 2016-05-06
10  * @author Cay Horstmann
11  */
12 public class EnumCombo<T> extends JComboBox<String>
13 {
14    private Map<String, T> table = new TreeMap<>();
15
16    /**
17     * Constructs an EnumCombo yielding values of type T.
18     * @param cl a class
19     * @param labels an array of strings describing static field names
20     * of cl that have type T
21     */
22    public EnumCombo(Class<?> cl, String... labels)
23    {
24       for (String label : labels)
25       {
26          String name = label.toUpperCase().replace(' ', '_');
27          try
28          {
29             java.lang.reflect.Field f = cl.getField(name);
30             @SuppressWarnings("unchecked") T value = (T) f.get(cl);
31             table.put(label, value);
32          }
```

```
33        catch (Exception e)
34        {
35           label = "(" + label + ")";
36           table.put(label, null);
37        }
38        addItem(label);
39     }
40     setSelectedItem(labels[0]);
41  }
42
43  /**
44   * Returns the value of the field that the user selected.
45   * @return the static field value
46   */
47  public T getValue()
48  {
49     return table.get(getSelectedItem());
50  }
51 }
```

---

java.time.format.DateTimeFormatter 8

- static DateTimeFormatter ofLocalizedDate(FormatStyle dateStyle)
- static DateTimeFormatter ofLocalizedTime(FormatStyle dateStyle)
- static DateTimeFormatter ofLocalizedDateTime(FormatStyle dateTimeStyle)
- static DateTimeFormatter ofLocalizedDate(FormatStyle dateStyle, FormatStyle timeStyle)

  returns DateTimeFormatter instances that format dates, times, or dates and times with the specified styles.

- DateTimeFormatter withLocale(Locale locale)

  returns a copy of this formatter with the given locale.

- String format(TemporalAccessor temporal)

  returns the string resulting from formatting the given date/time.

---

java.time.LocalDate 8
java.time.LocalTime 8
java.time.LocalDateTime 8
java.time.ZonedDateTime 8

- static *Xxx* parse(CharSequence text, DateTimeFormatter formatter)

  parses the given string and returns the LocalDate, LocalTime, LocalDateTime, or ZonedDateTime described in it. Throws a DateTimeParseException if parsing was not successful.

7.4 Collation and Normalization

Most programmers know how to compare strings with the compareTo method of the String class. Unfortunately, when interacting with human users, this method is not very useful. The compareTo method uses the values of the UTF-16 encoding of the string, which leads to absurd results, even in English. For example, the following five strings are ordered according to the compareTo method:

```
America
Zulu
able
zebra
Ångström
```

For dictionary ordering, you would want to consider upper case and lower case to be equivalent. To an English speaker, the sample list of words would be ordered as

```
able
America
Ångström
zebra
Zulu
```

However, that order would not be acceptable to a Swedish user. In Swedish, the letter Å is different from the letter A, and it is collated *after* the letter Z! That is, a Swedish user would want the words to be sorted as

```
able
America
zebra
Zulu
Ångström
```

To obtain a locale-sensitive comparator, call the static Collator.getInstance method:

```
Collator coll = Collator.getInstance(locale);
words.sort(coll); // Collator implements Comparator<Object>
```

Since the Collator class implements the Comparator interface, you can pass a Collator object to the List.sort(Comparator) method to sort a list of strings.

There are a couple of advanced settings for collators. You can set a collator's *strength* to select how selective it should be. Character differences are classified as *primary*, *secondary*, or *tertiary*. For example, in English, the difference between "A" and "Z" is considered primary, the difference between "A" and "Å" is secondary, and between "A" and "a" is tertiary.

By setting the strength of the collator to Collator.PRIMARY, you tell it to pay attention only to primary differences. By setting the strength to Collator.SECONDARY, you instruct the collator to take secondary differences into account. That is, two strings will be more likely to be considered different when the strength is set to "secondary" or "tertiary," as shown in Table 7.6.

Table 7.6 Collations with Different Strengths (English Locale)

Primary	Secondary	Tertiary
Angstrom = Ångström	Angstrom ≠ Ångström	Angstrom ≠ Ångström
Able = able	Able = able	Able ≠ able

When the strength has been set to Collator.IDENTICAL, no differences are allowed. This setting is mainly useful in conjunction with a rather technical collator setting, the *decomposition mode*, which we take up next.

Occasionally, a character or sequence of characters can be described in more than one way in Unicode. For example, an "Å" can be Unicode character U+00C5, or it can be expressed as a plain A (U+0065) followed by a ° ("combining ring above"; U+030A). Perhaps more surprisingly, the letter sequence "ffi" can be described with a single character "Latin small ligature ffi" with code U+FB03. (One could argue that this is a presentation issue that should not have resulted in different Unicode characters, but we don't make the rules.)

The Unicode standard defines four *normalization forms* (D, KD, C, and KC) for strings. See www.unicode.org/unicode/reports/tr15/tr15-23.html for the details. In the normalization form C, accented characters are always composed. For example, a sequence of A and a combining ring above ° is combined into a single character Å. In form D, accented characters are always decomposed into their base letters and combining accents: Å is turned into A followed by °. Forms KC and KD also decompose characters such as ligatures or the trademark symbol.

You can choose the degree of normalization that you want a collator to use. The value Collator.NO_DECOMPOSITION does not normalize strings at all. This option is faster, but it might not be appropriate for texts that express characters in multiple forms. The default, Collator.CANONICAL_DECOMPOSITION, uses the normalization form D. This is useful for texts that contain accents but not ligatures. Finally, "full decomposition" uses normalization form KD. See Table 7.7 for examples.

Table 7.7 Differences between Decomposition Modes

No Decomposition	Canonical Decomposition	Full Decomposition
Å ≠ A°	Å = A°	Å = A°
™ ≠ TM	™ ≠ TM	™ = TM

It is wasteful to have the collator decompose a string many times. If one string is compared against other strings many times, you can save the decomposition in a *collation* key object. The getCollationKey method returns a CollationKey object that you can use for further, faster comparisons. Here is an example:

```
String a = . . .;
CollationKey aKey = coll.getCollationKey(a);
if(aKey.compareTo(coll.getCollationKey(b)) == 0) // fast comparison
. . .
```

Finally, you might want to convert strings into their normalized forms even if you don't do collation—for example, to store strings in a database or communicate with another program. The java.text.Normalizer class carries out the normalization process. For example,

```
String name = "Ångström";
String normalized = Normalizer.normalize(name, Normalizer.Form.NFD); // uses normalization
                                                                     // form D
```

The normalized string contains ten characters. The "Å" and "ö" are replaced by "A°" and "o¨" sequences.

However, that is not usually the best form for storage and transmission. Normalization form C first applies decomposition and then combines the accents back in a standardized order. According to the W3C, this is the recommended mode for transferring data over the Internet.

The program in Listing 7.4 lets you experiment with collation order. Type a word into the text field and click the Add button to add it to the list of words. Each time you add another word, or change the locale, strength, or decomposition mode, the list of words is sorted again. An = sign indicates words that are considered identical (see Figure 7.3).

The locale names in the combo box are displayed in sorted order, using the collator of the default locale. If you run this program with the US English locale, note that "Norwegian (Norway,Nynorsk)" comes before "Norwegian (Norway)", even though the Unicode value of the comma character is greater than the Unicode value of the closing parenthesis.

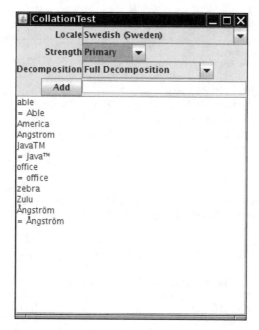

Figure 7.3 The CollationTest program

Listing 7.4 collation/CollationTest.java

```java
1 package collation;
2
3 import java.awt.*;
4 import java.awt.event.*;
5 import java.text.*;
6 import java.util.*;
7 import java.util.List;
8
9 import javax.swing.*;
10
11 /**
12  * This program demonstrates collating strings under various locales.
13  * @version 1.16 2018-05-01
14  * @author Cay Horstmann
15  */
16 public class CollationTest
17 {
18    public static void main(String[] args)
19    {
```

(Continues)

Listing 7.4 *(Continued)*

```
20        EventQueue.invokeLater(() ->
21           {
22              var frame = new CollationFrame();
23              frame.setTitle("CollationTest");
24              frame.setDefaultCloseOperation(JFrame.EXIT_ON_CLOSE);
25              frame.setVisible(true);
26           });
27     }
28 }
29
30 /**
31  * This frame contains combo boxes to pick a locale, collation strength and decomposition
32  * rules, a text field and button to add new strings, and a text area to list the collated
33  * strings.
34  */
35 class CollationFrame extends JFrame
36 {
37     private Collator collator = Collator.getInstance(Locale.getDefault());
38     private List<String> strings = new ArrayList<>();
39     private Collator currentCollator;
40     private Locale[] locales;
41     private JComboBox<String> localeCombo = new JComboBox<>();
42     private JTextField newWord = new JTextField(20);
43     private JTextArea sortedWords = new JTextArea(20, 20);
44     private JButton addButton = new JButton("Add");
45     private EnumCombo<Integer> strengthCombo = new EnumCombo<>(Collator.class, "Primary",
46        "Secondary", "Tertiary", "Identical");
47     private EnumCombo<Integer> decompositionCombo = new EnumCombo<>(Collator.class,
48        "Canonical Decomposition", "Full Decomposition", "No Decomposition");
49
50     public CollationFrame()
51     {
52        setLayout(new GridBagLayout());
53        add(new JLabel("Locale"), new GBC(0, 0).setAnchor(GBC.EAST));
54        add(new JLabel("Strength"), new GBC(0, 1).setAnchor(GBC.EAST));
55        add(new JLabel("Decomposition"), new GBC(0, 2).setAnchor(GBC.EAST));
56        add(addButton, new GBC(0, 3).setAnchor(GBC.EAST));
57        add(localeCombo, new GBC(1, 0).setAnchor(GBC.WEST));
58        add(strengthCombo, new GBC(1, 1).setAnchor(GBC.WEST));
59        add(decompositionCombo, new GBC(1, 2).setAnchor(GBC.WEST));
60        add(newWord, new GBC(1, 3).setFill(GBC.HORIZONTAL));
61        add(new JScrollPane(sortedWords), new GBC(0, 4, 2, 1).setFill(GBC.BOTH));
62
63        locales = (Locale[]) Collator.getAvailableLocales().clone();
64        Arrays.sort(locales,
65           (l1, l2) -> collator.compare(l1.getDisplayName(), l2.getDisplayName()));
```

```
66      for (Locale loc : locales)
67          localeCombo.addItem(loc.getDisplayName());
68      localeCombo.setSelectedItem(Locale.getDefault().getDisplayName());
69
70      strings.add("America");
71      strings.add("able");
72      strings.add("Zulu");
73      strings.add("zebra");
74      strings.add("\u00C5ngstr\u00F6m");
75      strings.add("A\u030angstro\u0308m");
76      strings.add("Angstrom");
77      strings.add("Able");
78      strings.add("office");
79      strings.add("o\uFB03ce");
80      strings.add("Java\u2122");
81      strings.add("JavaTM");
82      updateDisplay();
83
84      addButton.addActionListener(event ->
85         {
86             strings.add(newWord.getText());
87             updateDisplay();
88         });
89
90      ActionListener listener = event -> updateDisplay();
91
92      localeCombo.addActionListener(listener);
93      strengthCombo.addActionListener(listener);
94      decompositionCombo.addActionListener(listener);
95      pack();
96   }
97
98   /**
99    * Updates the display and collates the strings according to the user settings.
100   */
101  public void updateDisplay()
102  {
103     Locale currentLocale = locales[localeCombo.getSelectedIndex()];
104     localeCombo.setLocale(currentLocale);
105
106     currentCollator = Collator.getInstance(currentLocale);
107     currentCollator.setStrength(strengthCombo.getValue());
108     currentCollator.setDecomposition(decompositionCombo.getValue());
109
110     strings.sort(currentCollator);
111
112     sortedWords.setText("");
```

(Continues)

Listing 7.4 *(Continued)*

```
113      for (int i = 0; i < strings.size(); i++)
114      {
115         String s = strings.get(i);
116         if (i > 0 && currentCollator.compare(s, strings.get(i - 1)) == 0)
117            sortedWords.append("= ");
118         sortedWords.append(s + "\n");
119      }
120      pack();
121   }
122 }
```

---

java.text.Collator 1.1

- static Locale[] getAvailableLocales()

  returns an array of Locale objects for which Collator objects are available.

- static Collator getInstance()
- static Collator getInstance(Locale l)

  returns a collator for the default locale or the given locale.

- int compare(String a, String b)

  returns a negative value if a comes before b, 0 if they are considered identical, and a positive value otherwise.

- boolean equals(String a, String b)

  returns true if a and b are considered identical, false otherwise.

- void setStrength(int strength)
- int getStrength()

  sets or gets the strength of the collator. Stronger collators tell more words apart. Strength values are Collator.PRIMARY, Collator.SECONDARY, and Collator.TERTIARY.

- void setDecomposition(int decomp)
- int getDecompositon()

  sets or gets the decomposition mode of the collator. The more a collator decomposes a string, the more strict it will be in deciding whether two strings should be considered identical. Decomposition values are Collator.NO_DECOMPOSITION, Collator.CANONICAL_DECOMPOSITION, and Collator.FULL_DECOMPOSITION.

- CollationKey getCollationKey(String a)

  returns a collation key that contains a decomposition of the characters in a form that can be quickly compared against another collation key.

---

java.text.CollationKey 1.1

- int compareTo(CollationKey b)

  returns a negative value if this key comes before b, 0 if they are considered identical, and a positive value otherwise.

---

java.text.Normalizer 6

- static String normalize(CharSequence str, Normalizer.Form form)

  returns the normalized form of str. The form value is one of ND, NKD, NC, or NKC.

7.5 Message Formatting

The Java library has a MessageFormat class that formats text with variable parts. It is similar to formatting with the printf method, but it supports locales and formats for numbers and dates. We will examine that mechanism in the following sections.

7.5.1 Formatting Numbers and Dates

Here is a typical message format string:

```
"On {2}, a {0} destroyed {1} houses and caused {3} of damage."
```

The numbers in braces are placeholders for actual names and values. The static method MessageFormat.format lets you substitute values for the variables. It is a "varargs" method, so you can simply supply the parameters as follows:

```
String msg
  = MessageFormat.format("On {2}, a {0} destroyed {1} houses and caused {3} of damage.",
      "hurricane", 99, new GregorianCalendar(1999, 0, 1).getTime(), 10.0E8);
```

In this example, the placeholder {0} is replaced with "hurricane", {1} is replaced with 99, and so on.

The result of our example is the string

```
On 1/1/99 12:00 AM, a hurricane destroyed 99 houses and caused 100,000,000 of damage.
```

That is a start, but it is not perfect. We don't want to display the time "12:00 AM," and we want the damage amount printed as a currency value. The way we do this is by supplying an optional format for some of the placeholders:

"On **{2,date,long}**, a {0} destroyed {1} houses and caused **{3,number,currency}** of damage."

This example code prints:

On **January 1, 1999**, a hurricane destroyed 99 houses and caused **$100,000,000** of damage.

In general, the placeholder index can be followed by a *type* and a *style*. Separate the index, type, and style by commas. The type can be any of

```
number
time
date
choice
```

If the type is number, then the style can be

```
integer
currency
percent
```

or it can be a number format pattern such as $,##0. (See the documentation of the DecimalFormat class for more information about the possible formats.)

If the type is either time or date, then the style can be

```
short
medium
long
full
```

or a date format pattern such as yyyy-MM-dd. (See the documentation of the SimpleDateFormat class for more information about the possible formats.)

CAUTION: The static MessageFormat.format method uses the current locale to format the values. To format with an arbitrary locale, you have to work a bit harder because there is no "varargs" method that you can use. You need to place the values to be formatted into an Object[] array, like this:

```
var mf = new MessageFormat(pattern, loc);
String msg = mf.format(new Object[] { values });
```

---

java.text.MessageFormat 1.1

- MessageFormat(String pattern)
- MessageFormat(String pattern, Locale loc)

  constructs a message format object with the specified pattern and locale.

(Continues)

`java.text.MessageFormat` 1.1 *(Continued)*

- void applyPattern(String pattern)

  sets the pattern of a message format object to the specified pattern.
- void setLocale(Locale loc)
- Locale getLocale()

  sets or gets the locale to be used for the placeholders in the message. The locale is *only* used for subsequent patterns that you set by calling the applyPattern method.
- static String format(String pattern, Object... args)

  formats the pattern string by using args[i] as input for placeholder {i}.
- StringBuffer format(Object args, StringBuffer result, FieldPosition pos)

  formats the pattern of this MessageFormat. The args parameter must be an array of objects. The formatted string is appended to result, and result is returned. If pos equals new FieldPosition(MessageFormat.Field.ARGUMENT), its beginIndex and endIndex properties are set to the location of the text that replaces the {1} placeholder. Supply null if you are not interested in position information.

`java.text.Format` 1.1

- String format(Object obj)

  formats the given object, according to the rules of this formatter. This method calls format(obj, new StringBuffer(), new FieldPosition(1)).toString().

7.5.2 Choice Formats

Let's look closer at the pattern of the preceding section:

```
"On {2}, a {0} destroyed {1} houses and caused {3} of damage."
```

If we replace the disaster placeholder {0} with "earthquake", the sentence is not grammatically correct in English:

```
On January 1, 1999, a earthquake destroyed . . .
```

What we really want to do is integrate the article "a" into the placeholder:

```
"On {2}, {0} destroyed {1} houses and caused {3} of damage."
```

The {0} would then be replaced with "a hurricane" or "an earthquake". That is especially appropriate if this message needs to be translated into a language where the gender of a word affects the article. For example, in German, the pattern would be

```
"{0} zerstörte am {2} {1} Häuser und richtete einen Schaden von {3} an."
```

The placeholder would then be replaced with the grammatically correct combination of article and noun, such as "Ein Wirbelsturm" or "Eine Naturkatastrophe".

Now let us turn to the {1} parameter. If the disaster wasn't all that catastrophic, {1} might be replaced with the number 1, and the message would read:

```
On January 1, 1999, a mudslide destroyed 1 houses and . . .
```

Ideally, we would like the message to vary according to the placeholder value, so it would read

```
no houses
one house
2 houses
. . .
```

depending on the placeholder value. The choice formatting option was designed for this purpose.

A choice format is a sequence of pairs, each containing

- A *lower limit*
- A *format string*

The lower limit and format string are separated by a # character, and the pairs are separated by | characters.

For example,

```
{1,choice,0#no houses|1#one house|2#{1} houses}
```

Table 7.8 shows the effect of this format string for various values of {1}.

Table 7.8 String Formatted by Choice Format

{1}	Result	{1}	Result
0	"no houses"	3	"3 houses"
1	"one house"	-1	"no houses"

Why do we use {1} twice in the format string? When the message format applies the choice format to the {1} placeholder and the value is 2, the choice format returns "{1} houses". That string is then formatted again by the message format, and the answer is spliced into the result.

NOTE: This example shows that the designer of the choice format was a bit muddleheaded. If you have three format strings, you need two limits to separate them. In general, you need *one fewer limit* than you have format strings. As you saw in Table 7.8, the `MessageFormat` class ignores the first limit.

The syntax would have been a lot clearer if the designer of this class realized that the limits belong *between* the choices, such as

```
no houses|1|one house|2|{1} houses // not the actual format
```

You can use the < symbol to denote that a choice should be selected if the lower bound is strictly less than the value.

You can also use the ≤ symbol (expressed as the Unicode character code \u2264) as a synonym for #. If you like, you can even specify a lower bound of −∞ as -\u221E for the first value.

For example,

```
-∞<no houses|0<one house|2≤{1} houses
```

or, using Unicode escapes,

```
-\u221E<no houses|0<one house|2\u2264{1} houses
```

Let's finish our natural disaster scenario. If we put the choice string inside the original message string, we get the following format instruction:

```
String pattern = "On {2,date,long}, {0} destroyed {1,choice,0#no houses|1#one house|2#{1}
    houses}" + "and caused {3,number,currency} of damage.";
```

Or, in German,

```
String pattern
    = "{0} zerstörte am {2,date,long} {1,choice,0#kein Haus|1#ein Haus|2#{1} Häuser}"
        + "und richtete einen Schaden von {3,number,currency} an.";
```

Note that the ordering of the words is different in German, but the array of objects you pass to the `format` method is the *same*. The order of the placeholders in the format string takes care of the changes in the word ordering.

7.6 Text Input and Output

As you know, the Java programming language itself is fully Unicode-based. However, Windows and Mac OS X still support legacy character encodings such as Windows-1252 or Mac Roman in Western European countries, or Big5 in Taiwan. Therefore, communicating with your users through text is not as simple as it should be. The following sections discuss the complications that you may encounter.

7.6.1 Text Files

Nowadays, it is best to use UTF-8 for saving and loading text files. But you may need to work with legacy files. If you know the expected character encoding, you can specify it when writing or reading text files:

```
var out = new PrintWriter(filename, "Windows-1252");
```

For a guess of the best encoding to use, get the "platform encoding" by calling

```
Charset platformEncoding = Charset.defaultCharset();
```

7.6.2 Line Endings

This isn't an issue of locales but of platforms. On Windows, text files are expected to use \r\n at the end of each line, where UNIX-based systems only require a \n character. Nowadays, most Windows programs can deal with just a \n. The notable exception is Notepad. If it is important to you that users can double-click on a text file that your application produces and view it in Notepad, make sure that the text file has proper line endings.

Any line written with the println method will be properly terminated. The only problem is if you print strings that contain \n characters. They are not automatically modified to the platform line ending.

Instead of using \n in strings, you can use printf and the %n format specifier to produce platform-dependent line endings. For example,

```
out.printf("Hello%nWorld%n");
```

produces

```
Hello\r\nWorld\r\n
```

on Windows and

```
Hello\nWorld\n
```

everywhere else.

7.6.3 The Console

If you write programs that communicate with the user through System.in/System.out or System.console(), you have to face the possibility that the console may use a character encoding that is different from the platform encoding reported by Charset.defaultCharset(). This is particularly noticeable when working with the cmd shell on Windows. In the US version of Windows 10, the command shell still uses the archaic IBM437 encoding that originated with IBM personal computers in 1982. There is no official API for revealing that information. The Charset.defaultCharset() method will return the Windows-1252 character set, which is quite different. For example, the euro symbol € is present in Windows-1252 but not in IBM437. When you call

```
System.out.println("100 €");
```

the console will display

```
100 ?
```

You can advise your users to switch the character encoding of the console. In Windows, that is achieved with the chcp command. For example,

```
chcp 1252
```

changes the console to the Windows-1252 code page.

Ideally, of course, your users should switch the console to UTF-8. In Windows, the command is

```
chcp 65001
```

Unfortunately, that is not enough to make Java use UTF-8 in the console. It is also necessary to set the platform encoding with the unofficial file.encoding system property:

```
java -Dfile.encoding=UTF-8 MyProg
```

7.6.4 Log Files

When log messages from the java.util.logging library are sent to the console, they are written in the console encoding. You saw how to control that in the preceding section. However, log messages in a file use a FileHandler which, by default, uses the platform encoding.

To change the encoding to UTF-8, you need to change the log manager settings. In the logging configuration file, set

```
java.util.logging.FileHandler.encoding=UTF-8
```

7.6.5 The UTF-8 Byte Order Mark

As already mentioned, it is a good idea to use UTF-8 for text files when you can. However, if your application has to read UTF-8 text files created by other programs, you run into another potential problem. It is perfectly legal to add a "byte order mark" character U+FEFF as the first character of a file.

In the UTF-16 encoding, where each code unit is a two-byte quantity, the byte order mark tells a reader whether the file uses "big-endian" or "little-endian" byte ordering. UTF-8 is a single-byte encoding, so there is no need to specify a byte ordering. But if a file starts with bytes 0xEF 0xBB 0xBF (the UTF-8 encoding of U+FEFF), that is a strong indication that it uses UTF-8. For that reason, the Unicode standard encourages this practice. Any reader is supposed to discard an initial byte order mark.

There is just one fly in the ointment. The Oracle Java implementation stubbornly refuses to follow the Unicode standard, citing potential compatibility issues. That means that you, the programmer, must do what the platform won't do. When you read a text file and encounter a U+FEFF at the beginning, ignore it.

CAUTION: Unfortunately, the JDK implementors do not follow this advice. When you pass the `javac` compiler a valid UTF-8 source file that starts with a byte order mark, compilation fails with an error message "illegal character: \65279".

7.6.6 Character Encoding of Source Files

You, the programmer, will need to communicate with the Java compiler—and you do that with tools on your local system. For example, you can use the Chinese version of Notepad to write your Java source code files. The resulting source code files are *not portable* because they use the local character encoding (GB or Big5, depending on which Chinese operating system you use). Only the compiled class files are portable—they will automatically use the "modified UTF-8" encoding for identifiers and strings. That means that when a program is compiling and running, three character encodings are involved:

- Source files: platform encoding
- Class files: modified UTF-8
- Virtual machine: UTF-16

(See Chapter 1 for a definition of the modified UTF-8 and UTF-16 formats.)

TIP: You can specify the character encoding of your source files with the `-encoding` flag, for example:

```
javac -encoding UTF-8 Myfile.java
```

7.7 Resource Bundles

When localizing an application, you'll probably have a dauntingly large number of message strings, button labels, and so on, that all need to be translated. To make this task feasible, you'll want to define the message strings in an external location, usually called a *resource*. The person carrying out the translation can then simply edit the resource files without having to touch the source code of the program.

In Java, you can use property files to specify string resources, and you can implement classes for resources of other types.

 NOTE: Java technology resources are not the same as Windows or Macintosh resources. A Macintosh or Windows executable program stores resources, such as menus, dialog boxes, icons, and messages, in a section separate from the program code. A resource editor can inspect and update these resources without affecting the program code.

 NOTE: Volume I, Chapter 5 describes a concept of JAR file resources, whereby data files, sounds, and images can be placed in a JAR file. The getResource method of the class Class finds the file, opens it, and returns a URL to the resource. By placing your files into the JAR file, you leave the job of finding the files to the class loader—which already knows how to locate items in a JAR file. However, that mechanism has no locale support.

7.7.1 Locating Resource Bundles

When localizing an application, you produce a set of *resource bundles*. Each bundle is a property file or a class that describes locale-specific items (such as messages, labels, and so on). For each bundle, you have to provide versions for all locales that you want to support.

You need to use a specific naming convention for these bundles. For example, resources specific to Germany go into a file *baseName*_de_DE, whereas those shared by all German-speaking countries go into *baseName*_de. In general, use

   baseName_language_country

for all country-specific resources, and

   baseName_language

for all language-specific resources. Finally, as a fallback, you can put defaults into a file without any suffix.

To load a bundle, use the command

```
ResourceBundle currentResources = ResourceBundle.getBundle(baseName, currentLocale);
```

The getBundle method attempts to load the bundle that matches the current locale by language and country. If it is not successful, the country and the language are dropped in turn. Then the same search is applied to the default locale, and, finally, the default bundle file is consulted. If even that attempt fails, the method throws a MissingResourceException.

That is, the getBundle method tries to load the following bundles:

baseName_currentLocaleLanguage_currentLocaleCountry
baseName_currentLocaleLanguage
baseName_currentLocaleLanguage_defaultLocaleCountry
baseName_defaultLocaleLanguage
baseName

Once the getBundle method has located a bundle (say, *baseName*_de_DE), it will still keep looking for *baseName*_de and *baseName*. If these bundles exist, they become the *parents* of the *baseName*_de_DE bundle in a *resource hierarchy*. Later, when looking up a resource, the parents are searched if a lookup was not successful in the current bundle. That is, if a particular resource was not found in *baseName*_de_DE, then the *baseName*_de and *baseName* will be queried as well.

This is clearly a very useful service—and one that would be tedious to program by hand. The resource bundle mechanism of the Java programming language automatically locates the items that are the best match for a given locale. It is easy to add more and more localizations to an existing program—all you have to do is create additional resource bundles.

 NOTE: We simplified the discussion of resource bundle lookup. If a locale has a script or variant, the lookup is quite a bit more complex. See the documentation of the method ResourceBundle.Control.getCandidateLocales for the gory details.

 TIP: You need not place all resources for your application into a single bundle. You could have one bundle for button labels, one for error messages, and so on.

7.7.2 Property Files

Internationalizing strings is quite straightforward. You place all your strings into a property file such as MyProgramStrings.properties. This is simply a text file with one key/value pair per line. A typical file would look like this:

```
computeButton=Rechnen
colorName=black
defaultPaperSize=210×297
```

Then you name your property files as described in the preceding section, for example:

```
MyProgramStrings.properties
MyProgramStrings_en.properties
MyProgramStrings_de_DE.properties
```

You can load the bundle simply as

```
ResourceBundle bundle = ResourceBundle.getBundle("MyProgramStrings", locale);
```

To look up a specific string, call

```
String computeButtonLabel = bundle.getString("computeButton");
```

 CAUTION: Before Java 9, files for storing properties had to be ASCII files. If you are using an old Java version and need to place a Unicode character into a property file, encode it using the \uxxxx encoding. For example, to specify "colorName=Grün", use

```
colorName=Gr\u00FCn
```

You can use the native2ascii tool to generate these encodings.

7.7.3 Bundle Classes

To provide resources that are not strings, define classes that extend the ResourceBundle class. Use the standard naming convention to name your classes, for example

```
MyProgramResources.java
MyProgramResources_en.java
MyProgramResources_de_DE.java
```

Load the class with the same getBundle method that you use to load a property file:

```
ResourceBundle bundle = ResourceBundle.getBundle("MyProgramResources", locale);
```

 CAUTION: When searching for bundles, a bundle in a class is given preference over a property file when the two bundles have the same base names.

Each resource bundle class implements a lookup table. You need to provide a key string for each setting you want to localize, and use that key string to retrieve the setting. For example,

```
var backgroundColor = (Color) bundle.getObject("backgroundColor");
double[] paperSize = (double[]) bundle.getObject("defaultPaperSize");
```

The simplest way to implement resource bundle classes is to extend the ListResourceBundle class. The ListResourceBundle lets you place all your resources into an object array and then does the lookup for you. Follow this code outline:

```
public class baseName_language_country extends ListResourceBundle
{
   private static final Object[][] contents =
   {
      { key₁, value₂ },
      { key₂, value₂ },
      . . .
   }
   public Object[][] getContents() { return contents; }
}
```

For example,

```
public class ProgramResources_de extends ListResourceBundle
{
   private static final Object[][] contents =
   {
      { "backgroundColor", Color.black },
      { "defaultPaperSize", new double[] { 210, 297 } }
   }
   public Object[][] getContents() { return contents; }
}
public class ProgramResources_en_US extends ListResourceBundle
{
   private static final Object[][] contents =
   {
      { "backgroundColor", Color.blue },
      { "defaultPaperSize", new double[] { 216, 279 } }
   }
   public Object[][] getContents() { return contents; }
}
```

 NOTE: The paper sizes are given in millimeters. Everyone on the planet, with the exception of the United States and Canada, uses ISO 216 paper sizes. For more information, see www.cl.cam.ac.uk/~mgk25/iso-paper.html.

Alternatively, your resource bundle classes can extend the ResourceBundle class. Then you need to implement two methods, to enumerate all keys and to look up the value for a given key:

```
Enumeration<String> getKeys()
Object handleGetObject(String key)
```

The getObject method of the ResourceBundle class calls the handleGetObject method that you supply.

---

java.util.ResourceBundle 1.1

- static ResourceBundle getBundle(String baseName, Locale loc)
- static ResourceBundle getBundle(String baseName)

  loads the resource bundle class with the given name, for the given locale or the default locale, and its parent classes. If the resource bundle classes are located in a package, the base name must contain the full package name, such as "intl.ProgramResources". The resource bundle classes must be public so that the getBundle method can access them.

- Object getObject(String name)

  looks up an object from the resource bundle or its parents.

- String getString(String name)

  looks up an object from the resource bundle or its parents and casts it as a string.

- String[] getStringArray(String name)

  looks up an object from the resource bundle or its parents and casts it as a string array.

- Enumeration<String> getKeys()

  returns an enumeration object to enumerate the keys of this resource bundle. It enumerates the keys in the parent bundles as well.

- Object handleGetObject(String key)

  should be overridden to look up the resource value associated with the given key if you define your own resource lookup mechanism.

7.8 A Complete Example

In this section, we apply the material of this chapter to localize a retirement calculator. The program calculates whether or not you are saving enough money for your retirement. You enter your age, how much money you save every month, and so on (see Figure 7.4).

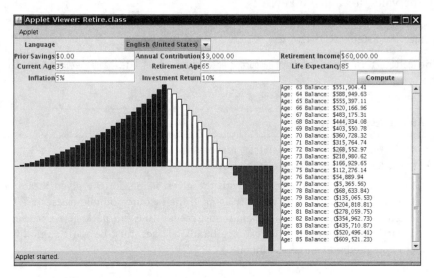

Figure 7.4 The retirement calculator in English

The text area and the graph show the balance of the retirement account for every year. If the numbers turn negative toward the later part of your life and the bars in the graph appear below the x axis, you need to do something—for example, save more money, postpone your retirement, die earlier, or be younger.

The retirement calculator works in three locales (English, German, and Chinese). Here are some of the highlights of the internationalization:

- The labels, buttons, and messages are translated into German and Chinese. You can find them in the classes RetireResources_de and RetireResources_zh. English is used as the fallback—see the RetireResources file.

- Whenever the locale changes, we reset the labels and reformat the contents of the text fields.

- The text fields handle numbers, currency amounts, and percentages in the local format.

- The computation field uses a MessageFormat. The format string is stored in the resource bundle of each language.

- Just to show that it can be done, we use different colors for the bar graph, depending on the language chosen by the user.

Listings 7.5 through 7.8 show the code. Listings 7.9 through 7.11 are the property files for the localized strings. Figures 7.5 and 7.6 show the outputs in German and Chinese, respectively. To see Chinese characters, be sure you have Chinese fonts installed and configured with your Java runtime. Otherwise, Chinese characters will show up as "missing character" icons.

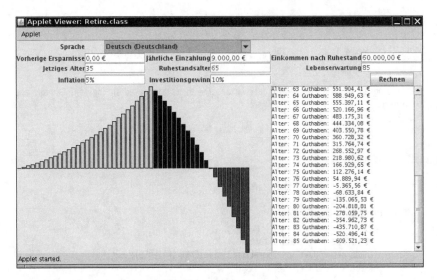

Figure 7.5 The retirement calculator in German

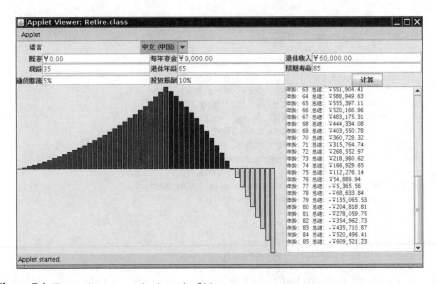

Figure 7.6 The retirement calculator in Chinese

Listing 7.5 retire/Retire.java

```
1  package retire;
2
3  import java.awt.*;
4  import java.awt.geom.*;
5  import java.text.*;
6  import java.util.*;
7
8  import javax.swing.*;
9
10 /**
11  * This program shows a retirement calculator. The UI is displayed in English, German, and
12  * Chinese.
13  * @version 1.25 2018-05-01
14  * @author Cay Horstmann
15  */
16 public class Retire
17 {
18    public static void main(String[] args)
19    {
20       EventQueue.invokeLater(() ->
21          {
22             var frame = new RetireFrame();
23             frame.setDefaultCloseOperation(JFrame.EXIT_ON_CLOSE);
24             frame.setVisible(true);
25          });
26    }
27 }
28
29 class RetireFrame extends JFrame
30 {
31    private JTextField savingsField = new JTextField(10);
32    private JTextField contribField = new JTextField(10);
33    private JTextField incomeField = new JTextField(10);
34    private JTextField currentAgeField = new JTextField(4);
35    private JTextField retireAgeField = new JTextField(4);
36    private JTextField deathAgeField = new JTextField(4);
37    private JTextField inflationPercentField = new JTextField(6);
38    private JTextField investPercentField = new JTextField(6);
39    private JTextArea retireText = new JTextArea(10, 25);
40    private RetireComponent retireCanvas = new RetireComponent();
41    private JButton computeButton = new JButton();
42    private JLabel languageLabel = new JLabel();
43    private JLabel savingsLabel = new JLabel();
44    private JLabel contribLabel = new JLabel();
45    private JLabel incomeLabel = new JLabel();
46    private JLabel currentAgeLabel = new JLabel();
47    private JLabel retireAgeLabel = new JLabel();
48    private JLabel deathAgeLabel = new JLabel();
```

```
49   private JLabel inflationPercentLabel = new JLabel();
50   private JLabel investPercentLabel = new JLabel();
51   private RetireInfo info = new RetireInfo();
52   private Locale[] locales = { Locale.US, Locale.CHINA, Locale.GERMANY };
53   private Locale currentLocale;
54   private JComboBox<Locale> localeCombo = new LocaleCombo(locales);
55   private ResourceBundle res;
56   private ResourceBundle resStrings;
57   private NumberFormat currencyFmt;
58   private NumberFormat numberFmt;
59   private NumberFormat percentFmt;
60
61   public RetireFrame()
62   {
63      setLayout(new GridBagLayout());
64      add(languageLabel, new GBC(0, 0).setAnchor(GBC.EAST));
65      add(savingsLabel, new GBC(0, 1).setAnchor(GBC.EAST));
66      add(contribLabel, new GBC(2, 1).setAnchor(GBC.EAST));
67      add(incomeLabel, new GBC(4, 1).setAnchor(GBC.EAST));
68      add(currentAgeLabel, new GBC(0, 2).setAnchor(GBC.EAST));
69      add(retireAgeLabel, new GBC(2, 2).setAnchor(GBC.EAST));
70      add(deathAgeLabel, new GBC(4, 2).setAnchor(GBC.EAST));
71      add(inflationPercentLabel, new GBC(0, 3).setAnchor(GBC.EAST));
72      add(investPercentLabel, new GBC(2, 3).setAnchor(GBC.EAST));
73      add(localeCombo, new GBC(1, 0, 3, 1));
74      add(savingsField, new GBC(1, 1).setWeight(100, 0).setFill(GBC.HORIZONTAL));
75      add(contribField, new GBC(3, 1).setWeight(100, 0).setFill(GBC.HORIZONTAL));
76      add(incomeField, new GBC(5, 1).setWeight(100, 0).setFill(GBC.HORIZONTAL));
77      add(currentAgeField, new GBC(1, 2).setWeight(100, 0).setFill(GBC.HORIZONTAL));
78      add(retireAgeField, new GBC(3, 2).setWeight(100, 0).setFill(GBC.HORIZONTAL));
79      add(deathAgeField, new GBC(5, 2).setWeight(100, 0).setFill(GBC.HORIZONTAL));
80      add(inflationPercentField, new GBC(1, 3).setWeight(100, 0).setFill(GBC.HORIZONTAL));
81      add(investPercentField, new GBC(3, 3).setWeight(100, 0).setFill(GBC.HORIZONTAL));
82      add(retireCanvas, new GBC(0, 4, 4, 1).setWeight(100, 100).setFill(GBC.BOTH));
83      add(new JScrollPane(retireText),
84         new GBC(4, 4, 2, 1).setWeight(0, 100).setFill(GBC.BOTH));
85
86      computeButton.setName("computeButton");
87      computeButton.addActionListener(event ->
88         {
89            getInfo();
90            updateData();
91            updateGraph();
92         });
93      add(computeButton, new GBC(5, 3));
94
95      retireText.setEditable(false);
96      retireText.setFont(new Font("Monospaced", Font.PLAIN, 10));
97
```

(Continues)

Listing 7.5 *(Continued)*

```
 98        info.setSavings(0);
 99        info.setContrib(9000);
100        info.setIncome(60000);
101        info.setCurrentAge(35);
102        info.setRetireAge(65);
103        info.setDeathAge(85);
104        info.setInvestPercent(0.1);
105        info.setInflationPercent(0.05);
106
107        int localeIndex = 0; // US locale is default selection
108        for (int i = 0; i < locales.length; i++)
109           // if current locale one of the choices, select it
110           if (getLocale().equals(locales[i])) localeIndex = i;
111        setCurrentLocale(locales[localeIndex]);
112
113        localeCombo.addActionListener(event ->
114           {
115              setCurrentLocale((Locale) localeCombo.getSelectedItem());
116              validate();
117           });
118        pack();
119     }
120
121     /**
122      * Sets the current locale.
123      * @param locale the desired locale
124      */
125     public void setCurrentLocale(Locale locale)
126     {
127        currentLocale = locale;
128        localeCombo.setLocale(currentLocale);
129        localeCombo.setSelectedItem(currentLocale);
130
131        res = ResourceBundle.getBundle("retire.RetireResources", currentLocale);
132        resStrings = ResourceBundle.getBundle("retire.RetireStrings", currentLocale);
133        currencyFmt = NumberFormat.getCurrencyInstance(currentLocale);
134        numberFmt = NumberFormat.getNumberInstance(currentLocale);
135        percentFmt = NumberFormat.getPercentInstance(currentLocale);
136
137        updateDisplay();
138        updateInfo();
139        updateData();
140        updateGraph();
141     }
142
143     /**
144      * Updates all labels in the display.
145      */
```

```
146   public void updateDisplay()
147   {
148       languageLabel.setText(resStrings.getString("language"));
149       savingsLabel.setText(resStrings.getString("savings"));
150       contribLabel.setText(resStrings.getString("contrib"));
151       incomeLabel.setText(resStrings.getString("income"));
152       currentAgeLabel.setText(resStrings.getString("currentAge"));
153       retireAgeLabel.setText(resStrings.getString("retireAge"));
154       deathAgeLabel.setText(resStrings.getString("deathAge"));
155       inflationPercentLabel.setText(resStrings.getString("inflationPercent"));
156       investPercentLabel.setText(resStrings.getString("investPercent"));
157       computeButton.setText(resStrings.getString("computeButton"));
158   }
159
160   /**
161    * Updates the information in the text fields.
162    */
163   public void updateInfo()
164   {
165       savingsField.setText(currencyFmt.format(info.getSavings()));
166       contribField.setText(currencyFmt.format(info.getContrib()));
167       incomeField.setText(currencyFmt.format(info.getIncome()));
168       currentAgeField.setText(numberFmt.format(info.getCurrentAge()));
169       retireAgeField.setText(numberFmt.format(info.getRetireAge()));
170       deathAgeField.setText(numberFmt.format(info.getDeathAge()));
171       investPercentField.setText(percentFmt.format(info.getInvestPercent()));
172       inflationPercentField.setText(percentFmt.format(info.getInflationPercent()));
173   }
174
175   /**
176    * Updates the data displayed in the text area.
177    */
178   public void updateData()
179   {
180       retireText.setText("");
181       var retireMsg = new MessageFormat("");
182       retireMsg.setLocale(currentLocale);
183       retireMsg.applyPattern(resStrings.getString("retire"));
184
185       for (int i = info.getCurrentAge(); i <= info.getDeathAge(); i++)
186       {
187           Object[] args = { i, info.getBalance(i) };
188           retireText.append(retireMsg.format(args) + "\n");
189       }
190   }
191
192   /**
193    * Updates the graph.
194    */
```

(Continues)

Listing 7.5 *(Continued)*

```
195    public void updateGraph()
196    {
197       retireCanvas.setColorPre((Color) res.getObject("colorPre"));
198       retireCanvas.setColorGain((Color) res.getObject("colorGain"));
199       retireCanvas.setColorLoss((Color) res.getObject("colorLoss"));
200       retireCanvas.setInfo(info);
201       repaint();
202    }
203
204    /**
205     * Reads the user input from the text fields.
206     */
207    public void getInfo()
208    {
209       try
210       {
211          info.setSavings(currencyFmt.parse(savingsField.getText()).doubleValue());
212          info.setContrib(currencyFmt.parse(contribField.getText()).doubleValue());
213          info.setIncome(currencyFmt.parse(incomeField.getText()).doubleValue());
214          info.setCurrentAge(numberFmt.parse(currentAgeField.getText()).intValue());
215          info.setRetireAge(numberFmt.parse(retireAgeField.getText()).intValue());
216          info.setDeathAge(numberFmt.parse(deathAgeField.getText()).intValue());
217          info.setInvestPercent(percentFmt.parse(investPercentField.getText()).doubleValue());
218          info.setInflationPercent(
219             percentFmt.parse(inflationPercentField.getText()).doubleValue());
220       }
221       catch (ParseException ex)
222       {
223          ex.printStackTrace();
224       }
225    }
226 }
227
228 /**
229  * The information required to compute retirement income data.
230  */
231 class RetireInfo
232 {
233    private double savings;
234    private double contrib;
235    private double income;
236    private int currentAge;
237    private int retireAge;
238    private int deathAge;
239    private double inflationPercent;
240    private double investPercent;
```

```
241    private int age;
242    private double balance;
243
244    /**
245     * Gets the available balance for a given year.
246     * @param year the year for which to compute the balance
247     * @return the amount of money available (or required) in that year
248     */
249    public double getBalance(int year)
250    {
251       if (year < currentAge) return 0;
252       else if (year == currentAge)
253       {
254          age = year;
255          balance = savings;
256          return balance;
257       }
258       else if (year == age) return balance;
259       if (year != age + 1) getBalance(year - 1);
260       age = year;
261       if (age < retireAge) balance += contrib;
262       else balance -= income;
263       balance = balance * (1 + (investPercent - inflationPercent));
264       return balance;
265    }
266
267    /**
268     * Gets the amount of prior savings.
269     * @return the savings amount
270     */
271    public double getSavings()
272    {
273       return savings;
274    }
275
276    /**
277     * Sets the amount of prior savings.
278     * @param newValue the savings amount
279     */
280    public void setSavings(double newValue)
281    {
282       savings = newValue;
283    }
284
285    /**
286     * Gets the annual contribution to the retirement account.
287     * @return the contribution amount
288     */
```

(Continues)

Listing 7.5 *(Continued)*

```
289    public double getContrib()
290    {
291       return contrib;
292    }
293
294    /**
295     * Sets the annual contribution to the retirement account.
296     * @param newValue the contribution amount
297     */
298    public void setContrib(double newValue)
299    {
300       contrib = newValue;
301    }
302
303    /**
304     * Gets the annual income.
305     * @return the income amount
306     */
307    public double getIncome()
308    {
309       return income;
310    }
311
312    /**
313     * Sets the annual income.
314     * @param newValue the income amount
315     */
316    public void setIncome(double newValue)
317    {
318       income = newValue;
319    }
320
321    /**
322     * Gets the current age.
323     * @return the age
324     */
325    public int getCurrentAge()
326    {
327       return currentAge;
328    }
329
330    /**
331     * Sets the current age.
332     * @param newValue the age
333     */
```

```
334     public void setCurrentAge(int newValue)
335     {
336        currentAge = newValue;
337     }
338
339     /**
340      * Gets the desired retirement age.
341      * @return the age
342      */
343     public int getRetireAge()
344     {
345        return retireAge;
346     }
347
348     /**
349      * Sets the desired retirement age.
350      * @param newValue the age
351      */
352     public void setRetireAge(int newValue)
353     {
354        retireAge = newValue;
355     }
356
357     /**
358      * Gets the expected age of death.
359      * @return the age
360      */
361     public int getDeathAge()
362     {
363        return deathAge;
364     }
365
366     /**
367      * Sets the expected age of death.
368      * @param newValue the age
369      */
370     public void setDeathAge(int newValue)
371     {
372        deathAge = newValue;
373     }
374
375     /**
376      * Gets the estimated percentage of inflation.
377      * @return the percentage
378      */
379     public double getInflationPercent()
380     {
381        return inflationPercent;
382     }
```

(Continues)

Listing 7.5 *(Continued)*

```java
383
384    /**
385     * Sets the estimated percentage of inflation.
386     * @param newValue the percentage
387     */
388    public void setInflationPercent(double newValue)
389    {
390       inflationPercent = newValue;
391    }
392
393    /**
394     * Gets the estimated yield of the investment.
395     * @return the percentage
396     */
397    public double getInvestPercent()
398    {
399       return investPercent;
400    }
401
402    /**
403     * Sets the estimated yield of the investment.
404     * @param newValue the percentage
405     */
406    public void setInvestPercent(double newValue)
407    {
408       investPercent = newValue;
409    }
410 }
411
412 /**
413  * This component draws a graph of the investment result.
414  */
415 class RetireComponent extends JComponent
416 {
417    private static final int PANEL_WIDTH = 400;
418    private static final int PANEL_HEIGHT = 200;
419    private static final Dimension PREFERRED_SIZE = new Dimension(800, 600);
420    private RetireInfo info = null;
421    private Color colorPre;
422    private Color colorGain;
423    private Color colorLoss;
424
425    public RetireComponent()
426    {
427       setSize(PANEL_WIDTH, PANEL_HEIGHT);
428    }
```

```
429
430    /**
431     * Sets the retirement information to be plotted.
432     * @param newInfo the new retirement info.
433     */
434    public void setInfo(RetireInfo newInfo)
435    {
436       info = newInfo;
437       repaint();
438    }
439
440    public void paintComponent(Graphics g)
441    {
442       var g2 = (Graphics2D) g;
443       if (info == null) return;
444
445       double minValue = 0;
446       double maxValue = 0;
447       int i;
448       for (i = info.getCurrentAge(); i <= info.getDeathAge(); i++)
449       {
450          double v = info.getBalance(i);
451          if (minValue > v) minValue = v;
452          if (maxValue < v) maxValue = v;
453       }
454       if (maxValue == minValue) return;
455
456       int barWidth = getWidth() / (info.getDeathAge() - info.getCurrentAge() + 1);
457       double scale = getHeight() / (maxValue - minValue);
458
459       for (i = info.getCurrentAge(); i <= info.getDeathAge(); i++)
460       {
461          int x1 = (i - info.getCurrentAge()) * barWidth + 1;
462          int y1;
463          double v = info.getBalance(i);
464          int height;
465          int yOrigin = (int) (maxValue * scale);
466
467          if (v >= 0)
468          {
469             y1 = (int) ((maxValue - v) * scale);
470             height = yOrigin - y1;
471          }
472          else
473          {
474             y1 = yOrigin;
475             height = (int) (-v * scale);
476          }
```

(Continues)

Listing 7.5 *(Continued)*

```
477
478            if (i < info.getRetireAge()) g2.setPaint(colorPre);
479            else if (v >= 0) g2.setPaint(colorGain);
480            else g2.setPaint(colorLoss);
481            var bar = new Rectangle2D.Double(x1, y1, barWidth - 2, height);
482            g2.fill(bar);
483            g2.setPaint(Color.black);
484            g2.draw(bar);
485         }
486      }
487
488      /**
489       * Sets the color to be used before retirement.
490       * @param color the desired color
491       */
492      public void setColorPre(Color color)
493      {
494         colorPre = color;
495         repaint();
496      }
497
498      /**
499       * Sets the color to be used after retirement while the account balance is positive.
500       * @param color the desired color
501       */
502      public void setColorGain(Color color)
503      {
504         colorGain = color;
505         repaint();
506      }
507
508      /**
509       * Sets the color to be used after retirement when the account balance is negative.
510       * @param color the desired color
511       */
512      public void setColorLoss(Color color)
513      {
514         colorLoss = color;
515         repaint();
516      }
517
518      public Dimension getPreferredSize() { return PREFERRED_SIZE; }
519 }
```

Listing 7.6 retire/RetireResources.java

```java
1  package retire;
2
3  import java.awt.*;
4
5  /**
6   * These are the English non-string resources for the retirement calculator.
7   * @version 1.21 2001-08-27
8   * @author Cay Horstmann
9   */
10 public class RetireResources extends java.util.ListResourceBundle
11 {
12    private static final Object[][] contents = {
13    // BEGIN LOCALIZE
14       { "colorPre", Color.blue }, { "colorGain", Color.white }, { "colorLoss", Color.red }
15    // END LOCALIZE
16    };
17
18    public Object[][] getContents()
19    {
20       return contents;
21    }
22 }
```

Listing 7.7 retire/RetireResources_de.java

```java
1  package retire;
2
3  import java.awt.*;
4
5  /**
6   * These are the German non-string resources for the retirement calculator.
7   * @version 1.21 2001-08-27
8   * @author Cay Horstmann
9   */
10 public class RetireResources_de extends java.util.ListResourceBundle
11 {
12    private static final Object[][] contents = {
13    // BEGIN LOCALIZE
14       { "colorPre", Color.yellow }, { "colorGain", Color.black }, { "colorLoss", Color.red }
15    // END LOCALIZE
16    };
17
18    public Object[][] getContents()
19    {
20       return contents;
21    }
22 }
```

Listing 7.8 retire/RetireResources_zh.java

```
1 package retire;
2
3 import java.awt.*;
4
5 /**
6  * These are the Chinese non-string resources for the retirement calculator.
7  * @version 1.21 2001-08-27
8  * @author Cay Horstmann
9  */
10 public class RetireResources_zh extends java.util.ListResourceBundle
11 {
12    private static final Object[][] contents = {
13    // BEGIN LOCALIZE
14        { "colorPre", Color.red }, { "colorGain", Color.blue }, { "colorLoss", Color.yellow }
15    // END LOCALIZE
16    };
17
18    public Object[][] getContents()
19    {
20       return contents;
21    }
22 }
```

Listing 7.9 retire/RetireStrings.properties

```
1 language=Language
2 computeButton=Compute
3 savings=Prior Savings
4 contrib=Annual Contribution
5 income=Retirement Income
6 currentAge=Current Age
7 retireAge=Retirement Age
8 deathAge=Life Expectancy
9 inflationPercent=Inflation
10 investPercent=Investment Return
11 retire=Age: {0,number} Balance: {1,number,currency}
```

Listing 7.10 retire/RetireStrings_de.properties

```
1 language=Sprache
2 computeButton=Rechnen
3 savings=Vorherige Ersparnisse
4 contrib=Jährliche Einzahlung
5 income=Einkommen nach Ruhestand
6 currentAge=Jetziges Alter
7 retireAge=Ruhestandsalter
```

```
 8 deathAge=Lebenserwartung
 9 inflationPercent=Inflation
10 investPercent=Investitionsgewinn
11 retire=Alter: {0,number} Guthaben: {1,number,currency}
```

Listing 7.11 retire/RetireStrings_zh.properties

```
 1 language=语言
 2 computeButton=计算
 3 savings=既存
 4 contrib=每年存金
 5 income=退休收入
 6 currentAge=现龄
 7 retireAge=退休年龄
 8 deathAge=预期寿命
 9 inflationPercent=通货膨涨
10 investPercent=投资报酬
11 retire=年龄: {0,number} 总结: {1,number,currency}
```

You have seen how to use the internationalization features of the Java language. You can now use resource bundles to provide translations into multiple languages, and use formatters and collators for locale-specific text processing.

In the next chapter, we will delve into scripting, compiling, and annotation processing.

Scripting, Compiling, and Annotation Processing

In this chapter

This chapter introduces three techniques for processing code. The scripting API lets you invoke code in a scripting language such as JavaScript or Groovy. You can use the compiler API when you want to compile Java code inside your application. Annotation processors operate on Java source or class files that contain annotations. As you will see, there are many applications for annotation processing, ranging from simple diagnostics to "bytecode engineering"—the insertion of bytecodes into class files or even running programs.

8.1 Scripting for the Java Platform

A scripting language is a language that avoids the usual edit/compile/link/run cycle by interpreting the program text at runtime. Scripting languages have a number of advantages:

- Rapid turnaround, encouraging experimentation
- Changing the behavior of a running program
- Enabling customization by program users

On the other hand, most scripting languages lack features that are beneficial for programming complex applications, such as strong typing, encapsulation, and modularity.

It is therefore tempting to combine the advantages of scripting and traditional languages. The scripting API lets you do just that for the Java platform. It enables you to invoke scripts written in JavaScript, Groovy, Ruby, and even exotic languages such as Scheme and Haskell, from a Java program. For example, the Renjin project (www.renjin.org) provides a Java implementation of the R programming language, which is commonly used for statistical programming, together with an "engine" of the scripting API.

In the following sections, we'll show you how to select an engine for a particular language, how to execute scripts, and how to make use of advanced features that some scripting engines offer.

8.1.1 Getting a Scripting Engine

A scripting engine is a library that can execute scripts in a particular language. When the virtual machine starts, it discovers the available scripting engines. To enumerate them, construct a ScriptEngineManager and invoke the getEngineFactories method. You can ask each engine factory for the supported engine names, MIME types, and file extensions. Table 8.1 shows typical values.

Table 8.1 Properties of Scripting Engine Factories

Engine	Names	MIME types	Extensions
Nashorn (included with the JDK)	nashorn, Nashorn, js, JS, JavaScript, javascript, ECMAScript, ecmascript	application/javascript, application/ecmascript, text/javascript, text/ecmascript	js
Groovy	groovy	None	groovy
Renjin	Renjin	text/x-R	R, r, S, s

Usually, you know which engine you need, and you can simply request it by name, MIME type, or extension. For example:

```
ScriptEngine engine = manager.getEngineByName("nashorn");
```

Java 8 introduced Nashorn, a JavaScript interpreter developed by Oracle. You can add more languages by providing the necessary JAR files on the class path.

---

javax.script.ScriptEngineManager 6

- `List<ScriptEngineFactory> getEngineFactories()`

  gets a list of all discovered engine factories.
- `ScriptEngine getEngineByName(String name)`
- `ScriptEngine getEngineByExtension(String extension)`
- `ScriptEngine getEngineByMimeType(String mimeType)`

  gets the script engine with the given name, script file extension, or MIME type.

---

javax.script.ScriptEngineFactory 6

- `List<String> getNames()`
- `List<String> getExtensions()`
- `List<String> getMimeTypes()`

  gets the names, script file extensions, and MIME types under which this factory is known.

8.1.2 Script Evaluation and Bindings

Once you have an engine, you can call a script simply by invoking

```
Object result = engine.eval(scriptString);
```

If the script is stored in a file, open a `Reader` and call

```
Object result = engine.eval(reader);
```

You can invoke multiple scripts on the same engine. If one script defines variables, functions, or classes, most scripting engines retain the definitions for later use. For example,

```
engine.eval("n = 1728");
Object result = engine.eval("n + 1");
```

will return 1729.

NOTE: To find out whether it is safe to concurrently execute scripts in multiple threads, call

```
Object param = factory.getParameter("THREADING");
```

The returned value is one of the following:

- `null`: Concurrent execution is not safe.
- `"MULTITHREADED"`: Concurrent execution is safe. Effects from one thread might be visible from another thread.
- `"THREAD-ISOLATED"`: In addition to `"MULTITHREADED"`, different variable bindings are maintained for each thread.
- `"STATELESS"`: In addition to `"THREAD-ISOLATED"`, scripts do not alter variable bindings.

You will often want to add variable bindings to the engine. A binding consists of a name and an associated Java object. For example, consider these statements:

```
engine.put("k", 1728);
Object result = engine.eval("k + 1");
```

The script code reads the definition of k from the bindings in the "engine scope." This is particularly important because most scripting languages can access Java objects, often with a syntax that is simpler than the Java syntax. For example,

```
engine.put("b", new JButton());
engine.eval("b.text = 'Ok'");
```

Conversely, you can retrieve variables that were bound by scripting statements:

```
engine.eval("n = 1728");
Object result = engine.get("n");
```

In addition to the engine scope, there is also a global scope. Any bindings that you add to the `ScriptEngineManager` are visible to all engines.

Instead of adding bindings to the engine or global scope, you can collect them in an object of type `Bindings` and pass it to the `eval` method:

```
Bindings scope = engine.createBindings();
scope.put("b", new JButton());
engine.eval(scriptString, scope);
```

This is useful if a set of bindings should not persist for future calls to the eval method.

 NOTE: You might want to have scopes other than the engine and global scopes. For example, a web container might need request and session scopes. However, then you are on your own. You will need to write a class that implements the ScriptContext interface, managing a collection of scopes. Each scope is identified by an integer number, and scopes with lower numbers should be searched first. (The standard library provides a SimpleScriptContext class, but it only holds global and engine scopes.)

---

javax.script.ScriptEngine 6

- Object eval(String script)
- Object eval(Reader reader)
- Object eval(String script, Bindings bindings)
- Object eval(Reader reader, Bindings bindings)

  evaluates the script given by the string or reader, subject to the given bindings.

- Object get(String key)
- void put(String key, Object value)

  gets or puts a binding in the engine scope.

- Bindings createBindings()

  creates an empty Bindings object suitable for this engine.

---

javax.script.ScriptEngineManager 6

- Object get(String key)
- void put(String key, Object value)

  gets or puts a binding in the global scope.

---

javax.script.Bindings 6

- Object get(String key)
- void put(String key, Object value)

  gets or puts a binding into the scope represented by this Bindings object.

8.1.3 Redirecting Input and Output

You can redirect the standard input and output of a script by calling the setReader and setWriter methods of the script context. For example,

```
var writer = new StringWriter();
engine.getContext().setWriter(new PrintWriter(writer, true));
```

Any output written with the JavaScript print or println functions is sent to writer.

The setReader and setWriter methods only affect the scripting engine's standard input and output sources. For example, if you execute the JavaScript code

```
println("Hello");
java.lang.System.out.println("World");
```

only the first output is redirected.

The Nashorn engine does not have the notion of a standard input source. Calling setReader has no effect.

---

javax.script.ScriptEngine 6

- ScriptContext getContext()

  gets the default script context for this engine.

---

javax.script.ScriptContext 6

- Reader getReader()
- void setReader(Reader reader)
- Writer getWriter()
- void setWriter(Writer writer)
- Writer getErrorWriter()
- void setErrorWriter(Writer writer)

  gets or sets the reader for input or writer for normal or error output.

8.1.4 Calling Scripting Functions and Methods

With many script engines, you can invoke a function in the scripting language without having to evaluate the actual script code. This is useful if you allow users to implement a service in a scripting language of their choice.

The script engines that offer this functionality implement the Invocable interface. In particular, the Nashorn engine implements Invocable.

To call a function, call the invokeFunction method with the function name, followed by the function parameters:

```
// Define greet function in JavaScript
engine.eval("function greet(how, whom) { return how + ', ' + whom + '!' }");

// Call the function with arguments "Hello", "World"
result = ((Invocable) engine).invokeFunction("greet", "Hello", "World");
```

If the scripting language is object-oriented, call invokeMethod:

```
// Define Greeter class in JavaScript
engine.eval("function Greeter(how) { this.how = how }");
engine.eval("Greeter.prototype.welcome = "
  + " function(whom) { return this.how + ', ' + whom + '!' }");

// Construct an instance
Object yo = engine.eval("new Greeter('Yo')");

// Call the welcome method on the instance
result = ((Invocable) engine).invokeMethod(yo, "welcome", "World");
```

 NOTE: For more information on how to define classes in JavaScript, see *JavaScript—The Good Parts* by Douglas Crockford (O'Reilly, 2008).

 NOTE: If the script engine does not implement the Invocable interface, you might still be able to call a method in a language-independent way. The getMethodCallSyntax method of the ScriptEngineFactory interface produces a string that you can pass to the eval method. For this, however, all method parameters must be bound to names, whereas invokeMethod can be called with arbitrary values.

You can go a step further and ask the scripting engine to implement a Java interface. Then you can call scripting functions and methods with the Java method call syntax.

The details depend on the scripting engine, but typically you need to supply a function for each method of the interface. For example, consider a Java interface

```
public interface Greeter
{
   String welcome(String whom);
}
```

If you define a global function with the same name in Nashorn, you can call it through this interface:

```
// Define welcome function in JavaScript
engine.eval("function welcome(whom) { return 'Hello, ' + whom + '!' }");

// Get a Java object and call a Java method
Greeter g = ((Invocable) engine).getInterface(Greeter.class);
result = g.welcome("World");
```

In an object-oriented scripting language, you can access a script class through a matching Java interface. For example, here is how to call an object of the JavaScript SimpleGreeter class with Java syntax:

```
Greeter g = ((Invocable) engine).getInterface(yo, Greeter.class);
result = g.welcome("World");
```

In summary, the Invocable interface is useful if you want to call scripting code from Java without worrying about the scripting language syntax.

---

javax.script.Invocable 6

- Object invokeFunction(String name, Object... parameters)
- Object invokeMethod(Object implicitParameter, String name, Object... explicitParameters)

  invokes the function or method with the given name, passing the given parameters.

- <T> T getInterface(Class<T> iface)

  returns an implementation of the given interface, implementing the methods with functions in the scripting engine.

- <T> T getInterface(Object implicitParameter, Class<T> iface)

  returns an implementation of the given interface, implementing the methods with the methods of the given object.

8.1.5 Compiling a Script

Some scripting engines can compile scripting code into an intermediate form for efficient execution. Those engines implement the Compilable interface. The following example shows how to compile and evaluate code contained in a script file:

```
var reader = new FileReader("myscript.js");
CompiledScript script = null;
if (engine implements Compilable)
    script = ((Compilable) engine).compile(reader);
```

Once the script is compiled, you can execute it. The following code executes the compiled script if compilation was successful, or the original script if the engine didn't support compilation:

```
if (script != null)
    script.eval();
else
    engine.eval(reader);
```

Of course, it only makes sense to compile a script if you need to execute it repeatedly.

---

javax.script.Compilable 6

- CompiledScript compile(String script)
- CompiledScript compile(Reader reader)

  compiles the script given by a string or reader.

---

javax.script.CompiledScript 6

- Object eval()
- Object eval(Bindings bindings)

  evaluates this script.

8.1.6 An Example: Scripting GUI Events

To illustrate the scripting API, we will write a sample program that allows users to specify event handlers in a scripting language of their choice.

Have a look at the program in Listing 8.1 that adds scripting to an arbitrary frame class. By default it reads the ButtonFrame class in Listing 8.2, which is similar to the event handling demo in Volume I, with two differences:

- Each component has its name property set.
- There are no event handlers.

The event handlers are defined in a property file. Each property definition has the form

componentName.eventName = scriptCode

For example, if you choose to use JavaScript, supply the event handlers in a file js.properties, like this:

```
yellowButton.action=panel.background = java.awt.Color.YELLOW
blueButton.action=panel.background = java.awt.Color.BLUE
redButton.action=panel.background = java.awt.Color.RED
```

The companion code also has files for Groovy and R.

The program starts by loading an engine for the language specified on the command line. If no language is specified, we use JavaScript.

We then process a script init.*language* if it is present. This is useful for the R and Scheme languages, which need some initializations that we did not want to include in every event handler script.

Next, we recursively traverse all child components and add the bindings (*name*, *object*) into a map of components. Then we add the bindings to the engine.

Next, we read the file *language*.properties. For each property, we synthesize an event handler proxy that causes the script code to be executed. The details are a bit technical. You might want to read the section on proxies in Volume I, Chapter 6, if you want to follow the implementation in detail. The essential part, however, is that each event handler calls

```
engine.eval(scriptCode);
```

Let us look at the yellowButton in more detail. When the line

```
yellowButton.action=panel.background = java.awt.Color.YELLOW
```

is processed, we find the JButton component with the name "yellowButton". We then attach an ActionListener with an actionPerformed method that executes the script

```
panel.background = java.awt.Color.YELLOW
```

if the scripting is done with Nashorn.

The engine contains a binding that binds the name "panel" to the JPanel object. When the event occurs, the setBackground method of the panel is executed, and the color changes.

You can run this program with the JavaScript event handlers simply by executing

```
java ScriptTest
```

For the Groovy handlers, use

```
java -classpath .:groovy/lib/\* ScriptTest groovy
```

Here, *groovy* is the directory into which you installed Groovy.

For the Renjin implementation of R, include the JAR files for Renjin Studio and the Renjin script engine on the classpath. Both are available at www.renjin.org /downloads.html.

This application demonstrates how to use scripting for Java GUI programming. One could go a step further and describe the GUI with an XML file, as you have seen in Chapter 3. Then our program would become an interpreter for GUIs that have their visual presentation defined in XML and behavior defined in a scripting language. Note the similarity to a dynamic HTML page or a dynamic server-side scripting environment.

Listing 8.1 script/ScriptTest.java

```java
1  package script;
2
3  import java.awt.*;
4  import java.beans.*;
5  import java.io.*;
6  import java.lang.reflect.*;
7  import java.util.*;
8  import javax.script.*;
9  import javax.swing.*;
10
11 /**
12  * @version 1.03 2018-05-01
13  * @author Cay Horstmann
14  */
15 public class ScriptTest
16 {
17     public static void main(String[] args)
18     {
19         EventQueue.invokeLater(() ->
20             {
21                 try
22                 {
23                     var manager = new ScriptEngineManager();
24                     String language;
25                     if (args.length == 0)
26                     {
27                         System.out.println("Available factories: ");
28                         for (ScriptEngineFactory factory : manager.getEngineFactories())
29                             System.out.println(factory.getEngineName());
30
31                         language = "nashorn";
32                     }
33                     else language = args[0];
```

(Continues)

Listing 8.1 *(Continued)*

```
34
35              final ScriptEngine engine = manager.getEngineByName(language);
36              if (engine == null)
37              {
38                 System.err.println("No engine for " + language);
39                 System.exit(1);
40              }
41
42              final String frameClassName
43                 = args.length < 2 ? "buttons1.ButtonFrame" : args[1];
44
45              var frame
46                 = (JFrame) Class.forName(frameClassName).getConstructor().newInstance();
47              InputStream in = frame.getClass().getResourceAsStream("init." + language);
48              if (in != null) engine.eval(new InputStreamReader(in));
49              var components = new HashMap<String, Component>();
50              getComponentBindings(frame, components);
51              components.forEach((name, c) -> engine.put(name, c));
52
53              var events = new Properties();
54              in = frame.getClass().getResourceAsStream(language + ".properties");
55              events.load(in);
56
57              for (Object e : events.keySet())
58              {
59                 String[] s = ((String) e).split("\\.");
60                 addListener(s[0], s[1], (String) events.get(e), engine, components);
61              }
62              frame.setTitle("ScriptTest");
63              frame.setDefaultCloseOperation(JFrame.EXIT_ON_CLOSE);
64              frame.setVisible(true);
65           }
66           catch (ReflectiveOperationException | IOException
67                 | ScriptException | IntrospectionException ex)
68           {
69              ex.printStackTrace();
70           }
71        });
72     }
73
74     /**
75      * Gathers all named components in a container.
76      * @param c the component
77      * @param namedComponents a map into which to enter the component names and components
78      */
```

```java
79   private static void getComponentBindings(Component c,
80         Map<String, Component> namedComponents)
81   {
82      String name = c.getName();
83      if (name != null) { namedComponents.put(name, c); }
84      if (c instanceof Container)
85      {
86         for (Component child : ((Container) c).getComponents())
87            getComponentBindings(child, namedComponents);
88      }
89   }
90
91   /**
92    * Adds a listener to an object whose listener method executes a script.
93    * @param beanName the name of the bean to which the listener should be added
94    * @param eventName the name of the listener type, such as "action" or "change"
95    * @param scriptCode the script code to be executed
96    * @param engine the engine that executes the code
97    * @param bindings the bindings for the execution
98    * @throws IntrospectionException
99    */
100  private static void addListener(String beanName, String eventName, final String scriptCode,
101        ScriptEngine engine, Map<String, Component> components)
102        throws ReflectiveOperationException, IntrospectionException
103  {
104     Object bean = components.get(beanName);
105     EventSetDescriptor descriptor = getEventSetDescriptor(bean, eventName);
106     if (descriptor == null) return;
107     descriptor.getAddListenerMethod().invoke(bean,
108        Proxy.newProxyInstance(null, new Class[] { descriptor.getListenerType() },
109           (proxy, method, args) ->
110              {
111                 engine.eval(scriptCode);
112                 return null;
113              }));
114  }
115
116  private static EventSetDescriptor getEventSetDescriptor(Object bean, String eventName)
117        throws IntrospectionException
118  {
119     for (EventSetDescriptor descriptor : Introspector.getBeanInfo(bean.getClass())
120           .getEventSetDescriptors())
121        if (descriptor.getName().equals(eventName)) return descriptor;
122     return null;
123  }
124 }
```

Listing 8.2 buttons1/ButtonFrame.java

```
1  package buttons1;
2
3  import javax.swing.*;
4
5  /**
6   * A frame with a button panel.
7   * @version 1.00 2007-11-02
8   * @author Cay Horstmann
9   */
10 public class ButtonFrame extends JFrame
11 {
12    private static final int DEFAULT_WIDTH = 300;
13    private static final int DEFAULT_HEIGHT = 200;
14
15    private JPanel panel;
16    private JButton yellowButton;
17    private JButton blueButton;
18    private JButton redButton;
19
20    public ButtonFrame()
21    {
22       setSize(DEFAULT_WIDTH, DEFAULT_HEIGHT);
23
24       panel = new JPanel();
25       panel.setName("panel");
26       add(panel);
27
28       yellowButton = new JButton("Yellow");
29       yellowButton.setName("yellowButton");
30       blueButton = new JButton("Blue");
31       blueButton.setName("blueButton");
32       redButton = new JButton("Red");
33       redButton.setName("redButton");
34
35       panel.add(yellowButton);
36       panel.add(blueButton);
37       panel.add(redButton);
38    }
39 }
```

8.2 The Compiler API

There are quite a few tools that need to compile Java code. Obviously, development environments and programs that teach Java programming are among them, as well as testing and build automation tools. Another example is the processing of JavaServer Pages—web pages with embedded Java statements.

8.2.1 Invoking the Compiler

It is very easy to invoke the compiler. Here is a sample call:

```
JavaCompiler compiler = ToolProvider.getSystemJavaCompiler();
OutputStream outStream = . . .;
OutputStream errStream = . . .;
int result = compiler.run(null, outStream, errStream,
    "-sourcepath", "src", "Test.java");
```

A result value of 0 indicates successful compilation.

The compiler sends its output and error messages to the provided streams. You can set these parameters to null, in which case System.out and System.err are used. The first parameter of the run method is an input stream. As the compiler takes no console input, you can always leave it as null. (The run method is inherited from a generic Tool interface, which allows for tools that read input.)

The remaining parameters of the run method are the arguments that you would pass to javac if you invoked it on the command line. These can be options or file names.

8.2.2 Launching a Compilation Task

You can have more control over the compilation process with a CompilationTask object. This can be useful if you want to supply source from string, capture class files in memory, or process the error and warning messages.

To obtain a CompilationTask, start with a compiler object as in the preceding section. Then call

```
JavaCompiler.CompilationTask task = compiler.getTask(
    errorWriter, // Uses System.err if null
    fileManager, // Uses the standard file manager if null
    diagnostics, // Uses System.err if null
    options, // null if no options
    classes, // For annotation processing; null if none
    sources);
```

The last three arguments are Iterable instances. For example, a sequence of options might be specified as

```
Iterable<String> options = List.of("-d", "bin");
```

The sources parameter is an Iterable of JavaFileObject instances. If you want to compile disk files, get a StandardJavaFileManager and call its getJavaFileObjects method:

```
StandardJavaFileManager fileManager = compiler.getStandardFileManager(null, null, null);
Iterable<JavaFileObject> sources
   = fileManager.getJavaFileObjectsFromStrings(List.of("File1.java", "File2.java"));
JavaCompiler.CompilationTask task = compiler.getTask(
   null, null, null, options, null, sources);
```

 NOTE: The `classes` parameter is only used for annotation processing. In that case, you also need to call `task.processors(annotationProcessors)` with a list of `Processor` objects. See Section 8.6, "Source-Level Annotation Processing," on p. 484 for an example of annotation processing.

The `getTask` method returns the task object but does not yet start the compilation process. The `CompilationTask` class extends `Callable<Boolean>`. You can pass it to an `ExecutorService` for concurrent execution, or you can just make a synchronous call:

```
Boolean success = task.call();
```

8.2.3 Capturing Diagnostics

To listen to error messages, install a `DiagnosticListener`. The listener receives a `Diagnostic` object whenever the compiler reports a warning or error message. The `DiagnosticCollector` class implements this interface. It simply collects all diagnostics so that you can iterate through them after the compilation is complete.

```
DiagnosticCollector<JavaFileObject> collector = new DiagnosticCollector<>();
compiler.getTask(null, fileManager, collector, null, null, sources).call();
for (Diagnostic<? extends JavaFileObject> d : collector.getDiagnostics())
{
   System.out.println(d);
}
```

A `Diagnostic` object contains information about the problem location (including file name, line number, and column number) as well as a human-readable description.

You can also install a `DiagnosticListener` to the standard file manager, in case you want to trap messages about missing files:

```
StandardJavaFileManager fileManager
   = compiler.getStandardFileManager(diagnostics, null, null);
```

8.2.4 Reading Source Files from Memory

If you generate source code on the fly, you can have it compiled from memory, without having to save files to disk. Use this class to hold the code:

```
public class StringSource extends SimpleJavaFileObject
{
```

```
   private String code;

   StringSource(String name, String code)
   {
      super(URI.create("string:///" + name.replace('.','/') + ".java"), Kind.SOURCE);
      this.code = code;
   }

   public CharSequence getCharContent(boolean ignoreEncodingErrors)
   {
      return code;
   }
}
```

Then generate the code for your classes and give the compiler a list of
StringSource objects:

```
List<StringSource> sources = List.of(
   new StringSource(className1, class1CodeString), . . .);
task = compiler.getTask(null, fileManager, diagnostics, null, null, sources);
```

8.2.5 Writing Byte Codes to Memory

If you compile classes on the fly, there is no need to save the class files to
disk. You can save them to memory and load them right away.

First, here is a class for holding the bytes:

```
public class ByteArrayClass extends SimpleJavaFileObject
{
   private ByteArrayOutputStream out;

   ByteArrayClass(String name)
   {
      super(URI.create("bytes:///" + name.replace('.','/') + ".class"), Kind.CLASS);
   }

   public byte[] getCode()
   {
      return out.toByteArray();
   }

   public OutputStream openOutputStream() throws IOException
   {
      out = new ByteArrayOutputStream();
      return out;
   }
}
```

Next, you need to configure the file manager to use these classes for output:

```
List<ByteArrayClass> classes = new ArrayList<>();
StandardJavaFileManager stdFileManager
   = compiler.getStandardFileManager(null, null, null);
JavaFileManager fileManager
   = new ForwardingJavaFileManager<JavaFileManager>(stdFileManager)
      {
         public JavaFileObject getJavaFileForOutput(Location location,
               String className, Kind kind, FileObject sibling)
               throws IOException
         {
            if (kind == Kind.CLASS)
            {
               ByteArrayClass outfile = new ByteArrayClass(className);
               classes.add(outfile);
               return outfile;
            }
            else
               return super.getJavaFileForOutput(location, className, kind, sibling);
         }
      };
```

To load the classes, you need a class loader (see Chapter 10):

```
public class ByteArrayClassLoader extends ClassLoader
{
   private Iterable<ByteArrayClass> classes;

   public ByteArrayClassLoader(Iterable<ByteArrayClass> classes)
   {
      this.classes = classes;
   }

   public Class<?> findClass(String name) throws ClassNotFoundException
   {
      for (ByteArrayClass cl : classes)
      {
         if (cl.getName().equals("/" + name.replace('.','/') + ".class"))
         {
            byte[] bytes = cl.getCode();
            return defineClass(name, bytes, 0, bytes.length);
         }
      }
      throw new ClassNotFoundException(name);
   }
}
```

After compilation has finished, call the Class.forName method with that class loader:

```
ByteArrayClassLoader loader = new ByteArrayClassLoader(classes);
Class<?> cl = Class.forName(className, true, loader);
```

8.2.6 An Example: Dynamic Java Code Generation

In the JSP technology for dynamic web pages, you can mix HTML with snippets of Java code, for example:

```
<p>The current date and time is <b><%= new java.util.Date() %></b>.</p>
```

The JSP engine dynamically compiles the Java code into a servlet. In our sample application, we use a simpler example and generate dynamic Swing code instead. The idea is that you use a GUI builder to lay out the components in a frame and specify the behavior of the components in an external file. Listing 8.4 shows a very simple example of a frame class, and Listing 8.5 shows the code for the button actions. Note that the constructor of the frame class calls an abstract method addEventHandlers. Our code generator will produce a subclass that implements the addEventHandlers method, adding an action listener for each line in the action.properties file. (We leave it as the proverbial exercise to the reader to extend the code generation to other event types.)

We place the subclass into a package with the name x, which we hope is not used anywhere else in the program. The generated code has the form

```
package x;
public class Frame extends SuperclassName
{
    protected void addEventHandlers()
    {
        componentName₁.addActionListener(event ->
            {
                code for event handler₁
            });
        // repeat for the other event handlers . . .
    }
}
```

The buildSource method in the program of Listing 8.3 builds up this code and places it into a StringSource object. That object is passed to the Java compiler.

As described in the preceding section, we use a ForwardingJavaFileManager that constructs a ByteArrayClass object for every compiled class. These objects capture the class files generated when the x.Frame class is compiled. The method adds each file object to a list before returning it so that we can locate the bytecodes later.

After compilation, we use the class loader from the preceding section to load the classes stored in this list. Then, we construct and display the application's frame class.

```
var loader = new ByteArrayClassLoader(classFileObjects);
var frame = (JFrame) loader.loadClass("x.Frame").getConstructor().newInstance();
frame.setVisible(true);
```

When you click the buttons, the background color changes in the usual way.
To see that the actions are dynamically compiled, change one of the lines in
action.properties, for example, like this:

```
yellowButton=panel.setBackground(java.awt.Color.YELLOW); yellowButton.setEnabled(false);
```

Run the program again. Now the Yellow button is disabled after you click it.
Also, have a look at the code directories. You will not find any source or class
files for the classes in the x package. This example demonstrates how you
can use dynamic compilation with in-memory source and class files.

Listing 8.3 compiler/CompilerTest.java

```
 1  package compiler;
 2
 3  import java.awt.*;
 4  import java.io.*;
 5  import java.nio.file.*;
 6  import java.util.*;
 7  import java.util.List;
 8
 9  import javax.swing.*;
10  import javax.tools.*;
11  import javax.tools.JavaFileObject.*;
12
13  /**
14   * @version 1.10 2018-05-01
15   * @author Cay Horstmann
16   */
17  public class CompilerTest
18  {
19     public static void main(final String[] args)
20           throws IOException, ReflectiveOperationException
21     {
22        JavaCompiler compiler = ToolProvider.getSystemJavaCompiler();
23
24        var classFileObjects = new ArrayList<ByteArrayClass>();
25        var diagnostics = new DiagnosticCollector<JavaFileObject>();
26
27        JavaFileManager fileManager = compiler.getStandardFileManager(diagnostics, null, null);
28        fileManager = new ForwardingJavaFileManager<JavaFileManager>(fileManager)
29           {
30              public JavaFileObject getJavaFileForOutput(Location location,
31                    String className, Kind kind, FileObject sibling) throws IOException
32              {
```

```
33            if (kind == Kind.CLASS)
34            {
35               var fileObject = new ByteArrayClass(className);
36               classFileObjects.add(fileObject);
37               return fileObject;
38            }
39            else return super.getJavaFileForOutput(location, className, kind, sibling);
40         }
41      };
42
43      String frameClassName = args.length == 0 ? "buttons2.ButtonFrame" : args[0];
44      //compiler.run(null, null, null, frameClassName.replace(".", "/") + ".java");
45
46      StandardJavaFileManager fileManager2 = compiler.getStandardFileManager(null, null, null);
47      var sources = new ArrayList<JavaFileObject>();
48      for (JavaFileObject o : fileManager2.getJavaFileObjectsFromStrings(
49            List.of(frameClassName.replace(".", "/") + ".java")))
50         sources.add(o);
51
52      JavaFileObject source = buildSource(frameClassName);
53      JavaCompiler.CompilationTask task = compiler.getTask(null, fileManager, diagnostics,
54         null, null, List.of(source));
55      Boolean result = task.call();
56
57      for (Diagnostic<? extends JavaFileObject> d : diagnostics.getDiagnostics())
58         System.out.println(d.getKind() + ": " + d.getMessage(null));
59      fileManager.close();
60      if (!result)
61      {
62         System.out.println("Compilation failed.");
63         System.exit(1);
64      }
65
66      var loader = new ByteArrayClassLoader(classFileObjects);
67      var frame = (JFrame) loader.loadClass("x.Frame").getConstructor().newInstance();
68
69      EventQueue.invokeLater(() ->
70         {
71            frame.setDefaultCloseOperation(JFrame.EXIT_ON_CLOSE);
72            frame.setTitle("CompilerTest");
73            frame.setVisible(true);
74         });
75   }
76
77   /*
78    * Builds the source for the subclass that implements the addEventHandlers method.
79    * @return a file object containing the source in a string builder
80    */
```

(Continues)

Listing 8.3 *(Continued)*

```
81    static JavaFileObject buildSource(String superclassName)
82        throws IOException, ClassNotFoundException
83    {
84       var builder = new StringBuilder();
85       builder.append("package x;\n\n");
86       builder.append("public class Frame extends " + superclassName + " {\n");
87       builder.append("protected void addEventHandlers() {\n");
88       var props = new Properties();
89       props.load(Files.newInputStream(Paths.get(
90           superclassName.replace(".", "/")).getParent().resolve("action.properties")));
91       for (Map.Entry<Object, Object> e : props.entrySet())
92       {
93          var beanName = (String) e.getKey();
94          var eventCode = (String) e.getValue();
95          builder.append(beanName + ".addActionListener(event -> {\n");
96          builder.append(eventCode);
97          builder.append("\n} );\n");
98       }
99       builder.append("} }\n");
100      return new StringSource("x.Frame", builder.toString());
101   }
102 }
```

Listing 8.4 buttons2/ButtonFrame.java

```
1 package buttons2;
2 import javax.swing.*;
3
4 /**
5  * A frame with a button panel.
6  * @version 1.00 2007-11-02
7  * @author Cay Horstmann
8  */
9 public abstract class ButtonFrame extends JFrame
10 {
11    public static final int DEFAULT_WIDTH = 300;
12    public static final int DEFAULT_HEIGHT = 200;
13
14    protected JPanel panel;
15    protected JButton yellowButton;
16    protected JButton blueButton;
17    protected JButton redButton;
18
19    protected abstract void addEventHandlers();
20
```

```
21   public ButtonFrame()
22   {
23      setSize(DEFAULT_WIDTH, DEFAULT_HEIGHT);
24
25      panel = new JPanel();
26      add(panel);
27
28      yellowButton = new JButton("Yellow");
29      blueButton = new JButton("Blue");
30      redButton = new JButton("Red");
31
32      panel.add(yellowButton);
33      panel.add(blueButton);
34      panel.add(redButton);
35
36      addEventHandlers();
37   }
38 }
```

Listing 8.5 buttons2/action.properties

```
1 yellowButton=panel.setBackground(java.awt.Color.YELLOW);
2 blueButton=panel.setBackground(java.awt.Color.BLUE);
```

---

javax.tools.Tool 6

- int run(InputStream in, OutputStream out, OutputStream err, String... arguments)

  runs the tool with the given input, output, and error streams and the given arguments. Returns 0 for success, a nonzero value for failure.

---

javax.tools.JavaCompiler 6

- StandardJavaFileManager getStandardFileManager(DiagnosticListener<? super JavaFileObject> diagnosticListener, Locale locale, Charset charset)

  gets the standard file manager for this compiler. You can supply null for default error reporting, locale, and character set.

- JavaCompiler.CompilationTask getTask(Writer out, JavaFileManager fileManager, DiagnosticListener<? super JavaFileObject> diagnosticListener, Iterable<String> options, Iterable<String> classesForAnnotationProcessing, Iterable<? extends JavaFileObject> sourceFiles)

  gets a compilation task that, when called, will compile the given source files. See the discussion in the preceding section for details.

---

javax.tools.StandardJavaFileManager 6

- Iterable<? extends JavaFileObject> getJavaFileObjectsFromStrings(Iterable<String> fileNames)
- Iterable<? extends JavaFileObject> getJavaFileObjectsFromFiles(Iterable<? extends File> files)

  translates a sequence of file names or files into a sequence of JavaFileObject instances.

---

javax.tools.JavaCompiler.CompilationTask 6

- Boolean call()

  performs the compilation task.

---

javax.tools.DiagnosticCollector<S> 6

- DiagnosticCollector()

  constructs an empty collector.

- List<Diagnostic<? extends S>> getDiagnostics()

  gets the collected diagnostics.

---

javax.tools.Diagnostic<S> 6

- S getSource()

  gets the source object associated with this diagnostic.

- Diagnostic.Kind getKind()

  gets the type of this diagnostic—one of ERROR, WARNING, MANDATORY_WARNING, NOTE, or OTHER.

- String getMessage(Locale locale)

  gets the message describing the issue raised in this diagnostic. Pass null for the default locale.

- long getLineNumber()
- long getColumnNumber()

  gets the position of the issue raised in this diagnostic.

---

javax.tools.SimpleJavaFileObject 6

- CharSequence getCharContent(boolean ignoreEncodingErrors)

  Override this method for a file object that represents a source file and produces the source code.

- OutputStream openOutputStream()

  Override this method for a file object that represents a class file and produces a stream to which the bytecodes can be written.

---

javax.tools.ForwardingJavaFileManager<M extends JavaFileManager> 6

- protected ForwardingJavaFileManager(M fileManager)

  constructs a JavaFileManager that delegates all calls to the given file manager.

- FileObject   getFileForOutput(JavaFileManager.Location   location,   String   className, JavaFileObject.Kind kind, FileObject sibling)

  Intercept this call if you want to substitute a file object for writing class files; kind is one of SOURCE, CLASS, HTML, or OTHER.

8.3 Using Annotations

Annotations are tags that you insert into your source code so that some tool can process them. The tools can operate on the source level, or they can process class files into which the compiler has placed annotations.

Annotations do not change the way in which your programs are compiled. The Java compiler generates the same virtual machine instructions with or without the annotations.

To benefit from annotations, you need to select a *processing tool*. Use annotations that your processing tool understands, then apply the processing tool to your code.

There is a wide range of uses for annotations, and that generality can be confusing at first. Here are some uses for annotations:

- Automatic generation of auxiliary files, such as deployment descriptors or bean information classes

- Automatic generation of code for testing, logging, transaction semantics, and so on

8.3.1 An Introduction into Annotations

We'll start our discussion of annotations with the basic concepts and put them to use in a concrete example, in which we will mark methods as event listeners for AWT components and show you an annotation processor that analyzes the annotations and hooks up the listeners. We'll then discuss the syntax rules in detail and finish the chapter with two advanced examples of annotation processing. One of them processes source-level annotations, the other uses the Apache Bytecode Engineering Library to process class files, injecting additional bytecodes into annotated methods.

Here is an example of a simple annotation:

```
public class MyClass
{
   . . .
   @Test public void checkRandomInsertions()
}
```

The annotation @Test annotates the checkRandomInsertions method.

In Java, an annotation is used like a *modifier* and is placed before the annotated item *without a semicolon*. (A modifier is a keyword such as public or static.) The name of each annotation is preceded by an @ symbol, similar to Javadoc comments. However, Javadoc comments occur inside the /** . . . */ delimiters, whereas annotations are part of the code.

By itself, the @Test annotation does not do anything. It needs a tool to be useful. For example, the JUnit testing tool (available at http://junit.org) calls all methods that are labeled @Test when testing a class. Another tool might remove all test methods from a class file so they are not shipped with the program after it has been tested.

Annotations can be defined to have *elements*, such as

```
@Test(timeout="10000")
```

These elements can be processed by the tools that read the annotations. Other forms of elements are possible; we'll discuss them later in this chapter.

Besides methods, you can annotate classes, fields, and local variables—an annotation can be anywhere you could put a modifier such as public or static. In addition, as you will see in Section 8.4, "Annotation Syntax," on p. 471, you can annotate packages, parameter variables, type parameters, and type uses.

Each annotation must be defined by an *annotation interface*. The methods of the interface correspond to the elements of the annotation. For example, the JUnit Test annotation is defined by the following interface:

```
@Target(ElementType.METHOD)
@Retention(RetentionPolicy.RUNTIME)
public @interface Test
{
    long timeout() default 0L;
    . . .
}
```

The @interface declaration creates an actual Java interface. Tools that process annotations receive objects that implement the annotation interface. A tool would call the timeout method to retrieve the timeout element of a particular Test annotation.

The Target and Retention annotations are *meta-annotations*. They annotate the Test annotation, marking it as an annotation that can be applied to methods only and is retained when the class file is loaded into the virtual machine. We'll discuss these in detail in Section 8.5.3, "Meta-Annotations," on p. 481.

You have now seen the basic concepts of program metadata and annotations. In the next section, we'll walk through a concrete example of annotation processing.

 NOTE: For a compelling use of annotations, check out JCommander (http://jcommander.org) and picocli (http://picocli.info). These libraries use annotations for the processing of command-line parameters.

8.3.2 An Example: Annotating Event Handlers

One of the more boring tasks in user interface programming is the wiring of listeners to event sources. Many listeners are of the form

```
myButton.addActionListener(() -> doSomething());
```

In this section, we'll design an annotation to reverse the wiring. The annotation, defined in Listing 8.8, is used as follows:

```
@ActionListenerFor(source="myButton") void doSomething() { . . . }
```

The programmer no longer has to make calls to addActionListener. Instead, each method is tagged with an annotation. Listing 8.7 shows the ButtonFrame class from Volume I, Chapter 10, reimplemented with these annotations.

We also need to define an annotation interface. The code is in Listing 8.8.

Of course, the annotations don't do anything by themselves. They sit in the source file. The compiler places them in the class file, and the virtual machine loads them. We now need a mechanism to analyze them and install action listeners. That is the job of the `ActionListenerInstaller` class. The `ButtonFrame` constructor calls

```
ActionListenerInstaller.processAnnotations(this);
```

The static `processAnnotations` method enumerates all methods of the object it received. For each method, it gets the `ActionListenerFor` annotation object and processes it.

```
Class<?> cl = obj.getClass();
for (Method m : cl.getDeclaredMethods())
{
   ActionListenerFor a = m.getAnnotation(ActionListenerFor.class);
   if (a != null) . . .
}
```

Here, we use the `getAnnotation` method defined in the `AnnotatedElement` interface. The classes `Method`, `Constructor`, `Field`, `Class`, and `Package` implement this interface.

The name of the source field is stored in the annotation object. We retrieve it by calling the `source` method, and then look up the matching field.

```
String fieldName = a.source();
Field f = cl.getDeclaredField(fieldName);
```

This shows a limitation of our annotation. The source element must be the name of a field. It cannot be a local variable.

The remainder of the code is rather technical. For each annotated method, we construct a proxy object, implementing the `ActionListener` interface, with an `actionPerformed` method that calls the annotated method. (For more information about proxies, see Volume I, Chapter 6.) The details are not important. The key observation is that the functionality of the annotations was established by the `processAnnotations` method.

Figure 8.1 shows how annotations are handled in this example.

In this example, the annotations were processed at runtime. It is also possible to process them at the source level: A source code generator would then produce the code for adding the listeners. Alternatively, the annotations can be processed at the bytecode level: A bytecode editor could inject the calls to `addActionListener` into the frame constructor. This sounds complex, but libraries are available to make this task relatively straightforward. You can see an example in Section 8.7, "Bytecode Engineering," on p. 489.

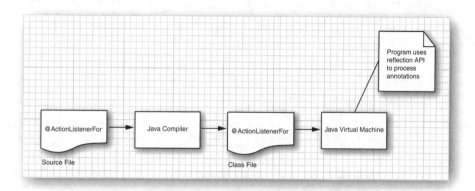

Figure 8.1 Processing annotations at runtime

Our example was not intended as a serious tool for user interface programmers. A utility method for adding a listener could be just as convenient for the programmer as the annotation. (In fact, the java.beans.EventHandler class tries to do just that. You could make the class truly useful by supplying a method that adds the event handler instead of just constructing it.)

However, this example shows the mechanics of annotating a program and of analyzing the annotations. Having seen a concrete example, you are now more prepared (we hope) for the following sections that describe the annotation syntax in complete detail.

Listing 8.6 runtimeAnnotations/ActionListenerInstaller.java

```
1  package runtimeAnnotations;
2
3  import java.awt.event.*;
4  import java.lang.reflect.*;
5
6  /**
7   * @version 1.00 2004-08-17
8   * @author Cay Horstmann
9   */
10 public class ActionListenerInstaller
11 {
12    /**
13     * Processes all ActionListenerFor annotations in the given object.
14     * @param obj an object whose methods may have ActionListenerFor annotations
15     */
```

(Continues)

Listing 8.6 *(Continued)*

```
16   public static void processAnnotations(Object obj)
17   {
18      try
19      {
20         Class<?> cl = obj.getClass();
21         for (Method m : cl.getDeclaredMethods())
22         {
23            ActionListenerFor a = m.getAnnotation(ActionListenerFor.class);
24            if (a != null)
25            {
26               Field f = cl.getDeclaredField(a.source());
27               f.setAccessible(true);
28               addListener(f.get(obj), obj, m);
29            }
30         }
31      }
32      catch (ReflectiveOperationException e)
33      {
34         e.printStackTrace();
35      }
36   }
37
38   /**
39    * Adds an action listener that calls a given method.
40    * @param source the event source to which an action listener is added
41    * @param param the implicit parameter of the method that the listener calls
42    * @param m the method that the listener calls
43    */
44   public static void addListener(Object source, final Object param, final Method m)
45         throws ReflectiveOperationException
46   {
47      var handler = new InvocationHandler()
48      {
49         public Object invoke(Object proxy, Method mm, Object[] args) throws Throwable
50         {
51            return m.invoke(param);
52         }
53      };
54
55      Object listener = Proxy.newProxyInstance(null,
56            new Class[] { java.awt.event.ActionListener.class }, handler);
57      Method adder = source.getClass().getMethod("addActionListener", ActionListener.class);
58      adder.invoke(source, listener);
59   }
60 }
```

Listing 8.7 buttons3/ButtonFrame.java

```
1  package buttons3;
2
3  import java.awt.*;
4  import javax.swing.*;
5  import runtimeAnnotations.*;
6
7  /**
8   * A frame with a button panel.
9   * @version 1.00 2004-08-17
10  * @author Cay Horstmann
11  */
12 public class ButtonFrame extends JFrame
13 {
14    private static final int DEFAULT_WIDTH = 300;
15    private static final int DEFAULT_HEIGHT = 200;
16
17    private JPanel panel;
18    private JButton yellowButton;
19    private JButton blueButton;
20    private JButton redButton;
21
22    public ButtonFrame()
23    {
24       setSize(DEFAULT_WIDTH, DEFAULT_HEIGHT);
25
26       panel = new JPanel();
27       add(panel);
28
29       yellowButton = new JButton("Yellow");
30       blueButton = new JButton("Blue");
31       redButton = new JButton("Red");
32
33       panel.add(yellowButton);
34       panel.add(blueButton);
35       panel.add(redButton);
36
37       ActionListenerInstaller.processAnnotations(this);
38    }
39
40    @ActionListenerFor(source = "yellowButton")
41    public void yellowBackground()
42    {
43       panel.setBackground(Color.YELLOW);
44    }
45
46    @ActionListenerFor(source = "blueButton")
```

(Continues)

Listing 8.7 *(Continued)*

```
47    public void blueBackground()
48    {
49       panel.setBackground(Color.BLUE);
50    }
51
52    @ActionListenerFor(source = "redButton")
53    public void redBackground()
54    {
55       panel.setBackground(Color.RED);
56    }
57 }
```

Listing 8.8 runtimeAnnotations/ActionListenerFor.java

```
1 package runtimeAnnotations;
2
3 import java.lang.annotation.*;
4
5 /**
6  * @version 1.00 2004-08-17
7  * @author Cay Horstmann
8  */
9 @Target(ElementType.METHOD)
10 @Retention(RetentionPolicy.RUNTIME)
11 public @interface ActionListenerFor
12 {
13    String source();
14 }
```

---

java.lang.reflect.AnnotatedElement 5.0

- boolean isAnnotationPresent(Class<? extends Annotation> annotationType)

  returns true if this item has an annotation of the given type.

- <T extends Annotation> T getAnnotation(Class<T> annotationType)

  gets the annotation of the given type, or null if this item has no such annotation.

- <T extends Annotation> T[] getAnnotationsByType(Class<T> annotationType) 8

  gets all annotations of a repeatable annotation type (see Section 8.5.3, "Meta-Annotations," on p. 481), or an array of length 0.

- Annotation[] getAnnotations()

  gets all annotations present for this item, including inherited annotations. If no annotations are present, an array of length 0 is returned.

(Continues)

---

java.lang.reflect.AnnotatedElement 5.0 *(Continued)*

* Annotation[] getDeclaredAnnotations()

  gets all annotations declared for this item, excluding inherited annotations. If no annotations are present, an array of length 0 is returned.

8.4 Annotation Syntax

In the following sections, we cover everything you need to know about the annotation syntax.

8.4.1 Annotation Interfaces

An annotation is defined by an annotation interface:

```
modifiers @interface AnnotationName
{
    elementDeclaration1
    elementDeclaration2
    . . .
}
```

Each element declaration has the form

```
type elementName();
```

or

```
type elementName() default value;
```

For example, the following annotation has two elements, assignedTo and severity:

```
public @interface BugReport
{
    String assignedTo() default "[none]";
    int severity();
}
```

All annotation interfaces implicitly extend the java.lang.annotation.Annotation interface. That interface is a regular interface, *not* an annotation interface. See the API notes at the end of this section for the methods provided by this interface. You cannot extend an annotation interface—in other words, all annotation interfaces directly extend java.lang.annotation.Annotation. You never supply classes that implement annotation interfaces.

The methods of an annotation interface have no parameters and no throws clauses. They cannot be default or static methods, and they cannot have type parameters.

The type of an annotation element is one of the following:

- A primitive type (int, short, long, byte, char, double, float, or boolean)
- String
- Class (with an optional type parameter such as Class<? extends MyClass>)
- An enum type
- An annotation type
- An array of the preceding types (an array of arrays is not a legal element type)

Here are examples of valid element declarations:

```
public @interface BugReport
{
    enum Status { UNCONFIRMED, CONFIRMED, FIXED, NOTABUG };
    boolean showStopper() default false;
    String assignedTo() default "[none]";
    Class<?> testCase() default Void.class;
    Status status() default Status.UNCONFIRMED;
    Reference ref() default @Reference(); // an annotation type
    String[] reportedBy();
}
```

---

java.lang.annotation.Annotation 5.0

- Class<? extends Annotation> annotationType()

    returns the Class object that represents the annotation interface of this annotation object. Note that calling getClass on an annotation object would return the actual class, not the interface.

- boolean equals(Object other)

    returns true if other is an object that implements the same annotation interface as this annotation object and if all elements of this object and other are equal.

- int hashCode()

    returns a hash code, compatible with the equals method, derived from the name of the annotation interface and the element values.

- String toString()

    returns a string representation that contains the annotation interface name and the element values, for example @BugReport(assignedTo=[none], severity=0).

8.4.2 Annotations

Each annotation has the format

$@AnnotationName(elementName_1=value_1, elementName_2=value_2, . . .)$

For example,

```
@BugReport(assignedTo="Harry", severity=10)
```

The order of the elements does not matter. The annotation

```
@BugReport(severity=10, assignedTo="Harry")
```

is identical to the preceding one.

The default value of the declaration is used if an element value is not specified. For example, consider the annotation

```
@BugReport(severity=10)
```

The value of the assignedTo element is the string "[none]".

 CAUTION: Defaults are not stored with the annotation; instead, they are dynamically computed. For example, if you change the default for the assignedTo element to "[]" and recompile the BugReport interface, the annotation @BugReport(severity=10) will use the new default, even in class files that have not been recompiled after the default changed.

Two special shortcuts can simplify annotations.

If no elements are specified, either because the annotation doesn't have any or because all of them use the default value, you don't need to use parentheses. For example,

```
@BugReport
```

is the same as

```
@BugReport(assignedTo="[none]", severity=0)
```

Such an annotation is called a *marker annotation*.

The other shortcut is the *single-value annotation*. If an element has the special name value and no other element is specified, you can omit the element name and the = symbol. For example, had we defined the ActionListenerFor annotation interface of the preceding section as

```
public @interface ActionListenerFor
{
   String value();
}
```

then the annotations could be written as

```
@ActionListenerFor("yellowButton")
```

instead of

```
@ActionListenerFor(value="yellowButton")
```

An item can have multiple annotations:

```
@Test
@BugReport(showStopper=true, reportedBy="Joe")
public void checkRandomInsertions()
```

If the author of an annotation declared it to be repeatable, you can repeat the same annotation multiple times:

```
@BugReport(showStopper=true, reportedBy="Joe")
@BugReport(reportedBy={"Harry", "Carl"})
public void checkRandomInsertions()
```

 NOTE: Since annotations are evaluated by the compiler, all element values must be compile-time constants. For example,

```
@BugReport(showStopper=true, assignedTo="Harry", testCase=MyTestCase.class,
    status=BugReport.Status.CONFIRMED, . . .)
```

 CAUTION: An annotation element can never be set to null. Not even a default of null is permissible. This can be rather inconvenient in practice. You will need to find other defaults, such as "" or Void.class.

If an element value is an array, enclose its values in braces:

```
@BugReport(. . ., reportedBy={"Harry", "Carl"})
```

You can omit the braces if the element has a single value:

```
@BugReport(. . ., reportedBy="Joe") // OK, same as {"Joe"}
```

Since an annotation element can be another annotation, you can build arbitrarily complex annotations. For example,

```
@BugReport(ref=@Reference(id="3352627"), . . .)
```

NOTE: It is an error to introduce circular dependencies in annotations. For example, `BugReport` has an element of the annotation type `Reference`, therefore `Reference` cannot have an element of type `BugReport`.

8.4.3 Annotating Declarations

There are many places where annotations can occur. They fall into two categories: *declarations* and *type uses*. Declaration annotations can appear at the declarations of

- Packages
- Classes (including `enum`)
- Interfaces (including annotation interfaces)
- Methods
- Constructors
- Instance fields (including `enum` constants)
- Local variables
- Parameter variables
- Type parameters

For classes and interfaces, put the annotations before the `class` or `interface` keyword:

```
@Entity public class User { . . . }
```

For variables, put them before the type:

```
@SuppressWarnings("unchecked") List<User> users = . . .;
public User getUser(@Param("id") String userId)
```

A type parameter in a generic class or method can be annotated like this:

```
public class Cache<@Immutable V> { . . . }
```

A package is annotated in a file `package-info.java` that contains only the package statement preceded by annotations.

```
/**
   Package-level Javadoc
*/
@GPL(version="3")
package com.horstmann.corejava;
import org.gnu.GPL;
```

NOTE: Annotations for local variables can only be processed at the source level. Class files do not describe local variables. Therefore, all local variable annotations are discarded when a class is compiled. Similarly, annotations for packages are not retained beyond the source level.

8.4.4 Annotating Type Uses

A declaration annotation provides some information about the item being declared. For example, in the declaration

```
public User getUser(@NonNull String userId)
```

it is asserted that the `userId` parameter is not null.

 NOTE: The `@NonNull` annotation is a part of the Checker Framework (https://checkerframework.org). With that framework, you can include assertions in your program—for example, that a parameter is non-null or that a `String` contains a regular expression. A static analysis tool then checks whether the assertions are valid in a given body of source code.

Now, suppose we have a parameter of type `List<String>`, and we want to express that all of the strings are non-null. That is where type use annotations come in. Place the annotation before the type argument: `List<@NonNull String>`.

Type use annotations can appear in the following places:

- With generic type arguments: `List<@NonNull String>`, `Comparator.<@NonNull String> reverseOrder()`.

- In any position of an array: `@NonNull String[][] words` (`words[i][j]` is not null), `String @NonNull [][] words` (`words` is not null), `String[] @NonNull [] words` (`words[i]` is not null).

- With superclasses and implemented interfaces: `class Warning extends @Localized Message`.

- With constructor invocations: `new @Localized String(. . .)`.

- With casts and `instanceof` checks: `(@Localized String) text`, `if (text instanceof @Localized String)`. (The annotations are only for use by external tools. They have no effect on the behavior of a cast or an `instanceof` check.)

- With exception specifications: `public String read() throws @Localized IOException`.

- With wildcards and type bounds: `List<@Localized ? extends Message>`, `List<? extends @Localized Message>`.

- With method and constructor references: `@Localized Message::getText`.

There are a few type positions that cannot be annotated:

```
@NonNull String.class // ERROR: Cannot annotate class literal
import java.lang.@NonNull String; // ERROR: Cannot annotate import
```

You can place annotations before or after other modifiers such as private and static. It is customary (but not required) to put type use annotations after other modifiers, and declaration annotations before other modifiers. For example,

```
private @NonNull String text; // Annotates the type use
@Id private String userId; // Annotates the variable
```

> **NOTE:** An annotation author needs to specify where a particular annotation can appear. If an annotation is permissible both for a variable and a type use, and it is used in a variable declaration, then both the variable and the type use are annotated. For example, consider
>
> ```
> public User getUser(@NonNull String userId)
> ```
>
> If @NonNull can apply both to parameters and to type uses, the userId parameter is annotated, and the parameter type is @NonNull String.

8.4.5 Annotating this

Suppose you want to annotate parameters that are not being mutated by a method.

```
public class Point
{
    public boolean equals(@ReadOnly Object other) { . . . }
}
```

Then a tool that processes this annotation would, upon seeing a call

```
p.equals(q)
```

reason that q has not been changed.

But what about p?

When the method is called, the this variable is bound to p. But this is never declared, so you cannot annotate it.

Actually, you can declare it, with a rarely used syntax variant, just so that you can add an annotation:

```
public class Point
{
    public boolean equals(@ReadOnly Point this, @ReadOnly Object other) { . . . }
}
```

The first parameter is called the *receiver parameter*. It must be named this. Its type is the class that is being constructed.

 NOTE: You can provide a receiver parameter only for methods, not for constructors. Conceptually, the this reference in a constructor is not an object of the
given type until the constructor has completed. Instead, an annotation placed
on the constructor describes a property of the constructed object.

A different hidden parameter is passed to the constructor of an inner class, namely the reference to the enclosing class object. You can make that parameter explicit as well:

```
public class Sequence
{
    private int from;
    private int to;

    class Iterator implements java.util.Iterator<Integer>
    {
        private int current;
        public Iterator(@ReadOnly Sequence Sequence.this)
        {
            this.current = Sequence.this.from;
        }
        . . .
    }
    . . .
}
```

The parameter must be named just like when you refer to it, *EnclosingClass*.this, and its type is the enclosing class.

8.5 Standard Annotations

A number of annotation interfaces are defined in the java.lang, java.lang.annotation, and javax.annotation packages. Four of them are meta-annotations that describe the behavior of annotation interfaces. The others are regular annotations that you can use to annotate items in your source code. Table 8.2 shows these annotations. We'll discuss them in detail in the following two sections.

Table 8.2 The Standard Annotations

Annotation Interface	Applicable To	Purpose
Deprecated	All	Marks item as deprecated.
SuppressWarnings	All but packages and annotations	Suppresses warnings of the given type.
SafeVarargs	Methods and constructors	Asserts that the varargs parameter is safe to use.
Override	Methods	Checks that this method overrides a superclass method.
FunctionalInterface	Interfaces	Marks an interface as functional (with a single abstract method).
PostConstruct PreDestroy	Methods	The marked method should be invoked immediately after construction or before removal.
Resource	Classes, interfaces, methods, fields	On a class or interface, marks it as a resource to be used elsewhere. On a method or field, marks it for "injection."
Resources	Classes, interfaces	Specifies an array of resources.
Generated	All	Marks an item as source code that has been generated by a tool.
Target	Annotations	Specifies the items to which this annotation can be applied.
Retention	Annotations	Specifies how long this annotation is retained.
Documented	Annotations	Specifies that this annotation should be included in the documentation of annotated items.
Inherited	Annotations	Specifies that this annotation, when applied to a class, is automatically inherited by its subclasses.
Repeatable	Annotations	Specifies that this annotation can be applied multiple times to the same item.

8.5.1 Annotations for Compilation

The @Deprecated annotation can be attached to any items whose use is no longer encouraged. The compiler will warn when you use a deprecated item. This annotation has the same role as the @deprecated Javadoc tag. However, the annotation persists until runtime.

 NOTE: The jdeprscan utility that is part of the JDK can scan a set of JAR files for deprecated elements.

The @SuppressWarnings annotation tells the compiler to suppress warnings of a particular type, for example:

```
@SuppressWarnings("unchecked")
```

The @Override annotation applies only to methods. The compiler checks that a method with this annotation really overrides a method from the superclass. For example, if you declare

```
public MyClass
{
    @Override public boolean equals(MyClass other);
    . . .
}
```

then the compiler will report an error. After all, the equals method does *not* override the equals method of the Object class because that method has a parameter of type Object, not MyClass.

The @Generated annotation is intended for use by code generator tools. Any generated source code can be annotated to differentiate it from programmer-created code. For example, a code editor can hide the generated code, or a code generator can remove older versions of generated code. Each annotation must contain a unique identifier for the code generator. A date string (in ISO 8601 format) and a comment string are optional. For example,

```
@Generated("com.horstmann.beanproperty", "2008-01-04T12:08:56.235-0700");
```

8.5.2 Annotations for Managing Resources

The @PostConstruct and @PreDestroy annotations are used in environments that control the lifecycle of objects, such as web containers and application servers. Methods tagged with these annotations should be invoked immediately after an object has been constructed or immediately before it is being removed.

The @Resource annotation is intended for resource injection. For example, consider a web application that accesses a database. Of course, the database access information should not be hardwired into the web application. Instead, the web container has some user interface for setting connection parameters and a JNDI name for a data source. In the web application, you can reference the data source like this:

```
@Resource(name="jdbc/mydb")
private DataSource source;
```

When an object containing this field is constructed, the container "injects" a reference to the data source.

8.5.3 Meta-Annotations

The @Target meta-annotation is applied to an annotation, restricting the items to which the annotation applies. For example,

```
@Target({ElementType.TYPE, ElementType.METHOD})
public @interface BugReport
```

Table 8.3 shows all possible values. They belong to the enumerated type ElementType. You can specify any number of element types, enclosed in braces.

Table 8.3 Element Types for the @Target Annotation

Element Type	Annotation Applies To
ANNOTATION_TYPE	Annotation type declarations
PACKAGE	Packages
TYPE	Classes (including enum) and interfaces (including annotation types)
METHOD	Methods
CONSTRUCTOR	Constructors
FIELD	Fields (including enum constants)
PARAMETER	Method or constructor parameters
LOCAL_VARIABLE	Local variables
TYPE_PARAMETER	Type parameters
TYPE_USE	Uses of a type

An annotation without an @Target restriction can be applied to any item. The compiler checks that you apply an annotation only to a permitted item. For example, if you apply @BugReport to a field, a compile-time error results.

The @Retention meta-annotation specifies how long an annotation is retained. You can specify at most one of the values in Table 8.4. The default is RetentionPolicy.CLASS.

Table 8.4 Retention Policies for the @Retention Annotation

Retention Policy	Description
SOURCE	Annotations are not included in class files.
CLASS	Annotations are included in class files, but the virtual machine need not load them.
RUNTIME	Annotations are included in class files and loaded by the virtual machine. They are available through the reflection API.

In Listing 8.8, the @ActionListenerFor annotation was declared with RetentionPolicy .RUNTIME because we used reflection to process annotations. In the following two sections, you will see examples of processing annotations at the source and class file levels.

The @Documented meta-annotation gives a hint to documentation tools such as Javadoc. Documented annotations should be treated just like other modifiers, such as protected or static, for documentation purposes. The use of other annotations is not included in the documentation. For example, suppose we declare @ActionListenerFor as a documented annotation:

```
@Documented
@Target(ElementType.METHOD)
@Retention(RetentionPolicy.RUNTIME)
public @interface ActionListenerFor
```

Now the documentation of each annotated method contains the annotation, as shown in Figure 8.2.

If an annotation is transient (such as @BugReport), you should probably not document its use.

 NOTE: It is legal to apply an annotation to itself. For example, the @Documented annotation is itself annotated as @Documented. Therefore, the Javadoc documentation for annotations shows whether they are documented.

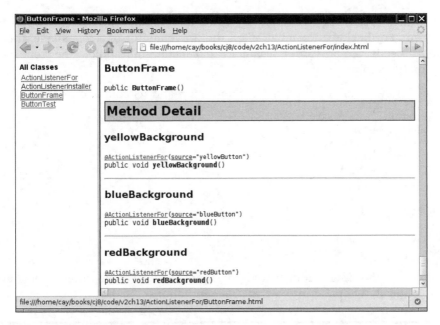

Figure 8.2 Documented annotations

The @Inherited meta-annotation applies only to annotations for classes. When a class has an inherited annotation, then all of its subclasses automatically have the same annotation. This makes it easy to create annotations that work as marker interfaces, such as Serializable.

In fact, an annotation @Serializable would be more appropriate than the Serializable marker interface with no methods. A class is serializable because there is runtime support for reading and writing its fields, not because of any principles of object-oriented design. An annotation describes this fact better than does interface inheritance. Of course, the Serializable interface was created in JDK 1.1, long before annotations existed.

Suppose you define an inherited annotation @Persistent to indicate that objects of a class can be saved in a database. Then the subclasses of persistent classes are automatically annotated as persistent.

```
@Inherited @interface Persistent { }
@Persistent class Employee { . . . }
class Manager extends Employee { . . . } // also @Persistent
```

When the persistence mechanism searches for objects to store in the database, it will detect both Employee and Manager objects.

As of Java 8, it is legal to apply the same annotation type multiple times to an item. For backward compatibility, the implementor of a repeatable annotation needs to provide a *container annotation* that holds the repeated annotations in an array.

Here is how to define the @TestCase annotation and its container:

```
@Repeatable(TestCases.class)
@interface TestCase
{
   String params();
   String expected();
}

@interface TestCases
{
   TestCase[] value();
}
```

Whenever the user supplies two or more @TestCase annotations, they are automatically wrapped into a @TestCases annotation.

 CAUTION: You have to be careful when processing repeatable annotations. If you call getAnnotation to look up a repeatable annotation, and the annotation was actually repeated, then you get null. That is because the repeated annotations were wrapped into the container annotation.

In that case, you should call getAnnotationsByType. That call "looks through" the container and gives you an array of the repeated annotations. If there was just one annotation, you get it in an array of length 1. With this method, you don't have to worry about the container annotation.

8.6 Source-Level Annotation Processing

In the preceding section, you saw how to analyze annotations in a running program. Another use for annotation is the automatic processing of source files to produce more source code, configuration files, scripts, or whatever else one might want to generate.

8.6.1 Annotation Processors

Annotation processing is integrated into the Java compiler. During compilation, you can *invoke annotation processors* by running

```
javac -processor ProcessorClassName₁,ProcessorClassName₂,. . . sourceFiles
```

The compiler locates the annotations of the source files. Each annotation processor is executed in turn and given the annotations in which it expressed an interest. If an annotation processor creates a new source file, the process is repeated. Once a processing round yields no further source files, all source files are compiled.

 NOTE: An annotation processor can only generate new source files. It cannot modify an existing source file.

An annotation processor implements the Processor interface, generally by extending the AbstractProcessor class. You need to specify which annotations your processor supports. In our case:

```
@SupportedAnnotationTypes("com.horstmann.annotations.ToString")
@SupportedSourceVersion(SourceVersion.RELEASE_8)
public class ToStringAnnotationProcessor extends AbstractProcessor
{
   public boolean process(Set<? extends TypeElement> annotations,
         RoundEnvironment currentRound)
   {
      . . .
   }
}
```

A processor can claim specific annotation types, wildcards such as "com.horstmann.*" (all annotations in the com.horstmann package or any subpackage), or even "*" (all annotations).

The process method is called once for each round, with the set of all annotations that were found in any files during this round, and a RoundEnvironment reference that contains information about the current processing round.

8.6.2 The Language Model API

Use the *language model* API for analyzing source-level annotations. Unlike the reflection API, which presents the virtual machine representation of classes and methods, the language model API lets you analyze a Java program according to the rules of the Java language.

The compiler produces a tree whose nodes are instances of classes that implement the javax.lang.model.element.Element interface and its subinterfaces: TypeElement, VariableElement, ExecutableElement, and so on. These are the compile-time analogs to the Class, Field/Parameter, Method/Constructor reflection classes.

I do not want to cover the API in detail, but here are the highlights that you need to know for processing annotations:

- The RoundEnvironment gives you a set of all elements annotated with a particular annotation. Call the method

  ```
  Set<? extends Element> getElementsAnnotatedWith(Class<? extends Annotation> a)
  ```

- The source-level equivalent of the AnnotateElement interface is AnnotatedConstruct. Use the methods

  ```
  A getAnnotation(Class<A> annotationType)
  A[] getAnnotationsByType(Class<A> annotationType)
  ```

  to get the annotation or repeated annotations for a given annotation class.

- A TypeElement represents a class or interface. The getEnclosedElements method yields a list of its fields and methods.

- Calling getSimpleName on an Element or getQualifiedName on a TypeElement yields a Name object that can be converted to a string with toString.

8.6.3 Using Annotations to Generate Source Code

As an example, we will use annotations to reduce the tedium of implementing toString methods. We can't put these methods into the original classes—annotation processors can only produce new classes, not modify existing ones.

Therefore, we'll add all methods into a utility class ToStrings:

```
public class ToStrings
{
   public static String toString(Point obj)
   {
      Generated code
   }
   public static String toString(Rectangle obj)
   {
      Generated code
   }
   . . .

   public static String toString(Object obj)
   {
      return Objects.toString(obj);
   }
}
```

We don't want to use reflection, so we annotate accessor methods, not fields:

```
@ToString
public class Rectangle
{
   . . .
   @ToString(includeName=false) public Point getTopLeft() { return topLeft; }
   @ToString public int getWidth() { return width; }
   @ToString public int getHeight() { return height; }
}
```

The annotation processor should then generate the following source code:

```
public static String toString(Rectangle obj)
{
   var result = new StringBuilder();
   result.append("Rectangle");
   result.append("[");
   result.append(toString(obj.getTopLeft()));
   result.append(",");
   result.append("width=");
   result.append(toString(obj.getWidth()));
   result.append(",");
   result.append("height=");
   result.append(toString(obj.getHeight()));
   result.append("]");
   return result.toString();
}
```

The "boilerplate" code is in gray. Here is an outline of the method that produces the toString method for a class with a given TypeElement:

```
private void writeToStringMethod(PrintWriter out, TypeElement te)
{
   String className = te.getQualifiedName().toString();
   Print method header and declaration of string builder
   ToString ann = te.getAnnotation(ToString.class);
   if (ann.includeName())
      Print code to add class name
   for (Element c : te.getEnclosedElements())
   {
      ann = c.getAnnotation(ToString.class);
      if (ann != null)
      {
         if (ann.includeName()) Print code to add field name
         Print code to append toString(obj.methodName())
      }
   }
   Print code to return string
}
```

And here is an outline of the process method of the annotation processor. It creates a source file for the helper class and writes the class header and one method for each annotated class.

```
public boolean process(Set<? extends TypeElement> annotations,
      RoundEnvironment currentRound)
{
   if (annotations.size() == 0) return true;
   try
   {
      JavaFileObject sourceFile = processingEnv.getFiler().createSourceFile(
          "com.horstmann.annotations.ToStrings");
      try (var out = new PrintWriter(sourceFile.openWriter()))
      {
         Print code for package and class
         for (Element e : currentRound.getElementsAnnotatedWith(ToString.class))
         {
            if (e instanceof TypeElement)
            {
               TypeElement te = (TypeElement) e;
               writeToStringMethod(out, te);
            }
         }
         Print code for toString(Object)
      }
      catch (IOException ex)
      {
         processingEnv.getMessager().printMessage(
             Kind.ERROR, ex.getMessage());
      }
   }
   return true;
}
```

For the tedious details, check the book's companion code.

Note that the process method is called in subsequent rounds with an empty list of annotations. It then returns immediately so it doesn't create the source file twice.

First, compile the annotation processor, and then compile and run the test program as follows:

```
javac sourceAnnotations/ToStringAnnotationProcessor.java
javac -processor sourceAnnotations.ToStringAnnotationProcessor rect/*.java
java rect.SourceLevelAnnotationDemo
```

TIP: To see the rounds, run the `javac` command with the `-XprintRounds` flag:

```
Round 1:
    input files: {rect.Point, rect.Rectangle,
        rect.SourceLevelAnnotationDemo}
    annotations: [sourceAnnotations.ToString]
    last round: false
Round 2:
    input files: {sourceAnnotations.ToStrings}
    annotations: []
    last round: false
Round 3:
    input files: {}
    annotations: []
    last round: true
```

This example demonstrates how tools can harvest source file annotations to produce other files. The generated files don't have to be source files. Annotation processors may choose to generate XML descriptors, property files, shell scripts, HTML documentation, and so on.

 NOTE: Some people have suggested using annotations to remove an even bigger drudgery. Wouldn't it be nice if trivial getters and setters were generated automatically? For example, the annotation

```
@Property private String title;
```

could produce the methods

```
public String getTitle() { return title; }
public void setTitle(String title) { this = title; }
```

However, those methods need to be added to the *same class*. This requires editing a source file, not just generating another file, and is beyond the capabilities of annotation processors. It would be possible to build another tool for this purpose, but such a tool would go beyond the mission of annotations. An annotation is intended as a description *about* a code item, not a directive for adding or changing code.

8.7 Bytecode Engineering

You have seen how annotations can be processed at runtime or at the source code level. There is a third possibility: processing at the bytecode level. Unless annotations are removed at the source level, they are present in the class files. The class file format is documented (see `http://docs.oracle.com/javase/specs/jvms/se10/html`). The format is rather complex, and it would be challenging to process class files without special libraries. One such library is the ASM library, available at `http://asm.ow2.org`.

8.7.1 Modifying Class Files

In this section, we use ASM to add logging messages to annotated methods. If a method is annotated with

```
@LogEntry(logger=loggerName)
```

then we add the bytecodes for the following statement at the beginning of the method:

```
Logger.getLogger(loggerName).entering(className, methodName);
```

For example, if you annotate the `hashCode` method of the `Item` class as

```
@LogEntry(logger="global") public int hashCode()
```

then a message similar to the following is printed whenever the method is called:

```
May 17, 2016 10:57:59 AM Item hashCode
FINER: ENTRY
```

To achieve this, we do the following:

1. Load the bytecodes in the class file.

2. Locate all methods.

3. For each method, check whether it has a `LogEntry` annotation.

4. If it does, add the bytecodes for the following instructions at the beginning of the method:

```
ldc loggerName
invokestatic
    java/util/logging/Logger.getLogger:(Ljava/lang/String;)Ljava/util/logging/Logger;
ldc className
ldc methodName
invokevirtual
    java/util/logging/Logger.entering:(Ljava/lang/String;Ljava/lang/String;)V
```

Inserting these bytecodes sounds tricky, but ASM makes it fairly straightforward. We don't describe the process of analyzing and inserting bytecodes in detail. The important point is that the program in Listing 8.9 edits a class file and inserts a logging call at the beginning of the methods annotated with the `LogEntry` annotation.

For example, here is how you add the logging instructions to Item.java in Listing 8.10, where *asm* is the directory into which you installed the ASM library:

```
javac set/Item.java
javac -classpath .:asm/lib/\* bytecodeAnnotations/EntryLogger.java
java -classpath .:asm/lib/\* bytecodeAnnotations.EntryLogger set.Item
```

Try running

```
javap -c set.Item
```

before and after modifying the Item class file. You can see the inserted instructions at the beginning of the hashCode, equals, and compareTo methods.

```
public int hashCode();
  Code:
  0: ldc #85; // String global
  2:    invokestatic    #80;
     // Method
     // java/util/logging/Logger.getLogger:(Ljava/lang/String;)Ljava/util/logging/Logger;
  5:    ldc     #86; //String Item
  7:    ldc     #88; //String hashCode
  9:    invokevirtual   #84;
     // Method java/util/logging/Logger.entering:(Ljava/lang/String;Ljava/lang/String;)V
  12:   bipush  13
  14:   aload_0
  15:   getfield        #2; // Field description:Ljava/lang/String;
  18:   invokevirtual   #15; // Method java/lang/String.hashCode:()I
  21:   imul
  22:   bipush  17
  24:   aload_0
  25:   getfield        #3; // Field partNumber:I
  28:   imul
  29:   iadd
  30:   ireturn
```

The SetTest program in Listing 8.11 inserts Item objects into a hash set. When you run it with the modified class file, you will see the logging messages.

```
May 17, 2016 10:57:59 AM Item hashCode
FINER: ENTRY
May 17, 2016 10:57:59 AM Item hashCode
FINER: ENTRY
May 17, 2016 10:57:59 AM Item hashCode
FINER: ENTRY
May 17, 2016 10:57:59 AM Item equals
FINER: ENTRY
[[description=Toaster, partNumber=1729], [description=Microwave, partNumber=4104]]
```

Note the call to equals when we insert the same item twice.

This example shows the power of bytecode engineering. Annotations are used to add directives to a program, and a bytecode editing tool picks up the directives and modifies the virtual machine instructions.

Listing 8.9 bytecodeAnnotations/EntryLogger.java

```java
1  package bytecodeAnnotations;
2
3  import java.io.*;
4  import java.nio.file.*;
5
6  import org.objectweb.asm.*;
7  import org.objectweb.asm.commons.*;
8
9  /**
10  * Adds "entering" logs to all methods of a class that have the LogEntry annotation.
11  * @version 1.21 2018-05-01
12  * @author Cay Horstmann
13  */
14  public class EntryLogger extends ClassVisitor
15  {
16     private String className;
17
18     /**
19      * Constructs an EntryLogger that inserts logging into annotated methods of a given class.
20      * @param cg the class
21      */
22     public EntryLogger(ClassWriter writer, String className)
23     {
24        super(Opcodes.ASM5, writer);
25        this.className = className;
26     }
27
28     public MethodVisitor visitMethod(int access, String methodName, String desc,
29           String signature, String[] exceptions)
30     {
31        MethodVisitor mv = cv.visitMethod(access, methodName, desc, signature, exceptions);
32        return new AdviceAdapter(Opcodes.ASM5, mv, access, methodName, desc)
33        {
34           private String loggerName;
35
36           public AnnotationVisitor visitAnnotation(String desc, boolean visible)
37           {
38              return new AnnotationVisitor(Opcodes.ASM5)
39              {
```

```
40          public void visit(String name, Object value)
41          {
42              if (desc.equals("LbytecodeAnnotations/LogEntry;")
43                      && name.equals("logger"))
44                  loggerName = value.toString();
45          }
46      };
47  }
48
49  public void onMethodEnter()
50  {
51      if (loggerName != null)
52      {
53          visitLdcInsn(loggerName);
54          visitMethodInsn(INVOKESTATIC, "java/util/logging/Logger", "getLogger",
55              "(Ljava/lang/String;)Ljava/util/logging/Logger;", false);
56          visitLdcInsn(className);
57          visitLdcInsn(methodName);
58          visitMethodInsn(INVOKEVIRTUAL, "java/util/logging/Logger", "entering",
59              "(Ljava/lang/String;Ljava/lang/String;)V", false);
60          loggerName = null;
61      }
62  }
63  };
64  }
65
66  /**
67   * Adds entry logging code to the given class.
68   * @param args the name of the class file to patch
69   */
70  public static void main(String[] args) throws IOException
71  {
72      if (args.length == 0)
73      {
74          System.out.println("USAGE: java bytecodeAnnotations.EntryLogger classfile");
75          System.exit(1);
76      }
77      Path path = Paths.get(args[0]);
78      var reader = new ClassReader(Files.newInputStream(path));
79      var writer = new ClassWriter(
80          ClassWriter.COMPUTE_MAXS | ClassWriter.COMPUTE_FRAMES);
81      var entryLogger = new EntryLogger(writer,
82          path.toString().replace(".class", "").replaceAll("[/\\\\]", "."));
83      reader.accept(entryLogger, ClassReader.EXPAND_FRAMES);
84      Files.write(Paths.get(args[0]), writer.toByteArray());
85  }
86  }
```

Listing 8.10 set/Item.java

```java
1  package set;
2
3  import java.util.*;
4  import bytecodeAnnotations.*;
5
6  /**
7   * An item with a description and a part number.
8   * @version 1.01 2012-01-26
9   * @author Cay Horstmann
10  */
11 public class Item
12 {
13    private String description;
14    private int partNumber;
15
16    /**
17     * Constructs an item.
18     * @param aDescription the item's description
19     * @param aPartNumber the item's part number
20     */
21    public Item(String aDescription, int aPartNumber)
22    {
23       description = aDescription;
24       partNumber = aPartNumber;
25    }
26
27    /**
28     * Gets the description of this item.
29     * @return the description
30     */
31    public String getDescription()
32    {
33       return description;
34    }
35
36    public String toString()
37    {
38       return "[description=" + description + ", partNumber=" + partNumber + "]";
39    }
40
41    @LogEntry(logger = "com.horstmann")
42    public boolean equals(Object otherObject)
43    {
44       if (this == otherObject) return true;
45       if (otherObject == null) return false;
```

```
46        if (getClass() != otherObject.getClass()) return false;
47        var other = (Item) otherObject;
48        return Objects.equals(description, other.description) && partNumber == other.partNumber;
49     }
50
51     @LogEntry(logger = "com.horstmann")
52     public int hashCode()
53     {
54        return Objects.hash(description, partNumber);
55     }
56  }
```

Listing 8.11 set/SetTest.java

```
1   package set;
2
3   import java.util.*;
4   import java.util.logging.*;
5
6   /**
7    * @version 1.03 2018-05-01
8    * @author Cay Horstmann
9    */
10  public class SetTest
11  {
12     public static void main(String[] args)
13     {
14        Logger.getLogger("com.horstmann").setLevel(Level.FINEST);
15        var handler = new ConsoleHandler();
16        handler.setLevel(Level.FINEST);
17        Logger.getLogger("com.horstmann").addHandler(handler);
18
19        var parts = new HashSet<Item>();
20        parts.add(new Item("Toaster", 1279));
21        parts.add(new Item("Microwave", 4104));
22        parts.add(new Item("Toaster", 1279));
23        System.out.println(parts);
24     }
25  }
```

8.7.2 Modifying Bytecodes at Load Time

In the last section, you saw a tool that edits class files. However, it can be cumbersome to add yet another tool into the build process. An attractive alternative is to defer the bytecode engineering until *load time*, when the class loader loads the class.

The *instrumentation API* has a hook for installing a bytecode transformer. The transformer must be installed before the main method of the program is called. You can meet this requirement by defining an *agent*, a library that is loaded to monitor a program in some way. The agent code can carry out initializations in a premain method.

Here are the steps required to build an agent:

1. Implement a class with a method

   ```
   public static void premain(String arg, Instrumentation instr)
   ```

   This method is called when the agent is loaded. The agent can get a single command-line argument, which is passed in the arg parameter. The instr parameter can be used to install various hooks.

2. Make a manifest file EntryLoggingAgent.mf that sets the Premain-Class attribute, for example:

   ```
   Premain-Class: bytecodeAnnotations.EntryLoggingAgent
   ```

3. Package the agent code and the manifest into a JAR file:

   ```
   javac -classpath .:asm/lib/\* bytecodeAnnotations/EntryLoggingAgent.java
   jar cvfm EntryLoggingAgent.jar bytecodeAnnotations/EntryLoggingAgent.mf \
       bytecodeAnnotations/Entry*.class
   ```

To launch a Java program together with the agent, use the following command-line options:

```
java -javaagent:AgentJARFile=agentArgument . . .
```

For example, to run the SetTest program with the entry logging agent, call

```
javac set/SetTest.java
java -javaagent:EntryLoggingAgent.jar=set.Item -classpath .:asm/lib/\* set.SetTest
```

The Item argument is the name of the class that the agent should modify.

Listing 8.12 shows the agent code. The agent installs a class file transformer. The transformer first checks whether the class name matches the agent argument. If so, it uses the EntryLogger class from the preceding section to modify the bytecodes. However, the modified bytecodes are not saved to a file. Instead, the transformer returns them for loading into the virtual machine (see Figure 8.3). In other words, this technique carries out "just in time" modification of the bytecodes.

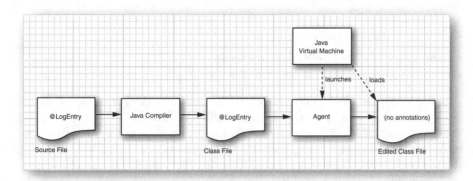

Figure 8.3 Modifying classes at load time

Listing 8.12 bytecodeAnnotations/EntryLoggingAgent.java

```
1  package bytecodeAnnotations;
2
3  import java.lang.instrument.*;
4
5  import org.objectweb.asm.*;
6
7  /**
8   * @version 1.11 2018-05-01
9   * @author Cay Horstmann
10  */
11 public class EntryLoggingAgent
12 {
13     public static void premain(final String arg, Instrumentation instr)
14     {
15         instr.addTransformer((loader, className, cl, pd, data) ->
16             {
17                 if (!className.replace("/", ".").equals(arg)) return null;
18                 var reader = new ClassReader(data);
19                 var writer = new ClassWriter(
20                     ClassWriter.COMPUTE_MAXS | ClassWriter.COMPUTE_FRAMES);
21                 var el = new EntryLogger(writer, className);
22                 reader.accept(el, ClassReader.EXPAND_FRAMES);
23                 return writer.toByteArray();
24             });
25     }
26 }
```

In this chapter, you have learned how to

- Add annotations to Java programs
- Design your own annotation interfaces
- Implement tools that make use of the annotations

You have seen three technologies for processing code: scripting, compiling Java programs, and processing annotations. The first two were quite straightforward. On the other hand, building annotation tools is undeniably complex and not something that most developers will need to tackle. This chapter gave you the background for understanding the inner workings of the annotation tools you will encounter, and perhaps piqued your interest in developing your own tools.

The following chapter discusses the Java Platform Module System, the key feature of Java 9 that is important for moving the Java platform forward.

The Java Platform Module System

In this chapter

An important characteristic of object-oriented programming is encapsulation. A class declaration consists of a public interface and a private implementation. A class can evolve by changing the implementation without affecting its users. A module system provides the same benefits for programming in the large. A module can make classes and packages selectively available so that its evolution can be controlled.

Several existing Java module systems rely on class loaders to isolate classes. However, Java 9 introduced a new system, called the Java Platform Module System, that is supported by the Java compiler and virtual machine. It was designed to modularize the large code base of the Java platform. You can, if you choose, use this system to modularize your own applications.

Whether or not you use Java platform modules in your own applications, you may be impacted by the modularized Java platform. This chapter shows you how to declare and use Java platform modules. You will also learn how to migrate your applications to work with the modularized Java platform and third-party modules.

9.1 The Module Concept

In object-oriented programming, the fundamental building block is the class. Classes provide encapsulation. Private features can only be accessed by code that has explicit permission—namely, the methods of the class. This makes it possible to reason about access. If a private variable has changed, you can produce a set of all possible culprits. If you need to modify the private representation, you know which methods are affected.

In Java, packages provide the next larger organizational grouping. A package is a collection of classes. Packages also provide a level of encapsulation. Any feature with package access (neither public nor private) is accessible only from methods in the same package.

However, in large systems, this level of access control is not enough. Any public feature (that is, a feature that is accessible outside a package) is accessible everywhere. Suppose you want to modify or drop a rarely used feature. Once it is public, there is no way to reason about the impact of that change.

This is the situation that the Java platform designers faced. Over twenty years, the JDK grew by leaps and bounds, but clearly some features are now essentially obsolete. Everyone's favorite example is CORBA. When was the last time you used it? Yet, the org.omg.corba package was shipped with every JDK until Java 10. As of Java 11, those few who still need it must add the required JAR files to their projects.

What about java.awt? It shouldn't be required in a server-side application, right? Except that the class java.awt.DataFlavor is used in the implementation of SOAP, an XML-based web services protocol.

The Java platform designers, faced with a giant hairball of code, decided that they needed a structuring mechanism that provides more control. They looked at existing module systems (such as OSGi) and found them unsuitable for their problem. Instead, they designed a new system, called the *Java Platform Module System*, that is now a part of the Java language and virtual machine. That system has been used successfully to modularize the Java API, and you can, if you so choose, use it with your own applications.

A Java platform module consists of

- A collection of packages
- Optionally, resource files and other files such as native libraries
- A list of the accessible packages in the module
- A list of all modules on which this module depends

The Java platform enforces encapsulation and dependencies, both at compile time and in the virtual machine.

Why should you consider using the Java Platform Module System for your own programs instead of following the traditional approach of using JAR files on the class path? There are two advantages.

1. Strong encapsulation: You can control which of your packages are accessible, and you don't have to worry about maintaining code that you didn't intend for public consumption.
2. Reliable configuration: You avoid common class path problems such as duplicate or missing classes.

There are some issues that the Java Platform Module System does not address, such as versioning of modules. There is no support for specifying which version of a module is required, or for using multiple versions of a module in the same program. These can be desirable features, but you must use mechanisms other than the Java Platform Module System if you need them.

9.2 Naming Modules

A module is a collection of packages. The package names in the module need not be related. For example, the module java.sql contains packages java.sql, javax.sql, and javax.transaction.xa. Also, as you can see from this example, it is perfectly acceptable for the module name to be the same as a package name.

Just like a path name, a module name is made up of letters, digits, underscores, and periods. Also, just as with path names, there is no hierarchical relationship between modules. If you had a module com.horstmann and another module com.horstmann.corejava, they would be unrelated, as far as the module system is concerned.

When creating a module for use by others, it is important to ensure that its name is globally unique. It is expected that most module names will follow the "reverse domain name" convention, just like package names.

The easiest approach is to name a module after the top-level package that the module provides. For example, the SLF4J logging façade has a module org.slf4j with packages org.slf4j, org.slf4j.spi, org.slf4j.event, and org.slf4j.helpers.

This convention prevents package name conflicts in modules. Any given package can only be placed in one module. If your module names are unique and your package names start with the module name, then your package names will also be unique.

You can use shorter module names for modules that are not meant to be used by other programmers, such as a module containing an application program. Just to show that it can be done, I will do the same in this chapter. Modules with what could plausibly be library code will have names such as com.horstmann.util, and modules containing programs (with a class that has a main method) will have catchy names such as v2ch09.hellomod.

 NOTE: Module names are only used in module declarations. In the source files for your Java classes, you never refer to module names; instead, use package names the way they have always been used.

9.3 The Modular "Hello, World!" Program

Let us put the traditional "Hello, World!" program into a module. First, we need to put the class into a package—the "unnamed package" cannot be contained in a module. Here it is:

```
package com.horstmann.hello;

public class HelloWorld
{
   public static void main(String[] args)
   {
      System.out.println("Hello, Modular World!");
   }
}
```

So far, nothing has changed. To make a module v2ch09.hellomod containing this package, you need to add a module declaration. You place it in a file named module-info.java, located in the base directory (that is, the same directory that contains the com directory). By convention, the name of the base directory is the same as the module name.

```
v2ch09.hellomod/
 └ module-info.java
   com/
   └ horstmann/
     └ hello/
       └ HelloWorld.java
```

The module-info.java file contains the module declaration:

```
module v2ch09.hellomod
{
}
```

This module declaration is empty because the module has nothing to offer to anyone, nor does it need anything.

Now, compile as usual:

```
javac v2ch09.hellomod/module-info.java v2ch09.hellomod/com/horstmann/hello/HelloWorld.java
```

The module-info.java file doesn't look like a Java source file, and of course there can't be a class with the name module-info, since class names cannot contain hyphens. The module keyword, as well as keywords requires, exports, and so on, that you will see in the following sections, are "restricted keywords" that have a special meaning only in module declarations. The file is compiled into a class file module-info.class that contains the module definition in binary form.

To run this program as a modular application, you specify the *module path*, which is similar to the class path but contains modules. You also specify the main class in the format *modulename/classname*:

```
java --module-path v2ch09.hellomod --module v2ch09.hellomod/com.horstmann.hello.HelloWorld
```

Instead of --module-path and --module, you can use the single-letter options -p and -m:

```
java -p v2ch09.hellomod -m v2ch09.hellomod/com.horstmann.hello.HelloWorld
```

Either way, the "Hello, Modular World" greeting will appear, demonstrating that you have successfully modularized your first application.

NOTE: When you compile this module, you get a warning:

```
warning: [module] module name component v2ch09 should avoid terminal digits
```

This warning is intended to discourage programmers from adding version numbers to module names. You can ignore the warning, or suppress it with an annotation:

```
@SuppressWarnings("module")
module v2ch09.hellomod
{
}
```

In this one respect, the `module` declaration is just like a class declaration: You can annotate it. (The annotation type must have target `ElementType.MODULE`.)

9.4 Requiring Modules

Let us make a new module `v2ch09.requiremod` in which a program uses a `JOptionPane` to show the "Hello, Modular World" message:

```
package com.horstmann.hello;

import javax.swing.JOptionPane;

public class HelloWorld
{
    public static void main(String[] args)
    {
        JOptionPane.showMessageDialog(null, "Hello, Modular World!");
    }
}
```

Now compilation fails with this message:

```
error: package javax.swing is not visible
  (package javax.swing is declared in module java.desktop,
  but module v2ch09.requiremod does not read it)
```

The JDK has been modularized, and the `javax.swing` package is now contained in the `java.desktop` module. Our module needs to declare that it relies on that module:

```
module v2ch09.requiremod
{
    requires java.desktop;
}
```

It is a design goal of the module system that modules are explicit about their requirements, so the virtual machine can ensure that all requirements are fulfilled before starting a program.

In the preceding section, the need for explicit requirements did not arise because we only used the java.lang and java.io packages. These packages are included in the java.base module which is required by default.

Note that our v2ch09.requiremod module lists only its own module requirements. It requires the java.desktop module so that it can use the javax.swing package. The java.desktop module itself declares that it requires three other modules, namely java.datatransfer, java.prefs, and java.xml.

Figure 9.1 shows the *module graph* whose nodes are modules. The edges of the graph—the arrows joining nodes—are either declared requirements or the implied requirement on java.base when none is declared.

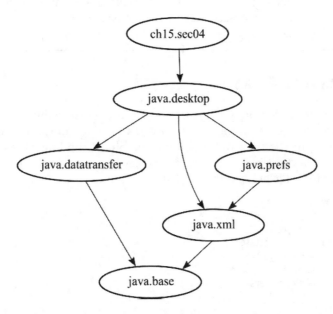

Figure 9.1 The module graph of the Swing "Hello, Modular World" application

You cannot have cycles in the module graph—that is, a module cannot directly or indirectly require itself.

A module does not automatically pass on access rights to other modules. In our example, the java.desktop module declares that it requires java.prefs, and the java.prefs module declares that it requires java.xml. That does not give java.desktop the right to use packages from the java.xml module. It needs to explicitly declare that requirement. In mathematical terms, the requires relationship is not "transitive." Generally, this behavior is desirable because it makes requirements explicit, but as you will see in Section 9.11, "Transitive and Static Requirements," on p. 519, you can relax it in some cases.

 NOTE: The error message at the beginning of this section stated that our v2ch09.requiremod module did not "read" the java.desktop module. In the parlance of the Java Platform Module System, module *M reads* module *N* in the following cases:

1. *M* requires *N*.

2. *M* requires a module that transitively requires *N* (see Section 9.11, "Transitive and Static Requirements," on p. 519).

3. *N* is *M* or java.base.

9.5 Exporting Packages

In the preceding section, you saw that a module must require another module if it wants to use its packages. However, that does not automatically make all packages in the required module available. A module states which of its packages are accessible, using the exports keyword. For example, here is a part of the module declaration for the java.xml module:

```
module java.xml
{
    exports javax.xml;
    exports javax.xml.catalog;
    exports javax.xml.datatype;
    exports javax.xml.namespace;
    exports javax.xml.parsers;
    . . .
}
```

This module makes many packages available, but hides others (such as jdk.xml.internal) by not exporting them.

When a package is exported, its public and protected classes and interfaces, and their public and protected members, are accessible outside the module. (As always, protected types and members are accessible only in subclasses.)

However, a package that is not exported is not accessible outside its own module. This is quite different from Java before modules. In the past, you were able to use public classes from any package, even if it was not part of the public API. For example, it was commonly recommended to use classes such as sun.misc.BASE64Encoder or com.sun.rowset.CachedRowSetImpl when the public API did not provide the appropriate functionality.

Nowadays, you can no longer access unexported packages from the Java platform API since all of them are contained inside modules. As a result, some programs will no longer run with Java 9. Of course, nobody ever committed to keeping non-public APIs available, so this should not come as a shock.

Let us put exports to use in a simple situation. We will prepare a module com.horstmann.greet that exports a package, also called com.horstmann.greet, following the convention that a module that provides code for others should be named after the top-level package inside it. There is also a package com.horstmann.greet .internal that we don't export.

A public Greeter interface is in the first package.

```
package com.horstmann.greet;

public interface Greeter
{
   static Greeter newInstance()
   {
      return new com.horstmann.greet.internal.GreeterImpl();
   }

   String greet(String subject);
}
```

The second package has a class that implements the interface. The class is public since it is accessed in the first package.

```
package com.horstmann.greet.internal;

import com.horstmann.greet.Greeter;

public class GreeterImpl implements Greeter
{
   public String greet(String subject)
   {
      return "Hello, " + subject + "!";
   }
}
```

The com.horstmann.greet module contains both packages but only exports the first:

```
module com.horstmann.greet
{
    exports com.horstmann.greet;
}
```

The second package is inaccessible outside the module.

We put our application into a second module, which will require the first module:

```
module v2ch09.exportedpkg
{
    requires com.horstmann.greet;
}
```

 NOTE: The `exports` statement is followed by a package name, whereas `requires` is followed by a module name.

Our application now uses a `Greeter` to obtain a greeting:

```
package com.horstmann.hello;

import com.horstmann.greet.Greeter;

public class HelloWorld
{
    public static void main(String[] args)
    {
        Greeter greeter = Greeter.newInstance();
        System.out.println(greeter.greet("Modular World"));
    }
}
```

Here is the source file structure for these two modules:

```
com.horstmann.greet
├ module-info.java
└ com
   └ horstmann
      └ greet
         ├ Greeter.java
         └ internal
            └ GreeterImpl.java
v2ch09.exportedpkg
├ module-info.java
└ com
   └ horstmann
      └ hello
         └ HelloWorld.java
```

To build this application, first compile the com.horstmann.greet module:

```
javac com.horstmann.greet/module-info.java \
    com.horstmann.greet/com/horstmann/greet/Greeter.java \
    com.horstmann.greet/com/horstmann/greet/internal/GreeterImpl.java
```

Then compile the application module with the first module on the module path:

```
javac -p com.horstmann.greet v2ch09.exportedpkg/module-info.java \
    v2ch09.exportedpkg/com/horstmann/hello/HelloWorld.java
```

Finally, run the program with both modules on the module path:

```
java -p v2ch09.exportedpkg:com.horstmann.greet \
    -m v2ch09.exportedpkg/com.horstmann.hello.HelloWorld
```

 TIP: To build this application with Eclipse, make a separate project for each module. In the v2ch09.exportedpkg project, edit the project properties. In the Projects tab, add the com.horstmann.greet module to the module path—see Figure 9.2.

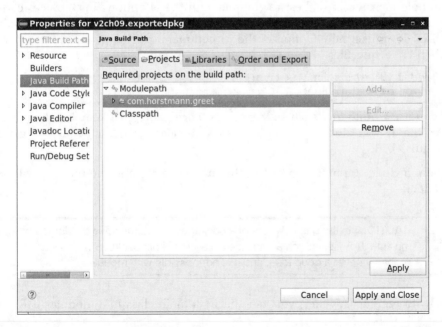

Figure 9.2 Adding a dependent module to an Eclipse project

You have now seen the `requires` and `exports` statements that form the backbone of the Java Platform Module System. As you can see, the module system is conceptually simple. Modules specify what modules they need, and which packages they offer to other modules. Section 9.12, "Qualified Exporting and Opening," on p. 521 shows a minor variation of the `exports` statement.

 CAUTION: A module does not provide a scope. You cannot have two packages with the same name in different modules. This is true even for hidden packages (that is, packages that are not exported.)

9.6 Modular JARs

So far, we have simply compiled modules into the directory tree of the source code. Clearly, that is not satisfactory for deployment. Instead, a module can be deployed by placing all its classes in a JAR file, with a `module-info.class` in the root. Such a JAR file is called a *modular* JAR.

To create a modular JAR file, use the `jar` tool in the usual way. If you have multiple packages, it is best to compile with the `-d` option which places class files into a separate directory. The directory is created if it doesn't already exists. Then use the `-C` option of the `jar` command to change to that directory when collecting files.

```
javac -d modules/com.horstmann.greet $(find com.horstmann.greet -name *.java)
jar -cvf com.horstmann.greet.jar -C modules/com.horstmann.greet .
```

If you use a build tool such as Maven, Ant, or Gradle, just keep building your JAR file as you always do. As long as `module-info.class` is included, you get a modular JAR.

Then, include the modular JAR in the module path, and the module will be loaded.

 CAUTION: In the past, classes of a package were sometimes distributed over multiple JAR files. (Such a package is called a "split package".) This was probably never a good idea, and it is not possible with modules.

As with regular JAR files, you can specify a main class in a modular JAR:

```
javac -p com.horstmann.greet.jar \
    -d modules/v2ch09.exportedpkg $(find v2ch09.exportedpkg -name *.java)
```

```
jar -c -v -f v2ch09.exportedpkg.jar -e com.horstmann.hello.HelloWorld \
  -C modules/v2ch09.exportedpkg .
```

When you launch the program, you specify the module containing the main class:

```
java -p com.horstmann.greet.jar:v2ch09.exportedpkg.jar -m v2ch09.exportedpkg
```

When creating a JAR file, you can optionally specify a version number. Use the `--module-version` parameter, and also add @ and the version number to the JAR file name:

```
jar -c -v -f com.horstmann.greet@1.0.jar --module-version 1.0 -C com.horstmann.greet .
```

As already discussed, the version number is not used by the Java Platform Module System for resolving modules, but it can be queried by other tools and frameworks.

 NOTE: You can find out the version number through the reflection API. In our example:

```
Optional<String> version = Greeter.class.getModule().getDescriptor().rawVersion();
```

yields an `Optional` containing the version string `"1.0"`.

 NOTE: The module equivalent to a class loader is a *layer*. The Java Platform Module System loads the JDK modules and application modules into the *boot layer*. A program can load other modules, using the layer API (which is not covered in this book). Such a program may choose to take module versions into account. Is is expected that developers of programs such as Java EE application servers will make use of the layer API to provide support for modules.

 TIP: If you want to load a module into JShell, include the JAR on the module path and use the `--add-modules` option:

```
jshell --module-path com.horstmann.greet@1.0.jar --add-modules com.horstmann.greet
```

9.7 Modules and Reflective Access

In the preceding sections, you saw that the module system enforces encapsulation. A module can only access explicitly exported packages from another module. In the past, it was always possible to overcome pesky access restrictions by using reflection. As you have seen in Chapter 5 of Volume I, reflection can access private members of any class.

However, in the modular world, that is no longer true. If a class is inside a module, reflective access to non-public members will fail. Specifically, recall how we accessed private fields:

```
Field f = obj.getClass().getDeclaredField("salary");
f.setAccessible(true);
double value = f.getDouble(obj);
f.setDouble(obj, value * 1.1);
```

The call f.setAccessible(true) succeeds unless a security manager disallows private field access. However, it is not common to run Java applications with security managers, and there are many libraries that use reflective access. Typical examples are object-relational mappers, such as JPA, that automatically persist objects in databases and libraries that convert between objects and XML or JSON, such as JAXB and JSON-B.

If you use such a library, and you also want to use modules, you have to be careful. To demonstrate this issue, let us place the ObjectAnalyzer class from Chapter 5 of Volume I into a module com.horstmann.util. That class has a toString method that prints the fields of an object, using reflection.

A separate v2ch09.openpkg module contains a simple Country class:

```
package com.horstmann.places;

public class Country
{
   private String name;
   private double area;

   public Country(String name, double area)
   {
      this.name = name;
      this.area = area;
   }
   // . . .
}
```

A short program demonstrates how to analyze a Country object:

```
package com.horstmann.places;

import com.horstmann.util.*;

public class Demo
{
```

```
public static void main(String[] args) throws ReflectiveOperationException
{
    var belgium = new Country("Belgium", 30510);
    var analyzer = new ObjectAnalyzer();
    System.out.println(analyzer.toString(belgium));
}
}
```

Now compile both modules and the Demo program:

```
javac com.horstmann.util/module-info.java \
    com.horstmann.util/com/horstmann/util/ObjectAnalyzer.java
javac -p com.horstmann.util v2ch09.openpkg/module-info.java \
    v2ch09.openpkg/com/horstmann/places/*.java
java -p v2ch09.openpkg:com.horstmann.util -m v2ch09.openpkg/com.horstmann.places.Demo
```

The program will fail with an exception:

```
Exception in thread "main" java.lang.reflect.InaccessibleObjectException:
    Unable to make field private java.lang.String com.horstmann.places.Country.name
    accessible: module v2ch09.openpkg does not "opens com.horstmann.places" to module
    com.horstmann.util
```

Of course, in pristine theory, it is wrong to violate encapsulation and poke around in the private members of an object. But mechanisms such as object-relational mapping or XML/JSON binding are so common that the module system must accommodate them.

Using the opens keyword, a module can *open* a package, which enables reflective access to all instances of classes in the given package. Here is what our module has to do:

```
module v2ch09.openpkg
{
    requires com.horstmann.util;
    opens com.horstmann.places;
}
```

With this change, the ObjectAnalyzer will work correctly.

A module can be declared as open, such as

```
open module v2ch09.openpkg
{
    requires com.horstmann.util;
}
```

An open module grants runtime access to all of its packages, as if all packages had been declared with exports and opens. However, only explicitly exported packages are accessible at compile time. Open modules combine the compile-time safety of the module system with the classic permissive runtime behavior.

Recall from Chapter 5 of Volume I that JAR files can contain, in addition to class files and a manifest, *file resources* which can be loaded with the method `Class.getResourceAsStream`, and now also with `Module.getResourceAsStream`. If a resource is stored in a directory that matches a package in a module, then the package must be opened to the caller. Resources in other directories, as well as the class files and manifest, can be read by anyone.

 NOTE: For a more realistic example, we could convert the `Country` object to XML or JSON. Java 9 and 10 included the `java.xml.bind` module for conversion to XML. That module has been removed from Java 11 (together with the modules `java.activation`, `java.corba`, `java.transaction`, `java.xml.ws`, and `java.xml.ws.annotation`). These modules contain packages that are also part of the Jakarta EE (formerly Java EE) specification, where the APIs are more encompassing than with Java SE. Enterprise application servers can not be modularized if the JDK has conflicting packages. Unfortunately, as this book is being written, there is no modularized replacement for XML binding.

However, the JSON-B implementation provides modular JAR files if one builds it from source. Hopefully, these JAR files will make it to Maven Central by the time you read this. Place the JAR files on the module path and run the `com.horstmann.places.Demo2` program. When the `com.horstmann.places` package is opened, conversion to JSON succeeds.

 NOTE: It is possible that future libraries will use *variable handles* instead of reflection for reading and writing fields. A `VarHandle` is similar to a `Field`. You can use it to read or write a specific field of any instance of a specific class. However, to obtain a `VarHandle`, the library code needs a `Lookup` object:

```
public Object getFieldValue(Object obj, String fieldName, Lookup lookup)
      throws NoSuchFieldException, IllegalAccessException
{
   Class<?> cl = obj.getClass();
   Field field = cl.getDeclaredField(fieldName);
   VarHandle handle = MethodHandles.privateLookupIn(cl, lookup)
      .unreflectVarHandle(field);
   return handle.get(obj);
}
```

This works provided the `Lookup` object is generated in the module that has the permission to access the field. Some method in the module simply calls `MethodHandles.lookup()`, which yields an object encapsulating the access rights of the caller. In this way, one module can give permission for accessing private members to another module. The practical issue is how those permissions can be given with a minimum of hassle.

9.8 Automatic Modules

You now know to put the Java Platform Module System to use. If you start with a brand-new project in which you write all the code yourself, you can design modules, declare module dependencies, and package your application into modular JAR files.

However, that is an extremely uncommon scenario. Almost all projects rely on third-party libraries. Of course, you can wait until the providers of all libraries have turned them into modules, and then modularize your own code.

But what if you don't want to wait? The Java Platform Module System provides two mechanisms for crossing the chasm that separates today's premodular world and fully modular applications: automatic modules and the unnamed module.

For migration purposes, you can turn any JAR file into a module simply by placing it onto a directory in the module path instead of the class path. A JAR without a `module-info.class` on the module path is called an *automatic module*. An automatic module has the following properties:

1. The module implicitly has a `requires` clause for all other modules.
2. All of its packages are exported and opened.
3. If there is an entry with key `Automatic-Module-Name` in the JAR file manifest `META-INF/MANIFEST.MF`, its value becomes the module name.
4. Otherwise the module name is obtained from the JAR file name, dropping any trailing version number and replacing sequences of non-alphanumeric characters with a dot.

The first two rules imply that the packages in the automatic module act as if they were on the class path. The reason for using the module path is for the benefit of other modules, allowing them to express dependencies on this module.

Suppose, for example, that you are implementing a module that processes CSV files and uses the Apache Commons CSV library. You would like to express in your `module-info.java` file that your module depends on Apache Commons CSV.

If you add `commons-csv-1.5.jar` onto the module path, then your modules can reference the module. Its name is `commons.csv` since the trailing version number -1.5 is removed and the non-alphanumeric character - is replaced by a dot.

This name might be an acceptable module name because Commons CSV is well known and it is unlikely that someone else will try to use the same name for a different module. But it would be better if the maintainers of this JAR file could quickly agree to reserve a reverse DNS name, preferably the top-level package name org.apache.commons.csv, as the module name. They just need to add a line

```
Automatic-Module-Name: org.apache.commons.csv
```

to the META-INF/MANIFEST.MF file inside the JAR. Eventually, hopefully, they will turn the JAR file into a true module by adding module-info.java with the reserved module name—and every other module that refers to the CSV module with that name will just continue to work.

 NOTE: The migration plan to modules is a great social experiment, and nobody knows whether it will end well. Before you put third-party JARs on the module path, check whether they are modular, and if not, whether their manifest has a module name. If not, you can still turn the JAR into an automatic module, but be prepared to update the module name later.

As this book is being written, version 1.5 of the Commons CSV JAR file does not have a module descriptor or an automatic module name. Nevertheless, it will work fine on the module path. You can download the library from https://commons.apache.org/proper/commons-csv. Uncompress and place the commons-csv-1.5.jar file into the directory of the v2ch9.automod module. That module contains a simple program that reads a CSV file with country data:

```java
package com.horstmann.places;

import java.io.*;
import org.apache.commons.csv.*;

public class CSVDemo
{
    public static void main(String[] args) throws IOException
    {
        var in = new FileReader("countries.csv");
        Iterable<CSVRecord> records = CSVFormat.EXCEL.withDelimiter(';')
            .withHeader().parse(in);
        for (CSVRecord record : records)
        {
            String name = record.get("Name");
            double area = Double.parseDouble(record.get("Area"));
            System.out.println(name + " has area " + area);
        }
    }
}
```

Since we will use `commons-csv-1.5.jar` as an automatic module, we need to require it:

```
@SuppressWarnings("module")
module v2ch09.automod
{
    requires commons.csv;
}
```

Here are the commands for compiling and running the program:

```
javac -p v2ch09.automod:commons-csv-1.5.jar \
    v2ch09.automod/com/horstmann/places/CSVDemo.java \
    v2ch09.automod/module-info.java
java -p v2ch09.automod:commons-csv-1.5.jar \
    -m v2ch09.automod/com.horstmann.places.CSVDemo
```

9.9 The Unnamed Module

Any class that is not on the module path is part of an *unnamed module*. Technically, there may be more than one unnamed module, but all of them together act as if they are a single module which is called *the* unnamed module. As with automatic modules, the unnamed module can access all other modules, and all of its packages are exported and opened.

However, *no explicit module* can access the unnamed module. (An explicit module is a module that is neither automatic nor unnamed—that is, a module with a `module-info.class` on the module path.) In other words, explicit modules are always free from the "class path hell."

Consider, for example, the program of the preceding section. Suppose you put `commons-csv-1.5.jar` onto the class path instead of the module path:

```
java --module-path v2ch09.automod \
    --class-path commons-csv-1.5.jar \
    -m v2ch09.automod/com.horstmann.places.CSVDemo
```

Now the program won't start:

```
Error occurred during initialization of boot layer
java.lang.module.FindException: Module commons.csv not found, required by v2ch09.automod
```

Therefore, migration to the Java Platform Module System is necessarily a bottom-up process:

1. The Java platform itself is modularized.
2. Next, libraries are modularized, either by using automatic modules or by turning them into explicit modules.

3. Once all libraries used by your application are modularized, you can turn the code of your application into a module.

 NOTE: Automatic modules *can* read the unnamed module, so their dependencies can go onto the class path.

9.10 Command-Line Flags for Migration

Even if your programs do not use modules, you cannot escape the modular world when using Java 9 and beyond. Even if the application code resides on the class path in an unnamed module and all packages are exported and opened, it interacts with the Java platform, which is modularized.

Up to Java 11, the default behavior is to permit illegal module access but to display a warning on the console for the first instance of each offense. In a future version of Java, the default behavior will change, and illegal access with be denied. In order to give you time to prepare for that change, you should test your applications with the --illegal-access flag. There are four possible settings:

1. --illegal-access=permit is the Java 9 default behavior, printing a message for the first instance of illegal access.
2. --illegal-access=warn prints a message for each illegal access.
3. --illegal-access=debug prints a message and stack trace for each illegal access.
4. --illegal-access=deny is the future default behavior, denying all illegal access.

Now is the time to test with --illegal-access=deny so you can be ready when that behavior becomes the default.

Consider an application that uses an internal API that is no longer accessible, such as com.sun.rowset.CachedRowSetImpl. The best remedy is to change the implementation. (As of Java 7, you can get a cached row set from a RowSetProvider.) But suppose you don't have access to the source code.

In that case, start the application with the --add-exports flag. Specify the module and the package that you want to export, and the module to which you want to export the package, which in our case is the unnamed module.

```
java --illegal-access=deny --add-exports java.sql.rowset/com.sun.rowset=ALL_UNNAMED \
   -jar MyApp.jar
```

Now, suppose your application uses reflection to access private fields or methods. Reflection inside the unnamed module is OK, but it is no longer possible to reflectively access non-public members of the Java platform classes. For example, some libraries that dynamically generate Java classes call the protected `ClassLoader.defineClass` method through reflection. If an application uses such a library, add the flag

```
--add-opens java.base/java.lang=ALL-UNNAMED
```

When adding all those command-line options to get a legacy app to work, you may well end up with the command line from hell. To better manage multiple options, you can put them in one or more files specified with an @ prefix. For example,

```
java @options1 @options2 -jar MyProg.java
```

where the files `options1` and `options2` contain options for the `java` command.

There are a few syntax rules for the options files:

- Separate options with spaces, tabs, or newlines.
- Use double quotes around arguments that include spaces, such as `"Program Files"`.
- A line ending in a \ is merged with the next line.
- Backslashes must be escaped, such as `C:\\Users\\Fred`.
- Comment lines start with #.

9.11 Transitive and Static Requirements

In Section 9.4, "Requiring Modules," on p. 504, you have seen the basic form of the `requires` statement. In this section, you will see two variants that are occasionally useful.

In some situation, it can be tedious for a user of a given module to declare all required modules. Consider, for example, the `javafx.controls` module that contains JavaFX user interface elements such as buttons. The `javafx.controls` requires the `javafx.base` module, and everyone using `javafx.controls` will also need `javafx.base`. (You can't do much with a user interface control such as a `Button` if you don't have packages from the `javafx.base` module available.) For that reason, the `javafx.controls` module declares the requirement with the `transitive` modifier:

```
module javafx.controls
{
    requires transitive javafx.base;
    . . .
}
```

Any module that declares a requirement on javafx.controls now automatically requires javafx.base.

 NOTE: Some programmers recommend that you should always use requires transitive when a package from another module is used in the public API. But that is not a rule of the Java language. Consider, for example, the java.sql module:

```
module java.sql
{
    requires transitive java.logging;
    . . .
}
```

There is a single use of a package from the java.logging module in the entire java.sql API, namely the java.sql.Driver.parentLogger method that returns a java.util.logging.Logger. It would have been perfectly acceptable to not declare this module requirement as transitive. Then, those modules—and only those—who actually use that method would need to declare that they require java.logging.

One compelling use of the requires transitive statement is an *aggregator* module—a module with no packages and only transitive requirements. One such module is the java.se module, declared like this:

```
module java.se
{
    requires transitive java.compiler;
    requires transitive java.datatransfer;
    requires transitive java.desktop;
    . . .
    requires transitive java.sql;
    requires transitive java.sql.rowset;
    requires transitive java.xml;
    requires transitive java.xml.crypto;
}
```

A programmer who isn't interested in fine-grained module dependencies can simply require java.se and get all modules of the Java SE platform.

Finally, there is an uncommon requires static variant that declares that a module must be present at compile time but is optional at runtime. There are two use cases:

1. To access an annotation that is processed at compile time and declared in a different module.

2. To use a class in a different module if it is available, and otherwise do something else, such as:

```
try
{
   new oracle.jdbc.driver.OracleDriver();
   . . .
}
catch (NoClassDefFoundError er)
{
   Do something else
}
```

9.12 Qualified Exporting and Opening

In this section, you will see a variant of the `exports` and `opens` statement that narrows their scope to a specified set of modules. For example, the `javafx.base` module contains a statement

```
exports com.sun.javafx.collections to
   javafx.controls, javafx.graphics, javafx.fxml, javafx.swing;
```

Such a statement is called a *qualified export*. The listed modules can access the package, but other modules cannot.

Excessive use of qualified exports can indicate a poor modular structure. Nevertheless, they can arise when modularizing an existing code base. Here, the Java platform designers distributed the code for JavaFX into multiple modules, which is a good idea because not all JavaFX applications need FXML or Swing interoperability. However, the JavaFX implementors liberally used internal classes such as `com.sun.javafx.collections.ListListenerHelper` in their code. In a greenfield project, one can instead design a more robust public API.

Similarly, you can restrict the `opens` statement to specific modules. For example, in Section 9.7, "Modules and Reflective Access," on p. 511 we could have used a qualified `opens` statement, like this:

```
module v2ch09.openpkg
{
   requires com.horstmann.util;
   opens com.horstmann.places to com.horstmann.util;
}
```

Now the `com.horstmann.places` package is only opened to the `com.horstmann.util` module.

9.13 Service Loading

The ServiceLoader class (see Chapter 6 of Volume I) provides a lightweight mechanism for matching up service interfaces with implementations. The Java Platform Module System makes this mechanism easier to use.

Here is a quick reminder of service loading. A service has an interface and one or more possible implementations. Here is a simple example of an interface:

```
public interface GreeterService
{
    String greet(String subject);
    Locale getLocale();
}
```

One or more modules provide implementations, such as

```
public class FrenchGreeter implements GreeterService
{
    public String greet(String subject) { return "Bonjour " + subject; }
    public Locale getLocale() { return Locale.FRENCH; }
}
```

The service consumer must pick an implementation among all offered implementations, based on whatever criteria it deems appropriate.

```
ServiceLoader<GreeterService> greeterLoader = ServiceLoader.load(GreeterService.class);
GreeterService chosenGreeter;
for (GreeterService greeter : greeterLoader)
{
    if (. . .)
    {
        chosenGreeter = greeter;
    }
}
```

In the past, implementations were offered by placing text files into the META-INF/services directory of the JAR file containing the implementation classes. The module system provides a better approach. Instead of text files, you can add statements to the module descriptors.

A module providing an implementation of a service adds a provides statement that lists the service interface (which may be defined in any module) and the implementing class (which must be a part of this module). Here is an example from the jdk.security.auth module:

```
module jdk.security.auth
{
    . . .
```

```
    provides javax.security.auth.spi.LoginModule with
        com.sun.security.auth.module.Krb5LoginModule,
        com.sun.security.auth.module.UnixLoginModule,
        com.sun.security.auth.module.JndiLoginModule,
        com.sun.security.auth.module.KeyStoreLoginModule,
        com.sun.security.auth.module.LdapLoginModule,
        com.sun.security.auth.module.NTLoginModule;
}
```

This is the equivalent of the META-INF/services file.

A consuming module contains a uses statement.

```
module java.base
{
    . . .
    uses javax.security.auth.spi.LoginModule;
}
```

When code in a consuming module calls ServiceLoader.load(*ServiceInterface*.class), the matching provider classes will be loaded, even though they may not be in accessible packages.

In our code example, we provide implementations for a German and French greeter in the package com.horstmann.greetsvc.internal. The service module exports the com.horstmann.greetsvc package, but not the package with the implementations. The provides statement declares the service and its implementing classes in the unexported package:

```
module com.horstmann.greetsvc
{
    exports com.horstmann.greetsvc;

    provides com.horstmann.greetsvc.GreeterService with
        com.horstmann.greetsvc.internal.FrenchGreeter,
        com.horstmann.greetsvc.internal.GermanGreeterFactory;
}
```

The v2ch09.useservice module consumes the service. Using the ServiceLoader facility, we iterate over the provided services and pick the one matching the desired language:

```
package com.horstmann.hello;

import java.util.*;
import com.horstmann.greetsvc.*;

public class HelloWorld
{
    public static void main(String[] args)
    {
```

```
ServiceLoader<GreeterService> greeterLoader
    = ServiceLoader.load(GreeterService.class);
String desiredLanguage = args.length > 0 ? args[0] : "de";
GreeterService chosenGreeter = null;
for (GreeterService greeter : greeterLoader)
{
    if (greeter.getLocale().getLanguage().equals(desiredLanguage))
        chosenGreeter = greeter;
}
if (chosenGreeter == null)
    System.out.println("No suitable greeter.");
else
    System.out.println(chosenGreeter.greet("Modular World"));
    }
}
```

The module declaration requires the service module and declares that the GreeterService is being used.

```
module v2ch09.useservice
{
    requires com.horstmann.greetsvc;
    uses com.horstmann.greetsvc.GreeterService;
}
```

As a result of the provides and uses declarations, the module that consumes the service is allowed access to the private implementation classes.

To build and run the program, first compile the service:

```
javac com.horstmann.greetsvc/module-info.java \
    com.horstmann.greetsvc/com/horstmann/greetsvc/GreeterService.java \
    com.horstmann.greetsvc/com/horstmann/greetsvc/internal/*.java
```

Then compile and run the consuming module:

```
javac -p com.horstmann.greetsvc \
    v2ch09.useservice/com/horstmann/hello/HelloWorld.java \
    v2ch09.useservice/module-info.java
java -p com.horstmann.greetsvc:v2ch09.useservice \
    -m v2ch09.useservice/com.horstmann.hello.HelloWorld
```

9.14 Tools for Working with Modules

The jdeps tool analyzes the dependencies of a given set of JAR files. Suppose, for example, that you want to modularize JUnit 4. Run

```
jdeps -s junit-4.12.jar hamcrest-core-1.3.jar
```

The -s flag generates a summary output:

```
hamcrest-core-1.3.jar -> java.base
junit-4.12.jar -> hamcrest-core-1.3.jar
junit-4.12.jar -> java.base
junit-4.12.jar -> java.management
```

That tells you the module graph:

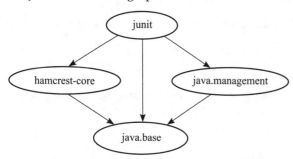

If you omit the -s flag, you get the module summary followed by a mapping from packages to required packages and modules. If you add the -v flag, the listing maps classes to required packages and modules.

The --generate-module-info option produces module-info files for each analyzed module:

```
jdeps --generate-module-info /tmp/junit junit-4.12.jar hamcrest-core-1.3.jar
```

 NOTE: There is also an option to generate graphical output in the "dot" language for describing graphs. Assuming you have the dot tool installed, run these commands:

```
jdeps -s -dotoutput /tmp/junit junit-4.12.jar hamcrest-core-1.3.jar
dot -Tpng /tmp/junit/summary.dot > /tmp/junit/summary.png
```

You get this summary.png image:

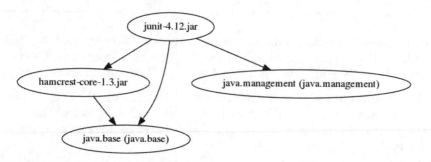

Use the jlink tool to produce an application that executes without a separate Java runtime. The resulting image is much smaller than the entire JDK. You specify the modules that you want to have included and an output directory.

```
jlink --module-path com.horstmann.greet.jar:v2ch09.exportedpkg.jar:$JAVA_HOME/jmods \
    --add-modules v2ch09.exportedpkg --output /tmp/hello
```

The output directory has a subdirectory bin with a java executable. If you run

```
bin/java -m v2ch09.exportedpkg
```

the main method of the module's main class is invoked.

The point of jlink is that it bundles up the minimal set of modules required to run the application. You can list them all:

```
bin/java --list-modules
```

In this example, the output is

```
v2ch09.exportedpkg
com.horstmann.greet
java.base@9
```

All modules are included in a *runtime image* file lib/modules. On my computer, that file is 23MB, whereas the runtime image of all JDK modules takes up 181MB. The entire application takes up 45MB, less than 10% of the JDK which is 486MB.

This can be the basis of a useful tool for packaging applications. You would still need to produce file sets for multiple platforms and launch scripts for the application.

 NOTE: You can inspect the runtime image with the jimage command. However, the format is internal to the JVM, and runtime images are not meant to be generated or used by other tools.

Finally, the jmod tool builds and inspects the module files that are included with the JDK. When you look into the jmods directory inside the JDK, you will find a file with extension jmod for each module. There is no longer a rt.jar file.

Like JAR files, these files contain class files. In addition, they can hold native code libraries, commands, header files, configuration files, and legal notices. The JMOD files use the ZIP format. You can inspect their contents with any ZIP tool.

Unlike JAR files, JMOD files are only useful for linking—that is, for producing runtime images. There is no need for you to produce JMOD files unless you also want to bundle binary files such as native code libraries with your modules.

 NOTE: Since the rt.jar and tools.jar files are no longer included with Java 9, you need to update any references to them. For example, if you referred to tools.jar in a security policy file, change it to a reference to the module:

```
grant codeBase "jrt:/jdk.compiler"
{
    permission java.security.AllPermission;
};
```

The jrt: syntax denotes the Java runtime file.

This brings us to the end of the chapter on the Java Platform Module System. The following chapter covers another important topic: security. Security has always been a core feature of the Java platform. As the world in which we live and compute gets more dangerous, a thorough understanding of Java security will be of increasing importance for many developers.

Security

In this chapter

When Java technology first appeared on the scene, the excitement was not about a well-crafted programming language but about the possibility of safely executing applets delivered over the Internet. Obviously, serving executable applets is only practical when the recipients can be sure the code won't wreak havoc on their machines. Security therefore was and is a major concern of both the designers and the users of Java technology. This means that unlike other languages and systems, where security was implemented as an afterthought or as a reaction to break-ins, security mechanisms are an integral part of Java technology.

Three mechanisms help ensure safety:

- Language design features (bounds checking on arrays, no unchecked type conversions, no pointer arithmetic, and so on).
- An access control mechanism that controls what the code can do (file access, network access, and so on).

- Code signing, whereby code authors can use standard cryptographic algorithms to authenticate Java code. Then, the users of the code can determine exactly who created the code and whether the code has been altered after it was signed.

We will first discuss *class loaders* that check class files for integrity when they are loaded into the virtual machine. We will demonstrate how that mechanism can detect tampering with class files.

For maximum security, both the default mechanism for loading a class and a custom class loader need to work with a *security manager* class that controls what actions code can perform. You'll see in detail how to configure Java platform security.

Finally, you'll see the cryptographic algorithms supplied in the java.security package, which enable code signing and user authentication.

As always, we'll focus on those topics that are of greatest interest to application programmers. For an in-depth view, we recommend the book *Inside Java™ 2 Platform Security: Architecture, API Design, and Implementation, Second Edition*, by Li Gong, Gary Ellison, and Mary Dageforde (Prentice Hall, 2003).

10.1 Class Loaders

A Java compiler converts source instructions into code for the Java virtual machine. The virtual machine code is stored in a class file with a .class extension. Each class file contains the definition and implementation code for one class or interface. In the following section, you will see how the virtual machine loads these class files.

10.1.1 The Class-Loading Process

The virtual machine loads only those class files that are needed for the execution of a program. For example, suppose program execution starts with MyProgram.class. Here are the steps that the virtual machine carries out:

1. The virtual machine has a mechanism for loading class files—for example, by reading the files from disk or by requesting them from the Web; it uses this mechanism to load the contents of the MyProgram class file.

2. If the MyProgram class has fields or superclasses of another class type, their class files are loaded as well. (The process of loading all the classes that a given class depends on is called *resolving* the class.)

3. The virtual machine then executes the main method in MyProgram (which is static, so no instance of a class needs to be created).

4. If the `main` method or a method that `main` calls requires additional classes, these are loaded next.

The class loading mechanism doesn't just use a single class loader, however. Every Java program has at least three class loaders:

*   The bootstrap class loader
*   The platform class loader
*   The system class loader (sometimes called the application class loader)

The bootstrap class loader loads the platform classes contained in the modules

```
java.base
java.datatransfer
java.desktop
java.instrument
java.logging
java.management
java.management.rmi
java.naming
java.prefs
java.rmi
java.security.sasl
java.xml
```

as well as a number of JDK-internal modules.

There is no `ClassLoader` object corresponding to the bootstrap class loader. For example,

```
StringBuilder.class.getClassLoader()
```

returns `null`.

Prior to Java 9, the Java platform classes were located in a file `rt.jar`. Nowadays, the Java platform is modular, and each platform module is contained in a JMOD file (see Chapter 9). The platform class loader loads all classes of the Java platform that are not loaded by the bootstrap class loader.

The system class loader loads application classes from the module path and class path.

NOTE: Prior to Java 9, an "extension class loader" loaded "standard extensions" from the *jre*/`lib`/`ext` directory, and an "endorsed standards override" mechanism provided a way of overriding certain platform classes (including the CORBA and XML implementations) with newer versions. Both of these mechanisms have been removed.

10.1.2 The Class Loader Hierarchy

Class loaders have a *parent/child* relationship. Every class loader except for the bootstrap one has a parent class loader. A class loader will give its parent a chance to load any given class and will only load it if the parent has failed. For example, when the system class loader is asked to load a system class (say, java.lang.StringBuilder), it first asks the platform class loader. That class loader first asks the bootstrap class loader. The bootstrap class loader finds and loads the class, so neither of the other class loaders searches any further.

Some programs have a plugin architecture in which certain parts of the code are packaged as optional plugins. If the plugins are packaged as JAR files, you can simply load the plugin classes with an instance of URLClassLoader.

```
var url = new URL("file:///path/to/plugin.jar");
var pluginLoader = new URLClassLoader(new URL[] { url });
Class<?> cl = pluginLoader.loadClass("mypackage.MyClass");
```

Since no parent was specified in the URLClassLoader constructor, the parent of the pluginLoader is the system class loader. Figure 10.1 shows the hierarchy.

 CAUTION: Prior to Java 9, the system class loader was an instance of URLClassLoader. Some programmers used a cast to access the getURLs method, or added JAR files to the class path by calling the protected addURLs method through reflection. This is no longer possible.

Most of the time, you don't have to worry about the class loader hierarchy. Generally, classes are loaded because they are required by other classes, and that process is transparent to you.

Occasionally, however, you need to intervene and specify a class loader. Consider this example:

• Your application code contains a helper method that calls Class.forName(classNameString).

• That method is called from a plugin class.

• The classNameString specifies a class that is contained in the plugin JAR.

The author of the plugin wants the class to be loaded. However, the helper method's class was loaded by the system class loader, and that is the class loader used by Class.forName. The classes in the plugin JAR are not visible. This phenomenon is called *classloader inversion*.

To overcome this problem, the helper method needs to use the correct class loader. It can require the class loader as a parameter. Alternatively, it can

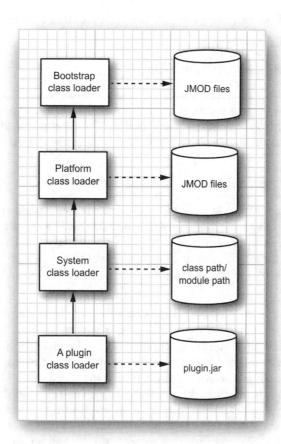

Figure 10.1 The class loader hierarchy

require that the correct class loader is set as the *context class loader* of the current thread. This strategy is used by many frameworks (such as JAXP and JNDI).

Each thread has a reference to a class loader, called the context class loader. The main thread's context class loader is the system class loader. When a new thread is created, its context class loader is set to the creating thread's context class loader. Thus, if you don't do anything, all threads will have their context class loaders set to the system class loader.

However, you can set any class loader by calling

```
Thread t = Thread.currentThread();
t.setContextClassLoader(loader);
```

The helper method can then retrieve the context class loader:

```
Thread t = Thread.currentThread();
ClassLoader loader = t.getContextClassLoader();
Class<?> cl = loader.loadClass(className);
```

 TIP: If you write a method that loads a class by name, it is a good idea to offer the caller the choice between passing an explicit class loader and using the context class loader. Don't simply use the class loader of the method's class.

10.1.3 Using Class Loaders as Namespaces

Every Java programmer knows that package names are used to eliminate name conflicts. There are two classes called Date in the standard library, but of course their real names are java.util.Date and java.sql.Date. The simple name is only a programmer convenience and requires the inclusion of appropriate import statements. In a running program, all class names contain their package names.

It might surprise you, however, that you can have two classes in the same virtual machine that have the same class *and package* name. A class is determined by its full name *and* the class loader. This technique is useful for loading code from multiple sources. For example, an application server uses separate class loaders for each application. This allows the virtual machine to separate classes from different applications, no matter what they are named. Figure 10.2 shows an example. Suppose an application server loads two different applications, and each has a class called Util. Since each class is loaded by a separate class loader, these classes are entirely distinct and do not conflict with each other.

10.1.4 Writing Your Own Class Loader

You can write your own class loader for specialized purposes. That lets you carry out custom checks before you pass the bytecodes to the virtual machine. For example, your class loader may refuse to load a class that has not been marked as "paid for."

To write your own class loader, simply extend the ClassLoader class and override the method

```
findClass(String className)
```

The loadClass method of the ClassLoader superclass takes care of the delegation to the parent and calls findClass only if the class hasn't already been loaded and if the parent class loader was unable to load the class.

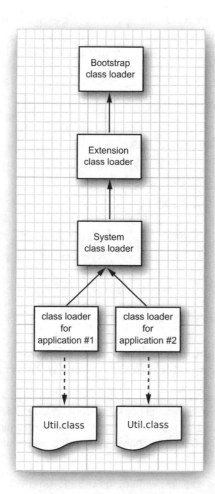

Figure 10.2 Two class loaders load different classes with the same name.

Your implementation of this method must do the following:

1. Load the bytecodes for the class from the local file system or some other source.
2. Call the defineClass method of the ClassLoader superclass to present the bytecodes to the virtual machine.

In the program of Listing 10.1, we implement a class loader that loads encrypted class files. The program asks the user for the name of the first class to load (that is, the class containing main) and the decryption key. It then uses a special class loader to load the specified class and calls the main method. The class loader decrypts the specified class and all nonsystem classes that are referenced by it. Finally, the program calls the main method of the loaded class (see Figure 10.3).

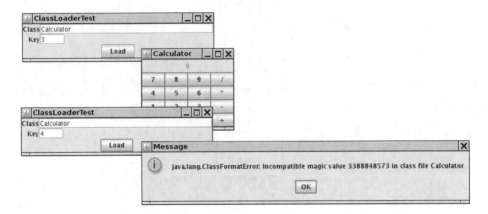

Figure 10.3 The ClassLoaderTest program

For simplicity, we ignore the 2,000 years of progress in the field of cryptography and use the venerable Caesar cipher for encrypting the class files.

 NOTE: David Kahn's wonderful book *The Codebreakers* (Macmillan, 1967, p. 84) refers to Suetonius as a historical source for the Caesar cipher. Caesar shifted the 24 letters of the Roman alphabet by 3 letters, which at the time baffled his adversaries.

When this chapter was first written, the U.S. government restricted the export of strong encryption methods. Therefore, we used Caesar's method for our example because it was clearly legal for export.

Our version of the Caesar cipher has as a key a number between 1 and 255. To decrypt, simply add that key to every byte and reduce modulo 256. The Caesar.java program of Listing 10.2 carries out the encryption.

To not confuse the regular class loader, we use a different extension, .caesar, for the encrypted class files.

To decrypt, the class loader simply subtracts the key from every byte. In the companion code for this book, you will find four class files, encrypted with a key value of 3—the traditional choice. To run the encrypted program, you'll need the custom class loader defined in our ClassLoaderTest program.

Encrypting class files has a number of practical uses (provided, of course, that you use something stronger than the Caesar cipher). Without the decryption key, the class files are useless. They can neither be executed by a standard virtual machine nor readily disassembled.

This means that you can use a custom class loader to authenticate the user of the class or to ensure that a program has been paid for before it will be allowed to run. Of course, encryption is only one application of a custom class loader. You can use other types of class loaders to solve other problems—for example, storing class files in a database.

Listing 10.1 classLoader/ClassLoaderTest.java

```java
1  package classLoader;
2
3  import java.io.*;
4  import java.lang.reflect.*;
5  import java.nio.file.*;
6  import java.awt.*;
7  import java.awt.event.*;
8  import javax.swing.*;
9
10 /**
11  * This program demonstrates a custom class loader that decrypts class files.
12  * @version 1.25 2018-05-01
13  * @author Cay Horstmann
14  */
15 public class ClassLoaderTest
16 {
17     public static void main(String[] args)
18     {
19         EventQueue.invokeLater(() ->
20             {
21                 var frame = new ClassLoaderFrame();
22                 frame.setTitle("ClassLoaderTest");
23                 frame.setDefaultCloseOperation(JFrame.EXIT_ON_CLOSE);
24                 frame.setVisible(true);
25             });
26     }
27 }
28
```

(Continues)

Listing 10.1 *(Continued)*

```
29  /**
30   * This frame contains two text fields for the name of the class to load and the decryption
31   * key.
32   */
33  class ClassLoaderFrame extends JFrame
34  {
35     private JTextField keyField = new JTextField("3", 4);
36     private JTextField nameField = new JTextField("Calculator", 30);
37     private static final int DEFAULT_WIDTH = 300;
38     private static final int DEFAULT_HEIGHT = 200;
39
40     public ClassLoaderFrame()
41     {
42        setSize(DEFAULT_WIDTH, DEFAULT_HEIGHT);
43        setLayout(new GridBagLayout());
44        add(new JLabel("Class"), new GBC(0, 0).setAnchor(GBC.EAST));
45        add(nameField, new GBC(1, 0).setWeight(100, 0).setAnchor(GBC.WEST));
46        add(new JLabel("Key"), new GBC(0, 1).setAnchor(GBC.EAST));
47        add(keyField, new GBC(1, 1).setWeight(100, 0).setAnchor(GBC.WEST));
48        var loadButton = new JButton("Load");
49        add(loadButton, new GBC(0, 2, 2, 1));
50        loadButton.addActionListener(event -> runClass(nameField.getText(), keyField.getText()));
51        pack();
52     }
53
54     /**
55      * Runs the main method of a given class.
56      * @param name the class name
57      * @param key the decryption key for the class files
58      */
59     public void runClass(String name, String key)
60     {
61        try
62        {
63           var loader = new CryptoClassLoader(Integer.parseInt(key));
64           Class<?> c = loader.loadClass(name);
65           Method m = c.getMethod("main", String[].class);
66           m.invoke(null, (Object) new String[] {});
67        }
68        catch (Throwable t)
69        {
70           JOptionPane.showMessageDialog(this, t);
71        }
72     }
73  }
```

```
74
75  /**
76   * This class loader loads encrypted class files.
77   */
78  class CryptoClassLoader extends ClassLoader
79  {
80     private int key;
81
82     /**
83      * Constructs a crypto class loader.
84      * @param k the decryption key
85      */
86     public CryptoClassLoader(int k)
87     {
88        key = k;
89     }
90
91     protected Class<?> findClass(String name) throws ClassNotFoundException
92     {
93        try
94        {
95           byte[] classBytes = null;
96           classBytes = loadClassBytes(name);
97           Class<?> cl = defineClass(name, classBytes, 0, classBytes.length);
98           if (cl == null) throw new ClassNotFoundException(name);
99           return cl;
100       }
101       catch (IOException e)
102       {
103          throw new ClassNotFoundException(name);
104       }
105    }
106
107    /**
108     * Loads and decrypt the class file bytes.
109     * @param name the class name
110     * @return an array with the class file bytes
111     */
112    private byte[] loadClassBytes(String name) throws IOException
113    {
114       String cname = name.replace('.', '/') + ".caesar";
115       byte[] bytes = Files.readAllBytes(Paths.get(cname));
116       for (int i = 0; i < bytes.length; i++)
117          bytes[i] = (byte) (bytes[i] - key);
118       return bytes;
119    }
120 }
```

Listing 10.2 classLoader/Caesar.java

```java
1  package classLoader;
2
3  import java.io.*;
4
5  /**
6   * Encrypts a file using the Caesar cipher.
7   * @version 1.02 2018-05-01
8   * @author Cay Horstmann
9   */
10 public class Caesar
11 {
12    public static void main(String[] args) throws Exception
13    {
14       if (args.length != 3)
15       {
16          System.out.println("USAGE: java classLoader.Caesar in out key");
17          return;
18       }
19
20       try (var in = new FileInputStream(args[0]);
21            var out = new FileOutputStream(args[1]))
22       {
23          int key = Integer.parseInt(args[2]);
24          int ch;
25          while ((ch = in.read()) != -1)
26          {
27             byte c = (byte) (ch + key);
28             out.write(c);
29          }
30       }
31    }
32 }
```

---

java.lang.Class   1.0

- ClassLoader getClassLoader()

  gets the class loader that loaded this class.

---

java.lang.ClassLoader   1.0

- ClassLoader getParent()   1.2

  returns the parent class loader, or null if the parent class loader is the bootstrap class loader.

(Continues)

---

java.lang.ClassLoader 1.0 *(Continued)*

- static ClassLoader getSystemClassLoader() 1.2

  gets the system class loader—that is, the class loader that was used to load the first application class.

- protected Class findClass(String name) 1.2

  should be overridden by a class loader to find the bytecodes for a class and present them to the virtual machine by calling the defineClass method. In the name of the class, use . as package name separator, and don't use a .class suffix.

- Class defineClass(String name, byte[] byteCodeData, int offset, int length)

  adds a new class to the virtual machine whose bytecodes are provided in the given data range.

---

java.net.URLClassLoader 1.2

- URLClassLoader(URL[] urls)
- URLClassLoader(URL[] urls, ClassLoader parent)

  constructs a class loader that loads classes from the given URLs. If the URL ends in a /, it is assumed to be a directory, otherwise it is assumed to be a JAR file.

---

java.lang.Thread 1.0

- ClassLoader getContextClassLoader() 1.2

  gets the class loader that the creator of this thread has designated as the most reasonable class loader to use when executing this thread.

- void setContextClassLoader(ClassLoader loader) 1.2

  sets a class loader for code in this thread to retrieve for loading classes. If no context class loader is set explicitly when a thread is started, the parent's context class loader is used.

10.1.5 Bytecode Verification

When a class loader presents the bytecodes of a newly loaded Java platform class to the virtual machine, these bytecodes are first inspected by a *verifier*. The verifier checks that the instructions cannot perform actions that are obviously damaging. All classes except for system classes are verified.

Here are some of the checks that the verifier carries out:

- Variables are initialized before they are used.
- Method calls match the types of object references.
- Rules for accessing private data and methods are not violated.
- Local variable accesses fall within the runtime stack.
- The runtime stack does not overflow.

If any of these checks fails, the class is considered corrupted and will not be loaded.

 NOTE: If you are familiar with Gödel's theorem, you might wonder how the verifier can prove that a class file is free from type mismatches, uninitialized variables, and stack overflows. Gödel's theorem states that it is impossible to design algorithms that process a program and decide whether it has a particular property (such as being free from stack overflows). Is this a conflict between the public relations department at Oracle and the laws of logic? No—in fact, the verifier is *not* a decision algorithm in the sense of Gödel. If the verifier accepts a program, it is indeed safe. However, the verifier might reject virtual machine instructions even though they would actually be safe. (You might have run into this issue when you were forced to initialize a variable with a dummy value because the verifier couldn't see that it was going to be properly initialized.)

This strict verification is an important security consideration. Accidental errors, such as uninitialized variables, can easily wreak havoc if they are not caught. More importantly, in the wide open world of the Internet, you must be protected against malicious programmers who create evil effects on purpose. For example, by modifying values on the runtime stack or by writing to the private data fields of system objects, a program can break through the security system of a browser.

You might wonder, however, why a special verifier is needed to check all these features. After all, the compiler would never allow you to generate a class file in which an uninitialized variable is used or in which a private data field is accessed from another class. Indeed, a class file generated by a compiler for the Java programming language always passes verification. However, the bytecode format used in the class files is well documented, and it is an easy matter for someone with experience in assembly programming and a hex editor to manually produce a class file containing valid but unsafe instructions for the Java virtual machine. The verifier is always guarding against maliciously altered class files—not just checking the class files produced by a compiler.

Here's an example of how to construct such an altered class file. We start with the program VerifierTest.java of Listing 10.3. This is a simple program that calls a method and displays the method's result. The program can be run both as a console program and as an applet. The fun method itself just computes 1 + 2.

```
static int fun()
{
   int m;
   int n;
   m = 1;
   n = 2;
   int r = m + n;
   return r;
}
```

As an experiment, try to compile the following modification of this program:

```
static int fun()
{
   int m = 1;
   int n;
   m = 1;
   m = 2;
   int r = m + n;
   return r;
}
```

Here, n is not initialized, so it could have any random value. Of course, the compiler detects that problem and refuses to compile the program. To create a bad class file, we have to work a little harder. First, run the javap program to find out how the compiler translates the fun method. The command

```
javap -c verifier.VerifierTest
```

shows the bytecodes in the class file in mnemonic form.

```
Method int fun()
   0 iconst_1
   1 istore_0
   2 iconst_2
   3 istore_1
   4 iload_0
   5 iload_1
   6 iadd
   7 istore_2
   8 iload_2
   9 ireturn
```

Use a hex editor to change instruction 3 from istore_1 to istore_0. That is, local variable 0 (which is m) is initialized twice, and local variable 1 (which is n) is not initialized at all. We need to know the hexadecimal values for these instructions; these values are readily available from the Java Virtual Machine specification (https://docs.oracle.com/javase/specs/jvms/se11/html/index.html).

```
0 iconst_1  04
1 istore_0  3B
2 iconst_2  05
3 istore_1  3C
4 iload_0   1A
5 iload_1   1B
6 iadd      60
7 istore_2  3D
8 iload_2   1C
9 ireturn   AC
```

You can use any hex editor to carry out the modification. In Figure 10.4, you see the class file VerifierTest.class loaded into the Gnome hex editor, with the bytecodes of the fun method highlighted.

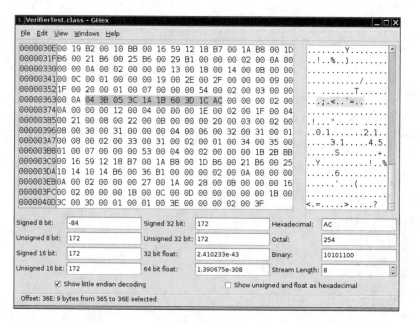

Figure 10.4 Modifying bytecodes with a hex editor

Change 3C to 3B and save the class file. Then try running the VerifierTest program. You get an error message:

Exception in thread "main" java.lang.VerifyError: (class: VerifierTest, method:fun signature: ()I) Accessing value from uninitialized register 1

That is good—the virtual machine detected our modification.

Now run the program with the -noverify (or -Xverify:none) option:

```
java -noverify verifier.VerifierTest
```

The fun method returns a seemingly random value. This is actually 2 plus the value that happened to be stored in the variable n, which was never initialized. Here is a typical printout:

```
1 + 2 == 15102330
```

Listing 10.3 verifier/VerifierTest.java

```java
1  package verifier;
2
3  import java.awt.*;
4
5  /**
6   * This application demonstrates the bytecode verifier of the virtual machine. If you use a
7   * hex editor to modify the class file, then the virtual machine should detect the tampering.
8   * @version 1.10 2018-05-05
9   * @author Cay Horstmann
10  */
11 public class VerifierTest
12 {
13    public static void main(String[] args)
14    {
15       System.out.println("1 + 2 == " + fun());
16    }
17
18    /**
19     * A function that computes 1 + 2.
20     * @return 3, if the code has not been corrupted
21     */
22    public static int fun()
23    {
24       int m;
25       int n;
26       m = 1;
27       n = 2;
28       // use hex editor to change to "m = 2" in class file
29       int r = m + n;
30       return r;
31    }
32 }
```

10.2 Security Managers and Permissions

Once a class has been loaded into the virtual machine and checked by the verifier, the second security mechanism of the Java platform springs into action: the *security manager*. This is the topic of the following sections.

10.2.1 Permission Checking

The security manager controls whether a specific operation is permitted. Operations checked by the security manager include the following:

- Creating a new class loader
- Exiting the virtual machine
- Accessing a field of another class by using reflection
- Accessing a file
- Opening a socket connection
- Starting a print job
- Accessing the system clipboard
- Accessing the AWT event queue
- Bringing up a top-level window

There are many other checks throughout the Java library.

The default behavior when running Java applications is to install *no* security manager, so all these operations are permitted. In contrast, applets relied on a very restrictive security policy. Stricter security also makes sense in other situations.

For example, suppose you run a Tomcat instance and allow collaborators or students to install servlets. You would not want any of them to call System.exit since this would terminate the Tomcat instance. You can set a security policy that causes calls to System.exit to throw a security exception instead of actually closing down the virtual machine. Here is what happens in detail. The exit method of the Runtime class calls the checkExit method of the security manager. Here is the entire code of the exit method:

```
public void exit(int status)
{
   SecurityManager security = System.getSecurityManager();
   if (security != null)
      security.checkExit(status);
   exitInternal(status);
}
```

The security manager now checks if the exit request came from the browser or an individual applet. If the security manager agrees with the exit request, the checkExit method simply returns and normal processing continues. However, if the security manager doesn't want to grant the request, the checkExit method throws a SecurityException.

The exit method continues only if no exception occurred. It then calls the *private native* exitInternal method that actually terminates the virtual machine. There is no other way to terminate the virtual machine, and since the exitInternal method is private, it cannot be called from any other class. Thus, any code that attempts to exit the virtual machine must go through the exit method and thus through the checkExit security check without triggering a security exception.

Clearly, the integrity of the security policy depends on careful coding. The providers of system services in the standard library must always consult the security manager before attempting any sensitive operation.

The security manager of the Java platform allows both programmers and system administrators fine-grained control over individual security permissions. We will describe these features in the following section. First, we'll summarize the Java 2 platform security model. We'll then show how you can control permissions with *policy files*. Finally, we'll explain how you can define your own permission types.

10.2.2 Java Platform Security

JDK 1.0 had a very simple security model: Local classes had full permissions, and remote classes were confined to the *sandbox*. Just like a child that can only play in a sandbox, remote code was only allowed to paint on the screen and interact with the user. The applet security manager denied all access to local resources. JDK 1.1 implemented a slight modification: Remote code that was signed by a trusted entity was granted the same permissions as local classes. However, both versions of the JDK used an all-or-nothing approach. Programs either had full access or they had to play in the sandbox.

Starting with Java 1.2, the Java platform has a much more flexible mechanism. A *security policy* maps *code sources to permission sets* (see Figure 10.5).

A *code source* is specified by a *code base* and a set of *certificates*. The code base specifies the origin of the code. For example, the code base of remote applet code is the HTTP URL from which the applet was loaded. The code base of code in a JAR file is the file's URL. A certificate, if present, is an assurance by some party that the code has not been tampered with. We'll cover certificates later in this chapter.

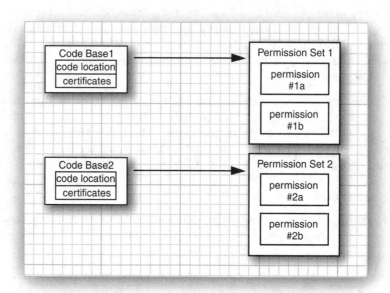

Figure 10.5 A security policy

A *permission* is any property that is checked by a security manager. The Java platform supports a number of permission classes, each encapsulating the details of a particular permission. For example, the following instance of the FilePermission class states that it is OK to read and write any file in the /tmp directory:

```
var p = new FilePermission("/tmp/*", "read,write");
```

More importantly, the default implementation of the Policy class reads permissions from a *permission file*. Inside a permission file, the same read permission is expressed as

```
permission java.io.FilePermission "/tmp/*", "read,write";
```

We'll discuss permission files in the next section.

Figure 10.6 shows the hierarchy of the permission classes that were supplied with Java 1.2. Many more permission classes have been added in subsequent Java releases.

In the preceding section, you saw that the SecurityManager class has security check methods such as checkExit. These methods exist only for the convenience of the programmer and for backward compatibility. They all map to standard

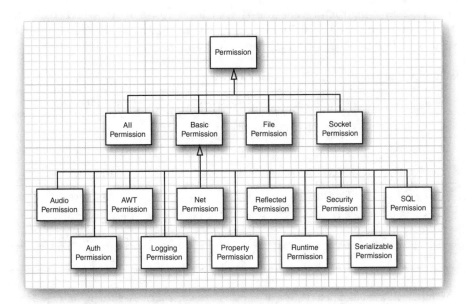

Figure 10.6 A part of the hierarchy of permission classes

permission checks. For example, here is the source code for the checkExit method:

```
public void checkExit()
{
    checkPermission(new RuntimePermission("exitVM"));
}
```

Each class has a *protection domain*—an object that encapsulates both the code source and the collection of permissions of the class. When the SecurityManager needs to check a permission, it looks at the classes of all methods currently on the call stack. It then gets the protection domains of all classes and asks each protection domain if its permission collection allows the operation currently being checked. If all domains agree, the check passes. Otherwise, a SecurityException is thrown.

Why do all methods on the call stack need to allow a particular operation? Let us work through an example. Suppose the init method of a servlet wants to open a file. It might call

```
var in = new FileReader(name);
```

The FileReader constructor calls the FileInputStream constructor, which calls the checkRead method of the security manager, which finally calls checkPermission with a FilePermission(name, "read") object. Table 10.1 shows the call stack.

Table 10.1 Call Stack During Permission Checking

Class	Method	Code Source	Permissions
SecurityManager	checkPermission	null	AllPermission
SecurityManager	checkRead	null	AllPermission
FileInputStream	Constructor	null	AllPermission
FileReader	Constructor	null	AllPermission
Servlet	init	Servlet code source	Tomcat web app permissions
. . .			

The FileInputStream and SecurityManager classes are *system classes* for which CodeSource is null and the permissions consist of an instance of the AllPermission class, which allows all operations. Clearly, their permissions alone can't determine the outcome of the check. As you can see, the checkPermission method must take into account the restricted permissions of the applet class. By checking the entire call stack, the security mechanism ensures that one class can never ask another class to carry out a sensitive operation on its behalf.

NOTE: This brief discussion of permission checking explains the basic concepts. However, we omit a number of technical details here. With security, the devil lies in the details, and we encourage you to read the book by Li Gong for more information. For a more critical view of the Java platform's security model, see the book *Securing Java: Getting Down to Business with Mobile Code, Second Edition*, by Gary McGraw and Ed W. Felten (Wiley, 1999). You can find an online version of that book at www.securingjava.com.

---

java.lang.SecurityManager 1.0

- void checkPermission(Permission p) 1.2

    checks whether this security manager grants the given permission. The method throws a SecurityException if the permission is not granted.

---

java.lang.Class 1.0

- ProtectionDomain getProtectionDomain() 1.2

  gets the protection domain for this class, or null if this class was loaded without a protection domain.

---

java.security.ProtectionDomain 1.2

- ProtectionDomain(CodeSource source, PermissionCollection permissions)

  constructs a protection domain with the given code source and permissions.
- CodeSource getCodeSource()

  gets the code source of this protection domain.
- boolean implies(Permission p)

  returns true if the given permission is allowed by this protection domain.

---

java.security.CodeSource 1.2

- Certificate[] getCertificates()

  gets the certificate chain for class file signatures associated with this code source.
- URL getLocation()

  gets the code base of class files associated with this code source.

10.2.3 Security Policy Files

The *policy manager* reads *policy files* that contain instructions for mapping code sources to permissions. Here is a typical policy file:

```
grant codeBase "http://www.horstmann.com/classes"
{
    permission java.io.FilePermission "/tmp/*", "read,write";
};
```

This file grants permission to read and write files in the /tmp directory to all code that was downloaded from www.horstmann.com/classes.

You can install policy files in standard locations. By default, there are two locations:

- The file java.policy in the Java platform's home directory

- The file .java.policy (notice the period at the beginning of the file name) in the user's home directory

NOTE: You can change the locations of these files in the java.security configuration file in the *jdk*/conf/security directory. The defaults are specified as

```
policy.url.1=file:${java.home}/lib/security/java.policy
policy.url.2=file:${user.home}/.java.policy
```

A system administrator can modify the java.security file and specify policy URLs that reside on another server and cannot be edited by users. There can be any number of policy URLs (with consecutive numbers) in the policy file. The permissions of all files are combined.

If you want to store policies outside the file system, you can implement a subclass of the Policy class that gathers the permissions. Then change the line

```
policy.provider=sun.security.provider.PolicyFile
```

in the java.security configuration file.

During testing, we don't like to constantly modify the standard policy files. Therefore, we prefer to explicitly name the policy file required for each application. Place the permissions into a separate file—say, MyApp.policy. To apply the policy, you have two choices. You can set a system property inside your application's main method:

```
System.setProperty("java.security.policy", "MyApp.policy");
```

Alternatively, you can start the virtual machine as

```
java -Djava.security.policy=MyApp.policy MyApp
```

In these examples, the MyApp.policy file is added to the other policies in effect. If you add a second equal sign, for example:

```
java -Djava.security.policy==MyApp.policy MyApp
```

then your application will use *only* the specified policy file, and the standard policy files will be ignored.

CAUTION: An easy mistake during testing is to accidentally leave a .java.policy file that grants a lot of permissions, perhaps even AllPermission, in the home directory. If you find that your application doesn't seem to pay attention to the restrictions in your policy file, check for a left-behind .java.policy file in your home directory. If you use a UNIX system, this is a particularly easy mistake to make because files with names that start with a period are not displayed by default.

As you saw previously, Java applications by default do not install a security manager. Therefore, you won't see the effect of policy files until you install one. You can, of course, add a line

```
System.setSecurityManager(new SecurityManager());
```

into your `main` method. Or you can add the command-line option `-Djava.security.manager` when starting the virtual machine.

```
java -Djava.security.manager -Djava.security.policy=MyApp.policy MyApp
```

In the remainder of this section, we'll show you in detail how to describe permissions in the policy file. We'll describe the entire policy file format except for code certificates which we cover later in this chapter.

A policy file contains a sequence of `grant` entries. Each entry has the following form:

```
grant codesource
{
    permission₁;
    permission₂;
    . . .
};
```

The code source contains a code base (which can be omitted if the entry applies to code from all sources) and the names of trusted principals and certificate signers (which can be omitted if signatures are not required for this entry).

The code base is specified as

```
codeBase "url"
```

If the URL ends in a /, it refers to a directory. Otherwise, it is taken to be the name of a JAR file. For example,

```
grant codeBase "www.horstmann.com/classes/" { . . . };
grant codeBase "www.horstmann.com/classes/MyApp.jar" { . . . };
```

The code base is a URL and should always contain forward slashes as file separators, even for file URLs in Windows. For example,

```
grant codeBase "file:C:/myapps/classes/" { . . . };
```

 NOTE: Everyone knows that `http` URLs start with two slashes (`http://`). But there is enough confusion about `file` URLs, so the policy file reader accepts two forms of file URLs—namely, `file://localFile` and `file:localFile`. Furthermore, a slash before a Windows drive letter is optional. That is, all of the following are acceptable:

```
file:C:/dir/filename.ext
file:/C:/dir/filename.ext
file://C:/dir/filename.ext
file:///C:/dir/filename.ext
```

Actually, in our tests, the `file:////C:/dir/filename.ext` is acceptable as well, and we have no explanation for that.

 NOTE: Consider an application that compiles some Java code, which requires a large number of permissions. Prior to JDK 9, you could have granted all permissions to the code in the `tools.jar` file. This JAR file doesn't exist anymore. Instead, give permissions to the appropriate module, like this:

```
grant codeBase "jrt:/jdk.compiler"
{
    permission java.security.AllPermission;
};
```

The permissions have the following structure:

```
permission className targetName, actionList;
```

The *className* is the fully qualified class name of the permission class (such as `java.io.FilePermission`). The *targetName* is a permission-specific value—for example, a file or directory name for the file permission, or a host and port for a socket permission. The *actionList* is also permission-specific. It is a list of actions, such as `read` or `connect`, separated by commas. Some permission classes don't need target names and action lists. Table 10.2 lists the commonly used permission classes and their actions.

Table 10.2 Permissions and Their Associated Targets and Actions

Permission	Target	Action
`java.io.FilePermission`	File target (see text)	read, write, execute, delete
`java.net.SocketPermission`	Socket target (see text)	accept, connect, listen, resolve
`java.util.PropertyPermission`	Property target (see text)	read, write

(Continues)

Table 10.2 *(Continued)*

Permission	Target	Action
java.lang.RuntimePermission	createClassLoader getClassLoader setContextClassLoader enableContextClassLoaderOverride createSecurityManager setSecurityManager exitVM getenv.variableName shutdownHooks setFactory setIO modifyThread stopThread modifyThreadGroup getProtectionDomain readFileDescriptor writeFileDescriptor loadLibrary.libraryName accessClassInPackage.packageName defineClassInPackage.packageName accessDeclaredMembers.className queuePrintJob getStackTrace setDefaultUncaughtExceptionHandler preferences usePolicy	None
java.awt.AWTPermission	showWindowWithoutWarningBanner accessClipboard accessEventQueue createRobot fullScreenExclusive listenToAllAWTEvents readDisplayPixels replaceKeyboardFocusManager watchMousePointer setWindowAlwaysOnTop setAppletStub	None

(Continues)

Table 10.2 *(Continued)*

Permission	Target	Action
java.net.NetPermission	setDefaultAuthenticator specifyStreamHandler requestPasswordAuthentication setProxySelector getProxySelector setCookieHandler getCookieHandler setResponseCache getResponseCache	None
java.lang.reflect.ReflectPermission	suppressAccessChecks	None
java.io.SerializablePermission	enableSubclassImplementation enableSubstitution	None
java.security.SecurityPermission	createAccessControlContext getDomainCombiner getPolicy setPolicy getProperty.keyName setProperty.keyName insertProvider.providerName removeProvider.providerName setSystemScope setIdentityPublicKey setIdentityInfo addIdentityCertificate removeIdentityCertificate printIdentity clearProviderProperties.providerName putProviderProperty.providerName removeProviderProperty.providerName getSignerPrivateKey setSignerKeyPair	None
java.security.AllPermission	None	None
javax.audio.AudioPermission	Play record	None

(Continues)

Table 10.2 *(Continued)*

Permission	Target	Action
javax.security.auth.AuthPermission	doAs doAsPrivileged getSubject getSubjectFromDomainCombiner setReadOnly modifyPrincipals modifyPublicCredentials modifyPrivateCredentials refreshCredential destroyCredential createLoginContext.contextName getLoginConfiguration setLoginConfiguration refreshLoginConfiguration	None
java.util.logging.LoggingPermission	control	None
java.sql.SQLPermission	setLog	None

As you can see from Table 10.2, most permissions simply permit a particular operation. You can think of the operation as the target with an implied action "permit". These permission classes all extend the BasicPermission class (see Figure 10.6). However, the targets for the file, socket, and property permissions are more complex, and we need to investigate them in detail.

File permission targets can have the following form:

file	A file
directory/	A directory
directory/*	All files in the directory
*	All files in the current directory
directory/-	All files in the directory or one of its subdirectories
-	All files in the current directory or one of its subdirectories
<<ALL FILES>>	All files in the file system

For example, the following permission entry gives access to all files in the directory /myapp and any of its subdirectories:

```
permission java.io.FilePermission "/myapp/-", "read,write,delete";
```

You must use the \\ escape sequence to denote a backslash in a Windows file name.

```
permission java.io.FilePermission "c:\\myapp\\-", "read,write,delete";
```

Socket permission targets consist of a host and a port range. Host specifications have the following form:

hostname or *IPaddress*	A single host
localhost or the empty string	The local host
*.domainSuffix	Any host whose domain ends with the given suffix
*	All hosts

Port ranges are optional and have the form:

:*n*	A single port
:*n*-	All ports numbered *n* and above
:-*n*	All ports numbered *n* and below
:*n1*-*n2*	All ports in the given range

Here is an example:

```
permission java.net.SocketPermission "*.horstmann.com:8000-8999", "connect";
```

Finally, property permission targets can have one of two forms:

property	A specific property
propertyPrefix.*	All properties with the given prefix

Examples are "java.home" and "java.vm.*".

For example, the following permission entry allows a program to read all properties that start with java.vm:

```
permission java.util.PropertyPermission "java.vm.*", "read";
```

You can use system properties in policy files. The token ${*property*} is replaced by the property value. For example, ${user.home} is replaced by the home directory of the user. Here is a typical use of this system property in a permission entry:

```
permission java.io.FilePermission "${user.home}", "read,write";
```

To create platform-independent policy files, it is a good idea to use the file.separator property instead of explicit / or \\ separators. To make this simpler, the special notation ${/} is a shortcut for ${file.separator}. For example,

```
permission java.io.FilePermission "${user.home}${/}-", "read,write";
```

is a portable entry for granting permission to read and write in the user's home directory and any of its subdirectories.

10.2.4 Custom Permissions

In this section, you'll see how you can supply your own permission class that users can refer to in their policy files.

To implement your permission class, extend the `Permission` class and supply the following methods:

- A constructor with two `String` parameters, for the target and the action list
- `String getActions()`
- `boolean equals(Object other)`
- `int hashCode()`
- `boolean implies(Permission other)`

The last method is the most important. Permissions have an *ordering*, in which more general permissions *imply* more specific ones. Consider the file permission

```
p1 = new FilePermission("/tmp/-", "read, write");
```

This permission allows reading and writing of any file in the /tmp directory and any of its subdirectories.

This permission implies other, more specific permissions:

```
p2 = new FilePermission("/tmp/-", "read");
p3 = new FilePermission("/tmp/aFile", "read, write");
p4 = new FilePermission("/tmp/aDirectory/-", "write");
```

In other words, a file permission p1 implies another file permission p2 if

1. The target file set of p1 contains the target file set of p2.
2. The action set of p1 contains the action set of p2.

Consider the following example of the use of the `implies` method. When the `FileInputStream` constructor wants to open a file for reading, it checks whether it has permission to do so. For that check, a *specific* file permission object is passed to the `checkPermission` method:

```
checkPermission(new FilePermission(fileName, "read"));
```

The security manager now asks all applicable permissions whether they imply this permission. If any one of them implies it, the check passes.

In particular, the AllPermission implies all other permissions.

If you define your own permission classes, you need to define a suitable notion of implication for your permission objects. Suppose, for example, that you define a TVPermission for a set-top box powered by Java technology. A permission

```
new TVPermission("Tommy:2-12:1900-2200", "watch,record")
```

might allow Tommy to watch and record television channels 2–12 between 19:00 and 22:00. You need to implement the implies method so that this permission implies a more specific one, such as

```
new TVPermission("Tommy:4:2000-2100", "watch")
```

10.2.5 Implementation of a Permission Class

In the next sample program, we implement a new permission for monitoring the insertion of text into a text area. The program ensures that you cannot add bad words such as *sex*, *drugs*, and C++ into a text area. We use a custom permission class so that the list of bad words can be supplied in a policy file.

The following subclass of JTextArea asks the security manager whether it is OK to add new text:

```
class WordCheckTextArea extends JTextArea
{
   public void append(String text)
   {
      var p = new WordCheckPermission(text, "insert");
      SecurityManager manager = System.getSecurityManager();
      if (manager != null) manager.checkPermission(p);
      super.append(text);
   }
}
```

If the security manager grants the WordCheckPermission, the text is appended. Otherwise, the checkPermission method throws an exception.

Word check permissions have two possible actions: insert (the permission to insert a specific text) and avoid (the permission to add any text that avoids certain bad words). You should run this program with the following policy file:

```
grant
{
   permission permissions.WordCheckPermission "sex,drugs,C++", "avoid";
};
```

This policy file grants the permission to insert any text that avoids the bad words *sex*, *drugs*, and C++.

When designing the WordCheckPermission class, we must pay particular attention to the implies method. Here are the rules that control whether permission p1 implies permission p2:

- If p1 has action avoid and p2 has action insert, then the target of p2 must avoid all words in p1. For example, the permission

  ```
  permissions.WordCheckPermission "sex,drugs,C++", "avoid"
  ```

  implies the permission

  ```
  permissions.WordCheckPermission "Mary had a little lamb", "insert"
  ```

- If p1 and p2 both have action avoid, then the word set of p2 must contain all words in the word set of p1. For example, the permission

  ```
  permissions.WordCheckPermission "sex,drugs", "avoid"
  ```

  implies the permission

  ```
  permissions.WordCheckPermission "sex,drugs,C++", "avoid"
  ```

- If p1 and p2 both have action insert, then the text of p1 must contain the text of p2. For example, the permission

  ```
  permissions.WordCheckPermission "Mary had a little lamb", "insert"
  ```

  implies the permission

  ```
  permissions.WordCheckPermission "a little lamb", "insert"
  ```

You can find the implementation of this class in Listing 10.4.

Note that to retrieve the permission target, you need to use the confusingly named getName method of the Permission class.

Since permissions are described by a pair of strings in policy files, permission classes need to be prepared to parse these strings. In particular, we use the following method to transform the comma-separated list of bad words of an avoid permission into a genuine Set:

```java
public Set<String> badWordSet()
{
   var set = new HashSet<String>();
   set.addAll(List.of(getName().split(",")));
   return set;
}
```

This code allows us to use the equals and containsAll methods to compare sets. As you saw in Chapter 9 of Volume I, the equals method of a set class finds two sets to be equal if they contain the same elements in any order. For example, the sets resulting from "sex,drugs,C++" and "C++,drugs,sex" are equal.

CAUTION: Make sure that your permission class is a public class. The policy file loader cannot load classes with package visibility, and it silently ignores any classes it cannot find.

The program in Listing 10.5 shows how the WordCheckPermission class works. Type any text into the text field and click the Insert button. If the security check passes, the text is appended to the text area. If not, an error message is displayed (see Figure 10.7).

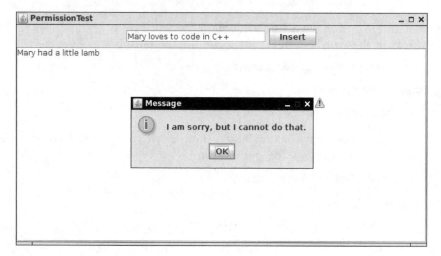

Figure 10.7 The PermissionTest program

You have now seen how to configure Java platform security. Most commonly, you will simply tweak the standard permissions. For additional control, you can define custom permissions that can be configured in the same way as the standard permissions.

Listing 10.4 permissions/WordCheckPermission.java

```
1 package permissions;
2
3 import java.security.*;
4 import java.util.*;
5
6 /**
7  * A permission that checks for bad words.
8  */
```

```
 9   public class WordCheckPermission extends Permission
10   {
11      private String action;
12
13      /**
14       * Constructs a word check permission.
15       * @param target a comma separated word list
16       * @param anAction "insert" or "avoid"
17       */
18      public WordCheckPermission(String target, String anAction)
19      {
20         super(target);
21         action = anAction;
22      }
23
24      public String getActions()
25      {
26         return action;
27      }
28
29      public boolean equals(Object other)
30      {
31         if (other == null) return false;
32         if (!getClass().equals(other.getClass())) return false;
33         var b = (WordCheckPermission) other;
34         if (!Objects.equals(action, b.action)) return false;
35         if ("insert".equals(action)) return Objects.equals(getName(), b.getName());
36         else if ("avoid".equals(action)) return badWordSet().equals(b.badWordSet());
37         else return false;
38      }
39
40      public int hashCode()
41      {
42         return Objects.hash(getName(), action);
43      }
44
45      public boolean implies(Permission other)
46      {
47         if (!(other instanceof WordCheckPermission)) return false;
48         var b = (WordCheckPermission) other;
49         if (action.equals("insert"))
50         {
51            return b.action.equals("insert") && getName().indexOf(b.getName()) >= 0;
52         }
53         else if (action.equals("avoid"))
54         {
55            if (b.action.equals("avoid")) return b.badWordSet().containsAll(badWordSet());
56            else if (b.action.equals("insert"))
57            {
```

(Continues)

Listing 10.4 *(Continued)*

```
58              for (String badWord : badWordSet())
59                  if (b.getName().indexOf(badWord) >= 0) return false;
60              return true;
61          }
62          else return false;
63      }
64      else return false;
65  }
66
67  /**
68   * Gets the bad words that this permission rule describes.
69   * @return a set of the bad words
70   */
71  public Set<String> badWordSet()
72  {
73      var set = new HashSet<String>();
74      set.addAll(List.of(getName().split(",")));
75      return set;
76  }
77 }
```

Listing 10.5 permissions/PermissionTest.java

```
1 package permissions;
2
3 import java.awt.*;
4
5 import javax.swing.*;
6
7 /**
8  * This class demonstrates the custom WordCheckPermission.
9  * @version 1.05 2018-05-01
10  * @author Cay Horstmann
11  */
12 public class PermissionTest
13 {
14    public static void main(String[] args)
15    {
16       System.setProperty("java.security.policy", "permissions/PermissionTest.policy");
17       System.setSecurityManager(new SecurityManager());
18       EventQueue.invokeLater(() ->
19          {
20             var frame = new PermissionTestFrame();
21             frame.setTitle("PermissionTest");
22             frame.setDefaultCloseOperation(JFrame.EXIT_ON_CLOSE);
23             frame.setVisible(true);
24          });
```

```
25    }
26 }
27
28 /**
29  * This frame contains a text field for inserting words into a text area that is protected
30  * from "bad words".
31  */
32 class PermissionTestFrame extends JFrame
33 {
34    private JTextField textField;
35    private WordCheckTextArea textArea;
36    private static final int TEXT_ROWS = 20;
37    private static final int TEXT_COLUMNS = 60;
38
39    public PermissionTestFrame()
40    {
41       textField = new JTextField(20);
42       var panel = new JPanel();
43       panel.add(textField);
44       var openButton = new JButton("Insert");
45       panel.add(openButton);
46       openButton.addActionListener(event -> insertWords(textField.getText()));
47
48       add(panel, BorderLayout.NORTH);
49
50       textArea = new WordCheckTextArea();
51       textArea.setRows(TEXT_ROWS);
52       textArea.setColumns(TEXT_COLUMNS);
53       add(new JScrollPane(textArea), BorderLayout.CENTER);
54       pack();
55    }
56
57    /**
58     * Tries to insert words into the text area. Displays a dialog if the attempt fails.
59     * @param words the words to insert
60     */
61    public void insertWords(String words)
62    {
63       try
64       {
65          textArea.append(words + "\n");
66       }
67       catch (SecurityException ex)
68       {
69          JOptionPane.showMessageDialog(this, "I am sorry, but I cannot do that.");
70          ex.printStackTrace();
71       }
72    }
73 }
```

(Continues)

Listing 10.5 *(Continued)*

```
74
75  /**
76   * A text area whose append method makes a security check to see that no bad words are added.
77   */
78  class WordCheckTextArea extends JTextArea
79  {
80     public void append(String text)
81     {
82        var p = new WordCheckPermission(text, "insert");
83        SecurityManager manager = System.getSecurityManager();
84        if (manager != null) manager.checkPermission(p);
85        super.append(text);
86     }
87  }
```

---

java.security.Permission 1.2

- `Permission(String name)`

  constructs a permission with the given target name.

- `String getName()`

  returns the target name of this permission.

- `boolean implies(Permission other)`

  checks whether this permission implies the other permission. That is the case if the other permission describes a more specific condition that is a consequence of the condition described by this permission.

10.3 User Authentication

The Java API provides a framework, called the Java Authentication and Authorization Service (JAAS), that integrates platform-provided authentication with permission management. We'll discuss the JAAS framework in the following sections.

10.3.1 The JAAS Framework

As you can tell from its name, the JAAS framework has two components. The "authentication" part is concerned with ascertaining the identity of a program user. The "authorization" part maps users to permissions.

JAAS is a "pluggable" API that isolates Java applications from the particular technology used to implement authentication. It supports, among others,

UNIX logins, Windows logins, Kerberos authentication, and certificate-based authentication.

Once a user has been authenticated, you can attach a set of permissions. For example, here we grant Harry a particular set of permissions that other users do not have:

```
grant principal com.sun.security.auth.UnixPrincipal "harry"
{
    permission java.util.PropertyPermission "user.*", "read";
    . . .
};
```

The com.sun.security.auth.UnixPrincipal class checks the name of the UNIX user who is running this program. Its getName method returns the UNIX login name, and we check whether that name equals "harry".

Use a LoginContext to allow the security manager to check such a grant statement. Here is the basic outline of the login code:

```
try
{
    System.setSecurityManager(new SecurityManager());
    var context = new LoginContext("Login1"); // defined in JAAS configuration file
    context.login();
    // get the authenticated Subject
    Subject subject = context.getSubject();
    . . .
    context.logout();
}
catch (LoginException exception) // thrown if login was not successful
{
    exception.printStackTrace();
}
```

Now the subject denotes the individual who has been authenticated.

The string parameter "Login1" in the LoginContext constructor refers to an entry with the same name in the JAAS configuration file. Here is a sample configuration file:

```
Login1
{
    com.sun.security.auth.module.UnixLoginModule required;
    com.whizzbang.auth.module.RetinaScanModule sufficient;
};

Login2
{
    . . .
};
```

Of course, the JDK contains no biometric login modules. The following modules are supplied in the `com.sun.security.auth.module` package:

```
UnixLoginModule
NTLoginModule
Krb5LoginModule
JndiLoginModule
KeyStoreLoginModule
```

A login policy consists of a sequence of login modules, each labeled `required`, `sufficient`, `requisite`, or `optional`. The meaning of these keywords is given by the following algorithm.

A login authenticates a *subject*, which can have multiple *principals*. A principal describes some property of the subject, such as the user name, group ID, or role. As you saw in the `grant` statement, principals govern permissions. The `com.sun.security.auth.UnixPrincipal` describes the UNIX login name, and the `UnixNumericGroupPrincipal` can test for membership in a UNIX group.

A `grant` clause can test for a principal, with the syntax

```
grant principalClass "principalName"
```

For example:

```
grant com.sun.security.auth.UnixPrincipal "harry"
```

When a user has logged in, you then run, in a separate access control context, the code that requires checking of principals. Use the static `doAs` or `doAsPrivileged` method to start a new `PrivilegedAction` whose `run` method executes the code.

Both of those methods execute an action by calling the `run` method of an object that implements the `PrivilegedAction` interface, using the permissions of the subject's principals:

```
PrivilegedAction<T> action = () ->
    {
        // run with permissions of subject principals
        . . .
    };
T result
    = Subject.doAs(subject, action); // or Subject.doAsPrivileged(subject, action, null)
```

If the actions can throw checked exceptions, you need to implement the `PrivilegedExceptionAction` interface instead.

The difference between the `doAs` and `doAsPrivileged` methods is subtle. The `doAs` method starts out with the current access control context, whereas the `doAsPrivileged` method starts out with a new context. The latter method allows

you to separate the permissions for the login code and the "business logic."
In our example application, the login code has permissions

```
permission javax.security.auth.AuthPermission "createLoginContext.Login1";
permission javax.security.auth.AuthPermission "doAsPrivileged";
```

The authenticated user has a permission

```
permission java.util.PropertyPermission "user.*", "read";
```

If we had used doAs instead of doAsPrivileged, then the login code would have
also needed that permission!

The program in Listings 10.6 and 10.7 demonstrates how to restrict permissions to certain users. The AuthTest program authenticates a user and runs
a simple action that retrieves a system property.

To make this example work, package the code for the login and the action
into two separate JAR files:

```
javac auth/*.java
jar cvf login.jar auth/AuthTest.class
jar cvf action.jar auth/SysPropAction.class
```

If you look at the policy file in Listing 10.8, you will see that the UNIX user
with the name harry has the permission to read all files. Change harry to your
login name. Then run the command

```
java -classpath login.jar:action.jar \
   -Djava.security.policy=auth/AuthTest.policy \
   -Djava.security.auth.login.config=auth/jaas.config \
   auth.AuthTest
```

Listing 10.9 shows the login configuration.

On Windows, change UnixPrincipal to NTUserPrincipal in AuthTest.policy and
UnixLoginModule to NTLoginModule in jaas.config. When running the program, use a
semicolon to separate the JAR files:

```
java -classpath login.jar;action.jar . . .
```

The AuthTest program should now display the value of the user.home property.
However, if you log in with a different name, a security exception should be
thrown because you no longer have the required permission.

 CAUTION: Be careful to follow these instructions *exactly*. It is very easy to get
the setup wrong by making seemingly innocuous changes.

Listing 10.6 auth/AuthTest.java

```
1  package auth;
2
3  import javax.security.auth.*;
4  import javax.security.auth.login.*;
5
6  /**
7   * This program authenticates a user via a custom login and then executes the SysPropAction
8   * with the user's privileges.
9   * @version 1.02 2018-05-01
10  * @author Cay Horstmann
11  */
12 public class AuthTest
13 {
14    public static void main(final String[] args)
15    {
16       System.setSecurityManager(new SecurityManager());
17       try
18       {
19          var context = new LoginContext("Login1");
20          context.login();
21          System.out.println("Authentication successful.");
22          Subject subject = context.getSubject();
23          System.out.println("subject=" + subject);
24          var action = new SysPropAction("user.home");
25          String result = Subject.doAsPrivileged(subject, action, null);
26          System.out.println(result);
27          context.logout();
28       }
29       catch (LoginException e)
30       {
31          e.printStackTrace();
32       }
33    }
34 }
```

Listing 10.7 auth/SysPropAction.java

```
1  package auth;
2
3  import java.security.*;
4
5  /**
6   * This action looks up a system property.
7   * @version 1.01 2007-10-06
8   * @author Cay Horstmann
9   */
```

```
10  public class SysPropAction implements PrivilegedAction<String>
11  {
12      private String propertyName;
13
14      /**
15          Constructs an action for looking up a given property.
16          @param propertyName the property name (such as "user.home")
17      */
18      public SysPropAction(String propertyName)
19      {
20          this.propertyName = propertyName;
21      }
22
23      public String run()
24      {
25          return System.getProperty(propertyName);
26      }
27  }
```

Listing 10.8 auth/AuthTest.policy

```
1  grant codebase "file:login.jar"
2  {
3      permission javax.security.auth.AuthPermission "createLoginContext.Login1";
4      permission javax.security.auth.AuthPermission "doAsPrivileged";
5  };
6
7  grant principal com.sun.security.auth.UnixPrincipal "harry"
8  {
9      permission java.util.PropertyPermission "user.*", "read";
10 };
```

Listing 10.9 auth/jaas.config

```
1  Login1
2  {
3      com.sun.security.auth.module.UnixLoginModule required;
4  };
```

---

javax.security.auth.login.LoginContext 1.4

- LoginContext(String name)

  constructs a login context. The name corresponds to the login descriptor in the JAAS configuration file.

(Continues)

---

javax.security.auth.login.LoginContext 1.4 *(Continued)*

- void login()

  establishes a login or throws LoginException if the login failed. Invokes the login method on the managers in the JAAS configuration file.

- void logout()

  logs out the subject. Invokes the logout method on the managers in the JAAS configuration file.

- Subject getSubject()

  returns the authenticated subject.

---

javax.security.auth.Subject 1.4

- Set<Principal> getPrincipals()

  gets the principals of this subject.

- static Object doAs(Subject subject, PrivilegedAction action)
- static Object doAs(Subject subject, PrivilegedExceptionAction action)
- static Object doAsPrivileged(Subject subject, PrivilegedAction action, AccessControlContext context)
- static Object doAsPrivileged(Subject subject, PrivilegedExceptionAction action, AccessControlContext context)

  executes the privileged action on behalf of the subject. Returns the return value of the run method. The doAsPrivileged methods execute the action in the given access control context. You can supply a "context snapshot" that you obtained earlier by calling the static method AccessController.getContext(), or you can supply null to execute the code in a new context.

---

java.security.PrivilegedAction 1.4

- Object run()

  You must define this method to execute the code that you want to have executed on behalf of a subject.

---

java.security.PrivilegedExceptionAction 1.4

- Object run()

  You must define this method to execute the code that you want to have executed on behalf of a subject. This method may throw any checked exceptions.

java.security.Principal 1.1

- `String getName()`

  returns the identifying name of this principal.

10.3.2 JAAS Login Modules

In this section, we'll look at a JAAS example that shows you

- How to implement your own login module
- How to implement *role-based* authentication

Supplying your own login module is useful if you store login information in a database. Even if you are happy with the default module, studying a custom module will help you understand the JAAS configuration file options.

Role-based authentication is essential if you manage a large number of users. It would be impractical to put the names of all legitimate users into a policy file. Instead, the login module should map users to roles such as "admin" or "HR", and the permissions should be based on these roles.

One job of the login module is to populate the principal set of the subject that is being authenticated. If a login module supports roles, it adds `Principal` objects that describe roles. The Java library does not provide a class for this purpose, so we wrote our own (see Listing 10.10). The class simply stores a description/value pair, such as `role=admin`. Its `getName` method returns that pair, so we can add role-based permissions into a policy file:

```
grant principal SimplePrincipal "role=admin" { . . . }
```

Our login module looks up users, passwords, and roles in a text file that contains lines like this:

```
harry|secret|admin
carl|guessme|HR
```

Of course, in a realistic login module, you would store this information in a database or directory.

You can find the code for the `SimpleLoginModule` in Listing 10.11. The `checkLogin` method checks whether the user name and password match a record in the password file. If so, we add two `SimplePrincipal` objects to the subject's principal set:

```
Set<Principal> principals = subject.getPrincipals();
principals.add(new SimplePrincipal("username", username));
principals.add(new SimplePrincipal("role", role));
```

The remainder of SimpleLoginModule is straightforward plumbing. The initialize method receives

- The Subject that is being authenticated
- A handler to retrieve login information
- A sharedState map that can be used for communication between login modules
- An options map that contains the name/value pairs that are set in the login configuration

For example, we configure our module as follows:

```
SimpleLoginModule required pwfile="password.txt";
```

The login module retrieves the pwfile settings from the options map.

The login module does not gather the user name and password; that is the job of a separate handler. This separation allows you to use the same login module without worrying whether the login information comes from a GUI dialog box, a console prompt, or a configuration file.

The handler is specified when you construct the LoginContext, for example:

```
var context = new LoginContext("Login1",
  new com.sun.security.auth.callback.DialogCallbackHandler());
```

The DialogCallbackHandler pops up a simple GUI dialog box to retrieve the user name and password. The com.sun.security.auth.callback.TextCallbackHandler class gets the information from the console.

However, in our application, we have our own GUI for collecting the user name and password (see Figure 10.8). We produce a simple handler that merely stores and returns that information (see Listing 10.12).

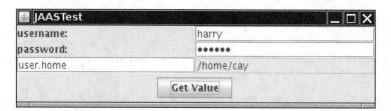

Figure 10.8 A custom login module

The handler has a single method, handle, that processes an array of Callback objects. A number of predefined classes, such as NameCallback and PasswordCallback, implement the Callback interface. You could also add your own class, such as

RetinaScanCallback. The handler code is a bit unsightly because it needs to analyze the types of the callback objects:

```
public void handle(Callback[] callbacks)
{
    for (Callback callback : callbacks)
    {
        if (callback instanceof NameCallback) . . .
        else if (callback instanceof PasswordCallback) . . .
        else . . .
    }
}
```

The login module prepares an array of the callbacks that it needs for authentication:

```
var nameCall = new NameCallback("username: ");
var passCall = new PasswordCallback("password: ", false);
callbackHandler.handle(new Callback[] { nameCall, passCall });
```

Then it retrieves the information from the callbacks.

The program in Listing 10.13 displays a form for entering the login information and the name of a system property. If the user is authenticated, the property value is retrieved in a PrivilegedAction. As you can see from the policy file in Listing 10.14, only users with the admin role have permission to read properties.

As in the preceding section, you must separate the login and action code. Create two JAR files:

```
javac *.java
jar cvf login.jar JAAS*.class Simple*.class
jar cvf action.jar SysPropAction.class
```

Then run the program as

```
java -classpath login.jar:action.jar \
    -Djava.security.policy=JAASTest.policy \
    -Djava.security.auth.login.config=jaas.config \
    JAASTest
```

Listing 10.15 shows the policy file.

NOTE: It is possible to support a more complex two-phase protocol, whereby a login is *committed* if all modules in the login configuration were successful. For more information, see the login module developer's guide at http://docs.oracle.com/javase/8/docs/technotes/guides/security/jaas/JAASLMDevGuide.html.

Listing 10.10 jaas/SimplePrincipal.java

```java
1  package jaas;
2
3  import java.security.*;
4  import java.util.*;
5
6  /**
7   * A principal with a named value (such as "role=HR" or "username=harry").
8   */
9  public class SimplePrincipal implements Principal
10 {
11    private String descr;
12    private String value;
13
14    /**
15     * Constructs a SimplePrincipal to hold a description and a value.
16     * @param descr the description
17     * @param value the associated value
18     */
19    public SimplePrincipal(String descr, String value)
20    {
21       this.descr = descr;
22       this.value = value;
23    }
24
25    /**
26     * Returns the role name of this principal.
27     * @return the role name
28     */
29    public String getName()
30    {
31       return descr + "=" + value;
32    }
33
34    public boolean equals(Object otherObject)
35    {
36       if (this == otherObject) return true;
37       if (otherObject == null) return false;
38       if (getClass() != otherObject.getClass()) return false;
39       var other = (SimplePrincipal) otherObject;
40       return Objects.equals(getName(), other.getName());
41    }
42
43    public int hashCode()
44    {
45       return Objects.hashCode(getName());
46    }
47 }
```

Listing 10.11 jaas/SimpleLoginModule.java

```
 1 package jaas;
 2
 3 import java.io.*;
 4 import java.nio.charset.*;
 5 import java.nio.file.*;
 6 import java.security.*;
 7 import java.util.*;
 8 import javax.security.auth.*;
 9 import javax.security.auth.callback.*;
10 import javax.security.auth.login.*;
11 import javax.security.auth.spi.*;
12
13 /**
14  * This login module authenticates users by reading usernames, passwords, and roles from
15  * a text file.
16  */
17 public class SimpleLoginModule implements LoginModule
18 {
19    private Subject subject;
20    private CallbackHandler callbackHandler;
21    private Map<String, ?> options;
22
23    public void initialize(Subject subject, CallbackHandler callbackHandler,
24          Map<String, ?> sharedState, Map<String, ?> options)
25    {
26       this.subject = subject;
27       this.callbackHandler = callbackHandler;
28       this.options = options;
29    }
30
31    public boolean login() throws LoginException
32    {
33       if (callbackHandler == null) throw new LoginException("no handler");
34
35       var nameCall = new NameCallback("username: ");
36       var passCall = new PasswordCallback("password: ", false);
37       try
38       {
39          callbackHandler.handle(new Callback[] { nameCall, passCall });
40       }
41       catch (UnsupportedCallbackException e)
42       {
43          var e2 = new LoginException("Unsupported callback");
44          e2.initCause(e);
45          throw e2;
46       }
```

(Continues)

Listing 10.11 *(Continued)*

```
47       catch (IOException e)
48       {
49          var e2 = new LoginException("I/O exception in callback");
50          e2.initCause(e);
51          throw e2;
52       }
53
54       try
55       {
56          return checkLogin(nameCall.getName(), passCall.getPassword());
57       }
58       catch (IOException ex)
59       {
60          var ex2 = new LoginException();
61          ex2.initCause(ex);
62          throw ex2;
63       }
64    }
65
66    /**
67     * Checks whether the authentication information is valid. If it is, the subject acquires
68     * principals for the user name and role.
69     * @param username the user name
70     * @param password a character array containing the password
71     * @return true if the authentication information is valid
72     */
73    private boolean checkLogin(String username, char[] password)
74          throws LoginException, IOException
75    {
76       try (var in = new Scanner(
77          Paths.get("" + options.get("pwfile")), StandardCharsets.UTF_8))
78       {
79          while (in.hasNextLine())
80          {
81             String[] inputs = in.nextLine().split("\\|");
82             if (inputs[0].equals(username)
83                   && Arrays.equals(inputs[1].toCharArray(), password))
84             {
85                String role = inputs[2];
86                Set<Principal> principals = subject.getPrincipals();
87                principals.add(new SimplePrincipal("username", username));
88                principals.add(new SimplePrincipal("role", role));
89                return true;
90             }
91          }
92          return false;
93       }
94    }
```

```
95
96    public boolean logout()
97    {
98       return true;
99    }
100
101   public boolean abort()
102   {
103      return true;
104   }
105
106   public boolean commit()
107   {
108      return true;
109   }
110 }
```

Listing 10.12 jaas/SimpleCallbackHandler.java

```
1 package jaas;
2
3 import javax.security.auth.callback.*;
4
5 /**
6  * This simple callback handler presents the given user name and password.
7  */
8 public class SimpleCallbackHandler implements CallbackHandler
9 {
10    private String username;
11    private char[] password;
12
13    /**
14     * Constructs the callback handler.
15     * @param username the user name
16     * @param password a character array containing the password
17     */
18    public SimpleCallbackHandler(String username, char[] password)
19    {
20       this.username = username;
21       this.password = password;
22    }
23
24    public void handle(Callback[] callbacks)
25    {
26       for (Callback callback : callbacks)
27       {
28          if (callback instanceof NameCallback)
29          {
```

(Continues)

Listing 10.12 *(Continued)*

```
30              ((NameCallback) callback).setName(username);
31          }
32          else if (callback instanceof PasswordCallback)
33          {
34              ((PasswordCallback) callback).setPassword(password);
35          }
36      }
37   }
38 }
```

Listing 10.13 jaas/JAASTest.java

```
1  package jaas;
2
3  import java.awt.*;
4  import javax.swing.*;
5
6  /**
7   * This program authenticates a user via a custom login and then looks up a system property
8   * with the user's privileges.
9   * @version 1.03 2018-05-01
10  * @author Cay Horstmann
11  */
12 public class JAASTest
13 {
14    public static void main(final String[] args)
15    {
16       System.setSecurityManager(new SecurityManager());
17       EventQueue.invokeLater(() ->
18          {
19             var frame = new JAASFrame();
20             frame.setDefaultCloseOperation(JFrame.EXIT_ON_CLOSE);
21             frame.setTitle("JAASTest");
22             frame.setVisible(true);
23          });
24    }
25 }
```

Listing 10.14 jaas/JAASTest.policy

```
1  grant codebase "file:login.jar"
2  {
3    permission java.awt.AWTPermission "showWindowWithoutWarningBanner";
4    permission java.awt.AWTPermission "accessEventQueue";
5    permission javax.security.auth.AuthPermission "createLoginContext.Login1";
6    permission javax.security.auth.AuthPermission "doAsPrivileged";
```

```
 7    permission javax.security.auth.AuthPermission "modifyPrincipals";
 8    permission java.io.FilePermission "jaas/password.txt", "read";
 9  };
10
11  grant principal jaas.SimplePrincipal "role=admin"
12  {
13    permission java.util.PropertyPermission "*", "read";
14  };
```

Listing 10.15 jaas/jaas.config

```
1  Login1
2  {
3    jaas.SimpleLoginModule required pwfile="jaas/password.txt" debug=true;
4  };
```

---

javax.security.auth.callback.CallbackHandler 1.4

* void handle(Callback[] callbacks)

  handles the given callbacks, interacting with the user if desired, and stores the security information in the callback objects.

---

javax.security.auth.callback.NameCallback 1.4

* NameCallback(String prompt)
* NameCallback(String prompt, String defaultName)

  constructs a NameCallback with the given prompt and default name.

* String getName()
* void setName(String name)

  gets or sets the name gathered by this callback.

* String getPrompt()

  gets the prompt to use when querying this name.

* String getDefaultName()

  gets the default name to use when querying this name.

---

javax.security.auth.callback.PasswordCallback 1.4

* PasswordCallback(String prompt, boolean echoOn)

  constructs a PasswordCallback with the given prompt and echo flag.

(Continues)

---

javax.security.auth.callback.PasswordCallback 1.4 *(Continued)*

- `char[] getPassword()`
- `void setPassword(char[] password)`

  gets or sets the password gathered by this callback.

- `String getPrompt()`

  gets the prompt to use when querying this password.

- `boolean isEchoOn()`

  gets the echo flag to use when querying this password.

---

javax.security.auth.spi.LoginModule 1.4

- `void initialize(Subject subject, CallbackHandler handler, Map<String,?> sharedState, Map<String,?> options)`

  initializes this `LoginModule` for authenticating the given `subject`. During login processing, uses the given handler to gather login information. Use the `sharedState` map for communicating with other login modules. The `options` map contains the name/value pairs specified in the login configuration for this module instance.

- `boolean login()`

  carries out the authentication process and populates the subject's principals. Returns `true` if the login was successful.

- `boolean commit()`

  is called after all login modules were successful, for login scenarios that require a two-phase commit. Returns `true` if the operation was successful.

- `boolean abort()`

  is called if the failure of another login module caused the login process to abort. Returns `true` if the operation was successful.

- `boolean logout()`

  logs out this subject. Returns `true` if the operation was successful.

10.4 Digital Signatures

As we said earlier, applets were what started the Java craze. In practice, people discovered that although they could write animated applets (like the famous "nervous text"), applets could not do a whole lot of useful stuff in the JDK 1.0 security model. For example, since applets under JDK 1.0 were so closely supervised, they couldn't do much good on a corporate intranet, even though relatively little risk attaches to executing an applet from your company's secure intranet. It quickly became clear to Sun that for applets to become truly useful, users need to be able to assign *different* levels of security, depending on where the applet originated. If an applet comes from a trusted supplier and has not been tampered with, the user of that applet can decide whether to give the applet more privileges.

To give more trust to an applet, we need to know two things:

- Where did the applet come from?
- Was the code corrupted in transit?

In the past 50 years, mathematicians and computer scientists have developed sophisticated algorithms for ensuring the integrity of data and for creating electronic signatures. The java.security package contains implementations of many of these algorithms. Fortunately, you don't need to understand the underlying mathematics to use the algorithms in the java.security package. In the next sections, we'll show you how message digests can detect changes in data files and how digital signatures can prove the identity of the signer.

10.4.1 Message Digests

A message digest is a digital fingerprint of a block of data. For example, the so-called SHA-1 (Secure Hash Algorithm #1) condenses any data block, no matter how long, into a sequence of 160 bits (20 bytes). As with real fingerprints, one hopes that no two different messages have the same SHA-1 fingerprint. Of course, that cannot be true—there are only 2^{160} SHA-1 fingerprints, so there must be some messages with the same fingerprint. But 2^{160} is so large that the probability of a collision is negligible. How negligible? According to James Walsh in *True Odds: How Risks Affect Your Everyday Life* (Merritt Publishing, 1996), the chance that you will die from being struck by lightning is about one in 30,000. Now, think of nine other people—for example, your nine least favorite managers or professors. The chance that you and *all of them* will die from lightning strikes is higher than that of a forged message having the same SHA-1 fingerprint as the original. (Of course, more than ten people, none of whom you are likely to know, *will* die from lightning strikes. However, we are talking about the far slimmer chance that *your particular choice* of people will be wiped out.)

A message digest has two essential properties:

- If one bit or several bits of the data are changed, the message digest also changes.

- A forger who is in possession of a given message cannot construct a fake message that has the same message digest as the original.

The second property is, again, a matter of probabilities. Consider the following message by the billionaire father:

"Upon my death, my property shall be divided equally among my children; however, my son George shall receive nothing."

That message (with a final newline) has an SHA-1 fingerprint of

```
12 5F 09 03 E7 31 30 19 2E A6 E7 E4 90 43 84 B4 38 99 8F 67
```

The distrustful father has deposited the message with one attorney and the fingerprint with another. Now, suppose George bribes the lawyer holding the message. He wants to change the message so that Bill gets nothing. Of course, that changes the fingerprint to a completely different bit pattern:

```
7D F6 AB 08 EB 40 EC CD AB 74 ED E9 86 F9 ED 99 D1 45 B1 57
```

Can George find some other wording that matches the fingerprint? If he had been the proud owner of a billion computers from the time the Earth was formed, each computing a million messages a second, he would not yet have found a message he could substitute.

A number of algorithms have been designed to compute such message digests. Among them are SHA-1, the secure hash algorithm developed by the National Institute of Standards and Technology, and MD5, an algorithm invented by Ronald Rivest of MIT. Both algorithms scramble the bits of a message in ingenious ways. For details about these algorithms, see, for example, *Cryptography and Network Security, Seventh Edition*, by William Stallings (Prentice Hall, 2017). However, subtle regularities have been discovered in both algorithms, and NIST recommends to switch to stronger alternatives. Java supports the SHA-2 and SHA-3 sets of algorithms.

The MessageDigest class is a *factory* for creating objects that encapsulate the fingerprinting algorithms. It has a static method, called getInstance, that returns an object of a class that extends the MessageDigest class. This means the MessageDigest class serves double duty:

- As a factory class
- As the superclass for all message digest algorithms

For example, here is how you obtain an object that can compute SHA fingerprints:

```
MessageDigest alg = MessageDigest.getInstance("SHA-1");
```

After you have obtained a `MessageDigest` object, feed it all the bytes in the message by repeatedly calling the `update` method. For example, the following code passes all bytes in a file to the `alg` object just created to do the fingerprinting:

```
InputStream in = . . .;
int ch;
while ((ch = in.read()) != -1)
    alg.update((byte) ch);
```

Alternatively, if you have the bytes in an array, you can update the entire array at once:

```
byte[] bytes = . . .;
alg.update(bytes);
```

When you are done, call the `digest` method. This method pads the input as required by the fingerprinting algorithm, does the computation, and returns the digest as an array of bytes.

```
byte[] hash = alg.digest();
```

The program in Listing 10.16 computes a message digest. You can specify the file and algorithm on the command line:

```
java hash.Digest hash/input.txt SHA-1
```

If you do not supply command-line arguments, you will be prompted for the file and algorithm name.

Listing 10.16 hash/Digest.java

```
1  package hash;
2
3  import java.io.*;
4  import java.nio.file.*;
5  import java.security.*;
6  import java.util.*;
7
8  /**
9   * This program computes the message digest of a file.
10  * @version 1.21 2018-04-10
11  * @author Cay Horstmann
12  */
13  public class Digest
14  {
15     /**
16      * @param args args[0] is the filename, args[1] is optionally the algorithm
17      * (SHA-1, SHA-256, or MD5)
18      */
```

(Continues)

Listing 10.16 *(Continued)*

```
19  public static void main(String[] args) throws IOException, GeneralSecurityException
20  {
21     var in = new Scanner(System.in);
22     String filename;
23     if (args.length >= 1)
24        filename = args[0];
25     else
26     {
27        System.out.print("File name: ");
28        filename = in.nextLine();
29     }
30     String algname;
31     if (args.length >= 2)
32        algname = args[1];
33     else
34     {
35        System.out.println("Select one of the following algorithms: ");
36        for (Provider p : Security.getProviders())
37           for (Provider.Service s : p.getServices())
38              if (s.getType().equals("MessageDigest"))
39                 System.out.println(s.getAlgorithm());
40        System.out.print("Algorithm: ");
41        algname = in.nextLine();
42     }
43     MessageDigest alg = MessageDigest.getInstance(algname);
44     byte[] input = Files.readAllBytes(Paths.get(filename));
45     byte[] hash = alg.digest(input);
46     for (int i = 0; i < hash.length; i++)
47        System.out.printf("%02X ", hash[i] & 0xFF);
48     System.out.println();
49  }
50 }
```

---

java.security.MessageDigest 1.1

- static MessageDigest getInstance(String algorithmName)

  returns a MessageDigest object that implements the specified algorithm. Throws NoSuchAlgorithmException if the algorithm is not provided.

- void update(byte input)
- void update(byte[] input)
- void update(byte[] input, int offset, int len)

  updates the digest, using the specified bytes.

(Continues)

`java.security.MessageDigest` 1.1 *(Continued)*

- `byte[] digest()`

  completes the hash computation, returns the computed digest, and resets the algorithm object.

- `void reset()`

  resets the digest.

10.4.2 Message Signing

In the last section, you saw how to compute a message digest—a fingerprint for the original message. If the message is altered, the fingerprint of the altered message will not match the fingerprint of the original. If the message and its fingerprint are delivered separately, the recipient can check whether the message has been tampered with. However, if both the message and the fingerprint were intercepted, it is an easy matter to modify the message and then recompute the fingerprint. After all, the message digest algorithms are publicly known, and they don't require secret keys. In that case, the recipient of the forged message and the recomputed fingerprint would never know that the message has been altered. Digital signatures solve this problem.

To help you understand how digital signatures work, we'll explain a few concepts from the field called *public key cryptography*. Public key cryptography is based on the notion of a *public* key and *private* key. The idea is that you tell everyone in the world your public key. However, only you hold the private key, and it is important that you safeguard it and don't release it to anyone else. The keys are matched by mathematical relationships, though the exact nature of these relationships is not important to us. (If you are interested, look it up in *The Handbook of Applied Cryptography* at www.cacr.math.uwaterloo.ca/hac.)

The keys are quite long and complex. For example, here is a matching pair of public and private Digital Signature Algorithm (DSA) keys.

Public key:

```
p: fca682ce8e12caba26efccf7110e526db078b05edecbcd1eb4a208f3ae1617ae01f35b91a47e6df63413c5e12
ed0899bcd132acd50d99151bdc43ee737592e17

q: 962eddcc369cba8ebb260ee6b6a126d9346e38c5

g: 678471b27a9cf44ee91a49c5147db1a9aaf244f05a434d6486931d2d14271b9e35030b71fd73da179069b32e2
935630e1c2062354d0da20a6c416e50be794ca4

y: c0b6e67b4ac098eb1a32c5f8c4c1f0e7e6fb9d832532e27d0bdab9ca2d2a8123ce5a8018b8161a760480fadd0
40b927281ddb22cb9bc4df596d7de4d1b977d50
```

Private key:

p: fca682ce8e12caba26efccf7110e526db078b05edecbcd1eb4a208f3ae1617ae01f35b91a47e6df63413c5e12
ed0899bcd132acd50d99151bdc43ee737592e17

q: 962eddcc369cba8ebb260ee6b6a126d9346e38c5

g: 678471b27a9cf44ee91a49c5147db1a9aaf244f05a434d6486931d2d14271b9e35030b71fd73da179069b32e2
935630e1c2062354d0da20a6c416e50be794ca4

x: 146c09f881656cc6c51f27ea6c3a91b85ed1d70a

It is believed to be practically impossible to compute one key from the other. That is, even though everyone knows your public key, they can't, in your lifetime, compute your private key, no matter how many computing resources they have available.

It may be difficult to believe that the private key can't be computed from the public key—but nobody has found an algorithm to do this for the encryption algorithms in common use today. If the keys are sufficiently long, brute force—simply trying all possible keys—would require more computers than can be built from all the atoms in the solar system, crunching away for thousands of years. Of course it is possible that someone could come up with algorithms for computing keys that are much more clever than brute force. For example, the RSA algorithm (the encryption algorithm invented by Rivest, Shamir, and Adleman) depends on the difficulty of factoring large numbers. For the last 20 years, many of the best mathematicians have tried to come up with good factoring algorithms, but so far with no success. For that reason, most cryptographers believe that keys with a "modulus" of 2,000 bits or more are currently completely safe from any attack. DSA is believed to be similarly secure.

Figure 10.9 illustrates how the process works in practice.

Suppose Alice wants to send Bob a message, and Bob wants to know this message came from Alice and not an impostor. Alice writes the message and *signs* the message digest with her private key. Bob gets a copy of her public key. Bob then applies the public key to *verify* the signature. If the verification passes, Bob can be assured of two facts:

- The original message has not been altered.
- The message was signed by Alice, the holder of the private key that matches the public key that Bob used for verification.

You can see why the security of private keys is so important. If someone steals Alice's private key, or if a government can require her to turn it over, then she is in trouble. The thief or a government agent can now impersonate her by sending messages, such as money transfer instructions, that others will believe came from Alice.

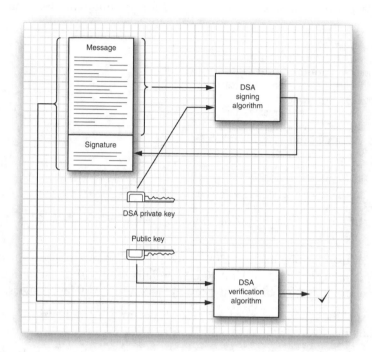

Figure 10.9 Public key signature exchange with DSA

10.4.3 Verifying a Signature

The JDK comes with the keytool program, which is a command-line tool to generate and manage a set of certificates. We expect that ultimately the functionality of this tool will be embedded in other, more user-friendly programs. But right now, we'll use keytool to show how Alice can sign a document and send it to Bob, and how Bob can verify that the document really was signed by Alice and not an impostor.

The keytool program manages *keystores*—databases of certificates and private/public key pairs. Each entry in the keystore has an *alias*. Here is how Alice creates a keystore, alice.certs, and generates a key pair with alias alice:

```
keytool -genkeypair -keystore alice.certs -alias alice
```

When creating or opening a keystore, you are prompted for a keystore password. For this example, just use secret. If you were to use the keytool-generated keystore for any serious purpose, you would need to choose a good password and safeguard this file.

When generating a key, you are prompted for the following information:

```
Enter keystore password: secret
Reenter new password: secret
What is your first and last name?
  [Unknown]: Alice Lee
What is the name of your organizational unit?
  [Unknown]: Engineering
What is the name of your organization?
  [Unknown]: ACME Software
What is the name of your City or Locality?
  [Unknown]: San Francisco
What is the name of your State or Province?
  [Unknown]: CA
What is the two-letter country code for this unit?
  [Unknown]: US
Is <CN=Alice Lee, OU=Engineering, O=ACME Software, L=San Francisco, ST=CA, C=US> correct?
  [no]: yes
```

The keytool uses names in the X.500 format, whose components are Common Name (CN), Organizational Unit (OU), Organization (O), Location (L), State (ST), and Country (C), to identify key owners and certificate issuers.

Finally, specify a key password, or press Enter to use the keystore password as the key password.

Suppose Alice wants to give her public key to Bob. She needs to export a certificate file:

```
keytool -exportcert -keystore alice.certs -alias alice -file alice.cer
```

Now Alice can send the certificate to Bob. When Bob receives the certificate, he can print it:

```
keytool -printcert -file alice.cer
```

The printout looks like this:

```
Owner: CN=Alice Lee, OU=Engineering, O=ACME Software, L=San Francisco, ST=CA, C=US
Issuer: CN=Alice Lee, OU=Engineering, O=ACME Software, L=San Francisco, ST=CA, C=US
Serial number: 470835ce
Valid from: Sat Oct 06 18:26:38 PDT 2007 until: Fri Jan 04 17:26:38 PST 2008
Certificate fingerprints:
    MD5:  BC:18:15:27:85:69:48:B1:5A:C3:0B:1C:C6:11:B7:81
    SHA1: 31:0A:A0:B8:C2:8B:3B:B6:85:7C:EF:C0:57:E5:94:95:61:47:6D:34
    Signature algorithm name: SHA1withDSA
    Version: 3
```

If Bob wants to check that he got the right certificate, he can call Alice and verify the certificate fingerprint over the phone.

> **NOTE:** Some certificate issuers publish certificate fingerprints on their web sites. For example, to check the DigiCert certificate in the keystore *jre*/lib/security/cacerts directory, use the -list option:
>
> ```
> keytool -list -v -keystore jre/lib/security/cacerts
> ```
>
> The password for this keystore is changeit. One of the certificates in this keystore is
>
> ```
> Owner: CN=DigiCert Assured ID Root G3, OU=www.digicert.com, O=DigiCert Inc, C=US
> Issuer: CN=DigiCert Assured ID Root G3, OU=www.digicert.com, O=DigiCert Inc, C=US
> Serial number: ba15afa1ddfa0b54944afcd24a06cec
> Valid from: Thu Aug 01 14:00:00 CEST 2013 until: Fri Jan 15 13:00:00 CET 2038
> Certificate fingerprints:
>         SHA1: F5:17:A2:4F:9A:48:C6:C9:F8:A2:00:26:9F:DC:0F:48:2C:AB:30:89
>         SHA256: 7E:37:CB:8B:4C:47:09:0C:AB:36:55:1B:A6:F4:5D:B8:40:68:0F:BA:
>                 16:6A:95:2D:B1:00:71:7F:43:05:3F:C2
> ```
>
> You can check that your certificate is valid by visiting the web site www.digicert.com/digicert-root-certificates.htm.

Once Bob trusts the certificate, he can import it into his keystore.

```
keytool -importcert -keystore bob.certs -alias alice -file alice.cer
```

> **CAUTION:** Never import into a keystore a certificate that you don't fully trust. Once a certificate is added to the keystore, any program that uses the keystore assumes that the certificate can be used to verify signatures.

Now Alice can start sending signed documents to Bob. The jarsigner tool signs and verifies JAR files. Alice simply adds the document to be signed into a JAR file.

```
jar cvf document.jar document.txt
```

She then uses the jarsigner tool to add the signature to the file. She needs to specify the keystore, the JAR file, and the alias of the key to use.

```
jarsigner -keystore alice.certs document.jar alice
```

When Bob receives the file, he uses the -verify option of the jarsigner program.

```
jarsigner -verify -keystore bob.certs document.jar
```

Bob does not need to specify the key alias. The jarsigner program finds the X.500 name of the key owner in the digital signature and looks for a matching certificate in the keystore.

If the JAR file is not corrupted and the signature matches, the jarsigner program prints

    jar verified.

Otherwise, the program displays an error message.

10.4.4 The Authentication Problem

Suppose you get a message from your friend Alice, signed with her private key, using the method we just showed you. You might already have her public key, or you can easily get it by asking her for a copy or by getting it from her web page. Then, you can verify that the message was in fact authored by Alice and has not been tampered with. Now, suppose you get a message from a stranger who claims to represent a famous software company, urging you to run a program attached to the message. The stranger even sends you a copy of his public key so you can verify that he authored the message. You check that the signature is valid. This proves that the message was signed with the matching private key and has not been corrupted.

Be careful: *You still have no idea who wrote the message.* Anyone can generate a pair of public and private keys, sign the message with the private key, and send the signed message and the public key to you. The problem of determining the identity of the sender is called the *authentication problem*.

The usual way to solve the authentication problem is simple. Suppose the stranger and you have a common acquaintance you both trust. Suppose the stranger meets your acquaintance in person and hands over a disk with the public key. Your acquaintance later meets you, assures you that he met the stranger and that the stranger indeed works for the famous software company, and then gives you the disk (see Figure 10.10). That way, your acquaintance vouches for the authenticity of the stranger.

In fact, your acquaintance does not actually need to meet you. Instead, he can use his private key to sign the stranger's public key file (see Figure 10.11).

When you get the public key file, you verify the signature of your friend, and because you trust him, you are confident that he did check the stranger's credentials before applying his signature.

However, you might not have a common acquaintance. Some trust models assume that there is always a "chain of trust"—a chain of mutual acquaintances—so that you trust every member of that chain. In practice, of course,

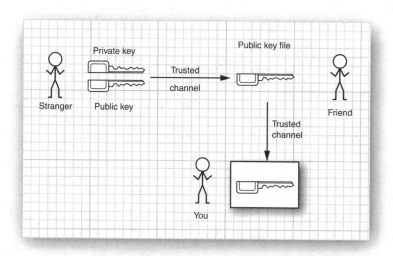

Figure 10.10 Authentication through a trusted intermediary

that isn't always true. You might trust your friend, Alice, and you know that Alice trusts Bob, but you don't know Bob and aren't sure that you trust him. Other trust models assume that there is a benevolent big brother—a company in which we all trust. Companies with confidence-inspiring names such as DigiCert, GlobalSign, and Entrust provide verification services.

You will often encounter digital signatures signed by one or more entities who will vouch for the authenticity, and you will need to evaluate to what degree you trust the authenticators. You might place a great deal of trust in a particular certificate authority, perhaps because you saw their logo on many web pages or because you heard that they require multiple people with black attaché cases to come together into a secure chamber whenever new master keys are to be minted.

However, you should have realistic expectations about what is actually being authenticated. You can get a "class 1" ID simply by filling out a web form and paying a small fee. The key is mailed to the e-mail address included in the certificate. Thus, you can be reasonably assured that the e-mail address is genuine, but the requestor could have filled in *any* name and organization. There are more stringent classes of IDs. For example, with a "class 3" ID, the certificate authority will require an individual requestor to appear before a notary public, and it will check the financial rating of a corporate requestor. Other authenticators will have different procedures. Thus, when you receive an authenticated message, it is important that you understand what, in fact, is being authenticated.

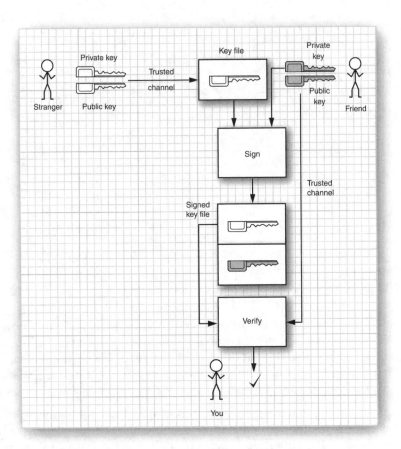

Figure 10.11 Authentication through a trusted intermediary's signature

10.4.5 Certificate Signing

In Section 10.4.3, "Verifying a Signature," on p. 589 you saw how Alice used a self-signed certificate to distribute a public key to Bob. However, Bob needed to ensure that the certificate was valid by verifying the fingerprint with Alice.

Suppose Alice wants to send her colleague Cindy a signed message, but Cindy doesn't want to bother with verifying lots of signature fingerprints. Now suppose there is an entity that Cindy trusts to verify signatures. In this example, Cindy trusts the Information Resources Department at ACME Software.

That department operates a *certificate authority* (CA). Everyone at ACME has the CA's public key in their keystore, installed by a system administrator who carefully checked the key fingerprint. The CA signs the keys of ACME employees. When they install each other's keys, the keystore will trust them implicitly because they are signed by a trusted key.

Here is how you can simulate this process. Create a keystore acmesoft.certs. Generate a key pair and export the public key:

```
keytool -genkeypair -keystore acmesoft.certs -alias acmeroot
keytool -exportcert -keystore acmesoft.certs -alias acmeroot -file acmeroot.cer
```

The public key is exported into a "self-signed" certificate. Then, add it to every employee's keystore:

```
keytool -importcert -keystore cindy.certs -alias acmeroot -file acmeroot.cer
```

For Alice to send messages to Cindy and to everyone else at ACME Software, she needs to bring her certificate to the Information Resources Department and have it signed. Unfortunately, this functionality is missing in the keytool program. In the book's companion code, we supply a CertificateSigner class to fill the gap. An authorized staff member at ACME Software would verify Alice's identity and generate a signed certificate as follows:

```
java CertificateSigner -keystore acmesoft.certs -alias acmeroot \
   -infile alice.cer -outfile alice_signedby_acmeroot.cer
```

The certificate signer program must have access to the ACME Software keystore, and the staff member must know the keystore password. Clearly, this is a sensitive operation.

Alice gives the file alice_signedby_acmeroot.cer to Cindy and to anyone else in ACME Software. Alternatively, ACME Software can simply store the file in a company directory. Remember, this file contains Alice's public key and an assertion by ACME Software that this key really belongs to Alice.

Now Cindy imports the signed certificate into her keystore:

```
keytool -importcert -keystore cindy.certs -alias alice -file alice_signedby_acmeroot.cer
```

The keystore verifies that the key was signed by a trusted root key that is already present in the keystore. Cindy is *not* asked to verify the certificate fingerprint.

Once Cindy has added the root certificate and the certificates of the people who regularly send her documents, she never has to worry about the keystore again.

10.4.6 Certificate Requests

In the preceding section, we simulated a CA with a keystore and the CertificateSigner tool. However, most CAs run more sophisticated software to manage certificates, and they use slightly different formats for certificates. This section shows the added steps required to interact with those software packages.

We will use the OpenSSL software package as an example. The software is preinstalled on many Linux systems and Mac OS X, and a Cygwin port for Windows is also available. You can download the software at www.openssl.org.

To create a CA, run the CA script. The exact location depends on your operating system. On Ubuntu, run

```
/usr/lib/ssl/misc/CA.pl -newca
```

This script creates a subdirectory called demoCA in the current directory. The directory contains a root key pair and storage for certificates and certificate revocation lists.

You will want to import the public key into the Java keystores of all employees, but it is in the Privacy Enhanced Mail (PEM) format, not the DER format that the keystore accepts easily. Copy the file demoCA/cacert.pem to a file acmeroot.pem and open that file in a text editor. Remove everything before the line

```
-----BEGIN CERTIFICATE-----
```

and after the line

```
-----END CERTIFICATE-----
```

Now you can import acmeroot.pem into each keystore in the usual way:

```
keytool -importcert -keystore cindy.certs -alias alice -file acmeroot.pem
```

It seems quite incredible that the keytool cannot carry out this editing operation itself.

To sign Alice's public key, start by generating a *certificate request* that contains the certificate in the PEM format:

```
keytool -certreq -keystore alice.store -alias alice -file alice.pem
```

To sign the certificate, run

```
openssl ca -in alice.pem -out alice_signedby_acmeroot.pem
```

As before, cut out everything outside the BEGIN CERTIFICATE/END CERTIFICATE markers from alice_signedby_acmeroot.pem. Then import it into the keystore:

```
keytool -importcert -keystore cindy.certs -alias alice -file alice_signedby_acmeroot.pem
```

You can use the same steps to have a certificate signed with a key that is issued by a certificate authority.

10.4.7 Code Signing

A common use of authentication technology is signing executable programs. If you download a program, you are naturally concerned about the damage it can do. For example, the program could have been infected by a virus. If you know where the code comes from *and* that it has not been tampered with since it left its origin, your comfort level will be a lot higher than without this knowledge.

In this section, we'll show you how to sign JAR files, and how you can configure Java to verify the signature. This capability was designed for applets and Java Web Start applications. These are no longer commonly used technologies, but you may still need to support them in legacy products.

When Java was first released, applets ran in the "sandbox," with limited permissions, as soon as they were loaded. If users wanted to use applets that can access the local file system, make network connections, and so on, they had to explicitly agree. To ensure that the applet code was not tampered with in transit, it had to be digitally signed.

Here is a specific example. Suppose that while surfing the Internet, you encounter a web site that offers to run an applet from an unfamiliar vendor, provided you grant it the permission to do so (see Figure 10.12). Such a program is signed with a *software developer* certificate issued by a certificate authority that the Java runtime trusts. The pop-up dialog box identifies the software developer and the certificate issuer. Now you need to decide whether to authorize the program.

What facts do you have at your disposal that might influence your decision? Here is what you know:

- Thawte sold a certificate to the software developer.
- The program really was signed with that certificate, and it hasn't been modified in transit.
- That certificate really was signed by Thawte—it was verified by the public key in the local cacerts file.

Of course, none of this tells you whether the code is safe to run. Can you trust a vendor if all you know is the vendor's name and the fact that Thawte sold them a software developer certificate? This approach never made much sense.

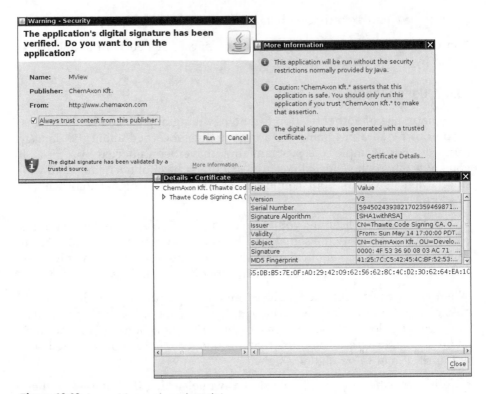

Figure 10.12 Launching a signed applet

For intranet deployment, certificates are more plausible. Administrators can install policy files and certificates on local machines so that no user interaction is required for launching trusted code. Whenever the Java plug-in tool loads signed code, it consults the policy file for the permissions and the keystore for signatures.

For the remainder of this section, we will describe how you can build policy files that grant specific permissions to trusted code.

Suppose ACME Software wants its employees to run certain programs that require local file access, and it wants to deploy these programs through a browser as Web Start applications.

As you saw earlier in this chapter, ACME could identify the programs by their code base. But that means ACME would need to update the policy files each time the programs are moved to a different web server. Instead, ACME decides to *sign* the JAR files that contain the program code.

First, ACME generates a root certificate:

```
keytool -genkeypair -keystore acmesoft.certs -alias acmeroot
```

Of course, the keystore containing the private root key must be kept in a safe place. Therefore, we create a second keystore client.certs for the public certificates and add the public acmeroot certificate into it.

```
keytool -exportcert -keystore acmesoft.certs -alias acmeroot -file acmeroot.cer
keytool -importcert -keystore client.certs -alias acmeroot -file acmeroot.cer
```

A trusted person at ACME runs the jarsigner tool to sign any application that they wish to sign, specifying the JAR file and the alias of the private key:

```
jarsigner -keystore acmesoft.certs ACMEApp.jar acmeroot
```

The signed Web Start application is now ready to be deployed on a web server.

Next, let us turn to the client machine configuration. A policy file must be distributed to each client machine.

To reference a keystore, a policy file starts with the line

```
keystore "keystoreURL", "keystoreType";
```

The URL can be absolute or relative. Relative URLs are relative to the location of the policy file. The type is JKS if the keystore was generated by keytool. For example,

```
keystore "client.certs", "JKS";
```

Then grant clauses can have suffixes signedBy "*alias*", such as this one:

```
grant signedBy "acmeroot"
{
    . . .
};
```

Any signed code that can be verified with the public key associated with the alias is now granted the permissions inside the grant clause.

10.5 Encryption

So far, we have discussed one important cryptographic technique implemented in the Java security API—namely, authentication through digital signatures. A second important aspect of security is *encryption*. Even when authenticated, the information itself is plainly visible. The digital signature merely verifies that the information has not been changed. In contrast, when information is encrypted, it is not visible. It can only be decrypted with a matching key.

Authentication is sufficient for code signing—there is no need to hide the code. However, encryption is necessary when applets or applications transfer confidential information, such as credit card numbers and other personal data.

In the past, patents and export controls prevented many companies from offering strong encryption. Fortunately, export controls are now much less stringent, and the patents for important algorithms have expired. Nowadays, Java provides excellent encryption support as a part of the standard library.

10.5.1 Symmetric Ciphers

The Java cryptographic extensions contain a class `Cipher` that is the superclass of all encryption algorithms. To get a cipher object, call the `getInstance` method:

```
Cipher cipher = Cipher.getInstance(algorithmName);
```

or

```
Cipher cipher = Cipher.getInstance(algorithmName, providerName);
```

The JDK comes with ciphers by the provider named `"SunJCE"`. It is the default provider used if you don't specify another provider name. You might want another provider if you need specialized algorithms that Oracle does not support.

The algorithm name is a string such as `"AES"` or `"DES/CBC/PKCS5Padding"`.

The Data Encryption Standard (DES) is a venerable block cipher with a key length of 56 bits. Nowadays, the DES algorithm is considered obsolete because it can be cracked with brute force. A far better alternative is its successor, the Advanced Encryption Standard (AES). See `https://nvlpubs.nist.gov/nistpubs/FIPS/NIST.FIPS.197.pdf` for a detailed description of the AES algorithm. We use AES for our example.

Once you have a cipher object, initialize it by setting the mode and the key:

```
int mode = . . .;
Key key = . . .;
cipher.init(mode, key);
```

The mode is one of

```
Cipher.ENCRYPT_MODE
Cipher.DECRYPT_MODE
Cipher.WRAP_MODE
Cipher.UNWRAP_MODE
```

The wrap and unwrap modes encrypt one key with another—see the next section for an example.

Now you can repeatedly call the update method to encrypt blocks of data:

```
int blockSize = cipher.getBlockSize();
var inBytes = new byte[blockSize];
. . . // read inBytes
int outputSize= cipher.getOutputSize(blockSize);
var outBytes = new byte[outputSize];
int outLength = cipher.update(inBytes, 0, outputSize, outBytes);
. . . // write outBytes
```

When you are done, you must call the doFinal method once. If a final block of input data is available (with fewer than blockSize bytes), call

```
outBytes = cipher.doFinal(inBytes, 0, inLength);
```

If all input data have been encrypted, instead call

```
outBytes = cipher.doFinal();
```

The call to doFinal is necessary to carry out *padding* of the final block. Consider the DES cipher. It has a block size of eight bytes. Suppose the last block of the input data has fewer than eight bytes. Of course, we can fill the remaining bytes with 0, to obtain one final block of eight bytes, and encrypt it. But when the blocks are decrypted, the result will have several trailing 0 bytes appended to it, and therefore will be slightly different from the original input file. To avoid this problem, we need a *padding scheme*. A commonly used padding scheme is the one described in the Public Key Cryptography Standard (PKCS) #5 by RSA Security, Inc. (https://tools.ietf.org/html/rfc2898).

In this scheme, the last block is not padded with a pad value of zero, but with a pad value that equals the number of pad bytes. In other words, if L is the last (incomplete) block, it is padded as follows:

```
L 01                          if length(L) = 7
L 02 02                       if length(L) = 6
L 03 03 03                    if length(L) = 5
. . .
L 07 07 07 07 07 07 07        if length(L) = 1
```

Finally, if the length of the input is actually divisible by 8, then one block

```
08 08 08 08 08 08 08 08
```

is appended to the input and encrypted. After decryption, the very last byte of the plaintext is a count of the padding characters to discard.

10.5.2 Key Generation

To encrypt, you need to generate a key. Each cipher has a different format for keys, and you need to make sure that the key generation is random. Follow these steps:

1. Get a KeyGenerator for your algorithm.
2. Initialize the generator with a source for randomness. If the block length of the cipher is variable, also specify the desired block length.
3. Call the generateKey method.

For example, here is how you generate an AES key:

```
KeyGenerator keygen = KeyGenerator.getInstance("AES");
var random = new SecureRandom(); // see below
keygen.init(random);
Key key = keygen.generateKey();
```

Alternatively, you can produce a key from a fixed set of raw data (perhaps derived from a password or the timing of keystrokes). Construct a SecretKeySpec (which implements the SecretKey interface) like this:

```
byte[] keyData = . . .; // 16 bytes for AES
var key = new SecretKeySpec(keyData, "AES");
```

When generating keys, make sure you use *truly random* numbers. For example, the regular random number generator in the Random class, seeded by the current date and time, is not random enough. Suppose the computer clock is accurate to 1/10 of a second. Then there are at most 864,000 seeds per day. If an attacker knows the day a key was issued (which can often be deduced from a message date or certificate expiration date), it is an easy matter to generate all possible seeds for that day.

The SecureRandom class generates random numbers that are far more secure than those produced by the Random class. You still need to provide a seed to start the number sequence at a random spot. The best method for doing this is to obtain random input from a hardware device such as a white-noise generator. Another reasonable source for random input is to ask the user to type away aimlessly on the keyboard, with each keystroke contributing only one or two bits to the random seed. Once you gather such random bits in an array of bytes, pass it to the setSeed method:

```
var secrand = new SecureRandom();
var b = new byte[20];
// fill with truly random bits
secrand.setSeed(b);
```

If you don't seed the random number generator, it will compute its own 20-byte seed by launching threads, putting them to sleep, and measuring the exact time when they are awakened.

 NOTE: This algorithm is *not* known to be safe. In the past, algorithms that relied on the timing of some components of the computer, such as hard disk access time, were shown not to be completely random.

The sample program at the end of this section puts the AES cipher to work (see Listing 10.17). The `crypt` utility method in Listing 10.18 will be reused in other examples. To use the program, you first need to generate a secret key. Run

```
java aes.AESTest -genkey secret.key
```

The secret key is saved in the file `secret.key`.

Now you can encrypt with the command

```
java aes.AESTest -encrypt plaintextFile encryptedFile secret.key
```

Decrypt with the command

```
java aes.AESTest -decrypt encryptedFile decryptedFile secret.key
```

The program is straightforward. The `-genkey` option produces a new secret key and serializes it in the given file. That operation takes a long time because the initialization of the secure random generator is time-consuming. The `-encrypt` and `-decrypt` options both call into the same `crypt` method that calls the `update` and `doFinal` methods of the cipher. Note how the `update` method is called so long as the input blocks have the full length, and the `doFinal` method is either called with a partial input block (which is then padded) or with no additional data (to generate one pad block).

Listing 10.17 aes/AESTest.java

```
1  package aes;
2
3  import java.io.*;
4  import java.security.*;
5  import javax.crypto.*;
6
```

(Continues)

Listing 10.17 *(Continued)*

```
7  /**
8   * This program tests the AES cipher. Usage:<br>
9   * java aes.AESTest -genkey keyfile<br>
10  * java aes.AESTest -encrypt plaintext encrypted keyfile<br>
11  * java aes.AESTest -decrypt encrypted decrypted keyfile<br>
12  * @author Cay Horstmann
13  * @version 1.02 2018-05-01
14  */
15 public class AESTest
16 {
17     public static void main(String[] args)
18         throws IOException, GeneralSecurityException, ClassNotFoundException
19     {
20        if (args[0].equals("-genkey"))
21        {
22           KeyGenerator keygen = KeyGenerator.getInstance("AES");
23           var random = new SecureRandom();
24           keygen.init(random);
25           SecretKey key = keygen.generateKey();
26           try (var out = new ObjectOutputStream(new FileOutputStream(args[1])))
27           {
28              out.writeObject(key);
29           }
30        }
31        else
32        {
33           int mode;
34           if (args[0].equals("-encrypt")) mode = Cipher.ENCRYPT_MODE;
35           else mode = Cipher.DECRYPT_MODE;
36
37           try (var keyIn = new ObjectInputStream(new FileInputStream(args[3]));
38                var in = new FileInputStream(args[1]);
39                var out = new FileOutputStream(args[2]))
40           {
41              var key = (Key) keyIn.readObject();
42              Cipher cipher = Cipher.getInstance("AES");
43              cipher.init(mode, key);
44              Util.crypt(in, out, cipher);
45           }
46        }
47     }
48 }
```

Listing 10.18 aes/Util.java

```java
1  package aes;
2
3  import java.io.*;
4  import java.security.*;
5  import javax.crypto.*;
6
7  public class Util
8  {
9     /**
10     * Uses a cipher to transform the bytes in an input stream and sends the transformed bytes
11     * to an output stream.
12     * @param in the input stream
13     * @param out the output stream
14     * @param cipher the cipher that transforms the bytes
15     */
16    public static void crypt(InputStream in, OutputStream out, Cipher cipher)
17          throws IOException, GeneralSecurityException
18    {
19       int blockSize = cipher.getBlockSize();
20       int outputSize = cipher.getOutputSize(blockSize);
21       var inBytes = new byte[blockSize];
22       var outBytes = new byte[outputSize];
23
24       int inLength = 0;
25       var done = false;
26       while (!done)
27       {
28          inLength = in.read(inBytes);
29          if (inLength == blockSize)
30          {
31             int outLength = cipher.update(inBytes, 0, blockSize, outBytes);
32             out.write(outBytes, 0, outLength);
33          }
34          else done = true;
35       }
36       if (inLength > 0) outBytes = cipher.doFinal(inBytes, 0, inLength);
37       else outBytes = cipher.doFinal();
38       out.write(outBytes);
39    }
40  }
```

---

javax.crypto.Cipher 1.4

- static Cipher getInstance(String algorithmName)
- static Cipher getInstance(String algorithmName, String providerName)

  returns a Cipher object that implements the specified algorithm. Throws a NoSuchAlgorithmException if the algorithm is not provided.

- int getBlockSize()

  returns the size (in bytes) of a cipher block, or 0 if the cipher is not a block cipher.

- int getOutputSize(int inputLength)

  returns the size of an output buffer that is needed if the next input has the given number of bytes. This method takes into account any buffered bytes in the cipher object.

- void init(int mode, Key key)

  initializes the cipher algorithm object. The mode is one of ENCRYPT_MODE, DECRYPT_MODE, WRAP_MODE, or UNWRAP_MODE.

- byte[] update(byte[] in)
- byte[] update(byte[] in, int offset, int length)
- int update(byte[] in, int offset, int length, byte[] out)

  transforms one block of input data. The first two methods return the output. The third method returns the number of bytes placed into out.

- byte[] doFinal()
- byte[] doFinal(byte[] in)
- byte[] doFinal(byte[] in, int offset, int length)
- int doFinal(byte[] in, int offset, int length, byte[] out)

  transforms the last block of input data and flushes the buffer of this algorithm object. The first three methods return the output. The fourth method returns the number of bytes placed into out.

---

javax.crypto.KeyGenerator 1.4

- static KeyGenerator getInstance(String algorithmName)

  returns a KeyGenerator object that implements the specified algorithm. Throws a NoSuchAlgorithmException if the algorithm is not provided.

- void init(SecureRandom random)
- void init(int keySize, SecureRandom random)

  initializes the key generator.

(Continues)

---

javax.crypto.KeyGenerator 1.4 *(Continued)*

- SecretKey generateKey()

  generates a new key.

---

javax.crypto.spec.SecretKeySpec 1.4

- SecretKeySpec(byte[] key, String algorithmName)

  constructs a key specification.

10.5.3 Cipher Streams

The JCE library provides a convenient set of stream classes that automatically encrypt or decrypt stream data. For example, here is how you can encrypt data to a file:

```
Cipher cipher = . . .;
cipher.init(Cipher.ENCRYPT_MODE, key);
var out = new CipherOutputStream(new FileOutputStream(outputFileName), cipher);
var bytes = new byte[BLOCKSIZE];
int inLength = getData(bytes); // get data from data source
while (inLength != -1)
{
   out.write(bytes, 0, inLength);
   inLength = getData(bytes); // get more data from data source
}
out.flush();
```

Similarly, you can use a CipherInputStream to read and decrypt data from a file:

```
Cipher cipher = . . .;
cipher.init(Cipher.DECRYPT_MODE, key);
var in = new CipherInputStream(new FileInputStream(inputFileName), cipher);
var bytes = new byte[BLOCKSIZE];
int inLength = in.read(bytes);
while (inLength != -1)
{
   putData(bytes, inLength); // put data to destination
   inLength = in.read(bytes);
}
```

The cipher stream classes transparently handle the calls to update and doFinal, which is clearly a convenience.

---

javax.crypto.CipherInputStream 1.4

- CipherInputStream(InputStream in, Cipher cipher)

  constructs an input stream that reads data from in and decrypts or encrypts them by using the given cipher.

- int read()
- int read(byte[] b, int off, int len)

  reads data from the input stream, which is automatically decrypted or encrypted.

---

javax.crypto.CipherOutputStream 1.4

- CipherOutputStream(OutputStream out, Cipher cipher)

  constructs an output stream that writes data to out and encrypts or decrypts them using the given cipher.

- void write(int ch)
- void write(byte[] b, int off, int len)

  writes data to the output stream, which is automatically encrypted or decrypted.

- void flush()

  flushes the cipher buffer and carries out padding if necessary.

10.5.4 Public Key Ciphers

The AES cipher that you have seen in the preceding section is a *symmetric* cipher. The same key is used for both encryption and decryption. The Achilles heel of symmetric ciphers is key distribution. If Alice sends Bob an encrypted method, Bob needs the same key that Alice used. If Alice changes the key, she needs to send Bob both the message and, through a secure channel, the new key. But perhaps she has no secure channel to Bob—which is why she encrypts her messages to him in the first place.

Public key cryptography solves that problem. In a public key cipher, Bob has a key pair consisting of a public key and a matching private key. Bob can publish the public key anywhere, but he must closely guard the private key. Alice simply uses the public key to encrypt her messages to Bob.

Actually, it's not quite that simple. All known public key algorithms are *much* slower than symmetric key algorithms such as DES or AES. It would not be practical to use a public key algorithm to encrypt large amounts of information. However, that problem can easily be overcome by combining a public key cipher with a fast symmetric cipher, like this:

1. Alice generates a random symmetric encryption key. She uses it to encrypt her plaintext.
2. Alice encrypts the symmetric key with Bob's public key.
3. Alice sends Bob both the encrypted symmetric key and the encrypted plaintext.
4. Bob uses his private key to decrypt the symmetric key.
5. Bob uses the decrypted symmetric key to decrypt the message.

Nobody but Bob can decrypt the symmetric key because only Bob has the private key for decryption. Thus, the expensive public key encryption is only applied to a small amount of key data.

The most commonly used public key algorithm is the RSA algorithm invented by Rivest, Shamir, and Adleman. Until October 2000, the algorithm was protected by a patent assigned to RSA Security, Inc. Licenses were not cheap—typically a 3% royalty, with a minimum payment of $50,000 per year. Now the algorithm is in the public domain.

To use the RSA algorithm, you need a public/private key pair. Use a KeyPairGenerator like this:

```
KeyPairGenerator pairgen = KeyPairGenerator.getInstance("RSA");
var random = new SecureRandom();
pairgen.initialize(KEYSIZE, random);
KeyPair keyPair = pairgen.generateKeyPair();
Key publicKey = keyPair.getPublic();
Key privateKey = keyPair.getPrivate();
```

The program in Listing 10.19 has three options. The -genkey option produces a key pair. The -encrypt option generates an AES key and *wraps* it with the public key.

```
Key key = . . .; // an AES key
Key publicKey = . . .; // a public RSA key
Cipher cipher = Cipher.getInstance("RSA");
cipher.init(Cipher.WRAP_MODE, publicKey);
byte[] wrappedKey = cipher.wrap(key);
```

It then produces a file that contains

*   The length of the wrapped key
*   The wrapped key bytes
*   The plaintext encrypted with the AES key

The -decrypt option decrypts such a file. To try the program, first generate the RSA keys:

```
java rsa.RSATest -genkey public.key private.key
```

Then encrypt a file:

```
java rsa.RSATest -encrypt plaintextFile encryptedFile public.key
```

Finally, decrypt it and verify that the decrypted file matches the plaintext:

```
java rsa.RSATest -decrypt encryptedFile decryptedFile private.key
```

Listing 10.19 rsa/RSATest.java

```
 1  package rsa;
 2
 3  import java.io.*;
 4  import java.security.*;
 5  import javax.crypto.*;
 6
 7  /**
 8   * This program tests the RSA cipher. Usage:<br>
 9   * java rsa.RSATest -genkey public private<br>
10   * java rsa.RSATest -encrypt plaintext encrypted public<br>
11   * java rsa.RSATest -decrypt encrypted decrypted private<br>
12   * @author Cay Horstmann
13   * @version 1.02 2018-05-01
14   */
15  public class RSATest
16  {
17     private static final int KEYSIZE = 512;
18
19     public static void main(String[] args)
20          throws IOException, GeneralSecurityException, ClassNotFoundException
21     {
22        if (args[0].equals("-genkey"))
23        {
24           KeyPairGenerator pairgen = KeyPairGenerator.getInstance("RSA");
25           var random = new SecureRandom();
26           pairgen.initialize(KEYSIZE, random);
27           KeyPair keyPair = pairgen.generateKeyPair();
28           try (var out = new ObjectOutputStream(new FileOutputStream(args[1])))
29           {
30              out.writeObject(keyPair.getPublic());
31           }
32           try (var out = new ObjectOutputStream(new FileOutputStream(args[2])))
33           {
34              out.writeObject(keyPair.getPrivate());
35           }
36        }
```

```
37      else if (args[0].equals("-encrypt"))
38      {
39         KeyGenerator keygen = KeyGenerator.getInstance("AES");
40         var random = new SecureRandom();
41         keygen.init(random);
42         SecretKey key = keygen.generateKey();
43
44         // wrap with RSA public key
45         try (var keyIn = new ObjectInputStream(new FileInputStream(args[3]));
46              var out = new DataOutputStream(new FileOutputStream(args[2]));
47              var in = new FileInputStream(args[1]) )
48         {
49            var publicKey = (Key) keyIn.readObject();
50            Cipher cipher = Cipher.getInstance("RSA");
51            cipher.init(Cipher.WRAP_MODE, publicKey);
52            byte[] wrappedKey = cipher.wrap(key);
53            out.writeInt(wrappedKey.length);
54            out.write(wrappedKey);
55
56            cipher = Cipher.getInstance("AES");
57            cipher.init(Cipher.ENCRYPT_MODE, key);
58            Util.crypt(in, out, cipher);
59         }
60      }
61      else
62      {
63         try (var in = new DataInputStream(new FileInputStream(args[1]));
64              var keyIn = new ObjectInputStream(new FileInputStream(args[3]));
65              var out = new FileOutputStream(args[2]))
66         {
67            int length = in.readInt();
68            var wrappedKey = new byte[length];
69            in.read(wrappedKey, 0, length);
70
71            // unwrap with RSA private key
72            var privateKey = (Key) keyIn.readObject();
73
74            Cipher cipher = Cipher.getInstance("RSA");
75            cipher.init(Cipher.UNWRAP_MODE, privateKey);
76            Key key = cipher.unwrap(wrappedKey, "AES", Cipher.SECRET_KEY);
77
78            cipher = Cipher.getInstance("AES");
79            cipher.init(Cipher.DECRYPT_MODE, key);
80
81            Util.crypt(in, out, cipher);
82         }
83      }
84   }
85 }
```

You have now seen how the Java security model allows controlled execution of code, which is a unique and increasingly important aspect of the Java platform. You have also seen the services for authentication and encryption that the Java library provides.

In the next chapter, we will delve into advanced Swing and graphics programming.

11

Advanced Swing and Graphics

In this chapter

In this chapter, we continue our discussion of the Swing user interface toolkit and AWT graphics from Volume I. We focus on techniques that are applicable to both client-side user interfaces and server-side generation of graphics and images. Swing has sophisticated components for rendering tables and trees. With the 2D graphics API, you can produce vector art of arbitrary complexity. The ImageIO API lets you manipulate raster images. Finally, you can use the printing API to generate printouts and PostScript files.

11.1 Tables

The JTable component displays a two-dimensional grid of objects. Tables are common in user interfaces, and the Swing team has put a lot of effort into the table control. Tables are inherently complex, but—perhaps more successfully than other Swing classes—the JTable component hides much of that complexity. You can produce fully functional tables with rich behavior by writing a few lines of code. You can also write more code and customize the display and behavior for your specific applications.

In the following sections, we will explain how to make simple tables, how the user interacts with them, and how to make some of the most common adjustments. As with the other complex Swing controls, it is impossible to cover all aspects in complete detail. For more information, look in *Graphic Java™*, *Third Edition*, by David M. Geary (Prentice Hall, 1999), or *Core Swing* by Kim Topley (Prentice Hall, 1999).

11.1.1 A Simple Table

A JTable does not store its own data but obtains them from a *table model*. The JTable class has a constructor that wraps a two-dimensional array of objects into a default model. That is the strategy that we use in our first example; later in this chapter, we will turn to table models.

Figure 11.1 shows a typical table, describing the properties of the planets of the solar system. (A planet is *gaseous* if it consists mostly of hydrogen and helium. You should take the "Color" entries with a grain of salt—that column was added because it will be useful in later code examples.)

As you can see from the code in Listing 11.1, the data of the table is stored as a two-dimensional array of Object values:

```
Object[][] cells =
{
   { "Mercury", 2440.0, 0, false, Color.YELLOW },
   { "Venus", 6052.0, 0, false, Color.YELLOW },
   . . .
}
```

Planet	Radius	Moons	Gaseous	Color
Mercury	2440.0	0	false	java.awt.C...
Venus	6052.0	0	false	java.awt.C...
Earth	6378.0	1	false	java.awt.C...
Mars	3397.0	2	false	java.awt.C...
Jupiter	71492.0	16	true	java.awt.C...
Saturn	60268.0	18	true	java.awt.C...
Uranus	25559.0	17	true	java.awt.C...
Neptune	24766.0	8	true	java.awt.C...

Figure 11.1 A simple table

NOTE: Here, we take advantage of autoboxing. The entries in the second, third, and fourth columns are automatically converted into objects of type `Double`, `Integer`, and `Boolean`.

The table simply invokes the `toString` method on each object to display it. That's why the colors show up as java.awt.Color[r=. . .,g=. . .,b=. . .].

Supply the column names in a separate array of strings:

```
String[] columnNames = { "Planet", "Radius", "Moons", "Gaseous", "Color" };
```

Then, construct a table from the cell and column name arrays:

```
var table = new JTable(cells, columnNames);
```

You can add scroll bars in the usual way—by wrapping the table in a JScrollPane:

```
var pane = new JScrollPane(table);
```

When you scroll the table, the table header doesn't scroll out of view.

Next, click on one of the column headers and drag it to the left or right. See how the entire column becomes detached (see Figure 11.2). You can drop it in a different location. This rearranges the columns *in the view only*. The data model is not affected.

TableTest				
Planet	Radius	ons	Gaseous	Color
Mercury	2440.0		false	java.awt.C...
Venus	6052.0		false	java.awt.C...
Earth	6378.0		false	java.awt.C...
Mars	3397.0		false	java.awt.C...
Jupiter	71492.0		true	java.awt.C...
Saturn	60268.0		true	java.awt.C...
Uranus	25559.0		true	java.awt.C...
Neptune	24766.0		true	java.awt.C...

Print

Figure 11.2 Moving a column

To *resize* columns, simply place the cursor between two columns until the cursor shape changes to an arrow. Then, drag the column boundary to the desired place (see Figure 11.3).

Users can select rows by clicking anywhere in a row. The selected rows are highlighted; you will see later how to get selection events. Users can also edit the table entries by clicking on a cell and typing into it. However, in this code example, the edits do not change the underlying data. In your programs,

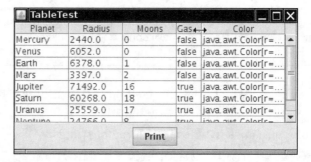

Figure 11.3 Resizing columns

you should either make cells uneditable or handle cell editing events and update your model. We will discuss those topics later in this section.

Finally, click on a column header. The rows are automatically sorted. Click again, and the sort order is reversed. This behavior is activated by the call

```
table.setAutoCreateRowSorter(true);
```

You can print a table with the call

```
table.print();
```

 CAUTION: If you don't wrap a table into a scroll pane, you need to explicitly add the header:

```
add(table.getTableHeader(), BorderLayout.NORTH);
```

Listing 11.1 table/TableTest.java

```
1  package table;
2
3  import java.awt.*;
4  import java.awt.print.*;
5
6  import javax.swing.*;
7
8  /**
9   * This program demonstrates how to show a simple table.
10  * @version 1.14 2018-05-01
11  * @author Cay Horstmann
12  */
```

```
13  public class TableTest
14  {
15     public static void main(String[] args)
16     {
17        EventQueue.invokeLater(() ->
18           {
19              var frame = new PlanetTableFrame();
20              frame.setTitle("TableTest");
21              frame.setDefaultCloseOperation(JFrame.EXIT_ON_CLOSE);
22              frame.setVisible(true);
23           });
24     }
25  }
26
27  /**
28   * This frame contains a table of planet data.
29   */
30  class PlanetTableFrame extends JFrame
31  {
32     private String[] columnNames = { "Planet", "Radius", "Moons", "Gaseous", "Color" };
33     private Object[][] cells =
34     {
35        { "Mercury", 2440.0, 0, false, Color.YELLOW },
36        { "Venus", 6052.0, 0, false, Color.YELLOW },
37        { "Earth", 6378.0, 1, false, Color.BLUE },
38        { "Mars", 3397.0, 2, false, Color.RED },
39        { "Jupiter", 71492.0, 16, true, Color.ORANGE },
40        { "Saturn", 60268.0, 18, true, Color.ORANGE },
41        { "Uranus", 25559.0, 17, true, Color.BLUE },
42        { "Neptune", 24766.0, 8, true, Color.BLUE },
43        { "Pluto", 1137.0, 1, false, Color.BLACK }
44     };
45
46     public PlanetTableFrame()
47     {
48        var table = new JTable(cells, columnNames);
49        table.setAutoCreateRowSorter(true);
50        add(new JScrollPane(table), BorderLayout.CENTER);
51        var printButton = new JButton("Print");
52        printButton.addActionListener(event ->
53           {
54              try { table.print(); }
55              catch (SecurityException | PrinterException ex) { ex.printStackTrace(); }
56           });
57        var buttonPanel = new JPanel();
58        buttonPanel.add(printButton);
59        add(buttonPanel, BorderLayout.SOUTH);
60        pack();
61     }
62  }
```

---

javax.swing.JTable 1.2

- `JTable(Object[][] entries, Object[] columnNames)`

  constructs a table with a default table model.
- `void print()` 5.0

  displays a print dialog box and prints the table.
- `boolean getAutoCreateRowSorter()` 6
- `void setAutoCreateRowSorter(boolean newValue)` 6

  gets or sets the `autoCreateRowSorter` property. The default is `false`. When set, a default row sorter is automatically set whenever the model changes.
- `boolean getFillsViewportHeight()` 6
- `void setFillsViewportHeight(boolean newValue)` 6

  gets or sets the `fillsViewportHeight` property. The default is `false`. When set, the table always fills the enclosing viewport.

11.1.2 Table Models

In the preceding example, the table data were stored in a two-dimensional array. However, you should generally not use that strategy in your own code. Instead of dumping data into an array to display it as a table, consider implementing your own table model.

Table models are particularly simple to implement because you can take advantage of the `AbstractTableModel` class that implements most of the required methods. You only need to supply three methods:

```
public int getRowCount();
public int getColumnCount();
public Object getValueAt(int row, int column);
```

There are many ways of implementing the `getValueAt` method. For example, if you want to display the contents of a `RowSet` that contains the result of a database query, simply provide this method:

```
public Object getValueAt(int r, int c)
{
   try
   {
      rowSet.absolute(r + 1);
      return rowSet.getObject(c + 1);
   }
```

```
    catch (SQLException e)
    {
        e.printStackTrace();
        return null;
    }
}
```

Our sample program is even simpler. We construct a table that shows some computed values—namely, the growth of an investment under different interest rate scenarios (see Figure 11.4).

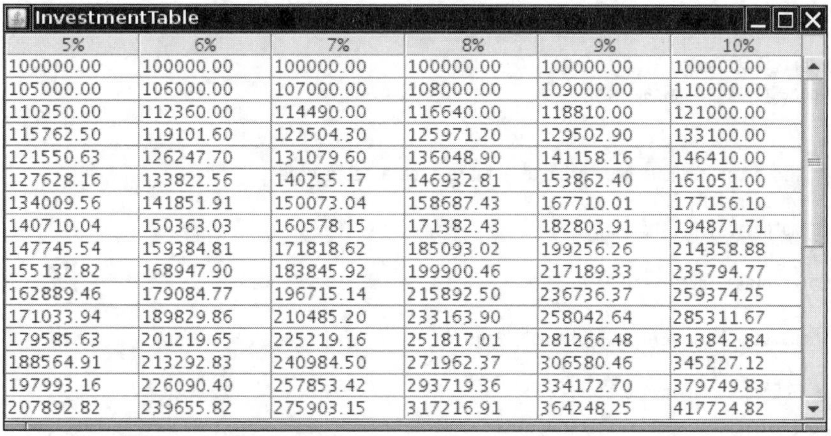

5%	6%	7%	8%	9%	10%
100000.00	100000.00	100000.00	100000.00	100000.00	100000.00
105000.00	106000.00	107000.00	108000.00	109000.00	110000.00
110250.00	112360.00	114490.00	116640.00	118810.00	121000.00
115762.50	119101.60	122504.30	125971.20	129502.90	133100.00
121550.63	126247.70	131079.60	136048.90	141158.16	146410.00
127628.16	133822.56	140255.17	146932.81	153862.40	161051.00
134009.56	141851.91	150073.04	158687.43	167710.01	177156.10
140710.04	150363.03	160578.15	171382.43	182803.91	194871.71
147745.54	159384.81	171818.62	185093.02	199256.26	214358.88
155132.82	168947.90	183845.92	199900.46	217189.33	235794.77
162889.46	179084.77	196715.14	215892.50	236736.37	259374.25
171033.94	189829.86	210485.20	233163.90	258042.64	285311.67
179585.63	201219.65	225219.16	251817.01	281266.48	313842.84
188564.91	213292.83	240984.50	271962.37	306580.46	345227.12
197993.16	226090.40	257853.42	293719.36	334172.70	379749.83
207892.82	239655.82	275903.15	317216.91	364248.25	417724.82

Figure 11.4 Growth of an investment

The getValueAt method computes the appropriate value and formats it:

```
public Object getValueAt(int r, int c)
{
    double rate = (c + minRate) / 100.0;
    int nperiods = r;
    double futureBalance = INITIAL_BALANCE * Math.pow(1 + rate, nperiods);
    return String.format("%.2f", futureBalance);
}
```

The getRowCount and getColumnCount methods simply return the number of rows and columns:

```
public int getRowCount() { return years; }
public int getColumnCount() {  return maxRate - minRate + 1; }
```

If you don't supply column names, the getColumnName method of the AbstractTableModel names the columns A, B, C, and so on. To change the default column names, override the `getColumnName` method. In this example, we simply label each column with the interest rate.

```
public String getColumnName(int c) { return (c + minRate) + "%"; }
```

You can find the complete source code in Listing 11.2.

Listing 11.2 tableModel/InvestmentTable.java

```
1  package tableModel;
2
3  import java.awt.*;
4
5  import javax.swing.*;
6  import javax.swing.table.*;
7
8  /**
9   * This program shows how to build a table from a table model.
10  * @version 1.04 2018-05-01
11  * @author Cay Horstmann
12  */
13 public class InvestmentTable
14 {
15    public static void main(String[] args)
16    {
17       EventQueue.invokeLater(() ->
18          {
19             var frame = new InvestmentTableFrame();
20             frame.setTitle("InvestmentTable");
21             frame.setDefaultCloseOperation(JFrame.EXIT_ON_CLOSE);
22             frame.setVisible(true);
23          });
24    }
25 }
26
27 /**
28  * This frame contains the investment table.
29  */
30 class InvestmentTableFrame extends JFrame
31 {
32    public InvestmentTableFrame()
33    {
34       var model = new InvestmentTableModel(30, 5, 10);
35       var table = new JTable(model);
36       add(new JScrollPane(table));
37       pack();
38    }
39 }
40
```

```
41  /**
42   * This table model computes the cell entries each time they are requested. The table contents
43   * shows the growth of an investment for a number of years under different interest rates.
44   */
45  class InvestmentTableModel extends AbstractTableModel
46  {
47     private static double INITIAL_BALANCE = 100000.0;
48
49     private int years;
50     private int minRate;
51     private int maxRate;
52
53     /**
54      * Constructs an investment table model.
55      * @param y the number of years
56      * @param r1 the lowest interest rate to tabulate
57      * @param r2 the highest interest rate to tabulate
58      */
59     public InvestmentTableModel(int y, int r1, int r2)
60     {
61        years = y;
62        minRate = r1;
63        maxRate = r2;
64     }
65
66     public int getRowCount()
67     {
68        return years;
69     }
70
71     public int getColumnCount()
72     {
73        return maxRate - minRate + 1;
74     }
75
76     public Object getValueAt(int r, int c)
77     {
78        double rate = (c + minRate) / 100.0;
79        int nperiods = r;
80        double futureBalance = INITIAL_BALANCE * Math.pow(1 + rate, nperiods);
81        return String.format("%.2f", futureBalance);
82     }
83
84     public String getColumnName(int c)
85     {
86        return (c + minRate) + "%";
87     }
88  }
```

---

javax.swing.table.TableModel 1.2

- `int getRowCount()`
- `int getColumnCount()`

  gets the number of rows and columns in the table model.

- `Object getValueAt(int row, int column)`

  gets the value at the given row and column.

- `void setValueAt(Object newValue, int row, int column)`

  sets a new value at the given row and column.

- `boolean isCellEditable(int row, int column)`

  returns true if the cell at the given row and column is editable.

- `String getColumnName(int column)`

  gets the column title.

11.1.3 Working with Rows and Columns

In this subsection, you will see how to manipulate the rows and columns in a table. As you read through this material, keep in mind that a Swing table is quite asymmetric—the operations that you can carry out on rows and columns are different. The table component was optimized to display rows of information with the same structure, such as the result of a database query, not an arbitrary two-dimensional grid of objects. You will see this asymmetry throughout this subsection.

11.1.3.1 Column Classes

In the next example, we again display our planet data, but this time we want to give the table more information about the column types. This is achieved by defining the method

```
Class<?> getColumnClass(int columnIndex)
```

of the table model to return the class that describes the column type.

The `JTable` class uses this information to pick an appropriate renderer for the class. Table 11.1 shows the default rendering actions.

You can see the checkboxes and images in Figure 11.5. (Thanks to Jim Evins for providing the planet images!)

To render other types, you can install a custom renderer—see Section 11.1.4, "Cell Rendering and Editing," on p. 639.

Table 11.1 Default Rendering Actions

Type	Rendered As
Boolean	Checkbox
Icon	Image
Object	String

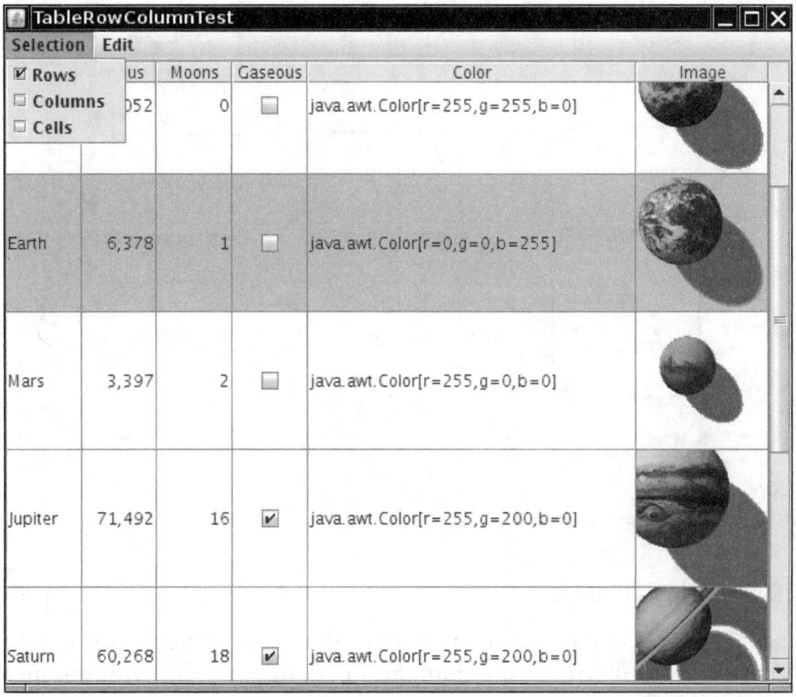

Figure 11.5 A table with planet data

11.1.3.2 Accessing Table Columns

The JTable class stores information about table columns in objects of type TableColumn. A TableColumnModel object manages the columns. (Figure 11.6 shows the relationships among the most important table classes.) If you don't want to insert or remove columns dynamically, you won't use the column model much. The most common use for the column model is simply to get a TableColumn object:

```
int columnIndex = . . .;
TableColumn column = table.getColumnModel().getColumn(columnIndex);
```

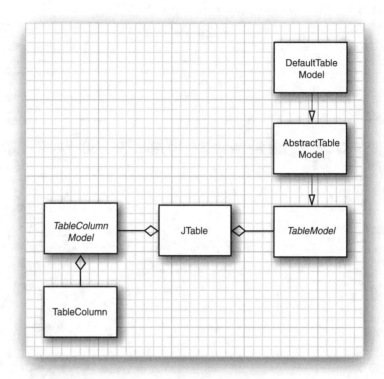

Figure 11.6 Relationship between table classes

11.1.3.3 Resizing Columns

The TableColumn class gives you control over the resizing behavior of columns. You can set the preferred, minimum, and maximum width with the methods

```
void setPreferredWidth(int width)
void setMinWidth(int width)
void setMaxWidth(int width)
```

This information is used by the table component to lay out the columns.

Use the method

```
void setResizable(boolean resizable)
```

to control whether the user is allowed to resize the column.

You can programmatically resize a column with the method

```
void setWidth(int width)
```

When a column is resized, the default is to leave the total size of the table unchanged. Of course, the width increase or decrease of the resized column must then be distributed over other columns. The default behavior is to change the size of all columns to the right of the resized column. That's a good default because it allows a user to adjust all columns to a desired width, moving from left to right.

You can set another behavior from Table 11.2 by using the method

```
void setAutoResizeMode(int mode)
```

of the JTable class.

Table 11.2 Resize Modes

Mode	Behavior
AUTO_RESIZE_OFF	Don't resize other columns; change the table width.
AUTO_RESIZE_NEXT_COLUMN	Resize the next column only.
AUTO_RESIZE_SUBSEQUENT_COLUMNS	Resize all subsequent columns equally; this is the default behavior.
AUTO_RESIZE_LAST_COLUMN	Resize the last column only.
AUTO_RESIZE_ALL_COLUMNS	Resize all columns in the table; this is not a good choice because it prevents the user from adjusting multiple columns to a desired size.

11.1.3.4 Resizing Rows

Row heights are managed directly by the JTable class. If your cells are taller than the default, you may want to set the row height:

```
table.setRowHeight(height);
```

By default, all rows of the table have the same height. You can set the heights of individual rows with the call

```
table.setRowHeight(row, height);
```

The actual row height equals the row height set with these methods, reduced by the row margin. The default row margin is 1 pixel, but you can change it with the call

```
table.setRowMargin(margin);
```

11.1.3.5 Selecting Rows, Columns, and Cells

Depending on the selection mode, the user can select rows, columns, or individual cells in the table. By default, row selection is enabled. Clicking inside a cell selects the entire row (see Figure 11.5). Call

```
table.setRowSelectionAllowed(false);
```

to disable row selection.

When row selection is enabled, you can control whether the user is allowed to select a single row, a contiguous set of rows, or any set of rows. You need to retrieve the *selection model* and use its setSelectionMode method:

```
table.getSelectionModel().setSelectionMode(mode);
```

Here, mode is one of the three values:

```
ListSelectionModel.SINGLE_SELECTION
ListSelectionModel.SINGLE_INTERVAL_SELECTION
ListSelectionModel.MULTIPLE_INTERVAL_SELECTION
```

Column selection is disabled by default. You can turn it on with the call

```
table.setColumnSelectionAllowed(true);
```

Enabling both row and column selection is equivalent to enabling cell selection. The user then selects ranges of cells (see Figure 11.7). You can also enable that setting with the call

```
table.setCellSelectionEnabled(true);
```

Run the program in Listing 11.3 to watch cell selection in action. Enable row, column, or cell selection in the Selection menu and watch how the selection behavior changes.

You can find out which rows and columns are selected by calling the getSelectedRows and getSelectedColumns methods. Both return an int[] array of the indexes of the selected items. Note that the index values are those of the table view, not the underlying table model. Try selecting rows and columns, then drag columns to different places and sort the rows by clicking on column headers. Use the Print Selection menu item to see which rows and columns are reported as selected.

If you need to translate the table index values to table model index values, use the JTable methods convertRowIndexToModel and convertColumnIndexToModel.

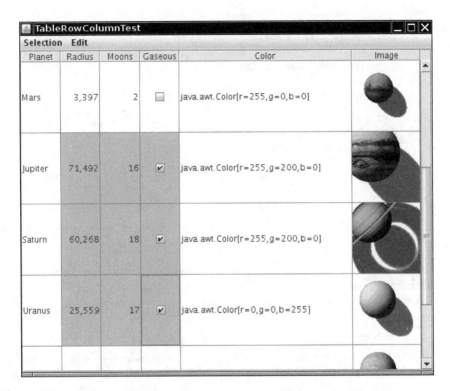

Figure 11.7 Selecting a range of cells

11.1.3.6 Sorting Rows

As you have seen in our first table example, it is easy to add row sorting to a JTable simply by calling the setAutoCreateRowSorter method. However, to have finer-grained control over the sorting behavior, install a TableRowSorter<M> object into a JTable and customize it. The type parameter M denotes the table model; it needs to be a subtype of the TableModel interface.

```
var sorter = new TableRowSorter<TableModel>(model);
table.setRowSorter(sorter);
```

Some columns should not be sortable, such as the image column in our planet data. Turn sorting off by calling

```
sorter.setSortable(IMAGE_COLUMN, false);
```

You can install a custom comparator for each column. In our example, we will sort the colors in the Color column by preferring blue and green over red. When you click on the Color column, you will see that the blue planets go to the bottom of the table. This is achieved with the following call:

```
sorter.setComparator(COLOR_COLUMN, new Comparator<Color>()
   {
      public int compare(Color c1, Color c2)
      {
         int d = c1.getBlue() - c2.getBlue();
         if (d != 0) return d;
         d = c1.getGreen() - c2.getGreen();
         if (d != 0) return d;
         return c1.getRed() - c2.getRed();
      }
   });
```

If you do not specify a comparator for a column, the sort order is determined as follows:

1. If the column class is String, use the default collator returned by Collator.getInstance(). It sorts strings in a way that is appropriate for the current locale. (See Chapter 7 for more information about locales and collators.)

2. If the column class implements Comparable, use its compareTo method.

3. If a TableStringConverter has been set for the sorter, sort the strings returned by the converter's toString method with the default collator. If you want to use this approach, define a converter as follows:

```
sorter.setStringConverter(new TableStringConverter()
   {
      public String toString(TableModel model, int row, int column)
      {
         Object value = model.getValueAt(row, column);
         convert value to a string and return it
      }
   });
```

4. Otherwise, call the toString method on the cell values and sort them with the default collator.

11.1.3.7 Filtering Rows

In addition to sorting rows, the TableRowSorter can also selectively hide rows—a process called *filtering*. To activate filtering, set a RowFilter. For example, to include all rows that contain at least one moon, call

```
sorter.setRowFilter(RowFilter.numberFilter(ComparisonType.NOT_EQUAL, 0, MOONS_COLUMN));
```

Here, we use a predefined number filter. To construct a number filter, supply

- The comparison type (one of EQUAL, NOT_EQUAL, AFTER, or BEFORE).
- An object of a subclass of Number (such as an Integer or Double). Only objects that have the same class as the given Number object are considered.
- Zero or more column index values. If no index values are supplied, all columns are searched.

The static RowFilter.dateFilter method constructs a date filter in the same way; you need to supply a Date object instead of the Number object.

Finally, the static RowFilter.regexFilter method constructs a filter that looks for strings matching a regular expression. For example,

```
sorter.setRowFilter(RowFilter.regexFilter(".*[^s]$", PLANET_COLUMN));
```

only displays those planets whose name doesn't end with an "s". (See Chapter 2 for more information on regular expressions.)

You can also combine filters with the andFilter, orFilter, and notFilter methods. To filter for planets not ending in an "s" with at least one moon, you can use this filter combination:

```
sorter.setRowFilter(RowFilter.andFilter(List.of(
   RowFilter.regexFilter(".*[^s]$", PLANET_COLUMN),
   RowFilter.numberFilter(ComparisonType.NOT_EQUAL, 0, MOONS_COLUMN))));
```

To implement your own filter, provide a subclass of RowFilter and implement an include method to indicate which rows should be displayed. This is easy to do, but the glorious generality of the RowFilter class makes it a bit scary.

The RowFilter<M, I> class has two type parameters—the types for the model and for the row identifier. When dealing with tables, the model is always a subtype of TableModel and the identifier type is Integer. (At some point in the future, other components might also support row filtering. For example, to filter rows in a JTree, one might use a RowFilter<TreeModel, TreePath>.)

A row filter must implement the method

```
public boolean include(RowFilter.Entry<? extends M, ? extends I> entry)
```

The RowFilter.Entry class supplies methods to obtain the model, the row identifier, and the value at a given index. Therefore, you can filter both by row identifier and by the contents of the row.

For example, this filter displays every other row:

```
var filter = new RowFilter<TableModel, Integer>()
{
   public boolean include(Entry<? extends TableModel, ? extends Integer> entry)
   {
      return entry.getIdentifier() % 2 == 0;
   }
};
```

If you wanted to include only those planets with an even number of moons, you would instead test for

```
((Integer) entry.getValue(MOONS_COLUMN)) % 2 == 0
```

In our sample program, we allow the user to hide arbitrary rows. We store the hidden row indexes in a set. The row filter shows all rows whose indexes are not in that set.

The filtering mechanism wasn't designed for filters with criteria changing over time. In our sample program, we keep calling

```
sorter.setRowFilter(filter);
```

whenever the set of hidden rows changes. Setting a filter causes it to be applied immediately.

11.1.3.8 Hiding and Displaying Columns

As you saw in the preceding section, you can filter table rows by either their contents or their row identifier. Hiding table columns uses a completely different mechanism.

The removeColumn method of the JTable class removes a column from the table view. The column data are not actually removed from the model—they are just hidden from view. The removeColumn method takes a TableColumn argument. If you have the column number (for example, from a call to getSelectedColumns), you need to ask the table model for the actual table column object:

```
TableColumnModel columnModel = table.getColumnModel();
TableColumn column = columnModel.getColumn(i);
table.removeColumn(column);
```

If you remember the column, you can later add it back in:

```
table.addColumn(column);
```

This method adds the column to the end. If you want it to appear elsewhere, call the moveColumn method.

You can also add a new column that corresponds to a column index in the table model, by adding a new TableColumn object:

```
table.addColumn(new TableColumn(modelColumnIndex));
```

You can have multiple table columns that view the same column of the model.

The program in Listing 11.3 demonstrates selection and filtering of rows and columns.

Listing 11.3 tableRowColumn/PlanetTableFrame.java

```
1  package tableRowColumn;
2
3  import java.awt.*;
4  import java.util.*;
5
6  import javax.swing.*;
7  import javax.swing.table.*;
8
9  /**
10  * This frame contains a table of planet data.
11  */
12 public class PlanetTableFrame extends JFrame
13 {
14    private static final int DEFAULT_WIDTH = 600;
15    private static final int DEFAULT_HEIGHT = 500;
16
17    public static final int COLOR_COLUMN = 4;
18    public static final int IMAGE_COLUMN = 5;
19
20    private JTable table;
21    private HashSet<Integer> removedRowIndices;
22    private ArrayList<TableColumn> removedColumns;
23    private JCheckBoxMenuItem rowsItem;
24    private JCheckBoxMenuItem columnsItem;
25    private JCheckBoxMenuItem cellsItem;
26
27    private String[] columnNames = { "Planet", "Radius", "Moons", "Gaseous", "Color", "Image" };
28
29    private Object[][] cells =
30    {
31       { "Mercury", 2440.0, 0, false, Color.YELLOW,
32          new ImageIcon(getClass().getResource("Mercury.gif")) },
33       { "Venus", 6052.0, 0, false, Color.YELLOW,
34          new ImageIcon(getClass().getResource("Venus.gif")) },
35       { "Earth", 6378.0, 1, false, Color.BLUE,
36          new ImageIcon(getClass().getResource("Earth.gif")) },
37       { "Mars", 3397.0, 2, false, Color.RED,
38          new ImageIcon(getClass().getResource("Mars.gif")) },
```

(Continues)

Listing 11.3 *(Continued)*

```
39        { "Jupiter", 71492.0, 16, true, Color.ORANGE,
40           new ImageIcon(getClass().getResource("Jupiter.gif")) },
41        { "Saturn", 60268.0, 18, true, Color.ORANGE,
42           new ImageIcon(getClass().getResource("Saturn.gif")) },
43        { "Uranus", 25559.0, 17, true, Color.BLUE,
44           new ImageIcon(getClass().getResource("Uranus.gif")) },
45        { "Neptune", 24766.0, 8, true, Color.BLUE,
46           new ImageIcon(getClass().getResource("Neptune.gif")) },
47        { "Pluto", 1137.0, 1, false, Color.BLACK,
48           new ImageIcon(getClass().getResource("Pluto.gif")) }
49     };
50
51     public PlanetTableFrame()
52     {
53        setSize(DEFAULT_WIDTH, DEFAULT_HEIGHT);
54
55        var model = new DefaultTableModel(cells, columnNames)
56           {
57              public Class<?> getColumnClass(int c)
58              {
59                 return cells[0][c].getClass();
60              }
61           };
62
63        table = new JTable(model);
64
65        table.setRowHeight(100);
66        table.getColumnModel().getColumn(COLOR_COLUMN).setMinWidth(250);
67        table.getColumnModel().getColumn(IMAGE_COLUMN).setMinWidth(100);
68
69        var sorter = new TableRowSorter<TableModel>(model);
70        table.setRowSorter(sorter);
71        sorter.setComparator(COLOR_COLUMN, Comparator.comparing(Color::getBlue)
72           .thenComparing(Color::getGreen).thenComparing(Color::getRed));
73        sorter.setSortable(IMAGE_COLUMN, false);
74        add(new JScrollPane(table), BorderLayout.CENTER);
75
76        removedRowIndices = new HashSet<>();
77        removedColumns = new ArrayList<>();
78
79        var filter = new RowFilter<TableModel, Integer>()
80           {
81              public boolean include(Entry<? extends TableModel, ? extends Integer> entry)
82              {
83                 return !removedRowIndices.contains(entry.getIdentifier());
84              }
85           };
86
```

```
87      // create menu
88
89      var menuBar = new JMenuBar();
90      setJMenuBar(menuBar);
91
92      var selectionMenu = new JMenu("Selection");
93      menuBar.add(selectionMenu);
94
95      rowsItem = new JCheckBoxMenuItem("Rows");
96      columnsItem = new JCheckBoxMenuItem("Columns");
97      cellsItem = new JCheckBoxMenuItem("Cells");
98
99      rowsItem.setSelected(table.getRowSelectionAllowed());
100     columnsItem.setSelected(table.getColumnSelectionAllowed());
101     cellsItem.setSelected(table.getCellSelectionEnabled());
102
103     rowsItem.addActionListener(event ->
104        {
105           table.clearSelection();
106           table.setRowSelectionAllowed(rowsItem.isSelected());
107           updateCheckboxMenuItems();
108        });
109     selectionMenu.add(rowsItem);
110
111     columnsItem.addActionListener(event ->
112        {
113           table.clearSelection();
114           table.setColumnSelectionAllowed(columnsItem.isSelected());
115           updateCheckboxMenuItems();
116        });
117     selectionMenu.add(columnsItem);
118
119     cellsItem.addActionListener(event ->
120        {
121           table.clearSelection();
122           table.setCellSelectionEnabled(cellsItem.isSelected());
123           updateCheckboxMenuItems();
124        });
125     selectionMenu.add(cellsItem);
126
127     var tableMenu = new JMenu("Edit");
128     menuBar.add(tableMenu);
129
130     var hideColumnsItem = new JMenuItem("Hide Columns");
131     hideColumnsItem.addActionListener(event ->
132        {
133           int[] selected = table.getSelectedColumns();
134           TableColumnModel columnModel = table.getColumnModel();
135
```

(Continues)

Listing 11.3 *(Continued)*

```
136            // remove columns from view, starting at the last
137            // index so that column numbers aren't affected
138
139            for (int i = selected.length - 1; i >= 0; i--)
140            {
141               TableColumn column = columnModel.getColumn(selected[i]);
142               table.removeColumn(column);
143
144               // store removed columns for "show columns" command
145
146               removedColumns.add(column);
147            }
148         });
149      tableMenu.add(hideColumnsItem);
150
151      var showColumnsItem = new JMenuItem("Show Columns");
152      showColumnsItem.addActionListener(event ->
153         {
154            // restore all removed columns
155            for (TableColumn tc : removedColumns)
156               table.addColumn(tc);
157            removedColumns.clear();
158         });
159      tableMenu.add(showColumnsItem);
160
161      var hideRowsItem = new JMenuItem("Hide Rows");
162      hideRowsItem.addActionListener(event ->
163         {
164            int[] selected = table.getSelectedRows();
165            for (int i : selected)
166               removedRowIndices.add(table.convertRowIndexToModel(i));
167            sorter.setRowFilter(filter);
168         });
169      tableMenu.add(hideRowsItem);
170
171      var showRowsItem = new JMenuItem("Show Rows");
172      showRowsItem.addActionListener(event ->
173         {
174            removedRowIndices.clear();
175            sorter.setRowFilter(filter);
176         });
177      tableMenu.add(showRowsItem);
178
179      var printSelectionItem = new JMenuItem("Print Selection");
180      printSelectionItem.addActionListener(event ->
181         {
182            int[] selected = table.getSelectedRows();
183            System.out.println("Selected rows: " + Arrays.toString(selected));
```

```
184            selected = table.getSelectedColumns();
185            System.out.println("Selected columns: " + Arrays.toString(selected));
186        });
187     tableMenu.add(printSelectionItem);
188  }
189
190  private void updateCheckboxMenuItems()
191  {
192     rowsItem.setSelected(table.getRowSelectionAllowed());
193     columnsItem.setSelected(table.getColumnSelectionAllowed());
194     cellsItem.setSelected(table.getCellSelectionEnabled());
195  }
196 }
```

---

javax.swing.table.TableModel 1.2

- Class getColumnClass(int columnIndex)

  gets the class for the values in this column. This information is used for sorting and rendering.

---

javax.swing.JTable 1.2

- TableColumnModel getColumnModel()

  gets the column model that describes the arrangement of the table columns.

- void setAutoResizeMode(int mode)

  sets the mode for automatic resizing of table columns.

  Parameters: mode   One of AUTO_RESIZE_OFF, AUTO_RESIZE_NEXT_COLUMN,
                                      AUTO_RESIZE_SUBSEQUENT_COLUMNS, AUTO_RESIZE_LAST_COLUMN,
                                      and AUTO_RESIZE_ALL_COLUMNS

- int getRowMargin()
- void setRowMargin(int margin)

  gets or sets the amount of empty space between cells in adjacent rows.

- int getRowHeight()
- void setRowHeight(int height)

  gets or sets the default height of all rows of the table.

- int getRowHeight(int row)
- void setRowHeight(int row, int height)

  gets or sets the height of the given row of the table.

(Continues)

`javax.swing.JTable` 1.2 *(Continued)*

- `ListSelectionModel getSelectionModel()`

  returns the list selection model. You need that model to choose between row, column, and cell selection.

- `boolean getRowSelectionAllowed()`
- `void setRowSelectionAllowed(boolean b)`

  gets or sets the rowSelectionAllowed property. If true, rows are selected when the user clicks on cells.

- `boolean getColumnSelectionAllowed()`
- `void setColumnSelectionAllowed(boolean b)`

  gets or sets the columnSelectionAllowed property. If true, columns are selected when the user clicks on cells.

- `boolean getCellSelectionEnabled()`

  returns true if both rowSelectionAllowed and columnSelectionAllowed are true.

- `void setCellSelectionEnabled(boolean b)`

  sets both rowSelectionAllowed and columnSelectionAllowed to b.

- `void addColumn(TableColumn column)`

  adds a column as the last column of the table view.

- `void moveColumn(int from, int to)`

  moves the column whose table index is from so that its index becomes to. Only the view is affected.

- `void removeColumn(TableColumn column)`

  removes the given column from the view.

- `int convertRowIndexToModel(int index)` 6
- `int convertColumnIndexToModel(int index)`

  returns the model index of the row or column with the given index. This value is different from index when rows are sorted or filtered, or when columns are moved or removed.

- `void setRowSorter(RowSorter<? extends TableModel> sorter)`

  sets the row sorter.

`javax.swing.table.TableColumnModel` 1.2

- `TableColumn getColumn(int index)`

  gets the table column object that describes the column with the given view index.

---

javax.swing.table.TableColumn 1.2

- TableColumn(int modelColumnIndex)

  constructs a table column for viewing the model column with the given index.
- void setPreferredWidth(int width)
- void setMinWidth(int width)
- void setMaxWidth(int width)

  sets the preferred, minimum, and maximum width of this table column to width.
- void setWidth(int width)

  sets the actual width of this column to width.
- void setResizable(boolean b)

  If b is true, this column is resizable.

---

javax.swing.ListSelectionModel 1.2

- void setSelectionMode(int mode)

  Parameters: mode   One of SINGLE_SELECTION, SINGLE_INTERVAL_SELECTION, and
  MULTIPLE_INTERVAL_SELECTION

---

javax.swing.DefaultRowSorter<M, I> 6

- void setComparator(int column, Comparator<?> comparator)

  sets the comparator to be used with the given column.
- void setSortable(int column, boolean enabled)

  enables or disables sorting for the given column.
- void setRowFilter(RowFilter<? super M,? super I> filter)

  sets the row filter.

---

javax.swing.table.TableRowSorter<M extends TableModel> 6

- void setStringConverter(TableStringConverter stringConverter)

  sets the string converter used for sorting and filtering.

---

javax.swing.table.TableStringConverter 6

- abstract String toString(TableModel model, int row, int column)

  converts the model value at the given location to a string; you can override
  this method.

---

javax.swing.RowFilter<M, I> 6

- `boolean include(RowFilter.Entry<? extends M,? extends I> entry)`

  specifies the rows that are retained; you can override this method.

- `static <M,I> RowFilter<M,I> numberFilter(RowFilter.ComparisonType type, Number number, int... indices)`
- `static <M,I> RowFilter<M,I> dateFilter(RowFilter.ComparisonType type, Date date, int... indices)`

  returns a filter that includes rows containing values that match the given comparison to the given number or date. The comparison type is one of EQUAL, NOT_EQUAL, AFTER, or BEFORE. If any column model indexes are given, only those columns are searched; otherwise, all columns are searched. For the number filter, the class of the cell value must match the class of number.

- `static <M,I> RowFilter<M,I> regexFilter(String regex, int... indices)`

  returns a filter that includes rows that have a string value matching the given regular expression. If any column model indexes are given, only those columns are searched; otherwise, all columns are searched. Note that the string returned by the getStringValue method of RowFilter.Entry is matched.

- `static <M,I> RowFilter<M,I> andFilter(Iterable<? extends RowFilter<? super M,? super I>> filters)`
- `static <M,I> RowFilter<M,I> orFilter(Iterable<? extends RowFilter<? super M,? super I>> filters)`

  returns a filter that includes the entries included by all filters, or at least one of the filters.

- `static <M,I> RowFilter<M,I> notFilter(RowFilter<M,I> filter)`

  returns a filter that includes the entries not included by the given filter.

---

javax.swing.RowFilter.Entry<M, I> 6

- `I getIdentifier()`

  returns the identifier of this row entry.

- `M getModel()`

  returns the model of this row entry.

- `Object getValue(int index)`

  returns the value stored at the given index of this row.

(Continues)

javax.swing.RowFilter.Entry<M, I> 6 *(Continued)*

- `int getValueCount()`

  returns the number of values stored in this row.

- `String getStringValue()`

  returns the value stored at the given index of this row, converted to a string. The TableRowSorter produces entries whose getStringValue calls the sorter's string converter.

11.1.4 Cell Rendering and Editing

As you saw in Section 11.1.3.2, "Accessing Table Columns," on p. 623, the column type determines how the cells are rendered. There are default renderers for the types Boolean and Icon that render a checkbox or icon. For all other types, you need to install a custom renderer.

11.1.4.1 Rendering Cells

Table cell renderers are similar to the list cell renderers that you saw earlier. They implement the TableCellRenderer interface that has a single method:

```
Component getTableCellRendererComponent(JTable table, Object value,
    boolean isSelected, boolean hasFocus, int row, int column)
```

That method is called when the table needs to draw a cell. You return a component whose paint method is then invoked to fill the cell area.

The table in Figure 11.8 contains cells of type Color. The renderer simply returns a panel with a background color that is the color object stored in the cell. The color is passed as the value parameter.

```
class ColorTableCellRenderer extends JPanel implements TableCellRenderer
{
    public Component getTableCellRendererComponent(JTable table, Object value,
        boolean isSelected, boolean hasFocus, int row, int column)
    {
        setBackground((Color) value);
        if (hasFocus)
            setBorder(UIManager.getBorder("Table.focusCellHighlightBorder"));
        else
            setBorder(null);
        return this;
    }
}
```

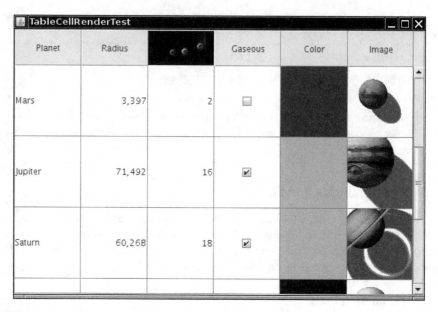

Figure 11.8 A table with cell renderers

As you can see, the renderer draws a border when the cell has focus. (We ask the `UIManager` for the correct border. To find the lookup key, we peeked into the source code of the `DefaultTableCellRenderer` class.)

 TIP: If your renderer simply draws a text string or an icon, you can extend the `DefaultTableCellRenderer` class. It takes care of rendering the focus and selection status for you.

You need to tell the table to use this renderer with all objects of type `Color`. The `setDefaultRenderer` method of the `JTable` class lets you establish this association. Supply a `Class` object and the renderer:

```
table.setDefaultRenderer(Color.class, new ColorTableCellRenderer());
```

That renderer is now used for all objects of the given type in this table.

If you want to select a renderer based on some other criterion, you need to subclass the `JTable` class and override the `getCellRenderer` method.

11.1.4.2 Rendering the Header

To display an icon in the header, set the header value:

```
moonColumn.setHeaderValue(new ImageIcon("Moons.gif"));
```

However, the table header isn't smart enough to choose an appropriate renderer for the header value. You have to install the renderer manually. For example, to show an image icon in a column header, call

```
moonColumn.setHeaderRenderer(table.getDefaultRenderer(ImageIcon.class));
```

11.1.4.3 Editing Cells

To enable cell editing, the table model must indicate which cells are editable by defining the isCellEditable method. Most commonly, you will want to make certain columns editable. In the example program, we allow editing in four columns.

```
public boolean isCellEditable(int r, int c)
{
   return c == PLANET_COLUMN || c == MOONS_COLUMN || c == GASEOUS_COLUMN
      || c == COLOR_COLUMN;
}
```

 NOTE: The AbstractTableModel defines the isCellEditable method to always return false. The DefaultTableModel overrides the method to always return true.

If you run the program (Listings 11.4 to 11.7), note that you can click the checkboxes in the Gaseous column and turn the check marks on and off. If you click a cell in the Moons column, a combo box appears (see Figure 11.9). You will shortly see how to install such a combo box as a cell editor.

Finally, click a cell in the first column. The cell gains focus. You can start typing, and the cell contents change.

What you just saw in action are the three variations of the DefaultCellEditor class. A DefaultCellEditor can be constructed with a JTextField, a JCheckBox, or a JComboBox. The JTable class automatically installs a checkbox editor for Boolean cells and a text field editor for all editable cells that don't supply their own renderer. The text fields let the user edit the strings that result from applying toString to the return value of the getValueAt method of the table model.

When the edit is complete, the edited value is retrieved by calling the getCellEditorValue method of your editor. That method should return a value of the correct type (that is, the type returned by the getColumnType method of the model).

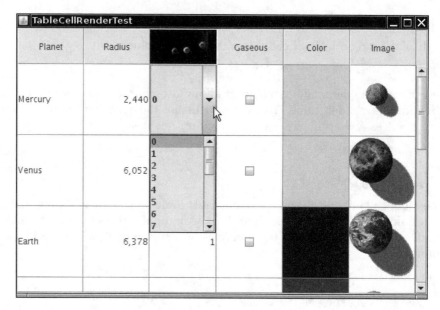

Figure 11.9 A cell editor

To get a combo box editor, set a cell editor manually—the JTable component has no idea what values might be appropriate for a particular type. For the Moons column, we wanted to enable the user to pick any value between 0 and 20. Here is the code for initializing the combo box:

```
var moonCombo = new JComboBox();
for (int i = 0; i <= 20; i++)
    moonCombo.addItem(i);
```

To construct a DefaultCellEditor, supply the combo box in the constructor:

```
var moonEditor = new DefaultCellEditor(moonCombo);
```

Next, we need to install the editor. Unlike the color cell renderer, this editor does not depend on the object *type*—we don't necessarily want to use it for all objects of type Integer. Instead, we need to install it into a particular column:

```
moonColumn.setCellEditor(moonEditor);
```

11.1.4.4 Custom Editors

Run the example program again and click a color. A *color chooser* pops up and lets you pick a new color for the planet. Select a color and click OK. The cell color is updated (see Figure 11.10).

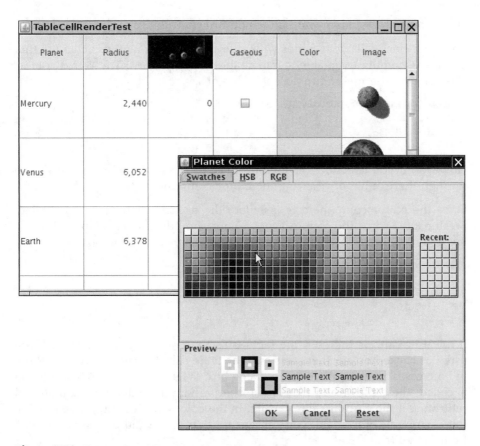

Figure 11.10 Editing the cell color with a color chooser

The color cell editor is not a standard table cell editor but a custom implementation. To create a custom cell editor, implement the TableCellEditor interface. That interface is a bit tedious, and as of Java SE 1.3, an AbstractCellEditor class is provided to take care of the event handling details.

The getTableCellEditorComponent method of the TableCellEditor interface requests a component to render the cell. It is exactly the same as the getTableCellRendererComponent method of the TableCellRenderer interface, except that there is no focus parameter. When the cell is being edited, it is presumed to have focus. The editor component temporarily *replaces* the renderer when the editing is in progress. In our example, we return a blank panel that is not colored. This is an indication to the user that the cell is currently being edited.

Next, you want to have your editor pop up when the user clicks on the cell.

The JTable class calls your editor with an event (such as a mouse click) to find out if that event is acceptable to initiate the editing process. The AbstractCellEditor class defines the method to accept all events.

```
public boolean isCellEditable(EventObject anEvent)
{
   return true;
}
```

However, if you override this method to return false, the table would not go through the trouble of inserting the editor component.

Once the editor component is installed, the shouldSelectCell method is called, presumably with the same event. You should initiate editing in this method—for example, by popping up an external edit dialog box.

```
public boolean shouldSelectCell(EventObject anEvent)
{
   colorDialog.setVisible(true);
   return true;
}
```

If the user cancels the edit, the table calls the cancelCellEditing method. If the user has clicked on another table cell, the table calls the stopCellEditing method. In both cases, you should hide the dialog box. When your stopCellEditing method is called, the table would like to use the partially edited value. You should return true if the current value is valid. In the color chooser, any value is valid. But if you edit other data, you can ensure that only valid data are retrieved from the editor.

Also, you should call the superclass methods that take care of event firing—otherwise, the editing won't be properly canceled.

```
public void cancelCellEditing()
{
   colorDialog.setVisible(false);
   super.cancelCellEditing();
}
```

Finally, you need a method that yields the value that the user supplied in the editing process:

```
public Object getCellEditorValue()
{
   return colorChooser.getColor();
}
```

To summarize, your custom editor should do the following:

1. Extend the AbstractCellEditor class and implement the TableCellEditor interface.
2. Define the getTableCellEditorComponent method to supply a component. This can either be a dummy component (if you pop up a dialog box) or a component for in-place editing such as a combo box or text field.
3. Define the shouldSelectCell, stopCellEditing, and cancelCellEditing methods to handle the start, completion, and cancellation of the editing process. The stopCellEditing and cancelCellEditing methods should call the superclass methods to ensure that listeners are notified.
4. Define the getCellEditorValue method to return the value that is the result of the editing process.

Finally, indicate when the user is finished editing by calling the stopCellEditing and cancelCellEditing methods. When constructing the color dialog box, we install the accept and cancel callbacks that fire these events.

```
colorDialog = JColorChooser.createDialog(null, "Planet Color", false, colorChooser,
    EventHandler.create(ActionListener.class, this, "stopCellEditing"),
    EventHandler.create(ActionListener.class, this, "cancelCellEditing"));
```

This completes the implementation of the custom editor.

You now know how to make a cell editable and how to install an editor. There is one remaining issue—how to update the model with the value that the user edited. When editing is complete, the JTable class calls the following method of the table model:

```
void setValueAt(Object value, int r, int c)
```

You need to override the method to store the new value. The value parameter is the object that was returned by the cell editor. If you implemented the cell editor, you know the type of the object you return from the getCellEditorValue method. In the case of the DefaultCellEditor, there are three possibilities for that value. It is a Boolean if the cell editor is a checkbox, a string if it is a text field, and, if the value comes from a combo box, it is the object that the user selected.

If the value object does not have the appropriate type, you need to convert it. That happens most commonly when a number is edited in a text field. In our example, we populated the combo box with Integer objects so that no conversion is necessary.

Listing 11.4 tableCellRender/TableCellRenderFrame.java

```
 1  package tableCellRender;
 2
 3  import java.awt.*;
 4  import javax.swing.*;
 5  import javax.swing.table.*;
 6
 7  /**
 8   * This frame contains a table of planet data.
 9   */
10  public class TableCellRenderFrame extends JFrame
11  {
12     private static final int DEFAULT_WIDTH = 600;
13     private static final int DEFAULT_HEIGHT = 400;
14
15     public TableCellRenderFrame()
16     {
17        setSize(DEFAULT_WIDTH, DEFAULT_HEIGHT);
18
19        var model = new PlanetTableModel();
20        var table = new JTable(model);
21        table.setRowSelectionAllowed(false);
22
23        // set up renderers and editors
24
25        table.setDefaultRenderer(Color.class, new ColorTableCellRenderer());
26        table.setDefaultEditor(Color.class, new ColorTableCellEditor());
27
28        var moonCombo = new JComboBox<Integer>();
29        for (int i = 0; i <= 20; i++)
30           moonCombo.addItem(i);
31
32        TableColumnModel columnModel = table.getColumnModel();
33        TableColumn moonColumn = columnModel.getColumn(PlanetTableModel.MOONS_COLUMN);
34        moonColumn.setCellEditor(new DefaultCellEditor(moonCombo));
35        moonColumn.setHeaderRenderer(table.getDefaultRenderer(ImageIcon.class));
36        moonColumn.setHeaderValue(new ImageIcon(getClass().getResource("Moons.gif")));
37
38        // show table
39
40        table.setRowHeight(100);
41        add(new JScrollPane(table), BorderLayout.CENTER);
42     }
43  }
```

Listing 11.5 tableCellRender/PlanetTableModel.java

```java
1  package tableCellRender;
2
3  import java.awt.*;
4  import javax.swing.*;
5  import javax.swing.table.*;
6
7  /**
8   * The planet table model specifies the values, rendering and editing properties for the
9   * planet data.
10  */
11 public class PlanetTableModel extends AbstractTableModel
12 {
13    public static final int PLANET_COLUMN = 0;
14    public static final int MOONS_COLUMN = 2;
15    public static final int GASEOUS_COLUMN = 3;
16    public static final int COLOR_COLUMN = 4;
17
18    private Object[][] cells =
19    {
20       { "Mercury", 2440.0, 0, false, Color.YELLOW,
21          new ImageIcon(getClass().getResource("Mercury.gif")) },
22       { "Venus", 6052.0, 0, false, Color.YELLOW,
23          new ImageIcon(getClass().getResource("Venus.gif")) },
24       { "Earth", 6378.0, 1, false, Color.BLUE,
25          new ImageIcon(getClass().getResource("Earth.gif")) },
26       { "Mars", 3397.0, 2, false, Color.RED,
27          new ImageIcon(getClass().getResource("Mars.gif")) },
28       { "Jupiter", 71492.0, 16, true, Color.ORANGE,
29          new ImageIcon(getClass().getResource("Jupiter.gif")) },
30       { "Saturn", 60268.0, 18, true, Color.ORANGE,
31          new ImageIcon(getClass().getResource("Saturn.gif")) },
32       { "Uranus", 25559.0, 17, true, Color.BLUE,
33          new ImageIcon(getClass().getResource("Uranus.gif")) },
34       { "Neptune", 24766.0, 8, true, Color.BLUE,
35          new ImageIcon(getClass().getResource("Neptune.gif")) },
36       { "Pluto", 1137.0, 1, false, Color.BLACK,
37          new ImageIcon(getClass().getResource("Pluto.gif")) }
38    };
39
40    private String[] columnNames = { "Planet", "Radius", "Moons", "Gaseous",
41       "Color", "Image" };
42
43    public String getColumnName(int c)
44    {
45       return columnNames[c];
46    }
47
```

(Continues)

Listing 11.5 *(Continued)*

```
48    public Class<?> getColumnClass(int c)
49    {
50        return cells[0][c].getClass();
51    }
52
53    public int getColumnCount()
54    {
55        return cells[0].length;
56    }
57
58    public int getRowCount()
59    {
60        return cells.length;
61    }
62
63    public Object getValueAt(int r, int c)
64    {
65        return cells[r][c];
66    }
67
68    public void setValueAt(Object obj, int r, int c)
69    {
70        cells[r][c] = obj;
71    }
72
73    public boolean isCellEditable(int r, int c)
74    {
75        return c == PLANET_COLUMN || c == MOONS_COLUMN || c == GASEOUS_COLUMN
76            || c == COLOR_COLUMN;
77    }
78 }
```

Listing 11.6 tableCellRender/ColorTableCellRenderer.java

```
1 package tableCellRender;
2
3 import java.awt.*;
4 import javax.swing.*;
5 import javax.swing.table.*;
6
7 /**
8  * This renderer renders a color value as a panel with the given color.
9  */
10 public class ColorTableCellRenderer extends JPanel implements TableCellRenderer
11 {
```

```
12   public Component getTableCellRendererComponent(JTable table, Object value,
13        boolean isSelected, boolean hasFocus, int row, int column)
14   {
15      setBackground((Color) value);
16      if (hasFocus) setBorder(UIManager.getBorder("Table.focusCellHighlightBorder"));
17      else setBorder(null);
18      return this;
19   }
20 }
```

Listing 11.7 tableCellRender/ColorTableCellEditor.java

```
1  package tableCellRender;
2
3  import java.awt.*;
4  import java.awt.event.*;
5  import java.beans.*;
6  import java.util.*;
7  import javax.swing.*;
8  import javax.swing.table.*;
9
10 /**
11  * This editor pops up a color dialog to edit a cell value.
12  */
13 public class ColorTableCellEditor extends AbstractCellEditor implements TableCellEditor
14 {
15    private JColorChooser colorChooser;
16    private JDialog colorDialog;
17    private JPanel panel;
18
19    public ColorTableCellEditor()
20    {
21       panel = new JPanel();
22       // prepare color dialog
23
24       colorChooser = new JColorChooser();
25       colorDialog = JColorChooser.createDialog(null, "Planet Color", false, colorChooser,
26             EventHandler.create(ActionListener.class, this, "stopCellEditing"),
27             EventHandler.create(ActionListener.class, this, "cancelCellEditing"));
28    }
29
30    public Component getTableCellEditorComponent(JTable table, Object value,
31          boolean isSelected, int row, int column)
32    {
33       // this is where we get the current Color value. We store it in the dialog in case the
34       // user starts editing
```

(Continues)

Listing 11.7 *(Continued)*

```
35        colorChooser.setColor((Color) value);
36        return panel;
37     }
38
39     public boolean shouldSelectCell(EventObject anEvent)
40     {
41        // start editing
42        colorDialog.setVisible(true);
43
44        // tell caller it is ok to select this cell
45        return true;
46     }
47
48     public void cancelCellEditing()
49     {
50        // editing is canceled--hide dialog
51        colorDialog.setVisible(false);
52        super.cancelCellEditing();
53     }
54
55     public boolean stopCellEditing()
56     {
57        // editing is complete--hide dialog
58        colorDialog.setVisible(false);
59        super.stopCellEditing();
60
61        // tell caller is is ok to use color value
62        return true;
63     }
64
65     public Object getCellEditorValue()
66     {
67        return colorChooser.getColor();
68     }
69  }
```

---

javax.swing.JTable 1.2

- TableCellRenderer getDefaultRenderer(Class<?> type)

  gets the default renderer for the given type.

- TableCellEditor getDefaultEditor(Class<?> type)

  gets the default editor for the given type.

---

javax.swing.table.TableCellRenderer 1.2

- Component getTableCellRendererComponent(JTable table, Object value, boolean selected, boolean hasFocus, int row, int column)

  returns a component whose paint method is invoked to render a table cell.

Parameters:	table	The table containing the cell to be rendered
	value	The cell to be rendered
	selected	true if the cell is currently selected
	hasFocus	true if the cell currently has focus
	row, column	The row and column of the cell

---

javax.swing.table.TableColumn 1.2

- void setCellEditor(TableCellEditor editor)
- void setCellRenderer(TableCellRenderer renderer)

  sets the cell editor or renderer for all cells in this column.

- void setHeaderRenderer(TableCellRenderer renderer)

  sets the cell renderer for the header cell in this column.

- void setHeaderValue(Object value)

  sets the value to be displayed for the header in this column.

---

javax.swing.DefaultCellEditor 1.2

- DefaultCellEditor(JComboBox comboBox)

  constructs a cell editor that presents the combo box for selecting cell values.

---

javax.swing.table.TableCellEditor 1.2

- Component getTableCellEditorComponent(JTable table, Object value, boolean selected, int row, int column)

  returns a component whose paint method renders a table cell.

Parameters:	table	The table containing the cell to be rendered
	value	The cell to be rendered
	selected	true if the cell is currently selected
	row, column	The row and column of the cell

---

javax.swing.CellEditor 1.2

- boolean isCellEditable(EventObject event)

  returns true if the event is suitable for initiating the editing process for this cell.

- boolean shouldSelectCell(EventObject anEvent)

  starts the editing process. Returns true if the edited cell should be *selected*. Normally, you want to return true, but you can return false if you don't want the editing process to change the cell selection.

- void cancelCellEditing()

  cancels the editing process. You can abandon partial edits.

- boolean stopCellEditing()

  stops the editing process, with the intent of using the result. Returns true if the edited value is in a proper state for retrieval.

- Object getCellEditorValue()

  returns the edited result.

- void addCellEditorListener(CellEditorListener l)
- void removeCellEditorListener(CellEditorListener l)

  adds or removes the obligatory cell editor listener.

11.2 Trees

Every computer user who has worked with a hierarchical file system has seen tree displays. Of course, directories and files are only one of the many examples of tree-like organizations. Many tree structures arise in everyday life, such as the hierarchy of countries, states, and cities shown in Figure 11.11.

As programmers, we often need to display tree structures. Fortunately, the Swing library has a JTree class for this purpose. The JTree class (together with its helper classes) takes care of laying out the tree and processing user requests for expanding and collapsing nodes. In this section, you will learn how to put the JTree class to use.

As with the other complex Swing components, we must focus on the common and useful cases and cannot cover every nuance. If you want to achieve something unusual, we recommend that you consult *Graphic Java*™, *Third Edition*, by David M. Geary or *Core Swing* by Kim Topley.

Before going any further, let's settle on some terminology (see Figure 11.12). A *tree* is composed of *nodes*. Every node is either a *leaf* or it has *child nodes*. Every node, with the exception of the root node, has exactly one *parent*. A tree has exactly one root node. Sometimes you have a collection of trees, each with its own root node. Such a collection is called a *forest*.

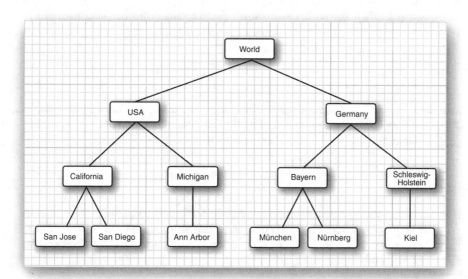

Figure 11.11 A hierarchy of countries, states, and cities

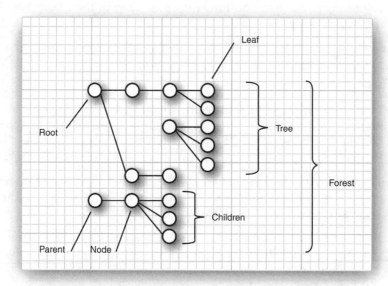

Figure 11.12 Tree terminology

11.2.1 Simple Trees

In our first example program, we will simply display a tree with a few nodes (see Figure 11.14). As with many other Swing components, you need to provide a model of the data, and the component displays it for you. To construct a JTree, supply the tree model in the constructor:

```
TreeModel model = . . .;
var tree = new JTree(model);
```

 NOTE: There are also constructors that construct trees out of a collection of elements:

```
JTree(Object[] nodes)
JTree(Vector<?> nodes)
JTree(Hashtable<?, ?> nodes) // the values become the nodes
```

These constructors are not very useful. They merely build a forest of trees, each with a single node. The third constructor seems particularly useless because the nodes appear in the seemingly random order determined by the hash codes of the keys.

How do you obtain a tree model? You can construct your own model by creating a class that implements the TreeModel interface. You will see later in this chapter how to do that. For now, we will stick with the DefaultTreeModel that the Swing library supplies.

To construct a default tree model, you must supply a root node.

```
TreeNode root = . . .;
var model = new DefaultTreeModel(root);
```

TreeNode is another interface. Populate the default tree model with objects of any class that implements the interface. For now, we will use the concrete node class that Swing supplies—namely, DefaultMutableTreeNode. This class implements the MutableTreeNode interface, a subinterface of TreeNode (see Figure 11.13).

A default mutable tree node holds an object—the *user object*. The tree renders the user objects for all nodes. Unless you specify a renderer, the tree displays the string that is the result of the toString method.

In our first example, we use strings as user objects. In practice, you would usually populate a tree with more expressive user objects. For example, when displaying a directory tree, it makes sense to use File objects for the nodes.

You can specify the user object in the constructor, or you can set it later with the setUserObject method.

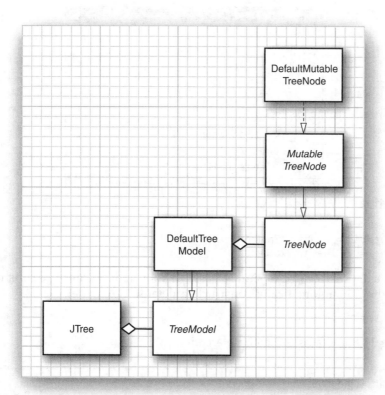

Figure 11.13 Tree classes

```
var node = new DefaultMutableTreeNode("Texas");
. . .
node.setUserObject("California");
```

Next, you need to establish the parent/child relationships between the nodes.
Start with the root node and use the add method to add the children:

```
var root = new DefaultMutableTreeNode("World");
var country = new DefaultMutableTreeNode("USA");
root.add(country);
var state = new DefaultMutableTreeNode("California");
country.add(state);
```

Figure 11.14 illustrates how the tree will look.

Link up all nodes in this fashion. Then, construct a DefaultTreeModel with the
root node. Finally, construct a JTree with the tree model.

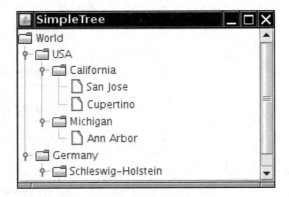

Figure 11.14 A simple tree

```
var treeModel = new DefaultTreeModel(root);
var tree = new JTree(treeModel);
```

Or, as a shortcut, you can simply pass the root node to the JTree constructor. Then the tree automatically constructs a default tree model:

```
var tree = new JTree(root);
```

Listing 11.8 contains the complete code.

Listing 11.8 tree/SimpleTreeFrame.java

```
 1 package tree;
 2
 3 import javax.swing.*;
 4 import javax.swing.tree.*;
 5
 6 /**
 7  * This frame contains a simple tree that displays a manually constructed tree model.
 8  */
 9 public class SimpleTreeFrame extends JFrame
10 {
11     private static final int DEFAULT_WIDTH = 300;
12     private static final int DEFAULT_HEIGHT = 200;
13
14     public SimpleTreeFrame()
15     {
16         setSize(DEFAULT_WIDTH, DEFAULT_HEIGHT);
17
18         // set up tree model data
19
20         var root = new DefaultMutableTreeNode("World");
21         var country = new DefaultMutableTreeNode("USA");
```

```
22        root.add(country);
23        var state = new DefaultMutableTreeNode("California");
24        country.add(state);
25        var city = new DefaultMutableTreeNode("San Jose");
26        state.add(city);
27        city = new DefaultMutableTreeNode("Cupertino");
28        state.add(city);
29        state = new DefaultMutableTreeNode("Michigan");
30        country.add(state);
31        city = new DefaultMutableTreeNode("Ann Arbor");
32        state.add(city);
33        country = new DefaultMutableTreeNode("Germany");
34        root.add(country);
35        state = new DefaultMutableTreeNode("Schleswig-Holstein");
36        country.add(state);
37        city = new DefaultMutableTreeNode("Kiel");
38        state.add(city);
39
40        // construct tree and put it in a scroll pane
41
42        var tree = new JTree(root);
43        add(new JScrollPane(tree));
44      }
45  }
```

When you run the program, the tree first looks as in Figure 11.15. Only the root node and its children are visible. Click on the circle icons (the *handles*) to open up the subtrees. The line sticking out from the handle icon points to the right when the subtree is collapsed and down when the subtree is expanded (see Figure 11.16). We don't know what the designers of the Metal look-and-feel had in mind, but we think of the icon as a door handle. You push down on the handle to open the subtree.

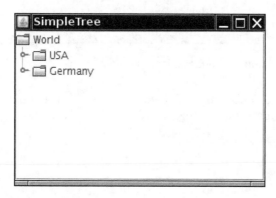

Figure 11.15 The initial tree display

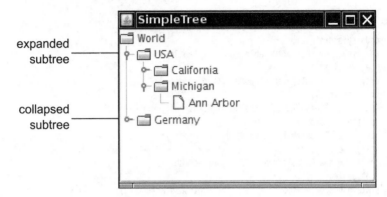

expanded subtree

collapsed subtree

Figure 11.16 Collapsed and expanded subtrees

NOTE: Of course, the display of the tree depends on the selected look-and-feel. We just described the Metal look-and-feel. In the Windows look-and-feel, the handles have the more familiar look—a "–" or "+" in a box (see Figure 11.17).

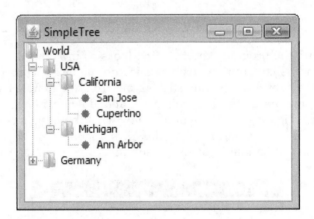

Figure 11.17 A tree with the Windows look-and-feel

You can use the following magic incantation to turn off the lines joining parents and children (see Figure 11.18):

```
tree.putClientProperty("JTree.lineStyle", "None");
```

Figure 11.18 A tree with no connecting lines

Conversely, to make sure that the lines are shown, use

```
tree.putClientProperty("JTree.lineStyle", "Angled");
```

Another line style, "Horizontal", is shown in Figure 11.19. The tree is displayed with horizontal lines separating only the children of the root. We aren't quite sure what it is good for.

Figure 11.19 A tree with the horizontal line style

By default, there is no handle for collapsing the root of the tree. If you like, you can add one with the call

```
tree.setShowsRootHandles(true);
```

Figure 11.20 shows the result. Now you can collapse the entire tree into the root node.

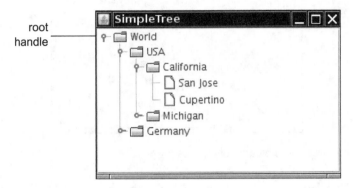

Figure 11.20 A tree with a root handle

Conversely, you can hide the root altogether. You will thus display a *forest*—a set of trees, each with its own root. You still must join all trees in the forest to a common root; then, hide the root with the instruction

```
tree.setRootVisible(false);
```

Look at Figure 11.21. There appear to be two roots, labeled "USA" and "Germany." The actual root that joins the two is made invisible.

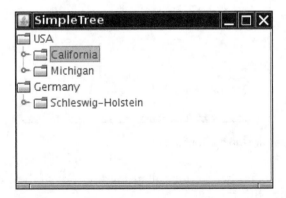

Figure 11.21 A forest

Let's turn from the root to the leaves of the tree. Note that the leaves have an icon different from the other nodes (see Figure 11.22).

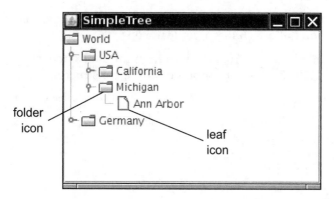

Figure 11.22 Leaf and folder icons

When the tree is displayed, each node is drawn with an icon. There are actually three kinds of icons: a leaf icon, an opened nonleaf icon, and a closed nonleaf icon. For simplicity, we refer to the last two as folder icons.

The node renderer needs to know which icon to use for each node. By default, the decision process works like this: If the isLeaf method of a node returns true, then the leaf icon is used; otherwise, a folder icon is used.

The isLeaf method of the DefaultMutableTreeNode class returns true if the node has no children. Thus, nodes with children get folder icons, and nodes without children get leaf icons.

Sometimes, that behavior is not appropriate. Suppose we added a node "Montana" to our sample tree, but we're at a loss as to what cities to add. We would not want the state node to get a leaf icon because, conceptually, only the cities are leaves.

The JTree class has no idea which nodes should be leaves. It asks the tree model. If a childless node isn't automatically a conceptual leaf, you can ask the tree model to use a different criterion for leafiness—namely, to query the "allows children" node property.

For those nodes that should not have children, call

```
node.setAllowsChildren(false);
```

Then, tell the tree model to ask the value of the "allows children" property to determine whether a node should be displayed with a leaf icon. Use the setAsksAllowsChildren method of the DefaultTreeModel class to set this behavior:

```
model.setAsksAllowsChildren(true);
```

With this decision criterion, nodes that allow children get folder icons, and nodes that don't allow children get leaf icons.

Alternatively, if you construct the tree from the root node, supply the setting for the "asks allows children" property in the constructor.

```
var tree = new JTree(root, true); // nodes that don't allow children get leaf icons
```

---

javax.swing.JTree 1.2

- JTree(TreeModel model)

  constructs a tree from a tree model.

- JTree(TreeNode root)
- JTree(TreeNode root, boolean asksAllowChildren)

  constructs a tree with a default tree model that displays the root and its children.

Parameters:	root	The root node
	asksAllowsChildren	true to use the "allows children" node property for determining whether a node is a leaf

- void setShowsRootHandles(boolean b)

  if b is true, the root node has a handle for collapsing or expanding its children.

- void setRootVisible(boolean b)

  if b is true, then the root node is displayed. Otherwise, it is hidden.

---

javax.swing.tree.TreeNode 1.2

- boolean isLeaf()

  returns true if this node is conceptually a leaf.

- boolean getAllowsChildren()

  returns true if this node can have child nodes.

---

javax.swing.tree.MutableTreeNode 1.2

- void setUserObject(Object userObject)

  sets the "user object" that the tree node uses for rendering.

---

javax.swing.tree.TreeModel 1.2

- boolean isLeaf(Object node)

  returns true if node should be displayed as a leaf node.

---

javax.swing.tree.DefaultTreeModel 1.2

- void setAsksAllowsChildren(boolean b)

  if b is true, nodes are displayed as leaves when their getAllowsChildren method returns false. Otherwise, they are displayed as leaves when their isLeaf method returns true.

---

javax.swing.tree.DefaultMutableTreeNode 1.2

- DefaultMutableTreeNode(Object userObject)

  constructs a mutable tree node with the given user object.

- void add(MutableTreeNode child)

  adds a node as the last child of this node.

- void setAllowsChildren(boolean b)

  if b is true, children can be added to this node.

---

javax.swing.JComponent 1.2

- void putClientProperty(Object key, Object value)

  adds a key/value pair to a small table that each component manages. This is an "escape hatch" mechanism that some Swing components use for storing properties specific to a look-and-feel.

11.2.1.1 Editing Trees and Tree Paths

In the next example program, you will see how to edit a tree. Figure 11.23 shows the user interface. If you click the Add Sibling or Add Child button, the program adds a new node (with title New) to the tree. If you click the Delete button, the program deletes the currently selected node.

To implement this behavior, you need to find out which tree node is currently selected. The JTree class has a surprising way of identifying nodes in a tree. It does not deal with tree nodes but with *paths of objects*, called *tree paths*. A

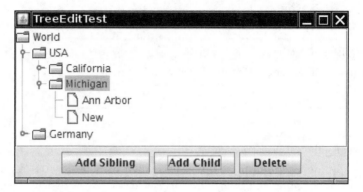

Figure 11.23 Editing a tree

tree path starts at the root and consists of a sequence of child nodes (see Figure 11.24).

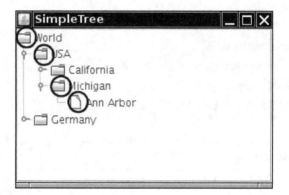

Figure 11.24 A tree path

You might wonder why the JTree class needs the whole path. Couldn't it just get a TreeNode and keep calling the getParent method? In fact, the JTree class knows nothing about the TreeNode interface. That interface is never used by the TreeModel interface; it is only used by the DefaultTreeModel implementation. You can have other tree models in which the nodes do not implement the TreeNode interface at all. If you use a tree model that manages other types of objects, those objects might not have getParent and getChild methods. They would of course need to have some other connection to each other. It is the job of the tree model to link nodes together. The JTree class itself has no clue about the nature of their linkage. For that reason, the JTree class always needs to work with complete paths.

The TreePath class manages a sequence of Object (not TreeNode!) references. A number of JTree methods return TreePath objects. When you have a tree path, you usually just need to know the terminal node, which you can get with the getLastPathComponent method. For example, to find out the currently selected node in a tree, use the getSelectionPath method of the JTree class. You will get a TreePath object back, from which you can retrieve the actual node.

```
TreePath selectionPath = tree.getSelectionPath();
var selectedNode = (DefaultMutableTreeNode) selectionPath.getLastPathComponent();
```

Actually, since this particular query is so common, there is a convenience method that gives the selected node immediately:

```
var selectedNode = (DefaultMutableTreeNode) tree.getLastSelectedPathComponent();
```

This method is not called getSelectedNode because the tree does not know that it contains nodes—its tree model deals only with paths of objects.

> **NOTE:** Tree paths are one of the two ways in which the JTree class describes nodes. Quite a few JTree methods take or return an integer index—the *row position*. A row position is simply the row number (starting with 0) of the node in the tree display. Only visible nodes have row numbers, and the row number of a node changes if other nodes before it are expanded, collapsed, or modified. For that reason, you should avoid row positions. All JTree methods that use row positions have equivalents that use tree paths instead.

Once you have the selected node, you can edit it. However, do not simply add children to a tree node:

```
selectedNode.add(newNode); // No!
```

If you change the structure of the nodes, you change the model but the associated view is not notified. You could send out a notification yourself, but if you use the insertNodeInto method of the DefaultTreeModel class, the model class takes care of that. For example, the following call appends a new node as the last child of the selected node and notifies the tree view:

```
model.insertNodeInto(newNode, selectedNode, selectedNode.getChildCount());
```

The analogous call removeNodeFromParent removes a node and notifies the view:

```
model.removeNodeFromParent(selectedNode);
```

If you keep the node structure in place but change the user object, you should call the following method:

```
model.nodeChanged(changedNode);
```

The automatic notification is a major advantage of using the DefaultTreeModel. If you supply your own tree model, you have to implement automatic notification by hand. (See *Core Swing* by Kim Topley for details.)

CAUTION: The DefaultTreeModel class has a reload method that reloads the entire model. However, don't call reload simply to update the tree after making a few changes. When the tree is regenerated, all nodes beyond the root's children are collapsed again. It will be quite disconcerting to your users if they have to keep expanding the tree after every change.

When the view is notified of a change in the node structure, it updates the display but does not automatically expand a node to show newly added children. In particular, if a user in our sample program adds a new child node to a node for which children are currently collapsed, the new node is silently added to the collapsed subtree. This gives the user no feedback that the command was actually carried out. In such a case, you should make a special effort to expand all parent nodes so that the newly added node becomes visible. Use the makeVisible method of the JTree class for this purpose. The makeVisible method expects a tree path leading to the node that should become visible.

Thus, you need to construct a tree path from the root to the newly inserted node. To get a tree path, first call the getPathToRoot method of the DefaultTreeModel class. It returns a TreeNode[] array of all nodes from a node to the root node. Pass that array to a TreePath constructor.

For example, here is how you make the new node visible:

```
TreeNode[] nodes = model.getPathToRoot(newNode);
var path = new TreePath(nodes);
tree.makeVisible(path);
```

NOTE: It is curious that the DefaultTreeModel class feigns almost complete ignorance of the TreePath class, even though its job is to communicate with a JTree. The JTree class uses tree paths a lot, and it never uses arrays of node objects.

Now, suppose your tree is contained inside a scroll pane. After the tree node expansion, the new node might still not be visible because it falls outside the viewport. To overcome that problem, call

```
tree.scrollPathToVisible(path);
```

instead of calling makeVisible. This call expands all nodes along the path and tells the ambient scroll pane to scroll the node at the end of the path into view (see Figure 11.25).

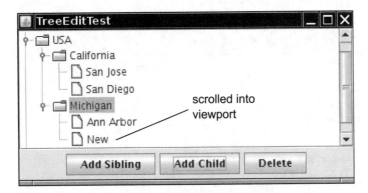

Figure 11.25 The scroll pane scrolls to display a new node.

By default, tree nodes cannot be edited. However, if you call

```
tree.setEditable(true);
```

the user can edit a node simply by double-clicking, editing the string, and pressing the Enter key. Double-clicking invokes the *default cell editor*, which is implemented by the DefaultCellEditor class (see Figure 11.26). It is possible to install other cell editors, using the same process that you have seen in our discussion of table cell editors.

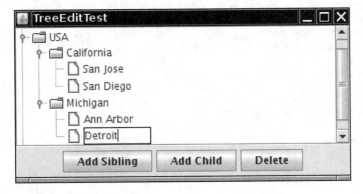

Figure 11.26 The default cell editor

Listing 11.9 shows the complete source code of the tree editing program. Run the program, add a few nodes, and edit them by double-clicking. Observe how collapsed nodes expand to show added children and how the scroll pane keeps added nodes in the viewport.

Listing 11.9 treeEdit/TreeEditFrame.java

```java
1   package treeEdit;
2
3   import java.awt.*;
4   import javax.swing.*;
5   import javax.swing.tree.*;
6
7   /**
8    * A frame with a tree and buttons to edit the tree.
9    */
10  public class TreeEditFrame extends JFrame
11  {
12     private static final int DEFAULT_WIDTH = 400;
13     private static final int DEFAULT_HEIGHT = 200;
14
15     private DefaultTreeModel model;
16     private JTree tree;
17
18     public TreeEditFrame()
19     {
20        setSize(DEFAULT_WIDTH, DEFAULT_HEIGHT);
21
22        // construct tree
23
24        TreeNode root = makeSampleTree();
25        model = new DefaultTreeModel(root);
26        tree = new JTree(model);
27        tree.setEditable(true);
28
29        // add scroll pane with tree
30
31        var scrollPane = new JScrollPane(tree);
32        add(scrollPane, BorderLayout.CENTER);
33
34        makeButtons();
35     }
36
37     public TreeNode makeSampleTree()
38     {
39        var root = new DefaultMutableTreeNode("World");
40        var country = new DefaultMutableTreeNode("USA");
41        root.add(country);
42        var state = new DefaultMutableTreeNode("California");
```

```
43        country.add(state);
44        var city = new DefaultMutableTreeNode("San Jose");
45        state.add(city);
46        city = new DefaultMutableTreeNode("San Diego");
47        state.add(city);
48        state = new DefaultMutableTreeNode("Michigan");
49        country.add(state);
50        city = new DefaultMutableTreeNode("Ann Arbor");
51        state.add(city);
52        country = new DefaultMutableTreeNode("Germany");
53        root.add(country);
54        state = new DefaultMutableTreeNode("Schleswig-Holstein");
55        country.add(state);
56        city = new DefaultMutableTreeNode("Kiel");
57        state.add(city);
58        return root;
59     }
60
61     /**
62      * Makes the buttons to add a sibling, add a child, and delete a node.
63      */
64     public void makeButtons()
65     {
66        var panel = new JPanel();
67        var addSiblingButton = new JButton("Add Sibling");
68        addSiblingButton.addActionListener(event ->
69           {
70              var selectedNode = (DefaultMutableTreeNode) tree.getLastSelectedPathComponent();
71
72              if (selectedNode == null) return;
73
74              var parent = (DefaultMutableTreeNode) selectedNode.getParent();
75
76              if (parent == null) return;
77
78              var newNode = new DefaultMutableTreeNode("New");
79
80              int selectedIndex = parent.getIndex(selectedNode);
81              model.insertNodeInto(newNode, parent, selectedIndex + 1);
82
83              // now display new node
84
85              TreeNode[] nodes = model.getPathToRoot(newNode);
86              var path = new TreePath(nodes);
87              tree.scrollPathToVisible(path);
88           });
89        panel.add(addSiblingButton);
90
91        var addChildButton = new JButton("Add Child");
```

(Continues)

Listing 11.9 *(Continued)*

```
92      addChildButton.addActionListener(event ->
93         {
94            var selectedNode = (DefaultMutableTreeNode) tree.getLastSelectedPathComponent();
95
96            if (selectedNode == null) return;
97
98            var newNode = new DefaultMutableTreeNode("New");
99            model.insertNodeInto(newNode, selectedNode, selectedNode.getChildCount());
100
101           // now display new node
102
103           TreeNode[] nodes = model.getPathToRoot(newNode);
104           var path = new TreePath(nodes);
105           tree.scrollPathToVisible(path);
106        });
107     panel.add(addChildButton);
108
109     var deleteButton = new JButton("Delete");
110     deleteButton.addActionListener(event ->
111        {
112           var selectedNode = (DefaultMutableTreeNode) tree.getLastSelectedPathComponent();
113
114           if (selectedNode != null && selectedNode.getParent() != null) model
115              .removeNodeFromParent(selectedNode);
116        });
117     panel.add(deleteButton);
118     add(panel, BorderLayout.SOUTH);
119  }
120 }
```

---

javax.swing.JTree 1.2

- TreePath getSelectionPath()

  gets the path to the currently selected node, or the path to the first selected node if multiple nodes are selected. Returns null if no node is selected.

- Object getLastSelectedPathComponent()

  gets the node object that represents the currently selected node, or the first node if multiple nodes are selected. Returns null if no node is selected.

- void makeVisible(TreePath path)

  expands all nodes along the path.

- void scrollPathToVisible(TreePath path)

  expands all nodes along the path and, if the tree is contained in a scroll pane, scrolls to ensure that the last node on the path is visible.

---

javax.swing.tree.TreePath 1.2

- Object getLastPathComponent()

  gets the last object on this path—that is, the node object that the path represents.

---

javax.swing.tree.TreeNode 1.2

- TreeNode getParent()

  returns the parent node of this node.

- TreeNode getChildAt(int index)

  looks up the child node at the given index. The index must be between 0 and getChildCount() − 1.

- int getChildCount()

  returns the number of children of this node.

- Enumeration children()

  returns an enumeration object that iterates through all children of this node.

---

javax.swing.tree.DefaultTreeModel 1.2

- void insertNodeInto(MutableTreeNode newChild, MutableTreeNode parent, int index)

  inserts newChild as a new child node of parent at the given index and notifies the tree model listeners.

- void removeNodeFromParent(MutableTreeNode node)

  removes node from this model and notifies the tree model listeners.

- void nodeChanged(TreeNode node)

  notifies the tree model listeners that node has changed.

- void nodesChanged(TreeNode parent, int[] changedChildIndexes)

  notifies the tree model listeners that all child nodes of parent with the given indexes have changed.

- void reload()

  reloads all nodes into the model. This is a drastic operation that you should use only if the nodes have changed completely because of some outside influence.

11.2.2 Node Enumeration

Sometimes you need to find a node in a tree by starting at the root and visiting all children until you have found a match. The DefaultMutableTreeNode class has several convenience methods for iterating through nodes.

The breadthFirstEnumeration and depthFirstEnumeration methods return enumeration objects whose nextElement method visits all children of the current node, using either a breadth-first or depth-first traversal. Figure 11.27 shows the traversals for a sample tree—the node labels indicate the order in which the nodes are traversed.

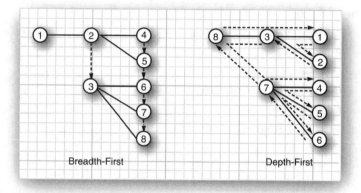

Figure 11.27 Tree traversal orders

Breadth-first enumeration is the easiest to visualize. The tree is traversed in layers. The root is visited first, followed by all of its children, then the grandchildren, and so on.

To visualize depth-first enumeration, imagine a rat trapped in a tree-shaped maze. It rushes along the first path until it comes to a leaf. Then, it backtracks and turns around to the next path, and so on.

Computer scientists also call this *postorder traversal* because the search process visits the children before visiting the parents. The postOrderEnumeration method is a synonym for depthFirstEnumeration. For completeness, there is also a preOrderEnumeration, a depth-first search that enumerates parents before the children.

Here is the typical usage pattern:

```
Enumeration breadthFirst = node.breadthFirstEnumeration();
while (breadthFirst.hasMoreElements())
    do something with breadthFirst.nextElement();
```

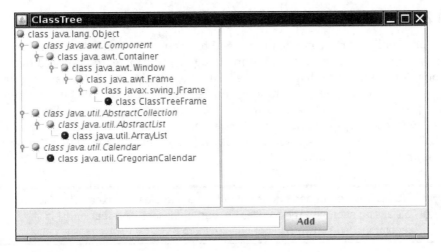

Figure 11.28 An inheritance tree

Finally, a related method, pathFromAncestorEnumeration, finds a path from an ancestor to a given node and enumerates the nodes along that path. That's no big deal— it just keeps calling getParent until the ancestor is found and then presents the path in reverse order.

In our next example program, we put node enumeration to work. The program displays inheritance trees of classes. Type the name of a class into the text field on the bottom of the frame. The class and all of its superclasses are added to the tree (see Figure 11.28).

In this example, we take advantage of the fact that the user objects of the tree nodes can be objects of any type. Since our nodes describe classes, we store Class objects in the nodes.

We don't want to add the same class object twice, so we need to check whether a class already exists in the tree. The following method finds the node with a given user object if it exists in the tree:

```
public DefaultMutableTreeNode findUserObject(Object obj)
{
   Enumeration e = root.breadthFirstEnumeration();
   while (e.hasMoreElements())
   {
      DefaultMutableTreeNode node = (DefaultMutableTreeNode) e.nextElement();
      if (node.getUserObject().equals(obj))
         return node;
   }
   return null;
}
```

11.2.3 Rendering Nodes

In your applications, you will often need to change the way a tree component draws the nodes. The most common change is, of course, to choose different icons for nodes and leaves. Other changes might involve changing the font of the node labels or drawing images at the nodes. All these changes are possible by installing a new *tree cell renderer* into the tree. By default, the JTree class uses DefaultTreeCellRenderer objects to draw each node. The DefaultTreeCellRenderer class extends the JLabel class. The label contains the node icon and the node label.

 NOTE: The cell renderer does not draw the "handles" for expanding and collapsing subtrees. The handles are part of the look-and-feel, and it is recommended that you do not change them.

You can customize the display in three ways.

- You can change the icons, font, and background color used by a DefaultTreeCellRenderer. These settings are used for all nodes in the tree.

- You can install a renderer that extends the DefaultTreeCellRenderer class and vary the icons, fonts, and background color for each node.

- You can install a renderer that implements the TreeCellRenderer interface to draw a custom image for each node.

Let us look at these possibilities one by one. The easiest customization is to construct a DefaultTreeCellRenderer object, change the icons, and install it into the tree:

```
var renderer = new DefaultTreeCellRenderer();
renderer.setLeafIcon(new ImageIcon("blue-ball.gif")); // used for leaf nodes
renderer.setClosedIcon(new ImageIcon("red-ball.gif")); // used for collapsed nodes
renderer.setOpenIcon(new ImageIcon("yellow-ball.gif")); // used for expanded nodes
tree.setCellRenderer(renderer);
```

You can see the effect in Figure 11.28. We just use the "ball" icons as place-holders—presumably your user interface designer would supply you with appropriate icons to use for your applications.

We don't recommend that you change the font or background color for an entire tree—that is really the job of the look-and-feel.

However, it can be useful to change the font of some nodes in a tree to highlight them. If you look carefully at Figure 11.28, you will notice that the *abstract* classes are set in italics.

To change the appearance of individual nodes, install a tree cell renderer. Tree cell renderers are very similar to the list cell renderers we discussed earlier in this chapter. The TreeCellRenderer interface has a single method:

```
Component getTreeCellRendererComponent(JTree tree, Object value, boolean selected,
        boolean expanded, boolean leaf, int row, boolean hasFocus)
```

The getTreeCellRendererComponent method of the DefaultTreeCellRenderer class returns this—in other words, a label. (The DefaultTreeCellRenderer class extends the JLabel class.) To customize the component, extend the DefaultTreeCellRenderer class. Override the getTreeCellRendererComponent method as follows: Call the superclass method so it can prepare the label data, customize the label properties, and finally return this.

```
class MyTreeCellRenderer extends DefaultTreeCellRenderer
{
    public Component getTreeCellRendererComponent(JTree tree, Object value, boolean selected,
        boolean expanded, boolean leaf, int row, boolean hasFocus)
    {
        Component comp = super.getTreeCellRendererComponent(tree, value, selected,
            expanded, leaf, row, hasFocus);
        DefaultMutableTreeNode node = (DefaultMutableTreeNode) value;
        look at node.getUserObject();
        Font font = appropriate font;
        comp.setFont(font);
        return comp;
    }
};
```

 CAUTION: The value parameter of the getTreeCellRendererComponent method is the *node* object, *not* the user object! Recall that the user object is a feature of the DefaultMutableTreeNode, and that a JTree can contain nodes of an arbitrary type. If your tree uses DefaultMutableTreeNode nodes, you must retrieve the user object in a second step, as we did in the preceding code sample.

 CAUTION: The DefaultTreeCellRenderer uses the *same* label object for all nodes, only changing the label text for each node. If you change the font for a particular node, you must set it back to its default value when the method is called again. Otherwise, all subsequent nodes will be drawn in the changed font! Look at the code in Listing 11.10 to see how to restore the font to the default.

The ClassNameTreeCellRenderer in Listing 11.10 sets the class name in either the normal or italic font, depending on the ABSTRACT modifier of the Class object. We don't want to set a particular font because we don't want to change whatever font the look-and-feel normally uses for labels. For that reason, we use the font from the label and *derive* an italic font from it. Recall that only a single shared `JLabel` object is returned by all calls. We need to hang on to the original font and restore it in the next call to the `getTreeCellRendererComponent` method.

Also, note how we change the node icons in the `ClassTreeFrame` constructor.

`javax.swing.tree.DefaultMutableTreeNode` 1.2

- Enumeration breadthFirstEnumeration()
- Enumeration depthFirstEnumeration()
- Enumeration preOrderEnumeration()
- Enumeration postOrderEnumeration()

returns enumeration objects for visiting all nodes of the tree model in a particular order. In breadth-first traversal, children that are closer to the root are visited before those that are farther away. In depth-first traversal, all children of a node are completely enumerated before its siblings are visited. The postOrderEnumeration method is a synonym for depthFirstEnumeration. The preorder traversal is identical to the postorder traversal except that parents are enumerated before their children.

`javax.swing.tree.TreeCellRenderer` 1.2

- Component getTreeCellRendererComponent(JTree tree, Object value, boolean selected, boolean expanded, boolean leaf, int row, boolean hasFocus)

returns a component whose paint method is invoked to render a tree cell.

Parameters:	tree	The tree containing the node to be rendered
	value	The node to be rendered
	selected	true if the node is currently selected
	expanded	true if the children of the node are visible
	leaf	true if the node needs to be displayed as a leaf
	row	The display row containing the node
	hasFocus	true if the node currently has input focus

`javax.swing.tree.DefaultTreeCellRenderer` 1.2

- void setLeafIcon(Icon icon)
- void setOpenIcon(Icon icon)
- void setClosedIcon(Icon icon)

sets the icon to show for a leaf node, an expanded node, and a collapsed node.

11.2.4 Listening to Tree Events

Most commonly, a tree component is paired with some other component. When the user selects tree nodes, some information shows up in another window. See Figure 11.29 for an example. When the user selects a class, the instance and static variables of that class are displayed in the text area to the right.

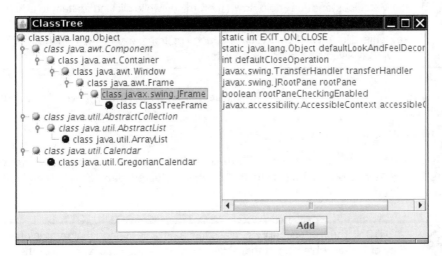

Figure 11.29 A class browser

To obtain this behavior, you need to install a *tree selection listener*. The listener must implement the TreeSelectionListener interface—an interface with a single method:

```
void valueChanged(TreeSelectionEvent event)
```

That method is called whenever the user selects or deselects tree nodes.

Add the listener to the tree in the normal way:

```
tree.addTreeSelectionListener(listener);
```

You can specify whether the user is allowed to select a single node, a contiguous range of nodes, or an arbitrary, potentially discontiguous, set of nodes. The JTree class uses a TreeSelectionModel to manage node selection. You need to retrieve the model to set the selection state to one of SINGLE_TREE_SELECTION, CONTIGUOUS_TREE_SELECTION, or DISCONTIGUOUS_TREE_SELECTION. (Discontiguous selection mode is the default.) For example, in our class browser, we want to allow selection of only a single class:

```
int mode = TreeSelectionModel.SINGLE_TREE_SELECTION;
tree.getSelectionModel().setSelectionMode(mode);
```

Apart from setting the selection mode, you need not worry about the tree selection model.

NOTE: How the user selects multiple items depends on the look-and-feel. In the Metal look-and-feel, hold down the Ctrl key while clicking an item to add it to the selection, or to remove it if it is currently selected. Hold down the Shift key while clicking an item to select a *range* of items, extending from the previously selected item to the new item.

To find out the current selection, query the tree with the getSelectionPaths method:

```
TreePath[] selectedPaths = tree.getSelectionPaths();
```

If you restricted the user to single-item selection, you can use the convenience method getSelectionPath which returns the first selected path or null if no path was selected.

CAUTION: The TreeSelectionEvent class has a getPaths method that returns an array of TreePath objects, but that array describes *selection changes*, not the current selection.

Listing 11.10 shows the frame class for the class tree program. The program displays inheritance hierarchies and customizes the display to show abstract classes in italics. (See Listing 11.11 for the cell renderer.) You can type the name of any class into the text field at the bottom of the frame. Press the Enter key or click the Add button to add the class and its superclasses to the tree. You must enter the full package name, such as java.util.ArrayList.

This program is a bit tricky because it uses reflection to construct the class tree. This work is done inside the addClass method. (The details are not that important. We use the class tree in this example because inheritance yields a nice supply of trees without laborious coding. When you display trees in your applications, you will have your own source of hierarchical data.) The method uses the breadth-first search algorithm to find whether the current class is already in the tree by calling the findUserObject method that we implemented in the preceding section. If the class is not already in the tree, we add the superclasses to the tree, then make the new class node a child and make that node visible.

When you select a tree node, the text area to the right is filled with the fields of the selected class. In the frame constructor, we restrict the user to single-item selection and add a tree selection listener. When the valueChanged method is called, we ignore its event parameter and simply ask the tree for the current selection path. As always, we need to get the last node of the path and look up its user object. We then call the getFieldDescription method which uses reflection to assemble a string with all fields of the selected class.

Listing 11.10 treeRender/ClassTreeFrame.java

```
1  package treeRender;
2
3  import java.awt.*;
4  import java.awt.event.*;
5  import java.lang.reflect.*;
6  import java.util.*;
7
8  import javax.swing.*;
9  import javax.swing.tree.*;
10
11 /**
12  * This frame displays the class tree, a text field, and an "Add" button to add more classes
13  * into the tree.
14  */
15 public class ClassTreeFrame extends JFrame
16 {
17    private static final int DEFAULT_WIDTH = 400;
18    private static final int DEFAULT_HEIGHT = 300;
19
20    private DefaultMutableTreeNode root;
21    private DefaultTreeModel model;
22    private JTree tree;
23    private JTextField textField;
24    private JTextArea textArea;
25
26    public ClassTreeFrame()
27    {
28       setSize(DEFAULT_WIDTH, DEFAULT_HEIGHT);
29
30       // the root of the class tree is Object
31       root = new DefaultMutableTreeNode(java.lang.Object.class);
32       model = new DefaultTreeModel(root);
33       tree = new JTree(model);
34
35       // add this class to populate the tree with some data
36       addClass(getClass());
37
```

(Continues)

Listing 11.10 *(Continued)*

```
38        // set up node icons
39        var renderer = new ClassNameTreeCellRenderer();
40        renderer.setClosedIcon(new ImageIcon(getClass().getResource("red-ball.gif")));
41        renderer.setOpenIcon(new ImageIcon(getClass().getResource("yellow-ball.gif")));
42        renderer.setLeafIcon(new ImageIcon(getClass().getResource("blue-ball.gif")));
43        tree.setCellRenderer(renderer);
44
45        // set up selection mode
46        tree.addTreeSelectionListener(event ->
47           {
48              // the user selected a different node--update description
49              TreePath path = tree.getSelectionPath();
50              if (path == null) return;
51              var selectedNode = (DefaultMutableTreeNode) path.getLastPathComponent();
52              Class<?> c = (Class<?>) selectedNode.getUserObject();
53              String description = getFieldDescription(c);
54              textArea.setText(description);
55           });
56        int mode = TreeSelectionModel.SINGLE_TREE_SELECTION;
57        tree.getSelectionModel().setSelectionMode(mode);
58
59        // this text area holds the class description
60        textArea = new JTextArea();
61
62        // add tree and text area
63        var panel = new JPanel();
64        panel.setLayout(new GridLayout(1, 2));
65        panel.add(new JScrollPane(tree));
66        panel.add(new JScrollPane(textArea));
67
68        add(panel, BorderLayout.CENTER);
69
70        addTextField();
71     }
72
73     /**
74      * Add the text field and "Add" button to add a new class.
75      */
76     public void addTextField()
77     {
78        var panel = new JPanel();
79
80        ActionListener addListener = event ->
81           {
82              // add the class whose name is in the text field
83              try
84              {
```

```
85          String text = textField.getText();
86          addClass(Class.forName(text)); // clear text field to indicate success
87          textField.setText("");
88        }
89        catch (ClassNotFoundException e)
90        {
91          JOptionPane.showMessageDialog(null, "Class not found");
92        }
93      };
94
95    // new class names are typed into this text field
96    textField = new JTextField(20);
97    textField.addActionListener(addListener);
98    panel.add(textField);
99
100   var addButton = new JButton("Add");
101   addButton.addActionListener(addListener);
102   panel.add(addButton);
103
104   add(panel, BorderLayout.SOUTH);
105 }
106
107 /**
108  * Finds an object in the tree.
109  * @param obj the object to find
110  * @return the node containing the object or null if the object is not present in the tree
111  */
112 public DefaultMutableTreeNode findUserObject(Object obj)
113 {
114   // find the node containing a user object
115   var e = (Enumeration<TreeNode>) root.breadthFirstEnumeration();
116   while (e.hasMoreElements())
117   {
118     var node = (DefaultMutableTreeNode) e.nextElement();
119     if (node.getUserObject().equals(obj)) return node;
120   }
121   return null;
122 }
123
124 /**
125  * Adds a new class and any parent classes that aren't yet part of the tree.
126  * @param c the class to add
127  * @return the newly added node
128  */
129 public DefaultMutableTreeNode addClass(Class<?> c)
130 {
131   // add a new class to the tree
132
```

(Continues)

Listing 11.10 *(Continued)*

```
133        // skip non-class types
134        if (c.isInterface() || c.isPrimitive()) return null;
135
136        // if the class is already in the tree, return its node
137        DefaultMutableTreeNode node = findUserObject(c);
138        if (node != null) return node;
139
140        // class isn't present--first add class parent recursively
141
142        Class<?> s = c.getSuperclass();
143
144        DefaultMutableTreeNode parent;
145        if (s == null) parent = root;
146        else parent = addClass(s);
147
148        // add the class as a child to the parent
149        var newNode = new DefaultMutableTreeNode(c);
150        model.insertNodeInto(newNode, parent, parent.getChildCount());
151
152        // make node visible
153        var path = new TreePath(model.getPathToRoot(newNode));
154        tree.makeVisible(path);
155
156        return newNode;
157    }
158
159    /**
160     * Returns a description of the fields of a class.
161     * @param the class to be described
162     * @return a string containing all field types and names
163     */
164    public static String getFieldDescription(Class<?> c)
165    {
166        // use reflection to find types and names of fields
167        var r = new StringBuilder();
168        Field[] fields = c.getDeclaredFields();
169        for (int i = 0; i < fields.length; i++)
170        {
171            Field f = fields[i];
172            if ((f.getModifiers() & Modifier.STATIC) != 0) r.append("static ");
173            r.append(f.getType().getName());
174            r.append(" ");
175            r.append(f.getName());
176            r.append("\n");
177        }
178        return r.toString();
179    }
180 }
```

Listing 11.11 treeRender/ClassNameTreeCellRenderer.java

```
1  package treeRender;
2
3  import java.awt.*;
4  import java.lang.reflect.*;
5  import javax.swing.*;
6  import javax.swing.tree.*;
7
8  /**
9   * This class renders a class name either in plain or italic. Abstract classes are italic.
10  */
11 public class ClassNameTreeCellRenderer extends DefaultTreeCellRenderer
12 {
13    private Font plainFont = null;
14    private Font italicFont = null;
15
16    public Component getTreeCellRendererComponent(JTree tree, Object value, boolean selected,
17          boolean expanded, boolean leaf, int row, boolean hasFocus)
18    {
19       super.getTreeCellRendererComponent(tree, value, selected, expanded, leaf,
20             row, hasFocus);
21       // get the user object
22       var node = (DefaultMutableTreeNode) value;
23       Class<?> c = (Class<?>) node.getUserObject();
24
25       // the first time, derive italic font from plain font
26       if (plainFont == null)
27       {
28          plainFont = getFont();
29          // the tree cell renderer is sometimes called with a label that has a null font
30          if (plainFont != null) italicFont = plainFont.deriveFont(Font.ITALIC);
31       }
32
33       // set font to italic if the class is abstract, plain otherwise
34       if ((c.getModifiers() & Modifier.ABSTRACT) == 0) setFont(plainFont);
35       else setFont(italicFont);
36       return this;
37    }
38 }
```

---

javax.swing.JTree 1.2

- TreePath getSelectionPath()
- TreePath[] getSelectionPaths()

  returns the first selected path, or an array of paths to all selected nodes. If no paths are selected, both methods return null.

---

javax.swing.event.TreeSelectionListener 1.2

- void valueChanged(TreeSelectionEvent event)

  is called whenever nodes are selected or deselected.

---

javax.swing.event.TreeSelectionEvent 1.2

- TreePath getPath()
- TreePath[] getPaths()

  gets the first path or all paths that have *changed* in this selection event. If you want to know the current selection, not the selection change, call JTree.getSelectionPaths instead.

11.2.5 Custom Tree Models

In the final example, we implement a program that inspects the contents of an object, just like a debugger does (see Figure 11.30).

Figure 11.30 An object inspection tree

Before going further, compile and run the example program. Each node corresponds to an instance field. If the field is an object, expand it to see *its* instance fields. The program inspects the contents of the frame window. If you poke around a few of the instance fields, you should be able to find some familiar classes. You'll also gain some respect for how complex the Swing user interface components are under the hood.

What's remarkable about the program is that the tree does not use the DefaultTreeModel. If you already have data that are hierarchically organized, you might not want to build a duplicate tree and worry about keeping both trees synchronized. That is the situation in our case—the inspected objects are already linked to each other through the object references, so there is no need to replicate the linking structure.

The TreeModel interface has only a handful of methods. The first group of methods enables the JTree to find the tree nodes by first getting the root, then the children. The JTree class calls these methods only when the user actually expands a node.

```
Object getRoot()
int getChildCount(Object parent)
Object getChild(Object parent, int index)
```

This example shows why the TreeModel interface, like the JTree class itself, does not need an explicit notion of nodes. The root and its children can be any objects. The TreeModel is responsible for telling the JTree how they are connected.

The next method of the TreeModel interface is the reverse of getChild:

```
int getIndexOfChild(Object parent, Object child)
```

Actually, this method can be implemented in terms of the first three—see the code in Listing 11.12.

The tree model tells the JTree which nodes should be displayed as leaves:

```
boolean isLeaf(Object node)
```

If your code changes the tree model, the tree needs to be notified so it can redraw itself. The tree adds itself as a TreeModelListener to the model. Thus, the model must support the usual listener management methods:

```
void addTreeModelListener(TreeModelListener l)
void removeTreeModelListener(TreeModelListener l)
```

You can see the implementations for these methods in Listing 11.13.

When the model modifies the tree contents, it calls one of the four methods of the TreeModelListener interface:

```
void treeNodesChanged(TreeModelEvent e)
void treeNodesInserted(TreeModelEvent e)
void treeNodesRemoved(TreeModelEvent e)
void treeStructureChanged(TreeModelEvent e)
```

The `TreeModelEvent` object describes the location of the change. The details of assembling a tree model event that describes an insertion or removal event are quite technical. You only need to worry about firing these events if your tree can actually have nodes added and removed. In Listing 11.12, we show how to fire one event by replacing the root with a new object.

 TIP: To simplify the code for event firing, use the `javax.swing.EventListenerList` convenience class that collects listeners. The last three methods of Listing 11.13 show how to use the class.

Finally, if the user edits a tree node, your model is called with the change:

```
void valueForPathChanged(TreePath path, Object newValue)
```

If you don't allow editing, this method is never called.

If you don't need to support editing, constructing a tree model is easily done. Implement the three methods:

```
Object getRoot()
int getChildCount(Object parent)
Object getChild(Object parent, int index)
```

These methods describe the structure of the tree. Supply routine implementations of the other five methods, as in Listing 11.12. You are then ready to display your tree.

Now let's turn to the implementation of the example program. Our tree will contain objects of type `Variable`.

 NOTE: Had we used the `DefaultTreeModel`, our nodes would have been objects of type `DefaultMutableTreeNode` with *user objects* of type `Variable`.

For example, suppose you inspect the variable

```
Employee joe;
```

That variable has a *type* `Employee.class`, a *name* `"joe"`, and a *value*—the value of the object reference `joe`. In Listing 11.14, we define a class `Variable` that describes a variable in a program:

```
var v = new Variable(Employee.class, "joe", joe);
```

If the type of the variable is a primitive type, you must use an object wrapper for the value.

```
new Variable(double.class, "salary", new Double(salary));
```

If the type of the variable is a class, the variable has *fields*. Using reflection, we enumerate all fields and collect them in an `ArrayList`. Since the `getFields` method of the `Class` class does not return the fields of the superclass, we need to call `getFields` on all superclasses as well. You can find the code in the `Variable` constructor. The `getFields` method of our `Variable` class returns the array of fields. Finally, the `toString` method of the `Variable` class formats the node label. The label always contains the variable type and name. If the variable is not a class, the label also contains the value.

 NOTE: If the type is an array, we do not display the elements of the array. This would not be difficult to do; we leave it as the proverbial "exercise for the reader."

Let's move on to the tree model. The first two methods are simple.

```
public Object getRoot()
{
   return root;
}

public int getChildCount(Object parent)
{
   return ((Variable) parent).getFields().size();
}
```

The `getChild` method returns a new `Variable` object that describes the field with the given index. The `getType` and `getName` methods of the `Field` class yield the field type and name. By using reflection, you can read the field value as `f.get(parentValue)`. That method can throw an `IllegalAccessException`. However, we made all fields accessible in the `Variable` constructor, so this won't happen in practice.

Here is the complete code of the `getChild` method:

```
public Object getChild(Object parent, int index)
{
   ArrayList fields = ((Variable) parent).getFields();
   var f = (Field) fields.get(index);
   Object parentValue = ((Variable) parent).getValue();
   try
   {
      return new Variable(f.getType(), f.getName(), f.get(parentValue));
   }
   catch (IllegalAccessException e)
   {
```

```
        return null;
    }
}
```

These three methods reveal the structure of the object tree to the JTree component. The remaining methods are routine—see the source code in Listing 11.13.

There is one remarkable fact about this tree model: It actually describes an *infinite* tree. You can verify this by following one of the WeakReference objects. Click on the variable named referent. It leads you right back to the original object. You get an identical subtree, and you can open its WeakReference object again, ad infinitum. Of course, you cannot *store* an infinite set of nodes; the tree model simply generates the nodes on demand as the user expands the parents. Listing 11.12 shows the frame class of the sample program.

Listing 11.12 treeModel/ObjectInspectorFrame.java

```java
 1  package treeModel;
 2
 3  import java.awt.*;
 4  import javax.swing.*;
 5
 6  /**
 7   * This frame holds the object tree.
 8   */
 9  public class ObjectInspectorFrame extends JFrame
10  {
11     private JTree tree;
12     private static final int DEFAULT_WIDTH = 400;
13     private static final int DEFAULT_HEIGHT = 300;
14
15     public ObjectInspectorFrame()
16     {
17        setSize(DEFAULT_WIDTH, DEFAULT_HEIGHT);
18
19        // we inspect this frame object
20
21        var v = new Variable(getClass(), "this", this);
22        var model = new ObjectTreeModel();
23        model.setRoot(v);
24
25        // construct and show tree
26
27        tree = new JTree(model);
28        add(new JScrollPane(tree), BorderLayout.CENTER);
29     }
30  }
```

Listing 11.13 treeModel/ObjectTreeModel.java

```
1  package treeModel;
2
3  import java.lang.reflect.*;
4  import java.util.*;
5  import javax.swing.event.*;
6  import javax.swing.tree.*;
7
8  /**
9   * This tree model describes the tree structure of a Java object. Children are the objects
10  * that are stored in instance variables.
11  */
12 public class ObjectTreeModel implements TreeModel
13 {
14    private Variable root;
15    private EventListenerList listenerList = new EventListenerList();
16
17    /**
18     * Constructs an empty tree.
19     */
20    public ObjectTreeModel()
21    {
22       root = null;
23    }
24
25    /**
26     * Sets the root to a given variable.
27     * @param v the variable that is being described by this tree
28     */
29    public void setRoot(Variable v)
30    {
31       Variable oldRoot = v;
32       root = v;
33       fireTreeStructureChanged(oldRoot);
34    }
35
36    public Object getRoot()
37    {
38       return root;
39    }
40
41    public int getChildCount(Object parent)
42    {
43       return ((Variable) parent).getFields().size();
44    }
45
46    public Object getChild(Object parent, int index)
47    {
```

(Continues)

Listing 11.13 *(Continued)*

```
48      ArrayList<Field> fields = ((Variable) parent).getFields();
49      var f = (Field) fields.get(index);
50      Object parentValue = ((Variable) parent).getValue();
51      try
52      {
53         return new Variable(f.getType(), f.getName(), f.get(parentValue));
54      }
55      catch (IllegalAccessException e)
56      {
57         return null;
58      }
59   }
60
61   public int getIndexOfChild(Object parent, Object child)
62   {
63      int n = getChildCount(parent);
64      for (int i = 0; i < n; i++)
65         if (getChild(parent, i).equals(child)) return i;
66      return -1;
67   }
68
69   public boolean isLeaf(Object node)
70   {
71      return getChildCount(node) == 0;
72   }
73
74   public void valueForPathChanged(TreePath path, Object newValue)
75   {
76   }
77
78   public void addTreeModelListener(TreeModelListener l)
79   {
80      listenerList.add(TreeModelListener.class, l);
81   }
82
83   public void removeTreeModelListener(TreeModelListener l)
84   {
85      listenerList.remove(TreeModelListener.class, l);
86   }
87
88   protected void fireTreeStructureChanged(Object oldRoot)
89   {
90      var event = new TreeModelEvent(this, new Object[] { oldRoot });
91      for (TreeModelListener l : listenerList.getListeners(TreeModelListener.class))
92         l.treeStructureChanged(event);
93   }
94 }
```

Listing 11.14 treeModel/Variable.java

```
1   package treeModel;
2
3   import java.lang.reflect.*;
4   import java.util.*;
5
6   /**
7    * A variable with a type, name, and value.
8    */
9   public class Variable
10  {
11     private Class<?> type;
12     private String name;
13     private Object value;
14     private ArrayList<Field> fields;
15
16     /**
17      * Construct a variable.
18      * @param aType the type
19      * @param aName the name
20      * @param aValue the value
21      */
22     public Variable(Class<?> aType, String aName, Object aValue)
23     {
24        type = aType;
25        name = aName;
26        value = aValue;
27        fields = new ArrayList<>();
28
29        // find all fields if we have a class type except we don't expand strings and
30        // null values
31
32        if (!type.isPrimitive() && !type.isArray() && !type.equals(String.class)
33              && value != null)
34        {
35           // get fields from the class and all superclasses
36           for (Class<?> c = value.getClass(); c != null; c = c.getSuperclass())
37           {
38              Field[] fs = c.getDeclaredFields();
39              AccessibleObject.setAccessible(fs, true);
40
41              // get all nonstatic fields
42              for (Field f : fs)
43                 if ((f.getModifiers() & Modifier.STATIC) == 0) fields.add(f);
44           }
45        }
46     }
47
```

(Continues)

Listing 11.14 *(Continued)*

```
48    /**
49     * Gets the value of this variable.
50     * @return the value
51     */
52    public Object getValue()
53    {
54       return value;
55    }
56
57    /**
58     * Gets all nonstatic fields of this variable.
59     * @return an array list of variables describing the fields
60     */
61    public ArrayList<Field> getFields()
62    {
63       return fields;
64    }
65
66    public String toString()
67    {
68       String r = type + " " + name;
69       if (type.isPrimitive()) r += "=" + value;
70       else if (type.equals(String.class)) r += "=" + value;
71       else if (value == null) r += "=null";
72       return r;
73    }
74 }
```

---

javax.swing.tree.TreeModel 1.2

- Object getRoot()

  returns the root node.

- int getChildCount(Object parent)

  gets the number of children of the parent node.

- Object getChild(Object parent, int index)

  gets the child node of the parent node at the given index.

- int getIndexOfChild(Object parent, Object child)

  gets the index of the child node in the parent node, or -1 if child is not a child of parent in this tree model.

(Continues)

---

javax.swing.tree.TreeModel 1.2 *(Continued)*

- boolean isLeaf(Object node)

  returns true if node is conceptually a leaf of the tree.
- void addTreeModelListener(TreeModelListener l)
- void removeTreeModelListener(TreeModelListener l)

  adds or removes listeners that are notified when the information in the tree model changes.
- void valueForPathChanged(TreePath path, Object newValue)

  is called when a cell editor has modified the value of a node.

  Parameters: path   The path to the node that has been edited

                    newValue   The replacement value returned by the editor

---

javax.swing.event.TreeModelListener 1.2

- void treeNodesChanged(TreeModelEvent e)
- void treeNodesInserted(TreeModelEvent e)
- void treeNodesRemoved(TreeModelEvent e)
- void treeStructureChanged(TreeModelEvent e)

  is called by the tree model when the tree has been modified.

---

javax.swing.event.TreeModelEvent 1.2

- TreeModelEvent(Object eventSource, TreePath node)

  constructs a tree model event.

  Parameters: eventSource   The tree model generating this event

                    node   The path to the node that is being changed

---

11.3 Advanced AWT

You can use the methods of the Graphics class to create simple drawings. Those methods are sufficient for simple applications, but they fall short when you need to create complex shapes or require complete control over the appearance of the graphics. The Java 2D API is a more sophisticated class library that you can use to produce high-quality drawings. In the following sections, we will give you an overview of that API.

11.3.1 The Rendering Pipeline

The original JDK 1.0 had a very simple mechanism for drawing shapes. You selected color and paint mode, and called methods of the Graphics class such as drawRect or fillOval. The Java 2D API supports many more options.

- You can easily produce a wide variety of *shapes.*
- You have control over the *stroke*—the pen that traces shape boundaries.
- You can *fill* shapes with solid colors, varying hues, and repeating patterns.
- You can use *transformations* to move, scale, rotate, or stretch shapes.
- You can *clip* shapes to restrict them to arbitrary areas.
- You can select *composition rules* to describe how to combine the pixels of a new shape with existing pixels.

To draw a shape, go through the following steps:

1. Obtain an object of the Graphics2D class. This class is a subclass of the Graphics class. Ever since Java SE 1.2, methods such as paint and paintComponent automatically receive an object of the Graphics2D class. Simply use a cast, as follows:

   ```
   public void paintComponent(Graphics g)
   {
      var g2 = (Graphics2D) g;
      . . .
   }
   ```

2. Use the setRenderingHints method to set *rendering hints*—trade-offs between speed and drawing quality.

   ```
   RenderingHints hints = . . .;
   g2.setRenderingHints(hints);
   ```

3. Use the setStroke method to set the *stroke.* The stroke draws the outline of the shape. You can select the thickness and choose among solid and dotted lines.

   ```
   Stroke stroke = . . .;
   g2.setStroke(stroke);
   ```

4. Use the setPaint method to set the *paint*. The paint fills areas such as the stroke or the interior of a shape. You can create solid color paint, paint with changing hues, or tiled fill patterns.

    ```
    Paint paint = . . .;
    g2.setPaint(paint);
    ```

5. Use the clip method to set the *clipping region*.

    ```
    Shape clip = . . .;
    g2.clip(clip);
    ```

6. Use the transform method to set a *transformation* from user space to device space. Use transformations if it is easier for you to define your shapes in a custom coordinate system than by using pixel coordinates.

    ```
    AffineTransform transform = . . .;
    g2.transform(transform);
    ```

7. Use the setComposite method to set a *composition rule* that describes how to combine the new pixels with the existing pixels.

    ```
    Composite composite = . . .;
    g2.setComposite(composite);
    ```

8. Create a shape. The Java 2D API supplies many shape objects and methods to combine shapes.

    ```
    Shape shape = . . .;
    ```

9. Draw or fill the shape. If you draw the shape, its outline is stroked. If you fill the shape, the interior is painted.

    ```
    g2.draw(shape);
    g2.fill(shape);
    ```

Of course, in many practical circumstances, you don't need all these steps. There are reasonable defaults for the settings of the 2D graphics context; change the settings only if you want to deviate from the defaults.

In the following sections, you will see how to describe shapes, strokes, paints, transformations, and composition rules.

The various set methods simply set the state of the 2D graphics context. They don't cause any drawing. Similarly, when you construct Shape objects, no drawing takes place. A shape is only rendered when you call draw or fill. At that time, the new shape is computed in a *rendering pipeline* (see Figure 11.31).

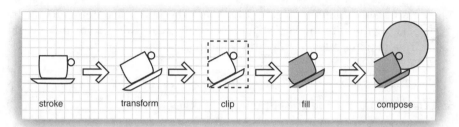

Figure 11.31 The rendering pipeline

In the rendering pipeline, the following steps take place to render a shape:

1. The path of the shape is stroked.
2. The shape is transformed.
3. The shape is clipped. If there is no intersection between the shape and the clipping area, the process stops.
4. The remainder of the shape after clipping is filled.
5. The pixels of the filled shape are composed with the existing pixels. (In Figure 11.31, the circle is part of the existing pixels, and the cup shape is superimposed over it.)

In the next section, you will see how to define shapes. Then, we will turn to the 2D graphics context settings.

---

java.awt.Graphics2D 1.2

- void draw(Shape s)

  draws the outline of the given shape with the current paint.
- void fill(Shape s)

  fills the interior of the given shape with the current paint.

11.3.2 Shapes

Here are some of the methods in the Graphics class to draw shapes:

```
drawLine
drawRectangle
drawRoundRect
draw3DRect
drawPolygon
drawPolyline
```

```
drawOval
drawArc
```

There are also corresponding fill methods. These methods have been in the Graphics class ever since JDK 1.0. The Java 2D API uses a completely different, object-oriented approach. Instead of methods, there are classes:

```
Line2D
Rectangle2D
RoundRectangle2D
Ellipse2D
Arc2D
QuadCurve2D
CubicCurve2D
GeneralPath
```

These classes all implement the Shape interface, which we will examine in the following sections.

11.3.2.1 The Shape Class Hierarchy

The Line2D, Rectangle2D, RoundRectangle2D, Ellipse2D, and Arc2D classes correspond to the drawLine, drawRectangle, drawRoundRect, drawOval, and drawArc methods. (The concept of a "3D rectangle" has died the death it so richly deserved—there is no analog to the draw3DRect method.) The Java 2D API supplies two additional classes, quadratic and cubic curves, that we will discuss in this section. There is no Polygon2D class; instead, the GeneralPath class describes paths made up from lines, quadratic and cubic curves. You can use a GeneralPath to describe a polygon; we'll show you how later in this section.

To draw a shape, first create an object of a class that implements the Shape interface and then call the draw method of the Graphics2D class.

The classes

```
Rectangle2D
RoundRectangle2D
Ellipse2D
Arc2D
```

all inherit from a common superclass RectangularShape. Admittedly, ellipses and arcs are not rectangular, but they have a *bounding rectangle* (see Figure 11.32).

Each of the classes with a name ending in "2D" has two subclasses for specifying coordinates as float or double quantities. In Volume I, you already encountered Rectangle2D.Float and Rectangle2D.Double.

The same scheme is used for the other classes, such as Arc2D.Float and Arc2D.Double.

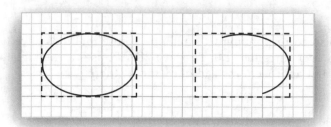

Figure 11.32 The bounding rectangle of an ellipse and an arc

Internally, all graphics classes use `float` coordinates because `float` numbers use less storage space but have sufficient precision for geometric computations. However, the Java programming language makes it a bit more tedious to manipulate `float` numbers. For that reason, most methods of the graphics classes use `double` parameters and return values. Only when constructing a 2D object you need to choose between the constructors with `float` and `double` coordinates. For example,

```
var floatRect = new Rectangle2D.Float(5F, 10F, 7.5F, 15F);
var doubleRect = new Rectangle2D.Double(5, 10, 7.5, 15);
```

The *Xxx*2D.Float and *Xxx*2D.Double classes are subclasses of the *Xxx*2D classes. After object construction, essentially no benefit accrues from remembering the subclass, and you can just store the constructed object in a superclass variable as in the code example above.

As you can see from the curious names, the *Xxx*2D.Float and *Xxx*2D.Double classes are also inner classes of the *Xxx*2D classes. That is just a minor syntactical convenience to avoid inflation of outer class names.

Finally, the `Point2D` class describes a point with an x and a y coordinate. Points are used to define shapes, but they aren't themselves shapes.

Figure 11.33 shows the relationships between the shape classes. However, the `Double` and `Float` subclasses are omitted. Legacy classes from the pre-2D library are marked with a gray fill.

11.3.2.2 Using the Shape Classes

You already saw how to use the `Rectangle2D`, `Ellipse2D`, and `Line2D` classes in Volume I, Chapter 10. In this section, you will learn how to work with the remaining 2D shapes.

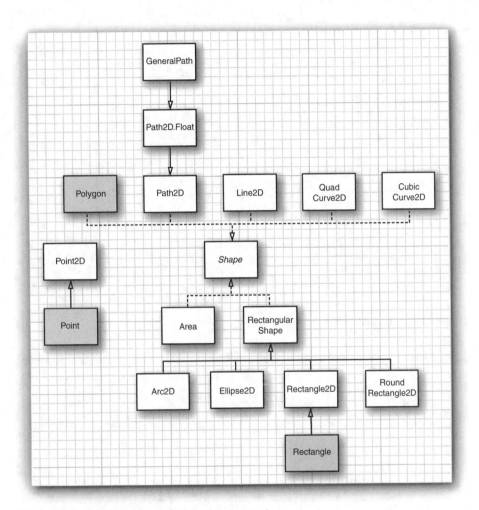

Figure 11.33 Relationships between the shape classes

For the `RoundRectangle2D` shape, specify the top left corner, width, height, and the x and y dimensions of the corner area that should be rounded (see Figure 11.34). For example, the call

```
var r = new RoundRectangle2D.Double(150, 200, 100, 50, 20, 20);
```

produces a rounded rectangle with circles of radius 20 at each of the corners.

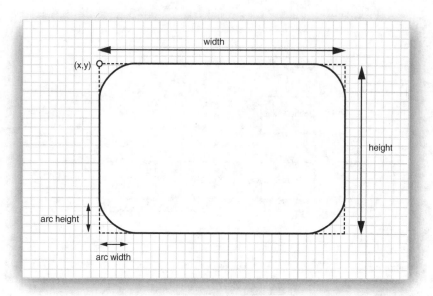

Figure 11.34 Constructing a RoundRectangle2D

To construct an arc, specify the bounding box, the start angle, the angle swept out by the arc (see Figure 11.35), and the closure type—one of Arc2D.OPEN, Arc2D.PIE, or Arc2D.CHORD.

```
var a = new Arc2D(x, y, width, height, startAngle, arcAngle, closureType);
```

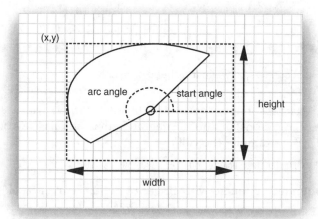

Figure 11.35 Constructing an elliptical arc

Figure 11.36 illustrates the arc types.

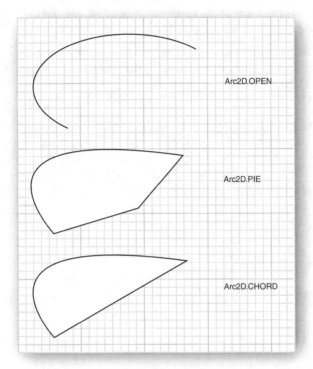

Figure 11.36 Arc types

CAUTION: If the arc is elliptical, the computation of the arc angles is not at all straightforward. The API documentation states: "The angles are specified relative to the nonsquare framing rectangle such that 45 degrees always falls on the line from the center of the ellipse to the upper right corner of the framing rectangle. As a result, if the framing rectangle is noticeably longer along one axis than the other, the angles to the start and end of the arc segment will be skewed farther along the longer axis of the frame." Unfortunately, the documentation is silent on how to compute this "skew." Here are the details:

Suppose the center of the arc is the origin and the point (x, y) lies on the arc. You can get a skewed angle with the following formula:

```
skewedAngle = Math.toDegrees(Math.atan2(-y * height, x * width));
```

The result is a value between -180 and 180. Compute the skewed start and end angles in this way. Then, compute the difference between the two skewed angles. If the start angle or the difference is negative, add 360 to the start angle. Then, supply the start angle and the difference to the arc constructor.

If you run the example program at the end of this section, you can visually check that this calculation yields the correct values for the arc constructor (see Figure 11.39).

The Java 2D API supports *quadratic* and *cubic* curves. In this chapter, we do not get into the mathematics of these curves. We suggest you get a feel for how the curves look by running the program in Listing 11.15. As you can see in Figures 11.37 and 11.38, quadratic and cubic curves are specified by two *end points* and one or two *control points*. Moving the control points changes the shape of the curves.

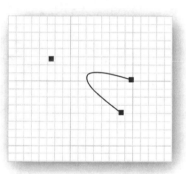

Figure 11.37 A quadratic curve

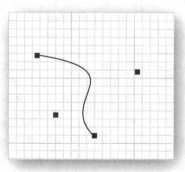

Figure 11.38 A cubic curve

To construct quadratic and cubic curves, give the coordinates of the end points and the control points. For example,

```
var q = new QuadCurve2D.Double(startX, startY, controlX, controlY, endX, endY);
var c = new CubicCurve2D.Double(startX, startY, control1X, control1Y,
   control2X, control2Y, endX, endY);
```

Quadratic curves are not very flexible, and they are not commonly used in practice. Cubic curves (such as the Bézier curves drawn by the `CubicCurve2D` class) are, however, very common. By combining many cubic curves so that the slopes at the connection points match, you can create complex, smooth-looking curved shapes. For more information, we refer you to *Computer Graphics: Principles and Practice, Third Edition*, by James D. Foley, Andries van Dam, Steven K. Feiner, et al. (Addison-Wesley, 2013).

You can build arbitrary sequences of line segments, quadratic curves, and cubic curves, and store them in a `GeneralPath` object. Specify the first coordinate of the path with the `moveTo` method, for example:

```
var path = new GeneralPath();
path.moveTo(10, 20);
```

You can then extend the path by calling one of the methods `lineTo`, `quadTo`, or `curveTo`. These methods extend the path by a line, a quadratic curve, or a cubic curve. To call `lineTo`, supply the end point. For the two curve methods, supply the control points, then the end point. For example,

```
path.lineTo(20, 30);
path.curveTo(control1X, control1Y, control2X, control2Y, endX, endY);
```

Close the path by calling the `closePath` method. It draws a straight line back to the starting point of the path.

To make a polygon, simply call `moveTo` to go to the first corner point, followed by repeated calls to `lineTo` to visit the other corner points. Finally, call `closePath` to close the polygon. The program in Listing 11.15 shows this in more detail.

A general path does not have to be connected. You can call `moveTo` at any time to start a new path segment.

Finally, you can use the `append` method to add arbitrary `Shape` objects to a general path. The outline of the shape is added to the end to the path. The second parameter of the `append` method is `true` if the new shape should be connected to the last point on the path, `false` otherwise. For example, the call

```
Rectangle2D r = . . .;
path.append(r, false);
```

appends the outline of a rectangle to the path without connecting it to the existing path. But

```
path.append(r, true);
```

adds a straight line from the end point of the path to the starting point of the rectangle, and then adds the rectangle outline to the path.

The program in Listing 11.15 lets you create sample paths. Figures 11.37 and 11.38 show sample runs of the program. You can pick a shape maker from the combo box. The program contains shape makers for

- Straight lines
- Rectangles, rounded rectangles, and ellipses
- Arcs (showing lines for the bounding rectangle and the start and end angles, in addition to the arc itself)
- Polygons (using a GeneralPath)
- Quadratic and cubic curves

Use the mouse to adjust the control points. As you move them, the shape continuously repaints itself.

The program is a bit complex because it handles multiple shapes and supports dragging of the control points.

An abstract superclass ShapeMaker encapsulates the commonality of the shape maker classes. Each shape has a fixed number of control points that the user can move around. The getPointCount method returns that value. The abstract method

```
Shape makeShape(Point2D[] points)
```

computes the actual shape, given the current positions of the control points. The toString method returns the class name so that the ShapeMaker objects can simply be dumped into a JComboBox.

To enable dragging of the control points, the ShapePanel class handles both mouse and mouse motion events. If the mouse is pressed on top of a rectangle, subsequent mouse drags move the rectangle.

The majority of the shape maker classes are simple—their makeShape methods just construct and return the requested shapes. However, the ArcMaker class needs to compute the distorted start and end angles. Furthermore, to demonstrate that the computation is indeed correct, the returned shape is a GeneralPath containing the arc itself, the bounding rectangle, and the lines from the center of the arc to the angle control points (see Figure 11.39).

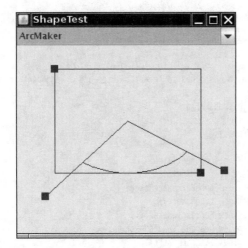

Figure 11.39 The ShapeTest program

Listing 11.15 shape/ShapeTest.java

```
1  package shape;
2
3  import java.awt.*;
4  import java.awt.event.*;
5  import java.awt.geom.*;
6  import java.util.*;
7  import javax.swing.*;
8
9  /**
10  * This program demonstrates the various 2D shapes.
11  * @version 1.04 2018-05-01
12  * @author Cay Horstmann
13  */
14  public class ShapeTest
15  {
16     public static void main(String[] args)
17     {
18        EventQueue.invokeLater(() ->
19           {
20              var frame = new ShapeTestFrame();
21              frame.setTitle("ShapeTest");
22              frame.setDefaultCloseOperation(JFrame.EXIT_ON_CLOSE);
23              frame.setVisible(true);
24           });
25     }
26  }
```

(Continues)

Listing 11.15   (Continued)

```
27
28  /**
29   * This frame contains a combo box to select a shape and a component to draw it.
30   */
31  class ShapeTestFrame extends JFrame
32  {
33     public ShapeTestFrame()
34     {
35        var comp = new ShapeComponent();
36        add(comp, BorderLayout.CENTER);
37        var comboBox = new JComboBox<ShapeMaker>();
38        comboBox.addItem(new LineMaker());
39        comboBox.addItem(new RectangleMaker());
40        comboBox.addItem(new RoundRectangleMaker());
41        comboBox.addItem(new EllipseMaker());
42        comboBox.addItem(new ArcMaker());
43        comboBox.addItem(new PolygonMaker());
44        comboBox.addItem(new QuadCurveMaker());
45        comboBox.addItem(new CubicCurveMaker());
46        comboBox.addActionListener(event ->
47           {
48              ShapeMaker shapeMaker = comboBox.getItemAt(comboBox.getSelectedIndex());
49              comp.setShapeMaker(shapeMaker);
50           });
51        add(comboBox, BorderLayout.NORTH);
52        comp.setShapeMaker((ShapeMaker) comboBox.getItemAt(0));
53        pack();
54     }
55  }
56
57  /**
58   * This component draws a shape and allows the user to move the points that define it.
59   */
60  class ShapeComponent extends JComponent
61  {
62     private static final Dimension PREFERRED_SIZE = new Dimension(300, 200);
63     private Point2D[] points;
64     private static Random generator = new Random();
65     private static int SIZE = 10;
66     private int current;
67     private ShapeMaker shapeMaker;
68
69     public ShapeComponent()
70     {
71        addMouseListener(new MouseAdapter()
72           {
73              public void mousePressed(MouseEvent event)
74              {
```

```
75              Point p = event.getPoint();
76              for (int i = 0; i < points.length; i++)
77              {
78                 double x = points[i].getX() - SIZE / 2;
79                 double y = points[i].getY() - SIZE / 2;
80                 var r = new Rectangle2D.Double(x, y, SIZE, SIZE);
81                 if (r.contains(p))
82                 {
83                    current = i;
84                    return;
85                 }
86              }
87           }
88
89           public void mouseReleased(MouseEvent event)
90           {
91              current = -1;
92           }
93        });
94     addMouseMotionListener(new MouseMotionAdapter()
95        {
96           public void mouseDragged(MouseEvent event)
97           {
98              if (current == -1) return;
99              points[current] = event.getPoint();
100             repaint();
101          }
102       });
103    current = -1;
104 }
105
106 /**
107  * Set a shape maker and initialize it with a random point set.
108  * @param aShapeMaker a shape maker that defines a shape from a point set
109  */
110 public void setShapeMaker(ShapeMaker aShapeMaker)
111 {
112    shapeMaker = aShapeMaker;
113    int n = shapeMaker.getPointCount();
114    points = new Point2D[n];
115    for (int i = 0; i < n; i++)
116    {
117       double x = generator.nextDouble() * getWidth();
118       double y = generator.nextDouble() * getHeight();
119       points[i] = new Point2D.Double(x, y);
120    }
121    repaint();
122 }
123
```

(Continues)

Listing 11.15 *(Continued)*

```
124    public void paintComponent(Graphics g)
125    {
126       if (points == null) return;
127       var g2 = (Graphics2D) g;
128       for (int i = 0; i < points.length; i++)
129       {
130          double x = points[i].getX() - SIZE / 2;
131          double y = points[i].getY() - SIZE / 2;
132          g2.fill(new Rectangle2D.Double(x, y, SIZE, SIZE));
133       }
134
135       g2.draw(shapeMaker.makeShape(points));
136    }
137
138    public Dimension getPreferredSize() { return PREFERRED_SIZE; }
139 }
140
141 /**
142  * A shape maker can make a shape from a point set. Concrete subclasses must return a shape in
143  * the makeShape method.
144  */
145 abstract class ShapeMaker
146 {
147    private int pointCount;
148
149    /**
150     * Constructs a shape maker.
151     * @param ointCount the number of points needed to define this shape
152     */
153    public ShapeMaker(int pointCount)
154    {
155       this.pointCount = pointCount;
156    }
157
158    /**
159     * Gets the number of points needed to define this shape.
160     * @return the point count
161     */
162    public int getPointCount()
163    {
164       return pointCount;
165    }
166
167    /**
168     * Makes a shape out of the given point set.
169     * @param p the points that define the shape
170     * @return the shape defined by the points
171     */
```

```
172    public abstract Shape makeShape(Point2D[] p);
173
174    public String toString()
175    {
176       return getClass().getName();
177    }
178 }
179
180 /**
181  * Makes a line that joins two given points.
182  */
183 class LineMaker extends ShapeMaker
184 {
185    public LineMaker()
186    {
187       super(2);
188    }
189
190    public Shape makeShape(Point2D[] p)
191    {
192       return new Line2D.Double(p[0], p[1]);
193    }
194 }
195
196 /**
197  * Makes a rectangle that joins two given corner points.
198  */
199 class RectangleMaker extends ShapeMaker
200 {
201    public RectangleMaker()
202    {
203       super(2);
204    }
205
206    public Shape makeShape(Point2D[] p)
207    {
208       var s = new Rectangle2D.Double();
209       s.setFrameFromDiagonal(p[0], p[1]);
210       return s;
211    }
212 }
213
214 /**
215  * Makes a round rectangle that joins two given corner points.
216  */
217 class RoundRectangleMaker extends ShapeMaker
218 {
219    public RoundRectangleMaker()
220    {
```

(Continues)

Listing 11.15 *(Continued)*

```
221        super(2);
222    }
223
224    public Shape makeShape(Point2D[] p)
225    {
226        var s = new RoundRectangle2D.Double(0, 0, 0, 0, 20, 20);
227        s.setFrameFromDiagonal(p[0], p[1]);
228        return s;
229    }
230 }
231
232 /**
233  * Makes an ellipse contained in a bounding box with two given corner points.
234  */
235 class EllipseMaker extends ShapeMaker
236 {
237    public EllipseMaker()
238    {
239        super(2);
240    }
241
242    public Shape makeShape(Point2D[] p)
243    {
244        var s = new Ellipse2D.Double();
245        s.setFrameFromDiagonal(p[0], p[1]);
246        return s;
247    }
248 }
249
250 /**
251  * Makes an arc contained in a bounding box with two given corner points, and with starting
252  * and ending angles given by lines emanating from the center of the bounding box and ending
253  * in two given points. To show the correctness of the angle computation, the returned shape
254  * contains the arc, the bounding box, and the lines.
255  */
256 class ArcMaker extends ShapeMaker
257 {
258    public ArcMaker()
259    {
260        super(4);
261    }
262
263    public Shape makeShape(Point2D[] p)
264    {
265        double centerX = (p[0].getX() + p[1].getX()) / 2;
266        double centerY = (p[0].getY() + p[1].getY()) / 2;
```

```
267        double width = Math.abs(p[1].getX() - p[0].getX());
268        double height = Math.abs(p[1].getY() - p[0].getY());
269
270        double skewedStartAngle = Math.toDegrees(Math.atan2(-(p[2].getY() - centerY) * width,
271           (p[2].getX() - centerX) * height));
272        double skewedEndAngle = Math.toDegrees(Math.atan2(-(p[3].getY() - centerY) * width,
273           (p[3].getX() - centerX) * height));
274        double skewedAngleDifference = skewedEndAngle - skewedStartAngle;
275        if (skewedStartAngle < 0) skewedStartAngle += 360;
276        if (skewedAngleDifference < 0) skewedAngleDifference += 360;
277
278        var s = new Arc2D.Double(0, 0, 0, 0,
279           skewedStartAngle, skewedAngleDifference, Arc2D.OPEN);
280        s.setFrameFromDiagonal(p[0], p[1]);
281
282        var g = new GeneralPath();
283        g.append(s, false);
284        var r = new Rectangle2D.Double();
285        r.setFrameFromDiagonal(p[0], p[1]);
286        g.append(r, false);
287        var center = new Point2D.Double(centerX, centerY);
288        g.append(new Line2D.Double(center, p[2]), false);
289        g.append(new Line2D.Double(center, p[3]), false);
290        return g;
291     }
292 }
293
294 /**
295  * Makes a polygon defined by six corner points.
296  */
297 class PolygonMaker extends ShapeMaker
298 {
299     public PolygonMaker()
300     {
301        super(6);
302     }
303
304     public Shape makeShape(Point2D[] p)
305     {
306        var s = new GeneralPath();
307        s.moveTo((float) p[0].getX(), (float) p[0].getY());
308        for (int i = 1; i < p.length; i++)
309           s.lineTo((float) p[i].getX(), (float) p[i].getY());
310        s.closePath();
311        return s;
312     }
313 }
314
```

(Continues)

Listing 11.15 *(Continued)*

```
315 /**
316  * Makes a quad curve defined by two end points and a control point.
317  */
318 class QuadCurveMaker extends ShapeMaker
319 {
320    public QuadCurveMaker()
321    {
322       super(3);
323    }
324
325    public Shape makeShape(Point2D[] p)
326    {
327       return new QuadCurve2D.Double(p[0].getX(), p[0].getY(), p[1].getX(), p[1].getY(),
328          p[2].getX(), p[2].getY());
329    }
330 }
331
332 /**
333  * Makes a cubic curve defined by two end points and two control points.
334  */
335 class CubicCurveMaker extends ShapeMaker
336 {
337    public CubicCurveMaker()
338    {
339       super(4);
340    }
341
342    public Shape makeShape(Point2D[] p)
343    {
344       return new CubicCurve2D.Double(p[0].getX(), p[0].getY(), p[1].getX(), p[1].getY(),
345          p[2].getX(), p[2].getY(), p[3].getX(), p[3].getY());
346    }
347 }
```

---

java.awt.geom.RoundRectangle2D.Double 1.2

- RoundRectangle2D.Double(double x, double y, double width, double height, double arcWidth, double arcHeight)

   constructs a rounded rectangle with the given bounding rectangle and arc dimensions. See Figure 11.34 for an explanation of the arcWidth and arcHeight parameters.

---

java.awt.geom.Arc2D.Double 1.2

- Arc2D.Double(double x, double y, double w, double h, double startAngle, double arcAngle, int type)

  constructs an arc with the given bounding rectangle, start and arc angle, and arc type. The startAngle and arcAngle are explained on p. 700. The type is one of Arc2D.OPEN, Arc2D.PIE, and Arc2D.CHORD.

---

java.awt.geom.QuadCurve2D.Double 1.2

- QuadCurve2D.Double(double x1, double y1, double ctrlx, double ctrly, double x2, double y2)

  constructs a quadratic curve from a start point, a control point, and an end point.

---

java.awt.geom.CubicCurve2D.Double 1.2

- CubicCurve2D.Double(double x1, double y1, double ctrlx1, double ctrly1, double ctrlx2, double ctrly2, double x2, double y2)

  constructs a cubic curve from a start point, two control points, and an end point.

---

java.awt.geom.GeneralPath 1.2

- GeneralPath()

  constructs an empty general path.

---

java.awt.geom.Path2D.Float 6

- void moveTo(float x, float y)

  makes (x, y) the *current point*—that is, the starting point of the next segment.

- void lineTo(float x, float y)
- void quadTo(float ctrlx, float ctrly, float x, float y)
- void curveTo(float ctrl1x, float ctrl1y, float ctrl2x, float ctrl2y, float x, float y)

  draws a line, quadratic curve, or cubic curve from the current point to the end point (x, y), and makes that end point the current point.

---

java.awt.geom.Path2D 6

- void append(Shape s, boolean connect)

  adds the outline of the given shape to the general path. If connect is true, the current point of the general path is connected to the starting point of the added shape by a straight line.

- void closePath()

  closes the path by drawing a straight line from the current point to the first point in the path.

11.3.3 Areas

In the preceding section, you saw how you can specify complex shapes by constructing general paths composed of lines and curves. By using a sufficient number of lines and curves, you can draw essentially any shape. For example, the shapes of characters in the fonts that you see on the screen and on your printouts are made up of lines and quadratic or cubic curves.

Occasionally, it is easier to describe a shape by composing it from *areas,* such as rectangles, polygons, or ellipses. The Java 2D API supports four *constructive area geometry* operations that combine two areas into a new area.

- add: The combined area contains all points that are in the first or the second area.
- subtract: The combined area contains all points that are in the first but not the second area.
- intersect: The combined area contains all points that are in the first and the second area.
- exclusiveOr: The combined area contains all points that are in either the first or the second area, but not in both.

Figure 11.40 shows these operations.

To construct a complex area, start with a default area object.

```
var a = new Area();
```

Then, combine the area with any shape.

```
a.add(new Rectangle2D.Double(. . .));
a.subtract(path);
. . .
```

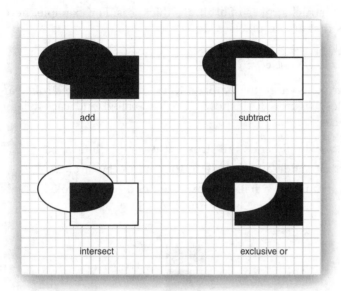

Figure 11.40 Constructive area geometry operations

The Area class implements the Shape interface. You can stroke the boundary of the area with the draw method or paint the interior with the fill method of the Graphics2D class.

---

java.awt.geom.Area

- void add(Area other)
- void subtract(Area other)
- void intersect(Area other)
- void exclusiveOr(Area other)

    carries out the constructive area geometry operation with this area and the other area and sets this area to the result.

11.3.4 Strokes

The draw operation of the Graphics2D class draws the boundary of a shape by using the currently selected *stroke*. By default, the stroke is a solid line that is 1 pixel wide. You can select a different stroke by calling the setStroke method and supplying an object of a class that implements the Stroke interface. The Java 2D API defines only one such class, called BasicStroke. In this section, we'll look at the capabilities of the BasicStroke class.

You can construct strokes of arbitrary thickness. For example, here is how to draw lines that are 10 pixels wide:

```
g2.setStroke(new BasicStroke(10.0F));
g2.draw(new Line2D.Double(. . .));
```

When a stroke is more than a pixel thick, the *end* of the stroke can have different styles. Figure 11.41 shows these so-called end cap styles. You have three choices:

- A *butt cap* simply ends the stroke at its end point.
- A *round cap* adds a half-circle to the end of the stroke.
- A *square cap* adds a half-square to the end of the stroke.

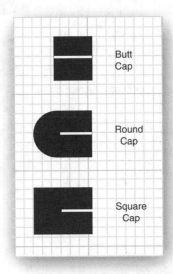

Figure 11.41 End cap styles

When two thick strokes meet, there are three choices for the *join style* (see Figure 11.42).

- A *bevel join* joins the strokes with a straight line that is perpendicular to the bisector of the angle between the two strokes.
- A *round join* extends each stroke to have a round cap.
- A *miter join* extends both strokes by adding a "spike."

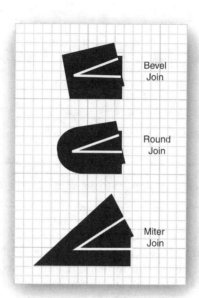

Figure 11.42 Join styles

If two lines come together in a miter join at a very small angle, a bevel join is used instead, preventing extremely long spikes. The *miter limit* controls this transition. Technically, this is the ratio of the distance of the inner and outer corners of the spike divided by the stroke width. The default miter limit of 10 corresponds to an angle of about 11 degrees.

You can specify these choices in the BasicStroke constructor, for example:

```
g2.setStroke(new BasicStroke(10.0F, BasicStroke.CAP_ROUND, BasicStroke.JOIN_ROUND));
g2.setStroke(new BasicStroke(10.0F, BasicStroke.CAP_BUTT, BasicStroke.JOIN_MITER,
   15.0F /* miter limit */));
```

Finally, you can create dashed lines by setting a *dash pattern*. In the program in Listing 11.16, you can select a dash pattern that spells out SOS in Morse code. The dash pattern is a float[] array that contains the lengths of the "on" and "off" intervals (see Figure 11.43).

You can specify the dash pattern and a *dash phase* when constructing the BasicStroke. The dash phase indicates where in the dash pattern each line should start. Normally, you set this value to 0.

```
float[] dashPattern = { 10, 10, 10, 10, 10, 10, 30, 10, 30, . . . };
g2.setStroke(new BasicStroke(10.0F, BasicStroke.CAP_BUTT, BasicStroke.JOIN_MITER,
   10.0F /* miter limit */, dashPattern, 0 /* dash phase */));
```

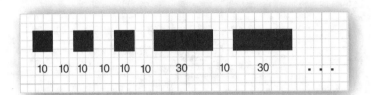

Figure 11.43 A dash pattern

 NOTE: End cap styles are applied to the ends of *each dash* in a dash pattern.

The program in Listing 11.16 lets you specify end cap styles, join styles, and dashed lines (see Figure 11.44). You can move the ends of the line segments to test the miter limit: Select the miter join, then move the line segment to form a very acute angle. You will see the miter join turn into a bevel join.

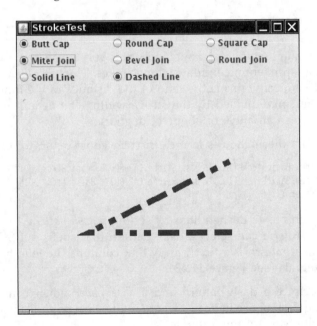

Figure 11.44 The StrokeTest program

The program is similar to the program in Listing 11.15. The mouse listener remembers your click on the end point of a line segment, and the mouse motion listener monitors the dragging of the end point. A set of radio buttons signal the user choices for the end cap style, join style, and solid or dashed line. The `paintComponent` method of the `StrokePanel` class constructs a `GeneralPath` consisting of the two line segments that join the three points which the user can move with the mouse. It then constructs a `BasicStroke`, according to the selections the user made, and finally draws the path.

Listing 11.16 `stroke/StrokeTest.java`

```
1  package stroke;
2
3  import java.awt.*;
4  import java.awt.event.*;
5  import java.awt.geom.*;
6  import javax.swing.*;
7
8  /**
9   * This program demonstrates different stroke types.
10  * @version 1.05 2018-05-01
11  * @author Cay Horstmann
12  */
13 public class StrokeTest
14 {
15    public static void main(String[] args)
16    {
17       EventQueue.invokeLater(() ->
18          {
19             var frame = new StrokeTestFrame();
20             frame.setTitle("StrokeTest");
21             frame.setDefaultCloseOperation(JFrame.EXIT_ON_CLOSE);
22             frame.setVisible(true);
23          });
24    }
25 }
26
27 /**
28  * This frame lets the user choose the cap, join, and line style, and shows the resulting
29  * stroke.
30  */
31 class StrokeTestFrame extends JFrame
32 {
33    private StrokeComponent canvas;
34    private JPanel buttonPanel;
35
```

(Continues)

Listing 11.16 *(Continued)*

```java
36  public StrokeTestFrame()
37  {
38     canvas = new StrokeComponent();
39     add(canvas, BorderLayout.CENTER);
40
41     buttonPanel = new JPanel();
42     buttonPanel.setLayout(new GridLayout(3, 3));
43     add(buttonPanel, BorderLayout.NORTH);
44
45     var group1 = new ButtonGroup();
46     makeCapButton("Butt Cap", BasicStroke.CAP_BUTT, group1);
47     makeCapButton("Round Cap", BasicStroke.CAP_ROUND, group1);
48     makeCapButton("Square Cap", BasicStroke.CAP_SQUARE, group1);
49
50     var group2 = new ButtonGroup();
51     makeJoinButton("Miter Join", BasicStroke.JOIN_MITER, group2);
52     makeJoinButton("Bevel Join", BasicStroke.JOIN_BEVEL, group2);
53     makeJoinButton("Round Join", BasicStroke.JOIN_ROUND, group2);
54
55     var group3 = new ButtonGroup();
56     makeDashButton("Solid Line", false, group3);
57     makeDashButton("Dashed Line", true, group3);
58  }
59
60  /**
61   * Makes a radio button to change the cap style.
62   * @param label the button label
63   * @param style the cap style
64   * @param group the radio button group
65   */
66  private void makeCapButton(String label, final int style, ButtonGroup group)
67  {
68     // select first button in group
69     boolean selected = group.getButtonCount() == 0;
70     var button = new JRadioButton(label, selected);
71     buttonPanel.add(button);
72     group.add(button);
73     button.addActionListener(event -> canvas.setCap(style));
74     pack();
75  }
76
77  /**
78   * Makes a radio button to change the join style.
79   * @param label the button label
80   * @param style the join style
81   * @param group the radio button group
82   */
```

```
83    private void makeJoinButton(String label, final int style, ButtonGroup group)
84    {
85       // select first button in group
86       boolean selected = group.getButtonCount() == 0;
87       var button = new JRadioButton(label, selected);
88       buttonPanel.add(button);
89       group.add(button);
90       button.addActionListener(event -> canvas.setJoin(style));
91    }
92
93    /**
94     * Makes a radio button to set solid or dashed lines.
95     * @param label the button label
96     * @param style false for solid, true for dashed lines
97     * @param group the radio button group
98     */
99    private void makeDashButton(String label, final boolean style, ButtonGroup group)
100    {
101       // select first button in group
102       boolean selected = group.getButtonCount() == 0;
103       var button = new JRadioButton(label, selected);
104       buttonPanel.add(button);
105       group.add(button);
106       button.addActionListener(event -> canvas.setDash(style));
107    }
108 }
109
110 /**
111  * This component draws two joined lines, using different stroke objects, and allows the user
112  * to drag the three points defining the lines.
113  */
114 class StrokeComponent extends JComponent
115 {
116    private static final Dimension PREFERRED_SIZE = new Dimension(400, 400);
117    private static int SIZE = 10;
118
119    private Point2D[] points;
120    private int current;
121    private float width;
122    private int cap;
123    private int join;
124    private boolean dash;
125
126    public StrokeComponent()
127    {
128       addMouseListener(new MouseAdapter()
129          {
```

(Continues)

Listing 11.16   *(Continued)*

```
130          public void mousePressed(MouseEvent event)
131          {
132             Point p = event.getPoint();
133             for (int i = 0; i < points.length; i++)
134             {
135                double x = points[i].getX() - SIZE / 2;
136                double y = points[i].getY() - SIZE / 2;
137                var r = new Rectangle2D.Double(x, y, SIZE, SIZE);
138                if (r.contains(p))
139                {
140                   current = i;
141                   return;
142                }
143             }
144          }
145
146          public void mouseReleased(MouseEvent event)
147          {
148             current = -1;
149          }
150       });
151
152    addMouseMotionListener(new MouseMotionAdapter()
153       {
154          public void mouseDragged(MouseEvent event)
155          {
156             if (current == -1) return;
157             points[current] = event.getPoint();
158             repaint();
159          }
160       });
161
162    points = new Point2D[3];
163    points[0] = new Point2D.Double(200, 100);
164    points[1] = new Point2D.Double(100, 200);
165    points[2] = new Point2D.Double(200, 200);
166    current = -1;
167    width = 8.0F;
168 }
169
170 public void paintComponent(Graphics g)
171 {
172    var g2 = (Graphics2D) g;
173    var path = new GeneralPath();
174    path.moveTo((float) points[0].getX(), (float) points[0].getY());
```

```
175        for (int i = 1; i < points.length; i++)
176           path.lineTo((float) points[i].getX(), (float) points[i].getY());
177        BasicStroke stroke;
178        if (dash)
179        {
180           float miterLimit = 10.0F;
181           float[] dashPattern = { 10F, 10F, 10F, 10F, 10F, 10F, 30F, 10F, 30F, 10F, 30F, 10F,
182                10F, 10F, 10F, 10F, 10F, 30F };
183           float dashPhase = 0;
184           stroke = new BasicStroke(width, cap, join, miterLimit, dashPattern, dashPhase);
185        }
186        else stroke = new BasicStroke(width, cap, join);
187        g2.setStroke(stroke);
188        g2.draw(path);
189     }
190
191     /**
192      * Sets the join style.
193      * @param j the join style
194      */
195     public void setJoin(int j)
196     {
197        join = j;
198        repaint();
199     }
200
201     /**
202      * Sets the cap style.
203      * @param c the cap style
204      */
205     public void setCap(int c)
206     {
207        cap = c;
208        repaint();
209     }
210
211     /**
212      * Sets solid or dashed lines.
213      * @param d false for solid, true for dashed lines
214      */
215     public void setDash(boolean d)
216     {
217        dash = d;
218        repaint();
219     }
220
221     public Dimension getPreferredSize() { return PREFERRED_SIZE; }
222  }
```

---

java.awt.Graphics2D 1.2

- void setStroke(Stroke s)

  sets the stroke of this graphics context to the given object that implements the Stroke interface.

---

java.awt.BasicStroke 1.2

- BasicStroke(float width)
- BasicStroke(float width, int cap, int join)
- BasicStroke(float width, int cap, int join, float miterlimit)
- BasicStroke(float width, int cap, int join, float miterlimit, float[] dash, float dashPhase)

  constructs a stroke object with the given attributes.

Parameters:	width	The width of the pen
	cap	The end cap style—one of CAP_BUTT, CAP_ROUND, and CAP_SQUARE
	join	The join style—one of JOIN_BEVEL, JOIN_MITER, and JOIN_ROUND
	miterlimit	The ratio between the outer and inner corners of the join and the stroke width, below which a miter join is rendered as a bevel join
	dash	An array of the lengths of the alternating filled and blank portions of a dashed stroke
	dashPhase	The "phase" of the dash pattern; a segment of this length, preceding the starting point of the stroke, is assumed to have the dash pattern already applied.

11.3.5 Paint

When you fill a shape, its inside is covered with *paint*. Use the setPaint method to set the paint style to an object whose class implements the Paint interface. The Java 2D API provides three such classes:

- The Color class implements the Paint interface. To fill shapes with a solid color, simply call setPaint with a Color object, such as

  ```
  g2.setPaint(Color.red);
  ```

- The GradientPaint class varies colors by interpolating between two given color values (see Figure 11.45).

Figure 11.45 Gradient paint

- The TexturePaint class fills an area with repetitions of an image (see Figure 11.46).

Figure 11.46 Texture paint

You can construct a GradientPaint object by specifying two points and the colors that you want at these two points.

```
g2.setPaint(new GradientPaint(p1, Color.RED, p2, Color.YELLOW));
```

Colors are interpolated along the line joining the two points. Colors are constant along lines perpendicular to that joining line. Points beyond an end point of the line are given the color at the end point.

Alternatively, if you call the GradientPaint constructor with true for the cyclic parameter:

```
g2.setPaint(new GradientPaint(p1, Color.RED, p2, Color.YELLOW, true));
```

Then, the color variation *cycles* and keeps varying beyond the end points.

To construct a `TexturePaint` object, specify a `BufferedImage` and an *anchor* rectangle.

```
g2.setPaint(new TexturePaint(bufferedImage, anchorRectangle));
```

We will introduce the `BufferedImage` class later in this chapter when we discuss images in detail. The simplest way of obtaining a buffered image is to read an image file:

```
bufferedImage = ImageIO.read(new File("blue-ball.gif"));
```

The anchor rectangle is extended indefinitely in x and y directions to tile the entire coordinate plane. The image is scaled to fit into the anchor and then replicated into each tile.

---

java.awt.Graphics2D 1.2

- `void setPaint(Paint s)`

  sets the paint of this graphics context to the given object that implements the Paint interface.

---

java.awt.GradientPaint 1.2

- `GradientPaint(float x1, float y1, Color color1, float x2, float y2, Color color2)`
- `GradientPaint(float x1, float y1, Color color1, float x2, float y2, Color color2, boolean cyclic)`
- `GradientPaint(Point2D p1, Color color1, Point2D p2, Color color2)`
- `GradientPaint(Point2D p1, Color color1, Point2D p2, Color color2, boolean cyclic)`

  constructs a gradient paint object that fills shapes with color such that the start point is colored with `color1`, the end point is colored with `color2`, and the colors in between are linearly interpolated. Colors are constant along lines perpendicular to the line joining the start and the end point. By default, the gradient paint is not cyclic—that is, points beyond the start and end points are colored with the same color as the start and end point. If the gradient paint is *cyclic*, then colors continue to be interpolated, first returning to the starting point color and then repeating indefinitely in both directions.

---

java.awt.TexturePaint 1.2

- `TexturePaint(BufferedImage texture, Rectangle2D anchor)`

  creates a texture paint object. The anchor rectangle defines the tiling of the space to be painted; it is repeated indefinitely in x and y directions, and the texture image is scaled to fill each tile.

11.3.6 Coordinate Transformations

Suppose you need to draw an object, such as an automobile. You know, from the manufacturer's specifications, the height, wheelbase, and total length. You could, of course, figure out all pixel positions, assuming some number of pixels per meter. However, there is an easier way: You can ask the graphics context to carry out the conversion for you.

```
g2.scale(pixelsPerMeter, pixelsPerMeter);
g2.draw(new Line2D.Double(coordinates in meters)); // converts to pixels and
                                                   // draws scaled line
```

The scale method of the Graphics2D class sets the *coordinate transformation* of the graphics context to a scaling transformation. That transformation changes *user coordinates* (user-specified units) to *device coordinates* (pixels). Figure 11.47 shows how the transformation works.

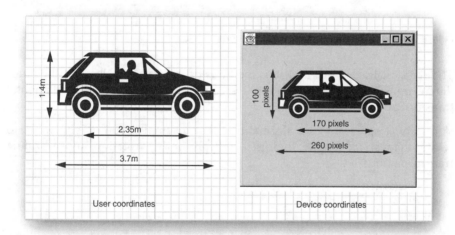

Figure 11.47 User and device coordinates

Coordinate transformations are very useful in practice. They allow you to work with convenient coordinate values. The graphics context takes care of the dirty work of transforming them to pixels.

There are four fundamental transformations.

- Scaling: blowing up, or shrinking, all distances from a fixed point
- Rotation: rotating all points around a fixed center
- Translation: moving all points by a fixed amount

- Shear: leaving one line fixed and "sliding" the lines parallel to it by an amount that is proportional to the distance from the fixed line

Figure 11.48 shows how these four fundamental transformations act on a unit square.

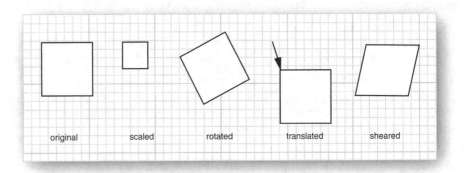

Figure 11.48 The fundamental transformations

The scale, rotate, translate, and shear methods of the Graphics2D class set the coordinate transformation of the graphics context to one of these fundamental transformations.

You can *compose* the transformations. For example, you might want to rotate shapes *and* double their size; supply both a rotation and a scaling transformation:

```
g2.rotate(angle);
g2.scale(2, 2);
g2.draw(. . .);
```

In this case, it does not matter in which order you supply the transformations. However, with most transformations, order does matter. For example, if you want to rotate and shear, then it makes a difference which of the transformations you supply first. You need to figure out what your intention is. The graphics context will apply the transformations in the order opposite to that in which you supplied them—that is, the last transformation you supply is applied first.

You can supply as many transformations as you like. For example, consider the following sequence of transformations:

```
g2.translate(x, y);
g2.rotate(a);
g2.translate(-x, -y);
```

The last transformation (which is applied first) moves the point (x, y) to the origin. The second transformation rotates with an angle a around the origin. The final transformation moves the origin back to (x, y). The overall effect is a rotation with center point (x, y)—see Figure 11.49. Since rotating about a point other than the origin is such a common operation, there is a shortcut:

```
g2.rotate(a, x, y);
```

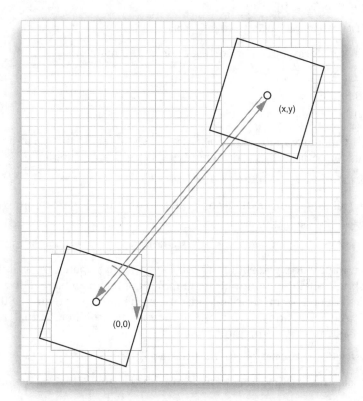

Figure 11.49 Composing transformations

If you know some matrix theory, you are probably aware that all rotations, translations, scalings, shears, and their compositions can be expressed by transformation matrices of the form:

$$\begin{bmatrix} x_{new} \\ y_{new} \\ 1 \end{bmatrix} = \begin{bmatrix} a & c & e \\ b & d & f \\ 0 & 0 & 1 \end{bmatrix} \cdot \begin{bmatrix} x \\ y \\ 1 \end{bmatrix}$$

Such a transformation is called an *affine transformation*. In the Java 2D API, the AffineTransform class describes such a transformation. If you know the components of a particular transformation matrix, you can construct it directly as

```
var t = new AffineTransform(a, b, c, d, e, f);
```

Additionally, the factory methods getRotateInstance, getScaleInstance, getTranslateInstance, and getShearInstance construct the matrices that represent these transformation types. For example, the call

```
t = AffineTransform.getScaleInstance(2.0F, 0.5F);
```

returns a transformation that corresponds to the matrix

$$
\begin{bmatrix}
2 & 0 & 0 \\
0 & 0.5 & 0 \\
0 & 0 & 1
\end{bmatrix}
$$

Finally, the instance methods setToRotation, setToScale, setToTranslation, and setToShear set a transformation object to a new type. Here is an example:

```
t.setToRotation(angle); // sets t to a rotation
```

You can set the coordinate transformation of the graphics context to an AffineTransform object.

```
g2.setTransform(t); // replaces current transformation
```

However, in practice, you shouldn't call the setTransform operation, as it replaces any existing transformation that the graphics context may have. For example, a graphics context for printing in landscape mode already contains a 90-degree rotation transformation. If you call setTransform, you obliterate that rotation. Instead, call the transform method.

```
g2.transform(t); // composes current transformation with t
```

It composes the existing transformation with the new AffineTransform object.

If you just want to apply a transformation temporarily, first get the old transformation, compose it with your new transformation, and finally restore the old transformation when you are done.

```
AffineTransform oldTransform = g2.getTransform(); // save old transform
g2.transform(t); // apply temporary transform
draw on g2
g2.setTransform(oldTransform); // restore old transform
```

java.awt.geom.AffineTransform 1.2

- AffineTransform(double a, double b, double c, double d, double e, double f)
- AffineTransform(float a, float b, float c, float d, float e, float f)

    constructs the affine transform with matrix

$$\begin{bmatrix} a & c & e \\ b & d & f \\ 0 & 0 & 1 \end{bmatrix}$$

- AffineTransform(double[] m)
- AffineTransform(float[] m)

    constructs the affine transform with matrix

$$\begin{bmatrix} m[0] & m[2] & m[4] \\ m[1] & m[3] & m[5] \\ 0 & 0 & 1 \end{bmatrix}$$

- static AffineTransform getRotateInstance(double a)

    creates a rotation around the origin by the angle a (in radians). The transformation matrix is

$$\begin{bmatrix} \cos(a) & -\sin(a) & 0 \\ \sin(a) & \cos(a) & 0 \\ 0 & 0 & 1 \end{bmatrix}$$

    If a is between 0 and $\pi\,/\,2$, the rotation moves the positive x axis toward the positive y axis.

- static AffineTransform getRotateInstance(double a, double x, double y)

    creates a rotation around the point (x,y) by the angle a (in radians).

- static AffineTransform getScaleInstance(double sx, double sy)

    creates a scaling transformation that scales the x axis by sx and the y axis by sy. The transformation matrix is

$$\begin{bmatrix} sx & 0 & 0 \\ 0 & sy & 0 \\ 0 & 0 & 1 \end{bmatrix}$$

(Continues)

`java.awt.geom.AffineTransform` 1.2 *(Continued)*

- `static AffineTransform getShearInstance(double shx, double shy)`

  creates a shear transformation that shears the x axis by shx and the y axis by shy. The transformation matrix is

$$
\begin{bmatrix}
1 & shx & 0 \\
shy & 1 & 0 \\
0 & 0 & 1
\end{bmatrix}
$$

- `static AffineTransform getTranslateInstance(double tx, double ty)`

  creates a translation that moves the x axis by tx and the y axis by ty. The transformation matrix is

$$
\begin{bmatrix}
1 & 0 & tx \\
0 & 1 & ty \\
0 & 0 & 1
\end{bmatrix}
$$

- `void setToRotation(double a)`
- `void setToRotation(double a, double x, double y)`
- `void setToScale(double sx, double sy)`
- `void setToShear(double sx, double sy)`
- `void setToTranslation(double tx, double ty)`

  sets this affine transformation to a basic transformation with the given parameters. See the getXxxInstance methods for an explanation of the basic transformations and their parameters.

`java.awt.Graphics2D` 1.2

- `void setTransform(AffineTransform t)`

  replaces the existing coordinate transformation of this graphics context with t.
- `void transform(AffineTransform t)`

  composes the existing coordinate transformation of this graphics context with t.
- `void rotate(double a)`
- `void rotate(double a, double x, double y)`
- `void scale(double sx, double sy)`
- `void shear(double sx, double sy)`
- `void translate(double tx, double ty)`

  composes the existing coordinate transformation of this graphics context with a basic transformation with the given parameters. See the AffineTransform .getXxxInstance methods for an explanation of the basic transformations and their parameters.

11.3.7 Clipping

By setting a *clipping shape* in the graphics context, you constrain all drawing operations to the interior of that clipping shape.

```
g2.setClip(clipShape); // but see below
g2.draw(shape); // draws only the part that falls inside the clipping shape
```

However, in practice, you don't want to call the setClip operation because it replaces any existing clipping shape that the graphics context might have. For example, as you will see later in this chapter, a graphics context for printing comes with a clip rectangle that ensures that you don't draw on the margins. Instead, call the clip method.

```
g2.clip(clipShape); // better
```

The clip method intersects the existing clipping shape with the new one that you supply.

If you just want to apply a clipping area temporarily, you should first get the old clip, add your new clip, and finally restore the old clip when you are done:

```
Shape oldClip = g2.getClip(); // save old clip
g2.clip(clipShape); // apply temporary clip
draw on g2
g2.setClip(oldClip); // restore old clip
```

In Figure 11.50, we show off the clipping capability with a rather dramatic drawing of a line pattern clipped by a complex shape—namely, the outline of a set of letters.

Figure 11.50 Using letter shapes to clip a line pattern

To obtain the character outlines, you need a *font render context*. Use the getFontRenderContext method of the Graphics2D class.

```
FontRenderContext context = g2.getFontRenderContext();
```

Next, using a string, a font, and the font render context, create a `TextLayout` object:

```
var layout = new TextLayout("Hello", font, context);
```

This text layout object describes the layout of a sequence of characters, as rendered by a particular font render context. The layout depends on the font render context—the same characters will look different on a screen and on a printer.

More important for our application, the `getOutline` method returns a `Shape` object that describes the shape of the outline of the characters in the text layout. The outline shape starts at the origin (0, 0), which might not be what you want. In that case, supply an affine transform to the `getOutline` operation to specify where you would like the outline to appear.

```
AffineTransform transform = AffineTransform.getTranslateInstance(0, 100);
Shape outline = layout.getOutline(transform);
```

Then, append the outline to the clipping shape.

```
var clipShape = new GeneralPath();
clipShape.append(outline, false);
```

Finally, set the clipping shape and draw a set of lines. The lines appear only inside the character boundaries.

```
g2.setClip(clipShape);
var p = new Point2D.Double(0, 0);
for (int i = 0; i < NLINES; i++)
{
   double x = . . .;
   double y = . . .;
   var q = new Point2D.Double(x, y);
   g2.draw(new Line2D.Double(p, q)); // lines are clipped
}
```

---

java.awt.Graphics 1.0

- void setClip(Shape s) 1.2

  sets the current clipping shape to the shape s.

- Shape getClip() 1.2

  returns the current clipping shape.

---

java.awt.Graphics2D 1.2

- void clip(Shape s)

  intersects the current clipping shape with the shape s.
- FontRenderContext getFontRenderContext()

  returns a font render context that is necessary for constructing TextLayout objects.

---

java.awt.font.TextLayout 1.2

- TextLayout(String s, Font f, FontRenderContext context)

  constructs a text layout object from a given string and font, using the font render context to obtain font properties for a particular device.
- float getAdvance()

  returns the width of this text layout.
- float getAscent()
- float getDescent()

  returns the height of this text layout above and below the baseline.
- float getLeading()

  returns the distance between successive lines in the font used by this text layout.

11.3.8 Transparency and Composition

In the standard RGB color model, every color is described by its red, green, and blue components. However, it is also convenient to describe areas of an image that are *transparent* or partially transparent. When you superimpose an image onto an existing drawing, the transparent pixels do not obscure the pixels under them at all, whereas partially transparent pixels are mixed with the pixels under them. Figure 11.51 shows the effect of overlaying a partially transparent rectangle on an image. You can still see the details of the image shine through from under the rectangle.

In the Java 2D API, transparency is described by an *alpha channel*. Each pixel has, in addition to its red, green, and blue color components, an alpha value between 0 (fully transparent) and 1 (fully opaque). For example, the rectangle in Figure 11.51 was filled with a pale yellow color with 50% transparency:

```
new Color(0.7F, 0.7F, 0.0F, 0.5F);
```

Figure 11.51 Overlaying a partially transparent rectangle on an image

Now let us look at what happens if you superimpose two shapes. You need to blend or *compose* the colors and alpha values of the source and destination pixels. Porter and Duff, two researchers in the field of computer graphics, have formulated 12 possible *composition rules* for this blending process. The Java 2D API implements all of these rules. Before going any further, we'd like to point out that only two of these rules have practical significance. If you find the rules arcane or confusing, just use the SRC_OVER rule. It is the default rule for a Graphics2D object, and it gives the most intuitive results.

Here is the theory behind the rules. Suppose you have a *source pixel* with alpha value a_S. In the image, there is already a *destination pixel* with alpha value a_D. You want to compose the two. The diagram in Figure 11.52 shows how to design a composition rule.

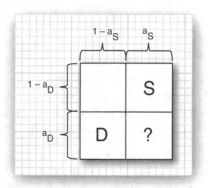

Figure 11.52 Designing a composition rule

Porter and Duff consider the alpha value as the probability that the pixel color should be used. From the perspective of the source, there is a probability a_S that it wants to use the source color and a probability of $1 - a_S$ that it doesn't care. The same holds for the destination. When composing the colors, let us assume that the probabilities are independent. Then there are four cases, as shown in Figure 11.52. If the source wants to use the source color and the destination doesn't care, then it seems reasonable to let the source have its way. That's why the upper right corner of the diagram is labeled "S". The probability for that event is $a_S \cdot (1 - a_D)$. Similarly, the lower left corner is labeled "D". What should one do if both destination and source would like to select their color? That's where the Porter–Duff rules come in. If we decide that the source is more important, we label the lower right corner with an "S" as well. That rule is called SRC_OVER. In that rule, you combine the source colors with a weight of a_S and the destination colors with a weight of $(1 - a_S) \cdot a_D$.

The visual effect is a blending of the source and destination, with preference given to the source. In particular, if a_S is 1, then the destination color is not taken into account at all. If a_S is 0, then the source pixel is completely transparent and the destination color is unchanged.

The other rules depend on what letters you put in the boxes of the probability diagram. Table 11.3 and Figure 11.53 show all rules that are supported by the Java 2D API. The images in the figure show the results of the rules when a rectangular source region with an alpha of 0.75 is combined with an elliptical destination region with an alpha of 1.0.

Table 11.3 The Porter–Duff Composition Rules

Rule	Explanation
CLEAR	Source clears destination.
SRC	Source overwrites destination and empty pixels.
DST	Source does not affect destination.
SRC_OVER	Source blends with destination and overwrites empty pixels.
DST_OVER	Source does not affect destination and overwrites empty pixels.
SRC_IN	Source overwrites destination.
SRC_OUT	Source clears destination and overwrites empty pixels.
DST_IN	Source alpha modifies destination.
DST_OUT	Source alpha complement modifies destination.
SRC_ATOP	Source blends with destination.
DST_ATOP	Source alpha modifies destination. Source overwrites empty pixels.
XOR	Source alpha complement modifies destination. Source overwrites empty pixels.

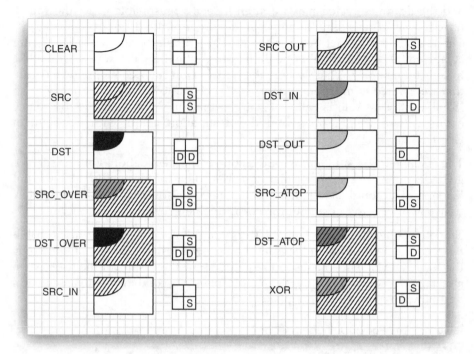

Figure 11.53 Porter–Duff composition rules

As you can see, most of the rules aren't very useful. Consider, as an extreme case, the DST_IN rule. It doesn't take the source color into account at all, but uses the alpha of the source to affect the destination. The SRC rule is potentially useful—it forces the source color to be used, turning off blending with the destination.

For more information on the Porter–Duff rules, see, for example, *Computer Graphics: Principles and Practice, Second Edition in C,* by James D. Foley, Andries van Dam, Steven K. Feiner, et al.

Use the setComposite method of the Graphics2D class to install an object of a class that implements the Composite interface. The Java 2D API supplies one such class, AlphaComposite, that implements all the Porter–Duff rules in Figure 11.53.

The factory method getInstance of the AlphaComposite class yields an AlphaComposite object. You supply the rule and the alpha value to be used for source pixels. For example, consider the following code:

```
int rule = AlphaComposite.SRC_OVER;
float alpha = 0.5f;
g2.setComposite(AlphaComposite.getInstance(rule, alpha));
g2.setPaint(Color.blue);
g2.fill(rectangle);
```

The rectangle is then painted with blue color and an alpha value of 0.5. Since the composition rule is SRC_OVER, it is transparently overlaid on the existing image.

The program in Listing 11.17 lets you explore these composition rules. Pick a rule from the combo box and use the slider to set the alpha value of the AlphaComposite object.

Furthermore, the program displays a verbal description of each rule. Note that the descriptions are computed from the composition rule diagrams. For example, a "DS" in the second row stands for "blends with destination."

The program has one important twist. There is no guarantee that the graphics context that corresponds to the screen has an alpha channel. (In fact, it generally does not.) When pixels are deposited to a destination without an alpha channel, the pixel colors are multiplied with the alpha value and the alpha value is discarded. Now, several of the Porter–Duff rules use the alpha values of the destination, which means a destination alpha channel is important. For that reason, we use a buffered image with the ARGB color model to compose the shapes. After the images have been composed, we draw the resulting image to the screen.

```
var image = new BufferedImage(getWidth(), getHeight(), BufferedImage.TYPE_INT_ARGB);
Graphics2D gImage = image.createGraphics();
// now draw to gImage
g2.drawImage(image, null, 0, 0);
```

Listings 11.17 and 11.18 show the frame and component class. The Rule class in Listing 11.19 provides a brief explanation for each rule—see Figure 11.54. As you run the program, move the alpha slider from left to right to see the effect on the composed shapes. In particular, note that the only difference between the DST_IN and DST_OUT rules is how the destination (!) color changes when you change the source alpha.

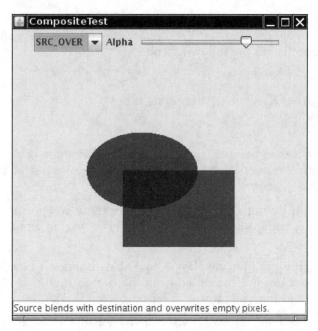

Figure 11.54 The CompositeTest program

Listing 11.17 composite/CompositeTestFrame.java

```
1 package composite;
2
3 import java.awt.*;
4 import javax.swing.*;
5
6 /**
7  * This frame contains a combo box to choose a composition rule, a slider to change the
8  * source alpha channel, and a component that shows the composition.
9  */
10 class CompositeTestFrame extends JFrame
11 {
12    private static final int DEFAULT_WIDTH = 400;
13    private static final int DEFAULT_HEIGHT = 400;
14
15    private CompositeComponent canvas;
16    private JComboBox<Rule> ruleCombo;
17    private JSlider alphaSlider;
18    private JTextField explanation;
19
20    public CompositeTestFrame()
21    {
22       setSize(DEFAULT_WIDTH, DEFAULT_HEIGHT);
```

```
23
24      canvas = new CompositeComponent();
25      add(canvas, BorderLayout.CENTER);
26
27      ruleCombo = new JComboBox<>(new Rule[] { new Rule("CLEAR", "  ", "  "),
28          new Rule("SRC", " S", " S"), new Rule("DST", " ", "DD"),
29          new Rule("SRC_OVER", " S", "DS"), new Rule("DST_OVER", " S", "DD"),
30          new Rule("SRC_IN", " ", " S"), new Rule("SRC_OUT", " S", " "),
31          new Rule("DST_IN", " ", " D"), new Rule("DST_OUT", " ", "D "),
32          new Rule("SRC_ATOP", " ", "DS"), new Rule("DST_ATOP", " S", " D"),
33          new Rule("XOR", " S", "D "), });
34      ruleCombo.addActionListener(event ->
35          {
36              var r = (Rule) ruleCombo.getSelectedItem();
37              canvas.setRule(r.getValue());
38              explanation.setText(r.getExplanation());
39          });
40
41      alphaSlider = new JSlider(0, 100, 75);
42      alphaSlider.addChangeListener(event -> canvas.setAlpha(alphaSlider.getValue()));
43      var panel = new JPanel();
44      panel.add(ruleCombo);
45      panel.add(new JLabel("Alpha"));
46      panel.add(alphaSlider);
47      add(panel, BorderLayout.NORTH);
48
49      explanation = new JTextField();
50      add(explanation, BorderLayout.SOUTH);
51
52      canvas.setAlpha(alphaSlider.getValue());
53      Rule r = ruleCombo.getItemAt(ruleCombo.getSelectedIndex());
54      canvas.setRule(r.getValue());
55      explanation.setText(r.getExplanation());
56    }
57 }
```

Listing 11.18 composite/CompositeComponent.java

```
1 package composite;
2
3 import java.awt.*;
4 import java.awt.geom.*;
5 import java.awt.image.*;
6 import javax.swing.*;
7
8 /**
9  * This component draws two shapes, composed with a composition rule.
10 */
```

(Continues)

Listing 11.18 *(Continued)*

```java
11  class CompositeComponent extends JComponent
12  {
13     private int rule;
14     private Shape shape1;
15     private Shape shape2;
16     private float alpha;
17
18     public CompositeComponent()
19     {
20        shape1 = new Ellipse2D.Double(100, 100, 150, 100);
21        shape2 = new Rectangle2D.Double(150, 150, 150, 100);
22     }
23
24     public void paintComponent(Graphics g)
25     {
26        var g2 = (Graphics2D) g;
27
28        var image = new BufferedImage(getWidth(), getHeight(), BufferedImage.TYPE_INT_ARGB);
29        Graphics2D gImage = image.createGraphics();
30        gImage.setPaint(Color.red);
31        gImage.fill(shape1);
32        AlphaComposite composite = AlphaComposite.getInstance(rule, alpha);
33        gImage.setComposite(composite);
34        gImage.setPaint(Color.blue);
35        gImage.fill(shape2);
36        g2.drawImage(image, null, 0, 0);
37     }
38
39     /**
40      * Sets the composition rule.
41      * @param r the rule (as an AlphaComposite constant)
42      */
43     public void setRule(int r)
44     {
45        rule = r;
46        repaint();
47     }
48
49     /**
50      * Sets the alpha of the source.
51      * @param a the alpha value between 0 and 100
52      */
53     public void setAlpha(int a)
54     {
55        alpha = (float) a / 100.0F;
56        repaint();
57     }
58  }
```

Listing 11.19 composite/Rule.java

```
1  package composite;
2
3  import java.awt.*;
4
5  /**
6   * This class describes a Porter-Duff rule.
7   */
8  class Rule
9  {
10    private String name;
11    private String porterDuff1;
12    private String porterDuff2;
13
14    /**
15     * Constructs a Porter-Duff rule.
16     * @param n the rule name
17     * @param pd1 the first row of the Porter-Duff square
18     * @param pd2 the second row of the Porter-Duff square
19     */
20    public Rule(String n, String pd1, String pd2)
21    {
22      name = n;
23      porterDuff1 = pd1;
24      porterDuff2 = pd2;
25    }
26
27    /**
28     * Gets an explanation of the behavior of this rule.
29     * @return the explanation
30     */
31    public String getExplanation()
32    {
33      var r = new StringBuilder("Source ");
34      if (porterDuff2.equals("  ")) r.append("clears");
35      if (porterDuff2.equals(" S")) r.append("overwrites");
36      if (porterDuff2.equals("DS")) r.append("blends with");
37      if (porterDuff2.equals(" D")) r.append("alpha modifies");
38      if (porterDuff2.equals("D ")) r.append("alpha complement modifies");
39      if (porterDuff2.equals("DD")) r.append("does not affect");
40      r.append(" destination");
41      if (porterDuff1.equals(" S")) r.append(" and overwrites empty pixels");
42      r.append(".");
43      return r.toString();
44    }
45
```

(Continues)

Listing 11.19 *(Continued)*

```
46    public String toString()
47    {
48       return name;
49    }
50
51    /**
52     * Gets the value of this rule in the AlphaComposite class.
53     * @return the AlphaComposite constant value, or -1 if there is no matching constant
54     */
55    public int getValue()
56    {
57       try
58       {
59          return (Integer) AlphaComposite.class.getField(name).get(null);
60       }
61       catch (Exception e)
62       {
63          return -1;
64       }
65    }
66 }
```

---

java.awt.Graphics2D 1.2

- void setComposite(Composite s)

  sets the composite of this graphics context to the given object that implements the Composite interface.

---

java.awt.AlphaComposite 1.2

- static AlphaComposite getInstance(int rule)
- static AlphaComposite getInstance(int rule, float sourceAlpha)

  constructs an alpha composite object. The rule is one of CLEAR, SRC, SRC_OVER, DST_OVER, SRC_IN, SRC_OUT, DST_IN, DST_OUT, DST, DST_ATOP, SRC_ATOP, XOR.

11.4 Raster Images

The Java2D API lets you create drawings that are made up of lines, curves, and areas. It is a "vector" API because you specify the mathematical properties of the shapes. However, for processing images that are made up of pixels, you want to work with a "raster" of color data. The following sections show you how to process raster images in Java.

11.4.1 Readers and Writers for Images

The javax.imageio package contains out-of-the-box support for reading and writing several common file formats, as well as a framework that enables third parties to add readers and writers for other formats. The GIF, JPEG, PNG, BMP (Windows bitmap), and WBMP (wireless bitmap) file formats are supported.

The basics of the library are extremely straightforward. To load an image, use the static read method of the ImageIO class:

```
File f = . . .;
BufferedImage image = ImageIO.read(f);
```

The ImageIO class picks an appropriate reader, based on the file type. It may consult the file extension and the "magic number" at the beginning of the file for that purpose. If no suitable reader can be found or the reader can't decode the file contents, the read method returns null.

Writing an image to a file is just as simple:

```
File f = . . .;
String format = . . .;
ImageIO.write(image, format, f);
```

Here the format string is a string identifying the image format, such as "JPEG" or "PNG". The ImageIO class picks an appropriate writer and saves the file.

11.4.1.1 Obtaining Readers and Writers for Image File Types

For more advanced image reading and writing operations that go beyond the static read and write methods of the ImageIO class, you first need to get the appropriate ImageReader and ImageWriter objects. The ImageIO class enumerates readers and writers that match one of the following:

- An image format (such as "JPEG")
- A file suffix (such as "jpg")
- A MIME type (such as "image/jpeg")

 NOTE: MIME is the Multipurpose Internet Mail Extensions standard. The MIME standard defines common data formats such as image/jpeg and application/pdf.

For example, you can obtain a reader that reads JPEG files as follows:

```
ImageReader reader = null;
Iterator<ImageReader> iter = ImageIO.getImageReadersByFormatName("JPEG");
if (iter.hasNext()) reader = iter.next();
```

The getImageReadersBySuffix and getImageReadersByMIMEType methods enumerate readers that match a file extension or MIME type.

It is possible that the ImageIO class can locate multiple readers that can all read a particular image type. In that case, you have to pick one of them, but it isn't clear how you can decide which one is the best. To find out more information about a reader, obtain its *service provider interface*:

```
ImageReaderSpi spi = reader.getOriginatingProvider();
```

Then you can get the vendor name and version number:

```
String vendor = spi.getVendor();
String version = spi.getVersion();
```

Perhaps that information can help you decide among the choices—or you might just present a list of readers to your program users and let them choose. For now, we assume that the first enumerated reader is adequate.

In the sample program in Listing 11.20, we want to find all file suffixes of all available readers so that we can use them in a file filter. Use the static ImageIO.getReaderFileSuffixes method for this purpose:

```
String[] extensions = ImageIO.getWriterFileSuffixes();
chooser.setFileFilter(new FileNameExtensionFilter("Image files", extensions));
```

For saving files, we have to work harder. We'd like to present the user with a menu of all supported image types. Unfortunately, the getWriterFormatNames of the ImageIO class returns a rather curious list with redundant names, such as

```
jpg, BMP, bmp, JPG, jpeg, wbmp, png, JPEG, PNG, WBMP, GIF, gif
```

That's not something one would want to present in a menu. What is needed is a list of "preferred" format names. We supply a helper method getWriterFormats for this purpose (see Listing 11.20). We look up the first writer associated with each format name. Then we ask it what its format names are, in the hope that it will list the most popular one first. Indeed, for the JPEG writer, this works fine—it lists "JPEG" before the other options. (The PNG writer, on the other hand, lists "png" in lower case before "PNG". We hope this behavior will be addressed at some point in the future. For now, we force all-lowercase names to upper case.) Once we pick a preferred name, we remove all alternate names from the original set. We keep going until all format names are handled.

11.4.1.2 Reading and Writing Files with Multiple Images

Some files—in particular, animated GIF files—contain multiple images. The read method of the ImageIO class reads a single image. To read multiple images, turn the input source (for example, an input stream or file) into an ImageInputStream.

```
InputStream in = . . .;
ImageInputStream imageIn = ImageIO.createImageInputStream(in);
```

Then, attach the image input stream to the reader:

```
reader.setInput(imageIn, true);
```

The second parameter indicates that the input is in "seek forward only" mode. Otherwise, random access is used, either by buffering stream input as it is read or by using random file access. Random access is required for certain operations. For example, to find out the number of images in a GIF file, you need to read the entire file. If you then want to fetch an image, the input must be read again.

This consideration is only important if you read from a stream, if the input contains multiple images, and if the image format doesn't have the information that you request (such as the image count) in the header. If you read from a file, simply use

```
File f = . . .;
ImageInputStream imageIn = ImageIO.createImageInputStream(f);
reader.setInput(imageIn);
```

Once you have a reader, you can read the images in the input by calling

```
BufferedImage image = reader.read(index);
```

where index is the image index, starting with 0.

If the input is in the "seek forward only" mode, you keep reading images until the read method throws an IndexOutOfBoundsException. Otherwise, you can call the getNumImages method:

```
int n = reader.getNumImages(true);
```

Here, the parameter indicates that you allow a search of the input to determine the number of images. That method throws an IllegalStateException if the input is in the "seek forward only" mode. Alternatively, you can set the "allow search" parameter to false. Then the getNumImages method returns -1 if it can't determine the number of images without a search. In that case, you'll have to switch to Plan B and keep reading images until you get an IndexOutOfBoundsException.

Some files contain thumbnails—smaller versions of an image for preview purposes. You can get the number of thumbnails of an image with the call

```
int count = reader.getNumThumbnails(index);
```

Then you get a particular index as

```
BufferedImage thumbnail = reader.getThumbnail(index, thumbnailIndex);
```

Sometimes you may want to get the image size before actually getting the image—in particular, if the image is huge or comes from a slow network connection. Use the calls

```
int width = reader.getWidth(index);
int height = reader.getHeight(index);
```

to get the dimensions of an image with a given index.

To write a file with multiple images, you first need an `ImageWriter`. The `ImageIO` class can enumerate the writers capable of writing a particular image format:

```
String format = . . .;
ImageWriter writer = null;
Iterator<ImageWriter> iter = ImageIO.getImageWritersByFormatName(format);
if (iter.hasNext()) writer = iter.next();
```

Next, turn an output stream or file into an `ImageOutputStream` and attach it to the writer. For example,

```
File f = . . .;
ImageOutputStream imageOut = ImageIO.createImageOutputStream(f);
writer.setOutput(imageOut);
```

You must wrap each image into an `IIOImage` object. You can optionally supply a list of thumbnails and image metadata (such as compression algorithms and color information). In this example, we just use `null` for both; see the API documentation for additional information.

```
var iioImage = new IIOImage(images[i], null, null);
```

To write out the *first* image, use the `write` method:

```
writer.write(new IIOImage(images[0], null, null));
```

For subsequent images, use

```
if (writer.canInsertImage(i))
    writer.writeInsert(i, iioImage, null);
```

The third parameter can contain an `ImageWriteParam` object to set image writing details such as tiling and compression; use `null` for default values.

Not all file formats can handle multiple images. In that case, the `canInsertImage` method returns `false` for i > 0, and only a single image is saved.

The program in Listing 11.20 lets you load and save files in the formats for which the Java library supplies readers and writers. The program displays multiple images (see Figure 11.55), but not thumbnails.

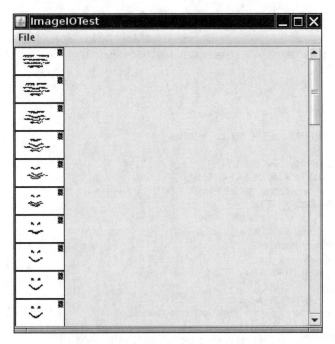

Figure 11.55 An animated GIF image

Listing 11.20 `imageIO/ImageIOFrame.java`

```java
1  package imageIO;
2
3  import java.awt.image.*;
4  import java.io.*;
5  import java.util.*;
6
7  import javax.imageio.*;
8  import javax.imageio.stream.*;
9  import javax.swing.*;
10 import javax.swing.filechooser.*;
11
```

(Continues)

Listing 11.20   *(Continued)*

```
12  /**
13   * This frame displays the loaded images. The menu has items for loading and saving files.
14   */
15  public class ImageIOFrame extends JFrame
16  {
17     private static final int DEFAULT_WIDTH = 400;
18     private static final int DEFAULT_HEIGHT = 400;
19
20     private static Set<String> writerFormats = getWriterFormats();
21
22     private BufferedImage[] images;
23
24     public ImageIOFrame()
25     {
26        setSize(DEFAULT_WIDTH, DEFAULT_HEIGHT);
27
28        var fileMenu = new JMenu("File");
29        var openItem = new JMenuItem("Open");
30        openItem.addActionListener(event -> openFile());
31        fileMenu.add(openItem);
32
33        var saveMenu = new JMenu("Save");
34        fileMenu.add(saveMenu);
35        Iterator<String> iter = writerFormats.iterator();
36        while (iter.hasNext())
37        {
38           final String formatName = iter.next();
39           var formatItem = new JMenuItem(formatName);
40           saveMenu.add(formatItem);
41           formatItem.addActionListener(event -> saveFile(formatName));
42        }
43
44        var exitItem = new JMenuItem("Exit");
45        exitItem.addActionListener(event -> System.exit(0));
46        fileMenu.add(exitItem);
47
48        var menuBar = new JMenuBar();
49        menuBar.add(fileMenu);
50        setJMenuBar(menuBar);
51     }
52
53     /**
54      * Open a file and load the images.
55      */
```

```
56    public void openFile()
57    {
58       var chooser = new JFileChooser();
59       chooser.setCurrentDirectory(new File("."));
60       String[] extensions = ImageIO.getReaderFileSuffixes();
61       chooser.setFileFilter(new FileNameExtensionFilter("Image files", extensions));
62       int r = chooser.showOpenDialog(this);
63       if (r != JFileChooser.APPROVE_OPTION) return;
64       File f = chooser.getSelectedFile();
65       Box box = Box.createVerticalBox();
66       try
67       {
68          String name = f.getName();
69          String suffix = name.substring(name.lastIndexOf('.') + 1);
70          Iterator<ImageReader> iter = ImageIO.getImageReadersBySuffix(suffix);
71          ImageReader reader = iter.next();
72          ImageInputStream imageIn = ImageIO.createImageInputStream(f);
73          reader.setInput(imageIn);
74          int count = reader.getNumImages(true);
75          images = new BufferedImage[count];
76          for (int i = 0; i < count; i++)
77          {
78             images[i] = reader.read(i);
79             box.add(new JLabel(new ImageIcon(images[i])));
80          }
81       }
82       catch (IOException e)
83       {
84          JOptionPane.showMessageDialog(this, e);
85       }
86       setContentPane(new JScrollPane(box));
87       validate();
88    }
89
90    /**
91     * Save the current image in a file.
92     * @param formatName the file format
93     */
94    public void saveFile(final String formatName)
95    {
96       if (images == null) return;
97       Iterator<ImageWriter> iter = ImageIO.getImageWritersByFormatName(formatName);
98       ImageWriter writer = iter.next();
99       var chooser = new JFileChooser();
100      chooser.setCurrentDirectory(new File("."));
101      String[] extensions = writer.getOriginatingProvider().getFileSuffixes();
102      chooser.setFileFilter(new FileNameExtensionFilter("Image files", extensions));
103
```

(Continues)

Listing 11.20   *(Continued)*

```
104      int r = chooser.showSaveDialog(this);
105      if (r != JFileChooser.APPROVE_OPTION) return;
106      File f = chooser.getSelectedFile();
107      try
108      {
109         ImageOutputStream imageOut = ImageIO.createImageOutputStream(f);
110         writer.setOutput(imageOut);
111
112         writer.write(new IIOImage(images[0], null, null));
113         for (int i = 1; i < images.length; i++)
114         {
115            var iioImage = new IIOImage(images[i], null, null);
116            if (writer.canInsertImage(i)) writer.writeInsert(i, iioImage, null);
117         }
118      }
119      catch (IOException e)
120      {
121         JOptionPane.showMessageDialog(this, e);
122      }
123   }
124
125   /**
126    * Gets a set of "preferred" format names of all image writers. The preferred format name
127    * is the first format name that a writer specifies.
128    * @return the format name set
129    */
130   public static Set<String> getWriterFormats()
131   {
132      var writerFormats = new TreeSet<String>();
133      var formatNames = List.of(ImageIO.getWriterFormatNames());
134      while (formatNames.size() > 0)
135      {
136         String name = formatNames.iterator().next();
137         Iterator<ImageWriter> iter = ImageIO.getImageWritersByFormatName(name);
138         ImageWriter writer = iter.next();
139         String[] names = writer.getOriginatingProvider().getFormatNames();
140         String format = names[0];
141         if (format.equals(format.toLowerCase())) format = format.toUpperCase();
142         writerFormats.add(format);
143         formatNames.removeAll(List.of(names));
144      }
145      return writerFormats;
146   }
147 }
```

javax.imageio.ImageIO 1.4

- static BufferedImage read(File input)
- static BufferedImage read(InputStream input)
- static BufferedImage read(URL input)

  reads an image from input.

- static boolean write(RenderedImage image, String formatName, File output)
- static boolean write(RenderedImage image, String formatName, OutputStream output)

  writes an image in the given format to output. Returns false if no appropriate writer was found.

- static Iterator<ImageReader> getImageReadersByFormatName(String formatName)
- static Iterator<ImageReader> getImageReadersBySuffix(String fileSuffix)
- static Iterator<ImageReader> getImageReadersByMIMEType(String mimeType)
- static Iterator<ImageWriter> getImageWritersByFormatName(String formatName)
- static Iterator<ImageWriter> getImageWritersBySuffix(String fileSuffix)
- static Iterator<ImageWriter> getImageWritersByMIMEType(String mimeType)

  gets all readers and writers that are able to handle the given format (e.g., "JPEG"), file suffix (e.g., "jpg"), or MIME type (e.g., "image/jpeg").

- static String[] getReaderFormatNames()
- static String[] getReaderMIMETypes()
- static String[] getWriterFormatNames()
- static String[] getWriterMIMETypes()
- static String[] getReaderFileSuffixes() 6
- static String[] getWriterFileSuffixes() 6

  gets all format names, MIME type names, and file suffixes supported by readers and writers.

- ImageInputStream createImageInputStream(Object input)
- ImageOutputStream createImageOutputStream(Object output)

  creates an image input or image output stream from the given object. The object can be a file, a stream, a RandomAccessFile, or another object for which a service provider exists. Returns null if no registered service provider can handle the object.

`javax.imageio.ImageReader` 1.4

- void setInput(Object input)
- void setInput(Object input, boolean seekForwardOnly)

  sets the input source of the reader.

  | *Parameters:* | input | An ImageInputStream object or another object that this reader can accept. |
  | | seekForwardOnly | true if the reader should read forward only. By default, the reader uses random access and, if necessary, buffers image data. |

- BufferedImage read(int index)

  reads the image with the given image index (starting at 0). Throws an IndexOutOfBoundsException if no such image is available.

- int getNumImages(boolean allowSearch)

  gets the number of images in this reader. If allowSearch is false and the number of images cannot be determined without reading forward, then -1 is returned. If allowSearch is true and the reader is in the "seek forward only" mode, then an IllegalStateException is thrown.

- int getNumThumbnails(int index)

  gets the number of thumbnails of the image with the given index.

- BufferedImage readThumbnail(int index, int thumbnailIndex)

  gets the thumbnail with index thumbnailIndex of the image with the given index.

- int getWidth(int index)
- int getHeight(int index)

  gets the image width and height. Throws an IndexOutOfBoundsException if no such image is available.

- ImageReaderSpi getOriginatingProvider()

  gets the service provider that constructed this reader.

`javax.imageio.spi.IIOServiceProvider` 1.4

- String getVendorName()
- String getVersion()

  gets the vendor name and version of this service provider.

---

javax.imageio.spi.ImageReaderWriterSpi 1.4

- String[] getFormatNames()
- String[] getFileSuffixes()
- String[] getMIMETypes()

  gets the format names, file suffixes, and MIME types supported by the readers or writers that this service provider creates.

---

javax.imageio.ImageWriter 1.4

- void setOutput(Object output)

  sets the output target of this writer.

  Parameters: output   An ImageOutputStream object or another object that this writer can accept
- void write(IIOImage image)
- void write(RenderedImage image)

  writes a single image to the output.
- void writeInsert(int index, IIOImage image, ImageWriteParam param)

  writes an image into a multi-image file.
- boolean canInsertImage(int index)

  returns true if it is possible to insert an image at the given index.
- ImageWriterSpi getOriginatingProvider()

  gets the service provider that constructed this writer.

---

javax.imageio.IIOImage 1.4

- IIOImage(RenderedImage image, List thumbnails, IIOMetadata metadata)

  constructs an IIOImage from an image, optional thumbnails, and optional metadata.

11.4.2 Image Manipulation

Suppose you have an image and you would like to improve its appearance. You then need to access the individual pixels of the image and replace them with other pixels. Or perhaps you want to compute the pixels of an image from scratch—for example, to show the result of physical measurements or a mathematical computation. The BufferedImage class gives you control over the pixels in an image, and the classes that implement the BufferedImageOp interface let you transform images.

 NOTE: JDK 1.0 had a completely different, and far more complex, imaging framework that was optimized for *incremental rendering* of images downloaded from the Web, a scan line at a time. However, it was difficult to manipulate those images. We do not discuss that framework in this book.

11.4.2.1 Constructing Raster Images

Most of the images that you manipulate are simply read in from an image file—they were either produced by a device such as a digital camera or scanner, or constructed by a drawing program. In this section, we'll show you a different technique for constructing an image—namely, building it up a pixel at a time.

To create an image, construct a BufferedImage object in the usual way.

```
image = new BufferedImage(width, height, BufferedImage.TYPE_INT_ARGB);
```

Now, call the getRaster method to obtain an object of type WritableRaster. You will use this object to access and modify the pixels of the image.

```
WritableRaster raster = image.getRaster();
```

The setPixel method lets you set an individual pixel. The complexity here is that you can't simply set the pixel to a Color value. You must know how the buffered image specifies color values. That depends on the *type* of the image. If your image has a type of TYPE_INT_ARGB, then each pixel is described by four values—red, green, blue, and alpha, each between 0 and 255. You have to supply them in an array of four integers:

```
int[] black = { 0, 0, 0, 255 };
raster.setPixel(i, j, black);
```

In the lingo of the Java 2D API, these values are called the *sample values* of the pixel.

CAUTION: There are also setPixel methods that take array parameters of types float[] and double[]. However, the values that you need to place into these arrays are *not* normalized color values between 0.0 and 1.0.

```
float[] red = { 1.0F, 0.0F, 0.0F, 1.0F };
raster.setPixel(i, j, red); // ERROR
```

You need to supply values between 0 and 255, no matter what the type of the array is.

You can supply a batch of pixels with the setPixels method. Specify the starting pixel position and the width and height of the rectangle that you want to set. Then, supply an array that contains the sample values for all pixels. For example, if your buffered image has a type of TYPE_INT_ARGB, supply the red, green, blue, and alpha values of the first pixel, then the red, green, blue, and alpha values for the second pixel, and so on.

```
var pixels = new int[4 * width * height];
pixels[0] = . . .; // red value for first pixel
pixels[1] = . . .; // green value for first pixel
pixels[2] = . . .; // blue value for first pixel
pixels[3] = . . .; // alpha value for first pixel
. . .
raster.setPixels(x, y, width, height, pixels);
```

Conversely, to read a pixel, use the getPixel method. Supply an array of four integers to hold the sample values.

```
var sample = new int[4];
raster.getPixel(x, y, sample);
var color = new Color(sample[0], sample[1], sample[2], sample[3]);
```

You can read multiple pixels with the getPixels method.

```
raster.getPixels(x, y, width, height, samples);
```

If you use an image type other than TYPE_INT_ARGB and you know how that type represents pixel values, you can still use the getPixel/setPixel methods. However, you have to know the encoding of the sample values in the particular image type.

If you need to manipulate an image with an arbitrary, unknown image type, then you have to work a bit harder. Every image type has a *color model* that can translate between sample value arrays and the standard RGB color model.

NOTE: The RGB color model isn't as standard as you might think. The exact look of a color value depends on the characteristics of the imaging device. Digital cameras, scanners, monitors, and LCD displays all have their own idiosyncrasies. As a result, the same RGB value can look quite different on different devices. The International Color Consortium (www.color.org) recommends that all color data be accompanied by an *ICC profile* that specifies how the colors map to a standard form such as the 1931 CIE XYZ color specification. That specification was designed by the Commission Internationale de l'Eclairage, or CIE (www.cie.co.at), the international organization in charge of providing technical guidance in all matters of illumination and color. The specification is a standard method for representing any color that the human eye can perceive as a triplet of coordinates called X, Y, Z. (See, for example, *Computer Graphics: Principles and Practice, Second Edition in C*, by James D. Foley, Andries van Dam, Steven K. Feiner, et al., Chapter 13, for more information on the 1931 CIE XYZ specification.)

ICC profiles are complex, however. A simpler proposed standard, called sRGB (www.w3.org/Images/Color/sRGB.html), specifies an exact mapping between RGB values and the 1931 CIE XYZ values that was designed to work well with typical color monitors. The Java 2D API uses that mapping when converting between RGB and other color spaces.

The getColorModel method returns the color model:

```
ColorModel model = image.getColorModel();
```

To find the color value of a pixel, call the getDataElements method of the Raster class. That call returns an Object that contains a color-model-specific description of the color value.

```
Object data = raster.getDataElements(x, y, null);
```

 NOTE: The object that is returned by the getDataElements method is actually an array of sample values. You don't need to know this to process the object, but it explains why the method is called getDataElements.

The color model can translate the object to standard ARGB values. The getRGB method returns an int value that has the alpha, red, green, and blue values packed in four blocks of eight bits each. You can construct a Color value out of that integer with the Color(int argb, boolean hasAlpha) constructor:

```
int argb = model.getRGB(data);
var color = new Color(argb, true);
```

To set a pixel to a particular color, reverse these steps. The getRGB method of the Color class yields an int value with the alpha, red, green, and blue values. Supply that value to the getDataElements method of the ColorModel class. The return value is an Object that contains the color-model-specific description of the color value. Pass the object to the setDataElements method of the WritableRaster class.

```
int argb = color.getRGB();
Object data = model.getDataElements(argb, null);
raster.setDataElements(x, y, data);
```

To illustrate how to use these methods to build an image from individual pixels, we bow to tradition and draw a Mandelbrot set, as shown in Figure 11.56.

The idea of the Mandelbrot set is that each point of the plane is associated with a sequence of numbers. If that sequence stays bounded, you color the point. If it "escapes to infinity," you leave it transparent.

Here is how you can construct the simplest Mandelbrot set. For each point (a, b), look at sequences that start with $(x, y) = (0, 0)$ and iterate:

$$x_{new} = x^2 - y^2 + a$$

$$y_{new} = 2 \cdot x \cdot y + b$$

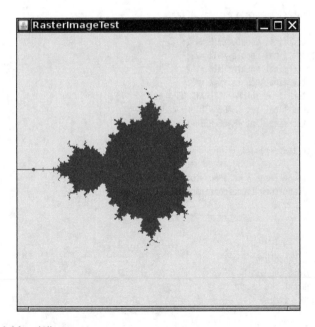

Figure 11.56 A Mandelbrot set

It turns out that if x or y ever gets larger than 2, then the sequence escapes to infinity. Only the pixels that correspond to points (a, b) leading to a bounded sequence are colored. (The formulas for the number sequences come ultimately from the mathematics of complex numbers; we'll just take them for granted.)

Listing 11.21 shows the code. In this program, we demonstrate how to use the ColorModel class for translating Color values into pixel data. That process is independent of the image type. Just for fun, change the color type of the buffered image to TYPE_BYTE_GRAY. You don't need to change any other code—the color model of the image automatically takes care of the conversion from colors to sample values.

Listing 11.21 rasterImage/RasterImageFrame.java

```
1  package rasterImage;
2
3  import java.awt.*;
4  import java.awt.image.*;
5  import javax.swing.*;
6
7  /**
8   * This frame shows an image with a Mandelbrot set.
9   */
10 public class RasterImageFrame extends JFrame
11 {
12    private static final double XMIN = -2;
13    private static final double XMAX = 2;
14    private static final double YMIN = -2;
15    private static final double YMAX = 2;
16    private static final int MAX_ITERATIONS = 16;
17    private static final int IMAGE_WIDTH = 400;
18    private static final int IMAGE_HEIGHT = 400;
19
20    public RasterImageFrame()
21    {
22       BufferedImage image = makeMandelbrot(IMAGE_WIDTH, IMAGE_HEIGHT);
23       add(new JLabel(new ImageIcon(image)));
24       pack();
25    }
26
27    /**
28     * Makes the Mandelbrot image.
29     * @param width the width
30     * @parah height the height
31     * @return the image
32     */
```

```
33   public BufferedImage makeMandelbrot(int width, int height)
34   {
35      var image = new BufferedImage(width, height, BufferedImage.TYPE_INT_ARGB);
36      WritableRaster raster = image.getRaster();
37      ColorModel model = image.getColorModel();
38
39      Color fractalColor = Color.RED;
40      int argb = fractalColor.getRGB();
41      Object colorData = model.getDataElements(argb, null);
42
43      for (int i = 0; i < width; i++)
44         for (int j = 0; j < height; j++)
45         {
46            double a = XMIN + i * (XMAX - XMIN) / width;
47            double b = YMIN + j * (YMAX - YMIN) / height;
48            if (!escapesToInfinity(a, b)) raster.setDataElements(i, j, colorData);
49         }
50      return image;
51   }
52
53   private boolean escapesToInfinity(double a, double b)
54   {
55      double x = 0.0;
56      double y = 0.0;
57      int iterations = 0;
58      while (x <= 2 && y <= 2 && iterations < MAX_ITERATIONS)
59      {
60         double xnew = x * x - y * y + a;
61         double ynew = 2 * x * y + b;
62         x = xnew;
63         y = ynew;
64         iterations++;
65      }
66      return x > 2 || y > 2;
67   }
68 }
```

---

java.awt.image.BufferedImage 1.2

• BufferedImage(int width, int height, int imageType)

constructs a buffered image object.

Parameters:	width, height	The image dimensions
	imageType	The image type. The most common types are TYPE_INT_RGB, TYPE_INT_ARGB, TYPE_BYTE_GRAY, and TYPE_BYTE_INDEXED.

(Continues)

`java.awt.image.BufferedImage` 1.2 *(Continued)*

- `ColorModel getColorModel()`

  returns the color model of this buffered image.

- `WritableRaster getRaster()`

  gets the raster for accessing and modifying pixels of this buffered image.

`java.awt.image.Raster` 1.2

- `Object getDataElements(int x, int y, Object data)`

  returns the sample data for a raster point, in an array whose element type and length depend on the color model. If data is not null, it is assumed to be an array that is appropriate for holding sample data, and it is filled. If data is null, a new array is allocated. Its element type and length depend on the color model.

- `int[] getPixel(int x, int y, int[] sampleValues)`
- `float[] getPixel(int x, int y, float[] sampleValues)`
- `double[] getPixel(int x, int y, double[] sampleValues)`
- `int[] getPixels(int x, int y, int width, int height, int[] sampleValues)`
- `float[] getPixels(int x, int y, int width, int height, float[] sampleValues)`
- `double[] getPixels(int x, int y, int width, int height, double[] sampleValues)`

  returns the sample values for a raster point, or a rectangle of raster points, in an array whose length depends on the color model. If sampleValues is not null, it is assumed to be sufficiently long for holding the sample values, and it is filled. If sampleValues is null, a new array is allocated. These methods are only useful if you know the meaning of the sample values for a color model.

`java.awt.image.WritableRaster` 1.2

- `void setDataElements(int x, int y, Object data)`

  sets the sample data for a raster point. data is an array filled with the sample data for a pixel. Its element type and length depend on the color model.

- `void setPixel(int x, int y, int[] sampleValues)`
- `void setPixel(int x, int y, float[] sampleValues)`
- `void setPixel(int x, int y, double[] sampleValues)`
- `void setPixels(int x, int y, int width, int height, int[] sampleValues)`
- `void setPixels(int x, int y, int width, int height, float[] sampleValues)`
- `void setPixels(int x, int y, int width, int height, double[] sampleValues)`

  sets the sample values for a raster point or a rectangle of raster points. These methods are only useful if you know the encoding of the sample values for a color model.

---

java.awt.image.ColorModel 1.2

- int getRGB(Object data)

  returns the ARGB value that corresponds to the sample data passed in the data array. Its element type and length depend on the color model.

- Object getDataElements(int argb, Object data);

  returns the sample data for a color value. If data is not null, it is assumed to be an array that is appropriate for holding sample data, and it is filled. If data is null, a new array is allocated. data is an array filled with the sample data for a pixel. Its element type and length depend on the color model.

---

java.awt.Color 1.0

- Color(int argb, boolean hasAlpha) 1.2

  creates a color with the specified combined ARGB value if hasAlpha is true, or the specified RGB value if hasAlpha is false.

- int getRGB()

  returns the ARGB color value corresponding to this color.

11.4.2.2 Filtering Images

In the preceding section, you saw how to build up an image from scratch. However, often you want to access image data for a different reason: You already have an image and you want to improve it in some way.

Of course, you can use the getPixel/getDataElements methods that you saw in the preceding section to read the image data, manipulate them, and write them back. Fortunately, the Java 2D API already supplies a number of *filters* that carry out common image processing operations for you.

The image manipulations all implement the BufferedImageOp interface. After you construct the operation, simply call the filter method to transform an image into another.

```
BufferedImageOp op = . . .;
BufferedImage filteredImage
   = new BufferedImage(image.getWidth(), image.getHeight(), image.getType());
op.filter(image, filteredImage);
```

Some operations can transform an image in place (op.filter(image, image)), but most can't.

Five classes implement the BufferedImageOp interface:

```
AffineTransformOp
RescaleOp
LookupOp
ColorConvertOp
ConvolveOp
```

The AffineTransformOp carries out an affine transformation on the pixels. For example, here is how you can rotate an image about its center:

```
AffineTransform transform = AffineTransform.getRotateInstance(Math.toRadians(angle),
    image.getWidth() / 2, image.getHeight() / 2);
var op = new AffineTransformOp(transform, interpolation);
op.filter(image, filteredImage);
```

The AffineTransformOp constructor requires an affine transform and an *interpolation* strategy. Interpolation is necessary to determine the target image pixels if the source pixels are transformed somewhere between target pixels. For example, if you rotate source pixels, they will generally not fall exactly onto target pixels. There are three interpolation strategies: AffineTransformOp.TYPE_BICUBIC, AffineTransformOp.TYPE_BILINEAR, and AffineTransformOp.TYPE_NEAREST_NEIGHBOR. Bicubic interpolation takes a bit longer but looks better than the other two.

The program in Listing 11.22 lets you rotate an image by 5 degrees (see Figure 11.57).

Figure 11.57 A rotated image

The RescaleOp carries out a rescaling operation

$$x_{\text{new}} = a \cdot x + b$$

for each of the color components in the image. (Alpha components are not affected.) The effect of rescaling with $a > 1$ is to brighten the image. Construct the RescaleOp by specifying the scaling parameters and optional rendering hints. In Listing 11.22, we use:

```
float a = 1.1f;
float b = 20.0f;
var op = new RescaleOp(a, b, null);
```

You can also supply separate scaling values for each color component—see the API notes.

The LookupOp operation lets you specify an arbitrary mapping of sample values. Supply a table that specifies how each value should be mapped. In the example program, we compute the *negative* of all colors, changing the color c to $255 - c$.

The LookupOp constructor requires an object of type LookupTable and a map of optional hints. The LookupTable class is abstract, with two concrete subclasses: ByteLookupTable and ShortLookupTable. Since RGB color values are bytes, a ByteLookupTable should suffice. However, because of the bug described in http://bugs.sun.com /bugdatabase/view_bug.do?bug_id=6183251, we will use a ShortLookupTable instead. Here is how we construct the LookupOp for the example program:

```
var negative = new short[256];
for (int i = 0; i < 256; i++) negative[i] = (short) (255 - i);
var table = new ShortLookupTable(0, negative);
var op = new LookupOp(table, null);
```

The lookup is applied to each color component separately, but not to the alpha component. You can also supply different lookup tables for each color component—see the API notes.

 NOTE: You cannot apply a LookupOp to an image with an indexed color model. (In those images, each sample value is an offset into a color palette.)

The ColorConvertOp is useful for color space conversions. We do not discuss it here.

The most powerful of the transformations is the ConvolveOp, which carries out a mathematical *convolution*. We won't get too deeply into the mathematical details, but the basic idea is simple. Consider, for example, the *blur filter* (see Figure 11.58).

The blurring is achieved by replacing each pixel with the *average* value from the pixel and its eight neighbors. Intuitively, it makes sense why this operation

Figure 11.58 Blurring an image

would blur out the picture. Mathematically, the averaging can be expressed as a convolution operation with the following *kernel:*

$$\begin{bmatrix} 1/9 & 1/9 & 1/9 \\ 1/9 & 1/9 & 1/9 \\ 1/9 & 1/9 & 1/9 \end{bmatrix}$$

The kernel of a convolution is a matrix that tells what weights should be applied to the neighboring values. The kernel above produces a blurred image. A different kernel carries out *edge detection*, locating the areas of color changes:

$$\begin{bmatrix} 0 & -1 & 0 \\ -1 & 4 & -1 \\ 0 & -1 & 0 \end{bmatrix}$$

Edge detection is an important technique for analyzing photographic images (see Figure 11.59).

To construct a convolution operation, first set up an array of the values for the kernel and construct a `Kernel` object. Then, construct a `ConvolveOp` object from the kernel and use it for filtering.

```
float[] elements =
  {
     0.0f, -1.0f, 0.0f,
    -1.0f,  4.f, -1.0f,
     0.0f, -1.0f, 0.0f
  };
```

Figure 11.59 Edge detection and inversion

```
var kernel = new Kernel(3, 3, elements);
var op = new ConvolveOp(kernel);
op.filter(image, filteredImage);
```

The program in Listing 11.22 allows a user to load in a GIF or JPEG image and carry out the image manipulations that we discussed. Thanks to the power of the operations provided by Java 2D API, the program is very simple.

Listing 11.22 imageProcessing/ImageProcessingFrame.java

```
1  package imageProcessing;
2
3  import java.awt.*;
4  import java.awt.geom.*;
5  import java.awt.image.*;
6  import java.io.*;
7
8  import javax.imageio.*;
9  import javax.swing.*;
10 import javax.swing.filechooser.*;
11
12 /**
13  * This frame has a menu to load an image and to specify various transformations, and a
14  * component to show the resulting image.
15  */
16 public class ImageProcessingFrame extends JFrame
17 {
18    private static final int DEFAULT_WIDTH = 400;
19    private static final int DEFAULT_HEIGHT = 400;
```

(Continues)

Listing 11.22   *(Continued)*

```
20
21     private BufferedImage image;
22
23     public ImageProcessingFrame()
24     {
25        setTitle("ImageProcessingTest");
26        setSize(DEFAULT_WIDTH, DEFAULT_HEIGHT);
27
28        add(new JComponent()
29           {
30              public void paintComponent(Graphics g)
31              {
32                 if (image != null) g.drawImage(image, 0, 0, null);
33              }
34           });
35
36        var fileMenu = new JMenu("File");
37        var openItem = new JMenuItem("Open");
38        openItem.addActionListener(event -> openFile());
39        fileMenu.add(openItem);
40
41        var exitItem = new JMenuItem("Exit");
42        exitItem.addActionListener(event -> System.exit(0));
43        fileMenu.add(exitItem);
44
45        var editMenu = new JMenu("Edit");
46        var blurItem = new JMenuItem("Blur");
47        blurItem.addActionListener(event ->
48           {
49              float weight = 1.0f / 9.0f;
50              float[] elements = new float[9];
51              for (int i = 0; i < 9; i++)
52                 elements[i] = weight;
53              convolve(elements);
54           });
55        editMenu.add(blurItem);
56
57        var sharpenItem = new JMenuItem("Sharpen");
58        sharpenItem.addActionListener(event ->
59           {
60              float[] elements = { 0.0f, -1.0f, 0.0f, -1.0f, 5.f, -1.0f, 0.0f, -1.0f, 0.0f };
61              convolve(elements);
62           });
63        editMenu.add(sharpenItem);
64
```

```
65    var brightenItem = new JMenuItem("Brighten");
66    brightenItem.addActionListener(event ->
67       {
68          float a = 1.1f;
69          float b = 20.0f;
70          var op = new RescaleOp(a, b, null);
71          filter(op);
72       });
73    editMenu.add(brightenItem);
74
75    var edgeDetectItem = new JMenuItem("Edge detect");
76    edgeDetectItem.addActionListener(event ->
77       {
78          float[] elements = { 0.0f, -1.0f, 0.0f, -1.0f, 4.f, -1.0f, 0.0f, -1.0f, 0.0f };
79          convolve(elements);
80       });
81    editMenu.add(edgeDetectItem);
82
83    var negativeItem = new JMenuItem("Negative");
84    negativeItem.addActionListener(event ->
85       {
86          short[] negative = new short[256 * 1];
87          for (int i = 0; i < 256; i++)
88             negative[i] = (short) (255 - i);
89          var table = new ShortLookupTable(0, negative);
90          var op = new LookupOp(table, null);
91          filter(op);
92       });
93    editMenu.add(negativeItem);
94
95    var rotateItem = new JMenuItem("Rotate");
96    rotateItem.addActionListener(event ->
97       {
98          if (image == null) return;
99          var transform = AffineTransform.getRotateInstance(Math.toRadians(5),
100                image.getWidth() / 2, image.getHeight() / 2);
101          var op = new AffineTransformOp(transform,
102                AffineTransformOp.TYPE_BICUBIC);
103          filter(op);
104       });
105    editMenu.add(rotateItem);
106
107    var menuBar = new JMenuBar();
108    menuBar.add(fileMenu);
109    menuBar.add(editMenu);
110    setJMenuBar(menuBar);
111 }
112
```

(Continues)

Listing 11.22 *(Continued)*

```
113    /**
114     * Open a file and load the image.
115     */
116    public void openFile()
117    {
118       var chooser = new JFileChooser(".");
119       chooser.setCurrentDirectory(new File(getClass().getPackage().getName()));
120       String[] extensions = ImageIO.getReaderFileSuffixes();
121       chooser.setFileFilter(new FileNameExtensionFilter("Image files", extensions));
122       int r = chooser.showOpenDialog(this);
123       if (r != JFileChooser.APPROVE_OPTION) return;
124
125       try
126       {
127          Image img = ImageIO.read(chooser.getSelectedFile());
128          image = new BufferedImage(img.getWidth(null), img.getHeight(null),
129                BufferedImage.TYPE_INT_RGB);
130          image.getGraphics().drawImage(img, 0, 0, null);
131       }
132       catch (IOException e)
133       {
134          JOptionPane.showMessageDialog(this, e);
135       }
136       repaint();
137    }
138
139    /**
140     * Apply a filter and repaint.
141     * @param op the image operation to apply
142     */
143    private void filter(BufferedImageOp op)
144    {
145       if (image == null) return;
146       image = op.filter(image, null);
147       repaint();
148    }
149
150    /**
151     * Apply a convolution and repaint.
152     * @param elements the convolution kernel (an array of 9 matrix elements)
153     */
154    private void convolve(float[] elements)
155    {
156       var kernel = new Kernel(3, 3, elements);
157       var op = new ConvolveOp(kernel);
158       filter(op);
159    }
160 }
```

---

java.awt.image.BufferedImageOp 1.2

- BufferedImage filter(BufferedImage source, BufferedImage dest)

  applies the image operation to the source image and stores the result in the destination image. If dest is null, a new destination image is created. The destination image is returned.

---

java.awt.image.AffineTransformOp 1.2

- AffineTransformOp(AffineTransform t, int interpolationType)

  constructs an affine transform operator. The interpolation type is one of TYPE_BILINEAR, TYPE_BICUBIC, or TYPE_NEAREST_NEIGHBOR.

---

java.awt.image.RescaleOp 1.2

- RescaleOp(float a, float b, RenderingHints hints)
- RescaleOp(float[] as, float[] bs, RenderingHints hints)

  constructs a rescale operator that carries out the scaling operation $x_{new} = a \cdot x + b$. When using the first constructor, all color components (but not the alpha component) are scaled with the same coefficients. When using the second constructor, you supply either the values for each color component, in which case the alpha component is unaffected, or the values for both alpha and color components.

---

java.awt.image.LookupOp 1.2

- LookupOp(LookupTable table, RenderingHints hints)

  constructs a lookup operator for the given lookup table.

---

java.awt.image.ByteLookupTable 1.2

- ByteLookupTable(int offset, byte[] data)
- ByteLookupTable(int offset, byte[][] data)

  constructs a lookup table for converting byte values. The offset is subtracted from the input before the lookup. The values in the first constructor are applied to all color components but not the alpha component. When using the second constructor, supply either the values for each color component, in which case the alpha component is unaffected, or the values for both alpha and color components.

---

java.awt.image.ShortLookupTable 1.2

- ShortLookupTable(int offset, short[] data)
- ShortLookupTable(int offset, short[][] data)

constructs a lookup table for converting short values. The offset is subtracted from the input before the lookup. The values in the first constructor are applied to all color components but not the alpha component. When using the second constructor, supply either the values for each color component, in which case the alpha component is unaffected, or the values for both alpha and color components.

---

java.awt.image.ConvolveOp 1.2

- ConvolveOp(Kernel kernel)
- ConvolveOp(Kernel kernel, int edgeCondition, RenderingHints hints)

constructs a convolution operator. The edge condition specified is one of EDGE_NO_OP and EDGE_ZERO_FILL. Edge values need to be treated specially because they don't have sufficient neighboring values to compute the convolution. The default is EDGE_ZERO_FILL.

---

java.awt.image.Kernel 1.2

- Kernel(int width, int height, float[] matrixElements)

constructs a kernel for the given matrix.

11.5 Printing

In the following sections, we will show you how you can easily print a drawing on a single sheet of paper, how you can manage a multipage printout, and how you can save a printout as a PostScript file.

11.5.1 Graphics Printing

In this section, we will tackle what is probably the most common printing situation: printing a 2D graphic. Of course, the graphic can contain text in various fonts or even consist entirely of text.

To generate a printout, you have to take care of these two tasks:

- Supply an object that implements the Printable interface
- Start a print job

The `Printable` interface has a single method:

```
int print(Graphics g, PageFormat format, int page)
```

That method is called whenever the print engine needs to have a page formatted for printing. Your code draws the text and the images to be printed onto the graphics context. The page format tells you the paper size and the print margins. The page number tells you which page to render.

To start a print job, use the `PrinterJob` class. First, call the static `getPrinterJob` method to get a print job object. Then set the `Printable` object that you want to print.

```
Printable canvas = . . .;
PrinterJob job = PrinterJob.getPrinterJob();
job.setPrintable(canvas);
```

CAUTION: The class `PrintJob` handles JDK 1.1-style printing. That class is now obsolete. Do not confuse it with the `PrinterJob` class.

Before starting the print job, you should call the `printDialog` method to display a print dialog box (see Figure 11.60). That dialog box gives the user a chance to select the printer to be used (in case multiple printers are available), the page range that should be printed, and various printer settings.

Collect printer settings in an object of a class that implements the `PrintRequestAttributeSet` interface, such as the `HashPrintRequestAttributeSet` class.

```
var attributes = new HashPrintRequestAttributeSet();
```

Add attribute settings and pass the `attributes` object to the `printDialog` method.

The `printDialog` method returns `true` if the user clicked OK and `false` if the user canceled the dialog box. If the user accepted, call the `print` method of the `PrinterJob` class to start the printing process. The `print` method might throw a `PrinterException`. Here is the outline of the printing code:

```
if (job.printDialog(attributes))
{
   try
   {
      job.print(attributes);
   }
   catch (PrinterException exception)
   {
      . . .
   }
}
```

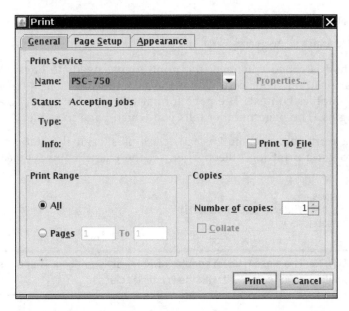

Figure 11.60 A cross-platform print dialog box

 NOTE: Prior to JDK 1.4, the printing system used the native print and page setup dialog boxes of the host platform. To show a native print dialog box, call the printDialog method with no parameters. (There is no way to collect user settings in an attribute set.)

During printing, the print method of the PrinterJob class makes repeated calls to the print method of the Printable object associated with the job.

Since the job does not know how many pages you want to print, it simply keeps calling the print method. As long as the print method returns the value Printable.PAGE_EXISTS, the print job keeps producing pages. When the print method returns Printable.NO_SUCH_PAGE, the print job stops.

 CAUTION: The page numbers that the print job passes to the print method start with page 0.

Therefore, the print job doesn't have an accurate page count until after the printout is complete. For that reason, the print dialog box can't display the correct page range—instead, it displays "Pages 1 to 1." You will see in the next section how to avoid this blemish by supplying a Book object to the print job.

During the printing process, the print job repeatedly calls the print method of the Printable object. The print job is allowed to make multiple calls *for the same page.* You should therefore not count pages inside the print method but always rely on the page number parameter. There is a good reason why the print job might call the print method repeatedly for the same page. Some printers, in particular dot-matrix and inkjet printers, use *banding.* They print one band at a time, advance the paper, and then print the next band. The print job might use banding even for laser printers that print a full page at a time—it gives the print job a way of managing the size of the spool file.

If the print job needs the Printable object to print a band, it sets the clip area of the graphics context to the requested band and calls the print method. Its drawing operations are clipped against the band rectangle, and only those drawing elements that show up in the band are rendered. Your print method need not be aware of that process, with one caveat: It should *not* interfere with the clip area.

 CAUTION: The Graphics object that your print method gets is also clipped against the page margins. If you replace the clip area, you can draw outside the margins. Especially in a printer graphics context, the clipping area must be respected. Call clip, not setClip, to further restrict the clipping area. If you must remove a clip area, make sure to call getClip at the beginning of your print method and restore that clip area.

The PageFormat parameter of the print method contains information about the printed page. The methods getWidth and getHeight return the paper size, measured in *points.* (One point is 1/72 of an inch; an inch equals 25.4 millimeters.) For example, A4 paper is approximately 595 × 842 points, and US Letter paper is 612 × 792 points.

Points are a common measurement in the printing trade in the United States. Much to the chagrin of the rest of the world, the printing package uses point units. There are two purposes for that: paper sizes and paper margins are measured in points, and points are the default unit for all print graphics contexts. You can verify that in the example program at the end of this section. The program prints two lines of text that are 72 units apart. Run the example program and measure the distance between the baselines; they are exactly 1 inch or 25.4 millimeters apart.

The getWidth and getHeight methods of the PageFormat class give you the complete paper size. Not all of the paper area is printable. Users typically select margins, and even if they don't, printers need to somehow grip the sheets of paper on which they print and therefore have a small unprintable area around the edges.

The methods getImageableWidth and getImageableHeight tell you the dimensions of the area that you can actually fill. However, the margins need not be symmetrical, so you must also know the top left corner of the imageable area (see Figure 11.61), which you obtain by the methods getImageableX and getImageableY.

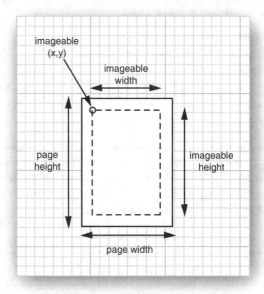

Figure 11.61 Page format measurements

 TIP: The graphics context that you receive in the print method is clipped to exclude the margins, but the origin of the coordinate system is nevertheless the top left corner of the paper. It makes sense to translate the coordinate system to the top left corner of the imageable area. Simply start your print method with

```
g.translate(pageFormat.getImageableX(), pageFormat.getImageableY());
```

If you want your users to choose the settings for the page margins or to switch between portrait and landscape orientation without setting other printing attributes, call the pageDialog method of the PrinterJob class:

```
PageFormat format = job.pageDialog(attributes);
```

NOTE: One of the tabs of the print dialog box contains the page setup dialog (see Figure 11.62). You might still want to give users an option to set the page format before printing, especially if your program presents a "what you see is what you get" display of the pages to be printed. The `pageDialog` method returns a `PageFormat` object with the user settings.

Figure 11.62 A cross-platform page setup dialog

The program in Listings 11.23 and 11.24 shows how to render the same set of shapes on the screen and on the printed page. A subclass of JPanel implements the Printable interface. Both the paintComponent and the print methods call the same method to carry out the actual drawing.

```
class PrintPanel extends JPanel implements Printable
{
   public void paintComponent(Graphics g)
   {
      super.paintComponent(g);
      var g2 = (Graphics2D) g;
      drawPage(g2);
   }

   public int print(Graphics g, PageFormat pf, int page) throws PrinterException
   {
      if (page >= 1) return Printable.NO_SUCH_PAGE;
      var g2 = (Graphics2D) g;
      g2.translate(pf.getImageableX(), pf.getImageableY());
```

```
        drawPage(g2);
        return Printable.PAGE_EXISTS;
    }

    public void drawPage(Graphics2D g2)
    {
        // shared drawing code goes here
        . . .
    }
    . . .
}
```

This example displays and prints the image shown in Figure 11.50—namely, the outline of the message "Hello, World" used as a clipping area for a pattern of lines.

Click the Print button to start printing, or click the Page setup button to open the page setup dialog box. Listing 11.23 shows the code.

NOTE: To show a native page setup dialog box, pass a default PageFormat object to the pageDialog method. The method clones that object, modifies it according to the user selections in the dialog box, and returns the cloned object.

```
PageFormat defaultFormat = printJob.defaultPage();
PageFormat selectedFormat = printJob.pageDialog(defaultFormat);
```

Listing 11.23 print/PrintTestFrame.java

```
1  package print;
2
3  import java.awt.*;
4  import java.awt.print.*;
5
6  import javax.print.attribute.*;
7  import javax.swing.*;
8
9  /**
10  * This frame shows a panel with 2D graphics and buttons to print the graphics and to set up
11  * the page format.
12  */
13 public class PrintTestFrame extends JFrame
14 {
15     private PrintComponent canvas;
16     private PrintRequestAttributeSet attributes;
17
18     public PrintTestFrame()
19     {
```

```
20        canvas = new PrintComponent();
21        add(canvas, BorderLayout.CENTER);
22
23        attributes = new HashPrintRequestAttributeSet();
24
25        var buttonPanel = new JPanel();
26        var printButton = new JButton("Print");
27        buttonPanel.add(printButton);
28        printButton.addActionListener(event ->
29           {
30              try
31              {
32                 PrinterJob job = PrinterJob.getPrinterJob();
33                 job.setPrintable(canvas);
34                 if (job.printDialog(attributes)) job.print(attributes);
35              }
36              catch (PrinterException ex)
37              {
38                 JOptionPane.showMessageDialog(PrintTestFrame.this, ex);
39              }
40           });
41
42        var pageSetupButton = new JButton("Page setup");
43        buttonPanel.add(pageSetupButton);
44        pageSetupButton.addActionListener(event ->
45           {
46              PrinterJob job = PrinterJob.getPrinterJob();
47              job.pageDialog(attributes);
48           });
49
50        add(buttonPanel, BorderLayout.NORTH);
51        pack();
52     }
53 }
```

Listing 11.24 print/PrintComponent.java

```
1 package print;
2
3 import java.awt.*;
4 import java.awt.font.*;
5 import java.awt.geom.*;
6 import java.awt.print.*;
7 import javax.swing.*;
8
9 /**
10 * This component generates a 2D graphics image for screen display and printing.
11 */
```

(Continues)

Listing 11.24 *(Continued)*

```
12  public class PrintComponent extends JComponent implements Printable
13  {
14     private static final Dimension PREFERRED_SIZE = new Dimension(300, 300);
15
16     public void paintComponent(Graphics g)
17     {
18        var g2 = (Graphics2D) g;
19        drawPage(g2);
20     }
21
22     public int print(Graphics g, PageFormat pf, int page) throws PrinterException
23     {
24        if (page >= 1) return Printable.NO_SUCH_PAGE;
25        var g2 = (Graphics2D) g;
26        g2.translate(pf.getImageableX(), pf.getImageableY());
27        g2.draw(new Rectangle2D.Double(0, 0, pf.getImageableWidth(), pf.getImageableHeight()));
28
29        drawPage(g2);
30        return Printable.PAGE_EXISTS;
31     }
32
33     /**
34      * This method draws the page both on the screen and the printer graphics context.
35      * @param g2 the graphics context
36      */
37     public void drawPage(Graphics2D g2)
38     {
39        FontRenderContext context = g2.getFontRenderContext();
40        var f = new Font("Serif", Font.PLAIN, 72);
41        var clipShape = new GeneralPath();
42
43        var layout = new TextLayout("Hello", f, context);
44        AffineTransform transform = AffineTransform.getTranslateInstance(0, 72);
45        Shape outline = layout.getOutline(transform);
46        clipShape.append(outline, false);
47
48        layout = new TextLayout("World", f, context);
49        transform = AffineTransform.getTranslateInstance(0, 144);
50        outline = layout.getOutline(transform);
51        clipShape.append(outline, false);
52
53        g2.draw(clipShape);
54        g2.clip(clipShape);
55
56        final int NLINES = 50;
57        var p = new Point2D.Double(0, 0);
```

```
58        for (int i = 0; i < NLINES; i++)
59        {
60           double x = (2 * getWidth() * i) / NLINES;
61           double y = (2 * getHeight() * (NLINES - 1 - i)) / NLINES;
62           var q = new Point2D.Double(x, y);
63           g2.draw(new Line2D.Double(p, q));
64        }
65     }
66
67     public Dimension getPreferredSize() { return PREFERRED_SIZE; }
68  }
```

---

java.awt.print.Printable 1.2

- int print(Graphics g, PageFormat format, int pageNumber)

  renders a page and returns PAGE_EXISTS, or returns NO_SUCH_PAGE.

  Parameters: g   The graphics context onto which the page is rendered
                   format   The format of the page to draw on
                   pageNumber   The number of the requested page

---

java.awt.print.PrinterJob 1.2

- static PrinterJob getPrinterJob()

  returns a printer job object.

- PageFormat defaultPage()

  returns the default page format for this printer.

- boolean printDialog(PrintRequestAttributeSet attributes)
- boolean printDialog()

  opens a print dialog box to allow a user to select the pages to be printed and to change print settings. The first method displays a cross-platform dialog box, the second a native dialog box. The first method modifies the attributes object to reflect the user settings. Both methods return true if the user accepts the dialog box.

- PageFormat pageDialog(PrintRequestAttributeSet attributes)
- PageFormat pageDialog(PageFormat defaults)

  displays a page setup dialog box. The first method displays a cross-platform dialog box, the second a native dialog box. Both methods return a PageFormat object with the format that the user requested in the dialog box. The first method modifies the attributes object to reflect the user settings. The second method does not modify the defaults object.

(Continues)

---

java.awt.print.PrinterJob 1.2 *(Continued)*

- void setPrintable(Printable p)
- void setPrintable(Printable p, PageFormat format)

  sets the Printable of this print job and an optional page format.

- void print()
- void print(PrintRequestAttributeSet attributes)

  prints the current Printable by repeatedly calling its print method and sending the rendered pages to the printer, until no more pages are available.

---

java.awt.print.PageFormat 1.2

- double getWidth()
- double getHeight()

  returns the width and height of the page.

- double getImageableWidth()
- double getImageableHeight()

  returns the width and height of the imageable area of the page.

- double getImageableX()
- double getImageableY()

  returns the position of the top left corner of the imageable area.

- int getOrientation()

  returns one of PORTRAIT, LANDSCAPE, or REVERSE_LANDSCAPE. Page orientation is transparent to programmers because the page format and graphics context settings automatically reflect the page orientation.

11.5.2 Multiple-Page Printing

In practice, you usually don't pass a raw Printable object to a print job. Instead, you should obtain an object of a class that implements the Pageable interface. The Java platform supplies one such class, called Book. A book is made up of sections, each of which is a Printable object. To make a book, add Printable objects and their page counts.

```
var book = new Book();
Printable coverPage = . . .;
Printable bodyPages = . . .;
book.append(coverPage, pageFormat); // append 1 page
book.append(bodyPages, pageFormat, pageCount);
```

Then, use the setPageable method to pass the Book object to the print job.

```
printJob.setPageable(book);
```

Now the print job knows exactly how many pages to print, so the print dialog box displays an accurate page range and the user can select the entire range or subranges.

 CAUTION: When the print job calls the print methods of the Printable sections, it passes the current page number of the *book*, and not of each *section*, as the current page number. That is a huge pain—each section must know the page counts of the preceding sections to make sense of the page number parameter.

From your perspective as a programmer, the biggest challenge of using the Book class is that you must know how many pages each section will have when you print it. Your Printable class needs a *layout algorithm* that computes the layout of the material on the printed pages. Before printing starts, invoke that algorithm to compute the page breaks and the page count. You can retain the layout information so you have it handy during the printing process.

You must guard against the possibility that the user has changed the page format. If that happens, you must recompute the layout, even if the information that you want to print has not changed.

Listing 11.26 shows how to produce a multipage printout. This program prints a message in very large characters on a number of pages (see Figure 11.63). You can then trim the margins and tape the pages together to form a banner.

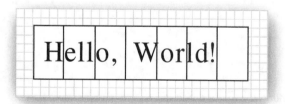

Figure 11.63 A banner

The layoutPages method of the Banner class computes the layout. We first lay out the message string in a 72-point font. We then compute the height of the resulting string and compare it with the imageable height of the page. We derive a scale factor from these two measurements. When printing the string, we magnify it by that scale factor.

CAUTION: To lay out your information precisely, you usually need access to the printer graphics context. Unfortunately, there is no way to obtain that graphics context before printing actually starts. In our example program, we make do with the screen graphics context and hope that the font metrics of the screen and printer match.

The getPageCount method of the Banner class first calls the layout method. Then it scales up the width of the string and divides it by the imageable width of each page. The quotient, rounded up to the next integer, is the page count.

It sounds like it might be difficult to print the banner because characters can be broken across multiple pages. However, thanks to the power of the Java 2D API, this turns out not to be a problem at all. When a particular page is requested, we simply use the translate method of the Graphics2D class to shift the top left corner of the string to the left. Then, we set a clip rectangle that equals the current page (see Figure 11.64). Finally, we scale the graphics context with the scale factor that the layout method computed.

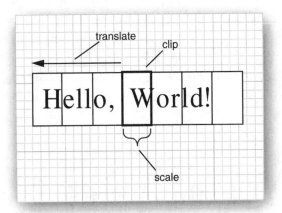

Figure 11.64 Printing a page of a banner

This example shows the power of transformations. The drawing code is kept simple, and the transformation does all the work of placing the drawing in the appropriate place. Finally, the clip cuts away the part of the image that falls outside the page. This program shows another compelling use of transformations—to display a print preview.

Listing 11.25 book/BookTestFrame.java

```java
 1  package book;
 2
 3  import java.awt.*;
 4  import java.awt.print.*;
 5
 6  import javax.print.attribute.*;
 7  import javax.swing.*;
 8
 9  /**
10   * This frame has a text field for the banner text and buttons for printing, page setup, and
11   * print preview.
12   */
13  public class BookTestFrame extends JFrame
14  {
15     private JTextField text;
16     private PageFormat pageFormat;
17     private PrintRequestAttributeSet attributes;
18
19     public BookTestFrame()
20     {
21        text = new JTextField();
22        add(text, BorderLayout.NORTH);
23
24        attributes = new HashPrintRequestAttributeSet();
25
26        var buttonPanel = new JPanel();
27
28        var printButton = new JButton("Print");
29        buttonPanel.add(printButton);
30        printButton.addActionListener(event ->
31           {
32              try
33              {
34                 PrinterJob job = PrinterJob.getPrinterJob();
35                 job.setPageable(makeBook());
36                 if (job.printDialog(attributes))
37                 {
38                    job.print(attributes);
39                 }
40              }
41              catch (PrinterException e)
42              {
43                 JOptionPane.showMessageDialog(BookTestFrame.this, e);
44              }
45           });
46
47        var pageSetupButton = new JButton("Page setup");
```

(Continues)

Listing 11.25 *(Continued)*

```
48        buttonPanel.add(pageSetupButton);
49        pageSetupButton.addActionListener(event ->
50           {
51              PrinterJob job = PrinterJob.getPrinterJob();
52              pageFormat = job.pageDialog(attributes);
53           });
54
55        var printPreviewButton = new JButton("Print preview");
56        buttonPanel.add(printPreviewButton);
57        printPreviewButton.addActionListener(event ->
58           {
59              var dialog = new PrintPreviewDialog(makeBook());
60              dialog.setVisible(true);
61           });
62
63        add(buttonPanel, BorderLayout.SOUTH);
64        pack();
65     }
66
67     /**
68      * Makes a book that contains a cover page and the pages for the banner.
69      */
70     public Book makeBook()
71     {
72        if (pageFormat == null)
73        {
74           PrinterJob job = PrinterJob.getPrinterJob();
75           pageFormat = job.defaultPage();
76        }
77        var book = new Book();
78        String message = text.getText();
79        var banner = new Banner(message);
80        int pageCount = banner.getPageCount((Graphics2D) getGraphics(), pageFormat);
81        book.append(new CoverPage(message + " (" + pageCount + " pages)"), pageFormat);
82        book.append(banner, pageFormat, pageCount);
83        return book;
84     }
85 }
```

Listing 11.26 book/Banner.java

```
1 package book;
2
3 import java.awt.*;
4 import java.awt.font.*;
5 import java.awt.geom.*;
6 import java.awt.print.*;
```

```
7
8  /**
9   * A banner that prints a text string on multiple pages.
10  */
11 public class Banner implements Printable
12 {
13    private String message;
14    private double scale;
15
16    /**
17     * Constructs a banner.
18     * @param m the message string
19     */
20    public Banner(String m)
21    {
22       message = m;
23    }
24
25    /**
26     * Gets the page count of this section.
27     * @param g2 the graphics context
28     * @param pf the page format
29     * @return the number of pages needed
30     */
31    public int getPageCount(Graphics2D g2, PageFormat pf)
32    {
33       if (message.equals("")) return 0;
34       FontRenderContext context = g2.getFontRenderContext();
35       var f = new Font("Serif", Font.PLAIN, 72);
36       Rectangle2D bounds = f.getStringBounds(message, context);
37       scale = pf.getImageableHeight() / bounds.getHeight();
38       double width = scale * bounds.getWidth();
39       int pages = (int) Math.ceil(width / pf.getImageableWidth());
40       return pages;
41    }
42
43    public int print(Graphics g, PageFormat pf, int page) throws PrinterException
44    {
45       var g2 = (Graphics2D) g;
46       if (page > getPageCount(g2, pf)) return Printable.NO_SUCH_PAGE;
47       g2.translate(pf.getImageableX(), pf.getImageableY());
48
49       drawPage(g2, pf, page);
50       return Printable.PAGE_EXISTS;
51    }
52
53    public void drawPage(Graphics2D g2, PageFormat pf, int page)
54    {
```

(Continues)

Listing 11.26 *(Continued)*

```
55     if (message.equals("")) return;
56     page--; // account for cover page
57
58     drawCropMarks(g2, pf);
59     g2.clip(new Rectangle2D.Double(0, 0, pf.getImageableWidth(), pf.getImageableHeight()));
60     g2.translate(-page * pf.getImageableWidth(), 0);
61     g2.scale(scale, scale);
62     FontRenderContext context = g2.getFontRenderContext();
63     var f = new Font("Serif", Font.PLAIN, 72);
64     var layout = new TextLayout(message, f, context);
65     AffineTransform transform = AffineTransform.getTranslateInstance(0, layout.getAscent());
66     Shape outline = layout.getOutline(transform);
67     g2.draw(outline);
68  }
69
70  /**
71   * Draws 1/2" crop marks in the corners of the page.
72   * @param g2 the graphics context
73   * @param pf the page format
74   */
75  public void drawCropMarks(Graphics2D g2, PageFormat pf)
76  {
77     final double C = 36; // crop mark length = 1/2 inch
78     double w = pf.getImageableWidth();
79     double h = pf.getImageableHeight();
80     g2.draw(new Line2D.Double(0, 0, 0, C));
81     g2.draw(new Line2D.Double(0, 0, C, 0));
82     g2.draw(new Line2D.Double(w, 0, w, C));
83     g2.draw(new Line2D.Double(w, 0, w - C, 0));
84     g2.draw(new Line2D.Double(0, h, 0, h - C));
85     g2.draw(new Line2D.Double(0, h, C, h));
86     g2.draw(new Line2D.Double(w, h, w, h - C));
87     g2.draw(new Line2D.Double(w, h, w - C, h));
88  }
89 }
90
91 /**
92  * This class prints a cover page with a title.
93  */
94 class CoverPage implements Printable
95 {
96    private String title;
97
98    /**
99     * Constructs a cover page.
100    * @param t the title
101    */
```

```
102    public CoverPage(String t)
103    {
104       title = t;
105    }
106
107    public int print(Graphics g, PageFormat pf, int page) throws PrinterException
108    {
109       if (page >= 1) return Printable.NO_SUCH_PAGE;
110       var g2 = (Graphics2D) g;
111       g2.setPaint(Color.black);
112       g2.translate(pf.getImageableX(), pf.getImageableY());
113       FontRenderContext context = g2.getFontRenderContext();
114       Font f = g2.getFont();
115       var layout = new TextLayout(title, f, context);
116       float ascent = layout.getAscent();
117       g2.drawString(title, 0, ascent);
118       return Printable.PAGE_EXISTS;
119    }
120 }
```

Listing 11.27 book/PrintPreviewDialog.java

```
1 package book;
2
3 import java.awt.*;
4 import java.awt.print.*;
5
6 import javax.swing.*;
7
8 /**
9  * This class implements a generic print preview dialog.
10  */
11 public class PrintPreviewDialog extends JDialog
12 {
13    private static final int DEFAULT_WIDTH = 300;
14    private static final int DEFAULT_HEIGHT = 300;
15
16    private PrintPreviewCanvas canvas;
17
18    /**
19     * Constructs a print preview dialog.
20     * @param p a Printable
21     * @param pf the page format
22     * @param pages the number of pages in p
23     */
```

(Continues)

Listing 11.27 *(Continued)*

```
24   public PrintPreviewDialog(Printable p, PageFormat pf, int pages)
25   {
26      var book = new Book();
27      book.append(p, pf, pages);
28      layoutUI(book);
29   }
30
31   /**
32    * Constructs a print preview dialog.
33    * @param b a Book
34    */
35   public PrintPreviewDialog(Book b)
36   {
37      layoutUI(b);
38   }
39
40   /**
41    * Lays out the UI of the dialog.
42    * @param book the book to be previewed
43    */
44   public void layoutUI(Book book)
45   {
46      setSize(DEFAULT_WIDTH, DEFAULT_HEIGHT);
47
48      canvas = new PrintPreviewCanvas(book);
49      add(canvas, BorderLayout.CENTER);
50
51      var buttonPanel = new JPanel();
52
53      var nextButton = new JButton("Next");
54      buttonPanel.add(nextButton);
55      nextButton.addActionListener(event -> canvas.flipPage(1));
56
57      var previousButton = new JButton("Previous");
58      buttonPanel.add(previousButton);
59      previousButton.addActionListener(event -> canvas.flipPage(-1));
60
61      var closeButton = new JButton("Close");
62      buttonPanel.add(closeButton);
63      closeButton.addActionListener(event -> setVisible(false));
64
65      add(buttonPanel, BorderLayout.SOUTH);
66   }
67 }
```

Listing 11.28 book/PrintPreviewCanvas.java

```java
1  package book;
2
3  import java.awt.*;
4  import java.awt.geom.*;
5  import java.awt.print.*;
6  import javax.swing.*;
7
8  /**
9   * The canvas for displaying the print preview.
10  */
11 class PrintPreviewCanvas extends JComponent
12 {
13    private Book book;
14    private int currentPage;
15
16    /**
17     * Constructs a print preview canvas.
18     * @param b the book to be previewed
19     */
20    public PrintPreviewCanvas(Book b)
21    {
22       book = b;
23       currentPage = 0;
24    }
25
26    public void paintComponent(Graphics g)
27    {
28       var g2 = (Graphics2D) g;
29       PageFormat pageFormat = book.getPageFormat(currentPage);
30
31       double xoff; // x offset of page start in window
32       double yoff; // y offset of page start in window
33       double scale; // scale factor to fit page in window
34       double px = pageFormat.getWidth();
35       double py = pageFormat.getHeight();
36       double sx = getWidth() - 1;
37       double sy = getHeight() - 1;
38       if (px / py < sx / sy) // center horizontally
39       {
40          scale = sy / py;
41          xoff = 0.5 * (sx - scale * px);
42          yoff = 0;
43       }
44       else
45       // center vertically
46       {
```

(Continues)

Listing 11.28 *(Continued)*

```
47          scale = sx / px;
48          xoff = 0;
49          yoff = 0.5 * (sy - scale * py);
50       }
51       g2.translate((float) xoff, (float) yoff);
52       g2.scale((float) scale, (float) scale);
53
54       // draw page outline (ignoring margins)
55       var page = new Rectangle2D.Double(0, 0, px, py);
56       g2.setPaint(Color.white);
57       g2.fill(page);
58       g2.setPaint(Color.black);
59       g2.draw(page);
60
61       Printable printable = book.getPrintable(currentPage);
62       try
63       {
64          printable.print(g2, pageFormat, currentPage);
65       }
66       catch (PrinterException e)
67       {
68          g2.draw(new Line2D.Double(0, 0, px, py));
69          g2.draw(new Line2D.Double(px, 0, 0, py));
70       }
71    }
72
73    /**
74     * Flip the book by the given number of pages.
75     * @param by the number of pages to flip by. Negative values flip backwards.
76     */
77    public void flipPage(int by)
78    {
79       int newPage = currentPage + by;
80       if (0 <= newPage && newPage < book.getNumberOfPages())
81       {
82          currentPage = newPage;
83          repaint();
84       }
85    }
86 }
```

11.5.3 Print Services

So far, you have seen how to print 2D graphics. However, the printing API introduced in Java SE 1.4 affords far greater flexibility. The API defines a number of data types and lets you find print services that are able to print them. Among the data types are

- Images in GIF, JPEG, or PNG format
- Documents in text, HTML, PostScript, or PDF format
- Raw printer code data
- Objects of a class that implements `Printable`, `Pageable`, or `RenderableImage`

The data themselves can be stored in a source of bytes or characters such as an input stream, a URL, or an array. A *document flavor* describes the combination of a data source and a data type. The `DocFlavor` class defines a number of inner classes for the various data sources. Each of the inner classes defines constants to specify the flavors. For example, the constant

```
DocFlavor.INPUT_STREAM.GIF
```

describes a GIF image that is read from an input stream. Table 11.4 lists the combinations.

Suppose you want to print a GIF image located in a file. First, find out whether there is a *print service* that is capable of handling the task. The static `lookupPrintServices` method of the `PrintServiceLookup` class returns an array of `PrintService` objects that can handle the given document flavor.

```
DocFlavor flavor = DocFlavor.INPUT_STREAM.GIF;
PrintService[] services = PrintServiceLookup.lookupPrintServices(flavor, null);
```

The second parameter of the `lookupPrintServices` method is `null` to indicate that we don't want to constrain the search by specifying printer attributes. We'll cover attributes in the next section.

If the lookup yields an array with more than one element, select from the listed print services. You can call the `getName` method of the `PrintService` class to get the printer names and let the user choose.

Next, get a document print job from the service:

```
DocPrintJob job = services[i].createPrintJob();
```

For printing, you need an object that implements the `Doc` interface. The Java library supplies a class `SimpleDoc` for that purpose. The `SimpleDoc` constructor requires the data source object, the document flavor, and an optional attribute set. For example,

```
var in = new FileInputStream(fileName);
var doc = new SimpleDoc(in, flavor, null);
```

Finally, you are ready to print:

```
job.print(doc, null);
```

As before, the `null` parameter can be replaced by an attribute set.

Table 11.4 Document Flavors for Print Services

Data Source	Data Type	MIME Type
INPUT_STREAM	GIF	image/gif
URL	JPEG	image/jpeg
BYTE_ARRAY	PNG	image/png
	POSTSCRIPT	application/postscript
	PDF	application/pdf
	TEXT_HML_HOST	text/html (using host encoding)
	TEXT_HTML_US_ASCII	text/html; charset=us-ascii
	TEXT_HTML_UTF_8	text/html; charset=utf-8
	TEXT_HTML_UTF_16	text/html; charset=utf-16
	TEXT_HTML_UTF_16LE	text/html; charset=utf-16le (little-endian)
	TEXT_HTML_UTF_16BE	text/html; charset=utf-16be (big-endian)
	TEXT_PLAIN_HOST	text/plain (using host encoding)
	TEXT_PLAIN_US_ASCII	text/plain; charset=us-ascii
	TEXT_PLAIN_UTF_8	text/plain; charset=utf-8
	TEXT_PLAIN_UTF_16	text/plain; charset=utf-16
	TEXT_PLAIN_UTF_16LE	text/plain; charset=utf-16le (little-endian)
	TEXT_PLAIN_UTF_16BE	text/plain; charset=utf-16be (big-endian)
	PCL	application/vnd.hp-PCL (Hewlett Packard Printer Control Language)
	AUTOSENSE	application/octet-stream (raw printer data)
READER	TEXT_HTML	text/html; charset=utf-16
STRING	TEXT_PLAIN	text/plain; charset=utf-16
CHAR_ARRAY		
SERVICE_FORMATTED	PRINTABLE	N/A
	PAGEABLE	N/A
	RENDERABLE_IMAGE	N/A

Note that this printing process is quite different from that of the preceding section. There is no user interaction through print dialog boxes. For example, you can implement a server-side printing mechanism in which users submit print jobs through a web form.

---

javax.print.PrintServiceLookup 1.4

- `PrintService[] lookupPrintServices(DocFlavor flavor, AttributeSet attributes)`

  looks up the print services that can handle the given document flavor and attributes.

Parameters:	flavor	The document flavor
	attributes	The required printing attributes, or `null` if attributes should not be considered

---

javax.print.PrintService 1.4

- `DocPrintJob createPrintJob()`

  creates a print job for printing an object of a class that implements the `Doc` interface, such as a `SimpleDoc`.

---

javax.print.DocPrintJob 1.4

- `void print(Doc doc, PrintRequestAttributeSet attributes)`

  prints the given document with the given attributes.

Parameters:	doc	The `Doc` to be printed
	attributes	The required printing attributes, or `null` if no printing attributes are required

---

javax.print.SimpleDoc 1.4

- `SimpleDoc(Object data, DocFlavor flavor, DocAttributeSet attributes)`

  constructs a `SimpleDoc` object that can be printed with a `DocPrintJob`.

Parameters:	data	The object with the print data, such as an input stream or a `Printable`
	flavor	The document flavor of the print data
	attributes	Document attributes, or `null` if attributes are not required

11.5.4 Stream Print Services

A print service sends print data to a printer. A stream print service generates the same print data but instead sends them to a stream, perhaps for delayed printing or because the print data format can be interpreted by other programs. In particular, if the print data format is PostScript, it may be useful to save the print data to a file because many programs can process PostScript files. The Java platform includes a stream print service that can produce PostScript output from images and 2D graphics. You can use that service on all systems, even if there are no local printers.

Enumerating stream print services is a bit more tedious than locating regular print services. You need both the DocFlavor of the object to be printed and the MIME type of the stream output. You then get a StreamPrintServiceFactory array of factories.

```
DocFlavor flavor = DocFlavor.SERVICE_FORMATTED.PRINTABLE;
String mimeType = "application/postscript";
StreamPrintServiceFactory[] factories
   = StreamPrintServiceFactory.lookupStreamPrintServiceFactories(flavor, mimeType);
```

The StreamPrintServiceFactory class has no methods that would help us distinguish any one factory from another, so we just take factories[0]. We call the getPrintService method with an output stream parameter to get a StreamPrintService object.

```
var out = new FileOutputStream(fileName);
StreamPrintService service = factories[0].getPrintService(out);
```

The StreamPrintService class is a subclass of PrintService. To produce a printout, simply follow the steps of the preceding section.

---

javax.print.StreamPrintServiceFactory 1.4

- StreamPrintServiceFactory[] lookupStreamPrintServiceFactories(DocFlavor flavor, String mimeType)

  looks up the stream print service factories that can print the given document flavor and produce an output stream of the given MIME type.

- StreamPrintService getPrintService(OutputStream out)

  gets a print service that sends the printing output to the given output stream.

The program in Listing 11.29 demonstrates how to use a stream print service to print Java 2D shapes to a PostScript file. You can replace the sample drawing code with code that generates any Java 2D shapes and have the shapes converted to PostScript. Then you can easily convert the result to PDF or EPS, using an external tool. (Unfortunately, Java does not support printing to PDF directly.)

 NOTE: In this example, we call a draw method that draws Java 2D shapes onto a Graphics2D object. If you want to draw the surface of a component (for example, a table or tree), use the following code:

```
private static int IMAGE_WIDTH = component.getWidth();
private static int IMAGE_HEIGHT = component.getHeight();
public static void draw(Graphics2D g2) { component.paint(g2); }
```

Listing 11.29 printService/PrintServiceTest.java

```
1  package printService;
2
3  import java.awt.*;
4  import java.awt.font.*;
5  import java.awt.geom.*;
6  import java.awt.print.*;
7  import java.io.*;
8  import javax.print.*;
9  import javax.print.attribute.*;
10
11 /**
12  * This program demonstrates the use of stream print services. The program prints
13  * Java 2D shapes to a PostScript file. If you don't supply a file name on the command
14  * line, the output is saved to out.ps.
15  * @version 1.0 2018-06-01
16  * @author Cay Horstmann
17  */
18 public class PrintServiceTest
19 {
20    // Set your image dimensions here
21    private static int IMAGE_WIDTH = 300;
22    private static int IMAGE_HEIGHT = 300;
23
24    public static void draw(Graphics2D g2)
25    {
26       // Your drawing instructions go here
27       FontRenderContext context = g2.getFontRenderContext();
28       var f = new Font("Serif", Font.PLAIN, 72);
29       var clipShape = new GeneralPath();
30
31       var layout = new TextLayout("Hello", f, context);
32       AffineTransform transform = AffineTransform.getTranslateInstance(0, 72);
33       Shape outline = layout.getOutline(transform);
```

(Continues)

Listing 11.29 *(Continued)*

```
34        clipShape.append(outline, false);
35
36        layout = new TextLayout("World", f, context);
37        transform = AffineTransform.getTranslateInstance(0, 144);
38        outline = layout.getOutline(transform);
39        clipShape.append(outline, false);
40
41        g2.draw(clipShape);
42        g2.clip(clipShape);
43
44        final int NLINES = 50;
45        var p = new Point2D.Double(0, 0);
46        for (int i = 0; i < NLINES; i++)
47        {
48           double x = (2 * IMAGE_WIDTH * i) / NLINES;
49           double y = (2 * IMAGE_HEIGHT * (NLINES - 1 - i)) / NLINES;
50           var q = new Point2D.Double(x, y);
51           g2.draw(new Line2D.Double(p, q));
52        }
53     }
54
55     public static void main(String[] args) throws IOException, PrintException
56     {
57        String fileName = args.length > 0 ? args[0] : "out.ps";
58        DocFlavor flavor = DocFlavor.SERVICE_FORMATTED.PRINTABLE;
59        var mimeType = "application/postscript";
60        StreamPrintServiceFactory[] factories
61           = StreamPrintServiceFactory.lookupStreamPrintServiceFactories(flavor, mimeType);
62        var out = new FileOutputStream(fileName);
63        if (factories.length > 0)
64        {
65           PrintService service = factories[0].getPrintService(out);
66           var doc = new SimpleDoc(new Printable()
67              {
68                 public int print(Graphics g, PageFormat pf, int page)
69                 {
70                    if (page >= 1) return Printable.NO_SUCH_PAGE;
71                    else
72                    {
73                       double sf1 = pf.getImageableWidth() / (IMAGE_WIDTH + 1);
74                       double sf2 = pf.getImageableHeight() / (IMAGE_HEIGHT + 1);
75                       double s = Math.min(sf1, sf2);
76                       var g2 = (Graphics2D) g;
77                       g2.translate((pf.getWidth() - pf.getImageableWidth()) / 2,
78                          (pf.getHeight() - pf.getImageableHeight()) / 2);
79                       g2.scale(s, s);
80
81                       draw(g2);
```

```
82              return Printable.PAGE_EXISTS;
83          }
84      }
85  }, flavor, null);
86  DocPrintJob job = service.createPrintJob();
87  var attributes = new HashPrintRequestAttributeSet();
88  job.print(doc, attributes);
89      }
90  else
91      System.out.println("No factories for " + mimeType);
92  }
93 }
```

11.5.5 Printing Attributes

The print service API contains a complex set of interfaces and classes to specify various kinds of attributes. There are four important groups of attributes. The first two specify requests to the printer.

• *Print request attributes* request particular features for all doc objects in a print job, such as two-sided printing or the paper size.

• *Doc attributes* are request attributes that apply only to a single doc object.

The other two attributes contain information about the printer and job status.

• *Print service attributes* give information about the print service, such as the printer make and model or whether the printer is currently accepting jobs.

• *Print job attributes* give information about the status of a particular print job, such as whether the job is already completed.

To describe the various attributes, there is an interface Attribute with subinterfaces:

```
PrintRequestAttribute
DocAttribute
PrintServiceAttribute
PrintJobAttribute
SupportedValuesAttribute
```

Individual attribute classes implement one or more of these interfaces. For example, objects of the Copies class describe the number of copies of a printout. That class implements both the PrintRequestAttribute and the PrintJobAttribute interfaces. Clearly, a print request can contain a request for multiple copies. Conversely, an attribute of the print job might be how many of these copies were actually printed. That number might be lower, perhaps because of printer limitations or because the printer ran out of paper.

The SupportedValuesAttribute interface indicates that an attribute value does not reflect actual request or status data but rather the capability of a service. For example, the CopiesSupported class implements the SupportedValuesAttribute interface. An object of that class might describe that a printer supports 1 through 99 copies of a printout.

Figure 11.65 shows a class diagram of the attribute hierarchy.

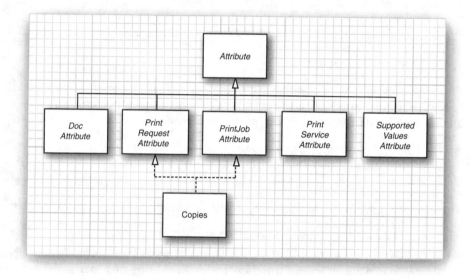

Figure 11.65 The attribute hierarchy

In addition to the interfaces and classes for individual attributes, the print service API defines interfaces and classes for attribute sets. A superinterface, AttributeSet, has four subinterfaces:

```
PrintRequestAttributeSet
DocAttributeSet
PrintServiceAttributeSet
PrintJobAttributeSet
```

Each of these interfaces has an implementing class, yielding the five classes:

```
HashAttributeSet
HashPrintRequestAttributeSet
HashDocAttributeSet
HashPrintServiceAttributeSet
HashPrintJobAttributeSet
```

Figure 11.66 shows a class diagram of the attribute set hierarchy.

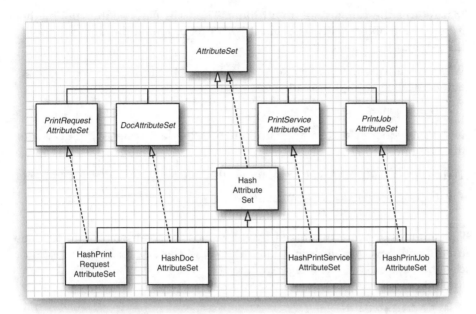

Figure 11.66 The attribute set hierarchy

For example, you can construct a print request attribute set like this:

```
var attributes = new HashPrintRequestAttributeSet();
```

After constructing the set, you are freed from worrying about the Hash prefix.

Why have all these interfaces? They make it possible to check for correct attribute usage. For example, a DocAttributeSet accepts only objects that implement the DocAttribute interface. Any attempt to add another attribute results in a runtime error.

An attribute set is a specialized kind of map where the keys are of type Class and the values belong to a class that implements the Attribute interface. For example, if you insert an object

```
new Copies(10)
```

into an attribute set, then its key is the Class object Copies.class. That key is called the *category* of the attribute. The Attribute interface declares a method

```
Class getCategory()
```

that returns the category of an attribute. The Copies class defines the method to return the object Copies.class, but it isn't a requirement that the category be the same as the class of the attribute.

When an attribute is added to an attribute set, the category is extracted automatically. Just add the attribute value:

```
attributes.add(new Copies(10));
```

If you subsequently add another attribute with the same category, it overwrites the first one.

To retrieve an attribute, you need to use the category as the key, for example:

```
AttributeSet attributes = job.getAttributes();
var copies = (Copies) attribute.get(Copies.class);
```

Finally, attributes are organized by the values they can have. The Copies attribute can have any integer value. The Copies class extends the IntegerSyntax class that takes care of all integer-valued attributes. The getValue method returns the integer value of the attribute, for example:

```
int n = copies.getValue();
```

The classes

```
TextSyntax
DateTimeSyntax
URISyntax
```

encapsulate a string, a date and time value, or a URI.

Finally, many attributes can take a finite number of values. For example, the PrintQuality attribute has three settings: draft, normal, and high. They are represented by three constants:

```
PrintQuality.DRAFT
PrintQuality.NORMAL
PrintQuality.HIGH
```

Attribute classes with a finite number of values extend the EnumSyntax class, which provides a number of convenience methods to set up these enumerations in a typesafe manner. You need not worry about the mechanism when using such an attribute. Simply add the named values to attribute sets:

```
attributes.add(PrintQuality.HIGH);
```

Here is how you check the value of an attribute:

```
if (attributes.get(PrintQuality.class) == PrintQuality.HIGH)
    . . .
```

Table 11.5 lists the printing attributes. The second column lists the superclass of the attribute class (for example, IntegerSyntax for the Copies attribute) or the set of enumeration values for the attributes with a finite set of values. The last four columns indicate whether the attribute class implements the DocAttribute (DA), PrintJobAttribute (PJA), PrintRequestAttribute (PRA), and PrintServiceAttribute (PSA) interfaces.

Table 11.5 Printing Attributes

Attribute	Superclass or Enumeration Constants	DA	PJA	PRA	PSA
Chromaticity	MONOCHROME, COLOR	✓	✓	✓	
ColorSupported	SUPPORTED, NOT_SUPPORTED				✓
Compression	COMPRESS, DEFLATE, GZIP, NONE	✓			
Copies	IntegerSyntax		✓	✓	
DateTimeAtCompleted	DateTimeSyntax		✓		
DateTimeAtCreation	DateTimeSyntax		✓		
DateTimeAtProcessing	DateTimeSyntax		✓		
Destination	URISyntax		✓	✓	
DocumentName	TextSyntax	✓			
Fidelity	FIDELITY_TRUE, FIDELITY_FALSE		✓	✓	
Finishings	NONE, STAPLE, EDGE_STITCH, BIND, SADDLE_STITCH, COVER, . . .	✓	✓	✓	
JobHoldUntil	DateTimeSyntax		✓	✓	
JobImpressions	IntegerSyntax		✓	✓	
JobImpressionsCompleted	IntegerSyntax		✓		
JobKOctets	IntegerSyntax		✓	✓	
JobKOctetsProcessed	IntegerSyntax		✓		
JobMediaSheets	IntegerSyntax		✓	✓	
JobMediaSheetsCompleted	IntegerSyntax		✓		
JobMessageFromOperator	TextSyntax		✓		
JobName	TextSyntax		✓	✓	

(Continues)

Table 11.5 *(Continued)*

Attribute	Superclass or Enumeration Constants	DA	PJA	PRA	PSA
JobOriginatingUserName	TextSyntax		✓		
JobPriority	IntegerSyntax		✓	✓	
JobSheets	STANDARD, NONE		✓	✓	
JobState	ABORTED, CANCELED, COMPLETED, PENDING, PENDING_HELD, PROCESSING, PROCESSING_STOPPED		✓		
JobStateReason	ABORTED_BY_SYSTEM, DOCUMENT_FORMAT_ERROR, many others				
JobStateReasons	HashSet		✓		
MediaName	ISO_A4_WHITE, ISO_A4_TRANSPARENT, NA_LETTER_WHITE, NA_LETTER_TRANSPARENT	✓	✓	✓	
MediaSize	ISO.A0–ISO.A10, ISO.B0–ISO.B10, ISO.C0–ISO.C10, NA.LETTER, NA.LEGAL, various other paper and envelope sizes				
MediaSizeName	ISO_A0–ISO_A10, ISO_B0–ISO_B10, ISO_C0–ISO_C10, NA_LETTER, NA_LEGAL, various other paper and envelope size names	✓	✓	✓	
MediaTray	TOP, MIDDLE, BOTTOM, SIDE, ENVELOPE, LARGE_CAPACITY, MAIN, MANUAL	✓	✓	✓	
MultipleDocumentHandling	SINGLE_DOCUMENT, SINGLE_DOCUMENT_NEW_SHEET, SEPARATE_DOCUMENTS_COLLATED_COPIES, SEPARATE_DOCUMENTS_UNCOLLATED_COPIES		✓	✓	
NumberOfDocuments	IntegerSyntax		✓		
NumberOfInterveningJobs	IntegerSyntax		✓		
NumberUp	IntegerSyntax	✓	✓	✓	
OrientationRequested	PORTRAIT, LANDSCAPE, REVERSE_PORTRAIT, REVERSE_LANDSCAPE	✓	✓	✓	

(Continues)

Table 11.5 *(Continued)*

Attribute	Superclass or Enumeration Constants	DA	PJA	PRA	PSA
OutputDeviceAssigned	TextSyntax		✓		
PageRanges	SetOfInteger	✓	✓	✓	
PagesPerMinute	IntegerSyntax				✓
PagesPerMinuteColor	IntegerSyntax				✓
PDLOverrideSupported	ATTEMPTED, NOT_ATTEMPTED				✓
PresentationDirection	TORIGHT_TOBOTTOM, TORIGHT_TOTOP, TOBOTTOM_TORIGHT, TOBOTTOM_TOLEFT, TOLEFT_TOBOTTOM, TOLEFT_TOTOP, TOTOP_TORIGHT, TOTOP_TOLEFT		✓	✓	
PrinterInfo	TextSyntax				✓
PrinterIsAcceptingJobs	ACCEPTING_JOBS, NOT_ACCEPTING_JOBS				✓
PrinterLocation	TextSyntax				✓
PrinterMakeAndModel	TextSyntax				✓
PrinterMessageFromOperator	TextSyntax				✓
PrinterMoreInfo	URISyntax				✓
PrinterMoreInfoManufacturer	URISyntax				✓
PrinterName	TextSyntax				✓
PrinterResolution	ResolutionSyntax	✓	✓	✓	
PrinterState	PROCESSING, IDLE, STOPPED, UNKNOWN				✓
PrinterStateReason	COVER_OPEN, FUSER_OVER_TEMP, MEDIA_JAM, and many others				
PrinterStateReasons	HashMap				
PrinterURI	URISyntax				✓
PrintQuality	DRAFT, NORMAL, HIGH	✓	✓	✓	
QueuedJobCount	IntegerSyntax				✓
ReferenceUriSchemesSupported	FILE, FTP, GOPHER, HTTP, HTTPS, NEWS, NNTP, WAIS				

(Continues)

Table 11.5 *(Continued)*

Attribute	Superclass or Enumeration Constants	DA	PJA	PRA	PSA
RequestingUserName	TextSyntax			✓	
Severity	ERROR, REPORT, WARNING				
SheetCollate	COLLATED, UNCOLLATED	✓	✓	✓	
Sides	ONE_SIDED, DUPLEX (= TWO_SIDED_LONG_EDGE), TUMBLE (= TWO_SIDED_SHORT_EDGE)	✓	✓	✓	

NOTE: As you can see, there are lots of attributes, many of which are quite specialized. The source for most of the attributes is the Internet Printing Protocol 1.1 (RFC 2911).

NOTE: An earlier version of the printing API introduced the `JobAttributes` and `PageAttributes` classes, whose purpose was similar to the printing attributes covered in this section. These classes are now obsolete.

---

javax.print.attribute.Attribute 1.4

- `Class getCategory()`

  gets the category of this attribute.
- `String getName()`

  gets the name of this attribute.

---

javax.print.attribute.AttributeSet 1.4

- `boolean add(Attribute attr)`

  adds an attribute to this set. If the set has another attribute with the same category, that attribute is replaced by the given attribute. Returns `true` if the set changed as a result of this operation.
- `Attribute get(Class category)`

  retrieves the attribute with the given category key, or `null` if no such attribute exists.

(Continues)

---

javax.print.attribute.AttributeSet 1.4 *(Continued)*

- `boolean remove(Attribute attr)`
- `boolean remove(Class category)`

    removes the given attribute, or the attribute with the given category, from the set. Returns true if the set changed as a result of this operation.

- `Attribute[] toArray()`

    returns an array with all attributes in this set.

---

javax.print.PrintService 1.4

- `PrintServiceAttributeSet getAttributes()`

    gets the attributes of this print service.

---

javax.print.DocPrintJob 1.4

- `PrintJobAttributeSet getAttributes()`

    gets the attributes of this print job.

You have now reached the end of this long chapter covering advanced Swing and AWT features. In the final chapter, we will turn to a different aspect of Java programming: interacting, on the same machine, with "native" code in a different programming language.

Native Methods

In this chapter

While a "100% Pure Java" solution is nice in principle, there are situations in which you will want to write (or use) code in another language. Such code is usually called *native* code.

Particularly in the early days of Java, many people assumed that it would be a good idea to use C or C++ to speed up critical parts of a Java application. However, in practice, this was rarely useful. A presentation at the 1996 JavaOne conference showed this clearly. The developers of the cryptography library at Sun Microsystems reported that a pure Java platform implementation of their cryptographic functions was more than adequate. It was true that the code was not as fast as a C implementation would have been, but it turned out not to matter. The Java platform implementation was far faster than the network I/O. This turned out to be the real bottleneck.

Of course, there are drawbacks to going native. If a part of your application is written in another language, you must supply a separate native library for every platform you want to support. Code written in C or C++ offers no protection against overwriting memory through invalid pointer usage. It is easy to write native methods that corrupt your program or infect the operating system.

Thus, we suggest using native code only when you need to. In particular, there are three reasons why native code might be the right choice:

- Your application requires access to system features or devices that are not accessible through the Java platform.
- You have substantial amounts of tested and debugged code in another language, and you know how to port it to all desired target platforms.
- You have found, through benchmarking, that the Java code is much slower than the equivalent code in another language.

The Java platform has an API for interoperating with native C code called the Java Native Interface (JNI). We'll discuss JNI programming in this chapter.

 C++ NOTE: You can also use C++ instead of C to write native methods. There are a few advantages—type checking is slightly stricter, and accessing the JNI functions is a bit more convenient. However, JNI does not support any mapping between Java and C++ classes.

12.1 Calling a C Function from a Java Program

Suppose you have a C function that does something you like and, for one reason or another, you don't want to bother reimplementing it in Java. For the sake of illustration, we'll start with a simple C function that prints a greeting.

The Java programming language uses the keyword native for a native method, and you will obviously need to place a method in a class. The result is shown in Listing 12.1.

The native keyword alerts the compiler that the method will be defined externally. Of course, native methods will contain no Java code, and the method header is followed immediately by a terminating semicolon. Therefore, native method declarations look similar to abstract method declarations.

Listing 12.1 helloNative/HelloNative.java

```
1  /**
2   * @version 1.11 2007-10-26
3   * @author Cay Horstmann
4   */
5  class HelloNative
6  {
7     public static native void greeting();
8  }
```

 NOTE: As in the previous chapter, we do not use packages here to keep examples simple.

In this particular example, the native method is also declared as static. Native methods can be both static and nonstatic. We'll start with a static method because we do not yet want to deal with parameter passing.

You can actually compile this class, but if you try to use it in a program, the virtual machine will tell you it doesn't know how to find greeting—reporting an UnsatisfiedLinkError. To implement the native code, write a corresponding C function. You must name that function *exactly* the way the Java virtual machine expects. Here are the rules:

1. Use the full Java method name, such as HelloNative.greeting. If the class is in a package, prepend the package name, such as com.horstmann.HelloNative .greeting.

2. Replace every period with an underscore, and append the prefix Java_. For example, Java_HelloNative_greeting or Java_com_horstmann_HelloNative_greeting.

3. If the class name contains characters that are not ASCII letters or digits—that is, '_', '$', or Unicode characters with codes greater than \u007F—replace them with _0xxxx, where *xxxx* is the sequence of four hexadecimal digits of the character's Unicode value.

 NOTE: If you *overload* native methods—that is, if you provide multiple native methods with the same name—you must append a double underscore followed by the encoded argument types. (We'll describe the encoding of the argument types later in this chapter.) For example, if you have a native method greeting and another native method greeting(int repeat), then the first one is called Java_HelloNative_greeting__ and the second, Java_HelloNative_greeting__I.

Actually, nobody does this by hand; instead, run `javac` with the `-h` flag, providing the directory in which the header files should be placed:

```
javac -h . HelloNative.java
```

This command creates a header file `HelloNative.h` in the current directory, as shown in Listing 12.2.

Listing 12.2 helloNative/HelloNative.h

```
1  /* DO NOT EDIT THIS FILE - it is machine generated */
2  #include <jni.h>
3  /* Header for class HelloNative */
4
5  #ifndef _Included_HelloNative
6  #define _Included_HelloNative
7  #ifdef __cplusplus
8  extern "C" {
9  #endif
10 /*
11  * Class:     HelloNative
12  * Method:    greeting
13  * Signature: ()V
14  */
15 JNIEXPORT void JNICALL Java_HelloNative_greeting
16   (JNIEnv *, jclass);
17
18 #ifdef __cplusplus
19 }
20 #endif
21 #endif
```

As you can see, this file contains the declaration of a function `Java_HelloNative_greeting`. (The macros `JNIEXPORT` and `JNICALL` are defined in the header file `jni.h`. They denote compiler-dependent specifiers for exported functions that come from a dynamically loaded library.)

Now, simply copy the function prototype from the header file into a source file and give the implementation code for the function, as shown in Listing 12.3.

In this simple function, ignore the `env` and `cl` arguments. You'll see their use later.

Listing 12.3 helloNative/HelloNative.c

```
1  /*
2     @version 1.10 1997-07-01
3     @author Cay Horstmann
4  */
5
6  #include "HelloNative.h"
7  #include <stdio.h>
8
9  JNIEXPORT void JNICALL Java_HelloNative_greeting(JNIEnv* env, jclass cl)
10 {
11     printf("Hello Native World!\n");
12 }
```

C++ NOTE: You can use C++ to implement native methods. However, you must then declare the functions that implement the native methods as extern "C". (This stops the C++ compiler from "mangling" the method name.) For example,

```
extern "C"
JNIEXPORT void JNICALL Java_HelloNative_greeting(JNIEnv* env, jclass cl)
{
    cout << "Hello, Native World!" << endl;
}
```

Compile the native C code into a dynamically loaded library. The details depend on your compiler.

For example, with the GNU C compiler on Linux, use these commands:

```
gcc -fPIC -I jdk/include -I jdk/include/linux -shared -o libHelloNative.so HelloNative.c
```

With the Microsoft compiler under Windows, the command is

```
cl -I jdk\include -I jdk\include\win32 -LD HelloNative.c -FeHelloNative.dll
```

Here, *jdk* is the directory that contains the JDK.

TIP: If you use the Microsoft compiler from a command shell, first run a batch file such as vsvars32.bat or vcvarsall.bat. That batch file sets up the path and the environment variables needed by the compiler. You can find it in the directory c:\Program Files\Microsoft Visual Studio 14.0\Common7\Tools or a similar monstrosity. Check the Visual Studio documentation for details.

You can also use the freely available Cygwin programming environment from www.cygwin.com. It contains the GNU C compiler and libraries for UNIX-style programming on Windows. With Cygwin, use the command

```
gcc -mno-cygwin -D __int64="long long" -I jdk/include/ -I jdk/include/win32 \
    -shared -Wl,--add-stdcall-alias -o HelloNative.dll HelloNative.c
```

 NOTE: The Windows version of the header file `jni_md.h` contains the type declaration

```
typedef __int64 jlong;
```

which is specific to the Microsoft compiler. If you use the GNU compiler, you might want to edit that file, for example,

```
#ifdef __GNUC__
    typedef long long jlong;
#else
    typedef __int64 jlong;
#endif
```

Alternatively, compile with `-D __int64="long long"`, as shown in the sample compiler invocation.

Finally, add a call to the `System.loadLibrary` method in your program. To ensure that the virtual machine will load the library before the first use of the class, use a static initialization block, as in Listing 12.4.

Listing 12.4 helloNative/HelloNativeTest.java

```
 1  /**
 2   * @version 1.11 2007-10-26
 3   * @author Cay Horstmann
 4   */
 5  class HelloNativeTest
 6  {
 7     public static void main(String[] args)
 8     {
 9        HelloNative.greeting();
10     }
11
12     static
13     {
14        System.loadLibrary("HelloNative");
15     }
16  }
```

Figure 12.1 gives a summary of the native code processing.

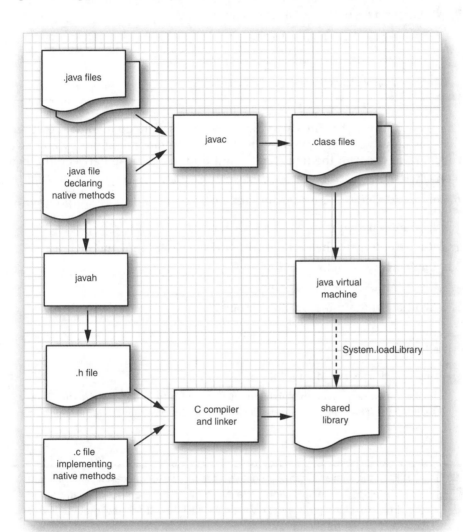

Figure 12.1 Processing native code

After you compile and run this program, the message "Hello, Native World!" is displayed in a terminal window.

NOTE: If you run Linux, you must add the current directory to the library path. Either set the `LD_LIBRARY_PATH` environment variable:

> `export LD_LIBRARY_PATH=.:$LD_LIBRARY_PATH`

or set the `java.library.path` system property:

> `java -Djava.library.path=. HelloNativeTest`

Of course, this is not particularly impressive by itself. Keep in mind, however, that this message is generated by the C `printf` command and not by any Java code. We have taken the first step toward bridging the gap between the two languages!

In summary, follow these steps to link a native method to a Java program:

1. Declare a native method in a Java class.
2. Run `javah` to get a header file with a C declaration for the method.
3. Implement the native method in C.
4. Place the code in a shared library.
5. Load that library in your Java program.

`java.lang.System` 1.0

*   void loadLibrary(String libname)

    loads the library with the given name. The library is located in the library search path. The exact method for locating the library depends on the operating system.

 NOTE: Some shared libraries for native code must execute certain initializations. You can place any initialization code into a `JNI_OnLoad` method. Similarly, when the virtual machine (VM) shuts down, it will call the `JNI_OnUnload` method if you provide it. The prototypes are

> `jint JNI_OnLoad(JavaVM* vm, void* reserved);`
> `void JNI_OnUnload(JavaVM* vm, void* reserved);`

The `JNI_OnLoad` method needs to return the minimum version of the VM it requires, such as `JNI_VERSION_1_2`.

12.2 Numeric Parameters and Return Values

When passing numbers between C and Java, you should understand which types correspond to each other. For example, although C does have data types called int and long, their implementation is platform-dependent. On some platforms, an int is a 16-bit quantity, on others it is a 32-bit quantity. On the Java platform, of course, an int is *always* a 32-bit integer. For that reason, JNI defines types jint, jlong, and so on.

Table 12.1 shows the correspondence between Java types and C types.

Table 12.1 Java Types and C Types

Java Programming Language	C Programming Language	Bytes
boolean	jboolean	1
byte	jbyte	1
char	jchar	2
short	jshort	2
int	jint	4
long	jlong	8
float	jfloat	4
double	jdouble	8

In the header file jni.h, these types are declared with typedef statements as the equivalent types on the target platform. That header file also defines the constants JNI_FALSE = 0 and JNI_TRUE = 1.

Until Java 5, Java had no direct analog of the C printf function. In the following examples, we will suppose you are stuck with an ancient JDK release and decide to implement the same functionality by calling the C printf function in a native method.

Listing 12.5 shows a class called Printf1 that uses a native method to print a floating-point number with a given field width and precision.

Notice that when the method is implemented in C, all int and double parameters are changed to jint and jdouble, as shown in Listing 12.6.

Listing 12.5 printf1/Printf1.java

```java
 1  /**
 2   * @version 1.10 1997-07-01
 3   * @author Cay Horstmann
 4   */
 5  class Printf1
 6  {
 7     public static native int print(int width, int precision, double x);
 8
 9     static
10     {
11        System.loadLibrary("Printf1");
12     }
13  }
```

Listing 12.6 printf1/Printf1.c

```c
 1  /**
 2     @version 1.10 1997-07-01
 3     @author Cay Horstmann
 4  */
 5
 6  #include "Printf1.h"
 7  #include <stdio.h>
 8
 9  JNIEXPORT jint JNICALL Java_Printf1_print(JNIEnv* env, jclass cl,
10        jint width, jint precision, jdouble x)
11  {
12     char fmt[30];
13     jint ret;
14     sprintf(fmt, "%%%d.%df", width, precision);
15     ret = printf(fmt, x);
16     fflush(stdout);
17     return ret;
18  }
```

The function simply assembles a format string "%w.pf" in the variable fmt, then calls printf. It returns the number of characters printed.

Listing 12.7 shows the test program that demonstrates the Printf1 class.

Listing 12.7 `printf1/Printf1Test.java`

```
1  /**
2   * @version 1.10 1997-07-01
3   * @author Cay Horstmann
4   */
5  class Printf1Test
6  {
7     public static void main(String[] args)
8     {
9        int count = Printf1.print(8, 4, 3.14);
10       count += Printf1.print(8, 4, count);
11       System.out.println();
12       for (int i = 0; i < count; i++)
13          System.out.print("-");
14       System.out.println();
15    }
16 }
```

12.3 String Parameters

Next, let's look at how to transfer strings to and from native methods. Strings are quite different in the two languages: In Java, they are sequences of UTF-16 code points, whereas C strings are null-terminated sequences of bytes. JNI has two sets of functions for manipulating strings: One converts Java strings to "modified UTF-8" byte sequences and another converts them to arrays of UTF-16 values—that is, to jchar arrays. (The UTF-8, "modified UTF-8," and UTF-16 formats were discussed in Chapter 2. Recall that the UTF-8 and "modified UTF-8" encodings leave ASCII characters unchanged, but all other Unicode characters are encoded as multibyte sequences.)

 NOTE: The standard UTF-8 encoding and the "modified UTF-8" encoding differ only for "supplementary" characters with codes higher than 0xFFFF. In the standard UTF-8 encoding, these characters are encoded as 4-byte sequences. In the "modified" encoding, each such character is first encoded as a pair of "surrogates" in the UTF-16 encoding, and then each surrogate is encoded with UTF-8, yielding a total of 6 bytes. This is clumsy, but it is a historical accident—the JVM specification was written when Unicode was still limited to 16 bits.

If your C code already uses Unicode, you'll want to use the second set of conversion functions. On the other hand, if all your strings are restricted to ASCII characters, you can use the "modified UTF-8" conversion functions.

A native method with a String parameter actually receives a value of an opaque type called jstring. A native method with a return value of type String must return a value of type jstring. JNI functions read and construct these jstring objects. For example, the NewStringUTF function makes a new jstring object out of a char array that contains ASCII characters or, more generally, "modified UTF-8"-encoded byte sequences.

JNI functions have a somewhat odd calling convention. Here is a call to the NewStringUTF function:

```
JNIEXPORT jstring JNICALL Java_HelloNative_getGreeting(JNIEnv* env, jclass cl)
{
   jstring jstr;
   char greeting[] = "Hello, Native World\n";
   jstr = (*env)->NewStringUTF(env, greeting);
   return jstr;
}
```

 NOTE: Unless explicitly mentioned otherwise, all code in this chapter is C code.

All calls to JNI functions use the env pointer that is the first argument of every native method. The env pointer is a pointer to a table of function pointers (see Figure 12.2). Therefore, you must prefix every JNI call with (*env)-> to actually dereference the function pointer. Furthermore, env is the first parameter of every JNI function.

 C++ NOTE: It is simpler to access JNI functions in C++. The C++ version of the JNIEnv class has inline member functions that take care of the function pointer lookup for you. For example, you can call the NewStringUTF function as

```
jstr = env->NewStringUTF(greeting);
```

Note that you omit the JNIEnv pointer from the parameter list of the call.

The NewStringUTF function lets you construct a new jstring. To read the contents of an existing jstring object, use the GetStringUTFChars function. This function returns a const jbyte* pointer to the "modified UTF-8" characters that describe

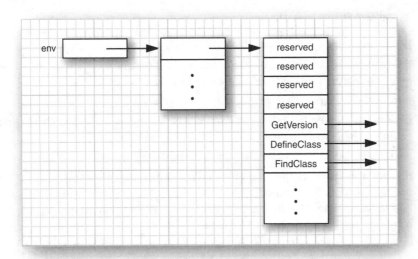

Figure 12.2 The env pointer

the character string. Note that a specific virtual machine is free to choose this character encoding for its internal string representation, so you might get a character pointer into the actual Java string. Since Java strings are meant to be immutable, it is *very* important that you treat the const seriously and do not try to write into this character array. On the other hand, if the virtual machine uses UTF-16 or UTF-32 characters for its internal string representation, this function call allocates a new memory block that will be filled with the "modified UTF-8" equivalents.

The virtual machine must know when you are finished using the string so that it can garbage-collect it. (The garbage collector runs in a separate thread, and it can interrupt the execution of native methods.) For that reason, you must call the ReleaseStringUTFChars function.

Alternatively, you can supply your own buffer to hold the string characters by calling the GetStringRegion or GetStringUTFRegion methods.

Finally, the GetStringUTFLength function returns the number of characters needed for the "modified UTF-8" encoding of the string.

 NOTE: You can find the JNI API at http://docs.oracle.com/javase/7/docs /technotes/guides/jni.

Accessing Java Strings from C Code

- `jstring NewStringUTF(JNIEnv* env, const char bytes[])`

  returns a new Java string object from a zero byte-terminated "modified UTF-8" byte sequence, or `NULL` if the string cannot be constructed.

- `jsize GetStringUTFLength(JNIEnv* env, jstring string)`

  returns the number of bytes required for the "modified UTF-8" encoding (not counting the zero byte terminator).

- `const jbyte* GetStringUTFChars(JNIEnv* env, jstring string, jboolean* isCopy)`

  returns a pointer to the "modified UTF-8" encoding of a string, or `NULL` if the character array cannot be constructed. The pointer is valid until `ReleaseStringUTFChars` is called. `isCopy` points to a jboolean filled with `JNI_TRUE` if a copy is made, or with `JNI_FALSE` otherwise.

- `void ReleaseStringUTFChars(JNIEnv* env, jstring string, const jbyte bytes[])`

  informs the virtual machine that the native code no longer needs access to the Java string through bytes (a pointer returned by `GetStringUTFChars`).

- `void GetStringRegion(JNIEnv *env, jstring string, jsize start, jsize length, jchar *buffer)`

  copies a sequence of UTF-16 double bytes from a string to a user-supplied buffer of size at least $2 \times$ `length`.

- `void GetStringUTFRegion(JNIEnv *env, jstring string, jsize start, jsize length, jbyte *buffer)`

  copies a sequence of "modified UTF-8" bytes from a string to a user-supplied buffer. The buffer must be long enough to hold the bytes. In the worst case, $3 \times$ `length` bytes are copied.

- `jstring NewString(JNIEnv* env, const jchar chars[], jsize length)`

  returns a new Java string object from a Unicode string, or `NULL` if the string cannot be constructed.

- `jsize GetStringLength(JNIEnv* env, jstring string)`

  returns the number of characters in the string.

- `const jchar* GetStringChars(JNIEnv* env, jstring string, jboolean* isCopy)`

  returns a pointer to the Unicode encoding of a string, or `NULL` if the character array cannot be constructed. The pointer is valid until `ReleaseStringChars` is called. `isCopy` is either `NULL` or points to a jboolean filled with `JNI_TRUE` if a copy is made, or with `JNI_FALSE` otherwise.

- `void ReleaseStringChars(JNIEnv* env, jstring string, const jchar chars[])`

  informs the virtual machine that the native code no longer needs access to the Java string through chars (a pointer returned by `GetStringChars`).

Let us put these functions to work and write a class that calls the C function sprintf. We would like to call the function as shown in Listing 12.8.

Listing 12.8 printf2/Printf2Test.java

```
1  /**
2   * @version 1.10 1997-07-01
3   * @author Cay Horstmann
4   */
5  class Printf2Test
6  {
7     public static void main(String[] args)
8     {
9        double price = 44.95;
10       double tax = 7.75;
11       double amountDue = price * (1 + tax / 100);
12
13       String s = Printf2.sprint("Amount due = %8.2f", amountDue);
14       System.out.println(s);
15    }
16 }
```

Listing 12.9 shows the class with the native sprint method.

Listing 12.9 printf2/Printf2.java

```
1  /**
2   * @version 1.10 1997-07-01
3   * @author Cay Horstmann
4   */
5  class Printf2
6  {
7     public static native String sprint(String format, double x);
8
9     static
10    {
11       System.loadLibrary("Printf2");
12    }
13 }
```

Therefore, the C function that formats a floating-point number has the prototype

```
JNIEXPORT jstring JNICALL Java_Printf2_sprint(JNIEnv* env, jclass cl,
    jstring format, jdouble x)
```

Listing 12.10 shows the code for the C implementation. Note the calls to GetStringUTFChars to read the format argument, NewStringUTF to generate the return value, and `ReleaseStringUTFChars` to inform the virtual machine that access to the string is no longer required.

Listing 12.10 printf2/Printf2.c

```
1  /**
2     @version 1.10 1997-07-01
3     @author Cay Horstmann
4  */
5
6  #include "Printf2.h"
7  #include <string.h>
8  #include <stdlib.h>
9  #include <float.h>
10
11 /**
12    @param format a string containing a printf format specifier
13    (such as "%8.2f"). Substrings "%%" are skipped.
14    @return a pointer to the format specifier (skipping the '%')
15    or NULL if there wasn't a unique format specifier
16 */
17 char* find_format(const char format[])
18 {
19    char* p;
20    char* q;
21
22    p = strchr(format, '%');
23    while (p != NULL && *(p + 1) == '%') /* skip %% */
24       p = strchr(p + 2, '%');
25    if (p == NULL) return NULL;
26    /* now check that % is unique */
27    p++;
28    q = strchr(p, '%');
29    while (q != NULL && *(q + 1) == '%') /* skip %% */
30       q = strchr(q + 2, '%');
31    if (q != NULL) return NULL; /* % not unique */
32    q = p + strspn(p, " -0+#"); /* skip past flags */
33    q += strspn(q, "0123456789"); /* skip past field width */
34    if (*q == '.') { q++; q += strspn(q, "0123456789"); }
35       /* skip past precision */
36    if (strchr("eEfFgG", *q) == NULL) return NULL;
37       /* not a floating-point format */
38    return p;
39 }
40
41 JNIEXPORT jstring JNICALL Java_Printf2_sprint(JNIEnv* env, jclass cl,
42       jstring format, jdouble x)
43 {
```

```
44    const char* cformat;
45    char* fmt;
46    jstring ret;
47
48    cformat = (*env)->GetStringUTFChars(env, format, NULL);
49    fmt = find_format(cformat);
50    if (fmt == NULL)
51       ret = format;
52    else
53    {
54       char* cret;
55       int width = atoi(fmt);
56       if (width == 0) width = DBL_DIG + 10;
57       cret = (char*) malloc(strlen(cformat) + width);
58       sprintf(cret, cformat, x);
59       ret = (*env)->NewStringUTF(env, cret);
60       free(cret);
61    }
62    (*env)->ReleaseStringUTFChars(env, format, cformat);
63    return ret;
64 }
```

In this function, we chose to keep error handling simple. If the format code to print a floating-point number is not of the form %w.pc, where c is one of the characters e, E, f, g, or G, then we simply do not format the number. We'll show you later how to make a native method throw an exception.

12.4 Accessing Fields

All the native methods you saw so far were static methods with number and string parameters. We'll now consider native methods that operate on objects. As an exercise, we will reimplement as native a method of the Employee class that was introduced in Volume I, Chapter 4. Again, this is not something you would normally want to do, but it does illustrate how to access fields from a native method when you need to do so.

12.4.1 Accessing Instance Fields

To see how to access instance fields from a native method, we will reimplement the raiseSalary method. Here is the code in Java:

```
public void raiseSalary(double byPercent)
{
   salary *= 1 + byPercent / 100;
}
```

Let us rewrite this as a native method. Unlike the previous examples of native methods, this is not a static method. Running `javac -h` gives the following prototype:

```
JNIEXPORT void JNICALL Java_Employee_raiseSalary(JNIEnv *, jobject, jdouble);
```

Note the second argument. It is no longer of type `jclass` but of type `jobject`. In fact, it is an equivalent of the `this` reference. Static methods obtain a reference to the class, whereas nonstatic methods obtain a reference to the implicit `this` argument object.

Now we access the `salary` field of the implicit argument. In the "raw" Java-to-C binding of Java 1.0, this was easy—a programmer could directly access object data fields. However, direct access requires all virtual machines to expose their internal data layout. For that reason, the JNI requires programmers to get and set the values of data fields by calling special JNI functions.

In our case, we need to use the `GetDoubleField` and `SetDoubleField` functions because the type of `salary` is `double`. There are other functions—`GetIntField`/`SetIntField`, `GetObjectField`/`SetObjectField`, and so on for other field types. The general syntax is:

```
x = (*env)->GetXxxField(env, this_obj, fieldID);
(*env)->SetXxxField(env, this_obj, fieldID, x);
```

Here, `fieldID` is a value of a special type, `jfieldID`, that identifies a field in a structure, and *Xxx* represents a Java data type (`Object`, `Boolean`, `Byte`, and so on). To obtain the `fieldID`, you must first get a value representing the class, which you can do in one of two ways. The `GetObjectClass` function returns the class of any object. For example:

```
jclass class_Employee = (*env)->GetObjectClass(env, this_obj);
```

The `FindClass` function lets you specify the class name as a string (curiously, with / characters instead of periods as package name separators).

```
jclass class_String = (*env)->FindClass(env, "java/lang/String");
```

Use the `GetFieldID` function to obtain the `fieldID`. You must supply the name of the field and its *signature,* an encoding of its type. For example, here is the code to obtain the field ID of the `salary` field:

```
jfieldID id_salary = (*env)->GetFieldID(env, class_Employee, "salary", "D");
```

The string `"D"` denotes the type `double`. You'll learn the complete rules for encoding signatures in the next section.

You might be thinking that accessing a data field is quite convoluted. The designers of the JNI did not want to expose the data fields directly, so they had to supply functions for getting and setting field values. To minimize the cost of these functions, computing the field ID from the field name—which is the most expensive step—is factored out into a separate step. That is, if you repeatedly get and set the value of a particular field, you can incur the cost of computing the field identifier only once.

Let us put all the pieces together. The following code reimplements the raiseSalary method as a native method:

```
JNIEXPORT void JNICALL Java_Employee_raiseSalary(JNIEnv* env, jobject this_obj,
      jdouble byPercent)
{
   /* get the class */
   jclass class_Employee = (*env)->GetObjectClass(env, this_obj);

   /* get the field ID */
   jfieldID id_salary = (*env)->GetFieldID(env, class_Employee, "salary", "D");

   /* get the field value */
   jdouble salary = (*env)->GetDoubleField(env, this_obj, id_salary);

   salary *= 1 + byPercent / 100;

   /* set the field value */
   (*env)->SetDoubleField(env, this_obj, id_salary, salary);
}
```

 CAUTION: Class references are only valid until the native method returns. You cannot cache the return values of GetObjectClass in your code. Do *not* store away a class reference for reuse in a later method call. You must call GetObjectClass every time the native method executes. If this is intolerable, you can lock the reference with a call to NewGlobalRef:

```
static jclass class_X = 0;
static jfieldID id_a;
. . .
if (class_X == 0)
{
   jclass cx = (*env)->GetObjectClass(env, obj);
   class_X = (*env)->NewGlobalRef(env, cx);
   id_a = (*env)->GetFieldID(env, cls, "a", ". . .");
}
```

Now you can use the class reference and field IDs in subsequent calls. When you are done using the class, make sure to call

```
(*env)->DeleteGlobalRef(env, class_X);
```

Listings 12.11 and 12.12 show the Java code for a test program and the Employee class. Listing 12.13 contains the C code for the native raiseSalary method.

Listing 12.11 employee/EmployeeTest.java

```java
1  /**
2   * @version 1.11 2018-05-01
3   * @author Cay Horstmann
4   */
5
6  public class EmployeeTest
7  {
8     public static void main(String[] args)
9     {
10        var staff = new Employee[3];
11
12        staff[0] = new Employee("Harry Hacker", 35000);
13        staff[1] = new Employee("Carl Cracker", 75000);
14        staff[2] = new Employee("Tony Tester", 38000);
15
16        for (Employee e : staff)
17           e.raiseSalary(5);
18        for (Employee e : staff)
19           e.print();
20     }
21  }
```

Listing 12.12 employee/Employee.java

```java
1  /**
2   * @version 1.10 1999-11-13
3   * @author Cay Horstmann
4   */
5
6  public class Employee
7  {
8     private String name;
9     private double salary;
10
11     public native void raiseSalary(double byPercent);
12
13     public Employee(String n, double s)
14     {
15        name = n;
16        salary = s;
17     }
```

```
18
19    public void print()
20    {
21       System.out.println(name + " " + salary);
22    }
23
24    static
25    {
26       System.loadLibrary("Employee");
27    }
28 }
```

Listing 12.13 employee/Employee.c

```
1  /**
2     @version 1.10 1999-11-13
3     @author Cay Horstmann
4  */
5
6  #include "Employee.h"
7
8  #include <stdio.h>
9
10 JNIEXPORT void JNICALL Java_Employee_raiseSalary(
11      JNIEnv* env, jobject this_obj, jdouble byPercent)
12 {
13    /* get the class */
14    jclass class_Employee = (*env)->GetObjectClass(env, this_obj);
15
16    /* get the field ID */
17    jfieldID id_salary = (*env)->GetFieldID(env, class_Employee, "salary", "D");
18
19    /* get the field value */
20    jdouble salary = (*env)->GetDoubleField(env, this_obj, id_salary);
21
22    salary *= 1 + byPercent / 100;
23
24    /* set the field value */
25    (*env)->SetDoubleField(env, this_obj, id_salary, salary);
26 }
27
```

12.4.2 Accessing Static Fields

Accessing static fields is similar to accessing nonstatic fields. Use the GetStaticFieldID and GetStatic*Xxx*Field/SetStatic*Xxx*Field functions that work almost identically to their nonstatic counterparts, with two differences:

- Since you have no object, you must use FindClass instead of GetObjectClass to obtain the class reference.
- You have to supply the class, not the instance object, when accessing the field.

For example, here is how you can get a reference to System.out:

```
/* get the class */
jclass class_System = (*env)->FindClass(env, "java/lang/System");

/* get the field ID */
jfieldID id_out = (*env)->GetStaticFieldID(env, class_System, "out",
    "Ljava/io/PrintStream;");

/* get the field value */
jobject obj_out = (*env)->GetStaticObjectField(env, class_System, id_out);
```

Accessing Fields

- jfieldID GetFieldID(JNIEnv *env, jclass cl, const char name[], const char fieldSignature[])

  returns the identifier of a field in a class.

- *Xxx* Get*Xxx*Field(JNIEnv *env, jobject obj, jfieldID id)

  returns the value of a field. The field type *Xxx* is one of Object, Boolean, Byte, Char, Short, Int, Long, Float, or Double.

- void Set*Xxx*Field(JNIEnv *env, jobject obj, jfieldID id, *Xxx* value)

  sets a field to a new value. The field type *Xxx* is one of Object, Boolean, Byte, Char, Short, Int, Long, Float, or Double.

- jfieldID GetStaticFieldID(JNIEnv *env, jclass cl, const char name[], const char fieldSignature[])

  returns the identifier of a static field in a class.

- *Xxx* GetStatic*Xxx*Field(JNIEnv *env, jclass cl, jfieldID id)

  returns the value of a static field. The field type *Xxx* is one of Object, Boolean, Byte, Char, Short, Int, Long, Float, or Double.

- void SetStatic*Xxx*Field(JNIEnv *env, jclass cl, jfieldID id, *Xxx* value)

  sets a static field to a new value. The field type *Xxx* is one of Object, Boolean, Byte, Char, Short, Int, Long, Float, or Double.

12.5 Encoding Signatures

To access instance fields and call methods defined in the Java programming language, you need to learn the rules for "mangling" the names of data types and method signatures. (A method signature describes the parameters and return type of the method.) Here is the encoding scheme:

B	byte
C	char
D	double
F	float
I	int
J	long
L*classname*;	a class type
S	short
V	void
Z	boolean

To describe an array type, use a [. For example, an array of strings is

```
[Ljava/lang/String;
```

A `float[][]` is mangled into

```
[[F
```

For the complete signature of a method, list the parameter types inside a pair of parentheses and then list the return type. For example, a method receiving two integers and returning an integer is encoded as

```
(II)I
```

The `sprint` method in Section 12.3, "String Parameters," on p. 819 has a mangled signature of

```
(Ljava/lang/String;D)Ljava/lang/String;
```

That is, the method receives a `String` and a `double` and returns a `String`.

Note that the semicolon at the end of the L expression is the terminator of the type expression, not a separator between parameters. For example, the constructor

```
Employee(java.lang.String, double, java.util.Date)
```

has a signature

```
"(Ljava/lang/String;DLjava/util/Date;)V"
```

Note that there is no separator between the D and Ljava/util/Date;. Also note that in this encoding scheme, you must use / instead of . to separate the package and class names. The V at the end denotes a return type of void. Even though you don't specify a return type for constructors in Java, you need to add a V to the virtual machine signature.

TIP: You can use the javap command with option -s to generate the method signatures from class files. For example, run

```
javap -s -private Employee
```

You will get the following output, displaying the signatures of all fields and methods:

```
Compiled from "Employee.java"
public class Employee extends java.lang.Object{
private java.lang.String name;
  Signature: Ljava/lang/String;
private double salary;
  Signature: D
public Employee(java.lang.String, double);
  Signature: (Ljava/lang/String;D)V
public native void raiseSalary(double);
  Signature: (D)V
public void print();
  Signature: ()V
static {};
  Signature: ()V
}
```

NOTE: There is no rationale whatsoever for forcing programmers to use this mangling scheme for signatures. The designers of the native calling mechanism could have just as easily written a function that reads signatures in the Java programming language style, such as void(int,java.lang.String), and encodes them into whatever internal representation they prefer. Then again, using the mangled signatures lets you partake in the mystique of programming close to the virtual machine.

12.6 Calling Java Methods

Of course, Java programming language functions can call C functions—that is what native methods are for. Can we go the other way? Why would we want to do this anyway? It often happens that a native method needs to request a service from an object that was passed to it. We'll first show you how to do it for instance methods, then for static methods.

12.6.1 Instance Methods

As an example of calling a Java method from native code, let's enhance the Printf class and add a method that works similarly to the C function fprintf. That is, it should be able to print a string on an arbitrary PrintWriter object. Here is the definition of the method in Java:

```
class Printf3
{
    public native static void fprint(PrintWriter out, String s, double x);
    . . .
}
```

We'll first assemble the string to be printed into a String object str, as in the sprint method that we already implemented. Then, from the C function that implements the native method, we'll call the print method of the PrintWriter class.

You can call any Java method from C by using the function call

(*env)->Call*Xxx*Method(env, *implicit parameter*, *methodID*, *explicit parameters*)

Replace *Xxx* with Void, Int, Object, and so on, depending on the return type of the method. Just as you need a fieldID to access a field of an object, you need a method ID to call a method. To obtain a method ID, call the JNI function GetMethodID and supply the class, the name of the method, and the method signature.

In our example, we want to obtain the ID of the print method of the PrintWriter class. The PrintWriter class has several overloaded methods called print. For that reason, you must also supply a string describing the parameters and the return value of the specific function that you want to use. For example, we want to use void print(java.lang.String). As described in the preceding section, we must now "mangle" the signature into the string "(Ljava/lang/String;)V".

Here is the complete code to make the method call:

```
/* get the class of the implicit parameter */
class_PrintWriter = (*env)->GetObjectClass(env, out);

/* get the method ID */
id_print = (*env)->GetMethodID(env, class_PrintWriter, "print", "(Ljava/lang/String;)V");

/* call the method */
(*env)->CallVoidMethod(env, out, id_print, str);
```

Listings 12.14 and 12.15 show the Java code for a test program and the Printf3 class. Listing 12.16 contains the C code for the native fprint method.

 NOTE: The numerical method IDs and field IDs are conceptually similar to Method and Field objects in the reflection API. You can convert between them with the following functions:

```
jobject ToReflectedMethod(JNIEnv* env, jclass class, jmethodID methodID);
    // returns Method object
methodID FromReflectedMethod(JNIEnv* env, jobject method);
jobject ToReflectedField(JNIEnv* env, jclass class, jfieldID fieldID);
    // returns Field object
fieldID FromReflectedField(JNIEnv* env, jobject field);
```

12.6.2 Static Methods

Calling static methods from native methods is similar to calling instance methods. There are two differences:

- Use the GetStaticMethodID and CallStaticXxxMethod functions
- Supply a class object, not an implicit parameter object, when invoking the method

As an example of this, let's make the call to the static method

```
System.getProperty("java.class.path")
```

from a native method. The return value of this call is a string that gives the current class path.

First, we have to find the class to use. As we have no object of the class System readily available, we use FindClass rather than GetObjectClass.

```
jclass class_System = (*env)->FindClass(env, "java/lang/System");
```

Next, we need the ID of the static getProperty method. The encoded signature of that method is

```
"(Ljava/lang/String;)Ljava/lang/String;"
```

because both the parameter and the return value are strings. Hence, we obtain the method ID as follows:

```
jmethodID id_getProperty = (*env)->GetStaticMethodID(env, class_System, "getProperty",
    "(Ljava/lang/String;)Ljava/lang/String;");
```

Finally, we can make the call. Note that the class object is passed to the CallStaticObjectMethod function.

```
jobject obj_ret = (*env)->CallStaticObjectMethod(env, class_System, id_getProperty,
    (*env)->NewStringUTF(env, "java.class.path"));
```

The return value of this method is of type jobject. If we want to manipulate it as a string, we must cast it to jstring:

```
jstring str_ret = (jstring) obj_ret;
```

 C++ NOTE: In C, the types jstring and jclass, as well as the array types to be introduced later, are all type-equivalent to jobject. The cast of the preceding example is therefore not strictly necessary in C. But in C++, these types are defined as pointers to "dummy classes" that have the correct inheritance hierarchy. For example, assigning a jstring to a jobject is legal without a cast in C++, but an assignment from a jobject to a jstring requires a cast.

12.6.3 Constructors

A native method can create a new Java object by invoking its constructor. Invoke the constructor by calling the NewObject function.

```
jobject obj_new = (*env)->NewObject(env, class, methodID, construction parameters);
```

You can obtain the method ID needed for this call from the GetMethodID function by specifying the method name as "<init>" and the encoded signature of the constructor (with return type void). For example, here is how a native method can create a FileOutputStream object:

```
const char[] fileName = ". . .";
jstring str_fileName = (*env)->NewStringUTF(env, fileName);
jclass class_FileOutputStream = (*env)->FindClass(env, "java/io/FileOutputStream");
jmethodID id_FileOutputStream
    = (*env)->GetMethodID(env, class_FileOutputStream, "<init>", "(Ljava/lang/String;)V");
jobject obj_stream
    = (*env)->NewObject(env, class_FileOutputStream, id_FileOutputStream, str_fileName);
```

Note that the signature of the constructor takes a parameter of type java.lang.String and has a return type of void.

12.6.4 Alternative Method Invocations

Several variants of the JNI functions can be used to call a Java method from native code. These are not as important as the functions that we already discussed, but they are occasionally useful.

The `CallNonvirtualXxxMethod` functions receive an implicit argument, a method ID, a class object (which must correspond to a superclass of the implicit argument), and explicit arguments. The function calls the version of the method in the specified class, bypassing the normal dynamic dispatch mechanism.

All call functions have versions with suffixes "A" and "V" that receive the explicit parameters in an array or a `va_list` (as defined in the C header `stdarg.h`).

Listing 12.14 `printf3/Printf3Test.java`

```java
1  import java.io.*;
2
3  /**
4   * @version 1.11 2018-05-01
5   * @author Cay Horstmann
6   */
7  class Printf3Test
8  {
9     public static void main(String[] args)
10    {
11       double price = 44.95;
12       double tax = 7.75;
13       double amountDue = price * (1 + tax / 100);
14       var out = new PrintWriter(System.out);
15       Printf3.fprint(out, "Amount due = %8.2f\n", amountDue);
16       out.flush();
17    }
18 }
```

Listing 12.15 `printf3/Printf3.java`

```java
1  import java.io.*;
2
3  /**
4   * @version 1.10 1997-07-01
5   * @author Cay Horstmann
6   */
7  class Printf3
8  {
9     public static native void fprint(PrintWriter out, String format, double x);
10
11    static
12    {
13       System.loadLibrary("Printf3");
14    }
15 }
```

Listing 12.16 `printf3/Printf3.c`

```
1  /**
2     @version 1.10 1997-07-01
3     @author Cay Horstmann
4  */
5
6  #include "Printf3.h"
7  #include <string.h>
8  #include <stdlib.h>
9  #include <float.h>
10
11 /**
12    @param format a string containing a printf format specifier
13    (such as "%8.2f"). Substrings "%%" are skipped.
14    @return a pointer to the format specifier (skipping the '%')
15    or NULL if there wasn't a unique format specifier
16 */
17 char* find_format(const char format[])
18 {
19    char* p;
20    char* q;
21
22    p = strchr(format, '%');
23    while (p != NULL && *(p + 1) == '%') /* skip %% */
24       p = strchr(p + 2, '%');
25    if (p == NULL) return NULL;
26    /* now check that % is unique */
27    p++;
28    q = strchr(p, '%');
29    while (q != NULL && *(q + 1) == '%') /* skip %% */
30       q = strchr(q + 2, '%');
31    if (q != NULL) return NULL; /* % not unique */
32    q = p + strspn(p, " -0+#"); /* skip past flags */
33    q += strspn(q, "0123456789"); /* skip past field width */
34    if (*q == '.') { q++; q += strspn(q, "0123456789"); }
35       /* skip past precision */
36    if (strchr("eEfFgG", *q) == NULL) return NULL;
37       /* not a floating-point format */
38    return p;
39 }
40
41 JNIEXPORT void JNICALL Java_Printf3_fprint(JNIEnv* env, jclass cl,
42       jobject out, jstring format, jdouble x)
43 {
44    const char* cformat;
45    char* fmt;
46    jstring str;
47    jclass class_PrintWriter;
```

(Continues)

Listing 12.16 *(Continued)*

```
48   jmethodID id_print;
49
50   cformat = (*env)->GetStringUTFChars(env, format, NULL);
51   fmt = find_format(cformat);
52   if (fmt == NULL)
53      str = format;
54   else
55   {
56      char* cstr;
57      int width = atoi(fmt);
58      if (width == 0) width = DBL_DIG + 10;
59      cstr = (char*) malloc(strlen(cformat) + width);
60      sprintf(cstr, cformat, x);
61      str = (*env)->NewStringUTF(env, cstr);
62      free(cstr);
63   }
64   (*env)->ReleaseStringUTFChars(env, format, cformat);
65
66   /* now call ps.print(str) */
67
68   /* get the class */
69   class_PrintWriter = (*env)->GetObjectClass(env, out);
70
71   /* get the method ID */
72   id_print = (*env)->GetMethodID(env, class_PrintWriter, "print", "(Ljava/lang/String;)V");
73
74   /* call the method */
75   (*env)->CallVoidMethod(env, out, id_print, str);
76 }
```

Executing Java Methods

- jmethodID GetMethodID(JNIEnv *env, jclass cl, const char name[], const char methodSignature[])

  returns the identifier of a method in a class.

- *Xxx* Call*Xxx*Method(JNIEnv *env, jobject obj, jmethodID id, args)
- *Xxx* Call*Xxx*MethodA(JNIEnv *env, jobject obj, jmethodID id, jvalue args[])
- *Xxx* Call*Xxx*MethodV(JNIEnv *env, jobject obj, jmethodID id, va_list args)

  calls a method. The return type *Xxx* is one of Object, Boolean, Byte, Char, Short, Int, Long, Float, or Double. The first function has a variable number of arguments—simply append the method parameters after the method ID. The second function receives the method arguments in an array of jvalue, where jvalue is a union defined as

Executing Java Methods *(Continued)*

```
typedef union jvalue
{
  jboolean z;
  jbyte b;
  jchar c;
  jshort s;
  jint i;
  jlong j;
  jfloat f;
  jdouble d;
  jobject l;
} jvalue;
```

The third function receives the method parameters in a va_list, as defined in the C header stdarg.h.

- *Xxx* CallNonvirtual*Xxx*Method(JNIEnv *env, jobject obj, jclass cl, jmethodID id, args)
- *Xxx* CallNonvirtual*Xxx*MethodA(JNIEnv *env, jobject obj, jclass cl, jmethodID id, jvalue args[])
- *Xxx* CallNonvirtual*Xxx*MethodV(JNIEnv *env, jobject obj, jclass cl, jmethodID id, va_list args)

calls a method, bypassing dynamic dispatch. The return type *Xxx* is one of Object, Boolean, Byte, Char, Short, Int, Long, Float, or Double. The first function has a variable number of arguments—simply append the method parameters after the method ID. The second function receives the method arguments in an array of jvalue. The third function receives the method parameters in a va_list, as defined in the C header stdarg.h.

- jmethodID GetStaticMethodID(JNIEnv *env, jclass cl, const char name[], const char methodSignature[])

returns the identifier of a static method in a class.

- *Xxx* CallStatic*Xxx*Method(JNIEnv *env, jclass cl, jmethodID id, args)
- *Xxx* CallStatic*Xxx*MethodA(JNIEnv *env, jclass cl, jmethodID id, jvalue args[])
- *Xxx* CallStatic*Xxx*MethodV(JNIEnv *env, jclass cl, jmethodID id, va_list args)

calls a static method. The return type *Xxx* is one of Object, Boolean, Byte, Char, Short, Int, Long, Float, or Double. The first function has a variable number of arguments—simply append the method parameters after the method ID. The second function receives the method arguments in an array of jvalue. The third function receives the method parameters in a va_list, as defined in the C header stdarg.h.

(Continues)

Executing Java Methods   *(Continued)*

- `jobject NewObject(JNIEnv *env, jclass cl, jmethodID id, args)`
- `jobject NewObjectA(JNIEnv *env, jclass cl, jmethodID id, jvalue args[])`
- `jobject NewObjectV(JNIEnv *env, jclass cl, jmethodID id, va_list args)`

  calls a constructor. The method ID is obtained from `GetMethodID` with a method name of `"<init>"` and a return type of `void`. The first function has a variable number of arguments—simply append the method parameters after the method ID. The second function receives the method arguments in an array of `jvalue`. The third function receives the method parameters in a `va_list`, as defined in the C header `stdarg.h`.

12.7 Accessing Array Elements

All array types of the Java programming language have corresponding C types, as shown in Table 12.2.

Table 12.2 Correspondence between Java Array Types and C Types

Java Type	C Type	Java Type	C Type
boolean[]	jbooleanArray	long[]	jlongArray
byte[]	jbyteArray	float[]	jfloatArray
char[]	jcharArray	double[]	jdoubleArray
int[]	jintArray	Object[]	jobjectArray
short[]	jshortArray		

 C++ NOTE: In C, all these array types are actually type synonyms of `jobject`. In C++, however, they are arranged in the inheritance hierarchy shown in Figure 12.3. The type `jarray` denotes a generic array.

The `GetArrayLength` function returns the length of an array.

```
jarray array = . . .;
jsize length = (*env)->GetArrayLength(env, array);
```

How you access elements in an array depends on whether the array stores objects or values of a primitive type (`bool`, `char`, or a numeric type). To access elements in an object array, use the `GetObjectArrayElement` and `SetObjectArrayElement` methods.

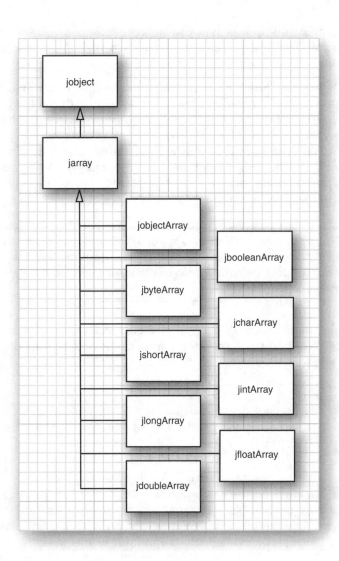

Figure 12.3 Inheritance hierarchy of array types

```
jobjectArray array = . . .;
int i, j;
jobject x = (*env)->GetObjectArrayElement(env, array, i);
(*env)->SetObjectArrayElement(env, array, j, x);
```

Although simple, this approach is also clearly inefficient; you want to be able to access array elements directly, especially when doing vector and matrix computations.

The GetXxxArrayElements function returns a C pointer to the starting element of an array. As with ordinary strings, you must remember to call the corresponding ReleaseXxxArrayElements function to tell the virtual machine when you no longer need that pointer. Here, the type Xxx must be a primitive type—that is, not Object. You can then read and write the array elements directly. However, since the pointer *might point to a copy*, any changes that you make are guaranteed to be reflected in the original array only after you call the corresponding ReleaseXxxArrayElements function!

 NOTE: You can find out if an array is a copy by passing a pointer to a jboolean variable as the third parameter to a GetXxxArrayElements method. The variable is filled with JNI_TRUE if the array is a copy. If you aren't interested in that information, just pass a NULL pointer.

Here is an example that multiplies all elements in an array of double values by a constant. We obtain a C pointer a into the Java array and then access individual elements as a[i].

```
jdoubleArray array_a = . . .;
double scaleFactor = . . .;
double* a = (*env)->GetDoubleArrayElements(env, array_a, NULL);
for (i = 0; i < (*env)->GetArrayLength(env, array_a); i++)
   a[i] = a[i] * scaleFactor;
(*env)->ReleaseDoubleArrayElements(env, array_a, a, 0);
```

Whether the virtual machine actually copies the array depends on how it allocates arrays and does its garbage collection. Some "copying" garbage collectors routinely move objects around and update object references. That strategy is not compatible with "pinning" an array to a particular location, because the collector cannot update the pointer values in native code.

 NOTE: In the Oracle JVM implementation, boolean arrays are represented as packed arrays of 32-bit words. The GetBooleanArrayElements method copies them into unpacked arrays of jboolean values.

To access just a few elements of a large array, use the GetXxxArrayRegion and SetXxxArrayRegion methods that copy a range of elements from the Java array into a C array and back.

You can create new Java arrays in native methods with the New*Xxx*Array function. To create a new array of objects, specify the length, the type of the array elements, and an initial element for all entries (typically, NULL). Here is an example:

```
jclass class_Employee = (*env)->FindClass(env, "Employee");
jobjectArray array_e = (*env)->NewObjectArray(env, 100, class_Employee, NULL);
```

Arrays of primitive types are simpler: Just supply the length of the array.

```
jdoubleArray array_d = (*env)->NewDoubleArray(env, 100);
```

The array is then filled with zeroes.

NOTE: The following methods are used for working with "direct buffers":

```
jobject NewDirectByteBuffer(JNIEnv* env, void* address, jlong capacity)
void* GetDirectBufferAddress(JNIEnv* env, jobject buf)
jlong GetDirectBufferCapacity(JNIEnv* env, jobject buf)
```

Direct buffers are used in the java.nio package to support more efficient input/output operations and to minimize the copying of data between native and Java arrays.

Manipulating Java Arrays

- jsize GetArrayLength(JNIEnv *env, jarray array)

  returns the number of elements in the array.

- jobject GetObjectArrayElement(JNIEnv *env, jobjectArray array, jsize index)

  returns the value of an array element.

- void SetObjectArrayElement(JNIEnv *env, jobjectArray array, jsize index, jobject value)

  sets an array element to a new value.

- *Xxx** Get*Xxx*ArrayElements(JNIEnv *env, jarray array, jboolean* isCopy)

  yields a C pointer to the elements of a Java array. The field type *Xxx* is one of Boolean, Byte, Char, Short, Int, Long, Float, or Double. The pointer must be passed to Release*Xxx*ArrayElements when it is no longer needed. isCopy is either NULL or points to a jboolean that is filled with JNI_TRUE if a copy is made, with JNI_FALSE otherwise.

- void Release*Xxx*ArrayElements(JNIEnv *env, jarray array, *Xxx* elems[], jint mode)

  notifies the virtual machine that a pointer obtained by Get*Xxx*ArrayElements is no longer needed. mode is one of 0 (free the elems buffer after updating the array elements), JNI_COMMIT (do not free the elems buffer after updating the array elements), or JNI_ABORT (free the elems buffer without updating the array elements).

(Continues)

Manipulating Java Arrays   *(Continued)*

- void Get*Xxx*ArrayRegion(JNIEnv *env, jarray array, jint start, jint length, *Xxx* elems[])

  copies elements from a Java array to a C array. The field type *Xxx* is one of Boolean, Byte, Char, Short, Int, Long, Float, or Double.

- void Set*Xxx*ArrayRegion(JNIEnv *env, jarray array, jint start, jint length, *Xxx* elems[])

  copies elements from a C array to a Java array. The field type *Xxx* is one of Boolean, Byte, Char, Short, Int, Long, Float, or Double.

12.8 Handling Errors

Native methods are a significant security risk to Java programs. The C runtime system has no protection against array bounds errors, indirection through bad pointers, and so on. It is particularly important that programmers of native methods handle all error conditions to preserve the integrity of the Java platform. In particular, when your native method diagnoses a problem it cannot handle, it should report this problem to the Java virtual machine.

Normally, you would throw an exception in this situation. However, C has no exceptions. Instead, you must call the Throw or ThrowNew function to create a new exception object. When the native method exits, the Java virtual machine throws that exception.

To use the Throw function, call NewObject to create an object of a subtype of Throwable. For example, here we allocate an EOFException object and throw it:

```
jclass class_EOFException = (*env)->FindClass(env, "java/io/EOFException");
jmethodID id_EOFException = (*env)->GetMethodID(env, class_EOFException, "<init>", "()V");
   /* ID of no-argument constructor */
jthrowable obj_exc = (*env)->NewObject(env, class_EOFException, id_EOFException);
(*env)->Throw(env, obj_exc);
```

It is usually more convenient to call ThrowNew, which constructs an exception object, given a class and a "modified UTF-8" byte sequence.

```
(*env)->ThrowNew(env, (*env)->FindClass(env, "java/io/EOFException"),
   "Unexpected end of file");
```

Both Throw and ThrowNew merely *post* the exception; they do not interrupt the control flow of the native method. Only when the method returns does the Java virtual machine throw the exception. Therefore, every call to Throw and ThrowNew should be immediately followed by a return statement.

> **C++ NOTE:** If you implement native methods in C++, you cannot throw a Java
> exception object in your C++ code. In a C++ binding, it would be possible to
> implement a translation between exceptions in C++ and Java; however, this is
> not currently done. Use `Throw` or `ThrowNew` to throw a Java exception in a native
> C++ method, and make sure your native methods throw no C++ exceptions.

Normally, native code need not be concerned with catching Java exceptions.
However, when a native method calls a Java method, that method might
throw an exception. Moreover, a number of the JNI functions throw exceptions
as well. For example, `SetObjectArrayElement` throws an `ArrayIndexOutOfBoundsException` if
the index is out of bounds, and an `ArrayStoreException` if the class of the stored
object is not a subclass of the element class of the array. In situations like
these, a native method should call the `ExceptionOccurred` method to determine
whether an exception has been thrown. The call

```
jthrowable obj_exc = (*env)->ExceptionOccurred(env);
```

returns `NULL` if no exception is pending, or a reference to the current exception
object. If you just want to check whether an exception has been thrown,
without obtaining a reference to the exception object, use

```
jboolean occurred = (*env)->ExceptionCheck(env);
```

Normally, a native method should simply return when an exception has occurred so that the virtual machine can propagate it to the Java code. However,
a native method *may* analyze the exception object to determine if it can
handle the exception. If it can, then the function

```
(*env)->ExceptionClear(env);
```

must be called to turn off the exception.

In our next example, we implement the `fprint` native method with all the
paranoia appropriate for a native method. Here are the exceptions that we
throw:

- A `NullPointerException` if the format string is `NULL`
- An `IllegalArgumentException` if the format string doesn't contain a `%` specifier
  that is appropriate for printing a `double`
- An `OutOfMemoryError` if the call to `malloc` fails

Finally, to demonstrate how to check for an exception when calling a Java
method from a native method, we send the string to the stream, a character
at a time, and call `ExceptionOccurred` after each call. Listing 12.17 shows the code
for the native method, and Listing 12.18 shows the definition of the class

containing the native method. Notice that the native method does not immediately terminate when an exception occurs in the call to PrintWriter.print—it first frees the cstr buffer. When the native method returns, the virtual machine again raises the exception. The test program in Listing 12.19 demonstrates how the native method throws an exception when the formatting string is not valid.

Listing 12.17 printf4/Printf4.c

```
1   /**
2      @version 1.10 1997-07-01
3      @author Cay Horstmann
4   */
5
6   #include "Printf4.h"
7   #include <string.h>
8   #include <stdlib.h>
9   #include <float.h>
10
11  /**
12     @param format a string containing a printf format specifier
13     (such as "%8.2f"). Substrings "%%" are skipped.
14     @return a pointer to the format specifier (skipping the '%')
15     or NULL if there wasn't a unique format specifier
16  */
17  char* find_format(const char format[])
18  {
19     char* p;
20     char* q;
21
22     p = strchr(format, '%');
23     while (p != NULL && *(p + 1) == '%') /* skip %% */
24        p = strchr(p + 2, '%');
25     if (p == NULL) return NULL;
26     /* now check that % is unique */
27     p++;
28     q = strchr(p, '%');
29     while (q != NULL && *(q + 1) == '%') /* skip %% */
30        q = strchr(q + 2, '%');
31     if (q != NULL) return NULL; /* % not unique */
32     q = p + strspn(p, " -0+#"); /* skip past flags */
33     q += strspn(q, "0123456789"); /* skip past field width */
34     if (*q == '.') { q++; q += strspn(q, "0123456789"); }
35        /* skip past precision */
36     if (strchr("eEfFgG", *q) == NULL) return NULL;
37        /* not a floating-point format */
38     return p;
39  }
```

```
40
41  JNIEXPORT void JNICALL Java_Printf4_fprint(JNIEnv* env, jclass cl,
42        jobject out, jstring format, jdouble x)
43  {
44      const char* cformat;
45      char* fmt;
46      jclass class_PrintWriter;
47      jmethodID id_print;
48      char* cstr;
49      int width;
50      int i;
51
52      if (format == NULL)
53      {
54         (*env)->ThrowNew(env,
55            (*env)->FindClass(env,
56            "java/lang/NullPointerException"),
57            "Printf4.fprint: format is null");
58         return;
59      }
60
61      cformat = (*env)->GetStringUTFChars(env, format, NULL);
62      fmt = find_format(cformat);
63
64      if (fmt == NULL)
65      {
66         (*env)->ThrowNew(env,
67            (*env)->FindClass(env,
68            "java/lang/IllegalArgumentException"),
69            "Printf4.fprint: format is invalid");
70         return;
71      }
72
73      width = atoi(fmt);
74      if (width == 0) width = DBL_DIG + 10;
75      cstr = (char*)malloc(strlen(cformat) + width);
76
77      if (cstr == NULL)
78      {
79         (*env)->ThrowNew(env,
80            (*env)->FindClass(env, "java/lang/OutOfMemoryError"),
81            "Printf4.fprint: malloc failed");
82         return;
83      }
84
85      sprintf(cstr, cformat, x);
86
87      (*env)->ReleaseStringUTFChars(env, format, cformat);
88
```

(Continues)

Listing 12.17 *(Continued)*

```
89     /* now call ps.print(str) */
90
91     /* get the class */
92     class_PrintWriter = (*env)->GetObjectClass(env, out);
93
94     /* get the method ID */
95     id_print = (*env)->GetMethodID(env, class_PrintWriter, "print", "(C)V");
96
97     /* call the method */
98     for (i = 0; cstr[i] != 0 && !(*env)->ExceptionOccurred(env); i++)
99        (*env)->CallVoidMethod(env, out, id_print, cstr[i]);
100
101    free(cstr);
102 }
```

Listing 12.18 printf4/Printf4.java

```
1 import java.io.*;
2
3 /**
4  * @version 1.10 1997-07-01
5  * @author Cay Horstmann
6  */
7 class Printf4
8 {
9    public static native void fprint(PrintWriter ps, String format, double x);
10
11    static
12    {
13       System.loadLibrary("Printf4");
14    }
15 }
```

Listing 12.19 printf4/Printf4Test.java

```
1 import java.io.*;
2
3 /**
4  * @version 1.11 2018-05-01
5  * @author Cay Horstmann
6  */
7 class Printf4Test
8 {
9    public static void main(String[] args)
10    {
```

```
11       double price = 44.95;
12       double tax = 7.75;
13       double amountDue = price * (1 + tax / 100);
14       var out = new PrintWriter(System.out);
15       /* This call will throw an exception--note the %% */
16       Printf4.fprint(out, "Amount due = %%8.2f\n", amountDue);
17       out.flush();
18    }
19 }
```

Handling Java Exceptions

- `jint Throw(JNIEnv *env, jthrowable obj)`

  prepares an exception to be thrown upon exiting from the native code. Returns 0 on success, a negative value on failure.

- `jint ThrowNew(JNIEnv *env, jclass cl, const char msg[])`

  prepares an exception of type `cl` to be thrown upon exiting from the native code. Returns 0 on success, a negative value on failure. `msg` is a "modified UTF-8" byte sequence denoting the `String` construction argument of the exception object.

- `jthrowable ExceptionOccurred(JNIEnv *env)`

  returns the exception object if an exception is pending, or `NULL` otherwise.

- `jboolean ExceptionCheck(JNIEnv *env)`

  returns true if an exception is pending.

- `void ExceptionClear(JNIEnv *env)`

  clears any pending exceptions.

12.9 Using the Invocation API

Up to now, we have considered programs in the Java programming language that made a few C calls, presumably because C was faster or allowed access to functionality inaccessible from the Java platform. Suppose you are in the opposite situation. You have a C or C++ program and would like to make calls to Java code. The *invocation API* enables you to embed the Java virtual machine into a C or C++ program. Here is the minimal code that you need to initialize a virtual machine:

```
JavaVMOption options[1];
JavaVMInitArgs vm_args;
JavaVM *jvm;
JNIEnv *env;

options[0].optionString = "-Djava.class.path=.";
```

```
memset(&vm_args, 0, sizeof(vm_args));
vm_args.version = JNI_VERSION_1_2;
vm_args.nOptions = 1;
vm_args.options = options;

JNI_CreateJavaVM(&jvm, (void**) &env, &vm_args);
```

The call to `JNI_CreateJavaVM` creates the virtual machine and fills in a pointer `jvm` to the virtual machine and a pointer `env` to the execution environment.

You can supply any number of options to the virtual machine. Simply increase the size of the `options` array and the value of `vm_args.nOptions`. For example,

```
options[i].optionString = "-Djava.compiler=NONE";
```

deactivates the just-in-time compiler.

 TIP: When you run into trouble and your program crashes, refuses to initialize the JVM, or can't load your classes, turn on the JNI debugging mode. Set an option to

```
options[i].optionString = "-verbose:jni";
```

You will see a flurry of messages that indicate the progress in initializing the JVM. If you don't see your classes loaded, check both your path and class path settings.

Once you have set up the virtual machine, you can call Java methods as described in the preceding sections. Simply use the `env` pointer in the usual way.

You'll need the `jvm` pointer only to call other functions in the invocation API. Currently, there are only four such functions. The most important one is the function to terminate the virtual machine:

```
(*jvm)->DestroyJavaVM(jvm);
```

Unfortunately, under Windows, it has become difficult to dynamically link to the `JNI_CreateJavaVM` function in the `jre/bin/client/jvm.dll` library, due to the changed linking rules in Vista and Oracle's reliance on an older C runtime library. Our sample program overcomes this problem by loading the library manually. This is the same approach used by the `java` program—see the file `launcher/java_md.c` in the `src.jar` file that is a part of the JDK.

The C program in Listing 12.20 sets up a virtual machine and calls the `main` method of the `Welcome` class, which was discussed in Volume I, Chapter 2. (Make sure to compile the `Welcome.java` file before starting the invocation test program.)

Listing 12.20 invocation/InvocationTest.c

```c
1   /**
2      @version 1.20 2007-10-26
3      @author Cay Horstmann
4   */
5
6   #include <jni.h>
7   #include <stdlib.h>
8
9   #ifdef _WINDOWS
10
11  #include <windows.h>
12  static HINSTANCE loadJVMLibrary(void);
13  typedef jint (JNICALL *CreateJavaVM_t)(JavaVM **, void **, JavaVMInitArgs *);
14
15  #endif
16
17  int main()
18  {
19     JavaVMOption options[2];
20     JavaVMInitArgs vm_args;
21     JavaVM *jvm;
22     JNIEnv *env;
23     long status;
24
25     jclass class_Welcome;
26     jclass class_String;
27     jobjectArray args;
28     jmethodID id_main;
29
30  #ifdef _WINDOWS
31     HINSTANCE hjvmlib;
32     CreateJavaVM_t createJavaVM;
33  #endif
34
35     options[0].optionString = "-Djava.class.path=.";
36
37     memset(&vm_args, 0, sizeof(vm_args));
38     vm_args.version = JNI_VERSION_1_2;
39     vm_args.nOptions = 1;
40     vm_args.options = options;
41
42  #ifdef _WINDOWS
43     hjvmlib = loadJVMLibrary();
44     createJavaVM = (CreateJavaVM_t) GetProcAddress(hjvmlib, "JNI_CreateJavaVM");
45     status = (*createJavaVM)(&jvm, (void **) &env, &vm_args);
```

(Continues)

Listing 12.20   *(Continued)*

```
46  #else
47     status = JNI_CreateJavaVM(&jvm, (void **) &env, &vm_args);
48  #endif
49
50     if (status == JNI_ERR)
51     {
52        fprintf(stderr, "Error creating VM\n");
53        return 1;
54     }
55
56     class_Welcome = (*env)->FindClass(env, "Welcome");
57     id_main = (*env)->GetStaticMethodID(env, class_Welcome, "main", "([Ljava/lang/String;)V");
58
59     class_String = (*env)->FindClass(env, "java/lang/String");
60     args = (*env)->NewObjectArray(env, 0, class_String, NULL);
61     (*env)->CallStaticVoidMethod(env, class_Welcome, id_main, args);
62
63     (*jvm)->DestroyJavaVM(jvm);
64
65     return 0;
66  }
67
68  #ifdef _WINDOWS
69
70  static int GetStringFromRegistry(HKEY key, const char *name, char *buf, jint bufsize)
71  {
72     DWORD type, size;
73
74     return RegQueryValueEx(key, name, 0, &type, 0, &size) == 0
75        && type == REG_SZ
76        && size < (unsigned int) bufsize
77        && RegQueryValueEx(key, name, 0, 0, buf, &size) == 0;
78  }
79
80  static void GetPublicJREHome(char *buf, jint bufsize)
81  {
82     HKEY key, subkey;
83     char version[MAX_PATH];
84
85     /* Find the current version of the JRE */
86     char *JRE_KEY = "Software\\JavaSoft\\Java Runtime Environment";
87     if (RegOpenKeyEx(HKEY_LOCAL_MACHINE, JRE_KEY, 0, KEY_READ, &key) != 0)
88     {
89        fprintf(stderr, "Error opening registry key '%s'\n", JRE_KEY);
90        exit(1);
91     }
92
```

```
93    if (!GetStringFromRegistry(key, "CurrentVersion", version, sizeof(version)))
94    {
95       fprintf(stderr, "Failed reading value of registry key:\n\t%s\\CurrentVersion\n",
96          JRE_KEY);
97       RegCloseKey(key);
98       exit(1);
99    }
100
101   /* Find directory where the current version is installed. */
102   if (RegOpenKeyEx(key, version, 0, KEY_READ, &subkey) != 0)
103   {
104      fprintf(stderr, "Error opening registry key '%s\\%s'\n", JRE_KEY, version);
105      RegCloseKey(key);
106      exit(1);
107   }
108
109   if (!GetStringFromRegistry(subkey, "JavaHome", buf, bufsize))
110   {
111      fprintf(stderr, "Failed reading value of registry key:\n\t%s\\%s\\JavaHome\n",
112         JRE_KEY, version);
113      RegCloseKey(key);
114      RegCloseKey(subkey);
115      exit(1);
116   }
117
118   RegCloseKey(key);
119   RegCloseKey(subkey);
120 }
121
122 static HINSTANCE loadJVMLibrary(void)
123 {
124   HINSTANCE h1, h2;
125   char msvcdll[MAX_PATH];
126   char javadll[MAX_PATH];
127   GetPublicJREHome(msvcdll, MAX_PATH);
128   strcpy(javadll, msvcdll);
129   strncat(msvcdll, "\\bin\\msvcr71.dll", MAX_PATH - strlen(msvcdll));
130   msvcdll[MAX_PATH - 1] = '\0';
131   strncat(javadll, "\\bin\\client\\jvm.dll", MAX_PATH - strlen(javadll));
132   javadll[MAX_PATH - 1] = '\0';
133
134   h1 = LoadLibrary(msvcdll);
135   if (h1 == NULL)
136   {
137      fprintf(stderr, "Can't load library msvcr71.dll\n");
138      exit(1);
139   }
140
```

(Continues)

Listing 12.20 *(Continued)*

```
141    h2 = LoadLibrary(javadll);
142    if (h2 == NULL)
143    {
144       fprintf(stderr, "Can't load library jvm.dll\n");
145       exit(1);
146    }
147    return h2;
148 }
149
150 #endif
```

To compile this program under Linux, use

```
gcc -I jdk/include -I jdk/include/linux -o InvocationTest \
  -L jdk/jre/lib/i386/client -ljvm InvocationTest.c
```

When compiling in Windows with the Microsoft compiler, use the command line

```
cl -D_WINDOWS -I jdk\include -I jdk\include\win32 InvocationTest.c \
  jdk\lib\jvm.lib advapi32.lib
```

You will need to make sure that the INCLUDE and LIB environment variables include the paths to the Windows API header and library files.

Using Cygwin, compile with

```
gcc -D_WINDOWS -mno-cygwin -I jdk\include -I jdk\include\win32 -D__int64="long long" \
  -I c:\cygwin\usr\include\w32api -o InvocationTest
```

Before you run the program under Linux/UNIX, make sure that the LD_LIBRARY_PATH contains the directories for the shared libraries. For example, if you use the bash shell on Linux, issue the following command:

```
export LD_LIBRARY_PATH=jdk/jre/lib/i386/client:$LD_LIBRARY_PATH
```

Invocation API Functions

- jint JNI_CreateJavaVM(JavaVM** p_jvm, void** p_env, JavaVMInitArgs* vm_args)

  initializes the Java virtual machine. The function returns 0 if successful, JNI_ERR on failure.

- jint DestroyJavaVM(JavaVM* jvm)

  destroys the virtual machine. Returns 0 on success, a negative number on failure. This function must be called through a virtual machine pointer, that is, (*jvm)->DestroyJavaVM(jvm).

12.10 A Complete Example: Accessing the Windows Registry

In this section, we describe a full, working example that covers everything we discussed in this chapter: using native methods with strings, arrays, objects, constructor calls, and error handling. We'll show you how to put a Java platform wrapper around a subset of the ordinary C-based APIs used to work with the Windows registry. Of course, the Windows registry being a Windows-specific feature, such a program is inherently nonportable. For that reason, the standard Java library has no support for the registry, and it makes sense to use native methods to gain access to it.

12.10.1 Overview of the Windows Registry

The Windows registry is a data depository that holds configuration information for the Windows operating system and application programs. It provides a single point for administration and backup of system and application preferences. On the downside, the registry is also a single point of failure—if you mess up the registry, your computer could malfunction or even fail to boot!

We don't suggest that you use the registry to store configuration parameters for your Java programs. The Java preferences API is a better solution (see Volume I, Chapter 10 for more information). We'll simply use the registry to demonstrate how to wrap a nontrivial native API into a Java class.

The principal tool for inspecting the registry is the *registry editor*. Because of the potential for error by naive but enthusiastic users, there is no icon for launching the registry editor. Instead, start a DOS shell (or open the Start → Run dialog box) and type regedit. Figure 12.4 shows the registry editor in action.

The left side shows the keys, which are arranged in a tree structure. Note that each key starts with one of the HKEY nodes like

```
HKEY_CLASSES_ROOT
HKEY_CURRENT_USER
HKEY_LOCAL_MACHINE
. . .
```

The right side shows the name/value pairs associated with a particular key. For example, if you installed Java 11, the key

```
HKEY_LOCAL_MACHINE\Software\JavaSoft\Java Runtime Environment
```

contains a name/value pair such as

```
CurrentVersion="11.0_10"
```

In this case, the value is a string. The values can also be integers or arrays of bytes.

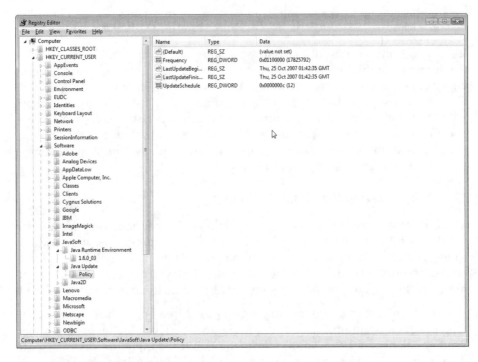

Figure 12.4 The registry editor

12.10.2 A Java Platform Interface for Accessing the Registry

We create a simple interface to access the registry from Java code, and then implement this interface with native code. Our interface allows only a few registry operations; to keep the code size down, we omitted some important operations such as adding, deleting, and enumerating keys. (It should be easy to add the remaining registry API functions.)

Even with the limited subset that we supply, you can

- Enumerate all names stored in a key
- Read the value stored with a name
- Set the value stored with a name

Here is the Java class that encapsulates a registry key:

```
public class Win32RegKey
{
    public Win32RegKey(int theRoot, String thePath) { . . . }
    public Enumeration names() { . . . }
    public native Object getValue(String name);
```

```
    public native void setValue(String name, Object value);

    public static final int HKEY_CLASSES_ROOT = 0x80000000;
    public static final int HKEY_CURRENT_USER = 0x80000001;
    public static final int HKEY_LOCAL_MACHINE = 0x80000002;
    . . .
}
```

The names method returns an enumeration that holds all the names stored with the key. You can get at them with the familiar hasMoreElements/nextElement methods. The getValue method returns an object that is either a string, an Integer object, or a byte array. The value parameter of the setValue method must also be of one of these three types.

12.10.3 Implementation of Registry Access Functions as Native Methods

We need to implement three actions:

- Get the value of a name
- Set the value of a name
- Iterate through the names of a key

In this chapter, you have seen essentially all the tools that are required, such as the conversion between Java strings and arrays and those of C. You also saw how to raise a Java exception in case something goes wrong.

Two issues make these native methods more complex than the preceding examples. The getValue and setValue methods deal with the type Object, which can be one of String, Integer, or byte[]. The enumeration object stores the state between successive calls to hasMoreElements and nextElement.

Let us first look at the getValue method. The method (shown in Listing 12.22) goes through the following steps:

1. Opens the registry key. To read their values, the registry API requires that keys be open.
2. Queries the type and size of the value associated with the name.
3. Reads the data into a buffer.
4. Calls NewStringUTF to create a new string with the value data if the type is REG_SZ (a string).
5. Invokes the Integer constructor if the type is REG_DWORD (a 32-bit integer).
6. Calls NewByteArray to create a new byte array, then SetByteArrayRegion to copy the value data into the byte array, if the type is REG_BINARY.

7. If the type is none of these or if an error occurred when an API function was called, throws an exception and releases all resources that had been acquired up to that point.

8. Closes the key and returns the object (String, Integer, or byte[]) that had been created.

As you can see, this example illustrates quite nicely how to generate Java objects of different types.

In this native method, coping with the generic return type is not difficult. The jstring, jobject, or jarray reference is simply returned as a jobject. However, the setValue method receives a reference to an Object and must determine the Object's exact type to save the Object as a string, integer, or byte array. We can make this determination by querying the class of the value object, finding the class references for java.lang.String, java.lang.Integer, and byte[], and comparing them with the IsAssignableFrom function.

If class1 and class2 are two class references, then the call

```
(*env)->IsAssignableFrom(env, class1, class2)
```

returns JNI_TRUE when class1 and class2 are the same class or when class1 is a subclass of class2. In either case, references to objects of class1 can be cast to class2. For example, when

```
(*env)->IsAssignableFrom(env, (*env)->GetObjectClass(env, value),
    (*env)->FindClass(env, "[B"))
```

is true, we know that value is a byte array.

Here is an overview of the steps in the setValue method:

1. Open the registry key for writing.
2. Find the type of the value to write.
3. Call GetStringUTFChars to get a pointer to the characters if the type is String.
4. Call the intValue method to get the integer stored in the wrapper object if the type is Integer.
5. Call GetByteArrayElements to get a pointer to the bytes if the type is byte[].
6. Pass the data and length to the registry.
7. Close the key.
8. Release the pointer to the data if the type is String or byte[].

Finally, let us turn to the native methods that enumerate keys. These are methods of the Win32RegKeyNameEnumeration class (see Listing 12.21). When the enumeration process starts, we must open the key. For the duration of the enumeration, we must retain the key handle—that is, the key handle must be stored with the enumeration object. The key handle is of type DWORD (a 32-bit quantity), so it can be stored in a Java integer. We store it in the hkey field of the enumeration class. When the enumeration starts, the field is initialized with SetIntField. Subsequent calls read the value with GetIntField.

In this example, we store three other data items with the enumeration object. When the enumeration first starts, we can query the registry for the count of name/value pairs and the length of the longest name, which we need so we can allocate C character arrays to hold the names. These values are stored in the count and maxsize fields of the enumeration object. Finally, the index field, initialized with -1 to indicate the start of the enumeration, is set to 0 once the other instance fields are initialized, and is incremented after every enumeration step.

Let's walk through the native methods that support the enumeration. The hasMoreElements method is simple:

1.   Retrieve the index and count fields.
2.   If the index is -1, call the startNameEnumeration function which opens the key, queries the count and maximum length, and initializes the hkey, count, maxsize, and index fields.
3.   Return JNI_TRUE if index is less than count, and JNI_FALSE otherwise.

The nextElement method needs to work a little harder:

1.   Retrieve the index and count fields.
2.   If the index is -1, call the startNameEnumeration function, which opens the key, queries the count and maximum length, and initializes the hkey, count, maxsize, and index fields.
3.   If index equals count, throw a NoSuchElementException.
4.   Read the next name from the registry.
5.   Increment index.
6.   If index equals count, close the key.

Before compiling, remember to run javac -h on both Win32RegKey and Win32RegKeyNameEnumeration. The complete command line for the Microsoft compiler is

```
cl -I jdk\include -I jdk\include\win32 -LD Win32RegKey.c advapi32.lib -FeWin32RegKey.dll
```

With Cygwin, use

```
gcc -mno-cygwin -D __int64="long long" -I jdk\include -I jdk\include\win32 \
   -I c:\cygwin\usr\include\w32api -shared -Wl,--add-stdcall-alias -o Win32RegKey.dll
Win32RegKey.c
```

As the registry API is specific to Windows, this program will not work on other operating systems.

Listing 12.23 shows a program to test our new registry functions. We add three name/value pairs, a string, an integer, and a byte array to the key

```
HKEY_CURRENT_USER\Software\JavaSoft\Java Runtime Environment
```

We then enumerate all names of that key and retrieve their values. The program will print

```
Default user=Harry Hacker
Lucky number=13
Small primes=2 3 5 7 11 13
```

Although adding these name/value pairs to that key probably does no harm, you might want to use the registry editor to remove them after running this program.

Listing 12.21 win32reg/Win32RegKey.java

```java
 1  import java.util.*;
 2
 3  /**
 4   * A Win32RegKey object can be used to get and set values of a registry key in the Windows
 5   * registry.
 6   * @version 1.00 1997-07-01
 7   * @author Cay Horstmann
 8   */
 9  public class Win32RegKey
10  {
11     public static final int HKEY_CLASSES_ROOT = 0x80000000;
12     public static final int HKEY_CURRENT_USER = 0x80000001;
13     public static final int HKEY_LOCAL_MACHINE = 0x80000002;
14     public static final int HKEY_USERS = 0x80000003;
15     public static final int HKEY_CURRENT_CONFIG = 0x80000005;
16     public static final int HKEY_DYN_DATA = 0x80000006;
17
18     private int root;
19     private String path;
20
21     /**
22      * Gets the value of a registry entry.
23      * @param name the entry name
24      * @return the associated value
25      */
26     public native Object getValue(String name);
27
```

```
28      /**
29       * Sets the value of a registry entry.
30       * @param name the entry name
31       * @param value the new value
32       */
33      public native void setValue(String name, Object value);
34
35      /**
36       * Construct a registry key object.
37       * @param theRoot one of HKEY_CLASSES_ROOT, HKEY_CURRENT_USER, HKEY_LOCAL_MACHINE,
38       * HKEY_USERS, HKEY_CURRENT_CONFIG, HKEY_DYN_DATA
39       * @param thePath the registry key path
40       */
41      public Win32RegKey(int theRoot, String thePath)
42      {
43         root = theRoot;
44         path = thePath;
45      }
46
47      /**
48       * Enumerates all names of registry entries under the path that this object describes.
49       * @return an enumeration listing all entry names
50       */
51      public Enumeration<String> names()
52      {
53         return new Win32RegKeyNameEnumeration(root, path);
54      }
55
56      static
57      {
58         System.loadLibrary("Win32RegKey");
59      }
60   }
61
62   class Win32RegKeyNameEnumeration implements Enumeration<String>
63   {
64      public native String nextElement();
65      public native boolean hasMoreElements();
66      private int root;
67      private String path;
68      private int index = -1;
69      private int hkey = 0;
70      private int maxsize;
71      private int count;
72
73      Win32RegKeyNameEnumeration(int theRoot, String thePath)
74      {
```

(Continues)

Listing 12.21 *(Continued)*

```
75        root = theRoot;
76        path = thePath;
77     }
78  }
79
80  class Win32RegKeyException extends RuntimeException
81  {
82     public Win32RegKeyException()
83     {
84     }
85
86     public Win32RegKeyException(String why)
87     {
88        super(why);
89     }
90  }
```

Listing 12.22 win32reg/Win32RegKey.c

```
1   /**
2      @version 1.00 1997-07-01
3      @author Cay Horstmann
4   */
5
6   #include "Win32RegKey.h"
7   #include "Win32RegKeyNameEnumeration.h"
8   #include <string.h>
9   #include <stdlib.h>
10  #include <windows.h>
11
12  JNIEXPORT jobject JNICALL Java_Win32RegKey_getValue(
13      JNIEnv* env, jobject this_obj, jobject name)
14  {
15     const char* cname;
16     jstring path;
17     const char* cpath;
18     HKEY hkey;
19     DWORD type;
20     DWORD size;
21     jclass this_class;
22     jfieldID id_root;
23     jfieldID id_path;
24     HKEY root;
25     jobject ret;
26     char* cret;
27
28     /* get the class */
```

```
29    this_class = (*env)->GetObjectClass(env, this_obj);
30
31    /* get the field IDs */
32    id_root = (*env)->GetFieldID(env, this_class, "root", "I");
33    id_path = (*env)->GetFieldID(env, this_class, "path", "Ljava/lang/String;");
34
35    /* get the fields */
36    root = (HKEY) (*env)->GetIntField(env, this_obj, id_root);
37    path = (jstring)(*env)->GetObjectField(env, this_obj, id_path);
38    cpath = (*env)->GetStringUTFChars(env, path, NULL);
39
40    /* open the registry key */
41    if (RegOpenKeyEx(root, cpath, 0, KEY_READ, &hkey) != ERROR_SUCCESS)
42    {
43       (*env)->ThrowNew(env, (*env)->FindClass(env, "Win32RegKeyException"),
44          "Open key failed");
45       (*env)->ReleaseStringUTFChars(env, path, cpath);
46       return NULL;
47    }
48
49    (*env)->ReleaseStringUTFChars(env, path, cpath);
50    cname = (*env)->GetStringUTFChars(env, name, NULL);
51
52    /* find the type and size of the value */
53    if (RegQueryValueEx(hkey, cname, NULL, &type, NULL, &size) != ERROR_SUCCESS)
54    {
55       (*env)->ThrowNew(env, (*env)->FindClass(env, "Win32RegKeyException"),
56          "Query value key failed");
57       RegCloseKey(hkey);
58       (*env)->ReleaseStringUTFChars(env, name, cname);
59       return NULL;
60    }
61
62    /* get memory to hold the value */
63    cret = (char*)malloc(size);
64
65    /* read the value */
66    if (RegQueryValueEx(hkey, cname, NULL, &type, cret, &size) != ERROR_SUCCESS)
67    {
68       (*env)->ThrowNew(env, (*env)->FindClass(env, "Win32RegKeyException"),
69          "Query value key failed");
70       free(cret);
71       RegCloseKey(hkey);
72       (*env)->ReleaseStringUTFChars(env, name, cname);
73       return NULL;
74    }
75
76    /* depending on the type, store the value in a string,
77       integer, or byte array */
```

(Continues)

Listing 12.22 *(Continued)*

```
78    if (type == REG_SZ)
79    {
80        ret = (*env)->NewStringUTF(env, cret);
81    }
82    else if (type == REG_DWORD)
83    {
84        jclass class_Integer = (*env)->FindClass(env, "java/lang/Integer");
85        /* get the method ID of the constructor */
86        jmethodID id_Integer = (*env)->GetMethodID(env, class_Integer, "<init>", "(I)V");
87        int value = *(int*) cret;
88        /* invoke the constructor */
89        ret = (*env)->NewObject(env, class_Integer, id_Integer, value);
90    }
91    else if (type == REG_BINARY)
92    {
93        ret = (*env)->NewByteArray(env, size);
94        (*env)->SetByteArrayRegion(env, (jarray) ret, 0, size, cret);
95    }
96    else
97    {
98        (*env)->ThrowNew(env, (*env)->FindClass(env, "Win32RegKeyException"),
99               "Unsupported value type");
100        ret = NULL;
101    }
102
103    free(cret);
104    RegCloseKey(hkey);
105    (*env)->ReleaseStringUTFChars(env, name, cname);
106
107    return ret;
108 }
109
110 JNIEXPORT void JNICALL Java_Win32RegKey_setValue(JNIEnv* env, jobject this_obj,
111        jstring name, jobject value)
112 {
113    const char* cname;
114    jstring path;
115    const char* cpath;
116    HKEY hkey;
117    DWORD type;
118    DWORD size;
119    jclass this_class;
120    jclass class_value;
121    jclass class_Integer;
122    jfieldID id_root;
123    jfieldID id_path;
124    HKEY root;
```

```
125    const char* cvalue;
126    int ivalue;
127
128    /* get the class */
129    this_class = (*env)->GetObjectClass(env, this_obj);
130
131    /* get the field IDs */
132    id_root = (*env)->GetFieldID(env, this_class, "root", "I");
133    id_path = (*env)->GetFieldID(env, this_class, "path", "Ljava/lang/String;");
134
135    /* get the fields */
136    root = (HKEY)(*env)->GetIntField(env, this_obj, id_root);
137    path = (jstring)(*env)->GetObjectField(env, this_obj, id_path);
138    cpath = (*env)->GetStringUTFChars(env, path, NULL);
139
140    /* open the registry key */
141    if (RegOpenKeyEx(root, cpath, 0, KEY_WRITE, &hkey) != ERROR_SUCCESS)
142    {
143       (*env)->ThrowNew(env, (*env)->FindClass(env, "Win32RegKeyException"),
144             "Open key failed");
145       (*env)->ReleaseStringUTFChars(env, path, cpath);
146       return;
147    }
148
149    (*env)->ReleaseStringUTFChars(env, path, cpath);
150    cname = (*env)->GetStringUTFChars(env, name, NULL);
151
152    class_value = (*env)->GetObjectClass(env, value);
153    class_Integer = (*env)->FindClass(env, "java/lang/Integer");
154    /* determine the type of the value object */
155    if ((*env)->IsAssignableFrom(env, class_value, (*env)->FindClass(env, "java/lang/String")))
156    {
157       /* it is a string--get a pointer to the characters */
158       cvalue = (*env)->GetStringUTFChars(env, (jstring) value, NULL);
159       type = REG_SZ;
160       size = (*env)->GetStringLength(env, (jstring) value) + 1;
161    }
162    else if ((*env)->IsAssignableFrom(env, class_value, class_Integer))
163    {
164       /* it is an integer--call intValue to get the value */
165       jmethodID id_intValue = (*env)->GetMethodID(env, class_Integer, "intValue", "()I");
166       ivalue = (*env)->CallIntMethod(env, value, id_intValue);
167       type = REG_DWORD;
168       cvalue = (char*)&ivalue;
169       size = 4;
170    }
171    else if ((*env)->IsAssignableFrom(env, class_value, (*env)->FindClass(env, "[B")))
172    {
173       /* it is a byte array--get a pointer to the bytes */
```

(Continues)

Listing 12.22 *(Continued)*

```
174       type = REG_BINARY;
175       cvalue = (char*)(*env)->GetByteArrayElements(env, (jarray) value, NULL);
176       size = (*env)->GetArrayLength(env, (jarray) value);
177   }
178   else
179   {
180       /* we don't know how to handle this type */
181       (*env)->ThrowNew(env, (*env)->FindClass(env, "Win32RegKeyException"),
182           "Unsupported value type");
183       RegCloseKey(hkey);
184       (*env)->ReleaseStringUTFChars(env, name, cname);
185       return;
186   }
187
188   /* set the value */
189   if (RegSetValueEx(hkey, cname, 0, type, cvalue, size) != ERROR_SUCCESS)
190   {
191       (*env)->ThrowNew(env, (*env)->FindClass(env, "Win32RegKeyException"),
192           "Set value failed");
193   }
194
195   RegCloseKey(hkey);
196   (*env)->ReleaseStringUTFChars(env, name, cname);
197
198   /* if the value was a string or byte array, release the pointer */
199   if (type == REG_SZ)
200   {
201       (*env)->ReleaseStringUTFChars(env, (jstring) value, cvalue);
202   }
203   else if (type == REG_BINARY)
204   {
205       (*env)->ReleaseByteArrayElements(env, (jarray) value, (jbyte*) cvalue, 0);
206   }
207 }
208
209 /* helper function to start enumeration of names */
210 static int startNameEnumeration(JNIEnv* env, jobject this_obj, jclass this_class)
211 {
212   jfieldID id_index;
213   jfieldID id_count;
214   jfieldID id_root;
215   jfieldID id_path;
216   jfieldID id_hkey;
217   jfieldID id_maxsize;
218
219   HKEY root;
220   jstring path;
```

```
221    const char* cpath;
222    HKEY hkey;
223    DWORD maxsize = 0;
224    DWORD count = 0;
225
226    /* get the field IDs */
227    id_root = (*env)->GetFieldID(env, this_class, "root", "I");
228    id_path = (*env)->GetFieldID(env, this_class, "path", "Ljava/lang/String;");
229    id_hkey = (*env)->GetFieldID(env, this_class, "hkey", "I");
230    id_maxsize = (*env)->GetFieldID(env, this_class, "maxsize", "I");
231    id_index = (*env)->GetFieldID(env, this_class, "index", "I");
232    id_count = (*env)->GetFieldID(env, this_class, "count", "I");
233
234    /* get the field values */
235    root = (HKEY)(*env)->GetIntField(env, this_obj, id_root);
236    path = (jstring)(*env)->GetObjectField(env, this_obj, id_path);
237    cpath = (*env)->GetStringUTFChars(env, path, NULL);
238
239    /* open the registry key */
240    if (RegOpenKeyEx(root, cpath, 0, KEY_READ, &hkey) != ERROR_SUCCESS)
241    {
242       (*env)->ThrowNew(env, (*env)->FindClass(env, "Win32RegKeyException"),
243           "Open key failed");
244       (*env)->ReleaseStringUTFChars(env, path, cpath);
245       return -1;
246    }
247    (*env)->ReleaseStringUTFChars(env, path, cpath);
248
249    /* query count and max length of names */
250    if (RegQueryInfoKey(hkey, NULL, NULL, NULL, NULL, NULL, NULL, &count, &maxsize,
251        NULL, NULL, NULL) != ERROR_SUCCESS)
252    {
253       (*env)->ThrowNew(env, (*env)->FindClass(env, "Win32RegKeyException"),
254           "Query info key failed");
255       RegCloseKey(hkey);
256       return -1;
257    }
258
259    /* set the field values */
260    (*env)->SetIntField(env, this_obj, id_hkey, (DWORD) hkey);
261    (*env)->SetIntField(env, this_obj, id_maxsize, maxsize + 1);
262    (*env)->SetIntField(env, this_obj, id_index, 0);
263    (*env)->SetIntField(env, this_obj, id_count, count);
264    return count;
265 }
266
267 JNIEXPORT jboolean JNICALL Java_Win32RegKeyNameEnumeration_hasMoreElements(JNIEnv* env,
268       jobject this_obj)
269 {
```

(Continues)

Listing 12.22 (Continued)

```
270    jclass this_class;
271    jfieldID id_index;
272    jfieldID id_count;
273    int index;
274    int count;
275    /* get the class */
276    this_class = (*env)->GetObjectClass(env, this_obj);
277
278    /* get the field IDs */
279    id_index = (*env)->GetFieldID(env, this_class, "index", "I");
280    id_count = (*env)->GetFieldID(env, this_class, "count", "I");
281
282    index = (*env)->GetIntField(env, this_obj, id_index);
283    if (index == -1) /* first time */
284    {
285       count = startNameEnumeration(env, this_obj, this_class);
286       index = 0;
287    }
288    else
289       count = (*env)->GetIntField(env, this_obj, id_count);
290    return index < count;
291 }
292
293 JNIEXPORT jobject JNICALL Java_Win32RegKeyNameEnumeration_nextElement(JNIEnv* env,
294       jobject this_obj)
295 {
296    jclass this_class;
297    jfieldID id_index;
298    jfieldID id_hkey;
299    jfieldID id_count;
300    jfieldID id_maxsize;
301
302    HKEY hkey;
303    int index;
304    int count;
305    DWORD maxsize;
306
307    char* cret;
308    jstring ret;
309
310    /* get the class */
311    this_class = (*env)->GetObjectClass(env, this_obj);
312
313    /* get the field IDs */
314    id_index = (*env)->GetFieldID(env, this_class, "index", "I");
315    id_count = (*env)->GetFieldID(env, this_class, "count", "I");
```

```
316    id_hkey = (*env)->GetFieldID(env, this_class, "hkey", "I");
317    id_maxsize = (*env)->GetFieldID(env, this_class, "maxsize", "I");
318
319    index = (*env)->GetIntField(env, this_obj, id_index);
320    if (index == -1) /* first time */
321    {
322       count = startNameEnumeration(env, this_obj, this_class);
323       index = 0;
324    }
325    else
326       count = (*env)->GetIntField(env, this_obj, id_count);
327
328    if (index >= count) /* already at end */
329    {
330       (*env)->ThrowNew(env, (*env)->FindClass(env, "java/util/NoSuchElementException"),
331             "past end of enumeration");
332       return NULL;
333    }
334
335    maxsize = (*env)->GetIntField(env, this_obj, id_maxsize);
336    hkey = (HKEY)(*env)->GetIntField(env, this_obj, id_hkey);
337    cret = (char*)malloc(maxsize);
338
339    /* find the next name */
340    if (RegEnumValue(hkey, index, cret, &maxsize, NULL, NULL, NULL, NULL) != ERROR_SUCCESS)
341    {
342       (*env)->ThrowNew(env, (*env)->FindClass(env, "Win32RegKeyException"),
343             "Enum value failed");
344       free(cret);
345       RegCloseKey(hkey);
346       (*env)->SetIntField(env, this_obj, id_index, count);
347       return NULL;
348    }
349
350    ret = (*env)->NewStringUTF(env, cret);
351    free(cret);
352
353    /* increment index */
354    index++;
355    (*env)->SetIntField(env, this_obj, id_index, index);
356
357    if (index == count) /* at end */
358    {
359       RegCloseKey(hkey);
360    }
361
362    return ret;
363 }
```

Listing 12.23 win32reg/Win32RegKeyTest.java

```java
1  import java.util.*;
2
3  /**
4     @version 1.03 2018-05-01
5     @author Cay Horstmann
6  */
7  public class Win32RegKeyTest
8  {
9     public static void main(String[] args)
10    {
11       var key = new Win32RegKey(
12          Win32RegKey.HKEY_CURRENT_USER, "Software\\JavaSoft\\Java Runtime Environment");
13
14       key.setValue("Default user", "Harry Hacker");
15       key.setValue("Lucky number", new Integer(13));
16       key.setValue("Small primes", new byte[] { 2, 3, 5, 7, 11 });
17
18       Enumeration<String> e = key.names();
19
20       while (e.hasMoreElements())
21       {
22          String name = e.nextElement();
23          System.out.print(name + "=");
24
25          Object value = key.getValue(name);
26
27          if (value instanceof byte[])
28             for (byte b : (byte[]) value) System.out.print((b & 0xFF) + " ");
29          else
30             System.out.print(value);
31
32          System.out.println();
33       }
34    }
35 }
```

Type Inquiry Functions

- jboolean IsAssignableFrom(JNIEnv *env, jclass cl1, jclass cl2)

  returns JNI_TRUE if objects of the first class can be assigned to objects of the second class, and JNI_FALSE otherwise. This tests if the classes are the same, or cl1 is a subclass of cl2, or cl2 represents an interface implemented by cl1 or one of its superclasses.

(Continues)

Type Inquiry Functions *(Continued)*

• jclass GetSuperclass(JNIEnv *env, jclass cl)

   returns the superclass of a class. If cl represents the class Object or an interface, returns NULL.

You have now reached the end of the second volume of *Core Java*, completing a long journey in which you encountered many advanced APIs. We started out with topics that every Java programmer needs to know: streams, XML, networking, databases, and internationalization. We concluded with very technical chapters on security, annotation processing, advanced graphics, and native methods. We hope that you enjoyed your tour through the vast breadth of the Java APIs, and that you will be able to apply your newly gained knowledge in your projects.

Index

Credits

Cover image: Chromakey/Shutterstock

Chapter 3: "The Extensible Markup Language (XML) has replaced Java, Design Patterns, and Object Technology as the software industry's solution to world hunger." Box, D., Skonnard, A., & Lam, J. (2000). *Essential XML: Beyond Markup*. Boston, Mass: Addison-Wesley.

Chapter 3, Figure 3.3: Screenshot of Mozilla Firefox © Mozilla Foundation

Chapter 4, Figures 4.1, 4.3, 4.4, 4.5: Screenshots from Microsoft Windows © Microsoft 2018

Chapter 4, Figure 4.6: Screenshot of Java © Oracle

Chapter 4, Figure 4.7: Screenshot of HTML form © 2018 USPS

Chapter 5, Figure 4.9: Screenshot of Mozilla Firefox © Mozilla Foundation

Chapter 5, Figures 5.3, 5.4: Screenshot of Ubuntu © 2018 Canonical Ltd. Ubuntu and Canonical are registered trademarks of Canonical Ltd.

Chapter 5, Figure 5.6: Screenshot of Java © Oracle

Chapter 7: "We have really everything ... except, of course, language." Oscar Wilde

Chapter 7, Figures 7.1, 7.2, 7.3, 7.4, 7.5, 7.6: Screenshot of Java © Oracle

Chapter 8, Figure 8.2: Screenshot of Mozilla Firefox © Mozilla Foundation

Chapter 9, Figure 9.2: Screenshot of Eclipse © Eclipse Foundation, Inc.

Chapter 10, Figures 10.3, 10.7, 10.8, 10.12: Screenshot of Java © Oracle

Chapter 10, Figure 10.4: Screenshot of hex editor © Jaka Mocnik and Chema Celorio

Chapter 11, Figures 11.1, 11.2, 11.3, 11.4, 11.5, 11.7, 11.8, 11.9, 11.10, 11.14, 11.15, 11.16, 11.17, 11.18, 11.19, 11.20, 11.21, 11.22, 11.23, 11.24, 11.25, 11.26, 11.28, 11.29, 11.30, 11.39, 11.44, 11.54, 11.55, 11.56, 11.60, 11.62: Screenshot of Java © Oracle

Chapter 11, Figure 11.51: Shao-Chun Wang/123RF

Chapter 11, Figure 11.57: Luca Trovato/The Image Bank/Getty Images

Chapter 11: Images of various planets courtesy of Jim Evins

Chapter 12, Figure 12.4: Screenshot of registry editor © Microsoft 2018

Register Your Product at informit.com/register

Access additional benefits and **save 35%** on your next purchase

- Automatically receive a coupon for 35% off your next purchase, valid for 30 days. Look for your code in your InformIT cart or the Manage Codes section of your account page.
- Download available product updates.
- Access bonus material if available.*
- Check the box to hear from us and receive exclusive offers on new editions and related products.

Registration benefits vary by product. Benefits will be listed on your account page under Registered Products.

InformIT.com—The Trusted Technology Learning Source

InformIT is the online home of information technology brands at Pearson, the world's foremost education company. At InformIT.com, you can:

- Shop our books, eBooks, software, and video training
- Take advantage of our special offers and promotions (informit.com/promotions)
- Sign up for special offers and content newsletter (informit.com/newsletters)
- Access thousands of free chapters and video lessons

Connect with InformIT—Visit informit.com/community

the trusted technology learning source

Addison-Wesley • Adobe Press • Cisco Press • Microsoft Press • Pearson IT Certification • Prentice Hall • Que • Sams • Peachpit Press

Ⓟ Pearson